SEVENTH EDITION

Total Learning

Developmental Curriculum for the Young Child

JOANNE HENDRICK
UNIVERSITY OF OKLAHOMA, EMERITA

PATRICIA WEISSMAN

PEARSON

Merrill
Prentice Hall

Upper Saddle River, New Jersey
Columbus, Ohio

Library of Congress Cataloging-in-Publication Data

Hendrick, Joanne.
  Total learning : developmental curriculum for the young child / Joanne Hendrick, Patricia Weissman.—7th ed.
    p. cm.
  Includes bibliographical references and indexes.
  ISBN 0-13-222566-2 (pbk.)
  1. Education, Preschool—Curricula. 2. Curriculum planning. 3. Child development. I. Weissman, Patricia. II. Title.
    LB1140.4.H45 2007
    372.19—dc22   2006005404

Vice President and Executive Publisher: Jeffery W. Johnston
Publisher: Kevin M. Davis
Acquisitions Editor: Julie Peters
Editorial Assistant: Tiffany Bitzel
Senior Production Editor: Linda Hillis Bayma
Production Coordination: Thistle Hill Publishing Services, LLC
Design Coordinator: Diane C. Lorenzo
Cover Designer: Ali Mohrman
Cover Image: SuperStock
Production Manager: Laura Messerly
Director of Marketing: David Gesell
Marketing Manager: Amy Judd
Marketing Coordinator: Brian Mounts

This book was set in Goudy by Carlisle Publishing Services. It was printed and bound by Von Hoffman Press, Inc. The cover was printed by Phoenix Color Corp.

Photo Credits: Sarah Futernick, p. iii (bottom); Joanne Hendrick, pp. 1, 6 (both), 21, 28, 50, 55, 59, 70, 112, 116, 120, 126 (both), 144, 169, 178, 184, 191, 204, 215, 234, 237 (both), 244 (both), 250, 269, 282, 308, 343; Boulder Journey School, pp. 7, 16, 30, 39, 40, 43, 61, 72, 84, 181, 271, 283, 293, 295, 302, 328, 332, 336; © Rob Lewine/Corbis, p. 4; White Oak School, pp. 37, 54; Leslie Gleim, pp. 76, 167, 333; Benjamin La Framboise, pp. 81, 91, 93, 99, 123, 128, 150, 219, 242, 289, 316; Krista Greco/Merrill, p. 95; Brigid McGinn, pp. 103, 185, 197, 304, 320; Dan Floss/Merrill, p. 133; Patrick Bates, pp. 146, 165; University of Michigan–Dearborn Child Development Center, p. 148; Anne Vega/Merrill, p. 171.

Pearson Prentice Hall™ is a trademark of Pearson Education, Inc.
Pearson® is a registered trademark of Pearson plc
Prentice Hall® is a registered trademark of Pearson Education, Inc.
Merrill® is a registered trademark of Pearson Education, Inc.

Pearson Education Ltd.   Pearson Education Australia Pty. Limited
Pearson Education Singapore Pte. Ltd.   Pearson Education North Asia Ltd.
Pearson Education Canada, Ltd.   Pearson Educación de Mexico, S.A. de C.V.
Pearson Education–Japan   Pearson Education Malaysia Pte. Ltd.

10 9 8 7 6 5 4 3 2
ISBN: 0-13-222566-2

Joanne Hendrick is professor emerita of early childhood education from the University of Oklahoma. In addition to raising four children of her own, her practical experience includes working with children at the Stanford Speech and Hearing Clinic, directing a parent–child workshop, working in Head Start, and chairing the early childhood areas at Santa Barbara City College and the University of Oklahoma. She holds an undergraduate degree from Stanford University in disorders of speech and hearing, and graduate degrees from the University of California in counseling and early childhood education. She is past president of the California Association for the Education of Young Children.

Her current interests include gardening, photography, traveling to exotic places, writing about young children, and enjoying her 10 grandchildren.

Patricia Weissman began her early childhood career as a family care provider for two infants. Having found her calling, she studied early childhood education in the master's program at San Francisco State University and received a doctorate of education from the University of San Francisco. During the past 25 years, she has worked as an infant caregiver, a preprimary teacher, a center director, a Child Development Associate (CDA) advisor, a professor of early childhood education, and a research associate in early childhood development at the Merrill-Palmer Institute of Wayne State University. She was the founding editor of the journal *Innovations in Early Education: The International Reggio Exchange*. Dr. Weissman also designed and consulted on the production of the Public Broadcasting Service video series titled *The Whole Child: A Caregiver's Guide to the First Five Years*.

Introduction

Total Learning is a practical book based on more than 40 years of teaching young children, their families, and student teachers, as well as on the authors' experiences with the preprimary schools in Reggio Emilia. The text advocates basing curriculum on the emerging interests of the children within a practical, flexible, thoughtful teacher-made plan.

Total Learning explains how to identify goals and objectives, how to incorporate them into a curriculum that meets individual needs, and how to assess the results in a developmentally appropriate way. Because this approach focuses on the children, the text is divided according to the physical, emotional, social, creative, and cognitive selves and explains how such topics as emergent literacy, cross-cultural understandings, and sound health practices can be incorporated to enhance those selves.

The text advocates curriculum that is age appropriate, nourished by play, and intended to encourage children to become independent, creative, thoughtful people.

Inviting Features of the Textbook

New to This Edition

- A new "Emergent Curriculum in Action" feature runs throughout the text, in which teachers in different types of programs and with students of different ages describe an example of how they used the emergent approach in planning curriculum.
- New material is included on the implications of recent research on the brain for educating young children.
- Because of current concerns, the issues of assessment and educational standards have been expanded, including discussion of the No Child Left Behind Act.
- New information has been added about teaching children in the K–3 primary grades.
- A new end-of-chapter section, "Related Organizations and Online Resources," provides students with resources to investigate the chapter topics further.

Continuing Features

- *Total Learning* includes a strong emphasis on multicultural, nonsexist, inclusive education.
- It emphasizes teaching the *whole* child—not just the child from the neck up.
- It explains Piaget's and Vygotsky's theories and their implications for early childhood education.
- It demonstrates how the *emergent* and the *conventional* approaches to teaching the cognitive self can work together for the benefit of the children.

- It includes extensive explanations of the Reggio Emilia approach together with many practical suggestions for integrating aspects of that philosophy into the curriculum.
- A series of videotapes originally made for *Total Learning*'s companion book, *The Whole Child*, funded by the Annenberg CPB Project, coordinates well with *Total Learning* and is available in both Spanish and English. These are available for purchase on the Annenberg Media website at *www.learner.org*
- The annotated references, a popular feature, include hundreds of new sources for further reading for both beginning and advanced students.
- "Food for Thought and Group Discussion" questions and "Self-Check Questions for Review" are provided as study aids at the end of each chapter.

Supplements to This Text

Online Instructor's Manual. For each chapter, this manual contains an Overview, Possible Focus for Teaching, a Checklist of Practical Teaching Skills, and Sample Assignments. This and other online supplements can be accessed from the Instructor's Resource Center at *www.prenhall.com*

Online Test Bank. The types of assessment items found in this manual include Essay, Situational Questions, Multiple Choice, and True/False.

TestGen. This test management software allows instructors to create customized tests from the collection of questions provided in the Test Bank.

Online PowerPoint Slides. These slides contain scenarios and challenging predicaments that teachers frequently face in their daily work. These narrative cases can be used to enhance class discussions and to support students as they learn to problem solve in teaching. Each scenario is followed by a question or questions requiring higher-level thinking skills.

Blackboard and WebCT cartridges. New to this edition, these online course cartridges contain the text bank, which has been converted into Blackboard and WebCT formats, and are accompanied by instructions for uploading the files into an existing course.

Acknowledgments

Writing and revising a book of this kind requires the work of the authors and also the support and contributions of many other people as well. In particular I want to thank the staff of the Children's Center at Santa Barbara City College: Donna Coffman, Clevonease Johnson, Marilyn Statucki, and Zoe Iverson. When I transferred to the University of Oklahoma, head teachers Cene Marquis, Jane Vaughn, Ruth Ann Ball, and Deb Parkinson also contributed mightily to my enlightenment. Over the years these people have shared so many ideas and suggestions, and our philosophies are now so entwined, that it would be impossible to say any longer who was responsible for what. The same can be said of the students: If students like this book, it is because of what former students taught me they needed and wanted—and many of their ideas and requests are incorporated here.

I am most indebted as well as thankful for the forbearance of the many staffs and children from a variety of children's centers and nursery schools who permitted me to invade their privacy by taking pictures for the book. These include the Institute of Child Development, University of Oklahoma; Children's Place of Integris Medical Hospital, Oklahoma City; the East and West Tinker Air Force Base Child Development Centers, Midwest City,

Oklahoma; the Metrotech Child Care Training Center, Oklahoma City; and the Starr King Parent Child Workshop, San Marcos Parent Child Workshop, Oaks Parent Child Workshop, and Discoveries, all located in Santa Barbara.

Of course, time does not stand still, so when the necessity for producing the seventh edition of *Total Learning* arrived—and I arrived at my 78th birthday—I continued to add to my list of essential collaborators. As this edition goes to press, they include the book's reviewers, who provided valuable input. In appreciation of their time and expertise, I would like to thank Vivian Harper, San Joaquin Delta College; Bernadette Haschke, Baylor University; Barbara Hatcher, Texas State University; Deborah Moberly, University of Memphis; and Marilyn Moore, Illinois State University.

Finally, the people at Merrill/Prentice Hall once again have been of great assistance. In particular I want to thank Kevin Davis, Publisher, and Julie Peters, Editor, for helping me welcome Patty Weissman, my congenial co-author.

While continuing the philosophy and practical approach that has characterized previous editions of *Total Learning,* Patty brings with her a fresh background of institutional and family child care. In addition, she is thoroughly acquainted with the Reggio Emilia approach because she was an early editor of *Innovations in Early Education: The International Reggio Exchange.*

As you enjoy the latest edition of *Total Learning,* I know you will come to respect Patty as much as I have and that you will agree I am leaving my precious book in good hands.

—Joanne Hendrick

I am forever grateful to Joanne Hendrick, not only for her faith in me as second author, but for all she has taught me through her writings and conversation. I feel very fortunate to have been graced with her friendship.

I am also thankful for the many wonderful teachers in my life, including Roz Saltz, Eli Saltz, Loris Malaguzzi, Carla Rinaldi, Lella Gandini, Amelia Gambetti, the many educators in Reggio Emilia—and my own children, Rose and Tony.

The beautiful new photographs in this book are courtesy of the following schools: Boulder Journey School, Boulder, Colorado; Carousel Center, Portsmouth, Ohio; Child Development Center, University of Michigan–Dearborn; Drayton Avenue Cooperative Nursery School, Ferndale, Michigan; Early Childhood Center, Wayne State University, Detroit; Merrill-Palmer Child Development Laboratory, Wayne State University, Detroit; St. Catherine's School, Richmond, Virginia; and White Oak School, Monticello, Illinois. I am particularly indebted to Patrick Bates, Leslie Gleim, Ellen Hall, Benjamin LaFramboise, Brigid McGinn, Lori Pickert, and Angi Primavera for sharing their work so generously.

Finally, I am grateful to the many people at Merrill/Prentice Hall whose expertise and insight made this book possible. Specifically, I'd like to thank Julie Peters, Carol Sykes, and Linda Bayma. Angela Urquhart at Thistle Hill Publishing Services also provided patient and invaluable assistance.

—Patricia Weissman

The Prentice Hall Companion Website: A Virtual Learning Environment

Technology is a constantly growing and changing aspect of our field that is creating a need for content and resources. To address this emerging need, Prentice Hall has developed an online learning environment for students and professors alike—Companion Websites—to support our textbooks.

In creating a Companion Website, our goal is to build on and enhance what the textbook already offers. For this reason, the content for each user-friendly website is organized by topic and provides the professor and student with a variety of meaningful resources. Common features of a Companion Website include:

- **Introduction**—General information about the topic and how it is covered in the website.
- **Web Links**—A variety of websites related to topic areas.
- **Timely Articles**—Links to online articles that enable you to become more aware of important issues in early childhood.
- **Learn by Doing**—Put concepts into action, participate in activities, examine strategies, and more.
- **Visit a School**—Visit a school's website to see concepts, theories, and strategies in action.
- **For Teachers/Practitioners**—Access information you will need to know as an educator, including information on materials, activities, and lessons.
- **Observation Tools**—A collection of checklists and forms to print and use when observing and assessing children's development.
- **Current Policies and Standards**—Find out the latest early childhood policies from the government and various organizations, and view state, federal, and curriculum standards.
- **Resources and Organizations**—Discover tools to help you plan your classroom or center and organizations to provide current information and standards for each topic.
- **Electronic Bluebook**—Paperless method of completing homework or essays assigned by a professor. Finished work can be sent to the professor via email.

To take advantage of these and other resources, please visit Merrill Education's **Early Childhood Education Resources Website.** Go to **www.prenhall.com/hendrick,** click on the book cover, and then click on "Enter" at the bottom of the next screen.

Teacher Preparation Classroom

TEACHER PREP

MERRILL
PRENTICE HALL

See a demo at
www.prenhall.com/teacherprep/demo

Your Class. Their Careers. Our Future. Will your students be prepared?

We invite you to explore our new, innovative and engaging website and all that it has to offer you, your course, and tomorrow's educators! Organized around the major courses pre-service teachers take, the Teacher Preparation site provides media, student/teacher artifacts, strategies, research articles, and other resources to equip your students with the quality tools needed to excel in their courses and prepare them for their first classroom.

This ultimate on-line education resource is available at no cost, when packaged with a Merrill text, and will provide you and your students access to:

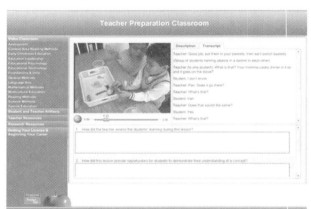

Online Video Library. More than 150 video clips—each tied to a course topic and framed by learning goals and Praxis-type questions—capture real teachers and students working in real classrooms, as well as in-depth interviews with both students and educators.

Student and Teacher Artifacts. More than 200 student and teacher classroom artifacts—each tied to a course topic and framed by learning goals and application questions—provide a wealth of materials and experiences to help make your study to become a professional teacher more concrete and hands-on.

Research Articles. Over 500 articles from ASCD's renowned journal *Educational Leadership*. The site also includes Research Navigator, a searchable database of additional educational journals.

Teaching Strategies. Over 500 strategies and lesson plans for you to use when you become a practicing professional.

Licensure and Career Tools. Resources devoted to helping you pass your licensure exam; learn standards, law, and public policies; plan a teaching portfolio; and succeed in your first year of teaching.

How to ORDER *Teacher Prep* for you and your students:
For students to receive a *Teacher Prep* Access Code with this text, instructors **must** provide a special value pack ISBN number on their textbook order form. To receive this special ISBN, please email **Merrill.marketing@pearsoned.com** and provide the following information:
- Name and Affiliation
- Author/Title/Edition of Merrill text

Upon ordering *Teacher Prep* for their students, instructors will be given a lifetime *Teacher Prep* Access Code.

BRIEF CONTENTS

CONTENTS

Chapter 2

Including Families in the Life of the School   21

Chapter 3

Play: The Integrative Force in Learning   37

Part II   *Planning for Total Learning*

Chapter 4
Designing the Supportive Environment   54

Chapter 5
Creating Supportive Curriculum Plans
and Schedules   70

Chapter 6
Getting to Know the Children by Keeping Track of What They're Learning   91

Chapter 7
Planning with Individual Children in Mind: Using Behavioral Objectives in the School   112

Part III   *Helping Young Children Relish Life
and Develop Healthy Bodies*

Chapter 8
Keeping Children Safe and Well Fed   123

Chapter 9
Developing Physical Competence   144

Chapter 10
Helping Children Understand and Value Life   165

Part IV *Fostering Emotional Health in Young Children*

Chapter 11
Achieving Emotional Competence 178

Part V   *Developing Social Competence and Healthy
Self-Identities*

Chapter 12
Getting Along Together: Achieving Competence in Interpersonal Relations   197

Chapter 13

Who Am I? Who Are You?: Coming to Terms with Multicultural, Gender, and Disability Issues   219

Part VI   *Encouraging Children to Be Creative*

Chapter 14
Freeing Children to Be Creative   242

Part VII　　*Fostering the Use of Language*

Chapter 15
Developing Verbal Competence　　*269*

Chapter 16
Taking the First Steps on the Road to Literacy   289

Part VIII   *Supporting Children's Cognitive Development*

Chapter 17
Helping Children Learn to Think for Themselves: Using the Emergent Approach   308

Chapter 18
Helping Children Develop Mental Abilities and Academic Competence: Using the Conventional Approach   328

Note: Every effort has been made to provide accurate and current Internet information in this book. However, the Internet and information on it are constantly changing, so it is inevitable that some of the Internet addresses listed in this textbook will change.

THE PURPOSE OF CURRICULUM

Have you ever . . .

- Felt you couldn't defend yourself when someone said you were "majoring in babysitting"?
- Wished you could be sure what you were teaching really mattered to the children?
- Wondered why other teachers kept referring to "all that new stuff about the brain"?

If you have, the material in this chapter will help you.

When it comes to working well with children, respect must be informed by understanding—understanding of children's development, children's needs, the individuality of each child, the way the world looks to a child, what childhood is all about. The more understanding there is, the greater the pleasure, the greater the delightful mystery of children.

Respect informed by understanding allows no place for seeing children as objects for our amusement, as "cute," as less than human. Respect informed by understanding leads to empowerment of children, even babies and toddlers.

—Ann Stonehouse (1995, p. 20)

The time is always right to do what is right.

—Martin Luther King, Jr.

This book concerns itself with answering the following questions: (a) What is the purpose of early education? and (b) What should curriculum for young children include?

WHAT IS THE PURPOSE OF EARLY EDUCATION?

The answers to these questions can be deceptively simple. The purpose of early education is to foster competence in young children, though not only competence in intellectual areas. Competence should be thought of as relating to all aspects of self: learning to live comfortably with others, learning to master and safely express one's feelings, and learning to love life and welcome new experience. The purpose of education, then, is to foster competence in dealing with life.

WHAT SHOULD CURRICULUM FOR YOUNG CHILDREN INCLUDE?

Curriculum, which is the design of experiences and activities developed by teachers to help children increase their competence, should be thought of as including *everything* that happens to children during their time at the preschool, primary school, family child care home, Head Start, or children's center. The teacher's task is to develop curriculum that enables such total learning to take place.

But how can teachers go about this? How is it possible to promote creativity, emotional health, physical prowess, social expertise, and cognitive skills in a few brief hours each day? Moreover, how is it possible to weave these into a consistent whole? At first glance it may appear an overwhelming task. However, if we break the task into smaller parts, we will see that it is possible to develop curriculum that does accomplish these goals and brings satisfaction and fulfillment to children and teachers.

The traditional way of breaking curriculum into parts is according to subject matter (Bredekamp & Rosegrant, 1995; Day, 1994; Seefeldt & Barbour, 1998). This approach may feel natural and sensible to us because we have been brought up in an educational tradition in which curriculum is divided according to that system. As children we moved from art class to science class to history class, seeing little relationship between subjects and often ignoring our feelings.

But life is not like that. In life many kinds of learnings happen together and affect each other. Feelings often strongly influence learning ability, and the need for social involvement takes priority over the acquisition of information. In real life all the selves of the child must be included and educated together. Nor does a child grow up in a vacuum—we must always remember to see that child as part of her family, complete with the intricate relationships and cultural values that family holds dear. Only when all these aspects of the person are recognized and provided for in the curriculum can true learning and competence develop.

For this reason, this book advocates designing curriculum that provides a variety of learning opportunities intended to develop competence for each of the selves. This life-oriented approach places the emphasis where it belongs—on the child in the context of the family, not on impersonal subject matter.

Curriculum Supports the Five "Selves"

In this book, the selves (often referred to as "domains") are identified as the physical, emotional, social, creative, and cognitive selves. The physical self is discussed first because a healthy body provides the foundation that enables the other selves to develop and flourish. Curriculum for the physical self covers not only recommendations for the development of physical abilities but also discussions regarding nutrition, cooking, caring for the body, and understanding the cycle of life and death.

The emotional self is emphasized because emotional stability contributes so much to children's sense of well-being and self-confidence. Emotionally healthy children do not need to put their energies into defending themselves from worries and insecurities; instead, they are free to channel their energy into developing their total being, thereby enriching the growth of all five selves. Curriculum for the emotional self involves the planning of experiences that inspire trust, autonomy, and initiative and that teach children to remain in contact with their feelings. Such curriculum uses dramatic play to clarify these emotions and help children understand that other people have feelings, too.

The social self is vital to consider because children must live with other people all their lives. The earlier children can gain skills that help them get along easily and happily with others, the more likely they are to enjoy life and to feel successful. Learning for the social self usually depends on interpersonal encounters between the child and other people, both grown-ups and children. Curriculum to aid such learning promotes the ability to control antisocial impulses. It helps children get along in a group, enjoy playing with other youngsters, and learn to lend a helping hand from time to time. If this curriculum is well presented, it encourages children to treasure their own ethnic and sexual identities and those of other people as well.

The creative self is another vital aspect because creativity greatly contributes to children's sense of self-worth and individuality and increases the probability of unique contributions that they may ultimately make to society. Curriculum for the creative self contains materials that encourage self-expression and pretend play and strategies that enhance the growth of original thought.

Finally, the curriculum for the cognitive self must be as carefully considered as the rest, because the ability to reason and put the results of this reasoning into words enhances children's potential for later intellectual development. Therefore, the cognitive self, though discussed last here, has an important place in school curriculum.

Such curriculum includes experiences and activities that enhance verbal fluency and elicit the use of particular mental abilities. Ideally, it should also encourage children to generate their own ideas and solutions to problems for themselves. Fostering this independent habit of mind is an invaluable aspect of developing the cognitive self.

Figure 1.1 illustrates the five selves of the whole child and some curricular ideas to support each self.

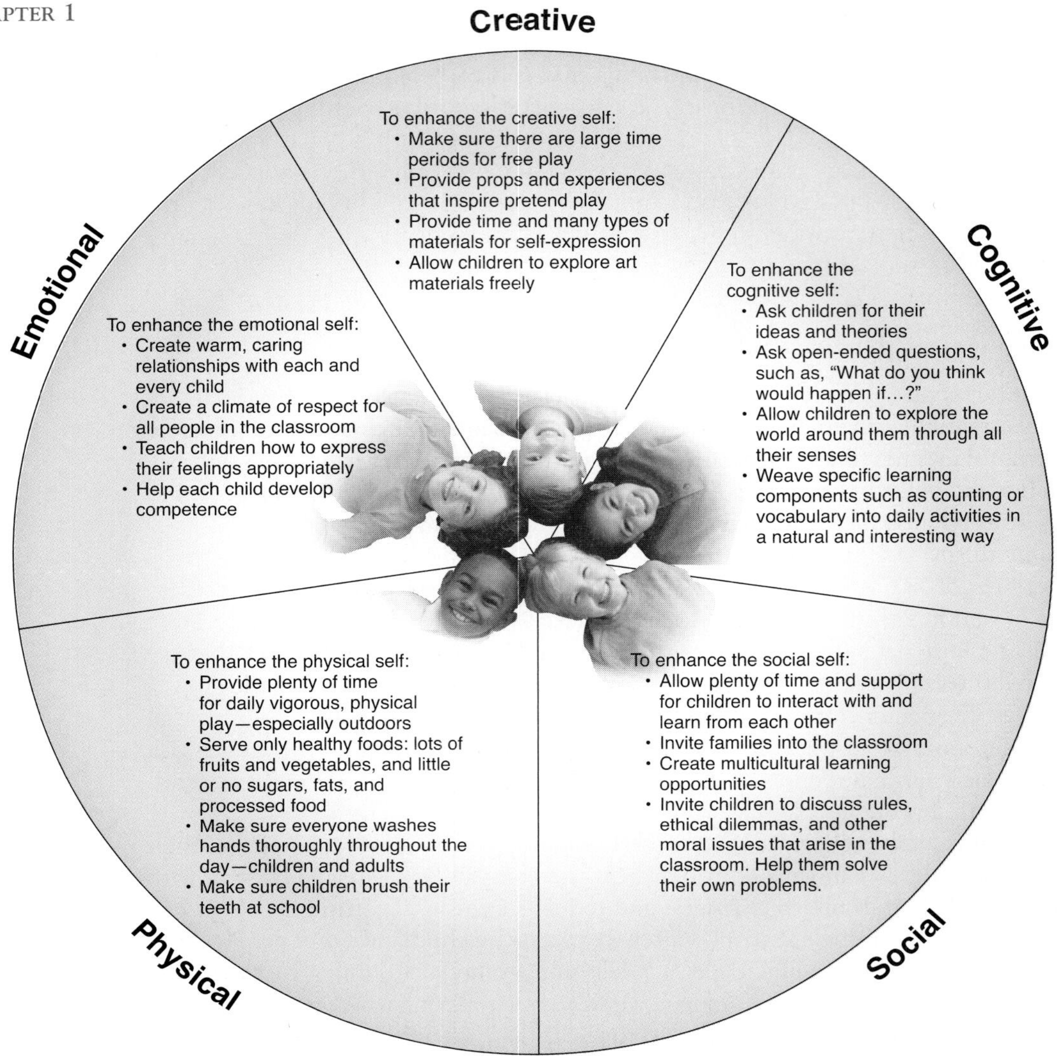

Creative

Emotional

Cognitive

To enhance the creative self:
- Make sure there are large time periods for free play
- Provide props and experiences that inspire pretend play
- Provide time and many types of materials for self-expression
- Allow children to explore art materials freely

To enhance the cognitive self:
- Ask children for their ideas and theories
- Ask open-ended questions, such as, "What do you think would happen if...?"
- Allow children to explore the world around them through all their senses
- Weave specific learning components such as counting or vocabulary into daily activities in a natural and interesting way

To enhance the emotional self:
- Create warm, caring relationships with each and every child
- Create a climate of respect for all people in the classroom
- Teach children how to express their feelings appropriately
- Help each child develop competence

To enhance the physical self:
- Provide plenty of time for daily vigorous, physical play—especially outdoors
- Serve only healthy foods: lots of fruits and vegetables, and little or no sugars, fats, and processed food
- Make sure everyone washes hands thoroughly throughout the day—children and adults
- Make sure children brush their teeth at school

To enhance the social self:
- Allow plenty of time and support for children to interact with and learn from each other
- Invite families into the classroom
- Create multicultural learning opportunities
- Invite children to discuss rules, ethical dilemmas, and other moral issues that arise in the classroom. Help them solve their own problems.

Physical

Social

Figure 1.1
The Five Selves of the Whole Child

Curriculum Should Be Integrated for Young Children

But while thinking of the individual selves, also remember that a sound curriculum not only provides opportunities to enhance the individual selves. In some ways, children are like bicycles: they are greater than the sum of their parts. It is the way the selves of the child operate together that produces the personality, just as gears and wheels operate together to become the bike. Therefore, a well-designed curriculum should be planned to foster this kind of wholeness by providing opportunities for integrating learning. Teachers should intend that every experience they include, whether it be cooking, carpentry, or caring for an animal, educates all the selves, even though it may emphasize only one in particular.

WHAT IS COMPETENCE?

This chapter began with the statement that the purpose of education is to foster competence in dealing with life. But what is competence, and why is it of such value? Competence can be defined as the wonderful feeling of assurance exemplified by the statements "I can do it," "I am able," "I know how," and "I am an effective person." These reveal a security and belief in oneself that are the fundamental cornerstones of self-esteem. The fortunate possessors of such confidence are willing to risk and explore for the sake of learning because they believe themselves to be worthwhile, competent people.

The desire for competence is one of the basic motivators of human behavior. In addition to needing to satisfy hunger, thirst, and other basic physiological needs, human beings have an inherent drive for mastery and competence. It is this drive that urges the infant on in the relentless practice of rolling over or sitting up, and it is the same drive that motivates many adults to pursue evening education classes after a long day's work. The drive for competence results in better academic achievement, better communication skills, and more positive behavioral outcomes (Alexander, 2000; Assets for Colorado Youth, 2002; Cooks & Watt, 2004; Fredericks & Eccles, 2002; White, 1968).

When individuals feel competent, they see themselves, at least to some degree, as in control of their own destinies, and as a result, they feel good about themselves. Bronson (2000) claims that the person who sees himself as competent expects that "under most conditions he is likely to encounter, he will be able to cope with whatever demands he meets, and to derive joy from the encounter" (p. 243). What a marvelous educational goal this is for teachers—to help children attain competence so they may experience joy. And what a powerful antidote this could be for children of the poor, whose abilities are often deemed inadequate as they enter the public school system.

HOW IS COMPETENCE ACQUIRED?

Given that competence is a fundamental goal desirable for education, the question remains: What do teachers need to know and do to foster competence in young children?

What Do Teachers Need to Know to Foster Competence?

Recognize the Family's Influence on Child Development
Teachers must realize that families are the most important influence in the child's development. Teachers sometimes fail to see that they have a limited role in the child's educational experience. The truth is that parents and the cultural/ethnic background of the home exert a much more profound influence than teachers do, particularly during the early stages of development (Bowman, 1997; Hildebrand, Phenice, Gray, & Hines, 2000; Mendoza, Katz, Robertson, & Rothenberg, 2003). This is true not only because of the greater amounts of time children and parents are likely to spend together but also because of the strong emotional bonds that exist between them. Teachers therefore need to keep their perspective about their relative importance and to realize the benefits of including families in the life of the school. As an aid to teachers, suggestions concerning this home–school cooperation are made throughout this book, and chapter 2 is devoted entirely to this subject.

Understand Children's General Capabilities and Interests at Each Age Level
Teachers need to understand the general capabilities and interests common to each age of childhood so they can plan curriculum that is neither so difficult it is discouraging, nor so

Hard to believe that 4-year-old Anthony could be this competent, but he performed this feat a number of times. (He is also the son of a basketball coach.)

easy it is uninteresting. Teachers need to know what constitutes these "typical" or average ages and sequences of growth, not because every child should reach an identical stage at an identical time but also because knowing developmental standards enables teachers to note when a child is markedly "out of sync" with the norm and do something about it. For example, maybe a 3-year-old is still only grunting and pointing when she wants something, or a 4-year-old consistently wets and messes her pants when her mother departs. In cases like these, knowledge of typical patterns is indispensable. A chart of developmental characteristics for the various selves of the child is included in appendix A.

Appreciate the Uniqueness of Each Child

Teachers also need to appreciate the uniqueness of individual children. Although charts can provide helpful baselines of developmental milestones, teachers also must rely on their own sensitivity and powers of observation to identify the variations in personality that make each child someone special.

Is a particular child impulsive or reserved? Easygoing or anxious? What tickles her funny bone? What's she particularly good at doing? What are her favorite pastimes? What might she be on the brink of learning?

How about the family? What do they prefer or anticipate that the school experience will be like? How do they seem to feel about the youngster? How do they define what is "being a good child"?

And what about the neighborhood? Can she play outdoors, or is it too dangerous? How much television does she watch, and what kinds of programs does she see? Who does she play with at home?

All these bits and pieces garnered by the teacher contribute to understanding the child and family and interpreting the child's behavior accurately. Actually, it is all these individual circumstances and variations that make teaching so fascinating.

Know How Young Children Learn

Teachers need to know how young children learn. Although recent evidence indicates that this is a complex question and that the answer varies from child to child, some basic principles about how all young children learn are generally regarded as true.

One such principle is that children pass through a series of developmental sequences as they grow. Children learn to sit up before they learn to stand, and learn to use their fingers before learning to hold a spoon. Such stage-related development has been substantiated by people with such diverse interests as Brittain (1979), Erikson (1963), Gallahue and Ozmun (2005), Piaget (1983), and Shore (1997).

Another related principle is that children learn things a step at a time. This step-by-step learning is often termed *hierarchical learning* because the child moves up a hierarchy rung by rung as skill is acquired. Teachers therefore should plan to teach skills gradually, first teaching simple skills and then more advanced ones as the children gain competence. An important implication of this principle for teaching is that the curriculum must offer a variety of levels of challenge concurrently, because different children in the same group are at different steps on the learning ladder during the same period.

Still another basic principle of learning is that children and adults learn best through actual experiences and participation. John Dewey's concept of learning by doing is as true today as it was in 1916. The truth of this can be seen by reflecting on the process of learning to teach. One can read forever about teaching, but all the reading and discussion in the world cannot substitute for the learning that results from actually encountering the liveliness and variability of young children in the classroom. It is learning by doing—not learning by talking about it—that makes the difference.

For young children who cannot read and for whom language is still new and tenuously grasped, the value of experience-based learning is even more crucial (Bardige, 2005; Fosnot, 2005; Neuman & Roskos, 2005; Piaget & Inhelder, 1969; Vygotsky, 1978). Discussion and verbal learning that are isolated from actual experience have little educative power for such young learners. Instead, learning must be accomplished through all the sensory channels. Children must live through, explore, and try things out to attach meaning to them.

The final principle to remember is that young children learn by using play to translate experience into understanding (Fromberg, 1999; Jones & Cooper, 2005; Paley, 2005; Piaget, 1962). As Frank (1968) remarks,

Children learn from experiences, active participation, and interactions with others.

- *Children pass through developmental sequences.* Infants babble before they form words, utter single words before forming complex sentences, and so forth. This developmental sequencing pertains to each of the five selves.
- *Children learn one step at a time.* A child learns to grasp a crayon and scribble. The child builds up a repertoire of experience before moving to the next stage of drawing, and then the next stage of forming letters. A child cannot master a higher level competency without first experiencing fully the earlier steps.
- *Children learn from experiences, active participation, and interaction with others.* Children learn best when they are able to touch, explore, question, converse, and use all their senses to interpret the world around them.
- *Children learn through play.* Freely chosen, child-directed play is the means by which children process the wealth of information they are gathering about the world: social norms, their own competencies, physical skills, emotions, and creative prowess.

Figure 1.2
Principles of How Children Learn

"Through play, children learn what no one can teach them" (p. 3). For young children, play is the lifeblood of learning, so it is vital that teachers provide extensive opportunities for children to learn through play every time they come to school.

Figure 1.2 summarizes these important principles of how children learn and should be kept in mind throughout the reading of this text.

Know How to Teach Young Children Effectively

Once teachers have a reasonable knowledge of what young children are like and how they learn, they need to understand how to teach them effectively, because the more easily children learn, the more competent they feel. The question of how to enable all children to learn as fully and completely as possible, without pushing them too hard or letting them drift into boredom, remains the continuing challenge of education. Because of a persistent pressure to push formal academic learning on young children before they are ready for it (Elkind, 1990a, 1990b; National Research Council and Institute of Medicine, 2000; Rescorla, Hyson, & Hirsh-Pasek, 1991; Stipek, 2005), teachers must be knowledgeable about what constitutes developmentally appropriate curriculum. In the current era of *standards-based education* in which schools must define "what children should learn and be able to do at certain age levels" (Neuman & Roskos, 2005, p.125), it is even more important that teachers understand the processes by which children learn.

Fortunately, the National Association for the Education of Young Children (NAEYC) has issued a publication titled *Developmentally Appropriate Practice in Early Childhood Programs Serving Children from Birth Through Age 8*, often termed "DAP," which spells out in detail what is and is not appropriate teaching practice for children of that age (Bredekamp & Copple, 1997; Bredekamp & Shepherd, 1990). In particular, the examples of appropriate and inappropriate teaching have helped people both in and out of the profession grasp what quality programs should provide. It has also stimulated development of standards for infants and toddlers (Lally et al., 2003) and for young children with special needs (Sandall, McLean, & Smith, 2000). Having this clearly written information readily available is an indispensable resource, as more and more public school administrators include preschool programs in their communities and need to understand what preschool programs should and should not include.

Meet Relevant Standards While Using Developmentally Appropriate Practice

Teachers need to understand and help children meet relevant standards while still using developmentally appropriate practice (DAP). It is especially important now for teachers to understand developmentally appropriate practice. Since the No Child Left Behind Act was passed in 2002, all public schools—elementary through high school—must adhere to federally mandated learning standards. In other words, all third-graders are expected to achieve a standard level of proficiency in subject areas such as math and language. The cornerstone of the law is standardized testing that requires each state to test children in grades 3 through 8 and at least once in high school (Gillespie, 2005; U.S. Department of Education, 2005). Although testing does not start until third grade, the move toward standards-based education is also gaining momentum in early childhood programs. Since 2003, another federal mandate requires Head Start to develop early learning standards and test every 4- and 5-year-old in the program to assess their abilities. Additionally, several federal initiatives require states to develop early learning standards for children ages 3 through 5 in language, literacy, and math. Forty-three states had developed such standards in the year 2005, compared to only 16 states with early learning standards in 2000 (Neuman & Roskos, 2005).

The movement for standards-based education has resulted in considerable debate within the education field. Although most of us would agree that there should be quality standards for children's education and care, there is disagreement about the appropriateness of mandated standards and testing, particularly with younger children (Meisels & Atkins-Burnett, 2005; Neuman & Roskos, 2005; Stipek, 2005). Fortunately, it is possible—and desirable—to incorporate standards-based education into developmentally appropriate practice. In 2003 the National Association for the Education of Young Children (NAEYC) and the National Association of Early Childhood Specialists in State Departments of Education (NAECS/SDE) issued a joint position statement, *Early Learning Standards: Creating the Conditions for Success*, which provides clear guidance for early childhood teachers. According to the statement, "early learning standards can be a valuable part of a comprehensive, high-quality system of services for young children, contributing to young children's educational experiences and to their future success. But these results can be achieved only if early learning standards emphasize significant, developmentally appropriate content and outcomes" (p. 1). Now, more than ever, early childhood teachers must understand which abilities and behaviors can be expected of children and at what ages.

What Do Teachers Need to Do?

Follow the Guidelines of the NAEYC Code of Ethics Behavior

First, teachers need to know and follow the guidelines for behavior that the National Association for the Education of Young Children has established in its Code of Ethical Conduct for the early childhood profession. These guidelines, updated in 2005, define what our ethical obligations are to families, the community, and above all to the young children in our care. It is helpful to turn to this code for guidance when difficult situations arise—for example, perhaps, as a newly hired aide, you see a teacher pinch a child on the back of the arm, and when she sees you looking at her she shrugs and says, "Don't worry about it! It's OK—I never pinch them hard enough to make a bruise." Of course, you don't want to lose your job, but you know it isn't right to hurt children, either. What should you do?

This example is just one of hundreds of dilemmas—many more difficult to solve than this one—the guidelines can help the teacher resolve.

Work Hard to Meet the Challenge

Teachers have to work hard. Occasional newcomers to the field of early childhood education have the impression that young children are easier to teach or less challenging to

9

control than older children. Of course, this is not true. Teaching young children requires very special energies. As Farnham-Diggory (1992) says so aptly:

> The common denominator of our good teachers is available, well-directed energy. Energy to notice and attend promptly to the individual needs of children; energy to be pleasant and cooperative despite numerous demands from the children; energy to direct aides and volunteers cheerfully and sufficiently; energy to plan, plan, and replan ways of keeping the children busy and independent; energy to keep track of the effectiveness of lessons and other kinds of activities, to keep notes and written guides; energy to explain details of the program to parents and administrators; and, above all, energy to respond warmly and sensitively to children. (p. 54)

The hours are long, and the responsibilities are great because research indicates it is during these very early years that much of the child's basic intellectual ability is formed. Indeed, neurologists now confirm what we early childhood teachers have known on a practical level for a long time. It is that successful development of the brain depends not only on adequate nutrition and health but also, crucially, on the quality and repetition of experience provided to the child during the preschool years (Gallagher, 2005; Nash, 1997; National Research Council and Institute of Medicine, 2000). We must never forget that the work of early childhood teachers and parents carries a very special responsibility with it—and the next day it is there to do all over again.

Take Pride in the Profession

Teachers should take pride in knowing that early education is important. It is a happy fact that during the past two decades research studies documenting the value of early childhood education have become too numerous to report in detail (Barnett & Boocock, 1998; Calman & Tarr-Whelan, 2005; Karoly & Bigelow, 2005; Peisner-Feinberg et al., 1999; Stipek, 2005.) Suffice it to summarize here the results of one pioneer study, still continuing, with a group of people who are now in their 40s. When compared with an equivalent group of children *not* enrolled in preschool, the findings about the Perry Preschool Project reveal that fewer of the children enrolled in the preschool had to repeat a grade in school, or were placed in special educational programs. More of them graduated from high school, and more of them had jobs after graduation. By age 40 they continued to have fewer arrests and higher incomes (Schweinhart, Montie, Yiang, Barnett, & Belfield, 2005).

Besides the studies that are directly related to the effects of preschool education, exciting evidence from an entirely different field of study is accumulating evidence that validates the worth of early learning experiences. This is the area of brain research, where investigators are studying how the human brain actually develops. Examples of those results are included in the following summary.

WHAT DOES RESEARCH ON THE BRAIN REVEAL ABOUT THE VALUE OF EARLY EDUCATION?

How Does the Brain Do Its Miraculous Work?

Although there is still a great deal to learn about how the brain functions, we do know some fundamental facts that all teachers need to understand about how it operates. The brain is composed of billions of specialized nerve cells called *neurons*. These special cells are present at birth. What is *not* present are most of the electrochemical impulses that "spark" across little tendrils (*axons* and *dendrites*) that connect the neurons. These connections are essential because they form networks that transmit impulses between and beyond the neurons to other neurons located in different areas of the brain where different functions are situated. *The more connections made between neurons (and one neuron can have thousands of connections!), the greater the ability of the brain to generate a variety of responses to the environment.* For

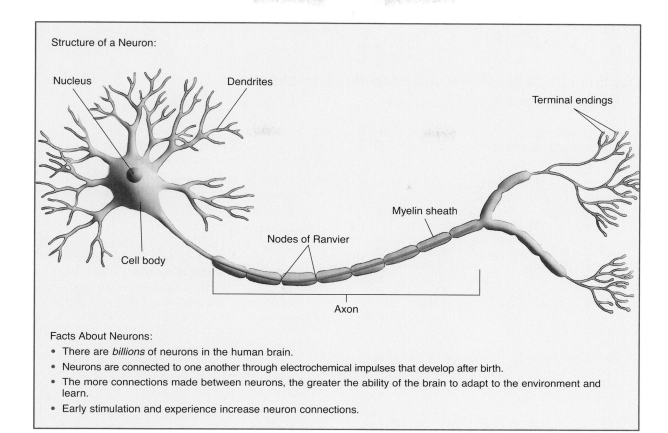

Structure of a Neuron:

Nucleus

Dendrites

Terminal endings

Myelin sheath

Nodes of Ranvier

Cell body

Axon

Facts About Neurons:

- There are *billions* of neurons in the human brain.
- Neurons are connected to one another through electrochemical impulses that develop after birth.
- The more connections made between neurons, the greater the ability of the brain to adapt to the environment and learn.
- Early stimulation and experience increase neuron connections.

Figure 1.3
What We Know About Neurons

example, most of the hearing function is located in one area of the brain, the language function in two others, and higher mental functioning in yet another. The more connections generated among these areas, the richer the potential for learning to use language and have ideas (Bardige, 2005; Gallagher, 2005; Hendrick & Weissman, 2006).

For a view of what a brain neuron actually looks like, see Figure 1.3.

Applying Brain Research to Teaching Young Children

Most of the early work on brain development and how to facilitate its growth was carried out on rats because it is unethical to perform such work on human beings. Although research with rats continues, new instruments now make it possible to do research on human subjects without causing them any pain or endangering them in any way. Such equipment as MRI (magnetic resonance imaging) and PET (positron emission tomography) allows us to see where and how much energy various areas of the brain are using at different times so we can tell when, how, and where development and/or activity is taking place. The increasing or decreasing energy levels thus revealed indicate when children are most likely able to acquire and use particular abilities. For example, the skills related to developing perception and vision have a "prime learning time" (sometimes called a *critical period*) of younger than age 4, and language, including learning a second language, is best acquired by age 10 (Bardige, 2005; Siegel, 1999). For more findings, see the Chapter Spotlight.

A Summary of Findings and Educational Implications Related to Recent Brain Research

Although space does not permit listing all the relevant findings of brain research, some of the most significant ones include the following:

Research Finding: "By the age of three, the brains of children are two and a half times more active than the brains of adults—and they stay that way throughout the first decade of life" (Shore, 1997, p. 21).

Implications for Teaching: The preschool age provides a "prime time" opportunity for learning, provided that learning is presented in appropriate ways.

Research Finding: Experience encourages and strengthens connections among neurons, thereby enhancing learning.

Implications for Teaching: Teachers and families should provide children with a wide variety of interesting experiences combined with many opportunities to repeat them.

Research Finding: Different areas of the brain develop at different times and at different rates.

Implications for Teaching: It is most effective to provide experiences at times when the brain has developed enough to make the best use of that experience. The NAEYC guidelines for developmentally appropriate practice provide teachers and parents with clues about when these periods are likely to occur.

Research Finding: Actual, hands-on experiences help learning "stick" inside the brain. Experience that uses a variety of sensory channels—hearing plus vision plus touch, for example—builds more connections than just looking at or talking about something does.

Implications for Teaching: Don't just talk or read about a subject to the children—provide real experiences whenever possible using as many avenues of sensory experience as possible.

Research Finding: Adding language to actual experiences makes connections even more numerous and thicker than experience alone does.

Implications for Teaching: Tie language and experience together whenever possible. One without the other is not as effective.

Research Finding: Emotional responses in the body affect how well the brain retains (remembers) information. When the body is overstressed and produces too much of a hormone called *cortisol,* some connections between neurons become weakened. However, strong positive emotional attachments have been found to promote and protect neural connections from the effects of too much cortisol.

Implications for Teaching: Keep anxiety levels low when working with young children and be sure to provide as warm and caring an environment as possible.

Research Finding: After age 10 the brain begins to discard unused or "extra" brain cells, but the ability to make and/or rebuild connections is retained throughout life.

Implications for Teaching: The adage "Use it or lose it" turns out to be true, but this does not necessarily mean "the sooner the better"—remember to take into consideration the information about critical periods as well. Also, never give up hope—people can learn at any age—even after "severe insults" to the brain, such as stroke.

Note: For further documentation of these findings, please see Bransford, Brown, & Cocking, 1999; Gallagher, 2005; Halfon, Shulman, & Hochstein, 2001; Shonkoff & Phillips, 1999; Shore, 1997; Siegel, 1999.

Teach Within a Climate of Caring

Teachers must present learning within a climate of caring. Although climate is composed of many elements, it is primarily a product of the teachers' attitudes toward the children and their work and the children's response to these feelings. We must ask ourselves, therefore, what kind of teacher attitude is most likely to promote learning in the classroom. Is it warmth or positive regard or even love? Surely all these qualities are of value in teaching.

Who would not prefer a warm teacher to a cold one, or an approving teacher to one who rejects children unless they conform to his or her demands?

The difficulty with advocating warmth and acceptance does not lie in whether these qualities are desirable. The difficulty lies in asking teachers to feel this way at times when they cannot do it sincerely—times, for example, when a child has deliberately twisted the rat's paw to see it wince or bitten another child hard enough to draw blood. In such circumstances can one feel warm or accepting? And if not, what is left? Is there, indeed, *any* genuine attitude that can be evoked in such highly charged situations, to promote positive growth for teacher and child?

It *is* possible, and that attitude is best described by the word *caring*. Perhaps it is really this quality that Harry Stack Sullivan (1940) has in mind when he comments, "Love exists when the satisfaction or security of another person becomes as significant to one as is one's own" (p. 20). We prefer to substitute the word *caring* for *love* because in our society the word *love* has so many connotations.

Thus, we can say that caring exists when the satisfaction or security of another person becomes as significant as one's own. This attitude fits even difficult circumstances, because it is possible for the teacher to continue to care, and to care intensely, about a youngster even while being appalled at what she has done. In tense confrontations, it is deeply reassuring to children to sense this true concern. It assures them that no matter what they have done, they are important to the teacher and the teacher will not abandon them. Moreover, this reaction has the additional virtue of being absolutely genuine, which thereby makes unnecessary such false declarations of approval as "I like *you* but not what you do."

One final aspect of the Sullivan definition requires comment. The definition states that caring exists when the well-being of another becomes as important as one's own. However, although good teachers give much of themselves to the children and families whom they serve, this should never be accomplished at the expense of caring for themselves. That is why it is so important to remember the second part of the definition, which makes it plain that it is necessary and acceptable to care for oneself as well as for other people. Caring should never be offered in a spirit of self-sacrifice, lest it become martyrdom.

Develop a Clear Philosophy of Teaching

Teachers need to develop a clear philosophy of teaching. This involves identifying those educational values they consider to be most worthwhile and determining the methods of instruction that will implement these values most effectively.

EDUCATIONAL PHILOSOPHIES

Two points of view about how children learn are particularly valuable for early childhood teachers to understand. These are the *behaviorist* approach and the *constructivist* approach. In actuality, no school is likely to be purely behaviorist or purely constructivist, rather, individual schools tend to follow one approach more than the other while remaining somewhat eclectic.

The Behaviorist Approach

The behaviorist approach maintains that the basic principles of learning operate according to the laws of classical operant conditioning. Proponents of this approach advocate using behavior modification techniques based on those principles.

The teachers' role is to select and reward behavior that they wish to continue and to ignore or negatively respond to behavior they wish to extinguish. Therefore, behaviorists recommend that teachers wishing to change a child's behavior should begin by carefully observing the current behavior, determining which rewards are preferred by that child, developing a description of what behavior would be more desirable, and developing and implementing a reinforcement plan or schedule that uses the preferred rewards to select and reinforce the more desirable behavior.

Nowadays it is particularly important to understand the value and uses of behavior modification as an educational approach because of the passage of the Americans with Disabilities Act (Turnbull & Cilley, 1999). This legislation not only mandates that more children with disabilities be included in ordinary school classrooms, but it also mandates that these children be provided with special support services. The vast majority of the specialists who constitute this support personnel use the behavior modification approach because they have found that it can have certain very positive results (Walker & Shea, 1999). Therefore, it is important for teachers to understand and accept the value of these strategies because they will be used increasingly as we welcome children with disabilities into our classrooms.

Although many early childhood teachers say they dislike this rather cut-and-dried, calculated approach to working with children, there is no denying that all teachers, either consciously or unconsciously, use the principles of positive reinforcement every time they smile in approval at what a child has done, just as they use negative reinforcement when they reprimand a child. One advantage of understanding behaviorist learning theory is that it may prevent naïve teachers from unwittingly causing unwanted behavior to continue because they fail to perceive and put a stop to the rewards a behavior holds for a child.

Another advantage of the behavior modification approach is that it encourages teachers to make careful observations of what the child is actually doing, develop clear-cut teaching goals, and formulate plans for how to reach those goals. The written individualized education plans (IEPs) that regulations require be used when working with children who have disabilities are classic examples of this sort of behavior-based goal setting and planning that often embrace the tenets of behavior modification to carry out the plan.

Despite these strengths, there are certain *limitations* to this approach that must also be noted. These include (a) whether specifically trained behaviors generalize to other behaviors, (b) how long the reinforced behavior is likely to continue once the reward is removed, and (c) how tangible rewards (such as candy or gold stars) can be exchanged for more intangible ones later on.

In addition, we raise the question of how such a reward system can create internal rather than external gratifications, so that the child ultimately becomes inner- rather than other-controlled. Also, this kind of extensive planning tends to kill any spontaneity and spur-of-the-moment learning that might otherwise occur. Indeed, Franklin and Biber (1977) comment that programs based on behavior modification techniques seemingly value the more traditional, academic forms of education. These programs often emphasize the use of learning drills and rote memory as educational techniques.

The Constructivist Approach

Because of such problems, many people believe that the strategies of behavior modification provide only partial explanations about how individuals learn, so they favor a *constructivist* approach that stems from the work of Piaget (1983) and Vygotsky (1978). Constructivists see the child as the source of action combined with interaction with the environment rather than being mainly manipulated from the outside as the behaviorists do. They maintain that as the child interacts with the environment, she gradually develops (constructs) inner cognitive structures that help her make sense of her world and that influence her response to the social and physical world in which she lives.

The earliest advocates of constructivism relied mainly on the philosophy of Piaget for support. Some examples of Piaget's contributions to constructivist theory include his emphasis on the value of direct exploration and handling of objects, his focus on the child's inner construction of what she knows, his identification of the various stages of cognitive and moral development, and his demonstrations that the thought processes of children and adults really do differ from each other. For these reasons Piaget's primary contributions to constructivism lie mainly in the cognitive realm.

Recently, as the work of Vygotsky has become more widely known, his theories have further enriched the constructivist base. While acknowledging the active role of the child in learning and developing meaning for herself, Vygotsky emphasized the social influences—the roles other people play—in what and how the child learns. He maintained that through discussion and experiences provided by other people—either children or adults—a child can be encouraged to reach beyond what she currently knows and move closer to the edge of what she "almost" knows, thereby adding to her store of knowledge. The art of teaching, then, is to perceive the child's current intellectual status and sensitively enable her to advance beyond that place through dialogue and questioning.

PHILOSOPHY OF THIS BOOK

Total Learning and its companion book *The Whole Child* (Hendrick & Weissman, 2006) are based primarily on the constructivist philosophy. The books emphasize the value of children figuring things out for themselves as they interact with the environment, and we support the idea that children construct their own knowledge of the world from their interaction with it and the people it contains.

This interpretation of the constructivist approach views interaction as taking place not only between the child and the environment but also among the various aspects or internal selves within the child. The way the child sees and feels about herself influences her ability to learn, just as her potential sense of mastery over cognitive materials increases her sense of self-worth.

It also incorporates the concept that children pass through a number of predictable, orderly sequences in their growth. It uses Erikson as the model for emotional development, Piaget and Vygotsky in relation to cognitive growth, and Gallahue and Ozmun (2005) for sequences of physical development.

The constructivist philosophy emphasizes that it is important to enhance the child's sense that she is a competent, autonomous person in all aspects of her being. The child who sees herself as socially adept, emotionally self-possessed, physically skilled, and intellectually able feels secure and masterful—ready to cope with changes in her environment as they occur, ready to relish life and welcome new experiences.

Although it is necessary to discuss these different aspects of the child's self individually as this book progresses, the overall intention is to blend the needs and education of all aspects together into an integrated, total curriculum and to deal with the child as a whole being. With such a philosophy, learning through play and actual experience is as essential to the curriculum as is the planning that provides for many choices within a carefully arranged yet flexible overall structure.

But do not think that "a carefully arranged structure" implies that a series of lesson plans should be written out months in advance. Instead, think of "curriculum" as an ongoing, developing plan that is sensitive to the children's interests and that incorporates those interests into the plan. This is what is meant by the term *responsive curriculum* because the subject matter is chosen in response to the children's interests and changes as their interests develop.

However, responsiveness is only one half of the curriculum equation. The other half is composed of the vital, more generalized skills the teacher also deems important. For example, these skills might include acquiring a new literacy concept, or becoming more aware of other's feelings, or experiencing the satisfaction of generating a new idea. The topics that well up from the children's interest provide the medium by which these overall concepts can be taught.

PUTTING IT INTO PRACTICE

It is all well and good to espouse an educational theory designed to provide the best opportunities for our children—in fact, it's essential! But the even trickier part is the daily implementation of that philosophy once it comes face-to-face with the children, families, colleagues, and classrooms that make up the educational systems in which we work. How then can we put our well-founded, well-intentioned ideals into actual practice?

Emergent Curriculum

In chapter 17 the emergent approach to curriculum is discussed more extensively. We feel it is important to introduce this approach from the beginning, however, so that as you read the next chapters, ideas for incorporating the emergent approach might percolate. After all, here is an approach that relies on the creativity of the teacher—so curriculum planning becomes interesting and often just plain fun!

The emergent approach is characterized by teacher and children collaborating together to pursue a common interest. The teacher contributes his ideas and information and also listens carefully to the children's comments and questions. He bases decisions about what should happen in the curriculum for the cognitive self as well as for the other selves on what these comments and behaviors reveal to him. That is why this approach is termed *emergent*—it develops gradually (in the same way a water turtle first pokes his head out of the water and then gradually becomes more visible as his body emerges). As the teacher questions the children and elicits their input, a richly developed focus of interest emerges and the investigations or projects can last for weeks or even months (Helm & Beneke, 2003; Helm & Katz, 2001).

Emergent curriculum is an approach well supported by the brain research discussed earlier. A report by Mind in the Making (2005), which summarizes the science of early learning, states:

> Studies across different scientific fields show that young children are most likely to learn: When they are interested and actively engaged; When they are connected to the significant adults in their lives; and When the adult *follows the child's lead*, extending and elaborating on what the child is working on. (p. 4)

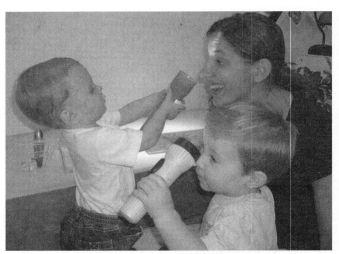

The emergent approach is characterized by teacher and children collaborating together to pursue a common interest.

Occasionally the emergent approach is misinterpreted by novices who conclude that all the ideas must come from the children and that the teacher blindly follows wherever they lead, "just letting the children do whatever they want." But that is not actually the way it works. What really happens is that the teacher may (or may not) have in mind some possibilities to begin with. He discusses potentially interesting subjects with the children and pays careful attention to their comments and questions. Then he analyzes what these reveal so he can selectively choose what he thinks might be the most productive possibilities to pursue further. In the Vygotskian view, the teacher acts as a mentor to the child, suggesting curriculum experiences that start with the child's current knowledge and propel her further into learning something new. As the project develops, the teacher repeats this process many times and adjusts the curriculum accordingly.

In the 35 preprimary schools in the Italian town of Reggio Emilia, the emergent approach has been used for more than 30 years with notable success. Some of the most interesting of the classroom investigations have been documented in beautiful display panels that show the children's drawings, dialogues, photographs, sculpture, and many other creative forms of expression. The documentation panels have been organized into an exhibit touring the United States, titled "The Hundred Languages of Children." The exhibit is moving testimony to the power and beauty of *listening to children* to plan curriculum in an emergent way.

Examples from Reggio Emilia—particularly in the areas of creativity and cognitive development—are provided in *Total Learning* to acquaint the reader with some of the possibilities that the Reggio approach employs.

The Emergent Curriculum in Action feature illustrates how teachers in a Reggio-inspired school in the United States listen to children and collaborate with them in co-constructing emergent curriculum.

Emergent Curriculum in Action

Toddlers' Investigation of Light and Shadow
by Jennifer Sieminski and Ellen Hall
Boulder Journey School, Boulder, Colorado

Context Information:

- There were a total of 11 toddlers in the classroom and two teachers.
- The experience was documented through photographs and notes. Video taping was also used as a source of documentation.

In the beginning of the school year, the teachers noted that even the youngest children were intrigued by light and shadow. The teachers observed children following moving patches of light on the ceiling and floor, attempting to catch the light, touch it, hold it, and taste it. As a result of their observations, the teachers anticipated that light and shadow could be a possible area for research with the children and thus decided to dedicate a space in the classroom for light and shadow exploration. The teachers incorporated an overhead projector, a light table, and flashlights as possible sources of light. As expected, the children were drawn to this space and a deeper investigation of light and shadow naturally emerged. The children were curious about the sources of light—both artificial and natural. They also demonstrated interest in the projection of light onto various surfaces, the movement of light, the interaction of light with other materials, the tangibility of light, and the absence of light—that is, shadows. They also demonstrated interest in the projection of light onto various surfaces, the movement of light, the interaction of light with other materials, the tangibility of light, and the

absence of light—that is, shadows. The following narrative closely examines one piece of this investigation that involved the construction of theories about shadows. This experience occurred throughout the summer of 2004.

The children were truly excited about shadows. When these mysterious dark figures appeared on the shadow screen, the teachers noticed numerous reactions: Some children stared in wonder, other children sought out more physical interactions with the shadows through simple touches and hugs, some children labeled the shadows as "shadow," some children called out their own names when referring to the shadows, and others waved to them. The teachers wondered what they could do to support and extend the children's play and developing theories around shadows. Families had shared that their children were discovering their shadows outside. So as a new provocation, the teachers invited the children outside on a sunny day, hoping that one of the children who had already discovered his shadow outside of school would discover it at school in the company of his classmates, and he did!

Immediately, other children began to discover their shadows. Later in the experience, the shadows surprised the children: One second, the shadows were right below the children's feet, and the next second, the children would look down and their shadows were gone. The children hypothesized that they couldn't see them anymore, because they were hiding. The teachers listened as the children

(Continued)

formulated many theories about where the shadows were hiding—"over the fence," "in the trees," "in the grass," and "up high in the sky."

Outside became a natural playground to test theories about hiding shadows. The teachers researched the position of shadows during various times of day so they knew when to take the children out to look for hiding shadows, both their own shadows and the shadows cast by other objects. The class went outside in all kinds of weather—rainy, cloudy, and windy. The children hypothesized that they would not find shadows outside in the rain because, "It's cold, and they do not like to be wet." On cloudy days the children searched high and low, seeking the shadows' secret hiding places. The days when the clouds moved in and out of the sun in a manner of minutes were best, because sometimes the shadows were visible and sometimes they were not. The children were absolutely ecstatic on these days. In their eyes, the shadows were truly playing a game of hide and seek. The children spent the entire summer outside, chasing shadows and trying to reveal their secrets.

The children and teachers were all learners in the process of supporting a curriculum that would naturally emerge and unfold through the interests of the children. The teachers learned the importance of letting go of their desire to "teach" the children about shadows, specifically about the relationship between shadows and the position of the sun. By offering the children the time and space to investigate shadows outside, they developed a great deal of knowledge about shadows. However, their learning extended far beyond shadow knowledge. The children learned how to work together, how to listen to each other's theories, and how to debate each other's theories. Through this process, they became better able to articulate their ideas. The experience offered authentic opportunities for the children to experiment with their theories that could be either confirmed or disconfirmed. Relationships among the children developed and strengthened as they realized the joy inherent in discovering together and sharing their discoveries with one another. The children and teachers discovered the excitement that results when learning is meaningful, emerging from common interests and curiosities.

Summary

The fundamental purpose of education is to foster competence in all aspects of life, so curriculum should provide opportunities for learning that educate the total self. This is best accomplished by including the five aspects of the child's personality (the physical, emotional, social, creative, and cognitive selves) when planning curriculum.

Total Learning favors a somewhat eclectic approach to early childhood education that acknowledges the contribution of behaviorism but also notes its many limitations. Therefore, while taking that theory into account where relevant, the book generally advocates a more constructivist approach. That approach emphasizes the child's role in constructing what she knows as she interacts with the world around her. To put this philosophy into practice, teachers need to value the family as the most important educational influence in the child's life. They need to know what children are like. They must be knowledgeable about developmental sequences, cultural influences, and individual differences to keep the curriculum both age- and child-appropriate. They need to remember that children learn things a step at a time, learn best through experience, and use play to interiorize knowledge.

Teachers need to comply with the code of ethics that defines their profession. They need to work hard. They must keep up on state and federal initiatives to develop standards and assessments in the schools.

Finally, teachers need to develop a clear philosophy of teaching and to present it in a climate of caring in which the well-being of the children is as important to them as their own. It is this climate of caring that is fundamental to the growth of competence. A powerful way of expressing a climate of caring to children is by listening to them and collaborating with them in developing emergent curriculum.

Food for Thought and Group Discussions

1. Nobody is competent at everything. Think of an area in which you do not regard yourself as skilled, such as playing tennis, using a power tool, or giving a talk. How do you respond when asked to participate in such an activity? And how do you feel when forced to participate?

2. Watch closely the next time you teach. See if you can spot any circumstances in which a child feels incompetent. Was there some way you could have helped him or her cope more satisfactorily? What might be the best thing to say or do when a child says, "I can't"?

3. Considering the opposite of what should be done often stimulates thought. For this reason, suppose you wanted to make children feel as helpless as possible. What could you do to make them feel this way? Give several everyday examples.

4. A family has just entered their child in your preschool. They ask whether he will be learning to write his name, the alphabet, and other skills that he will need before entering elementary school. How would you explain the program at your school so that the family understands what kinds of learning will take place?

5. Do you agree that caring is the most valuable attitude for a teacher to express? What other attitudes are important to project to children?

6. Think of an ethical problem you have encountered or imagine you might encounter as a teacher. Discuss how you feel the problem should be handled.

Self-Check Questions for Review

Content-Related Questions

1. Name the five selves, and mention some areas of curriculum that belong to the separate selves.

2. Name three important principles about how all young children learn. Why do teachers need to know these principles and how to apply them?

3. Describe some recent research findings in the areas of early childhood education and brain development that support the value of early childhood education.

4. Give a brief description of the strengths and weaknesses of the behaviorist philosophy of education.

5. Describe some cornerstones of the constructivist approach that underlie teaching young children. Give some examples of how you would put the constructivist approach into practice.

Integrative Questions

1. Select one activity, such as playing with blocks, and give examples of how creativity, emotional health, physical prowess, social expertise, and cognitive skills can be enhanced while the children are participating in that activity.

2. Taking into account the factors discussed in chapter 1, discuss your own personal requirements that you think a school should meet before you could accept a staff position.

3. You are brown-bagging it with some of your college friends when one of them laughingly comments, "Well—of course, we don't all have it as easy as you— just majoring in that babysitting stuff." What would you reply to convince your friend that early childhood education is a very important profession?

References for Further Reading

Pick of the Litter

Note: The "Pick of the Litter" selection that begins most of the reference lists in this book is a special, often offbeat book the reader might not otherwise encounter or one that is of such importance it must not be missed. We hope you will enjoy them!

Hatton, S. D. (2005). *Teaching by heart: The Foxfire interviews.* New York: Teachers College Press. Renowned educators share their personal stories and insights about teaching. *Fascinating reading!*

Overviews

Bredekamp, S., & Copple, C. (Eds.). (1997). *Developmentally appropriate practice in early childhood programs* (Rev. ed.). Washington, DC: National Association for the Education of Young Children. This book remains one of the most valuable resources in the field. It includes developmental overviews and clear-cut examples of appropriate and inappropriate practice. *An absolutely indispensable reference.*

Curtis, D., & Carter, M. (2005). *Reflecting children's lives: A handbook for planning child-centered curriculum.* (Redleaf Press Series). Upper Saddle River, NJ: Merrill/Prentice Hall. The authors provide many practical suggestions for creating a child-centered curriculum.

Standards

Seefeldt, C. (2005). *How to work with standards in the early childhood classroom.* New York: Teachers College Press.

Wein, C. A. (2004) *Negotiating standards in the primary classroom: The teacher's dilemma.* New York: Teachers College Press.

Here are two helpful guides for early childhood and primary teachers who wish to comply with standards-based regulations while remaining developmentally appropriate.

Competence

Hauser-Cram, P. (1998). I think I can, I think I can: Understanding and encouraging mastery motivation in young children. *Young Children, 53*(4), 67–71. This review of research emphasizes that mastery and competence are integral components of self-worth.

Descriptions of Representative Programs and Philosophies

Helm, J. H., & Beneke, S. (2003). *The power of projects: Meeting contemporary challenges in early childhood classrooms.* Washington, DC: National Association for the Education of Young Children. The authors present detailed discussion and examples of how to use projects as emergent curriculum.

Hendrick, J. (Ed.). (1997). *First steps toward teaching the Reggio way.* Upper Saddle River, NJ: Merrill/Prentice Hall. This book includes clear descriptions of the Reggio approach followed by many chapters depicting actual practices in Reggio-inspired American classrooms.

Roopnarine, J. L., & Johnson, J. E. (Eds.). (2005). *Approaches to early childhood education* (4th ed.). Upper Saddle River, NJ: Merrill/Prentice Hall. This valuable book presents discussions of educational theories/philosophies and descriptions of programs that exemplify the theories.

Professional Ethics

Feeney, S., & Freeman, N. K. (2005). *Ethics and the early childhood educator: Using the National Association for the Education of Young Children code* (2005 Code ed.). Washington, DC: National Association for the Education of Young Children. The authors include the code and discussion of difficult ethical dilemmas with real examples from classrooms.

Information About the Development of the Brain

Bergen, D., & Coscia, J. (2001). *Brain research and childhood education.* Olney, MD: Association for Childhood Education International. The authors summarize the research on brain development and suggest ways to put the findings into practice.

Shore, R. (1997). *Rethinking the brain: New insights into early development.* New York: Families and Work Institute & National Association for the Education of Young Children. This book demonstrates how important early stimulation and education are to fostering the positive development of the brain.

For the Advanced Student

Barnett, W. S., & Boocock, S. S. (1998). *Early care and education for children in poverty: Promises, programs, and long-term results.* Albany: State University of New York. This invaluable reference provides an extensive summary of long-term effects of early education programs on children of the poor. *Highly recommended.*

Nager, N., & Shapiro, E. K. (Eds.). (2000). *Revisiting a progressive pedagogy: The Developmental Interaction Approach.* Albany: State University of New York. Several articles are included describing this delightful early childhood approach to education begun in the 1930s that still has much to offer the contemporary early childhood scene.

Related Organizations and Online Resources

Please note that the organizations listed provide free downloads of their position statements. All childhood educators, in both preprimary and primary grades, should be familiar with the recommendations of these leadership organizations with regard to appropriate teaching in the various subject areas. Those who must follow federal or state guidelines for education standards will find these position statements to be essential reading.

The International Reading Association (IRA) is the world's leading organization of literacy professionals. In 1996, the IRA and National Council of Teachers of English published Standards for the English-language arts to provide guidance in ensuring that all students are proficient language users. In 1998, the IRA and the National Association for the Education of Young Children issued a joint position statement, *Learning to Read and Write: Developmentally Appropriate Practices for Young Children.* http://www.reading.org

The National Association for the Education of Young Children (NAEYC) is the largest membership organization of early childhood professionals. NAEYC sponsors an annual conference, publishes the journal *Young Children,* publishes books, and makes position statements on issues most pressing to early childhood educators. *All NAEYC position statements are available online and are highly recommended.* http//:www.naeyc.org

The National Council of Teachers of Mathematics (NCTM) was founded in 1920 and is the largest mathematics education organization. A joint position statement of the NCTM and NAEYC, *Early Childhood Mathematics: Promoting Good Beginnings,* is available online. http://www.nctm.org.

The National Science Teachers Association (NSTA), founded in 1944, is the largest organization for science teaching. NSTA is part of an ongoing effort to implement the National Science Education Standards, produced by the National Research Council in 1995, in all primary through high school classrooms across the country. http://www.nsta.org

INCLUDING FAMILIES IN THE LIFE OF THE SCHOOL

Have you ever . . .

- Wanted to get to know the family members in your center better but didn't know how to bridge that gap?
- Gotten angry when a parent criticized your program?
- Worried over how to conduct a parent–teacher conference?

If you have, the material in this chapter will help you.

Glooskap and the Baby

*Now it came to pass when Glooskap had conquered all his enemies, even the Kewahqu',
who were giants and sorcerers, and the M'teoulin, who were magicians, and the
Pamola, who is the evil spirit of the night air, and all manner of ghosts, witches, devils,
cannibals, and goblins, that he thought upon what he had done, and wondered if his
work was at an end.*

*And he said this to a certain woman. But she replied, "Not so fast, master, for there yet
remains one whom no one has ever conquered or got the better of in any way, and who will
remain unconquered to the end of time."*

"And who is he?" inquired Glooskap.

*"It is the mighty Wasis," she replied, "and there he sits; and I warn you that if you med-
dle with him you will be sorry."*

*Now Wasis was a baby. And he sat on the floor sucking a piece of maple sugar, greatly
contented and troubling no one.*

*As Glooskap had never married or had a child, he knew little of the way of managing
children. But he was quite certain, as such people are, that he knew all about it. So he
turned to the baby with a bewitching smile and bade him come to him.*

*The baby smiled again, but did not budge. And the Master spoke sweetly and made his
voice like that of the summer bird, but it was of no avail, for Wasis sat still and sucked his
maple sugar.*

*Then the Master frowned and spoke terribly, and ordered Wasis to come crawling to him
immediately. The baby burst out crying and yelling, but did not move for all that.*

*Then, since he could do but one thing more, the Master turned to magic. He used his
most awful spells, and sang the songs which raise the dead and scare the devils. The Wasis
sat and looked admiringly, and seemed to find it very interesting, but all the same he never
moved an inch.*

*So Glooskap gave up in despair, and Wasis, sitting on the floor in the sunshine, went
"Goo! Goo!" and crowed.*

*And to this day when you see a baby well contented, going "Goo! Goo!" and crowing,
and no one can tell why, you will know it is because he remembers the time when he over-
came the Master who had conquered all the world. For of all the beings that have ever been
since the beginning, the baby is alone the only invincible one.**

—Penobscot Indian Legend

There can be no doubt the family is the most important influence on the way children grow
and develop (Berger, 2004; Carter & McGoldrick, 1999; Eliot, 1999; Mendoza, Katz,
Robertson, & Rothenberg, 2003). This is true not only because parents provide the environment that surrounds the child most consistently, but also because profound emotional
ties exist between parents and children. When that potent influence is combined in a positive way with what goes on in the school, the outcome for the child is enhanced even
further (Gonzalez-Mena & Eyer, 2004; Honig, 2002; McBride, 1999). This is the reason

---

* From *Glooskap's Children* (pp. 14–15), by P. Anastas, 1973, Boston: Beacon Press, 1973. Copyright © 1973 by Peter
Anastas.

Total Learning begins with a discussion of practical ways teachers can welcome families into the life of the school from the first days of their teaching careers.

It is also true that beginning teachers do not always welcome the added complexity of relating to parents. Simply getting through group time, managing various behavior difficulties, and putting the children back on the Head Start bus seem like more than enough to cope with without thinking about parent conferencing and home visiting. Indeed, many teachers might prefer not to deal with families at all.

But we must recognize that such a choice is not possible. Teachers need to acknowledge there is an ever-increasing trend in the United States that advocates building a consistent closeness between families and those of us who care for their children outside the home.

Building that closeness can take many forms, ranging from encouraging more volunteer participation by families in the classroom to maintaining toy-lending libraries. Some newer ways to build closeness are even resulting in new kinds of jobs for early childhood teachers. For instance, resource and referral agencies are increasing all over the United States. These agencies serve a variety of functions for parents and caregivers by providing information on child-care vacancies, training for providers, and other benefits. A number of states have also instituted programs of home visitors who regularly visit families in their homes to offer suggestions about how to help the children develop to their fullest potential.

Still another way of building closeness between families and schools comes under the heading *family support systems*. This newer approach stresses the importance of coordinating agency services to families for the sake of not only convenience and better service but also greater economy (Raver, 2005).

Such programs make it plain that parents can no longer be ignored or relegated to a minor role in education. That is why this chapter is devoted to discussing ways of building bonds between home and school so that children will feel their world is a consistent whole rather than split into the unrelated halves termed *home* and *school*.

There are many ways of enriching this family–school bond, and strategies must necessarily vary to suit individual school situations. But all early childhood settings—whether they are half-day preschools, family child care, full-day child-care centers, or grades K through 3—should strengthen and weave together three basic home–school strands: strands of human relationships that let families know we care about them and their children, strands that accept help from families so that the lives of the children at the center are enriched, and strands that offer help to families to strengthen family life.

LETTING FAMILIES KNOW WE CARE ABOUT THEM AND THEIR CHILDREN

Building a Climate of Trust

There is no substitute for the gradual establishment of trust that can be built between teacher and parent when it is based on easygoing, consistent daily contact between them. It takes time and personal contact to make friends. To accomplish this, the teacher should make deliberate plans to be available while children are arriving, to make each youngster personally welcome and have a friendly word with the parent, too (Gonzalez-Mena & Eyer, 2004; Honig, 2002; Lally et al., 2003).

Strange as it may seem at first thought, the very beginning of the day is *not* the time for the teacher to be preoccupied with the children. If families are truly part of the life of the school, this transition should be thought of as being the part of the daily curriculum intentionally devoted to "family time." This is the part of the day when the teacher takes a genuine interest in the small details of each family's life. Needless to say, it takes a good memory to remember to ask about the anticipated kittens or how the grandparents' visit is coming along, but doing this helps build the friendliness that fosters trust. It also makes it more likely that the family will have opportunities to share helpful information about the child. Maybe Rosie has just gotten a new pair of shoes, or Tony has lost a tooth. Perhaps the parent is worried because a youngster has been having nightmares, or the child is very tired because he stayed up late to meet his father's plane the night before. These tidbits can contribute a lot to the teacher's understanding of the child's behavior, as well as build bridges of deepened understanding between the home and center.

Building trust also means that the teacher refrains from talking about a family's affairs with other people. This requires good judgment, as sometimes families are in a position to help each other if they know that such help is needed.

Making Visits to the Children's Homes

When "home visiting" is mentioned, two kinds of visits come to mind. The first involves regular, repeated contact in the home by specially trained people. These home visitors often provide a combination of information, comfort, and support to the home caregiver—typically the mother—and provide activities and encouragement for the children, too (Gomby, Culross, & Behrman, 1999; Raver, 2005).

In the majority of early childhood programs (aside from Head Start, which has a home visit component), visits happen less frequently—partly because of the time and expense involved and partly because of teachers' shyness and other responsibilities. Even though such visits take time and extra effort, it is also true that making even occasional home visits is one of the best ways to build trust and make friends with the families.

Although space does not permit a lengthy discussion of how to conduct successful visits, a few reminders can help get visitors off to a good start. For one thing, always let families know before stopping by—this can be done by telephone, e-mail, or even postcard if other means are not available. Remember, it is the family's right to refuse, and occasionally people consider such visitors intrusive spies, not friendly guests. During the visit, anticipate that the child will be thrilled and after some initial hesitancy will want to show you personal treasures. A new child will enjoy receiving a name tag, pencil, or some other token from you to help bridge the gap between home and that unfamiliar place called school.

It is also helpful to have in mind a handful of nonthreatening, get-acquainted questions to ask family members about the child—perhaps what his favorite foods are, what he likes to do best, and how you can help him feel comfortable at school. This is also a fine time to explain that the family members are always welcome to come to the school too, and to encourage them to remain until the child feels at ease.

If refreshments are offered, be sure to accept them freely—even if it means consuming three pieces of cake, a brownie, and a glass of wine all in one afternoon—as it is likely the parent has gone to special trouble to provide them.

Finally, for the sake of the teacher's time and also the family's, it is important to limit the length of each encounter. If the teacher politely mentions at the beginning of the visit she can stay only half an hour and has just stopped by to get acquainted, that will help the family know what to expect and not feel slighted when it is time to go.

Keeping Families Informed

A somewhat more impersonal but still useful way of emphasizing that the school cares about families, as well as the children, is by providing information to parents about what the children are doing in school. Many schools use a bulletin board by the sign-in sheet for this purpose, but some parents never seem to read this—and they certainly will not continue to check it unless the material is eye-catching and frequently changed. When kept current and relevant, bulletin boards have real, practical value. For example, it is constantly necessary to make certain that parents understand that early childhood education is purposeful, and a weekly curriculum chart posted on the bulletin board will emphasize that teachers are not babysitters.

Many centers also make use of a monthly newsletter, and these are excellent public relations vehicles (Diffily & Morrison, 1996; Power, 1999). One month a newsletter might concentrate on the cognitive skills the school is developing, and another could focus on ways the school fosters emotional health. In addition, it might include a calendar of events, recipes from the potluck dinner, general news about what the children will be doing during the coming month, or requests for "freebies" for the school. If bilingual families are part of the school, it is important to include material in both languages to make them feel welcome and let them know what is happening. Otherwise the language barrier may persist and perpetuate a feeling of being outside and apart from the school (Barrera, 2001).

Another method of keeping families informed about the children's activities comes from the schools of Reggio Emilia. Teachers there document children's projects with photographs, artwork, and transcribed pieces of dialogue, using them to create attractive displays in the school. When families enter the classroom they are drawn into the children's work and can see for themselves the depth of learning that takes place (Edwards, Gandini, & Forman, 1993, 1998).

ACCEPTING HELP FROM FAMILIES TO ENRICH THE LIVES OF CHILDREN AT THE CENTER

Fortunately, research supports the impression that parents and teachers agree on the skills that are most important for young children to acquire—and that agreement is not limited just to parents and teachers in the United States. Following a careful analysis of expectations in 12 countries, Weikart (1999) reported that both families and teachers identified developing skills with peers, language skills, and self-sufficiency skills as being the most important skills for young children to acquire.

Accepting and Using Criticism

There are also times, of course, when families and teachers *do not* agree. When that disagreement takes the form of criticism, many teachers become so upset and angry they are blinded to the possibility the comments could be helpful. Despite the initial reaction, it is important to pay attention to families when they express such concerns and to benefit from what they have to say. Sometimes, if teachers listen instead of rushing in with a lot of defensive remarks, such information can lead to changes that are more satisfactory for everyone. Teachers should remember that if one parent complains, possibly others are also dissatisfied but are too intimidated to speak up. For example, recently, a parent complained to us after her little boy arrived home for the third time in 2 weeks wearing someone else's sneakers. (At least one other family must have been unhappy!) She had a well-taken point, which was ultimately solved by color-coding 11 identical pairs of dark blue sneakers with dabs of tape so that children could match them up themselves.

Sometimes parents criticize policies because they do not understand what is going on. A father may be uneasy when he finds his little boy dressed up in a dance tutu or frilly dress. Another parent may wonder (as many do) when the children are "really going to learn something." It is best to view such critical-sounding queries as opportunities for explaining the educational purposes behind what is going on at school. Families are entitled to such information. *If, by chance, teachers find themselves unable to produce sound reasons for the inclusion of particular activities, perhaps they should think further about whether something else might be more profitably substituted for these activities in the future.*

Of course, it is not always possible for family and school values to coincide. The staff of our center believes that parents' wishes should be honored whenever possible, and so we are willing to cut naps short when a parent tells us her 4-year-old will not go to bed until 10 if we do not, or to help children follow religious dietary rules, or to change an occasional youngster into school clothes before letting him play in the mud.

On the other hand, we would not be willing to allow a child to roam around the room during lunch, eating as he goes, nor would we ever spank a child who has messed his pants, no matter what the family advised. When this kind of conflict occurs between home and school values and, for one reason or another, neither side feels it can compromise, we just say clearly to the child, "Well, there are home rules, and that's what you do at home, and there are school rules, and this is what the rules say you do here." In other words, when necessary, we are frank about the fact that different places have different rules. This is not too difficult for children to understand, and we believe that it is better than undercutting families by secretly defying their standards or cultural practices or implying to the children that the school is totally right and their homes are totally wrong.

Drawing on Families as Resources

Examples are cited throughout this book of ways parents can serve as resources for enriching the children's lives, so we will provide only an overview of such possibilities here. It is remarkable the kinds of contacts families have within the community and the amount of help families can offer once they are aware of what is needed. When asking about such resources, remember to be precise about what is needed and to furnish examples so that people really understand what you are looking for.

In addition to unearthing sources of free materials, parents often know of special animals, or they are acquainted with people who would be of interest to the children, or they may know of a fascinating place to visit, such as the back room of a bakery or a goat farm, and will help make the arrangements. Then, too, families themselves are so varied and have so many talents that it would be a pity to overlook them. Remember that family members include grandparents, aunts and uncles, and brothers and sisters, as well as parents, and these people often have special talents and free time they enjoy sharing with the children. During a recent few weeks, our center has welcomed a flute player, the owner of a large snake, and members of a Boy Scout troop, while these guests' young relatives basked in the reflected glory.

Family Members as Volunteers

Not all family members like working directly in the school (after all, a perfectly valid reason for sending children to school is so mothers and fathers can have time to themselves, and most parents work all day), so it makes sense to emphasize to families that volunteering can take many different forms. Producing the resources we discussed earlier is such a variation. Serving on a family advisory board, working on a potluck, or participating in a cleanup and painting day are other valuable contributions.

Participating in the Classroom. When family members do want to participate directly with the children, several basic things can be done to make them feel truly accepted and welcome. Always bear in mind that the primary purpose of having the volunteer at school is to provide a situation that *both the volunteer and children will enjoy* and not just to comply with a mandated family involvement component. This means that whatever activity is selected, it has to be something that does not entail a lot of potential discipline problems, it should not be demeaning (cleaning the animal cages, for example), and it should not be something that demands expertise the visitor may not have (such as being in charge of an entire group time).

It *should* capitalize on the interests and strengths of the volunteer—and if you have made a consistent point of becoming acquainted with the families, you can usually develop a pretty good idea of what these abilities are.

It works best to get volunteers together ahead of time to talk over basic school ground rules and ask them what they would like to do. A list of possibilities can help stimulate ideas. These might include reading to the children, cooking something with them, bringing a baby to share, or coming along as the additional adult needed on a field trip. If the volunteers can choose what they prefer doing, they will be more at ease than if such activities are simply assigned to them.

When volunteers come to school, it is important to pay attention to them so they feel truly welcome. Wachter's book *Classroom Volunteers: Uh-Oh! or Right On!* (1999) is packed with useful suggestions about how to do this even when the teachers are very busy.

Teachers sometimes fail to appreciate that being a volunteer is stressful. To feel competent, volunteers need specific instructions about what to do, and they also deserve to be thanked sincerely upon departure. Probably the best advice to give teachers working with volunteers is that they should ask themselves from time to time how *they* would feel if they were the volunteer and what they would say the staff could do that would make them want to return for another day. Then, of course, those teachers should accept their own advice and proceed accordingly.

OFFERING HELP TO FAMILIES TO STRENGTHEN FAMILY LIFE

Suggestions for Conferences with Families

Private conferences with families are one of the most satisfactory ways of providing help on a personal basis, but they do have the unfortunate tendency to make both teacher and families nervous. Realizing that this nervousness is typical and acknowledging this recognition to the families can help overcome such feelings. The daily informal chats recommended earlier help, too, but it really takes more than one conference to get past this hurdle.

Conferences are primarily useful because they provide private, uninterrupted opportunities for conversation, and there is no chance that the child might overhear the discussion. They are appropriate places to review the youngster's progress and to produce the checklists, observations, or portfolios that document that development. If begun early in the year when the teacher is just becoming acquainted with the child, conferences can help establish mutual respect between teacher and family. This is because the family can be cast in the role of knowing more about the child than the teacher can possibly know at this point.

Inevitably, conferences are also used to discuss problems, and, if that is the case, it is sensible for the teacher to avoid giving the impression of taking the parents to task for their child's foibles. Each child has a unique temperament from the time of birth, and it is not always within the family's ability to change some of these characteristics. The child is a powerful agent in creating his or her own behavior no matter how diligently parents may attempt to change it. That is why this chapter opens with the Glooskap legend; it is intended to remind adults to retain their sense of proportion and remain aware of that personal, individual power that comes from within each person.

More productive than indulging in the shaming-blaming syndrome (which is likely to elicit a similar retaliatory attack on the teacher by the family) is using conference time for the mutual purpose of sharing information and discussing alternative solutions.

In general, the teacher who has a listening ear and a quiet tongue will find the most positive changes taking place for the children and the families, should changes be needed. Parents often know deep inside what would be a good solution; the well-done conference can provide families with the chance to talk the situation through, weigh alternatives, and

Conferences should present an opportunity for sharing information and discussing alternative solutions.

decide for themselves what action to take. Only in this way are changes really brought about. Listening more than talking, however, does not mean that teachers should not contribute suggestions and ideas drawn from professional experience and training—they should. It *does* mean that the right to make the decisions rests with the families.

Meetings About Parenting

Many parents also benefit from opportunities to learn more about children in a general way, and, for this reason, parenting meetings are an additional helpful service offered by many schools. Some cooperative schools meet every week for discussion, which provides splendid opportunities to develop an informed population of parents who form close bonds with the other families as well as with the school. Families in most schools do not meet that frequently, so special attention must be paid to keeping the thread of relationships and continuity stretching from one meeting to the next.

Finding Appropriate Topics

Because *Total Learning* is, basically, a book about curriculum, a few suggestions about curriculum for family meetings are in order. An appealing topic to begin the fall might be a discussion of the curriculum and philosophy of the school, replete with visual aids such as pictures of their children involved in the activities. It often works well to ask families what they would like to discuss at the next meeting and to build continuing meetings from their input. Additional topics that are usually of interest include building inner controls in children (or themselves), understanding the father's influence in children's development, coping with jealousy in youngsters, defining nonsexist education, learning how to teach sharing, helping children through crisis situations, being a single parent, recognizing the characteristics of good toys, and fostering mental ability in young children.

We have found that using a relevant videotape as a basis for discussion is particularly helpful early in the year, because it gives a group who may not be acquainted with each other something in common to talk about. Such media are readily available from various catalogs, such as the one from the National Association for the Education of Young Children. There are also 13 half-hour videotapes that accompany *The Whole Child: Developmental Education for the Early Years* (Hendrick & Weissman, 2006), which cover a range of topics of interest to families.

Another effective way to entice families to attend a program is to use slides of their children participating at school. This is an especially effective approach when discussing why various activities are included during the school day—just remember that families will be looking for pictures of *their* child, so a wise teacher makes certain that every youngster is included.

Presenting the Topic

Many teachers feel anxious about leading such meetings and so, time after time, fall back on guest speakers. Although such visitors can bring special expertise and information, they have no way of knowing the people in the group and the significance of questions they may ask. The presence of visitors also reduces the chance for families and teachers to talk together about a topic of general mutual interest.

For these reasons, it is more desirable for teachers to pluck up their courage and lead the meetings themselves. They must remember that these meetings do not have to be, and really *should not* be, presented as lectures, anyway. People learn much more from discussing and sharing information than they do from just sitting and listening.

The secret of leading successful discussions is identifying the important points for people to learn before beginning, making certain that these points are covered during the discussions, developing a good selection of thought-provoking questions to pose to the group, and having the patience and courage to wait for the replies, particularly at the beginning of the discussion when people are feeling shy. Summarizing at the close is also helpful. It is really the same strategy recommended in chapter 17, in which the generation of creative thinking skills is discussed in relation to young children and to emergent curriculum.

Role playing, breaking into small groups to discuss special points, and participating in panel discussions are additional effective ways to produce interesting family nights, particularly after people are fairly well acquainted.

It is also effective to give families the opportunity to explore the same materials, such as clay and finger paints, as the children. At the New City Center in Chicago, families and community members are invited "to be a part of what we're doing, a part of our setting" (Kaminsky, 2001, p. 9). According to center director Kelsie-Miller:

> The parents feel valued. I remember an open house when the teachers set out activities for the parents. In one classroom, a father made a car out of clay. The next day, he brought his son to school and showed him what he had done. His son was so proud that the father decided to make another car. He was amazed at his son's reaction and thrilled that we displayed his work with that of the children. This father was one of the parents who didn't come into the school that much. After that, he began to come into the school more often. (Kaminsky, 2001, p. 9)

Including Time for Socializing to Take Place

Although education is often the ostensible reason for holding community meetings, another important value should not be overlooked. Meetings can also provide valuable social opportunities for families. These are especially nice for homemakers, particularly single parents, who may not get out much and are feeling isolated and lonely. The chance to be with other people who have similar problems and concerns can furnish real emotional support for such people, as well as simply providing fun. Therefore, part of every meeting should allow time for human friendliness. Refreshments offered beforehand or at a break give people something to do with their hands so they feel less self-conscious and furnish chances for them to become acquainted, too.

Sometimes it can be worthwhile to dispense with the program altogether and have a potluck dinner instead. There is no better way to build a comfortable, relaxed bond between home and school than by eating together.

WEAVING ALL THREE STRANDS TOGETHER

This chapter began by identifying three important strands to include when weaving together the fabric of children, teachers, and family: letting families know we care about them and their children, accepting help from them to enrich the lives of the children at the center, and offering help to strengthen family life.

It is so important to let families know we care about them and their children.

It seems the majority of American schools and children's centers are most comfortable letting parents know they care about them and their families, asking them to provide resources, and offering help to them. They are much less comfortable accepting criticism, requests, suggestions for change, or other forms of "interference" with the way the center operates.

The question then becomes: But how can we overcome this discomfort and empower families to participate more fully? What if we genuinely wish to strengthen the thread of welcoming more family input? Are there places right now where power is shared more equally between families and teachers, thus weaving the tapestry of the child's life into a more consistent design? The answer is: Yes, there are! The Chapter Spotlights on pages 31 and 32 provide examples of how two very different children's centers incorporate that stronger teacher–family strand into the life of their schools.

HELPING FAMILIES IN NONTRADITIONAL SETTINGS

Nowadays families come in a fascinating array of configurations, and it is absolutely vital for the teachers of young children to take these variations into account as they welcome them into the life of the school. The old, stereotyped picture of Father going off to work while Mother stays home and bakes cookies lies far from current reality for many people. (Refer to chapter 11 for a discussion of handling crises such as divorce, and to chapter 13 for information on families from various cultural and ethnic backgrounds.)

Some information garnered by the Children's Defense Fund (2004) from the Bureau of Labor Statistics and the Census Bureau include the following points:

- Despite the overwhelming prosperity of the United States, one child in five is born into poverty.
- One out of every three children will live in poverty at some point in their childhood.
- A quarter of all children live with only one parent.
- 60% of preschoolers have their mother in the labor force.
- One in five children is an immigrant or has immigrant parents.
- One in every eight is born to a teenage mother.

The Parent-Resource Strand in the Preprimary Schools of Reggio Emilia

Reggio Emilia is a moderate-size city in northern Italy that has sponsored a remarkable collection of infant, toddler, and preprimary full-day children's centers since the end of World War II. These are the schools whose philosophy has been exemplified by the "Hundred Languages of Children" exhibit that has toured the United States since 1987.

Since additional aspects of that philosophy will be described in more detail from time to time, suffice it here to provide an introduction by quoting Edwards, Gandini, and Forman (1998):

> Young children are encouraged to explore their environment and express themselves through all of their available "expressive, communicative, and cognitive languages," whether they be words, movement, drawing, painting, building, sculpture, shadow play, collage, dramatic play, or music to name a few. From the beginning there has been an explicit recognition of the relationship or partnership among parents, educators, and children. Classrooms are organized to support a highly collaborative problem-solving approach to learning. (p. 7)

Because the teachers remain with the same group for the 3 years the children attend the preprimary center, there are rich, ongoing opportunities for families and staff to become closely tied to one another. Families, children, and staff are viewed as three corners of a triangle wherein each corner supports the others. The emphasis is on communication and collaboration, so the well-being of everyone is valued and taken into account. Feelings of warmth and concern are evident throughout.

Management of the centers is inextricably intertwined with decisions by elected advisory councils at the local school and citywide level in which parents have a vital participatory role, and communication and collaboration are the keynotes. Individual family participation includes additional opportunities to talk and collaborate—including classroom and small group meetings, work sessions, and participation in celebrations, excursions, and parent education round tables and lectures. The focus of these activities is always on ways to enhance the well-being and wholesome growth of the children.

Note: For further information, refer to *First Steps Toward Teaching the Reggio Way,* by J. Hendrick, 1997, Upper Saddle River, NJ: Merrill/Prentice Hall.

Families in Which Both Parents Work Outside the Home

Compared with a generation ago, it is no longer unusual for both parents to work outside the home. Thus, considerable effort must be made to accommodate the circumstances of so many families today, including the following suggestions:

- Adapt center hours as much as possible to meet families' needs in a realistic way.

- Plan events so that working parents can attend. Perhaps a Saturday visiting day could be included; night meetings are also helpful.

- Set aside an evening or early morning for parent conferences. If conference times are planned for late afternoon, be sure to provide a bite to eat during the conference to reduce fatigue.

- Develop a list of people willing to care for children who are ill, and make this list available to families. (A handful of schools make provision for sick-child care on their own premises.)

- Be careful to keep the emergency call list for each child up-to-date so that permission is on file when parents have someone else pick up the child from school.

The Parent-Resource Strand in the Parent–Child Workshops of Santa Barbara, California

There are four parent–child workshops in Santa Barbara sponsored by the adult education division of the local community college that have flourished for more than half a century. The workshops are cooperative half-day nursery schools. Each school features two salaried staff—a director and assistant director—enhanced by parents who, along with the staff, assume direct teaching responsibilities. Children may attend daily, and an adult from each family participates twice weekly—once during the morning and again at an evening meeting.

The children's program is based on the philosophy that play is the mode through which children learn most naturally, and the curriculum emphasizes the value of positive social learnings, emotional health, opportunities for creative expression and development of language and cognitive abilities.

The parent–family program offers unique opportunities during daytime participation for the directors to model desirable ways to interact with children and to encourage family members to try different approaches. Families are encouraged to serve as curriculum resources for the children's program, and the variety of learning that takes place as a result is wonderful to see. The evening programs provide additional opportunities for adults to talk and learn together—these might feature informative discussions, videos, panels, and talks related to parent interests, work nights, planning for special events, and so forth.

Note: For further information, refer to "*It's the Camaraderie*": *A History of Parent Cooperative Preschools,* by D. Hewes, 1998, Davis: Center for Cooperatives, University of California.

- Reassure families that good parenting is a matter of spending "quality time" with their children and does not depend on the total amount of time—and help them define "quality time."

- Keep informed on tax information so that you can furnish correct information about the Earned Income Credit and the Child and Dependent Care Credit for parents who ask about them.*

- Make it clear that you respect whatever kind of work the parents do. If possible, arrange for a group of children to visit the workplaces. Encourage family members to come and explain their jobs to children at the school.

Families Headed by a Single Parent

Despite current trends, a stigma is still attached to being divorced. Therefore, try to overcome whatever critical feelings you may have about the pros and cons of divorce. Problems related to that situation are complex enough for the parents without having to deal with your prejudice, too. The following are some suggestions:

- Avoid using such terms as *broken home* and *fatherless children*. A more acceptable term could be *single-parent family*, because being a family does not necessarily depend on having a mother and father present in the home.

- Avoid taking sides with one parent or the other; it is likely that neither is all right or all wrong.

---

* Contact the Internal Revenue Service (http://www.irs.gov), or the National Women's Law Center, 11 Dupont Circle NW, Suite 800, Washington, DC 20036 (http://www.nwlc.org/).

- Remember that single-parent families are very likely to have low incomes. Newly divorced families may experience special problems in this regard and will benefit from referral to appropriate social agencies.

- Many single parents are lonely; they find themselves gradually excluded from contact with couples and at a loss to know how to handle holidays without a spouse. Suggestions and information can be very welcome if tactfully presented.

- Notices about community activities such as meetings of Parents Without Partners or We Care (for those whose spouse has died) should be routinely posted.

- Make it a point to introduce single parents to each other. They could be encouraged to develop a support group of their own within the school.

- Avoid deploring the fact the parents are divorced. Instead, be on the lookout for the strengths demonstrated by the single parents and comment on these in an encouraging way.

- Be sure to send notices offering conferences to *both* parents. Occasionally both will attend the same meeting, but frequently the parents prefer to come separately, and so conferences will require more of your time.

- *Be sure you are aware of the custody provisions for the child.* Know who is permitted to take the child from the school. Although this is often a friendly arrangement between divorced parents, sometimes it is not, and the school is legally responsible for the child's safety while on those premises.

Blended Families

Often considerable stress arises when parents remarry and blend families together. Schools can at least avoid contributing to such stress by doing some of the following:

- Understand that children going through the blending process may be confused or upset. They have to deal with feelings related to loyalty, jealousy, anger about possible rejection, confusion over authority, and so forth (and so do all the parents).

- Joining a blended family often means a child's birth order shifts dramatically. For example, a former "only" child might become a middle child with older and younger siblings.

- Be aware that stepparents often are not legally entitled to grant permission for medical treatment. Clarify this with the families *before* an emergency happens.

- Offer the children the opportunity to make something for both stepparents and natural parents at holiday times.

- Remember to include the stepparents in school functions. They are often ignored, and it should be their choice and the child's whether they will attend.

- Avoid the temptation to pass judgment on which reconstituted side of the family is doing the better job with the child in your care.

Families Who Have Very Low Incomes

Low-income families have specific needs that the school environment can and should address, as follows:

- Be matter-of-fact, not condescending or pitying.

- Be especially careful not to offend family members. Families on food stamps may not appreciate artwork made from macaroni or chocolate pudding finger painting. Nor do they feel comfortable with pictures of children who have heaps of presents around them during the holidays.

- Process agency papers, such as applications for child-care vouchers, as quickly as you can. Families' reimbursement or income may depend on your efficient paperwork.

- Be particularly aware of community resources—when and where food stamps are available and what the hours are for the county health clinic, for example.

- Deliberately build your own acquaintance with various social agencies. A friendly call from you will often help a parent use the system more effectively.

- Provide a clothing exchange for outgrown but not worn-out children's clothing.

- Offer a food coupon exchange in which people can leave or take whatever coupons they wish.

- Acquaint yourself with the state welfare aid regulations. There may be portions of those regulations that families do not know about that could benefit their children if used.

Families Who Have a Child with a Disability

The enactment of the Individuals with Disabilities Education Act (IDEA) combined with the Americans with Disabilities Act (ADA) means that more and more schools are gathering children with disabilities and their families into their schools, so some suggestions for helping those families fit comfortably into the group are worthwhile to include here. (Please note that many additional recommendations are incorporated throughout the text to help these children participate successfully as part of the group.)

- Always remember that children with disabilities are more like other children than they are different. It is important to see past the atypical qualities of the child to the typical qualities as well.

- Remember that participation in your program may be the first major encounter the family has with an organized group of typically developing children. These first encounters are often particularly stressful for the families because of contrasts in behaviors or abilities that may be apparent between their children and others in the group.

- Provide brief, matter-of-fact explanations of the child's disability to the other children and/or their parents to satisfy their concerns and curiosity about the child's brace, inability to hear, or unusual behavior, for example.

- It is vital to be truthful as well as kind and gentle when discussing the child's accomplishments with the family. Although it is delightful to rejoice in what the child has learned, it is also important to acknowledge limitations to keep reality in focus.

- Be aware that the child's siblings, who may also be attending your school, may be suffering from an intense and painful mixture of feelings about the child with special needs. These emotions can include protectiveness, jealousy, feeling left out, plus a multitude of other ambivalent feelings. Such conflicting emotions, often expressed as anger or a high level of frustration, may require special patience and attention from the teacher.

SUMMARY

Families are a tremendously significant part of the child's life, and children's centers should make every effort to weave bonds between home and school that make the fabric of that life complete and whole. The first strand in this process is letting families know that teachers care about them and their children. This can be accomplished by establishing a condition of trust between home and school through consistent, daily contact; handling separations with caring concern; and keeping families posted on school activities by means of bulletin boards, newsletters, and other forms of documentation.

The second strand in our tapestry—accepting help from families—is not always easy, particularly when the help comes in the form of critical comments and questions, but even these can benefit the school and the family–teacher relationship if handled maturely. Two other less threatening ways family members can offer the school help are by providing resources of various kinds and by participating directly in the school with staff and children. Such participation requires special preparation and planning by staff so that the volunteers and children gain feelings of competence and happiness as a result of that experience.

The third way of drawing families and teachers together is by offering help to strengthen family life. This should include adjusting the center's services for those who do not fit the traditional middle-class stereotypes of family life. Conducting individual conferences is one way of providing such help; making friendly visits to the home and sponsoring meetings on parenting concerns can also be effective. Potluck suppers and visiting days at school offer additional excellent opportunities for staff and families to become better acquainted so that more interchange can take place.

Food for Thought and Group Discussions

1. Do you think all teachers should be required to have families participate in their rooms? What might be some of the drawbacks to such a requirement?
2. One of your friends, who is in her first year of teaching, and feeling depressed, calls you. She went to some lengths to plan a special community meeting, and only half the families showed up that night. What would be your response to her disappointment?
3. The next time your college class is shown a video, take a few minutes and develop questions based on it that would encourage good discussion in a parenting group.
4. Think of a policy families might legitimately complain about at a children's center or at the school where you are teaching. Now try role-playing various responses to such complaints. These responses could include attacking back, refusing to listen, reflecting parent feelings, and explaining the reasons for the school policy.

Self-Check Questions for Review

Content-Related Questions

1. Why should teachers not be preoccupied with children at the beginning of the center day?
2. List some practical things teachers can do to help establish a feeling of trust between themselves and families.
3. Describe some important points to remember when planning a family education meeting.
4. What does the author suggest teachers should do when home and school policies cannot agree?
5. Select an example of a nontraditional family, and provide some suggestions about how the school could help the family function effectively.

Integrative Questions

1. Suppose that a teacher did not want to have much contact with families. Suggest some ways she could arrange her program so that it would be difficult for families to have informal chats with her.
2. You are now the teacher in a Head Start center, and you want to keep the families informed about what is happening in your classroom. If you could not use a newsletter to do this, what other practical means of communication could you use to relay news to the families?
3. In your opinion what might be the advantages of using either the Reggio or Santa Barbara approach as a basis for family involvement? What might be the limitations or disadvantages of each of the approaches?

Coordinating Videotape

Listening to families. Tape #6. *The whole child: A caregiver's guide to the first five years.* The Annenberg/CPB Collection, P.O. Box 2345, South Burlington, VT 05407-2345. *Listening to Families* prepares caregivers to welcome families into the life of the children's center. It demonstrates both ineffective and more desirable ways to conduct parent interviews and suggests ways to help families and children deal with everyday problems and life crises. The video programs in this collection were taped in a variety of real, working children's programs.

References for Further Reading

Pick of the Litter

Ispa, J., Thornburg, K., & Fine, M. (2006). *Keepin' on: The everyday struggles of young families in poverty.* Baltimore, MD: Brookes. This book is the result of a 5-year research project that studied the lives of nine single mothers living in poverty. It explores their strengths and challenges as well as research, practice, and policy issues related to families in poverty.

Overviews

Berger, E. H. (2004). *Parents as partners in education: Families and schools working together* (6th ed.). Upper Saddle River, NJ: Merrill/Prentice Hall. This comprehensive textbook provides in-depth discussions of ways to generate positive teacher–parent partnerships. *Highly recommended.*

Encouraging Volunteers

Barhyte, D. M. (2000). Keep volunteers invested in your program. *Child Care Information Exchange, 136,* 12–14. Practical advice about how to increase the comfort of volunteers is included here.

Working with Families

Barrera, R. M. (2001). Bringing home to school. *Scholastic Early Childhood Today, 16*(3), 44–50. The author offers practical suggestions for involving all families in the school and respecting the diversity of families.

Keyser, J. (2001). Creating partnerships with families: Problem-solving through communication. *Child Care Information Exchange, 138,* 44–47. For an excellent example of how to listen and respond to parents having a problem, this article provides practical examples of how to listen to and re-state parental feelings in a respectful way.

Szinovacz, M. E. (Ed.). (1998). *Handbook on grandparenthood.* Westport, CT: Greenwood Press. A comprehensive book on a seldom-addressed aspect of family life, the authors explore grandparents' diverse roles in our society.

Turbiville, V. P., Umbarger, G. T., & Guthrie, A. C. (2000). Fathers' involvement in programs for young children. *Young Children, 55*(4), 74–79. Basing their recommendations on a research study, the authors identify the kinds of inclusive approaches most preferred by fathers. *Highly recommended.*

Information Regarding Families with Special Concerns

Casper, V., & Schultz, S. B. (1999). *Gay parents, straight schools.* New York: Teachers College Press. The title is self-explanatory.

Harvey, J. H., & Fine, M. A. (2004). *Children of divorce: Stories of loss and growth.* Mahwah, NJ: Erlbaum. In addition to presenting current research on divorce, the authors highlight the real struggles and successes that divorcing families experience.

Hildebrand, V., Phenice, L. A., Gray, M. M., & Hines, R. P. (2007). *Knowing and serving diverse families* (3rd ed.). Upper Saddle River, NJ: Merrill/Prentice Hall. This book should be in every teacher's library because it offers information on family backgrounds ranging from various ethnic groups to single parents and gay and lesbian families.

Pareete, H. P., & Petch-Hogan, B. (2000). Approaching families: Facilitating culturally/linguistically diverse family involvement. *Teaching Exceptional Children, 33*(2), 4–10. Although the emphasis here is on consulting with families of children with disabilities and who come from cultures other than that of the teacher, the recommendations for good practice (in convenient checklist form) apply to all families.

For the Advanced Student

Children's Defense Fund. (2005). *Year book 2005: The state of America's children.* Washington, DC: Children's Defense Fund, 25 E Street NW, Washington, DC. This publication presents child-relevant statistics in both chart and paragraph form—an indispensable resource.

Reggio Children & Project Zero. (2001). *Making learning visible: Children as individual and group learners.* Reggio Emilia, Italy: Reggio Children. Educators from Reggio Emilia and researchers from Harvard's Project Zero illuminate ways in which documentation can foster learning. The many photographs show beautiful examples of how documentation is used in Reggio as a means of communication with families.

Related Organizations and Online Resources

The Child Trends Web site contains reports, fact sheets, and data related to a comprehensive list of early childhood topics, including fatherhood, family strengths, and poverty. http://www.childtrends.org

The Children's Defense Fund (CDF) works toward reducing the number of neglected, sick, uneducated, and poor children in the United States. The Web site provides information and resources for families and teachers. http://www.childrensdefense.org

The Council on Contemporary Families (CCF) is a nonprofit organization with a membership consisting of family researchers, mental health and social work practitioners, and clinicians dedicated to discussing what families need and how these needs can best be met. The site includes articles, fact sheets, suggested reading, and educational outreach. http://www.contemporaryfamilies.org

Zero to Three is dedicated to promoting the healthy development of infants and toddlers by supporting and strengthening the nation's families, communities, and those who work on their behalf. http://www.zerotothree.org

CHAPTER *three*

PLAY

The Integrative Force in Learning

Have you ever . . .

- Fumbled for words when a parent says, "Well, I'm glad they're having fun, but when do you really teach them something?"
- Known that play was an important avenue for learning social skills but doubted whether it contributed much to mental development?
- Wondered how you could encourage the children to get more out of their play experiences?

If you have, the material in this chapter will help you.

In play a child is always above his average age, above his daily behavior; in play, it is as though he were a head taller than himself. As in the focus of a magnifying glass, play contains all developmental tendencies in a condensed form; in play, it is as though the child were trying to jump above the level of his normal behavior.

—Lev Vygotsky (1966, p. 16)

Protecting the child's right to play is no easy job. It goes far beyond setting up an environment where play can occur. It includes knowing a great deal. It means knowing what goes on when children play, so that the environment can, in a sense, grow with the children, both as a group and as individuals. It means knowing when and how to intervene in the play and when to stay on the sidelines. It means comprehending the limits of play, knowing when play is not enough, knowing when children need the satisfaction of accomplishment in the real world and when soaring on the imaginations of others is more appropriate.

—Patricia Monighan-Nourot, Barbara Scales, and
Judith Van Hoorn, with Millie Almy (1987, p. 9)

Play is as fundamental a human disposition as loving and working. . . . It is important for us to communicate to families, administrators, and legislators that children's play is a biological imperative, essential to healthy early childhood growth and development. For young children, play is not, as it is for adults, an optional activity.

—David Elkind (2005, p. 40)

Chapter 1 advocates not only planning curriculum for each of the child's selves but also considering the child as a whole, because the whole is more than the sum of the individual parts. We never want to lose sight of the child as being this complete human being. So, as we plan our teaching, we must ask ourselves: What method do we use to bring about this sense of wholeness for children? What glue can we supply that will stick the parts of that small person together to form a complete, fully functioning person?

To answer this perplexing question, we have only to go to the children and observe what they use to accomplish this integration. The answer is that children use play to achieve this goal. Play provides children with unparalleled opportunities for integrating their personalities, because when children play, all the selves are used simultaneously. Thus, a child taking the parent's role in house play is developing the physical self by practicing eye–hand coordination as she pours pretend juice, is practicing social skills as she ingratiates herself with the group, is developing emotional insight when the recalcitrant baby protests "No! No! Baby not go to bed," and is using her cognitive creative abilities as she substitutes a necktie for a leash while walking the family dog. No other experience in the child's life provides the same opportunity for all the selves to interact and grow simultaneously as does the opportunity for play.

Play further acts as an integrative force by providing opportunities for children to clarify who they are and who they are not. Playing the role of a police officer, mother, baby, or bus driver is one way of doing this, of course, but the ordinary social interactions that occur during play also help children form concepts of their total self. During play they may define themselves, or may be defined by others, as someone who is liked, or disliked, or good at climbing, or a crybaby, or myriad other things. Such labels tend to push a child into a particular mold or framework that can be desirable or undesirable.

Play also acts as an integrative force by helping children discriminate not only between who they are and who they are not but also between what is real and what is not. Two- and 3-year-olds, in particular, may require the teacher's help in remembering that dramatic play is "just pretend" and that they are acting "as if" something were true. For example, we once helped a child work out some of his fear of dogs by allowing him to hit a stuffed dog at nursery school while stuttering out all the terrible things he would like to do to it because it had bitten him. Suddenly he stopped and said uncertainly, "But if I bite him, he won't bite back, will he?" He needed to be reminded "Is the puppy real?" before he could continue with his play. That moment of uncertainty demonstrated how thin the line can be between reality and fantasy in young children's play and how important the teacher is in providing reassurance when it is necessary.

Play provides opportunities for the child to clarify who she is and who she is not.

As children mature, they learn to handle the real–not real continuum themselves and need less frequent support from the teacher. Garvey (1983) explains that they do this by developing ways of signaling between themselves when they begin to play and make the transition from reality to pretend. For example, they may begin an interchange with "Pretend that . . ." or "I'll be the mommy and you be the daddy, OK?" This kind of gambit is an accepted social signal among preschoolers that they are entering a period where literalness is suspended and imaginative play substituted in its place.

BUT WHAT IS PLAY?

There are as many differing theories and definitions of play as there are people who write about it, and the discussions continue (Frost, Wortham, & Reifel, 2005; Spodek & Saracho, 1998). Schwartzman (1978) was, and still is, accurate when she said, "Today we are still flying theoretical 'kites' in the study of play—only now there are more of them. This is as it should be because play requires a multiperspective approach . . . and resists any attempts to define it rigidly" (p. 325).

Definitions range from Montessori's "Play is a child's work" to Dewey's "Play is what we enjoy while we are doing it. Work is what we enjoy when we have accomplished it." Views on the purpose of play also vary, ranging from Freud's contention that play provides opportunities to clarify and master emotions to Piaget's proposal that play enables children to substitute symbols in place of reality (Frost, Wortham, & Reifel, 2005). As we see in the chapter opening quote, Vygotsky contends that play is valuable because it enables the child to approach the growing edge of the *zone of proximal development (ZPD)*—to go just beyond her current level of development and incorporate new, more advanced skills into her repertoire. He maintains such advancement is most likely to occur when the play is guided by an adult (Bodrova & Leong, 1996). Like Piaget, Vygotsky values play because it encourages children to substitute pretend objects for real ones, thereby helping them separate thought from concrete objects.

When broadly defined, play may be thought of as taking place in many areas of the center—such as the art or music and dance areas or when playing simple games. For the purposes of this chapter, however, the discussion will be limited to a kind of play best described as free or pretend or dramatic play, because it is that sort of play that provides the richest opportunities for the full exercise of the children's imaginative powers.

The long-standing definition by Johnson and Ershler (1982) offers a definition of particular merit when thinking about the ingredients of this kind of play. They say, "Play may be defined as behavior that is intrinsically motivated, freely chosen, process-oriented, and pleasurable" (p. 137). This definition is useful because it provides a set of standards against which we can measure the play activity in our classrooms. We simply have to translate these standards into a series of questions. For example:

- *Play is intrinsically motivated*—(interpretation) Will children choose to become involved in the curriculum I have planned because the activities are inherently satisfying, or because they will be rewarded by the teacher?
- *Play is freely chosen*—(interpretation) Does this play allow children to choose freely what they wish to do for at least a portion of the time they are at school? Does it encourage them to use their own ideas?
- *Play is process-oriented*—(interpretation) Will children find satisfaction while doing the activity and not just in the end result?
- *Play is pleasurable*—(interpretation) Will the children enjoy what they are doing while they are participating in the activity?

We need to ask ourselves these questions continually because all too often teachers lose sight of them when planning to include play in the curriculum. For example, teachers may set up a block corner to carry out a particular theme, such as farm animals or transportation, and restrict the play to that theme thereby stifling the children's opportunities for freely choosing how they wish to play with blocks that day.

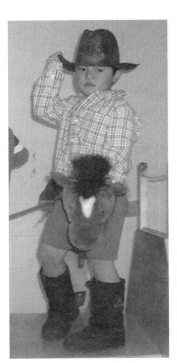

Pretend play provides the richest opportunities for the full exercise of the child's imaginative powers.

Sutton-Smith (1987) speaks of such guided play as the "domestication of early childhood play." He suggests that some teachers tend to see "educational play" as being the only really good, worthwhile kind and the more spontaneous, vigorous, child-instigated play as less desirable and hence not worthy of encouragement. Although there can be a place for controlled play experiences in the curriculum, we must always remember that guided play *does not meet the criteria of being child generated or freely chosen* because teachers tend to push children into following the theme and the teacher's idea.

Children are no fools about this—in fact, the most salient way they define the difference between work and play is that work is something you *have* to do whereas play is something freely chosen you *want* to do (Wing, 1995). So, if we wish children to feel they are genuinely playing, we must provide many opportunities for them to play freely and spontaneously as their own ideas and internal states dictate. It is only when such open opportunities abound that children can fully develop their own ideas and passions. It is this kind of open play that provides the best opportunities for integration of all the selves.

Stages of Play

Researchers do agree that play passes through a series of developmental stages, although once again they differ in their categorization of these (Bergen, 1998).

One tried-and-true categorization still in use today, which investigates the social aspects of play, was developed by Parten (1932, 1996). She viewed play as advancing from *solitary play* (playing alone, with little reference to what other children nearby are doing—characteristic of very young children), to *parallel play* (playing beside but not with a companion child with toys that are similar—often seen in the play of 2- and 3-year-olds), to *associative play* (playing together but not subordinating their individual interests to a common goal—often witnessed in the play of 3½ to 4½-year-old children), and finally to *cooperative play* (playing together for a common purpose—often apparent in the play of 4- and 5-year-olds who organize themselves into a group). These stages are not mutually exclusive, however. Rubin (1977) demonstrated that solitary play can be quite sophisticated and that the same child may use various forms and combinations of these stages at different times of the day and in various circumstances throughout early childhood. Therefore, at the preschool level, teachers should not view solitary and parallel play as necessarily being evidence of immaturity.

Another well-known way of categorizing stages of development in play was developed by Smilansky (1968) following Piagetian theory. This categorization has also been widely used by researchers (Henniger, 1985; Howe, Moller, & Chambers, 1994; Roopnarine, Bright, & Riegraf, 1994). Smilansky divides play according to *functional play* (making simple use of movements to provide exercise—characteristic of infants and young toddlers), *constructive play* (working toward a goal of some sort, such as completing a puzzle or picture—characteristic of children up to about 3½ years), and *sociodramatic play* (assuming roles and using language for pretending). By age 7 the child reaches the stage of *games with rules*, which is described as the highest form of cognitive play.

Smilansky used one of the Piagetian stages, *sociodramatic play*, in her research study cited in this chapter. It is mentioned here not only because the results are valuable but also because her work pioneered an entire new generation of research studies on play and is still widely cited today.

The value of understanding and identifying these stages is that it allows teachers to plan play activities that are appropriate for the ages of the children they are teaching. It is as inappropriate to expect a 2-year-old to understand how to play duck-duck-goose as it is to expect a 4-year-old to be satisfied with a rattle and set of nesting blocks. Knowledge of developmental levels prevents boredom or frustration in young children because it enables teachers to suit experiences to the child's developmental capabilities.

PRACTICAL WAYS TO ENCOURAGE FREELY CHOSEN PRETEND PLAY

Play flourishes best in an atmosphere of acceptance and approval (Ghafouri & Wein, 2005). Children sense when teachers are not fully convinced of the worth of play and just tolerate rather than accept it in a wholehearted way. On the other hand, teachers who fully understand that play is a productive avenue for learning and thus make a commitment to it subtly convey this message to children. In this climate, play and all its attendant benefits thrive and children lead rich, engrossed, and happy lives at school.

In addition to commitment, some more obvious and generally applicable principles can be incorporated into the teaching repertoire by teachers who wish to encourage play. One such principle is that *planning enough time for play to be generated is essential*. It takes time for children to develop their play ideas fully—to move all the way in their play from packing their suitcases to trundling them through the school, visiting their friends, pretending to have a snack, and finally returning.

Equipment Must Be Stored in Readily Accessible Areas

Teachers should feel free to move with the children's play and produce materials on request rather than say, "It's in the shed (or school storage or closet)—we'll get it tomorrow."

Plentiful materials also encourage children to play freely because having enough equipment to go around promotes comfortable, harmonious play. This does not mean it is necessary to have 20 little red cars so that everyone can have one, but it does mean it is wise to try to have at least two of whatever items are very popular.

Equipment Should Be Age Appropriate

For children to get the full benefit of their play experience, the manipulative toys, books and recordings, art supplies, and other equipment they use must be suitable for their developmental level. Appendix B offers many suggestions for the kinds of age-appropriate materials and equipment children love to use in their play.

Teachers Should Seek to Continue and Extend Children's Play

We sometimes think of pretend play as occurring only in the housekeeping area or in the block corner, and it is true that these are highly popular places for such activity to take place. However, play can occur anywhere: in the sandbox as children imagine they are digging to the bottom of the earth, on the climbing gym as it becomes an eagle's nest, or at the manipulative table as they play zoo with small models and cubical counting blocks. Play can also be a wagon transformed into an ambulance, a young parent nursing a doll, or two children laughing together as they do stunts on the crawl-through blocks.

Nourishing such play requires a delicate balance between knowing when to intervene and knowing when not to. Too intrusive, insensitive interventions by adults can actually spoil it, as the research by Fiese (1990) reveals. She found that when mothers did too much questioning and were too intrusive with their suggestions, their children retreated to less mature, simple play. In their zeal to use play to advance learning, it seems that proponents of Vygotskian theory need to be particularly sensitive to this kind of excessive intrusion.

On the other hand, research by Howes and Clements (1994) reports that most teachers do not intervene enough: "Teachers used free play and outdoor times in the child care center to step back and visit with their own peers. They tended to monitor peer play *only for safety believing that children learn best when they solve their own peer problems*" [italics added] (p. 33). Clearly, if the children are to obtain maximum benefit from playing together, either extreme of over- or underinvolvement should be avoided.

Encouraging play is like pulling taffy. Just as the accomplished taffy puller can stretch and bend the candy as far apart as his arms will reach, so the accomplished teacher can do the same thing with play—drawing it forth, stretching it out, extending it, so that children can obtain the maximum benefit from the experience.

To do this successfully, the teacher should anticipate what the children might go on to next in their play. Offering a mild suggestion as the play begins to wane or falter can save and continue it by adding an additional episode. ("Well, here you are, sitting at the cash register! Has anyone phoned in an order? Oh, here comes Ryan. Are you the man picking up the hamburgers?") Teachers can find inspiration by assuming the children's perspective and asking themselves what they would enjoy doing next if they were that age.

A note of caution: Be prepared to accept rejection of your idea by the children without feeling offended. Remember, it is *their* play and you are the supporter, not the creator, of it.

Teachers Must Allow Some Space Between Themselves and the Children

Youngsters may feel suffocated by too much close attention. Yet, at the same time, it is necessary to *remain alert and willing to set limits* when these are needed. Two- and 3-year-olds may require intervention for their own safety. Four-year-olds are more likely to benefit from restraints for the sake of others' safety, as when they are involved in such activities as monster play.

When children are involved in play, the ideal attitude for teachers to assume is that of attentive approval. Teachers with this attitude remain aware of what is happening, are willing to contribute ideas and materials when this seems desirable, can clarify and interpret the children's actions to each other should this be necessary, and appreciate the value of this activity as the play unfolds.

Offer a Variety of Possibilities to Stimulate Pretend Play and/or Attract Different Players

The Chapter Spotlight suggests a few of many possible ideas that can spark free dramatic play among the children. Remember that additional possibilities abound—for example, when furnished with a variety of accessories, the block area is a wonderful source for stimulating imaginative play, as is the outdoor play area. Stay open, too, to special family interests as a source of variety and enrichment. For example, our center recently did a lot of mountaineering play when we learned one child's mother was a geologist who was interested in rock climbing. (Pickaxes were a big favorite!) Cross-cultural items familiar to some of the children but not to all of them can also enliven interest. The baptism play so familiar to many of the children in our Oklahoma community, for instance, was welcomed by our Muslim children—could it have been the lavish use of water that play involved? Books, movies, and television shows can be additional sources, although such play may be less creative if the children just repeat what they have seen or favor the more violent episodes to reenact. Of course, if they've been frightened, playing out those concerns has the merit of possibly helping them come to terms with their worries.

Remember, too, that although setting out a few "props" can spark the fun, beware of falling into the trap of supplying every realistic detail. Leaving as much as possible for pretending places children more in control of their play and encourages them to think up plots, ideas, and solutions for themselves as they draw on their imaginations' own resources.

ADDITIONAL BENEFITS OF PLAY

If the integrative function of play were its only value to children, this would be reason enough to include it as a basic element in planning curriculum. But, when analyzed, play provides many additional benefits (see Table 3.1). When children play, they are more completely themselves than at any other time. Play leaves children free to express ideas and to play things out safely with no penalties attached. While playing, they make choices and decisions for themselves, they assume command, they are masterful and in control of what is happening, and they are able to seize endless opportunities to try out, experiment, and explore. Moreover, they can subtly regulate their play, so that it offers challenges that are neither too difficult nor too easy.

Knowledge of these benefits is important to teachers, because they need to be able to explain to parents and administrators why play is a vital ingredient when planning learning

In sociodramatic play, the child assumes roles and uses language for pretending.

43

Surefire Pretend Play Activities

Here are a few suggestions for settings that will spark dramatic play among the children:

- *Playing house*—A trustly standby that holds endless appeal for children. Try an apartment set up with two houses side by side made from hollow blocks; this often facilitates social interaction among groups of children and quells arguments as well. A nice variation on this play can be moving to a new house or apartment. Children decide where they would rather have the house be, use wagons to transport furniture, and so forth.
- *Grocery store*—Offer paper bags, empty cans and boxes, imitation fruits and vegetables, play money, and something to use as shopping carts (doll buggies, wagons, etc.). Children enjoy both the buyer and seller roles. Grocery store works well as an enrichment to house play.
- *Running a fast-food restaurant*—Although some of us may deplore certain aspects of this industry, there is no denying that children are familiar with placing orders, take-out features, and the virtues of "with pickles or without." Ride 'em trucks or possibly trikes, as well as cash registers, trays, sacks, containers, order blanks, and hats, add joy to the play.
- *Camping*—Bedspread tents hung on A-frames and whatever camping equipment is available such as canteens, firewood, or sleeping bags make this play lots of fun. Flashlights also add delight.
- *Hospital*—Children are deeply interested in participating in this activity. Inclusion of a stethoscope, some kind of shot needle (turkey basters or large eyedroppers can be used to represent these), and masking tape and gauze for bandages add interest. When one of our students assembled a transfusion unit from a plastic bottle and tubing, the children played with it repeatedly.
- *Business office*—Old typewriters or computers past the possibility of repair, calculators, stamps with stamp pads, used envelopes, paper clips, and surplus paper bring appeal and realism to this play.
- *Baby washing*—Baby play combines the delights of water play with family life. Because boys often can be enticed into this activity, it is particularly valuable as a way of providing experience in a nurturing role. Towels, bar soap, cornstarch powder, and diaper wipes add reality. Provide baby dolls of all races and all skin colors.
- *Birthday party*—Boxes (either with or without something inside) and recycled party wrappings, cards, pretend birthday cakes (foam bases with candles stuck in them), paper plates and cups, and possibly hats provide a surprising amount of rather ritualized, yet satisfying, play on this theme. Children enjoy wrapping up the "presents" as much as unwrapping them—perhaps because adults often restrict such activity so that gifts will "look nice."
- *Taking a trip*—Children find great pleasure in packing suitcases and lugging them around. Play may include plane tickets, maps, magazines, peanuts or pretzels for snack, and special hats for the pilots and flight attendants to wear. Discussions about destinations, possible weather anticipated there, and so forth, can encourage children to do a little thinking and planning ahead. If children from your school travel to visit grandparents or other family members' homes in other countries, such as the Philippines or Mexico, such travel might instigate child-initiated play with gentle teacher questioning.
- *Baptism*—A student suggested we name and baptize out newest doll. To my surprise several of our children were both knowledgeable and enthusiastic about the process and played it repeatedly. The combination of dressing up plus copious amounts of water and snack served as a "party" was irresistible.

situations for young children. In addition, teachers must be able to align play activities with government-mandated standards.

Developing the Physical Self Through Play

The joy, freedom, and vigor that are so characteristic of children as they use their bodies in physical play is certain evidence of how deeply satisfying this is to them. Knowing what

Table 3.1
Potential Learning Benefits from Pretend (Dramatic) Free Play

Creative	Emotional	Social	Physical	Cognitive
Encourages:	**Encourages:**	**Encourages:**	**Encourages:**	**Encourages:**
Enjoyment of process, not product	Clarification and better understanding of own personal feelings	Ability to get what child wants by peaceful means: negotiating, bargaining, trading, waiting, using a substitute	Practice of newly emerging physical skills	Use of language to express ideas to others during play
Generation of new possibilities and ideas	Ability to express and control own feelings	Generation of skills related to entering an ongoing group	Use of small-muscle skills such as buttoning doll's dress or pouring water	Ability to extend and expand on ideas and to solve problems
Use of the mental process of imagination	Expression of feelings in "safe" nonretaliatory environment	Development of cooperative skills: taking other people's desires and needs into account, sharing leadership role with others, sharing equipment	Use of large-muscle skills, particularly on climbing or balancing apparatus	Use of symbols in place of real objects (emergent cognitive and literacy skill)
Flexibility of thought	Feelings of delight and satisfaction		Coordination of subskills	Ability to tell real from pretend
Problem-solving skills: "How can we?" "What could we use for . . .?"	Feelings of relief when anxieties are played through		Attempts at more challenging new skills while pretending (e.g., sliding down pole while playing firefighter)	Ability to use imagination
Expression of personal uniqueness—self-expression	Feelings of freedom from adult standards and expectations	Grasp of social roles such as doctor, teacher, mother, and rules that govern each role	Acquisition of new motor skills	Development of advance plans and scenarios (e.g., "You be the cat doctor, and my cat just throwed up!")
Use of pretend and "as if" situations	Sense of mastery and control over what's happening		Experimentation with taking risks while in a safe environment	Clarification of information about world beyond the home
Increase breadth of repertoire of possible responses to situations	Development of empathy, insight into how other people feel	Differentiation between self and others: who child really is or is not	Integration of language with physical action (directions, finger plays, etc.)	Experimentation and drawing conclusions from trying things out
Unfamiliar uses of familiar equipment		Insights about others' cultures if teacher encourages this (see chapter 13)		Use of signs and labels (emergent literacy skill)
Creation of new roles				

one's body can do and feeling physically confident enhances the basic feelings of security and self-esteem in a special way.

With the growing rate of childhood obesity and overweight, along with the decrease in time spent in physical activity or recess at school, it is imperative that teachers encourage vigorous, physical play every day (Oliver & Klugman, 2005; Stegelin, 2005). By providing sufficient time each day for active play and exercise, teachers can help children avoid many of the problems that are associated with childhood obesity. These include both physical and psychological problems, from high blood pressure and diabetes to social rejection and school failure (Stegelin, 2005).

How Can Teachers Help? It is important to maintain a reasonable balance between allowing children to experiment with taking risks and practicing commonsense control.

A sound rule to follow is to intervene in any play that is genuinely dangerous to the child or to others nearby while encouraging as much movement and freedom as possible. More protection is necessary for 2-year-olds than for 4-year-olds because the former are less experienced and consequently have poorer judgment. Although 4-year-olds are thirsty for risks and infatuated with challenges, they can be asked to evaluate dangers for themselves rather than being constantly controlled by the teacher.

Adding variety to the possibilities for outdoor play will also support it in a positive way. When the same trikes, swings, and climbers are present day after day, no wonder children succumb to boredom and wild behavior. However, a bedspread tent over the climber or lengths of hose and a ladder combined with the tricycles can suggest new play potential that will sustain their interest and cultivate new ideas, as well as encourage continued physical effort.

Finally, play emphasizing physical activity between children can be influenced by the choice of equipment available. Large, portable items they can haul together, such as boards and hollow blocks, encourage cooperative, physical play. These open-ended materials (sometimes called "loose parts") allow children to work together to construct all kinds of play situations, which constitutes an added bonus for the creative self. (For further discussion of curriculum for the physical self, please refer to chapters 8 and 9.)

Enhancing the Emotional Self Through Play

We hear repeatedly that play can be the great reliever of feelings, and there is no denying the truth of that statement. Play does permit unacceptable impulses to be expressed in acceptable ways. Its value for the emotional self goes far beyond that, however. Playing out difficult situations provides prime opportunities for reducing stress and feelings of anxiety (Frost, 2005; Isenberg & Jalongo, 2001). For example, when opportunities for play are provided to children who are hospitalized, Kampe (1990) makes this point:

> Play provides a context for understanding and creating meaning, for regaining a sense of self-control in a strange environment, for building relationships, for learning new information, and for making pain and discomfort more bearable or waiting more tolerable. (p. 168)

On a more positive note, play promotes feelings of healthy delight. What fun it is to become absorbed in building an oven in which to bake the sandbox cookies, or to feel satisfied when at last the blocks balance or the car runs through the tunnel all the way. What joy it is to play with another child and feel she has become your friend.

Of course, other feelings also arise in play: anger, when someone else becomes dominant; pain, when one is left out; fear, when an activity becomes too scary. The virtue is that play allows children to experience this wide range of emotion under relatively safe circumstances and to learn to deal with these feelings bit by bit. How valuable it is to learn that sadness and anger can be coped with and that they do not last forever.

How Can Teachers Help? First, teachers can allow the expression of feelings while drawing the line when necessary between feeling like doing something and actually doing it (see chapter 11). It is just as acceptable to feel angry while playing as it is to feel silly or happy or excited. As a matter of fact, a child most probably will experience all these emotions when playing with other children. It is far better to realize this and to encourage children to express their emotions safely through words than to insist they conceal or suppress such feelings, thus causing children to act them out by hurting someone else.

Second, teachers can help the child's emotional self grow during play by providing play experiences that draw out a problem when a child seems blocked from dealing with it independently (Alat, 2002; Fenichel, 2002; Frost, 2005; Levin, 2003). Perhaps, for unknown reasons, a child has become afraid of the dark. The teacher might provide some large boxes and flashlights in a darkened corner of the playroom so that the youngster can control the situation and play through her fear. Of course, if the fear appears to be increasing or extreme, the teacher would take additional steps besides providing opportunities for such play. Depending on the severity of the behavior, these steps might include talking with the child, reading some stories during group time about how other children coped with similar concerns, or having a parent conference.

Usually, however, providing appropriate play opportunities will clarify feelings and provide relief, particularly when teachers realize how helpful such experiences can be. Teachers should also remain aware of their limitations in such circumstances. They are not professional psychologists. When a child's play appears to be anxiety ridden or highly ritualized and repetitious, they should recognize these signals as calls for help that go beyond their training. At this point, referring the family for psychological consultation is usually the wisest step.

Helping the Social Self Develop Through Play

Although children gain many benefits from playing by themselves (solitary play) or side by side (parallel play), it is when they play together in associative or cooperative play that the social self benefits most because these kinds of play provide the richest opportunities for social learning. Preschool teachers typically spend a large part of each day helping children develop this aspect of themselves. During such play, children learn about getting along together; entering a group; handling exclusion and dominance; sharing power, space, and ideas with other people; making compromises; driving bargains; and cooperating to gain satisfaction.

Children also learn about the social world that lies beyond childhood as they assume the role of a mother or a teacher or Godzilla during play. Moreover, some researchers (Rubin & Howe, 1986) maintain that such role-taking has the additional benefit of allowing children to put themselves in another's place, which probably encourages children to understand other people's feelings and to develop their ability to feel empathy for them. Social play therefore presents an unsurpassable means by which the social self can develop (Bodrova & Leong, 2005; Ghafouri & Wein, 2005).

How Can Teachers Help?   The most important contribution teachers can make to social play is to pay attention to what is happening so they can facilitate in a beneficial way. Perhaps one child is hovering on the edge of the play and needs a suggestion on how to enter the group; perhaps an argument is brewing over who will drive the truck and who will ride; perhaps someone is crying angrily because she thinks her friend tripped her on purpose. To deal with these situations, teachers must act as arbitrator, negotiator, and clarifier. At the same time, they model strategies that the children will eventually learn to use for themselves as teachers gradually encourage them to take over the demonstrated roles.

When seeking to facilitate social play, teachers have to walk a fine line between being at the center of attention and withdrawing too far from what is going on. The teacher's behavior must vary with the needs of the group. Some children, as Smilansky (1968) and Smilansky and Shefatya (1990) point out, are so inexperienced that they need help even to begin play. For such youngsters it may be necessary for the teacher to participate very directly by suggesting possibilities for play ("My goodness! It looks like there are some babies here that need to be fed. What shall we make them for dinner? Shredded wheat? Oh, that would be delicious. What can you use for bowls?"). For other inexperienced children, supplying equipment as the need arises is the answer. For older 4-year-olds it may be sufficient to extend their play by asking questions, such as "Now you've got the carriages loaded up—are you guys going on a trip, or what?" Through it all, teachers should remember the goal of promoting play *among* the children rather than between the children and themselves. They should be ready to intervene quickly when it is necessary but remain attentive observers when it is not.

Some kinds of activities and equipment appear to promote social interaction among children, whereas others do not. For example, Rubin (1977) reports that children usually engage in solitary or parallel play while using play dough, clay, or sand and water. On the other hand, some equipment invites or even requires participation by more than one child to be maximally satisfying. Parachutes, rocking boats, balls, long jump ropes (for slightly older children), wagon and trike combinations, and horizontally hung tire swings are all examples of equipment that encourage play by more than one child at a time. Teachers who wish to foster cooperative social interaction among children and help them develop their social selves as fully as possible should search for and acquire such equipment.

Fostering the Creative and Cognitive Selves Through Play

Reviews of research concerned with finding a possible link between *divergent thinking* (the ability to produce more than one answer to a problem) and play report that children who have been involved in free play before being asked to participate in situations requiring divergent thinking produce more various and creative answers to those problems than do children who were exposed to structured experiences before the problem was posed to them (Görlitz & Wohlwill, 1987; Johnson, 1990; Russ, 1996).

Research has shown a link between play and several areas of cognitive development, including memory, language development, self-regulation, literacy skills, school adjustment, and academic learning (Bodrova & Leong, 2005). In addition, recent brain research indicates that active, stimulating play promotes optimal development in the growing brain (Stegelin, 2005).

How Can Teachers Help? The most important thing to do is to remain open-minded about possibilities and recognize the value of creative ideas as they appear in such free play. Such positive support by teachers reinforces and encourages this kind of behavior in children.

Welcome the Unconventional Use of Equipment Whenever Possible

Have you ever watched a number of youngsters playing with one of those velvet-covered ropes that banks use to designate where people should stand? Although adults may see only this functional purpose for the rope, children see a number of other possibilities: They will brush their hands back and forth along it (a blissful sensory experience), play follow-the-leader and wind back and forth between its poles, hit it with a little stick to make it swing, and run under it in a game of tag. Children bring their playful, creative powers to almost any situation.

Teachers should generally accept unconventional uses of equipment by young children, because these are of great value to the children's creative selves. Thus, children should be permitted to ride tricycles backward, balance along the handle of a broom left on the sidewalk, or go down the slide toboggan-style on a bit of carpet.

Unfortunately, however, the same inexperience that enables children to perceive unusual possibilities in the equipment may also make it difficult for them to assess potential dangers, so teachers must remain alert to potentially dangerous situations if they arise. The child who attempts to convert a tier of dresser drawers into a set of stairs may be in for a painful surprise.

Encourage Imaginative Substitutions

Although children's activity can at times genuinely cause harm or destroy property and teachers must intervene, far more often the unconventional, original use of equipment would not be damaging or dangerous, and teachers need not discourage the children's idea. For example, there is really no reason that unit blocks cannot be used on a table instead of the floor or a hat cannot double as a shopping bag.

Sometimes this original, unconventional approach is expressed by the imaginative substitution of something for something else. Piaget (1983) terms this activity *symbolic play* and maintains that this representation of reality on a symbolic level is an important step in mental development. Pretend play almost always makes use of this kind of creative imagination at some point. For instance, the guinea pig might represent a lion, the doll carriage might become a hospital cart, or an oatmeal carton can become a drum. By age 4, children often do not need the object at all, and we see pretend coffee being poured into a nonexistent cup or an imaginary rocket taking off with all the appropriate sound effects.

Such creative, symbolic play can be particularly encouraged if the school makes a point of offering unstructured equipment, because the less structured (less reality bound) the equipment is, the more imagination the children are free to put into it. This is because whenever something looks like something in particular, it generally will be used as the thing it resembles, which thus restricts the children's imaginations. If a series of boxes in the play yard is painted to look like a series of quaint houses, the children are likely to play house in them, but not as likely to think of turning them over and converting them into a boat or train, as they would if the boxes were plain and accompanied by some boards, blocks, and old tires.

One February, for example, our staff decided that the housekeeping corner was not attracting children anymore despite its enchanting array of beds, artificial fruit, lifelike replicas of stoves and iceboxes, and charming little dishes. So we took it all away. In its place we set out boards and large, hollow blocks and sawhorses and then neatly laid out a few dolls, blankets, and dishes on one of the boards. We said nothing and just waited. It was really interesting to see the children expand on the possibilities. The creative play began at a very primitive level, with the "furniture" consisting of a bed of blankets arranged on a couple of blocks and a kind of picnic set up on the floor. Over the weeks the children played more and more intensely and for longer periods of time as they developed and extended their ideas and perceived additional possibilities. Their play varied on different days and included the construction of an elaborate, two-room house, a two-deck camper, and an operating room. As their enthusiasm mounted, they added unit blocks, cubical counting blocks, pictures from our file, and rug scraps. This became one of the most satisfying experiences for the children at our school.

Rasmussen (1979) sums it up well:

> Perhaps the most incalculable error that adults make in respect to children's play is assuming that expensive, fixed structures are somehow better than inexpensive or discarded raw materials. Such notions could be dispelled if adults would open their eyes to children at play and see for themselves the genius of imaginative creative minds at work, transforming the simplest material into the stuff of excitement and joy. (p. 39)

Ask Questions That Encourage Children to Think for Themselves

Free play time is the time par excellence to foster the development of thinking by asking children questions. The right question (or *provocation*, as our Reggio friends might term it) at the right time can stimulate creative solutions by children and also allows them to realize that the teacher values their ideas. Some examples of provocations that can encourage young children to think creatively include "We don't have a truck. What could you use instead?" or "Is there some way I could help you? Something I could get for you?" and "I've been wondering, how are you going to figure that out?"

HELPING CHILDREN WITH DISABILITIES JOIN IN THE PLAY

Although space does not permit extensive discussion of ways to facilitate the play of children who have specific disabilities, some principles are worthwhile to bear in mind.

The most basic of these is that fostering play for children with disabilities is of *great value* (Frost, Wortham, & Reifel, 2005). This is because a common educational pattern for these youngsters is divided schooling, in which they spend part of their time in classes where they receive special instruction adapted to their unique needs and the remainder of their time mainstreamed with groups of their typically developing peers. Observation has taught us that in the special instruction classes, children with disabilities can be expected to work particularly hard at tasks that may be quite difficult for them. That is why the relief provided by the free-play situations offered in the second school setting is especially precious for them. Free, pretend play provides the indispensable balance to other pressures to learn and achieve.

Welcoming children with special needs into their play also benefits typically developing children. As recent legislation concerning fair treatment of people with disabilities reminds us, the time is past when people who differ from the usual are hidden away or regarded as helpless. In the United States everyone is to be welcomed and employed according to their abilities, and there is no better time to instill that truth than in the early childhood years.

However, it is not enough to simply place a child who has a disability in the company of more typical children and expect play to automatically occur—and yet Tobias (1994) found this to be the typical expectation of adults she observed during free play. She found that without adult assistance the children did not mix much, less play together. Tobias concluded that teachers have to provide opportunities that are deliberately planned and structured to include all the children if such play is actually to take place. Otherwise, little benefit accrues from the experience for anyone.

Adapting Play to Fit the Capabilities of Children with Special Needs

The most obvious way to adapt play situations is to change the physical environment. For example, adding a nonslip surface to a ramp plus a lower railing makes it possible for a child with

Welcoming children with special needs into an activity benefits all the children.

braces to walk down unassisted, or reducing the noise level of the room can keep a child who is blind from becoming overly distracted. The references and online resources at the end of this chapter provide several sources of more information on this subject.

Even more important than physical adjustments, however, is adapting teacher expectations to the level of the child's particular abilities. The teacher must think of the child in terms of mental or physical developmental level, not in terms of actual chronological age. Unfortunately this is harder to do than to talk about. Who, for instance, has not fallen into the trap of expecting more mature social behavior from a child just because she was taller than the other children?

It can be even more difficult to remember this when children have disabilities because some of their needs may not be immediately apparent, either. For example, a 4-year-old who cannot hear well or who is developmentally delayed may appear "perfectly normal" and yet may need special help working her way into the group playing dragons. Fortunately, many play activities such as water play, housekeeping, and blocks adapt well to the differing levels of ability of all kinds of children as long as the teacher remembers to suit expectations to what the particular child is ready to learn next. Perhaps a child is just learning to trade something rather than grab it or to wait a little while for a turn. The teacher should commend these newly acquired skills instead of expecting the youngster to propose a more complicated bargain.

At the same time, do not make too many allowances for the child. It is as easy to underestimate abilities as it is to overestimate them. Either extreme breeds unfortunate results. It is as true for children with special needs as for more typical children that part of the teacher's responsibility is providing opportunities for consistent but not impossible growth.

Facilitating Play with Other Children

Of course, children are wary of individuals who look or act unusual, but a matter-of-fact explanation that Jamie's eyes look funny because he needs very thick glasses so he can see to string the beads will help reduce the uneasiness. Reducing feelings of apprehension goes a long way toward increasing the acceptability of the child who seems different.

Children do tend to be frank about their feelings, but they can also be taught that such frankness may hurt other people's feelings. A 4-year-old should no more be permitted to tell another youngster, "You're too dumb to do that" than be permitted to use a racial epithet. It is best to take the speaker aside and explain the child's difficulty while pointing out it makes her feel bad to be called dumb and it is unkind to hurt someone's feelings.

Fortunately, even young children can be genuinely kind and sympathetic to those who need their help if the teacher models that behavior and offers suggestions about ways to be thoughtful. Perhaps the teacher can point out how important it is to face a child who is hard of hearing when telling her something, or can thank a youngster who agrees to let a child who is developmentally delayed hold the hoop while the others roll the ball through it.

SUMMARY

As Frank (1968) remarks, "Play is how children learn what no one can teach them." To this we would add that the activity of free play is what children use to integrate their experiences and themselves into a meaningful whole.

Many definitions and purposes are ascribed to play, and all reflect some degree of truth. One definition is especially useful for teachers: "Play may be defined as behavior that is intrinsically motivated, freely chosen, process-oriented, and pleasurable" (Johnson & Ershler, 1982, p. 137). Teachers can profit by using the elements of this definition as standards against which to measure the freedom and richness of play in their schools.

Investigators agree that play develops through a series of stages as children mature. Two examples of these stage theories are presented in the text because an understanding of them helps teachers plan age-appropriate play experiences for the children.

Some general ways teachers can encourage rich, full play include creating an atmosphere of acceptance and approval, providing enough time for play to develop fully, storing equipment in accessible places, providing enough of it, and extending and prolonging play.

Teachers can foster the development of the physical self through play by helping children keep a reasonable balance between taking risks and being safe, adding variety to outdoor activities, and providing equipment that encourages children to use their bodies in different ways. Play that promotes the development of the emotional self can be encouraged by providing ample opportunities for play and permitting the expression and ownership of the full range of feelings by children. Teachers can enhance the social self by paying close attention to play and teaching social skills to children as the need arises. While doing this, teachers must avoid becoming the center of attention, yet they must be ready to stimulate and extend play if it begins to falter.

Play offers excellent opportunities for children to develop their creative and intellectual faculties. This is particularly true when teachers remain open-minded about unconventional but harmless uses of equipment, establish a climate of acceptance and admiration for the children's ideas, provide plenty of unstructured equipment, ask helpful questions, and avoid distracting the children by interrupting too often.

When drawing a child with disabilities into play activities, the teacher should try to adapt the play situation to make it as usable by the child as possible. This should include keeping activities physically accessible and developmentally appropriate to enhance their attractiveness. It is also important to encourage the other children to welcome the child with a disability into their play. This is best accomplished by matter-of-fact acceptance and explanation of the child's disabilities and by stressing the role of kindness and helpfulness by the other children.

Food for Thought and Group Discussions

1. You are planning your first family meeting of the year, and you want to base it on play and its value as a mode of learning. Think of two or three different ways you might present this topic so that it would be genuinely interesting to the families.

2. You have a group of young Mexican American boys in your room who spend most of their time playing "Bullee, Bullee" (a game where one boy acts the part of the bull by holding finger horns at the side of his head, and the other boys play matador). What, if anything, would you do about this kind of play? Does it encourage cruelty to animals? Is it too aggressive? What about the other children who do not join in?

3. Take time to observe some children playing at the water table. Record what they do. Then identify what they are learning from the activity while enjoying themselves. Compare your notes with others who have also observed the activity.

4. A new 3-year-old who has cerebral palsy will be joining the children in your group two mornings a week. You have met her and think she will fit in all right except you are worried that her unusual way of moving—her movements are somewhat uncoordinated, and sometimes she drools a little—will attract the other children's curiosity. Do you think you should discuss this child with the children before her arrival? What should you say? Do the parents need preparation? What if someone makes an unkind remark?

Self-Check Questions for Review
Content-Related Questions

1. One of the practical ways to encourage play is for the teacher to accept its value in a wholehearted way. Name four or five additional practical ways to encourage play that were discussed in the text.

2. Pretend you are giving a talk to a group of parents and you wish to explain to them why play is important in the lives of young children. (You will probably give this talk many times during your teaching career!) Give some examples that illustrate how play benefits the physical, emotional, social, creative, and cognitive selves of the child.

3. What are some practical things teachers can do to foster play for each of the child's five selves? (These are

the physical, social, emotional, creative, and cognitive selves.)

4. Why is it especially valuable to offer play opportunities to children with disabilities?

Integrative Questions

1. On a field trip, the children visited a family that raises rabbits. Upon return, the teacher passes out rabbit-ear hats and encourages the children to hop around like rabbits. What do you think Sutton-Smith would say about that activity?

2. Compare the suggestions about what teachers can do to help foster emotional growth in play with suggestions for fostering physical growth through play. How do the suggestions differ?

3. Propose two ways you might adjust an ordinary 4-year-old classroom to accommodate the needs of a child in a wheelchair. Now propose two ways you might modify the same room to accommodate a child who requires crutches to get around. Would the same adjustments facilitate the play of both children? If not, how might they differ?

Coordinating Videotape

Creativity and play. Tape # 11. The whole child: A caregiver's guide to the first five years. The Annenberg/CPB Collection, P.O. Box 2345, South Burlington, VT 05407-2345. *Creativity and Play* outlines the role of creativity in healthy child development, provides examples of how to encourage it, and devotes the second half of the tape to explaining why play is vital for healthy development and how to encourage it to flourish.

References for Further Reading
Pick of the Litter

Paley, V. G. (2004). *A child's work: The importance of fantasy play.* Chicago, IL: University of Chicago Press. A gem of a little book with a big message: Fantasy play is critical for children's full psychological, intellectual, and social development.

Overview

Isenberg, J. P., & Jalongo, M. R. (2006). *Creative thinking and arts-based learning: Preschool through fourth grade* (4th ed.). Upper Saddle River, NJ: Merrill/Prentice Hall. This book is filled with practical suggestions about incorporating play and self-expressive materials into the classroom.

Taking Cultural Differences into Account

Hyun, E. (1998). *Making sense of developmentally and culturally appropriate practice (DCAP) in early childhood education.* New York: Lang. In a valuable chapter, Hyun identifies different attitudes toward play sometimes held by various cultural groups. *Highly recommended.*

Special Help for Teachers

Widerstrom, A. H. (2005). *Achieving learning goals through play: Teaching young children with special needs* (2nd ed.). Baltimore, MD: Brookes. The authors offer many practical suggestions for using play-based activities to include all children in the life of the classroom.

Help for Elementary Teachers

Bronson, M. B. (2004). Choosing play materials for primary school children. In D. Koralek (Ed.), *Spotlight on young children and play* (pp. 22–23). Washington, DC: National Association for the Education of Young Children. Title is self-explanatory.

For the Advanced Student

Frost, J. L., Wortham, S. C., & Reifel, S. (2005). *Play and child development.* Upper Saddle River, NJ: Merrill/Prentice Hall. The authors devote nearly 600 pages to a definitive, comprehensive presentation of play in its many facets.

Piaget, J. (1962). *Play, dreams, and imitation in childhood.* New York: Norton. In his classic description, Piaget discusses how children assimilate knowledge of the world around them by means of imitation and the use of symbolic play. Rather difficult but interesting reading.

Related Organizations and Online Resources

International Association for the Child's Right to Play publishes various materials, such as the *PlayRights* quarterly newsletter, and conducts meetings that champion the child's right to play. http://www.ipausa.org/

Lekotek is a nonprofit organization that makes the world of play accessible to children with all types of disabilities. Nationwide, there are 33 Lekotek sites that offer family play sessions, toy lending libraries, and family computer centers. http://www.lekotek.org/

The Association for the Study of Play (TASP) is a multidisciplinary organization whose purpose is to promote the study of play. TASP publishes a newsletter that includes book reviews, research updates, and other information. TASP also publishes the *Annual Volume of Play and Culture Studies.* http://www.csuchico.edu/kine/tasp/index.html

DESIGNING THE SUPPORTIVE ENVIRONMENT

Have you ever . . .

- Felt torn between choosing something cheaper and practical or something beautiful for the children to use?
- Gone 3 weeks in a row without changing a thing in the room environment?
- Felt sick and tired of the children just running around when they went outside?

If you have, the material in this chapter will help you.

The aesthetics in a children's setting are, as is everything else, a tradeoff of cost, convenience, and health concerns. Plants and animals require tending. Fluorescent lighting is cost effective; uniform lighting results in maximum flexibility. Washable surfaces are healthier and more functional: water, earth, and clay are messy, and so on. Too often the tradeoffs don't take into account equally important concerns—appreciation for the rich, sensual nature of children and the importance of beauty in our lives.

—Jim Greenman (1998, p. 109)

SOME YARDSTICK QUESTIONS TO ASK

When thinking about the environment in which the children and staff will live while at the center, teachers can ask some helpful yardstick questions. These are closely related to what the teacher believes is most important about the purpose of curriculum and how young children learn. For example, if teachers believe the purpose of education is to increase competence for each of the child's selves, they might apply the following yardstick question to evaluate the environment: *Will this arrangement help children be competent and successful?* Accomplishing the goal implied by this question might involve something as simple as placing a row of tires as a barrier between the tricycle activity and the sandbox area so that riders need not be continually reprimanded for intruding on the diggers' space, thereby preserving their self-esteem by avoiding criticism of their behavior. It also might involve using small, transparent pitchers at snack time to make it easier for children to pour skillfully without spilling. Or it might involve enlarging the block corner so that children are less likely to antagonize each other by stumbling over each other's constructions.

If teachers believe that children learn best when all their senses are involved, they will continually incorporate these kinds of opportunities into the physical environment. They will tie visual experiences to concrete ones whenever possible. Perhaps they will start by opening a book to an exquisite drawing of a growing plant and placing it beside plants that the children have started for themselves. Perhaps they will encourage the children to listen to the silkworms chewing on their leaves and to feel their soft, dry bodies as well as to look at them. Good yardstick questions to ask here might be: *Does this environment appeal to all the senses? What will the*

Children learn best when all their senses are involved.

55

children be able to do with what is set out here? If the answer is "Just look," this is a clue that something should be modified.

If teachers believe that curriculum topics should respond to the children's interests, they will listen to these concerns carefully and create not only a curriculum that responds to these interests but also a physical environment that reflects them. A good question to ask here is: *Where did this idea come from?* Did it come from the children, or is it simply a piece of "embalmed" curriculum the teacher finds convenient to get out once again? Although physical settings often benefit from the use of resources accumulated from past years, they also derive great benefits from the addition of new resources that enhance the current children's interests. Adding these fresh items sustains both the teachers' and children's interest in the subject and helps ensure that teaching materials will be relevant to the current group of youngsters.

If teachers believe that parents are an indispensable part of the children's lives, and, hence, of the school's, they will ask themselves: *Is this a place that makes parents truly welcome?* Is there a comfortable place for them to sit when they come in? Does staff take time to chat and listen to their comments and suggestions? Is their participation sincerely welcomed, or merely endured?

If teachers are convinced that children learn to appreciate beauty by experiencing it, they will ask themselves these questions regarding the overall environment:

- What does the room look like today? Is it colorful but not garish?

- Is it orderly and clean but not bare or stark?

- Is it interesting without being overwhelming?

- Is it beautiful?

- Is it comfortable and homey?

Finally, if teachers believe that emotional comfort is as important to the developing whole child as physical needs, they will pay particular attention to the emotional climate that is expressed—both explicitly and implicitly—in the school. The Chapter Spotlight on page 58 discusses further how teachers can provide a comfortable environment for the emotional self.

PLANNING THE INDOOR ENVIRONMENT

Another Question: What Kind of Impression Will the Room Make on the Children?

Before getting down to the functional practicalities of room arrangement, a vital question to consider is what the room says to the children when they walk in the door.

Once the word *school* is mentioned, it is so easy to think in terms of chalkboards, tables, and chairs with a few bookshelves and possibly an easel scattered around the edge. But what does that setting say to young children? When they see mostly tables and chairs, what does that tell them about comfort and naturalness? When they see a great big room—larger than anything they live in at home—what does this suggest about friendliness and intimacy?

The truth is that children don't like environments that are littered with tables. There is even a delightful, old-time study recounting an experiment in which the children were invited to rearrange their room as they saw fit. They hardly used any tables in their redesign. Moreover, the staff reported that—as they paid closer attention to what the children were telling them, and as they encouraged the children to carry out their own ideas—the amount of conflict among children was reduced, and they began to solve more of their social difficulties for themselves (Pfluger & Zola, 1972). Wouldn't this be an interesting experiment to try out in your own classroom?

What children prefer instead of the tables and large, unfriendly spaces are smaller, cozy situations combined with sufficient room in which to move freely. A smaller space feels more homey and welcoming. Perhaps it includes a couch or some soft pillows tucked in a corner by the bookshelves, a generous yet sheltered space for blocks, a work-in-process area, an intriguing pretend area, another near the sink for messing about with paint and clay, and soft surfaces, color, and warmth to complete this cheerful, homelike, comfortable setting.

Planning Environments for Aesthetic Appeal

Not only should the children's space be comfortable and homey, but it should also be beautiful and appealing. Olds (1998) sums it up well when she says:

> Children live according to the information provided by their senses, and feast upon the nuances of color, light, sound, touch, texture, volume, movement, visual and kinesthetic vibration, form, and rhythm, by which they come to know the world. Their play is largely a response to variations in the environment. As the Hindus claim, "Sarvam annam,"—everything is food. Environments must be consciously and lovingly created to uplift the spirit and honor children's heightened sensibility. It is not sufficient that a setting be adequate. It must, instead, be beautiful.[*]

It is not necessary to put off improving the environment until a good fairy produces a flush budget for us. A bright pillow, a lovely painting, or a blooming plant can enliven a room with fresh color that delights both heart and eye during the day. We must never forget that the next generation's taste is being formed by the environment with which we surround them.

Wall coverings such as bulletin boards deserve special mention here when discussing environments because some teachers put so much emphasis on their design. If well done, these boards can tell children something valuable about how the school views their abilities. When their work is attractively presented and changed frequently, they can see that their work is valued and respected. In the Reggio schools, for example, the teachers take many photographs of the children's work to document its progress and mount these on boards so everyone can remember and appreciate what is happening.

The material on bulletin boards should be placed low enough that short people (that is, children) can see it easily. Often adults unthinkingly place items of interest at their own height, and the children do not benefit from such displays if they must crane their necks to see them. It is a sound principle to get right down to the children's height when planning wall arrangements and take a look at them from the children's position—the results can sometimes be surprising.

In their delightful books on teaching-learning environments, Jones (1977) and Jones and Prescott (1978) speak of the hardness–softness dimensions in the school environment. Softness should surely be a part of the aesthetics of the center, they say. Cozy furniture, carpeting, sand, rocking chairs, and laps all fall into this category, as do play dough, animals, and strap swings. These might all be thought of as simply "soft to touch," but the authors define their common quality in a different way: They describe a "soft" environment as one that is sensorily responsive. For example, a playground with grass, sand, and tires to bounce on is more sensorily responsive than is an asphalt one with metal play equipment. If we wish to make this sensorial responsiveness part of the room itself as well as part of the curriculum, we must strive for an overall effect that is homey and comfortable—"soft" in every sense of the word.

Some examples of ideal environments are found in the Italian city of Reggio Emilia where outstanding preschool education has been developing since the end of World War II (Ceppi & Zini, 1998; Hendrick, 1997; Hendrick, 2004). Briefly stated, the child-centered

[*]From "Places of Beauty," by A. R. Olds, 1998, in D. Bergen (Ed.), *Play as a Medium for Learning and Development* (p. 124), Olney, MD: Association for Childhood Education International. Copyright 1998 by Association for Childhood Education International. Reprinted with permission.

Providing Comfortable Environments for the Emotional Self

The primary emphasis in this chapter is on creating the most desirable physical setting for the children and staff to enjoy while living together at the school. But, at the same time, we cannot overlook another important aspect of environment. That component is the climate—in this case, the *emotional* climate—because it colors and affects everything that happens within that physical setting. So it is appropriate here to provide a preview of some basic elements of a comfortable emotional climate that will be discussed in more detail later in the book.

The first of these is the feeling of respect for everyone that should pervade the school. Such respect is conveyed by paying careful attention to what people, both children and adults, are saying to the teacher—hearing not only their words but who they really are and what they are feeling on the inside, and then responding to that feeling as sensitively and respectfully as possible.

Being able to have such interchanges implies the presence of the second element: an overall sense that there is plenty of time for such communion to take place. Of course, we all know there are many times during the day when all the children want everything at the same time, but well-planned schedules also provide interludes that allow time enough for one-to-one encounters. Such intimate moments let each person know that who they are and what they feel is valued.

The third basic ingredient of an emotionally comfortable climate is the sense that the environment is stable and reasonable. The children can generally predict what will happen next and can depend on teachers to help it happen. They can rely on the teachers to follow through on their promises, enforce the rules, and remain steady and in control of themselves while doing this—and, also, the children can count on them to intervene when situations escalate beyond their control.

Finally, this stability must be balanced by an openness to change and new ideas. Openness is a crucial aspect of the climate because feeling comfortable with innovation lies at the heart of implementing the responsive curriculum—curriculum that is sensitive to the interests of the children and follows those leads while also incorporating valuable educational goals identified by the teacher.

Granted, reality often falls short of this ideal—the teacher's feet hurt, three children are squabbling over the fire truck, and Henry has hidden his shoes (again!) and his mother is waiting. Trying circumstances such as these cause us to lose sight of our ideals temporarily. But even though glitches get in the way from time to time, it is still important to keep the long-term ideal in view. Teachers who cultivate a vision of respect embedded in unhurried time combined with stability and a responsive curriculum are most likely to provide the benign emotional climate that is such an important part of the overall environment.

philosophy of these schools is based on respect for the child that emphasizes collaborative learning among child, teacher, and family. The physical environment of the school is seen as a vital element in facilitating the relationship of children to the world around them, and teachers often comment that "the environment is the third teacher."

For this reason, the schools are designed with much emphasis on reducing the sense of barrier between outdoors and indoors through the use of large windows, airy ceilings, white walls, and pale woodwork. There are often windows between interior spaces as well, and even talking tubes are included between rooms to facilitate communication. The rooms themselves are colorful and filled with light while not seeming gaudy. Examples of the children's work are displayed throughout the buildings. Mirrors abound and are set at many unusual (to us) angles to encourage children to familiarize themselves with more than simple frontal views of their bodies. Everywhere there is a sense of space, color, light, joy, and growing things. What inspiration these rooms can provide if we, too, give thought to the important role beauty plays

Why should children have to put up with an environment that is not beautiful? What does a situation like this communicate to the children?

as we create room environments for our children. Sergio Spaggiari, director of the Reggio preprimary schools, puts it like this:

> In our experience, we have also placed a great deal of importance to aesthetics and beauty. We have never been able to understand why children should have to put up with an environment that is not beautiful. . . . It is very important to take care of the quality of the environment. The environment has a silent language, which interacts with the child and can facilitate processes of living, of learning and of relating to others. (2004, p. 4)

Including Multicultural Elements in the Design

It also contributes to the feeling of homeyness and comfort when the ethnic and cultural backgrounds of children are matter-of-factly represented in the physical environment of the school (Barrera, 2001). The inclusion of multiethnic pictures, books, and artifacts will contribute to the children's overall feelings of being valued for their own cultural richness, but *the inclusion of such things should constitute just the bare beginnings of multicultural experiences.* Opportunities for learning about other cultures, as discussed further in chapter 13, should be provided on a continuing basis throughout the year and should stress two things: first, that all people have many things in common—they get sleepy, feel hungry, and sometimes are sad or happy; and second, that everyone has different, unique, and valuable contributions to make to the life of the group.

Even though teachers should be casual and matter-of-fact in teaching these values, they should be persistent in planning for their inclusion as part of the environment. For example, the fact that all kinds of people have some needs in common could be taught by borrowing a tatami mat and quilts from a Japanese friend and encouraging the children to play "going to bed" using the Japanese bed and also using a Western-style sleeping bag. Meanwhile, the teacher could point out that everyone gets tired and sleepy and that they satisfy this need in different but equally practical and comfortable ways.

Total Learning begins with the statement that the purpose of education is to increase competence, and that statement is as true for children with disabilities as for more typical youngsters. When such children are mainstreamed into the ordinary school, one of the easiest ways to increase their competence is to take a good look at the physical environment and do everything possible to maximize the mainstreamed child's independence and ability to be self-sufficient.

It is good to realize that making such adjustments is no longer a matter of choice since the Americans with Disabilities Act became law. The act requires all public agencies, including children's centers, to make their services accessible to all people with disabilities (Cook, Tessier, & Klein, 2004). Part of being accessible has to do with removing physical barriers to access. For example, an obvious barrier might be a flight of steps up to the school—so it might be necessary to build a ramp to replace it. Or it might be necessary to rearrange the room to make it easier to maneuver a wheelchair around the other furniture.

Although space does not permit extensive recommendations on adapting environments for specific disabilities, there are some useful general principles to remember. More specific recommendations may be found in the References for Further Reading at the end of the chapter.

Common sense coupled with keen observation by the teacher are indispensable when seeking solutions for special problems. For instance, we had a 4-year-old who was partially sighted at the Institute, who always sat on the stairs and inched her way down them on her bottom despite the fact that there was a rail nearby. When we took a closer look at the stairs, we realized they were painted gray and all blended together. Adding a black strip at the edge of each step made them much more visible (and safer for everyone), and the sharper contrast enabled her to walk down them with confidence because she could see where the edge was.

Another helpful thing to do is to ask the family and the child development team for suggestions. These people are usually gold mines of ideas. Or they may have access to references that would be helpful.

It is also valuable to make a special effort to reduce confusion and clutter wherever possible. Some teachers, for example, keep music playing all day long or are insensitive to an escalating volume of noise. Such environments are particularly difficult for children who do not hear well or are exceptionally distractible. Other teachers unthinkingly allow a clutter of abandoned dress-up clothes or blocks to accumulate, which will surely trip up a child who cannot see. Sometimes a special piece of equipment, such as a U-shaped table to accommodate a wheelchair, will enable a child with special needs to participate more readily.

On the other hand, some youngsters who are developing more slowly than most do not require special equipment but just need materials that are appropriate for their developmental level (for example, puzzles with fewer, larger pieces or climbing equipment that does not require careful judgment about potential risks).

Whatever physical changes are contemplated, there is one most important thing to remember when thinking about modifying the environment: Be sure to ask yourself the right question. That question is *not* How can I keep this child protected and safe?—although safety for all children is important. The most important question to ask is: *How can I help each child be successful today?* Effective modification of the physical environment offers great potential for accomplishing that goal.

Arranging the Indoor Environment To Function Well

Can the physical arrangement of the room really make a difference in children's behavior? The answer is yes—and for this reason, in addition to considering the aesthetic, multicultural, and special-needs requirements related to arranging indoor environments, teachers should consider room arrangement. The way the environment is arranged definitely affects children's and adult's behavior, as confirmed by a number of studies (Babcock, Hartle, & Lamme, 1995; Petrakos & Howe, 1996).

For example, researchers found that the size of an activity area made a substantial difference in the length of time children played in the activity and how quickly they became involved in complex play. Small and sheltered was definitely better (Tegano, Moran, DeLong, Brickey, & Ramassini, 1996). The researchers make a good case for including nooks and crannies, a loft, screening, or even a closet with the door removed as potential sheltered spaces. At the Institute, we used an old fireplace filled with pillows to partially satisfy this need. The children loved it.

Children love small, cozy spaces.

As mentioned previously, including the children in planning the environment can also have beneficial effects. Witness the delight Karen Haigh describes when the children were encouraged to furnish their own cubbies—and consider what satisfying, personal, homey touches such embellishments must have contributed to her center:

> Children took weeks to think about, plan, purchase, bring from home, or make items to put in their cubbies. This was an excellent example of looking at the image of the child. Most often the teachers decide what will be in the child's cubbies: usually some type of sign for a name or some kind of symbol, but when thinking about children's capabilities, if children are supported and their ideas are respected, they are more than capable of planning and decorating their own cubbies. This is a small example of allowing the children to do for themselves what they are capable of doing and not robbing them of an opportunity. The children had many ideas for their cubbies as evidenced by photos of families, drawn pictures, cut-out pictures from magazines, miniature mobiles, miniature painted wood cut-outs, stuffed animals, and mirrors. Everyone wanted a mirror installed in their cubby. (Haigh, 1997, p. 161)

Indoor Activity Areas

Particular indoor activity areas commonly include the unit block area, a reading and story corner, one or more places for dramatic play (this usually includes a housekeeping area but should be able to accommodate many other pretend play situations from time to time), space for creative self-expressive activities and tabletop activities, and an investigation-in-process area that varies with the current focus of interest.

Of course, many areas in the children's center serve more than one purpose during the day. The carpeted block area, for instance, readily converts to a comfortable group time spot, and most full-day centers must use all available floor space for cots and mats at nap time.

Remember, too, to provide space for families that includes a comfortable place to sit, helpful resources, and, from time to time, a cup of coffee or cold drink.

Getting Started: Things to Consider

Unchangeable Items. Suppose that you, the teacher, are stepping into your room for the first time, and it is completely empty. (Sometimes when teachers have been teaching in the same room for awhile, they find it worthwhile to put everything out in the hall and simply experience the empty space while thinking about it and the children who will occupy it.) Now take note of unchangeable items such as the location of doors, windows, built-in cabinets, water facilities, and electric outlets, and examine how these "givens" affect the way things must ultimately be arranged in the room. (For example, the most convenient place for the cooking table is near both the sink and a power supply.)

Traffic Patterns.   Next, think about the traffic patterns. Can furniture be arranged to provide unimpeded pathways to the "go-home" door, bathrooms, and outdoor play areas? Can it be used as buffers and dividers to prevent undesirable patterns from developing, so that block and book corners and the dramatic play area are protected from unnecessary intrusions?

Available Furniture.   Then go out in the hall and look at the available furniture with a fresh perspective. Try to see the playhouse stove or the book cabinet in terms of its potential as an area demarcator or as an empty space on which a child's picture could be displayed or as a countertop for holding an interesting exhibit. Sometimes it is helpful to play the game "If I couldn't . . . " ("If I couldn't use this cabinet as a bookcase, what else could I use it for?"). Doing this can allow you to discover new possibilities in even the most mundane furnishings.

Noise Levels.   Noise levels must be considered, too. It is wisest to separate noisy areas as far from each other as possible. For example, if carpentry cannot be done outside, consider placing it at one end of the room, which will keep it out of the traffic pattern and will prevent (at least partially) the sound of hammering from rocketing through the school. Consider also whether it might be possible to use part of the hall for this purpose; as long as a teacher must devote undivided attention to it anyway, moving the activity to the hallway will not take a teacher from her duties.

Quiet Areas.   Quiet areas must be created to balance the more noisy, high-activity ones. Consider how tiring it is even for an adult to be in the constant company of other people. Although we think of children as generally seeking the company of other children, they find it equally exhausting to endure the continual stimulation and adjustments from constant contact with other people. Children need quieter, somewhat secluded places to which they can withdraw when they have had a surfeit of contact. Such arrangements may vary from a comfortable sofa with books nearby to an unused fireplace where children snuggle down into a mass of pillows.

Placement of Activities.   Finally, think about the various activities you want to include and where these would be most sensibly placed, taking into consideration the unchangeable givens, the desirable and undesirable traffic patterns, the need for noise and stimulation control, and the available equipment. Remember also to place activity areas with an eye to the accessibility of storage, the level of illumination needed, and the desirability of distributing activities throughout the room. Plan also for open spaces into which activities and children can spread as needed.

Evaluate and Reevaluate the Results

Once you have decided where everything should be placed, have included the aesthetic and multiethnic ingredients, have adapted the environment for children with special needs, and have kept practicality in mind, then it is time to try out the arrangement. Observe how the staff and children live within this environment together. Ask yourself if the plan is achieving the desired purposes. If not, why not? Perhaps it just requires waiting a bit longer for the changes to seem natural, or perhaps there are some unanticipated glitches that require correction. Never hesitate to rearrange things once again to achieve the educational goals you deem most desirable.

The *Infant/Toddler Environment Rating Scale* (Harms, Cryer, & Clifford, 2003), the *Early Childhood Environment Rating Scale* (Harms, Clifford, & Cryer, 2004), and the *Early Childhood Program Standards and Accreditation Performance Criteria* (National Association for the Education of Young Children, 2005) provide useful standards and methods of assessing the quality of a school's physical environment. These criteria have been tried and true over the years and work well with most state and federal standards.

PLANNING THE OUTDOOR ENVIRONMENT

The outdoor play area is just as valuable and important to plan and arrange wisely as is the indoor area. Too often teachers who take pains over their interior rooms think of outdoor play as primarily having large-muscle values, but a well-arranged play yard includes opportunities for the development of all the child's selves (Frost, Wortham, & Reifel, 2005). Therefore, in addition to swings, sandboxes, slides, and wheeled toys, outdoor areas should contain gardens, animals, and places for water and mud play. Opportunities for pretend play can be especially rich outdoors if a plentiful supply of sturdy boxes, boards, ladders, and perhaps a parachute is available. Science activities, particularly those in natural science and physics, fit in well outside if equipment such as water, pulleys, ropes, and living materials is included in the environment. Many art activities such as finger painting are also better suited to the more easily cleaned and less restrictive outdoor area.

Schools in colder climates lack the freedom of having some of these activities take place outside in winter months, but they do possess the advantage of vastly changing weather conditions, which can provide an appetizing variety of activities—if teacher and children dress warmly enough! In addition to grassy areas, a well-planned winter environment contains dry outdoor playing areas that are larger than usual and surfaced with asphalt, cement, or shredded bark so that the children do not become wet and chilled. Particular attention should be given to wind protection so that the children can spend considerable time outdoors almost every day.

Things to Consider

When arranging and developing the outdoor activity areas to increase their potential for richer play, teachers should ask themselves these questions:

- What direction is the play taking? What is there in reserve that might be added to deepen and extend it as it progresses?
- How can I involve the children in concocting solutions to items needed in their play?
- What is there on the playground that could be combined or recombined to produce a *complex* or *super unit* instead of several simple ones?
- How can I arrange this area so the children will be encouraged to play together?
- Is there a way to modify the setting to make it more accessible for our children with disabilities?

The Playground.

Many of the principles mentioned in regard to indoor planning apply equally to outdoor planning. It is important to provide clear pathways that invite children to move to different areas. Planning to prevent congestion by dispersing interesting areas throughout the yard is also valuable, and placing activities near their storage units makes effective use of equipment more probable. Shaded areas and a diversity of surfacing materials where possible are important to consider, too.

Outdoor Equipment.   In addition, the analysis of kinds of outdoor equipment done by Kritchevsky, Prescott, and Walling (1996) has particular merit, because there tend to be many more "simple" units used outdoors than inside. According to these researchers, a *simple unit* has "one obvious use and does not have sub-parts or a juxtaposition of materials which enable a child to manipulate or improvise. (Examples: swings, jungle gym, rocking horse, tricycle)" (Kritchevsky et al., 1996, p. 146). This kind of equipment is limited in play value because of the number of children it can interest at one time and the length of time it is likely to keep even one child occupied.

A *complex unit*, on the other hand, is defined as one "with sub-parts or juxtaposition of two essentially different play materials which enable the child to manipulate or improvise. (Examples: sand table with digging equipment; play house with supplies.) Also included in this category are single play materials and objects which encourage substantial improvisation and/or have a considerable element of unpredictability. (Examples: all art activities such as dough or paints; a table with books to look at; an area with animals such as a dog, guinea pigs, or ducks)" (p. 146). A *super unit* is a complex unit that has "one or more additional play materials, i.e., three or more play materials, juxtaposed. (Examples: sand box with play materials and water; dough table with tools; tunnel, movable climbing boards and box, and large crates)" (p. 146).

These units can involve more children at the same time and sustain each child's interest longer. Jones (1977) reported in another publication that "a super unit is about eight times as effective in holding a child's attention as a simple unit; a complex unit about four times as effective" (p. 12).

Certainly teachers who wish to promote positive social action, creative problem solving, and richer play as part of their outdoor curriculum will do well to assess the outdoor play equipment and convert it to complex and super units where possible. One of the easiest and most productive ways of doing this is to acquire the supply of boards, sawhorses, crawl-through blocks, mattresses, and large hollow blocks recommended in chapter 9. If these are moved to various areas at different times and are used in conjunction with other, less movable equipment, they add instant complexity and play possibilities to areas as diverse as the sandbox and jungle gym. Adding dramatic play props such as dolls, housekeeping paraphernalia, or fire hats and hoses is another easy way to change a simple unit to a complex or super one and in so doing enrich the children's outdoor play experience.

MAINTAINING THE TOTAL ENVIRONMENT IN GOOD ORDER

Another aspect of the development of the physical environment is worth considering: the overall impression that the physical environment conveys. Mundane as it may seem, orderliness and cleanliness play vital roles in that impression.

Of course, some items, such as the plastic cover used at the clay table, are better left uncleaned. Maintaining good order should not become a fetish in a children's center, but cleanliness is appreciated by experienced visitors who have all too often come across schools with sticky chairs, smudged blocks, and grubby puzzles with missing pieces. Days at a center move at a quick and ever-changing pace, which makes it difficult, though not impossible, to keep things looking fresh and well maintained. Table 4.1 contains many suggestions for keeping maintenance simple and for saving money, too.

Table 4.1
Money-Saving Tips on Maintaining and Preserving Equipment

Preservation and Maintenance	Additional Comments

Furniture

Buy varnished or lacquered shelves, cabinets, and so on, rather than painted ones. They require less frequent refurbishing.

Look for easily cleaned plastic surfaces on tabletops and chairs. Chairs, in particular, soil easily, so purchase ones that will hold up under frequent washing and do not require repainting; ones with plastic backs and seats are good choices.

Check all furniture regularly to make certain that nuts and bolts are tight.

Wax all wood and plastic furniture with paste wax before using initially and after washing. This cuts work and saves surfaces. (Children like to help polish the result.)

Buy furniture with casters when possible to aid movement. Avoid "built-ins" when you can; they reduce flexibility.

Scratched and marred surfaces can be recovered with plastic similar to Formica, but which can be cut with scissors and glued with a special adhesive.

Buy good-quality, substantial items or have them made; it saves money in the long run.

Haunt thrift shops and rummage sales for low dressers, shelves, old tables, and so forth. Tables are easy to shorten—all it takes is a saw, muscles, and careful measurement. It makes money go further.

Floors

Use linoleum as the basic surface (carpeting is impossible to keep clean in eating or art areas), but provide carpeted spaces where possible. (Keep carpets away from outdoor entries.)

An old-fashioned carpet sweeper is very handy for quick rug cleanup by children or teachers.

String mops are more effective than sponge mops after water play.

A drain in the bathroom floor facilitates frequent cleaning and disinfecting; it makes indoor water play more welcome.

Carpeting adds warmth, comfort, noise control, and "softness" to the room; tightly woven ones are best for easy vacuuming. Small area rugs that can be shaken out and moved easily are nice if they do not wrinkle too much; use nonskid mats underneath.

Files (Picture, Poetry, Flannel Boards, Songs)

Mount them on stiff cardboard or mat board. (Rubber cement is a most satisfactory adhesive.)

Spray with clear, flat, acrylic spray.

File under topic headings for easy identification.

These files are invaluable educational resources, cost relatively little, and provide instant access to curriculum when a sudden interest arises from the children.

Books

Purchase durable, library-grade bindings to start with or cover with clear contact paper.

Repair books promptly with mending tape.

Teach children to handle books with loving care.

It adds variety to put some books away for use another day.

Keeping books sorted according to some simple classification system makes finding that "special" book easier.

Stack on shelves according to kind; never dump in bins.

Unit Blocks

Wax with paste wax before use.

It is occasionally necessary to wash really dirty blocks. Do *not* soak. Dry immediately to avoid roughening and raising grain.

Use on flat, "tight" carpeting: It deadens noise, is warmer for children to sit on, and protect corners of the blocks.

(Continued)

65

Table 4.1

(*continued*)

Preservation and Maintenance	Additional Comments
	Use homemade soft wood blocks as money stretchers. They do not wear well but will do in a pinch—so will sealed and stapled milk cartons if money is really tight. Be sure you provide a lot of them.

Tabletop Activity Materials

Preservation and Maintenance	Additional Comments
Mend broken corners of storage boxes immediately. Children can help.	Storage in see-through plastic boxes is ideal.
Have a special, centrally located little pot or box, and drop stray bits and pieces into it for weekly sorting; include nuts bolts, Tinkertoys, puzzle knobs, and so forth.	Presenting some items, such as colored bears, pegs, and cubical counting blocks, in a shallow basket makes them readily visible and appealing.
Label puzzle pieces with individual symbols on back for rapid sorting and reassembly.	When cardboard boxes are used for storage, draw a picture on the side or top so children can "read" what is inside.
Teach children to keep small, many-pieced items on the table; do not permit these to scatter. Using carpet squares, one per child, helps keep an activity focused in one place.	
Count pieces of some items before setting out, mark quantities on box, and recount before putting away (e.g., doctor's kit and simple games).	
Protect teacher-made activities with acrylic spray or clear contact paper.	
Inspect all items regularly for cleanliness, and wash when necessary.	

Tools (Cooking, Woodworking, Gardening)

Preservation and Maintenance	Additional Comments
Keep tools out of the weather, and keep them oiled and painted when necessary.	Purchase sturdy equipment that really works.
Teach children to use them for their intended purpose; do not discourage experimentation, but do not permit destructive abuse.	Store tools of all kinds with care; do not just dump in a box.

Self-Expressive Materials

Preservation and Maintenance	Additional Comments
Present messy activities away from carpeted areas.	Stack large sheets of paper on a series of narrow shelves rather than on one deep one for easy access; paper is heavy to lift.
Store cleanup materials used together in the same place; for example, keep sponges, detergent, and scrub brushes assembled in the finger painting bucket.	Store construction paper in closed cabinets to reduce fading.
Wash glue- and paintbrushes thoroughly, every time; store on end, wood tips down.	Sort donated materials as they arrive.
	Buy art materials in quantity whenever possible (test quality first; tempera paint varies a good deal, as does paper).
	Consider forming a purchasing co-op with other schools; bargain for discounts.

Wheel Toys

Preservation and Maintenance	Additional Comments
Always store under cover.	In the long run it pays to buy the expensive school-grade quality to this equipment; check warranties.
When possible, buy toys that do not require painting.	
Check nuts and bolts frequently; oil occasionally.	

Outdoor Equipment (Swings and Slides)

Avoid buying painted equipment; if you have it, sand, prime, and paint it regularly.	Inspect rigorously for safety.
Repair instantly, for safety's sake and to discourage further abuse.	Purchase removable, fiber swing seats with extra hooks.
Wooden jungle gyms placed on grass or dirt rot quickly.	If affordable, rubber matting under such equipment is wonderful.

Hollow Blocks, Boards, Sawhorses, Boxes, and So On

These should be lacquered with a product such as Deft every year.	Some brands of large plastic blocks are reported to bow in or out or to be too slippery to be satisfactory for climbing on and for stacking.
Use only on grass or carpet to prevent splintering (indoor-outdoor carpeting or artificial turf can be used for this purpose when the entire play area is paved).	Store molded plastic items in a warm place and wooden equipment in a dry place.

Animal Cages

Bottoms should be made of mesh to be self-cleaning. No animal should live in squalor.	Outdoor cages require shade, wind protection, and ventilation.
	Protect from vandals by keeping cages carefully mended and using quality padlocks.

Recommendations for the actual presentation of various materials to children are included throughout this book, so here in closing we will content ourselves with the remarks by Harms (1972) on the importance of how materials are maintained and displayed:

> Everything present in the environment, even the spatial arrangement, communicates to the child how to live in that setting. Materials that are in good condition and placed on open shelves tell a child that the materials are valued, that they are meant to be considered, and that a child may take them off the shelf by himself. When they are taken off the shelf, they leave a big empty space so it is easy to put them back where they belong. What kind of message does a child get from open shelves crowded with an odd assortment of materials, few with all the pieces put together? What kind of message does he get from a closed cupboard? (p. 59)

When materials are plentiful, whether they be collage supplies or blocks, this tells children they need not pinch and scramble for their share, which thus allows them to be more generous. When materials are changed regularly, this tells them that school is a varied and challenging place. When games, supplies, and other materials are complete and well cared for, this teaches children to take care also. When they are in good taste or, better yet, beautiful, this helps form children's taste for things of beauty and quality. When materials are multiethnic and nonsexist, this reminds children repeatedly of the fundamental equality and worth of every human being.

Summary

When planning the arrangement of indoor and outdoor space in the school, it is important to consider immovable givens, traffic patterns, noise levels, and ways to control the level of stimulation. Beauty and a comfortable emotional climate are also important components. Special thought should be devoted to including multiethnic and nonsexist areas, and the needs of children with disabilities must also be taken into consideration.

All of these factors are involved in the careful arrangement of the physical setting and contribute in substantial ways to the overall effect, the *ambience*, of the school. But, like the children themselves, ambience is more than the sum of its parts. Ambience is composed of many things: It includes the intangible glow the staff radiates in the morning, the feeling that there is time for everyone, the splash of color on the walls, the rocking chair in the corner, and the blooming plant on the windowsill. These all contribute to the sense of caring, personal concern, and beauty that careful planning and sound arrangement convey to the children.

Food for Thought and Group Discussions

1. You are now the teacher and you have six Vietnamese children as part of your group. In terms of creating the physical environment, what multiethnic touches would you add from their culture to help them feel at home?

2. You have just been employed as the teacher of fifteen 4-year-old children and you have been provided with a reasonably well-furnished, rectangular preschool classroom. Make a list of the most typical activities you anticipate occurring in your room—remember to plan for nap, group, toileting and meal times as well as items such as the book corner, cooking area, and so forth. Now, sketch out a plan showing how you would arrange the room to accommodate those activities.

3. What is the best storage idea you have observed in a child-care center? Share it with the class.

Self-Check Questions for Review

Content-Related Questions

1. Several yardstick questions are recommended to use when evaluating the environment. What are those questions? Why are they worthwhile to ask?

2. List some points that should be considered when arranging equipment in a classroom, and give practical examples of how equipment could be arranged to take these factors into consideration. For example, suggest a variety of purposes a bookcase might fulfill in addition to holding books.

3. What are some ways a teacher could add touches of beauty to the room?

4. Why are complex and super play units valuable to include both indoors and outside?

5. Name four basic elements that contribute to a comfortable emotional climate and explain why each is valuable.

Integrative Questions

1. Select a piece of outdoor play equipment and explain how a simple unit could be transformed into a complex or super play unit.

2. The text emphasizes that the environment should reflect the teacher's underlying philosophy. Give four examples of the way you would set up an early childhood room so that it would reflect your philosophy.

3. If using the bulletin board areas as spaces for sharing what the children have made conveys the message their work is valued, what might the use of the cardboard, cartoonlike characters such as Power Rangers or Disney-type animals convey as messages?

4. You have agreed to welcome a 4-year-old boy who has partial vision into your group. He can tell dark from light and is aware of large objects when these are in his path. Using your common sense, suggest several ways you could adapt your room environment to make it possible for him to function as independently as possible.

References for Further Reading

Pick of the Litter

Ceppi, G., & Zini, M. (Eds.). (1998). *Children, spaces, relations: Metaproject for an environment for young children.* Reggio Emilia, Italy: Reggio Children. The pictures and explanatory text convey the beauty, spirit, and vitality that pervade the preschools in Reggio. Readers may come away seeing the potential offered by environments in a new and inspiring way.

Overviews

Greenman, J. (2005). *Caring spaces, learning places: Children's environments that work* (Rev. ed.). Redmond, WA:

Exchange Press. Greenman provides wonderful ideas for anyone redesigning or designing space for children. The book is delightful to read—written with humor and experienced insight.

Planning the Indoor Space

Decker, C. A., & Decker, J. R. (2005). *Planning and administering early childhood programs* (8th ed.). Upper Saddle River, NJ: Merrill/Prentice Hall. For a comprehensive discussion of designing and furnishing a children's center, this is the place to start. Interesting, too, because it offers contrasting plans showing how rooms and playgrounds should be planned differently for preschool and elementary age children.

Planning the Outdoor Space

Frost, J. L., Brown, P., Sutterby, J. A., & Thorton, C. D. (2004). *The developmental benefits of playgrounds*. Olney, MD: Association for Childhood Education International. Beginning with theoretical discussions of play, and brain research that shows the importance of play, the authors offer a wealth of practical information for creating healthy, appropriate play spaces for young children. *An indispensable reference.*

Adapting Environments for Children with Disabilities

Gould, P., & Sullivan, J. (2005). *The inclusive early childhood classroom. Easy ways to adopt learning center for all*. Upper Saddle River, NJ: Merrill/Prentice Hall/Gryphon House. Here is a book geared to what real teachers need to know when working with real-life children who have various disabilities—and the disabilities themselves are also discussed. We can't recommend this book highly enough.

Information About Equipment

Bronson, M. B. (1995). *The right stuff for children birth to 8: Selecting play materials to support development*. Washington, DC: National Association for the Education of Young Children. Bronson opens each chapter with a list of developmental characteristics, and then recommends equipment for six ages according to various categories.

Evaluating Preschool Settings

Harms, T., Clifford, R. M., & Cryer, D. (2004). *Early childhood environment rating scale*. (Rev. ed.), New York: Teachers Press.

Harms, T., Cryer, D., & Clifford, R. M. (2003). *Infant/toddler environment rating scale* (Rev. ed.). New York: Teachers College Press. The Harms/Clifford Scales are simple to use and cover personal-care routines of children and creative activities to how well the needs of the adults are met.

National Association for the Education of Young Children. (2005). *Early childhood program standards and accreditation performance criteria* (Rev. ed.). Washington, DC: Author. This is another very useful set of criteria for measuring many aspects of quality programs, including the physical environment.

For the Advanced Student

Consumer Product Safety Commission. (1997). *Handbook for public playground safety*. Washington, DC: Author. This is the basic reference in the field for all playgrounds, preschool ones included. *Indispensable.*

Related Organizations and Online Resources

The National Program for Playground Safety (NPSS) is a nonprofit organization that serves as a national resource for educational and research information on playground safety. Many excellent resources are available on the Web site, including a newsletter and recommended equipment and suppliers. http://www.playgroundsafety.org/home.htm

Reggio Emilia can be found at more than one Internet location. To learn more about the importance of environment in the Reggio Emilia schools, visit their Web site. http://zerosei.comune.re.it/inter/

To catch a glimpse of some of the Reggio-inspired environments in North American schools, visit the Web site of the North American Reggio Emilia Alliance. http://www.reggioalliance.org/index.php

CHAPTER *five*

CREATING SUPPORTIVE CURRICULUM PLANS AND SCHEDULES

Have you ever . . .

- Had exciting ideas of what to offer the children but been puzzled about how to go about it?
- Needed an example of a basic schedule for a children's program?
- Wondered what the terms *child-centered* and *emergent curriculum* mean in terms of your own curriculum planning?

If you have, the material in this chapter will help you.

At no other level of education does a teacher have so much freedom and so few constraints concerning content, method and expected outcomes. Inherent in this freedom is both challenge and responsibility for careful, imaginative, resourceful planning for the education of young children.

—Oralie McAfee (1981)

Traditionally, I had made monthly plans, consistently fine-tuning procedures to make them more developmentally appropriate and process oriented. Materials were usually brought out for only one day, with new activities being introduced daily with hopes of keeping the children's interest stimulated. The ideas were teacher generated and carefully planned to avoid problems and keep conflict among the children to a minimum.

Inspired by Reggio, I totally abandoned this carefully worked out curriculum. One of the most important things that we did when making this change was slow down and tackle fewer activities on which we could emphasize more in-depth research.

—Cheryl Breig-Allen (1997, p. 128)

You got to be very careful if you don't know where you are going because you might not get there.

—Yogi Berra, as quoted in M. P. Zuckerman (1992, p. 88)

Chapter 4 discussed constructing wholesome environments for children—the *where* of what will happen. Now it is time to concentrate on planning curriculum—*what* and *how* it will happen—and scheduling it—*when* it will happen.

THE BASIC INGREDIENTS: WHAT SHOULD BE INCLUDED IN THE CURRICULUM?

Know What You Want the Children to Learn for All the Selves

The first chapter of *Total Learning* states that the basic purpose of education is to enhance children's feelings of being competent and cared for. Later chapters describe in detail how to achieve such feelings of security and self-worth for each of the five selves. We will content ourselves here with presenting a basic list of competencies, intended only as a summary of the most valuable skills children should begin to acquire as they move through a well-planned day at school. Teachers need to be aware of these skills so they can include them consistently when planning curriculum, particularly in view of today's standards-based education.

Developing the Physical Self. In addition to activities that provide for the health and safety of the children and help them understand and value life, there are activities specifically for the physical self that should be included in the curriculum. These include activities that provide practice in the following areas:

- Participating in movement and locomotion activities
- Practicing static and dynamic balance
- Developing body and space awareness
- Practicing rebound and airborne activities

71

- Fostering rhythm and temporal awareness
- Engaging in throwing and catching activities
- Using daily motor skills
- Participating in relaxation and tension-releasing activities

Developing the Emotional Self. A curriculum that favors the development of emotional health in children should include opportunities for learning to do the following:

- Separating comfortably from their families
- Achieving the basic attitudes of trust, autonomy, initiative, and industry (depending on age)
- Remaining in contact with their feelings while maintaining emotional control
- Using dramatic play and other self-expressive materials to come to terms with emotional problems
- Facing reality
- Beginning to understand how other people feel and feel empathy for them

Developing the Social Self. Curriculum for children's social selves should encompass the following:

- Learning to feel what they want but control what they do
- Acquiring socially acceptable strategies for getting what they want
- Learning to function successfully as a member of a group
- Finding satisfaction in helping each other
- Finding pleasure in accomplishing meaningful work
- Understanding their place in the world, and feeling good about their gender roles and cultural/ethnic heritages

Developing the Creative Self. Opportunities for children to develop their creative selves should include the following:

- Using a wide range of self-expressive activities
- Participating in imaginative dramatic play
- Engaging in creative thinking and problem solving

The social self is enhanced when children learn to function successfully as part of a group.

Developing the Cognitive Self. Finally, the children's cognitive selves should be enhanced by the following:

- Fostering *verbal ability* by (a) putting their ideas into words throughout the day and enjoying communicating with other people and (b) participating in carefully planned group times
- Developing *cognitive skills* by (a) pursuing interesting subjects (pathways) in depth, (b) analyzing choices and making decisions, and (c) figuring out answers for themselves
- Using the *midlevel mental abilities* of matching, perceiving common relations, grouping, temporal ordering, graduated ordering (seriation), and determining simple cause- and-effect relationships

Decide How to Incorporate the *What* and *How* into an Overall Plan

It is vital to realize right from the start of this discussion of curriculum planning that developing the plan requires a combination of structure and flexibility.

Careful structuring is the more usual, conventional aspect of planning curriculum content. This structure is essential because it ensures that all aspects of the self are covered. But there is another side to good content planning in addition to this structured approach. *Really good planning* also allows the curriculum to develop and change in a flexible way as the children's interests develop and take direction.

This is often called a *responsive* or *emergent curriculum* because it responds to the children's interests and emerges and is negotiated between teacher and children as the topic develops (Jones & Nimmo, 1994). It is this willingness to move with the children's interests—while at the same time analyzing those interests and singling some of them out to focus on—that provides the best opportunities for learning. At the same time, although it is extremely worthwhile to follow these burgeoning interests, this does not mean that overall curriculum plans should be abandoned. In the words of Rinaldi (1994), it is best to regard plans as a compass, not a train schedule. The Chapter Spotlight illustrates how such an interest might develop as the children think through various problems and possible solutions.

PLANNING WHAT WILL HAPPEN: DEVISING THE CURRICULUM PLAN

Developing a curriculum plan is accomplished most easily by identifying a subject stemming from the children's interests and considering several directions that subject might take the group over a period of time. Identifying overall possible directions is the best place to start because it is the overall direction that ultimately provides the momentum so important for generating continuing interest in the subject. After the steps for identifying that pathway have been accomplished and the long-term core pathway has been agreed on by the teacher and children, then additional related activities can be added to assure all the selves are provided with opportunities for their development, too.

Developing the pathway is most easily accomplished if the process is divided into a series of steps.

Step 1: Discover the Children's Interests

Begin with an aspect of the world that has caught the children's interests. The spontaneous interests of children vary widely. They might include tornadoes, or baby brothers and sisters, or what to do about Funny Bunny now that he's getting so big. But whatever it turns out to be, that interest should be the magnet that draws teacher and children together when considering a subject to pursue.

Sad to say, there are many situations where this is not the case. For example, witness the teacher whom Maloney (2000) describes in a discussion of classroom rituals:

> Helen adhered to a very strict regime over the year. She had developed a sequential structure for her yearly program, which had become a long-standing tradition for her. She had identified a set of topics and repeated these on a yearly basis with very little variation in the 20 years she had been teaching at Radford Pre-School. When I returned to her classroom one year later, she was talking about the same topic, using the same resources, and implementing the same activities. (p. 147)

An important philosophical aspect is contained in our curriculum planning choices. In the above example of embalmed curriculum, what message is given to the children about their ideas and interests? In order to develop a curriculum based on the interests of the children, one must first *really listen to the children*. As discussed in chapter 4, the emotional environment of the school is just as important as a beautiful physical environment. By co-constructing an emergent curriculum along with the children, teachers convey their respect for the children's ideas and abilities.

Contrast the embalmed curriculum approach with that of a Reggio-inspired teacher in Ohio:

> My take on themes vs. projects . . . themes are very cutesy oriented, driven by the teacher in what she feels is important: apples in September, pumpkins and Pilgrims fall. I feel the learning becomes surface level and limited, as we must not think outside the theme. Themes are often given a predetermined time length when they occur and their duration. . . .
>
> Projects (as based upon Reggio projects) are not predictable when they happen. They cannot be brought out of box nor are there directions. Teaching is always fresh! The life of a project is not predetermined . . . in that it is about having the children journey into a deeper place in their work and thinking.
>
> I would advise learning to slow down, as a tool for learning how to document and as a means for us to learn about children—not through a developmental chart which causes our focus to be very narrow and thus leads to that theme-like mindset—but looking at ordinary moments as revealing the child's thinking: their theories and strategies of how the world works which lends to the extraordinary projects that are exemplified in the project work of Reggio. (Gleim, 2005)

Step 2: Look for a Topic That Can Be Developed

Remember, when formulating curriculum plans, simply picking an interesting subject is not enough! Look for a topic that offers a core of continuing interest that could be developed.

Some might think it sufficient if teachers focus on a topic of interest to the children that would tie the curriculum together in a consistent way. Thus a "Rabbit Unit" might include reading books about rabbits, raising a baby rabbit, experimenting with what rabbits like to eat, comparing the texture of rabbit fur with that of other animals, analyzing the differences between rabbits and guinea pigs, and so forth. An array of activities could be carefully selected to make certain that all five selves—particularly cognitive ones—are included and developed. The result might be a rich, reasonably comprehensive array of activities focusing on one subject—rabbits, for instance—based on the children's interests but depending mostly on the teacher for their development and presentation.

The problem and limitation of this approach is that the curriculum has no ongoing momentum to it. No matter how many thought questions and problems are included, it really consists of just a series of topic-related experiences of mainly one or two days's duration.

What should be done instead is to include a core of longer-term, sustained interest that increases as the children's involvement grows. This core could be

In order to base curriculum on the children's interests and ideas, we must first observe and really listen to them.

an investigative experience where the children seek information and answers to questions, such as in Reggio where they explored how water actually reaches the fountain and what becomes of it after that. Or it could be an experience where they plan and construct something, as when the Reggio youngsters planned and constructed an amusement park for birds (Forman & Gandini, 1994).

There are two great advantages to providing this core. The first is that the extended time inherent in this approach allows opportunities for a rich array of problems to arise for discussion and solution as the pathway develops. The second advantage is the amount of mental stimulation at an appropriate developmental level this core provides for the children.

Some people prefer to think of such "cores" as being projects for the children to develop (Katz & Chard, 2000). Although we like and often use the word *project*, we prefer to picture this core as a *pathway* down which teacher and children venture together. For many people, *project* implies a finite, preplanned unit the children are expected to complete, whereas *pathway* implies an adventurous journey. As the path rounds a bend, sometimes unanticipated visions of learning possibilities are revealed to both teacher and children. But whether *project* or *pathway* is preferred, the necessity for building curriculum around a core of a continuing interest remains the same.

Step 3: Brainstorm with the Children About the Topic

Once a promising topic has been singled out, brainstorm with the children several directions the pathways of interest might take. Try not to settle on just one choice, however, in case it turns out to be a dead end, and consider breaking into smaller interest groups. Brainstorming is the crucial step in curriculum development where imagination and fancy should be allowed to wander and entertain all sorts of possibilities without evaluation or restriction.

For example, many children in Oklahoma are very interested in and afraid of tornadoes because they occur so frequently there. A teacher of 4-year-olds might list some of these possible pathways to investigate:

- What can tornadoes do?
- Practice safe tornado drills.
- Compare fire drills and tornado drills.
- How can we tell how hard the wind is blowing?
- Talk about places to go to be safe from tornadoes.
- Can you draw a tornado sound?
- Visit a TV station and see weather-reporting equipment.
- Experiment with different kinds of fans—handheld, electric, and so forth.
- Make a rain gauge to measure the amount of rain in a storm.
- Buy an anemometer to measure wind speed and have the children help hook it up.
- Where does wind come from? What makes wind?
- Can we make wind ourselves?
- How can we make wind blow harder or more gently?
- Fly kites with no wind and with some wind.
- Investigate bubbles—through straws in water, soap bubbles, balloons.
- How do you know whether a tornado is coming?
- Can we see wind?

How a Potential Pathway Might Develop with 4-Year-Olds:
Planning a Larger Pen for Funny Bunny

Potential Provocations *Things to Find Out* *Problems to Solve*	*Suggestions from Children and/or Teacher for Possible* *Ways to Find Out Answers or Produce Solutions*
Is Funny Bunny getting too big for his cage? How do we know whether the cage is still big enough? *Conclusion:* Cage is too small.	Compare previous pictures of F.B. with his current size. Let F.B. out and see if he does different things outside his cage.
How can we provide him with enough room so he can move more freely? Can we get a cage that's big enough?	Buy a bigger cage. Visit pet store. Look in catalogs.
How big is big enough . . . how big will F.B. turn out to be? *Conclusion:* Have to find out what breed of rabbit F.B. is.	Look up rabbits in books and on Internet. Different kinds of rabbits grow to different sizes.
How do we decide what kind of rabbit F.B. is? *Conclusion:* F.B. is a "regular" rabbit; i.e., not Angora or Lop-Eared.	Look at pictures of different breeds.
So . . . how big will he get? How can we measure a grown-up rabbit? *Conclusion:* So that's how big F.B. will grow.	Look up in book. Visit rabbit farm belonging to child's family. Measure grown rabbit with tape measure. Bring along stuffed animals and choose one the same size as a live grown-up "regular" bunny.

If he's going to grow to be that big, how big should his cage be?
    Is a cage really big enough for him to jump and hop around in?
Conclusion: F.B. needs more room than a cage provides—at least
    some of the time.
	Take similar size stuffed animal to pet store and see how it fits
	    in various size cages.

How can we fix it so F.B. has space to jump around?
Conclusion: F.B. chewed on table legs; wet on rug (although rabbits
    can be litter-box trained, he didn't "catch on"); rabbit droppings got
    stepped on; he spent most of the day hiding; having F.B. loose in
    room doesn't work, though he *did* get more exercise.
	Let him hop around the room.

If it doesn't work to let him loose in the room—what can we do instead? *Conclusion:* Give him away—too cruel; we love F.B. and want to keep him. *Conclusion:* He's too hard to catch outside; couldn't find him.	Let him hop around outside but not too far.
Could we pen him up some way? *Conclusion:* Sand box sides are too low—he jumps out; there were "B.M.s" in the sand; but pen would be a good idea.	Put F.B. in the sand box to keep him penned in.
Could we make a special pen with higher sides? How high should the sides be?	Watch F.B. hop and jump—make sides higher than that.
What could we make the pen out of? How can we decide?	Suggest various materials—boards, wire or plastic fencing; rope, etc. Visit hardware store—look at possibilities.
How can we make it? How can we hold up the sides?	Talk about possibilities. Draw ideas. Make models using clay for ground, sticks, wire mesh, netting; other materials as requested.
Where should we put it? Sun or shade? Grass, cement, or back porch?	Make patterns of paper as big as pen. Move pattern around different places—see where the shade moves.
Can we make it ourselves? How much help do we need?	

Examples of Cognitive, Verbal, and Creative Skills Used During Discussions

Have ideas; make comparisons; try out ideas; draw conclusions.

Figure out how to measure and record cage sizes.
Concept of money—how much cages cost; facing realities.
Literacy skill: Look up cages in catalog; "read" information, translate numbers into actual measurements.

Generate awareness of different ways to obtain information.
Learn how to acquire information.

Compare F.B. to pictures of rabbits.
Decide which picture goes most closely with real rabbit.

Understand numbers on measuring tape can be written down for later reference.
Creative idea: Use stuffed animal to visualize real size-equivalency.
Measure F.B. with tape—compare to same breed of fully grown rabbit.

Compare size of rabbit with size of cage.
Draw conclusions.
Make decisions.
Develop prediction skills.

Try out (experiment with) ideas.
Evaluate result of experiment.

Experiment: Draw conclusions; evaluate; decide.
Persistence in problem solving; generate alternative ideas.

Generate alternative ideas.
Experiment: Evaluate; draw conclusion.

Generate another alternative idea.
Observe: Estimate how high F.B. jumps—high as a tabletop? Knee? A chair seat?

Generate ideas.
Gather facts.

Gathering facts.
Put ideas into concrete form.
Transfer from one medium (words) into another form (concrete example).

Acquire information on shadows related to position of sun.
Evaluate grass/cement possibilities.

Evaluate possibilities and resources.

Other children might be equally interested in (though not as afraid of) rain. Potential pathways might be these:

- What would rain-type music sound like? Could you write it down some way?
- Where does the rain go that falls on the streets?
- What if it never rained—what could we do to get water?
- If we did not have boots and slickers, what could we use to stay dry?
- Are hail and snow really rain?
- How can we tell how much it has rained?
- What makes puddles dry up? Do they dry up faster in the sunshine, or under a tree?
- Why does it rain only when there are clouds in the sky?
- Experiment with different size holes in cans to make softer or harder rain.
- Use squirt bottles to discover how to make water pressure.
- See if we can make water fall up instead of down.
- Change water into its different forms—ice, steam.
- Can we make a rainbow?
- What could we use to make a rainy picture?

Or the children in the 3-year-old room might be particularly interested in babies because of new little brothers and sisters. Possible pathways for them might include the following:

- How do mothers take care of babies? (You might want to consider various animal mothers as well as humans.)
- Do rat mothers and bird mothers care for their babies the same way?
- Read books about babies.
- Talk about how it feels to be a baby.
- How can we take good care of baby animals?
- Bathing babies: Have Father visit and do this.
- How could we tell whether a baby is growing?
- How are babies different from children?
- Get out baby equipment and play house.
- Try on baby clothes—see how children have grown.
- Keep track of new skills as baby acquires them.
- Use picture puzzles of baby animals and their mothers.
- Invite Mom to school to feed baby with bottle and by nursing.
- Serve baby food at snack.
- Do all babies eat the same thing—animals and humans? How are the foods alike and different?
- Explore feelings that siblings may have about baby brothers or sisters.

Again, the importance of listening to the children's ideas, questions, and theories cannot be emphasized enough. Many teachers have found it useful to tape-record children's discussions and listen to them later to try to better pinpoint the children's interests.

Step 4: Evaluate the Realities of Pathways Under Consideration

The next step is to narrow the possibilities by recognizing what is possible and what is not, and then make tentative choices about which pathways to pursue further. In the process, several realities must be considered.

Reality 1: Which Ideas Are Most Developmentally Appropriate for the Children in the Group?

Older 4s might feel reassured by talking to the meteorologist and finding out how he or she keeps everyone safe during a storm, whereas young 3s would rather know that a safe place to go is available that will protect them. Two-year-olds are likely to be intrigued with actually trying on baby clothes and seeing how much they have grown, whereas 4-year-olds may think the answer so obvious that the idea is silly. On the other hand, the 4s might enjoy thinking of additional ways to measure and keep track of the baby's growth, whereas this might be too difficult a concept for young 3s to explore.

Reality 2: How Feasible Is the Idea?

How far away is the TV station? Does the teacher know where to locate fertile eggs to hatch? What if there are no mothers available who are willing to nurse a baby in front of an audience?

Reality 3: Which Topics Offer the Most Promising Potential for Developing Extended Pathways?

The lists of interests included under step 3 could all be potential starting points for investigations but, when considered further, some of them offer greater possibilities for more extensive development and "provocations" by the teacher than others do. For example, perhaps a preliminary investigation centering on whether puddles dry up faster in sun or shade might continue to hypothesizing about where that water goes or, perhaps, to figuring out what to do when there's too much water, and so forth.

When considering future directions a pathway might take, the teacher should also beware that sometimes pathways become so diffuse there is no focus or common avenue or theme that ties the information together. This is the problem that sometimes arises with *webbing* (Workman & Anziamo, 1996). When ideas are too loosely webbed or linked together, the pathway is lost sight of and teacher and children just wander around in ever-widening circles. For example, the children might be interested in how to find out what their guinea pig prefers to eat; this widens to how to grow plants for them, which then spreads to ideas about celebrating the harvest, which branches out to a discussion about Pilgrims.

The teacher's responsibility is to keep things on track while at the same time remaining sensitive to developing the areas that catch fire from the children's enthusiasm. Therefore, the teacher must consider whether some wonderful but extraneous ideas could best be used at another time. Perhaps the ideas about harvest and Pilgrims would fit in someplace else, for example.

Reality 4: Could This Pathway Offer Possible Short-Term Activities for the Five Selves?

For example, a continuing pathway or core experience related to tornadoes might be investigating various kinds and strengths of winds and how to make them happen, thereby offering a particularly rich reservoir of possibilities for developing the cognitive self in the realm of language and mental development. The creative self would be enriched by opportunities for children to represent their ideas about tornadoes by using various self-expressive materials. Because of the anxieties involved, the subject would also offer opportunities for dealing with emotional concerns. Planning about safety precautions for themselves and others could meet social and emotional needs, and physical activities would involve both small- and large-muscle skills as the children construct apparatus and run about trying to generate wind themselves.

Reality 5: Could This Pathway Be Used to Promote a Multiethnic or Nonsexist Approach?

If the subject is babies, sharing a cradle board during group time and explaining how Hopi mothers carry their babies on them, for instance, would satisfy the multiethnic requirement. Teaching about the role of both parents in conception would satisfy the nonsexist aspect (see chapter 10 for more details).

Reality 6: Could the Potential Pathway Take the Needs of Individual Children into Consideration?

Perhaps the teacher could ask the shy child to bring his baby sister to school. Or the unpopular youngster who tends to bully the weaker children could be asked to help those youngsters punch holes in the cans when doing the water investigation. Is there some way a particularly intelligent girl can pursue an interest related to the topic in more depth? Perhaps she would enjoy measuring the amount of rainfall over a month's time and making a flannel-board graph that shows the results. Or perhaps she might like to videotape different kinds of clouds and learn to identify each type by its special name.

Step 5: Find a Pathway That Appeals to Both the Teacher and the Children

After the realities of planning are considered, the teacher removes some ideas from the list, defers some, and adds others as inspiration strikes. The next step of the process is to find a pathway that the teacher sees as promising and that also appeals to the children. However, at this stage the teacher should keep options open. Are there alternative possible pathways available for discussion?

Step 5 can be fraught with peril because, once the teacher has evaluated the potential of various pathways, eliminating some and becoming excited about others, the temptation can be overwhelming to barge ahead without allowing for more input from the children. It is true that the children may be swept along quite comfortably in the wake of the teacher's enthusiasm, but barging ahead that way undercuts the real purpose of mutually defining curriculum. The ideal to strive for is to negotiate with the children so that both teacher and children settle on a pathway that is mutually acceptable.

Of course, it is also necessary to consider the developmental ages of the children when discussing alternatives with them. Fours and 5s are quite capable of talking over a selection of possibilities and relish the opportunities to discuss which one appeals to them most. (Often this resolves itself into choosing which one they want to pursue first, with the others held in the background for future investigation.) Younger 3s and 2s require more concrete experiences and a teacher who determines what to continue with by observing which activities particularly attract the children and keep them involved the longest.

Step 6: Embark on the Pathway Together

Once children and teacher have agreed on a topic of mutual interest, they are ready to follow the pathway. The Chapter Spotlight on pages 76–77 illustrates one direction a pathway might take. It also makes it plain that the project will need to continue for a number of weeks as the children gradually think through what they need to know and do to provide enough exercise space for Funny Bunny. Note how, throughout that extended period of time, the teacher maintains the primary direction by proposing questions that *provoke* the children into having ideas and proposing solutions.

Note, also, how one provocation and solution/conclusion leads the group to consider yet another provocation, and then to another provocation with still another solution/conclusion.

Thus the question about how much space Funny Bunny needs leads to figuring out where to get that information—perhaps visiting a family's rabbit farm, or looking up the information in a book or on the Internet—which leads to realizing that different kinds of rabbits grow to different sizes, then having to find out what kind of rabbit Funny Bunny is, and then investigating whether the pet store has a cage that is really big enough for him to jump and hop around in.

And finally, note that the teacher in the Spotlight example has kept the group centered on a particular pathway to pursue. This is an important point to remember because it is that continuing focus that generates the long-term momentum in place of the less desirable 1- to 2-day series of more loosely related activities.

Step 7: Add Related Activities That Will Include All the Selves

Once the core experience pathway has been selected, then include additional related activities to ensure all the selves are addressed in the curriculum. Referring to the Spotlight feature, the two selves receiving the most direct benefit from the Funny Bunny project are the cognitive/verbal self and the creative self, because of the need to create ideas and potential solutions and put them into words. Children also use other forms of communicating their ideas, such as making patterns and models. Additional cognitive skills include finding out relevant facts, developing various literacy and numerical concepts, trying out ideas (experimenting), evaluating the results, making decisions, and so forth.

What remains to be added are the activities that provide for the enhancement of the remaining selves—the physical, social, and emotional aspects of the children's development. Fortunately, there are innumerable examples of shorter-term activities available to nourish those selves. For example, social skills are needed as the children learn to listen to everyone's ideas and to work toward a common goal; kindness actually forms the basis for the entire project because of the children's concern for Funny Bunny's welfare, and the physical self is developed because of the numerous small-muscle skills needed to accomplish the project. In addition it might be interesting to eat bunny-type food for a snack, or compare the ears and noses of various animals and see how form is related to function, gather angora rabbit hair and try spinning it into yarn, or do rabbit puzzles.

Every activity should be included for a specific educational purpose—and because it is enjoyable.

Just remember that every activity should be included for a specific educational purpose as well as because it is enjoyable. Thus jumping as rabbits not only provides insight into how it might feel to be a rabbit, but also encourages the children to use both sides of their body together, and to appreciate how powerful the rabbit's legs must be for him to be able to jump higher than his head.

Also remember that all these activities need not be crammed into just one or two weeks. The continuing development of the core pathway means that related topics can be included over a longer period of time, too, as well as allowing the inclusion of other shorter-term, unrelated activities stemming from additional interests and/or needs of various youngsters.

It should also be noted that this sort of planning need not include all the children all the time. As our Reggio colleagues have demonstrated, clustering children into small groups based on a common interest allows for closer relationships, deeper conversations, and more extended investigations.

Step 8: Evaluate What Happened and Decide How to Improve the Activities Next Time

Nothing is more satisfying than finishing a day with children and knowing that it was a good one—that the children learned something worthwhile and that everyone has grown a little toward decency and happiness. When that happens, it can be a temptation to leave well enough alone and simply bask in the pleasure of work well done.

On the other hand, everyone has days when just the opposite occurs and nothing seems to go right. The temptation then is to wallow in misery and see everything in shades of gloom.

Actually, neither of these responses is desirable. What is preferable to either of them is taking a more clear-sighted view of how the children responded to each activity and then asking oneself what can be done next time to make the activity more effective.

PLANNING WHEN IT WILL HAPPEN: DEVISING THE DAILY SCHEDULE

Once the potential content of the curriculum has been identified, it is time to fit it into the schedule. Remember, a schedule is *not* a curriculum plan. The schedule is the pattern of the day during which the activities take place.

Such schedules can be a blessing if they are used to help teachers and children know what comes next and to contribute to the feeling of security such knowledge produces. Or they can be a burden if they are allowed to dominate the day in a rigid, minute-by-minute fashion that ignores the children's needs and prevents teachers from exercising good judgment. A well-designed schedule not only provides for orderly planning but also allows for flexibility so that time periods can be extended or contracted depending on whether the children are deeply occupied or particularly restless.

Meeting the Needs of the Children

Provide for Alternating Periods of Quiet and More Active Experiences
A sound schedule provides a daily pattern of activities that reduces the possibility of excitement escalating to the point of wild exhaustion. This is accomplished by interspersing quieter times, such as group or snack, with more vigorous experiences, such as outdoor play or dance.

In addition to this overall alternation, it is also important to plan for a variety of quieter and more vigorous activities within the larger time block, because individual children have different activity level requirements. Sometimes, for example, a child needs to be allowed to leave the group early, just as another youngster may relish the chance to withdraw to a shelter of blocks when the rest are rolling giddily down the hill outside. All schools should provide cozy book corners and rocking chairs to which children can retire when they wish to find peace and quiet.

Provide for Indoor and Outdoor Play

While thinking about the value of alternative quiet and active learning situations, it also makes sense to consider whether the schedule will require all the children to be inside or outdoors at once, or whether they will be free to move in and out as they desire.

If the staff is large enough and weather permits, allowing children to go in and out at will provides the best mix of large- and small-muscle activities. Schools in warm climates often operate on this kind of plan year-round, but schools situated in more wintry areas usually prefer to go through the routine of snowsuits, boots, and mittens only once a morning and afternoon. What these colder-climate schools sometimes forget, however, is that it might be possible to operate on a more open plan during early fall and late spring. If the staff is limited in number, part of the indoor and outdoor areas can be blocked off so that supervision remains adequate. The increased freedom and reduction of tension that results can make the effort of modifying the schedule well worth the trouble.

Sometimes, however, all-indoor or all-outdoor scheduling is necessary. Staff who must operate according to this plan should take special pains in planning the schedule to see to it that some large-muscle activities are planned for inside and some small-muscle activities are included outside to maintain a satisfactory balance in the curriculum.

Provide for a Reasonable Pace Throughout the Day

This section began by mentioning the beneficial effects of adjusting the tempo of particular days to the needs of the children as these become apparent, but it is necessary also to allow enough time overall, every day, in the schedule to permit children to become truly engrossed in what they are doing. Plans that cause children to be constantly shifted back and forth from one thing to another reduce their chances for concentration and deep involvement, to say nothing of the general feeling of harassment they promote throughout the school.

Besides planning long enough activity periods, think about planning transitions from one activity to another. Too many of these during the day can be exhausting for children and staff. As Neugebauer (1988) points out:

> Each day we must make many transitions from one space or activity or interaction to another—reorganizing our thoughts and emotions to deal with each situation. How much does each of these transitions cost us, in terms of psychological and emotional energy? How many transitions can we withstand in one day? If we agree that they're hard on us, how many should we expect children to make?
>
> *Maria has a daily schedule for her class posted on the bulletin board—it looks interesting, filled with activity and movement. If we count the transitions, there are over 18 that children in her class must deal with every day—from one classroom to another, from inside to outside, from circle to free play, from bathroom to snack time, from home to center and back. Many of these transitions are compounded by staffing rotations.*
>
> How much energy does each transition cost a child? How many of these transitions are really necessary? How can we make each transition less taxing? (p. 31)

Transitions also require time. Children do not "hurry" well. It takes time for them to shift gears from one activity to the next, and the wise teacher allows for this when making out the schedule. Particularly at the beginning of the year or in complicated change situations, a transition may require as long as 15 minutes.

A reasonable pace for transitions also means that staff has time to create those intimate moments of relationship with each youngster that lie at the heart of the learning experience—a truly vital ingredient in early education.

Provide a Balance Between Individual Experience and Group Experience

Finally, the schedule should provide for a balance between individual self-selected learning experiences and participation in more regulated group experiences. Another way of saying this is that the day should provide a combination of self-selected, open-choice activities combined with more whole-group participation. Whole-group activities include such experiences as eating together and circle time. The open-choice times are desirable so that children learn to make responsible choices, develop their autonomy, and have many opportunities to pursue their long-term interests in particular areas. The more structured group experiences are needed to help them learn to function as members of a group and to ensure comprehensive coverage of some areas of curriculum that might otherwise be shortchanged.

Meeting the Needs of the Adults

Adults, as well as children, have needs, and it is important that the schedule take these into consideration as well. For example, beware of the schedule that assumes the same staff member will be at the same place at the same time each day. Adults need variety just as children do. Changing areas frequently and encouraging staff to decide among themselves in which area they will be teaching during the coming week can help ensure cooperation and enthusiastic participation.

Particularly in full-day centers, teachers also need respite from being constantly with the children. They need this not only to go to the restroom, take a coffee break, or talk to a colleague, but they also need time to prepare materials and hold staff meetings. Unless such opportunities are deliberately included in the schedule, such times are often nibbled away, morale and energy decline, and both teachers and children suffer from the results.

Finally, as noted in chapter 2, the schedule must provide time for teachers to greet and chat with parents at the beginning and end of the day. These friendly, comfortable contacts are indispensable in creating the bonds between home and school.

Teachers need time to work and collaborate together away from the children.

Reviewing the Schedule from Time to Time

Children change during the year, and a schedule that suits them in the fall more than likely requires modification in the spring. For example, the time allocated to large group probably should be lengthened as the children's abilities to concentrate and get along together increase, and transition times can be shortened because the children have learned to move easily through such routines.

It is also useful to examine the schedule from time to time for spots where things are not going smoothly and consider whether an adjustment might alleviate the difficulty. Perhaps congestion and scuffling in the toilet room might be reduced by sending the 3-year-olds first and feeding them a little sooner than the 4-year-olds. Restlessness at group time might be alleviated by offering it earlier in the morning when the children are less tired. Remember, it is always possible to experiment with a variation for a week or two and then go back to the previous pattern if the change fails to solve the difficulty.

Some Comments on Half-Day and Full-Day Schedules

Half-day schedules, in particular, require attention to the comments about pacing the day well. If long enough blocks of time are to be included, the pattern that usually works best is two large time periods divided in the middle by snack and group time.

Short days also mean that most of the preparation must be done before the children arrive or after they go home—and, to be realistic, staff time for this purpose should be scheduled and paid for.

A Schedule for a Half-Day Center for 2-Year-Olds

Here is an example of a schedule for 2-year-olds. The teacher who shared this with us stressed that it is just the latest in a continuing revision based on the children's changing needs and the dictates of the classroom environment. For example, she commented that she changed group time from starting in the morning until later on because, to reach the group time area, the 2s had to walk across the activity areas and were beguiled by those attractions, thereby finding it difficult to come to group. Later on, she is thinking about rearranging the room, and the schedule may change in accordance with that rearrangement. Her goal is to have as few transitions as possible during the morning.

9:00–9:15 or later
    Arrival
9:00–10:15
    Self-select activities: art, gross-motor, blocks, cooking, dramatic play, book and writing corner, woodworking, and so forth
10:15–10:25
    Cleanup and transition to group
10:25–10:35
    Group (may last longer)
10:35–10:50
    Snack (includes washing hands)
10:50–11:00
    Transition to outdoors (allows time for outdoor dressing)
11:00–11:30
    Outside activities and go home

A Schedule for a Full-Day Center

Full-day centers are blessed with many scheduling advantages: Among these are the leisurely pace the longer day affords, combined with plenty of time for involving children in activities and for forming close relationships with them.

7:30–9:00
Children arrive, play indoors until it warms up; time of going outside varies, also, in accordance with children's energy needs

9:00–9:15
Transition: wash hands, toileting, move to snack tables

9:15–9:45
Breakfast or substantial snack—everyone sits down together; transition, including brief large-muscle activity

9:45–10:15
Planned experience group time (most intellectually challenging group time of day presented at this point)

10:15–11:45
Activity time, indoors and out; pursue special pathways, field trips, and so on

11:45–12:00
Transition: cleanup, toileting, everyone wash hands, gather for lunch

12:00–12:30
Lunch

12:30–12:45 or 1:00
Toileting, everyone wash hands again, brush teeth, gradually settle down for nap

1:00–2:30
Nap: children are expected to at least rest quietly for 30 to 45 minutes (most will sleep a bit longer than that); children get up gradually as they waken

3:00
Last child up by this time

2:30–3:15
Snack set out: children may come to table and eat as they are ready

2:30–4:30
Activity time, indoors and out; includes opportunities for field trips, purposeful play, and so forth

4:30–5:15
Story time for those who desire it, quiet play, get cleaned up with hands washed, hair smoothed, ready to go home with families

The major scheduling problem that full-day centers must take into account is that of monotony and lack of variety in curriculum that results from teacher fatigue and burnout. This is likely to be particularly true in the afternoon when all too often children are simply turned loose on the playground for hours at a time.

Rather than allowing this to happen, the staff should face the problem of teacher burnout squarely and attempt to solve it in two ways. First, make certain that the schedule provides respite for teachers from continual contact with children. The second effective scheduling strategy is to combine full-time and half-time staff so that some half-time people arrive in the afternoon armed with new ideas and the energy to see these through. (Young teachers in training and volunteers are both good sources for such afternoon help, but if these resources are drawn on, supervising teachers must play fair and make certain they provide them with sufficient guidance and support.)

Translated into an actual full-day schedule, the plan might appear as shown in Table 5.1.

Table 5.1
Activity Schedule for Fifteen 4-Year-Olds in a Full-Day Center

Date: Tuesday, November 6, 2001

Topic or theme for week: Babies and hospitals (chosen because of new baby in one family and because another child is due for a hernia repair the next week)

Time	Staff	Activity	Purpose and Notes
7:30–9:00	Two staff	*Welcome children*	Ease transition to school; conduct health check.
		Collecting baby pictures	Use pictures for bulletin board and group discussion—continues interest from yesterday.
		Tabletop activities, including books about babies	
		Outdoor play for awhile if warm enough	Weather is nice, better take advantage of it.
9:00–9:15	Two staff	*Transition*	Everyone to toilet if necessary and wash hands; get one adult seated with children as quickly as possible; make sure cook has breakfast ready as children sit down.
9:15–9:45	Two staff	*Breakfast (or snack)* Fruit, cereal, and milk with buttered toast	Special event: serve fruit in baby food jars, baby cereal, and milk to fit baby theme.
9:45–10:15	Two staff with divided group, or one adult sets up while other conducts group	*Planned experience time* Book: *Curious George Goes to the Hospital*	Generate questions about hospital; may read half of book, rest later if too long; during hospital discussion point out that doctors and nurses can be of either sex.
		Song: "Rock A Bye Baby"	Use *B* sound at beginning of each word for fun and for auditory training.
		Discussion: What was it like when you were a baby?	Use baby pictures to discuss "now and then" (temporal ordering).
		Poem: "Five Little Monkeys"	Use flannel board— may lead to doctor discussion; also talk about bouncing on mattress, which the children will do later outside.
		Transition—dismissal from group	Dismiss according to who is wearing sneakers, jeans, and so forth; provides practice in mental abilities of grouping or matching.

(Continued)

Table 5.1
(continued)

Date: Tuesday, November 6, 2001

Topic or theme for week: Babies and hospitals (chosen because of new baby in one family and because another child is due for a hernia repair the following week)

Time	Staff	Activity	Purpose and Notes
10:15–11:45	Two staff	*Highlights of self-select activity time*	Set up outside if weather permits.
		Hospital and baby play Blocks	Accessories: ambulance and multi-racial wooden medical figures.
		Make salad	Salad made with children's help if cook has time.
		Dough	Made by children with a little teacher help; illustrated recipe encourages left-to-right "reading" and provides practice in temporal ordering.
		Outside: swings, trikes, dampened sand, and obstacle course	Balance on low wall, jump off onto mattress, bounce, throw ball into tire, run up ramp, repeat (while they are jumping, remind children of "Five Little Monkeys"); practice in dynamic balance, locomotion, rhythm, rebound, throwing and catching activities.
11:45–12:00	Two staff	*Transition*	Toilet, wash hands (teachers, too), calm down, move transition along by singing and discussing what is for lunch.
12:00–12:30	Two staff	*Lunch* Tortillas with beans, green salad, yogurt with fresh fruits for dessert, milk	See if cook has time for children to help make salad during self-select; meal is multicultural emphasis for day—use one of the Mexican American family's recipes for beans.
12:30–12:45 or 1:00	Two staff	*Transition to nap*	Toilet, wash hands, brush teeth, emphasize quiet.
1:00–2:30	One staff during nap; two staff as children wake up (in nap room)	*Nap*	Children get up gradually as they wake up. Second staff preparation time.
2:30–3:00	One staff	*Transition*	Last child up by this time; toilet, wash hands.
2:30–3:15	Two staff	*Snack* Orange quarters and raisins; water if desired	Children come to eat as they get up and move on to play; second staff member sets up afternoon.
2:30–4:30	Two staff (after supervising nap and snack)	*Self-select activity time* Water play outdoors; then get out baby buggies, plus usual outdoor activities	Wading pool with hoses (requires supervision with both staff); fun, coolness, social play, and facts about volume and what the power of water can do.
4:30–5:15	Two staff and visitor	*Indoor activity time* Story time, quiet play; children cleaned up to go home	Offer drinks of water to thirsty children. As crowd diminishes, one staff sets up for morning activities.

Time	Staff	Activity	Purpose and Notes
		Special visit fro mother of African American twins who brings their baby book to share with the group	Builds self-esteem of twins who are shy and tend just to play together; provides practice in concept of matching (do the twins look the same as babies and now?) and cross-cultural learning.

Note: Group is composed of seven Anglos, four Mexican Americans (all English-speaking), and four African American children (including a set of twins). The identity of staff changes as their shifts are completed.

SUMMARY

Careful, flexible planning lies at the heart of all well-run early childhood programs. To accomplish this task, teachers need to do two things. First they must remain open to moving with the children's interests and questions as they venture down a variety of investigatory pathways together. Second, they must also plan curriculum so that it includes activities that foster the development of all five selves of the child.

Drawing up an effective curriculum plan involves going through a series of steps. These include identifying an aspect of the world that has caught the children's interest, selecting a topic offering a core of continuing interest that runs as a bright thread through the fabric of the days, brainstorming directions that interest might take, evaluating the realities of possible choices, finding out which possible pathways also appeal to the children, embarking on the pathway, adding related activities that enhance all the selves, and evaluating the results.

Once the *what* of the curriculum has been identified, then the *when* must be considered. A sound daily schedule provides for alternating periods of quiet and active experience, proceeds at a reasonable pace throughout the day, and includes a balance between self-selected and group times. Examples of schedules and plans complete the chapter.

Food for Thought and Group Discussions

1. Is there anything wrong with turning children loose on the playground in the afternoon? After all, don't they need this free time to generate creative play ideas?
2. Observe some of the children in your school. Pay particular attention to what they are interested in. Brainstorm some pathways related to these topics. What would be your next step in developing pathways to support the children's interests?
3. Are there some consistent trouble spots (times of day when teachers seem consistently to discipline or control the children) in teaching situations you have observed or in which you have worked? Share some of these with the class and consider possible rearrangements of the schedule that might alleviate these situations.

Self-Check Questions for Review

Content-Related Questions

1. Think of the five selves and list some competencies for each of them that should be included in a curriculum plan.
2. Why is it most satisfactory to select a topic for a curriculum theme drawn from the children's interests?
3. Describe the eight steps to follow when developing a curriculum plan. Why is each important?
4. Why is it valuable for teachers to pinpoint the purpose or reason why they are offering a particular activity for the children to do?
5. When planning the schedule, what are some of the children's needs the teacher should take into account? And what are some of the adult's needs that must also be considered?

Integrative Questions

1. Assume that you are teaching a group of 2-year-olds and that you intend to use birds as a theme because one of the children wants to bring her pet canary to school. Read through the following list of activities and evaluate them in terms of the six realities discussed in the text. Which ideas would you select? Which ones would you discard? Explain your reasons for each decision.*
   - Use a stuffed or dead bird for close observation.
   - Ask children to discuss the differences between robins and eagles.
   - Put a bird feeder outside the window for the children to check on every few days.
   - Raise a baby wild bird that has fallen from its nest.
   - Provide tubs of feathers and other objects to contrast how they feel on the children's feet or hands.
   - Offer a snack (popcorn and water) in flat bowls so that children can eat and drink as birds do without using their hands.
   - Visit the bird room in the museum.
   - Have children make a birdhouse to put in play yard.
   - Emphasize the Native American culture, because birds have always held a place of importance in that culture.
2. Think of a topic and pathway down which you and the children in your group might journey and propose several directions that could be investigated.

Coordinating Videotape

It's the little things. Tape #1. The whole child: A caregiver's guide to the first five years. The Annenburg/CPB Collection, P.O. Box 2345, South Burlington, VT 05407-2345. *It's the Little Things* discusses the significance of plans and schedules and illustrates the importance of a well-ordered, predictable environment where arrivals, departures, toileting, meals, and naps are managed consistently and warmly by caregivers and parents.

References for Further Reading

Pick of the Litter

Helm, J. H., & Katz, L. (2001). *Young investigators: The Project Approach in the early years.* New York: Teachers College Press. The authors explain one approach to using projects as the center of curriculum in preschool and primary grades. Many illustrations and explanations of actual projects enrich and inspire the text.

Developmentally Appropriate Planning

Bredekamp, S., & Copple, C. (Eds.). (1997). *Developmentally appropriate practice in early childhood programs serving children from birth through age 8* (Rev. ed.). Washington, DC: National Association for the Education of Young Children. Although this work has been cited previously, it is such a

valuable reference that it merits noting again because of its emphasis on planning curriculum that is developmentally appropriate for children.

Developing Responsive Emergent Curriculum

Jones, E., & Nimmo, J. (1994). *Emergent curriculum.* Washington, DC: National Association for the Education of Young Children. An open, enthusiastic example of how to make emergent curriculum work is provided here.

Developing Schedules

Downing, J. E., & Peckham-Hardin, K. D. (2001). Daily schedules: A helpful learning tool. *Teaching Exceptional Children, 33*(3), 62–68. This article suggests how to construct schedules for children with disabilities by using pictures or other media so the children can "read" them for themselves.

Greenberg, P. (2000). The value of classroom rituals and routines. *Scholastic Early Childhood Today, 15*(1), 32–39. Practical reasons and examples of sound routines are provided here.

For the Advanced Student

Bredekamp, S., & Rosegrant, T. (Eds.). (1995). *Reaching potentials: Transforming early childhood curriculum and assessment* (Vol. 2). Washington, DC: National Association for the Education of Young Children. Citing national curriculum standards developed by a variety of professional disciplines, this book provides discussions and examples illustrating how those standards can be appropriately implemented when teaching children age 3 to 8 years.

Hendrick, J. (Ed.). (1997). *First steps toward teaching the Reggio way.* Upper Saddle River, NJ: Merrill/Prentice Hall. Various authors explain how and where they are beginning their attempts to integrate some of the emergent Reggio approach into their own philosophy and practice.

Related Organizations and Online Resources

Early Childhood Research and Practice is a bilingual Internet journal on the development, care, and education of young children. Each biannual issue includes a presentation of a project or investigation that took place in classroom of varying ages across the country. http://ecrp.uiuc.edu/index.html

The Project Approach home page, developed by Sylvia Chard, contains links to a wealth of information about the theory and planning of projects, as well as documented projects in early childhood programs. http://www.project-approach.com/

REGGIO-L is a discussion board where early childhood educators, researchers, students, parents, and others who have an ongoing interest in the Reggio Emilia approach to early education can discuss the essential elements of the Reggio educational philosophy and Reggio-inspired explorations in North America. To subscribe, send an e-mail message to listserv@listserv.uiuc.edu. Leave the subject line blank. Just type "subscribe REGGIO-L YourFirstName YourLastName" in the first line of the message (using your real name, not your login name).

---

* Bird ideas kindness of Cené Marquis, Head Teacher, Institute of Child Development, University of Oklahoma.

GETTING TO KNOW THE CHILDREN BY KEEPING TRACK OF WHAT THEY'RE LEARNING

Have you ever . . .

- Had a parent ask you how her child was getting along and been unable to say anything concrete or specific in reply?
- Read an advertisement for a new assessment test and wondered how to tell whether it was any good?
- Been asked to prove that the children in your group were really learning something?

If you have, the material in this chapter will help you.

When we neglect to see who children really are, we deprive ourselves of deeper sources of delight. We miss the opportunity to witness the profound process of human development that is unfolding before our eyes. Becoming a careful observer of young children reminds us that what might seem ordinary at a superficial glance is actually quite extraordinary.

—Deb Curtis and Margie Carter (2000, p. xiii)

Now that a framework describing the overall environment and curriculum has been established, it is time to tailor that framework to the actual children in the group because teachers really don't know what to plan in detail until they know who they are planning for. But how do they do that? When planning curriculum, how do they find out what particular children are good at doing, what their potentials are, and who is interested in learning what next? The answer is that teachers need to have a systematic procedure for collecting information about the individual children to make those plans fit them well.

Is KEEPING SYSTEMATIC TRACK OF THE CHILDREN'S DEVELOPMENT REALLY WORTH THE TIME AND EFFORT IT REQUIRES?

Keeping such records requires a lot of time and energy, and, of course, there are some teachers who maintain they don't need to keep written records because they keep a running record in their heads. But the truth is that unless records are written down, teachers may find it all too easy to forget how much the children have changed over a period of time, or to focus on the needs of a few youngsters and overlook the ones who are getting along more smoothly. Additionally, many teachers are *required* to keep track of children's progress. Head Start, public elementary schools, and many state-sponsored early childhood programs now require that children are tested to assess their developmental progress.

Record's Document Children's Progress

Keeping records over a period of time reveals children's progress or lack thereof. Making time to systematically keep track of how individual children are coming along serves two purposes. First, it describes the child's current abilities, and second, if repeated at a later time, it can show ways the child has changed over a period of time—it is hoped for the better, but any change, whether desirable or not, is important to be aware of.

The careful observation these records require can also pinpoint particular behaviors and encourage the teacher to think of possible solutions should that be necessary. For example, a staff member at our center noted in her ongoing observations that one of her lively little boys never seemed to sit still during lunch time. After she kept track of how many times during just one lunch she told him to sit down and finish his meal, she resolved to change her approach. Instead, she asked him to be the kitchen messenger. This individualized activity empowered him do something helpful for the group, increased his self-esteem, and gave him the chance to move around. As a result, the wiggling was reduced and lunch became a more pleasant experience for everyone at the table.

Records Help Focus Curriculum on Children's Interests and Needs

Keeping systematic records can increase the quality and specificity of the curriculum by focusing on special interests and needs. Once the degree of the children's skills is known and their strengths and weaknesses are identified, the planning of a curriculum becomes easier and more focused. For example, the majority of the children in a group might be evaluated in September as "enjoying field trips." However, the majority also might be placed in the "hardly ever" category on "able to tell a connected story." A curriculum that uses the group's strength (enjoys field trips) to help remedy the weakness (inability to tell a connected story) could then be planned. Perhaps one such activity would be a field trip in which the teacher takes the children to visit a car wash and afterward asks them to tell what happened when the car went through the wash and she forgot to roll up the windows.

Records Enhance Conferences with Families

Keeping systematic records provides valuable and interesting information to use when talking with families. Families are always concerned about the welfare of their young children at school and like to know how they are getting along. In addition to the daily chats that are such a valuable part of binding home and school together, occasional conferences are also helpful. There is an obvious advantage to being able to produce carefully kept records at such times. Families really appreciate having the information, and they are also reassured when shown evidence that the teacher has cared enough to make this special effort to know about their child.

Records Can Improve Teacher Morale

Keeping systematic records can improve teacher morale. It is surprising how easy it is to forget in May what a child was like in September. Many teachers have been left at the end of the year with only the hazy impression that the children have learned a good deal and a few more specific memories, such as Matthew no longer bites or Kendra no longer screams when her mother leaves. But if we measure the children's abilities in the fall and again in the spring, for instance, we have tangible records of progress that can raise teacher morale by substituting concrete evidence for a handful of memories.

Records Provide Data for Funding Requests

Keeping systematic records provides invaluable data when applying for funding. When information on a number of children is combined, the results provide a picture of how they're doing now as well as how they have changed since the previous assessment. When such changes are for the better, as we hope they are, such information can provide substantial encouragement for funding to continue. For example, numerous long-term studies documenting the positive effects of various preschool programs have been instrumental in winning legislatures over to providing support for Head Start and other early childhood programs.

IMPORTANT PRINCIPLES TO REMEMBER

Children's Records Are Private and Should Be Kept Confidential

This means that they must never be left lying around for someone to pick up and read even while the teacher is working on them. The competence of individual children should never be discussed with people outside the school or with other parents who do not have a right to know about it.

Be Sure to Carry Out Evaluations More than One Time

Sometimes teachers employ measures of evaluation only at the end of the year. This provides a summing up for the family and for the next teacher (who may or may not read it) but is of little value to the teacher who has done the work. It is more useful to employ evaluative measures shortly after the child enters the program and again later on. Early assessment helps the teacher quickly become acquainted with the child and plan around the youngster's needs and interests. It also provides a record to be used as a comparison at the middle and end of the year. Without this measurement at the beginning, there is no way to show how much the child has learned during his time at school.

Be Careful to Take Varying Ethnic/Cultural Backgrounds into Account

Unfortunately, taking differing cultural characteristics into account is easier said than done by most teachers who are expected to assess people with backgrounds different from their own. A beginning has been made in the realm of some commercial tests that are now normed on populations that represent a wider assortment of children than former ones did. Much remains to be done in this area, however (Impara & Plake, 1998, 2000).

A special advantage early childhood teachers have is that we are likely to become well acquainted with families as well as their children, and, if we are at all open-minded, over time we have the opportunity to become comfortable with and knowledgeable about differing cultural values that influence the children's behavior. For example, traditional American teachers often value children's ability to sit quietly and raise their hands when they have something to say, whereas the children in Reggio Emilia are encouraged to benefit from sharing their ideas through lively discussions, even heated arguments. As G. Forman has remarked (personal communication, October 1994), "When people argue in the United States, the conversation is over; when people argue in Reggio, the conversation is just beginning." Young Japanese children are socialized into the importance of blending in and not "having their heads stick out above their friends" to a degree that would be unheard of in most American homes. Many Russians view the American habit of easy smiling as being close to dimwittedness. It is easy to see how these behaviors could be regarded as positive or negative aspects of behavior when viewed by a teacher who lacks cultural awareness (Frank, 1999).

Be sensitive to cultural differences when analyzing children's behavior.

Records Should Include Information About All Five Selves

The purpose of keeping track is to help the teacher see the whole child, not just the problem areas. For this reason, it is important to look at the child's abilities for all five selves—physical, emotional, social, creative, and cognitive—so a balanced picture of who the child is can be obtained. Not only will this positive, comprehensive approach endear the teacher to the parents at conference time, it will also help her identify and build on current strengths to mitigate some possible weaker areas of development.

Above All, Results of Evaluations Should Be Interpreted with Caution and Mercy

There are two reasons for remembering this recommendation. The first is that every form of assessing children has limitations and weaknesses. The second is that it is very possible the teacher may have reached an incorrect conclusion about what the results mean—all our assessments, after all, are subjective interpretations about the child's visible behaviors, not absolute objective fact.

SOME INFORMAL WAYS TO KEEP TRACK OF THE CHILDREN'S DEVELOPMENT

It is all too easy when discussing teacher-kept records to advocate methods that, though excellent in many respects, are simply not practical for regular use by most teachers. If record keeping requires too much time and effort, it is almost certain to be dropped by the wayside as the year progresses, and the teacher puts it off in favor of preparing for the potluck or Valentine's Day. Occasionally schools have access to extra help (parent cooperatives and laboratory schools are particularly fortunate in this regard) and are able to employ a more elaborate system of recording behavior, but this is not the case in most situations.

Fortunately, there are a variety of record-keeping possibilities that most teachers can adopt. Three quite different methods are selected here to illustrate the variety of approaches and suggest how each method might suit a particular one of the child's selves: anecdotal observations, child interviews and conversations, and checklists identifying specific skills and accomplishments.

Dean W.; birth date: August 2, 1997; entry to school: September 2001; observer: H.B.J.

Week 1: September 5

Dean is new to Center. Tall for age, slender, a little pale. First day stayed by door with mother, looked uncertain—stoic. Mother took off work to spend morning with D. She took him home after lunch, which he was unable to eat. Hid head when urged to say good-bye. During week, hardly knew he was there. Quiet, watchful, and attracted to book corner. Liked *Billy Goats Gruff* story a lot.

Summary: D. seems anxious, not sure he likes Center. Has made little contact with other children.

Objective: I want him to feel more at home and join in some of the activities this coming week.

Plan: Build bond with him myself. Talk with him about books he likes; suggest he bring one of his favorites to school for me to read to children. Don't push him too hard to join in.

Week 2: September 11

D. refused to bring book. However, at group time he brought me *Billy Goats Gruff* from our shelf and was delighted when I read it and told the children he had chosen it for the group. Spends most of time alone; used easel as vantage point for watching other activities. Able to eat more at lunch, especially bread and milk. Played a long time in blocks at end of day when Charlie (a vigorous block builder) had gone home.

Summary: D. is still a loner but is becoming interested in what is going on. Eating better so he's probably less anxious. Likes blocks.

Objective: I hope he will move into activities more and relax.

Plan: Make sure there's as much bread and milk as he wants until he's comfortable enough to eat the rest of the meal. Work on security bond. Read him special story. He likes trucks; add them to block corner. Invite him to go with small group to story hour at library.

Week 3: September 18

Turned down library—not surprising. Blocks are D.'s passion. Used trucks and blocks, built bridge. Said trucks were billy goats and they would fool the ogre. Later in week built elaborate structure; it was near 5:00 and he couldn't finish so left it for the next day. He arrived *smiling* and set to work; Charlie joined him. Boys worked together until every block in school was used. Dean was even noisy as they knocked it down afterward.

Figure 6.1
Example of an Informal, Anecdotal Record

Using Informal Observations to Gather Information About the Social and Emotional Selves

Basically, informal anecdotal observations are the notes made by teachers that record events and behaviors they think are particularly important to remember about individual children. Of the three informal methods, this is the easiest to use regularly. As a matter of fact, it is so easy that many teachers tell me they use it once a week, and they like it particularly because it reminds them to think about each individual child.

All that is required is the discipline to sit at the computer once a week and add notes for each child—or, if computer-shy, keep records on individual cards. Be sure to head each file with the name, birth date, and date of admission to the center. Also, include the name or initials of the observer and the date of each entry. Some teachers make a point of starting at one end of the alphabet one week and the other the next.

Figure 6.1 shows an example of anecdotal record keeping (names have been changed to protect the children's privacy). Note how informal the style is—rather like the form of a diary—with the additional benefit that each episode includes a summary, an informal objective, and a brief plan of action calculated to help the child attain that objective. Although such observations can encompass all the selves, this method is especially

Summary: Seems D. is mastering anxiety by playing out the *Billy Goat's Gruff* theme. Wonderful he's making friends with Charlie; relationship would be a good balance for each.

Objective: I hope D. will play with Charlie at least some of the time next week.

Plan: Suggest boys feel free to use cardboard blocks and boards with unit blocks if they need more scope. Show them pictures of other children building with all sorts of blocks in *The Complete Block Book* (Provenzo & Brett, 1983) to encourage them. Seat them together at lunch table.

Week 4: September 25

Had a setback with Dean. At mention of the practice fire drill he began to look anxious. Since everyone else wanted to hear the alarm, I turned it on. D. covered ears, scrunched down to bury head in carpet. I told him it was only practice, but he still looked worried. Retreated to book corner. Next morning cried as he came in door. I tried to reassure him. When drill came, I took his hand and he huddled against me. That afternoon he told his mother he didn't want to come anymore. I explained what had happened. She said she would explain at home, too.

Summary: The noise and fire talk frightened him—reawakened his anxiety. I think maybe I would have been smarter to have had fire drill right after hearing the alarm so that he wouldn't worry about it over the night.

Objective: I want D. to play through his fears about fire so he wants to come to the Center again.

Plan: Not sure, but must be careful not to make things worse. Start gently with fireman book. Be steady and not act overly concerned. Stress we can keep ourselves safe by knowing what to do when we hear the alarm.

Week 5: October 2

D. wouldn't let me read the fire book to him, but did look at it behind the bookcase by himself. What really worked was Charlie, Heaven bless him! He asked for the fire trucks to use in the block area. Dean hovered on the sidelines. Charlie said, "Hey, Deano—I'm squirtin' you with the hose," and he made fire siren sounds. Instead of retreating, D. said, "No you ain't—I'm squirtin' *you*," and he grabbed up another truck and shoved it at Charlie. They laughed hysterically at this, rolling on the floor (I could see Dean's relief on his face). Played in blocks with fire trucks, staked out fire area. Wouldn't let anyone else come in to get burned up. Play lasted intermittently rest of the week.

Summary: Never underestimate the power of play. I'm relieved for him. He is mastering his anxiety once again and building a friendship, too.

Objective: I want Dean to continue to play through his fear of fire and his anxiety during the coming week— and to play with Charlie.

Plan: Get out fire hats and some hoses. See if children will use them with the trikes when they go outside to play.

appropriate for gathering information about the child's social and emotional selves, as the figure illustrates.

Using Conversations and Interviews to Gather Information About the Cognitive Self

Nothing beats sitting down and talking with people to find out what they know and what they're thinking about. As we saw in chapter 2, talking with parents often provides invaluable information about the child that might otherwise take months for teachers to discover on their own. This is true, too, when talking directly with the children because interviews and conversations reveal so much about what is going on in the cognitive self.

For example, conversations can provide opportunities for posing *provocations*, as the Reggio teachers would say—in other words, opportunities for the teacher to provoke the children into thinking up ways to solve problems.[*]

---

[*] The following episodes are transcribed from *Growing Minds*, Tape #13 of *The Whole Child: A Caregiver's Guide to the First Five Years*, South Burlington, VT: Annenberg/CPB Collection.

Several 4-year-olds and their teacher have gathered around Funny Bunny's cage and are looking at him while the rabbit placidly munches lettuce. As the scene opens, they have been talking about how big he's getting.

> **Teacher:** Is he still the same size?
> **Claire:** No, he's getting bigger! (she gestures—showing how much bigger)
> **Teacher:** He *is* big!
> **Claire:** Yes! And he's growing *bigger!*
> **Teacher:** Then what will we have to do about his cage?
> **Tommy:** We'll have to get him a bigger one!
> **Teacher:** (nodding) But where'd we go to get it?
> **Tommy:** (authoritatively) Go to the pet store. (a pause while everyone thinks this over)
> **Teacher:** Could we build one ourselves?
> **Tommy and Jeremy:** We could build one ourselves! (waxing enthusiastic over their ideas) A big cage—as big as the whole world—get a big box and put it on the bottom and that will make it big and strong—and a top roof—and put in some chips—and put in some food—and put in some water—and put in Funny Bunny in there! (everyone laughs)
> **Teacher:** Do you think that will make him happy?
> **Children in chorus:** Yeah!

The conversation continues discussing the purposes of fur and whiskers.

Besides opportunities for provocations, conversations can provide insight into what the children are thinking about and what they know about a subject. Note how the following account also illustrates the way the student teacher uses that information to propose possible new pathways for curriculum development:

> The project that emerged while I was observing the water table was that two of the boys had found toothbrushes set out in the housekeeping corner and had brought them over. "What's going on?" I asked. "They're swimming and brushing their teeth" the boys explained while scrubbing on the whales. So I just started asking them some questions and one of the first questions I asked was, "Do animals brush their own teeth?" And so we got into this discussion about how we take care of our teeth and how animals take care of their teeth, and it was so interesting to hear Alex's ideas about how animals *do* take care of their teeth and about the dentist and brushing *his* teeth. And some overlaps into the whale world where he's convinced that animals *do* get their teeth brushed actually by humans who pull them up on fishing poles. But here was an opportunity to go to the other teachers and say these are some of the things Alex is talking about—he's talking about the dentist, and how animals get their teeth taken care of. The conversation lasted about 15 minutes. One child thought they drilled your teeth if you have something in them, and another said you just hold water in your mouth and spit it out. Maybe they can have another opportunity where they can exchange their ideas, and maybe we can have someone come in and talk—which is different from an ordinary classroom where you have a predetermined lesson plan you have to stick to.

Advantages and Drawbacks of Using the Conversational Approach

The problem with this approach can be keeping track of the conversation. Ideally it is wonderful to record the actual discussion either by having someone take notes on the spot or by transcribing an audiotape or videotape later—a strategy frequently employed in Reggio-type settings (Cadwell, 1997). Teachers who take this amount of time and effort are often astonished at comments they initially overlooked that were actually of great significance. Then, too, this kind of detailed recording makes it possible to use the records when sharing insights with other adults about the children's knowledge as well as providing a precise record of their language skills.

Even when such detailed recording is impossible, notes about the children's comments and interests *are* possible—and, realistically, are indispensable, because without that information, there is no way to embark on the joint construction of curriculum advocated throughout *Total Learning.*

A Few Suggestions for Conducting Productive Conversations

When talking with children, the most helpful way to nourish conversation is to make a habit of listening to them rather than telling them some facts you hope they will remember. In short, instead of *telling,* try *wondering*—wondering what they'll say next and providing time for them to say it. Paying unhurried, careful attention when anyone—child or adult—is talking is a very effective way of drawing them out and encouraging them to share more of their ideas.

Another good suggestion is to take advantage of opportunities when small groups are gathered together to generate conversation. Of course, having individual conversations is ideal, but it is also possible to have interesting discussions whenever and wherever small groups of children are gathered during snack or lunch or at the sandbox or water table. This is a good time to generate discussions among the children, as well as between the teacher and an individual child.

Finally, make notes as soon as possible about what was said. Also jot down how those ideas might be incorporated into the curriculum.

Using Checklists to Gather Information About the Physical Self

Checklists are another practical way to keep track of what the children have or have not learned. Because the items on such lists tend to be precise and single out specific accomplishments, they lend themselves particularly well to measuring behaviors the teacher can actually see happening such as physical attributes—for example, measurements of weight and height—and physical accomplishments—hopping on one foot, for example, or catching a ball. It is a simple matter to compile such checklists by referring to readily available charts of physical development.

But checklists, although particularly useful for evaluating the status of the physical self, need not be limited to these kinds of items. As shown in Figure 6.1 on pages 96–97, they can also be useful for identifying social abilities and emotional behaviors.

Paying unhurried, careful attention is an effective way for drawing the child out and encouraging him to share more of his ideas.

Advantages and Disadvantages of Using Checklists

Disadvantages include the problem that singling out a few behaviors narrows and restricts the amount of information that is gathered, and sometimes causes important skills to be overlooked while unimportant ones that are easier to "see" are included. The advantages are that checklists are quick and easy to use, they make certain the same behavior is observed for all the children, the results are easy to count—to quantify—for use in reports, and, if thoughtfully selected, can single out behaviors the staff has identified as being of particular value. Finally, they offer an excellent way to find out whether the teacher's hopes and intentions about what she wants the children to learn are bearing fruit. For example, referring again to Figure 6.1, one of the objectives in Dean's observation during week 2 was, "I want him to move into activities more and relax." This would make an appropriate checklist item not only for Dean but for many other children. It is readily observable, it has a worthwhile value for the social and emotional selves, and it is developmentally appropriate.

How to Develop and Use a Checklist

A checklist should be thought of as just that! It is not a test; it is a convenient way to keep track of how children are progressing and to remind the teacher of what goals have been selected as worthwhile curriculum goals for the year. When constructing such lists, the place to start is by listing each of these broad goals, and then including several examples of observable behaviors likely to be present when the goal is achieved. (Chapter 7, explains effective ways to write these goals and behaviors in greater detail.) Levels of reaching the behaviors should always be couched in optimistic terms such as "not yet accomplished," "occasionally accomplished," and "consistently accomplished."

Thus, when the staff of our children's center chose the general goal of fostering emotional health in the children, the following were selected as representing several coping behaviors related to emotional health: "able to express liking for other children and adults," "able to express anger in a way that does not damage people or equipment," "able to confront an adult directly when the adult has caused the child to feel angry," "able to maintain sustained friendships with other children."

Next, the process of making the checklist was refined by including measures of how often the behavior occurs. For our purposes we selected the following categories of frequency as quantitative measures we could all understand: "no opportunity to observe," "not yet accomplished," "occasionally accomplished," and "consistently accomplished." The addition of these measures of frequency changed our modest checklist into a more useful measure—a checklist rating scale.

Because we knew how desirable it is to assess the child's abilities shortly after school begins, as well as at midyear and year's end, we found it helpful to allow space for the three evaluation periods on one sheet of paper. This made comparison simpler and also reduced the bulkiness of the file for each youngster.

Finally, additional items were added to cover other aspects of the emotional and social selves that the staff felt were important. Bear in mind that there is nothing holy about this particular list; other staffs would select other items suited to their own goals and children. The final form of our chart looked like the one in Figure 6.2.

Suggestions for Compiling Checklists

Although going through the checklists of other schools to garner ideas is often helpful, each school should really develop its own set, because each school has its own philosophies about what teachers think is most important. The checklists should be designed to fit these objectives. It is astonishingly easy to become trapped into evaluating children on skills that

	Not able to observe	Not yet accomplished	Occasionally accomplished	Consistently accomplished	Not able to observe	Not yet accomplished	Occasionally accomplished	Consistently accomplished	Not able to observe	Not yet accomplished	Occasionally accomplished	Consistently accomplished
Social Competence												
Able to share teacher with others												
Willing to bargain to attain goals												
Able to share when he or she has enough for him- or herself												
Able to show or express concern for other people												
TOTAL												
Coping Techniques												
Able to express liking for other children and adults												
Able to express anger in a way that does not damage people or equipment												
Able to confront adult directly when adult has caused child to feel angry												
Able to maintain sustained friendships with other children												
TOTAL												
Self-Confidence												
Able to hold his or her own when challenged (confident, not unduly intimidated)												
Likes to try new things												
Takes criticism and reprimands in stride												
Able to adjust to change in routines or people in the center												
TOTAL												
Autonomy and Independence												
Enters into center activity within 10 minutes after mother's departure												
Spends more time with own age group than with adults												
Relates to more than one adult at school												
Appears independent—when given the opportunity, able to make decisions for him- or herself												
TOTAL												
GRAND TOTAL												

Name _____

Date of Birth _____

Date: _____   Date: _____   Date: _____
Recorder: _____   Recorder: _____   Recorder: _____

Figure 6.2

A Sampling of Some Social-Emotional Competencies for 4-Year-Olds

Note: From Santa Barbara City College Children's Center.

have not been emphasized in the curriculum. Results of such mismatched evaluations can only be disappointing.

The teacher should be as explicit and clear as possible when describing the behaviors that will be evaluated. For example, suppose that the following formal educational objective has been selected by the school: "Following an initial period of adjustment, the child will demonstrate emotional independence by tolerating separation from meaningful family members during his day at the center." Which of the following checklist items should be selected as the most explicit to use as a measure that the child is achieving independence?

1. The child rarely demonstrates his anxiety.

2. The child can wave good-bye to his mother without undue stress.

3. The child enters into a nursery school activity within 10 minutes after his mother's departure.

4. The child exhibits a favorable attitude toward his teachers.

Items 1 and 4 are not clearly related to the stated goal. Item 2 is probably a good one to use, although the phrase "without undue stress" may vary in interpretation from teacher to teacher. Item 3 is the clearest statement of the four and should be the one included on the list.

When composing such lists, the teacher also must stay within reason in terms of developmental levels. It can be frustrating and discouraging to both child and teacher if the teacher expects behavior that lies beyond the child's developmental ability to achieve. For this reason, it cannot be recommended too strongly that developmental charts, such as the one included in appendix A, be consulted when checklists are being constructed. Several resources are listed at the end of this chapter. Where such material is not available, the lists should be based on recommendations of experienced early childhood teachers.

One final admonition about the construction of checklists must be added. If the list is to be used in the manner suggested at the end of this chapter to summarize data for fiscal reports, it is necessary to phrase the behavior items so they are all positive behaviors that the teacher desires to have increase during the school year. An item should be phrased "able to share teacher with others" rather than "clings to teacher, fights other children off from her." If a positive form is not followed and a mixture of positive and negative descriptions is used, some of the behaviors will be marked as increasing and others as decreasing during the year. The result should be that the losses and gains cancel each other out, and no improvement could be revealed by the final scores.

Consistency in Presenting Checklist Material

Be careful to present checklist material to each child in the same way. Sometimes it can be a temptation to change the way a checklist item is presented in accord with the personality or skills of a particular child. For instance, a teacher might unconsciously take a few steps forward to shorten the distance when throwing a ball to a younger child, or in recording balance beam walking she might allow more accomplished children to walk on the narrow beam but use the wider side for a less able child, yet she will mark all the children as successful on the checklist. Such inconsistencies make comparison between children impossible and spoil the accuracy of the group report. Hard-hearted as it may seem at first, if a specific measure of accomplishment is included, it is essential to measure all the children against the same standard. The way to adjust a checklist to include less skilled children is to provide several different task levels, ranging from easier to more difficult, for the children to attempt. In the case of the balance beam, this might mean that all children are asked to try both the broad and narrow beams.

Sometimes also the teacher gradually changes the method of presenting a checklist item as she becomes more experienced using it and figures out a "better" way to do it. This tendency must also be avoided. Every item must be presented in the same manner from the first test to the last if comparisons are to be drawn between subjects or even if comparisons are to be made between early and later performances of the same child. To draw valid conclusions, the teacher must compare the same behaviors, not different ones.

Beware of the Getting-Better-and-Better Syndrome

Although it is a happy fact that many children will make progress, it is also true that some children will not, at least not in all areas. To avoid tester bias, which may view every child as getting better and better all the time, the teacher must discipline herself to observe behavior objectively so that she sees it as it is rather than as she wishes it to be. The development of explicit descriptions of behavior as checklist items will help the teacher be objective in her judgment. It is also helpful to have another teacher participate in the evaluation when possible.

A different kind of tester bias that must also be guarded against is the tendency of some teachers to check the same level of accomplishment for most items on a child's checklist. This is sometimes termed the *halo effect*. Again, the teacher must discipline herself to consider each item on the list on its own merits to resist the influence of the halo effect as much as possible.

Assembling the Results

Using Documentation Boards to Compile the Results and Record Information

The term *documentation* has come to have a particular meaning in recent years as a descriptor for a method of assessment used in the schools of Reggio Emilia (Gandini, 1997; Oken-Wright, 2001; Tarini, 1997). The teachers there keep track of what the children are doing by consistently recording dialogues and comments made by children and adults, taking frequent photographs of what the children are doing, and saving actual concrete examples of what they have made. This material is then compiled on "documentation boards" hung throughout the school. The result is a beautiful, colorful, respectful record of how the curriculum is developing and what the children are learning about that everyone can share.

Keeping track of children's development and learning in this fashion offers many advantages—one of the foremost being the record of the creative self such documentation provides. The boards stimulate the children to further effort by recognizing what they have already achieved; they help the children recall how their ideas developed; they inform families and other visitors about what the children and teachers are accomplishing together; and they contribute a great deal to the general impression of beauty and excitement that pervades these Italian schools.

Using Portfolios to Compile Information About Individual Children

Whereas documentation boards tend to illustrate how the children are working together and what the group is accomplishing as a whole (or a small group of children investigating a pathway together), portfolios keep track of what the children are learning individually. The word *portfolio* may sound fancy, but actually it just means collecting information about the child during the year from all sorts of sources and keeping it together for easy reference when needed to assess the child's achievements, deepen the teacher's and family's understanding of the child, and project future possibilities for learning. This collection should be started promptly in the fall so that the child's beginning level of accomplishments can be used as a point for comparisons as skills develop during the year.

The observations, conversations, and checklists discussed previously are good examples of teacher-produced records that are typically included, but the ingredients of the child's portfolio should

Documentation results in a beautiful, respectful record of how the children are thinking and learning, and how the curriculum is developing. This piece of documentation was used as an entry in the World Trade Center Memorial Competition. The children spent a year designing a park to memorialize the victims of 9/11.

never be limited to only that kind of material. Suggestions of what to include are as rich and varied as the imagination and energy of the teacher (and available storage space) permit. For example, the following items might be included:

Teacher-Produced Records

Informal observations

Conversations and investigations

Checklists

Photographs

Video and audiotapes

Health records—vaccinations, height, weight, possibly attendance

Summaries of family interviews

Evaluation of achievements defined by IEPs

Results of standardized commercial tests

Child-Produced Material

Photographs of block structures

Self-expressive efforts such as paintings, drawings, collages, and so forth

Dictated stories

Interviews with the child: favorite books, pets, things to do

Family-Produced Material

Questionnaires about child's development, preferences, and health

Summaries of conferences

Noteworthy family events

List of family members who are emotionally significant to the child

Emergency contact list

Anecdotes and other information the family wants to include

Records from Community Resources

Physician reports: immunizations, allergies, other relevant information

Information from the Child Development Team and IEPs, if the child uses these services

Some Helpful Suggestions for Reducing the Work of Collecting Portfolio Material. The advantage of many of the suggested items in the foregoing list is that quite a few such as health records, summaries of parent–teacher interviews, and results of the child's self-expressive activities require no more extra work than simply putting them in the portfolio.

Contributions by families make relatively effort-free additions. It is both fun and enlightening to send a return-mail postcard home once a month asking parents to note some way their child has developed during the month and something he has particularly enjoyed doing. When objectives have been previously agreed on by families and teachers together, it may also provide a helpful check about carryover of the behavior at home as well as at school.

Admittedly, it does take a certain amount of self-discipline to keep up with the filing, and it would be delightful if that tiresome task could be handed to a classroom volunteer. However, allowing a volunteer access to personal records violates students' ethical right to privacy, so that is one task teachers must do themselves.

The informal methods of observations, conversations, checklists, documentation boards, and portfolios discussed previously have many virtues: They are uniquely suited to learning about individual children and, if done by a well-informed teacher, can take cultural and ethnic backgrounds into account. They also can select whatever abilities and qualities of the children the teacher thinks are important to emphasize. These informal methods can be carried out as time permits and do not require a high degree of specialized training. Best of all, they are appropriate to use for the developmental levels of the children being assessed, and so do not make the children anxious.

Despite these numerous virtues, however, reality forces us to admit there is also a serious problem with relying on them. The problem is that, with the exception of checklists, *the results of these measures cannot be quantified*—that is, added up as a score (even checklists, if teacher-composed, can be used only as a comparison for that particular group of children).

This, of course, is a prime virtue of standardized tests—they all produce numerical scores. "But," one might ask, "since I hear there are so many drawbacks to using them, why are these numerical scores important?" The answer is that they are important because administrators, legislators, and the public understandably want to have some "solid" indicators of progress when funding programs, and they perceive statistical data as providing objective, scientific evidence that a program is producing worthwhile results (Fuller, Holloway, & Bozzi, 1997). Since future funding of programs often depends on such results, it behooves teachers to understand the pros and cons of standardized measures and learn the rudiments of identifying good quality, more appropriate ones where these exist.

Pros and Cons of Using Standardized, Commercially Produced Tests

Advantages of Using Standardized Tests

Standardized tests present the same task the same way to every child; they are scored the same way and provide comparison tables that reveal how other children performed on the same items (Goodwin & Goodwin, 1997). This quality of sameness is the reason they are referred to as being "standardized," and it often reassures the public they are "fair."

Because the tests themselves do not vary, their use makes it possible to compare the performance of the tested group or individual with a larger, national sample. Although this practice is often criticized because it may encourage teachers to teach to the test instead of to the needs of the children, the truth is that many school systems require this kind of numerical data as part (or all) of their accountability procedures.

Using a standardized test also makes it possible to compare the performance of one child with that of a group of children of similar age, gender, and so forth. Such comparisons can be quick and helpful assets in screening situations where pronounced deviations from the average can identify youngsters who will benefit from being offered whatever special help that deviation requires.

Disadvantages of Using Standardized Tests

Of course, the very advantage of "sameness" cited earlier is also a disadvantage because such tests are unable to adjust for the fact that children are never the same. When such differences—particularly differences related to race, gender, language, economic level, or cultural background—are not taken into consideration, the test is unable to measure the children's true abilities and becomes unfair (Wortham, 2005).

Because these kinds of tests require individual administration and special training when used with preschool children, they are typically administered by someone the child doesn't know in an unfamiliar setting performing unfamiliar tasks—hardly circumstances under which a "best" performance can be expected. It is difficult to find commercial preschool tests of good quality that meet adequate standards of reliability and/or validity; they are expensive to purchase; and tests that measure exactly what the early childhood teacher wishes to measure can be difficult or impossible to locate (Impara & Plake, 1998, 2000; Mantzicopoulos, 1999).

Additional objections cited by the National Association for the Education of Young Children (1988) and the Southern Early Childhood Association (1990) in their position papers on testing include the assertions that such tests provide extremely narrow assessments of skills, the form of the tests and methods of administration are often developmentally inappropriate, people put too much trust in the results, tests tend to label children unfairly or prematurely, and the testing situations are unrealistic.

A recent report from the National Research Council (Bowman, Donovan, & Burns, 2001) puts it in a nutshell when it cautions:

> The first five years of life are a time of incredible growth and learning, but the course of development is uneven and sporadic. The status of a child's development as of any given day can change very rapidly. Consequently, *assessment results—in particular, standardized test scores that reflect a given point in time—can easily misrepresent children's learning.* (p. 9, emphasis added)

Mandated Assessments

Regardless of advantages or disadvantages, many teachers—including those in Head Start programs and public elementary schools—are *required* to use specific standardized tests. Critics maintain that mandated testing of children, particularly at younger ages, is not appropriate and often leads to poorer teaching methods such as teaching to the test. Nevertheless, teachers should familiarize themselves with the assessments they must use and find ways to integrate them into the curriculum in a developmentally appropriate way (see the Online Resources at the end of this chapter to find out about your program or state's standards). The References for Further Reading at the end of the chapter will also help teachers in this situation.

Alternative Commercially Produced Approaches to Evaluating Young Children

In response to the criticisms of current approaches coupled with the continuing need for accountability, several attempts have been made to produce alternative measures, providing a broader view of children's abilities. Kritchevsky lists three of these possibilities: *The Child Observation Record for Ages 2½ to 6* (High/Scope Educational Research Foundation, 1992), the *Work Sampling System* (Meisels et al., 1994), and the *Project Spectrum* approach (Kritchevsky, 1998). Although each of these systems uses differing strategies for acquiring information about young children's development, they all represent heartening trends in the area of assessment.

Criteria for Selecting Commercial Tests

It is never safe to assume that just because a test has been published somewhere or is offered in a glossy brochure it is good quality.

Select Evaluation Measures That Match the Educational Goals and Objectives of the School

The dangerous results from the early days of Head Start—when tests that were *not related to the curriculum* were used to measure the program's effectiveness—remind us just how vital it is to select measures that are closely related to what the teachers are teaching. Head Start was almost scuttled as a result of those early, incorrectly selected tests (Cicerelli, Evans, & Schiller, 1969; Smith & Bissell, 1970), and the results haunt us still: Nearly four decades later, some elected representatives continue to cite that 1969 research as evidence that preschool programs are "no good."

Make Certain the Test Meets Adequate Standards of Population Sampling, Validity, and Reliability

Well-developed tests will always include demographic information on the children as well as how many were included in the original standardization of the test. For the test to be fair, it is of great importance that this original sample include an adequate mix of youngsters from various economic levels and ethnic groups in our society.

High-quality tests also make a point of reporting *validity* and *reliability*. The *content validity* of a test has to do with whether the test measures what it says it does. For example, if the test claims that it measures self-esteem, is that what it really measures? Another kind of validity, known as *predictive validity*, has to do with how well the test predicts future outcomes (for example, how well the test might predict future performance of the child in school). *Reliability* is the degree to which test scores can be counted on to be consistent when the test is repeated. For example, if the same child took the test again within a few days, would the score be about the same?

Occasionally tests publish this information in their brochures, but usually it is necessary to write to the publisher and request data on the test's population sample, reliability, and validity. These reports should be shown to someone who is knowledgeable about test construction and administration. School psychologists, for instance, are usually glad to help with this kind of evaluation and can determine whether the standards are high enough to make the test of real value.

Several Different Kinds of Commercial Tests

Generally speaking, there are four kinds of commercial tests used to assess young children; the first two listed here are of special concern to early childhood teachers (adapted from National Association for the Education of Young Children, 1988, p. 45):

- *Screening tests* (also called *developmental screening tests*)—Tests used to identify children who may be in need of special services, as a first step in identifying children in need of further diagnosis; focus on the child's ability to acquire skills. It is very desirable to include hearing and vision assessments as part of the screening procedures.

- *Readiness tests*—Assessments of child's level of preparedness for a specific academic or preacademic program. Screening tests and readiness tests typically measure skills and behaviors previously found to be typical of a large group of children of the same chronological age.

- *Achievement tests*—Tests that measure the extent to which a person has mastery over a certain body of information or possesses a certain skill after instruction has taken place.

- *Intelligence and other diagnostic tests*—A series of tasks yielding a score indicative of cognitive or other types of functioning.

The Pros and Cons of Using Screening and Readiness Tests

The purpose of screening tests is to assist administrators in finding children with disabilities who need special services and in identifying those children who are "developmentally immature" and not ready for kindergarten. Once children who appear to be lagging behind their peers are identified, they can be provided with whatever special services they require. That function is particularly useful when conducting "Child Find" searches intended to locate youngsters who would benefit from special services because they have a disability of some type.

However, the other purpose—determining maturity and readiness for kindergarten entry—remains the subject of considerable controversy. For example, the position paper on school readiness of the National Association for the Education of Young Children (1995) states:

> It is often assumed that tests exist to reliably determine which children are "ready" to enter school. Because of the nature of child development and how children learn, it is extremely difficult to develop reliable and valid measures of young children's abilities. When tests are used to make decisions which have such considerable impact on children's lives as denial of entry or assignment to a special class, they must offer the highest assurance of reliability and validity. No existing readiness measure meets these criteria. *Therefore, the only legally and ethically defensible criterion for determining school entry is whether the child has reached the legal chronological age of school entry.* (p. 22, emphasis added)

On the other hand, as the prevalence of junior kindergartens attest, other people continue to argue in favor of providing extra time for a child to mature. This is thought to be particularly true for boys born during the second half of the year before kindergarten entry. Just about every teacher can cite examples of children who made satisfying growth during that extra year—growth that enabled the children to function more effectively when they entered more formal schooling a year later.

This argument over the value of delayed admission is not completely settled, and because both sides have merit, it remains up to the reader to decide with which faction to agree. But whichever side is selected, it is important to remember that when a screening test singles out a particular child as needing help, the screening test must be regarded as just the first step in the diagnostic process.

The special committee from the National Education Goals Panel (Shepard, Kagan, & Wurtz, 1998) sums it up well when, while agreeing that "individual children with possible developmental delays should be referred for in-depth assessment" (p. 53), it also reminds us that:

> Before age eight, standardized achievement measures are not sufficiently accurate to be used for high-stakes decisions about individual children and schools. Therefore, high-stakes assessments intended for accountability purposes should be delayed until the end of third grade (or preferably fourth grade). (p. 53)

PUTTING THE COLLECTED INFORMATION TO GOOD USE

Developing an Individualized Curriculum

Because keeping track of the children's abilities and how they are developing requires so much persistent effort over the entire year, it is important to make certain that the results are put to good use.

Foremost among these uses is drawing on the information to tailor the curriculum to the individual children's interests and needs. This is best done by reviewing the entire collection of information. Teachers are sometimes surprised at how such a review not only sums up the child's current status and needs but also produces new insights into possible reasons for the child's behavior.

For example, when the teacher looked over Jeannie's checklist, she was alerted to the fact that she had several "hardly ever" ratings on a portion of the Social-Emotional Competence Scale. A further perusal of the anecdotal records contributed to the picture of a 4-year-old girl who was new to school and who, though appearing to like the other children, stuck close to the teacher and was unable to share whatever she played with. The parent interview added the information that Jeannie was an only child who lived in a neighborhood where there were no other children. When these pieces of information were put together, Jeannie emerged as being a socially inexperienced 4-year-old rather than the "spoiled little girl" she might have seemed at face value. The information not only increased the teacher's understanding but also her fondness for the child. It also helped her plan a curriculum that was built on Jeannie's liking of other people and that sought to develop her confidence and trust. This enabled Jeannie to gradually let go of teachers and equipment more easily and make friends with the other youngsters.

Making Reports to the Family

Preparation for a conference is much easier when records have been kept in a systematic manner. The material is already at the teacher's fingertips and needs only to be reviewed before the family's arrival. Such records may be referred to in a general, summarizing way or in terms of more specific behaviors as the occasion warrants. When these materials are shared with the parents and, hopefully, the parents have also contributed to the array, the resulting discussion can be much more revealing and satisfactory than merely presenting the family with a report card.

Indeed, when we think of "report" cards, a quotation from John Gatto's book *Dumbing Us Down* (1992) comes to mind:

> A monthly report, impressive in its provision, is sent into a student's home to elicit approval or mark exactly, down to a single percentage point, how dissatisfied with the child a parent should be. The ecology of "good" schooling depends on perpetuating dissatisfaction. . . . Although some people might be surprised how little time or reflection goes into making up these mathematical records, the cumulative weight of these objective-seeming documents establishes a profile that compels children to arrive at certain decisions about themselves and their futures based on the casual judgment of strangers. (p. 10)

It would do no harm if every teacher would read this quote over before every conference.

SUMMARY

Keeping track of the children's development is a valuable process that early childhood teachers can use for describing children and measuring changes in their behavior. However, great care must be taken when selecting such measures. Teachers must not place too much confidence in any one measure and must interpret all results with caution.

Practical, informal methods of recording and evaluating behavior include the use of observations, conversations and interviews with children and families, and developmentally relevant checklists. These are often compiled into documentation boards and individual portfolios.

Standardized, commercial tests provide more formal methods of assessment. Although they have some important strengths, such tests also have many significant weaknesses when used to measure the abilities of preschool children. Therefore, they should be carefully evaluated and used with great discretion when assessing such youngsters.

Evaluation that is systematically carried out increases knowledge of the individual child, facilitates planning an individualized curriculum, and makes reporting to parents a simple matter. It also provides useful data on which to base reports to advisory boards and funding agencies.

Food for Thought and Group Discussions

1. Testing and keeping informal anecdotal records and checklists are a lot of work and also time-consuming. Are these activities really worth the time and trouble? What other equally satisfactory methods might be employed in place of these?

2. Your school is funded by a state that requires you to administer a variety of pretests and posttests to the children to determine the effectiveness of the program. This year you are horrified to discover that the posttest results indicate that the children have made little improvement in language development when compared with the national norm included with the test information. You are in charge of the program. What would you do about this result?

3. If you were the teacher and had written the following notes in Patty's anecdotal record, how would you summarize her behavior? What objective might you pick for the following week, and what plans would you suggest to implement that objective?

> When Willie hit Patty and grabbed the book she was holding, she said, "You stupid! Give it back!" Later on I heard her call someone else a "dummy" because they wouldn't play with her. Last week she called a teacher a "nerd" because he wouldn't let her go outside.

Self-Check Questions for Review

Content-Related Questions

1. What are the advantages or reasons for keeping systematic track of children's development?
2. Name four important principles to remember when gathering records about how the children are developing.
3. Commercial tests can be helpful to use, but they also have potential drawbacks. Discuss the pros and cons of using such tests with young children.
4. What are the desirable and undesirable aspects of using screening tests with young children?

Integrative Questions

1. The text has already cited conversations as being a valuable informal method of finding out information about the cognitive self. Suggest some items that could be included on a checklist of cognitive skills that would draw on information obtained via conversations.
2. Compare checklists and rating scales. How are they alike and how do they differ?

References for Further Reading

Pick of the Litter

Curtis, D., & Carter, M. (2000). *The art of awareness: How observation can transform your teaching.* St. Paul, MN: Redleaf. This not-to-be-missed book combines inspiration with lots of practical advice about observing young children and recording what they do.

Overviews

National Association for the Education of Young Children. (2004). Assessment. *Young Children, 59*(1), entire issue. This cluster of articles gives a good overview of how assessment is used in the field today (see Online Resources).

Discussions of Specific Approaches for Keeping Track of Development and Abilities

Beaty, J. J. (2002). *Observing development of the young child* (5th ed.). Upper Saddle River, NJ: Merrill/Prentice Hall. Beaty offers many examples of appropriate developmental checklist items.

Bentzen, W. R., & Gaylord, T. (2000). *Seeing young children: A guide to observing and recording behavior* (4th ed.). Albany, NY: Delmar. This is a how-to book distinguished by the inclusion of lists of developmental characteristics.

Meisels, S. J., & Atkins-Burnett, S. (2005). *Developmental screening in early childhood* (5th ed.). Washington, DC: National Association for the Education of Young Children. This overview describes how to use developmental screening in early childhood programs and provides good examples.

Building Sensitivity to Cultural and Ethnic Differences

Santos, R. (2004). Ensuring culturally and linguistically appropriate assessment of young children. *Young Children, 59*(1), 48–50. Title is self-explanatory. Suggestions for resources are included.

Mandated Standards and Assessment

Jones, J. (2005). Using someone else's standards. *Exchange, 164,* 71–73. A concise article that offers good advice for adopting mandated standards and assessment in a developmentally appropriate way.

For the Advanced Student

Kohn, A. (2000). *The case against standardized testing: Raising the scores, ruining the schools.* Portsmouth, NH: Heinemann. As the title implies, this impassioned essay itemizes the most cogent objections to using standardized tests and provides practical suggestions for how to resist their use.

Related Organizations and Online Resources

Beyond the Journal is the online resource for articles published in *Young Children*. The January 2004 issue is devoted to assessment and provides a wealth of resource information. http://www.journal.naeyc.org/btj/200401/

Culturally and Linguistically Appropriate Services (CLAS) provides descriptions of assessments, screening tools, and appropriate practices for children with and without disabilities from culturally and linguistically diverse backgrounds. http://clas.uiuc.edu/special/evaltools/

Head Start Performance Standards went into effect in 1998. The revised standards define the services that Early Head Start and Head Start must offer families and children from birth to age 5. http://www.ehsnrc.org/Information Resources/HeadstartPerfStandards.htm

The National Institute for Early Education Research includes a state data bank that gives information for each state with regard to standards, assessment, and initiatives for early childhood education. http://www.nieer.org/states

No Child Left Behind (NCLB) is the legislation that mandates standards and assessment in the public schools. http://www.ed.gov/nclb/landing.jhtml?src=ln

PLANNING WITH INDIVIDUAL CHILDREN IN MIND

Using Behavioral Objectives in the School

Have you ever . . .

- Heard someone mention behavioral objectives and wondered what they were?
- Had trouble translating general goals for children into specific curriculum?
- Wanted to make a plan to help a particular child behave better?
- Welcomed a child with a disability into your class and been suddenly confronted with an IEP?

If you have, the material in this chapter will help you.

Once upon a time the animals had a school. The curriculum consisted of running, climbing, flying, and swimming, and all the animals took part in all the subjects.

The Duck was good in swimming, better, in fact, than his instructor, and he made passing grades in flying, but he was practically hopeless in running. Because he was low in this subject, he was made to stay after school and drop his swimming class in order to practice running. He kept this up until he was only average in swimming. But average is acceptable, so nobody worried about that except the Duck.

The Eagle was considered a problem pupil and was disciplined severely. He beat all the others to the top of the tree in climbing class, but he used his own way of getting there.

The Rabbit started out at the top of the class in running, but he had a nervous breakdown and had to drop out of school on account of so much makeup work in swimming.

The Squirrel led the climbing class, but his flying teacher made him start his flying lessons from the ground instead of the top of the tree down, and he developed charley horses from overexertion at the takeoff and began getting C's in climbing and D's in running.

The practical Prairie Dogs apprenticed their offspring to a Badger when the school authorities refused to add digging to the curriculum.

At the end of the year, the abnormal Eel that could swim well, run, climb, and fly a little was made valedictorian.

—Anonymous

Now that we have looked at the overall schedule and environment in terms of the entire group of children, and learned how to find out what individual children know and can do, it is time to think about individual children and their needs. Many teachers store an informal list of such needs and the ways they intend to meet these in their heads. Some examples might include the following:

- Next time I'll turn over the rocking boat, creating an arch of stairs, to give Cecile (who is 2 years old) practice in alternating her feet as she climbs up them.
- I think I'll serve soba (Japanese noodles) for snack to help Fumie feel more at home with us.

These teachers believe that such mental notes are sufficient and that they allow them to be flexible and adjust quickly to children's needs as they change from week to week.

For some teachers, however, such casual lists of what they intend to do about a problem do not suffice. They make a good case for the value of pinpointing what individual children need to learn. They maintain that, once these needs are clearly stated, it is much easier to make individualized curriculum plans that will help particular children acquire specific skills and become more competent. For example, a teacher who prefers this more definite approach might add the following objective to a child's record: "When Miles builds in the block area, he will do it with another child twice a week." Then, as was suggested in chapter 6, the teacher might include a few notes or a plan for helping Miles play with others in this area:

1. Suggest that another child carry some blocks over to help him build.
2. Get out the large boards that require two children to lift them together.
3. Add the small cars to block play—these seem to encourage interaction between the children.

When children's learning needs are stated in this specific way, they are called *educational* or *behavioral objectives*.

After a decline in the 1980s, the ability to understand and compose these more specific objectives has once again increased in importance. This is because of recent legislation that mandates inclusion of children with disabilities into typical school settings, including pre-school settings. Additional legislation also requires these youngsters be equipped with individualized education plans (IEPs) that specify what each child is supposed to learn next (Walsh, Smith, & Taylor, 2000). These expectations are typically written in the form of educational objectives. Teachers who welcome such youngsters into their classrooms will find they are often expected to help formulate such objectives for the children in their care or, at the very least, understand what they are and be able to translate the stipulated behaviors into reality. It is for this reason that the classic, "purist" approach to writing objectives is discussed in detail in this chapter. The Chapter Spotlight explains IEPs further.

CHAPTER SPOTLIGHT

Just What Is an IEP and Why Do Teachers Have to Care About It?

How Come We Teachers Are Involved?

The 1997 revision of the Individual with Disabilities Education Act (IDEA—Public Law 105-17) mandated that several increased services be made available to infants, toddlers, and preschoolers who have disabilities. Chief among these from the teacher's point of view was the requirement that an early childhood teacher—preferably the child's classroom teacher—must be included in the conferences where the educational plan is developed outlining what the child with the disability should learn next. This plan is called an individualized education plan (IEP).

How Are IEPs Developed? Where Do They Come From?

The IEP is the result of a two-part process.

Part I: Assuming the child and family have been through the often painful experience of realizing the youngster has a disability that would benefit from extra help, a thorough investigation is required to find out what services will be needed to help the child develop to her full potential. This process is based on the individual child's apparent needs and may involve everything from a neurological or psychological evaluation, to a hearing test or an eye examination, to gathering information from the teacher and parents about how the child is functioning at school and home.

Part II: Once that information has been assembled, a meeting is scheduled to discuss the results and reach agreement about what should be done next to best foster the child's further development. The law requires that certain people attend that meeting. First and foremost among these is the family. Also included are relevant specialists (for example, the psychologist who did the psychological assessment); the special education teacher who will consult with the teacher; the teacher, if the child has one; an administrator who sets various services in motion; and any additional people the family or school desire to have attend. It is during this meeting that the IEP is negotiated and agreed on by the family and other attendees.

Aha! At Last the Reason Becomes Clear Why It Is So Important for Teachers to Understand How to Write Worthwhile, Correct Educational Objectives!

The reason for understanding objectives and how to write them is that an IEP is *always* stated as a series of goals and objectives identifying behavior that exemplifies those goals. If the teacher and special education consultant want those objectives to be worthwhile and implementable in the regular classroom they'd better be prepared to suggest practical, well-written objectives. This is because it will be up to these two teachers to figure out activities to provide practice opportunities for the child that enable her to reach those objectives and, hence, reach the goals the conference people identified as important.

_____

Note: There is, of course, a great deal more to be said about the process of developing an adequate IEP than space permits here—the Spotlight is intended only to provide a brief explanation of the role educational objectives play in its development.

PROS AND CONS OF USING BEHAVIORAL OBJECTIVES

Objections to the Use of Behavioral Objectives

Since the 1970s, the pros and cons of using such objectives have been hotly debated (Ebel, 1970; Eisner, 1969), and the argument continues today (Howe, 1995; Neisworth, 2000). Some believe that using them stifles and narrows educational programs. They disapprove of objectives because they believe that they encourage a cut-and-dried approach to teaching based mainly on the principles of behavior modification and that such intensive preplanning deadens spontaneity. Others argue that some of the more valuable kinds of social and emotional learning cannot be made specific in behavioral terms.

Responses to These Arguments

There is no denying that objectives can be miswritten or misused. However, when objectives are correctly employed, they can also help teachers think seriously about which have the greatest value and how to tell when they have been accomplished. The clear-sightedness that results is a welcome antidote to the high-minded pronouncements that abound in education and that give the reader a pleasant glow but do not actually mean much when given careful attention.

Consider the following excerpt from a center brochure: "Our little school, nestled amid the rustic pines and hills of _____ , has as its goal the development of the whole child—we want him to be mentally healthy, physically able, authentically creative, and socially sensitive." There is nothing wrong with this statement as a long-range foundation for an educational program. But many teachers never bother to ask themselves seriously what practical steps they will take to translate such lofty goals into the daily reality of the children's lives. Behavioral objectives can help teachers bridge this gap between broadly stated, general goals and the actuality of everyday teaching.

Another difficulty teachers cite is that objectives deaden spontaneity and make responding to the children's developing ideas impossible. But this is not necessarily true. A softer word for *objectives* is *intentions*. If we think about objectives as crystallizing our intentions, as illustrated in chapter 6 and described later in this chapter in the discussion of constructing informal objectives, then it is easy to see how the teacher's desire to remain responsive to shifting interests need not interfere with her educational intentions and hopes regarding the development of individual children. The fact that the children's interests have changed from hatching ducklings to solving the problem of how to provide a pool for them does not change the teacher's intention, for example, that Sean needs to learn to *ask* another child for a toy (or duckling!) instead of just grabbing it.

DEFINITION OF FORMAL BEHAVIORAL OBJECTIVES

Formal behavioral objectives are not as appalling as they may sound. An *objective* is simply a clear statement that identifies a behavior the teacher deems important. It usually consists of one or two sentences describing how the child will behave or perform when he has reached the desired behavior. The outstanding characteristic of behavioral objectives is that *they must be based on behavior that the teacher can actually see*.

Objectives can and should cover many areas of learning rather than just the cognitive domain (Gronlund, 2000; Meisels & Atkins-Burnett, 2005). Thus, a teacher who believes that originality of ideas is important might write this objective: "When presented with a problem that requires a solution, Claire will think of and try out a variety of ways to solve it

Note how the climbing ladder has been lowered so this child with Down syndrome can enjoy (and practice) balancing across it in a safe way.

until she has found an effective solution. For example, when unable to get into a swing that is too high, she will think of and try out several ways to reach the seat until she achieves success." Another teacher who believes that physical development is valuable might compose this objective: "Given one or two trials, Ben will be able to catch a large ball thrown to him from a distance of 5 feet."

The worst pitfall for beginning teachers is a tendency to select insignificant behaviors to document (Edmiaston, Dolezal, Doolittle, Erickson, & Merritt, 2000). This is probably because certain behaviors, such as finger snapping or color naming, are easy to observe and count. Fortunately, it is equally possible to write behavioral objectives for the affective or cognitive domain that identify richer, more significant behaviors, as illustrated by the examples throughout this chapter.

Moreover, it is not necessary to write objectives in a stiffly classical form for them to be explicit and useful. Although that approach is included in this book because it is still required by many school systems as being the standard form for writing IEPs, this chapter also illustrates how to write objectives that say the same thing in a less stilted manner more palatable to teachers.

Steps in Writing Behavioral Objectives

There are four steps to writing an objective. The first step is to identify the desired, broad goal. The next step is to translate this goal into several behaviors that reflect the accomplishment of the goal and to write specific objectives for the most significant of these behaviors. The third step is to add the conditions and performance levels of the objectives—that is, where, when, and how often the child must exhibit the behavior for the teacher to decide he or she has attained the objective. The final step—which may or may not be included because it is not really a part of the objective—is a list of activities the teacher could use to help the youngster reach the objective.

Step 1: Select the Broad, General Goal

Selecting a broad goal is the most logical starting point because this requires teachers to think carefully about what they really want children to learn. For example, if they consider the area of mental health important, then they must identify a series of broad goals that are fundamental to having sound mental health. Identifying these long-term goals also helps ensure that they cover every area of curriculum it is deemed valuable to include.

One approach that helps ensure thorough coverage is to use outlines of educational goals. These outlines are often called *taxonomies* (several are listed in the references at the end of this chapter). But it is not necessary to use taxonomies devised by other people. The staffs of many centers believe they are quite capable of developing their own outlines. Working together to write them has the advantage of tailoring the goals to the specific philosophy of the school and to the particular desires of the children's families as well.

Some examples of broad goals that could be part of a fuller taxonomy include the following:

Physical Development

1. The child will be able to demonstrate or acquire physical skills appropriate to his age.

2. He will develop a sense of himself as being physically competent both in relation to his personal aspirations and in comparison with his peers.

Emotional Stability and Mental Health

1. The child will remain in touch with the full range of feelings, including positive and negative ones, within herself and will be encouraged to recognize and acknowledge their presence and express them in appropriate ways.

2. The child will develop a sense of identity by learning who she is in relation to other members of her family and their cultural background, and in relation to the children and staff in the school.

Creative Self-Expression

1. The child will express his own ideas and feelings through the use of self-expressive materials and play.

2. He will use a variety of different media (such as paint, play, dance, and collage) to express himself.

Social Competence

1. The child will gain the ability to care about the rights and needs of other people.

2. She will develop the ability to play with other children by accepting leadership from others on occasion and also by contributing her own ideas when desirable.

Language and Cognitive Development

1. The child will be able to express himself verbally by increasing his vocabulary and by gradually extending the length and complexity of his syntax.

2. He will increase his communication skills by learning to listen to other people and grasp what they mean.

3. He will learn to produce alternative solutions to problems when this is necessary.

Step 2: Compose an Objective That Describes the Desired Behavior

After identifying the broad goals, the next step is formulating the objectives. This involves deciding what behaviors can be used to indicate that the child has reached the goal. For example, in the first goal from the area of social competence ("The child will gain the ability to care about the rights and needs of other people"), it is necessary to think of several more specific situations that would require the child to consider the rights and needs of other people. One such occasion might be lunch time when everyone is entitled to a fair share of food. Other possibilities include respecting the privacy of other children's cubbies, being quiet at nap time so that all may sleep, not breaking other children's toys, or refraining from constantly demanding to be the center of attention. Let us suppose that sharing food at lunch time has been picked as one of the situations to use when assessing whether the goal of caring about the rights of others is being attained.

Write the Objective. After considerable trial and error, an objective to fit lunch time is developed: "When given a bowl of a favorite food, Max will show he cares about the rights of others by serving himself a portion and leaving enough for the other children, too."

117

There are two special points to note about this objective. The first is that the teacher used *action* verbs to describe the way Max will behave when he has accomplished the goal; that is, instead of the objective being written as "Max will *think* of others and *be aware* that everyone is hungry at lunch time," it is written as "Max will *show* he cares . . . by serving himself . . . and leaving enough food. . . ." Good verbs to use when writing objectives include *identify, name, describe, show, tell about, construct, arrange in order, show what comes next,* and *demonstrate.* These are far superior to verbs like *think, be aware, understand,* or *appreciate* because action verbs such as *show* and *demonstrate* describe behavior that can actually be seen; they make it unnecessary to guess at what is happening.

The second point to note about this objective is that it does *not* explain how the child will learn to take some and leave some. Because teachers are likely to be teachers before they become objective writers, they often fall into the trap of trying to explain how the goal will be reached. Such teachers might formulate the following objective: "The child will learn to share food at lunch time by having to wait until last when he grabs out of turn." Aside from whether this describes a sound teaching technique, it explains how the teacher intends to reach the goal of teaching social concern. This is incorrect. *An objective should state only the desired outcome, not the means by which it is to be attained.* It specifies only how the child will behave once he or she has reached the objective.

Here is an objective written by a hard-pressed aide with a particular child in mind: "At snack time Kenny will wait until the basket of fruit is passed to him. He is not to grab or yell 'Give me!' If he can usually wait until the basket has been passed to two other children before him, the goal is accomplished." Note how specific her goal is. Note also that the objective does not describe how to teach him not to grab or yell "Give me!" Note particularly the last sentence of this objective because it is an example of the final items that must be included to make an objective complete.

Step 3: State the Conditions and Performance Level of the Objective

Once the desired behavior is identified, two more items must be added to make the objective complete: the conditions and levels of performance the child is expected to reach to accomplish the objective. In Kenny's case the condition is that he can "wait until the basket has been passed to two other children before him," and the level, or frequency, of performance is "usually."

This portion of the objective, which stipulates when and how frequently a child must display the behavior, can be one of the most significant parts of writing objectives, because such statements of expectations force teachers to examine underlying values as well as standards of performance. Consider an objective that states, "The child will provide evidence that she likes to eat by eating everything on her plate at each meal." Another example, written for a group of 3-year-olds, might be, "The children will sit quietly during story time. They will never interrupt the reader or talk to their neighbor while the story is being read." But are "eating everything on her plate" and "sitting quietly during story time" truly desirable educational goals? Are there more desirable ones that could be selected in place of these? What are the most fundamental values that should be stressed and turned into goals?

Consider also the level of expectation in these examples. No one can be expected to be perfect. It is unreasonable to demand that a child *always* clear her plate or that a group of 3-year-olds *always* sit quietly during story hour. Unless these objectives are modified, they imply an expectation of perfection. For the behavioral objective to be successful (and to enhance the self-esteem of the children), it is necessary to take the children's developmental level into account and to set a reasonable standard of performance for them to attain.

Step 4: Create a Plan of Action to Help the Child Reach the Objective

After teachers have formulated an objective for a child, they often go on to develop a plan for reaching it. When such a plan of action is desired, it should be included as a separate, fourth step. Remember, it is not technically a part of the objective per se. For the objective we have been discussing ("When given a bowl of a favorite food, Max will show he cares about the rights of others by serving himself a portion and leaving enough for the other children"), a plan might include the following:

1. I will check the kitchen and make sure the amount of food supplied will be plentiful.

2. I will delegate Max as the one person to return to the kitchen for seconds to show him there is plenty.

3. When the food is passed, I will remind him to take some and leave some, showing him what I mean if necessary.

4. I will make sure he has a second helping when he wants one.

5. I will praise Max when he does help himself and remembers to leave enough for the other children.

CREATING INFORMAL OBJECTIVES

Writing objectives in the manner described here often seems so cold and unnatural to teachers that they become hostile to the whole idea. As mentioned previously, this view is particularly unfortunate because it may color teachers' attitudes when working with children for whom such objectives are required. That hostility may also blind teachers to the genuine virtue of objectives, which is that they *do* pin down what the child needs to learn.

As proposed earlier, one solution to this problem is to retain the fundamental concept of using objectives while thinking of them as representing your hope and intention and then write them in a more informal way to express that intention. When doing this, it often works well to begin with the words *I want* followed by what you want the child to learn.

For example, a formal objective might be phrased, "While playing in the sandbox, Jasmine will add her own ideas to our play activities two times each day." When this same objective is translated into an informal objective, it might be phrased, "I want Jasmine to be more confident and tell us her ideas a couple of times a day when the children play together in the sandbox."

The joy of this more informal approach is that it lends itself to a final step that feels natural, too. It is the addition of a plan of action for the teacher that clarifies what she intends to do to turn the objective into reality. In this case it could be, "I'll watch for a problem-solving situation—Jasmine is so smart—and ask her what she'd do about it. Maybe the children will need to carry water, or something like that, and they'll need a way to transport it. I think if I asked her directly, she wouldn't be too shy to tell or show me what she thinks."

Note that the less formal way of writing the objective still focuses on what the child will actually be doing when she has reached the objective, it says how frequently the behavior is expected to take place, and it tells the circumstances in which the behavior will occur. Note that the informal objectives also keep the plan of action separated from the objective by including it as a separate step.

Following are a few more examples illustrating the two forms of objective writing:

Formal objective for child: Maggie will participate in an interpersonal activity with at least two other people this week.

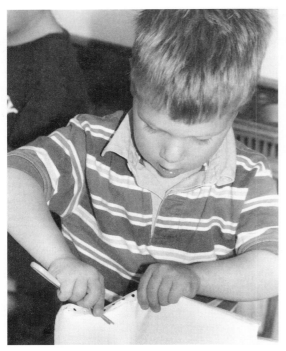

How would you phrase a formal and an informal objective for this child?

Informal objective or intention for child: I want Maggie to play with a couple of other children sometime during the week.

Plan of action: I'll invite Maggie, Mike, and Lisa to tell me what we need to play "going camping." I'll see if I can generate some togetherness that way.

Formal objective for child: Jonelle will try out the medium slide at least once or twice this month.

Informal objective or intention for child: I want Jonelle to overcome her fear of the medium slide and be willing to use it when we go outdoors, I hope by the end of this month.

Plan of action: I must think of some way to help Jonelle understand that going down slides is fun and that she doesn't need to be scared. I guess I'll start with sliding the dolls down the little slide. I'll also offer to slide down with Jonelle on my lap. I have to remember to take it easy and not push her too hard.

Formal objective for child: Brad will ask for a toy when he wants it at least once today.

Informal objective or intention for child: I want Brad to learn to ask instead of grabbing everything he wants at least once a day.

Plan of action: I will stay with Brad when he plays in the block area. When the chance comes up and I can see that he wants a block another child has, I'll coach him how to get it instead of just grabbing it and point out how much more friendly the other child acts when he behaves that way.

CARRYING THE OBJECTIVES THROUGH: FINAL COMMENTS

Remember that objectives, whether formally or informally stated, must be viewed as being continually "in process." As the children's abilities increase and their interests and needs change, objectives must change, too. The clarity that the use of objectives can provide, coupled with flexibility and the willingness to change them as the children change, is a hallmark of effective teaching.

Also remember that in addition to keeping pace with the children's development, goals and objectives will have little effect on the actual program unless they are reviewed from time to time to make certain the curriculum is focusing on them. If the review indicates that they do not match what is actually being taught in the school, then they should be rewritten in terms of the actual program, or the program should be modified to reflect the desired goals.

SUMMARY

The use of behavioral goals and objectives in curriculum planning can be a helpful strategy. If properly developed, they can help teachers examine their value systems, select goals they consider significant, and translate lofty ideas into practical behavioral expectations for the children in their groups.

A well-written objective confines itself to specifying behavior that can be readily observed and to stating the frequency and conditions under which the behavior is expected to take place. Although many school districts and IEPs require that teachers use more formal objectives, they may also be written according to a less formal style and phrased in terms of what the teacher wants the child to accomplish. When objectives are accompanied by an action plan designed to reach those objectives, the resulting changes in behavior can be very rewarding.

However, it is not sufficient only to write objectives. Checks must be made during the year to find out whether the objectives are being implemented in the actual curriculum, and evaluations of children's behavior should be carried out to determine whether the teaching has been effective.

Food for Thought and Group Discussions

1. Identify and explain the differences between the broad goals listed in the first part of the chapter and the behavioral objectives discussed later.
2. Select one of the broad goals listed in the chapter and practice identifying specific activities that would represent the goal in action, then write objectives based on the satisfactory performance of these activities.
3. One of the most effective ways to learn to write good objectives is to use negative practice; therefore, write the very worst objective you can think of. Be sure to make it an objective that is difficult to observe and that represents a value you feel would be inconsequential. Share these morsels with the class.
4. Which of the two forms of writing objectives do you prefer? Explain why this is the case. What might be the advantage of using your unpreferred form?

Self-Check Questions for Review

Content-Related Questions

1. List some pros and cons for using behavioral objectives.
2. Explain the difference between a goal and an objective, and give an example of a goal. Then show how you might change that goal into several objectives.
3. There are two special points to remember when writing an objective. One is that it is important to use action verbs. List some action verbs. Also list some that should be avoided because they are not verbs that describe behavior that can be seen.
4. What is the second important point to remember when writing an objective?
5. Write a formal objective. Then demonstrate how it could be turned into an informal objective. Next, write a plan of action for the teacher to accompany the informal objective.

Integrative Questions

1. Read over the parable at the beginning of the chapter. What is the meaning or moral of this tale?
2. Write a goal and an objective for some aspect of social behavior. Compare them and explain what they have in common. Also explain how they differ from each other.

References for Further Reading

Pick of the Litter

Pretti-Frontczak, K., & Bricker, D. (2000). Enhancing the quality of individualized education plan (IEP) goals and objectives. *Journal of Early Intervention*, 23(2), 92–105. This work provides a rare opportunity to cite a research article as our Pick of the Litter. It is particularly noteworthy because of the criteria it includes for telling quality IEPs apart from inferior ones.

Overviews

Walsh, S., Smith, B. J., & Taylor, R. C. (2000). *IDEA requirements for preschoolers with disabilities: IDEA early childhood policy and practice guide*. Reston, VA: Council for Exceptional Children. This publication lists the IDEA requirements and also includes the recommendations about how they should be interpreted when working with children.

Writing Effective Objectives

Edmiaston, R., Dolezal, V., Doolittle, S., Erickson, C., & Merritt, S. (2000). Developing individualized education programs for children in inclusive settings: A developmentally appropriate framework. *Young Children*, 55(4), 36–41. The authors explain how objectives can be written to reflect early childhood philosophy while also conforming to the IEP requirements.

Gronlund, N. E. (2004). *Writing instructional objectives for teaching and assessment* (7th ed.). Upper Saddle River,

NJ: Merrill/Prentice Hall. This sensible book describes in plain language how to write objectives for a variety of selves.

Rosenkoetter, S. E., & Squires, S. (2000). Writing outcomes that make a difference for children and families. *Young Exceptional Children, 4*(1), 2–8. This collaboration written by a professor and a parent provides practical standards for evaluating the usefulness of an objective from the family's point of view and explains standards for writing them for children from birth to age 3.

Taxonomies

Beaty, J. J. (2002). *Observing development of the young child* (5th ed.). Upper Saddle River, NJ: Merrill/Prentice Hall. Beaty begins each chapter with a list of skills children should acquire. She then suggests many activities that might be provided for practice in skill acquisition.

Beaty, J. J. (2004). *Skills for preschool teachers* (7th ed.). Upper Saddle River, NJ: Merrill/Prentice Hall. This text lists specific objectives for teachers for many areas of curriculum.

For the Advanced Student

Tyler, R. W. (1950). *Basic principles of curriculum and instruction*. Chicago: University of Chicago Press. Tyler's work is a famous classic example of the behavioral objectives movement.

Related Organizations and Online Resources

The Council for Exceptional Children (CEC) is a non-profit organization for people who work with children with special needs. The Division for Early Childhood (DEC) branch focuses on children birth through age 8. A wealth of resources and information about IDEA and the regulations for IEPs can be found at the CEC Web site. http://www.cec.sped.org and http://www.dec-sped.org

The National Dissemination Center for Children with Disabilities (NICHCY) is a national clearinghouse for information on disabilities in infants, children, and youth. The Web site has information on specific disabilities, IDEA regulations, and research. http://www.nichcy.org

KEEPING CHILDREN SAFE AND WELL FED

Have you ever . . .

- Worried how to tell whether something was safe for the children to do?
- Wondered whether there was any way to stem the tide of colds sweeping your center—and hope you didn't catch one?
- Wanted to include cooking for the 2s but thought they were too young to do it?

If you have, the material in this chapter will help you.

Sittin' in a High Chair
(To be sung to the tune "Shortnin' Bread")

Sittin' in a high chair, big chair, my chair,
Sittin' in a high chair, bang my spoon!
Sittin' in a high chair, big chair, my chair,
Sittin' in a high chair, feed me soon!!
Bring on the plate, bring on the cup,
Never going to fill this baby up!
Bring on bananas, bring on the bread,
Mama's gotta get this baby fed!

Sittin' in a high chair, big chair, my chair,
Sittin' in a high chair, bang my spoon!
Sittin' in a high chair, big chair, my chair,
Sittin' in a high chair, feed me soon!
Bring on the carrots, bring on the peas,
Mama come serve this baby please!
Bring on the pancakes stacked in a pile,
Papa's going to make this baby smile!

Sittin' in a high chair, big chair, my chair,
Sittin' in a high chair, bang my spoon!
Sittin' in a high chair, big chair, my chair,
Sittin' in a high chair, feed me soon!
Bring on the napkins, bring on the sponge,
Clean me up cuz I'm all done!

Hap Palmer and Martha Cheney (1984)

This song is so delightful because of its zest for enjoyment. If only we can convey this same sense of gusto and delight to children, we will transmit a worthwhile value about the pleasures their bodies can provide.

There are really two ways of helping children feel good about their bodies. The first consists of all the things we do to foster good health, safety, and sound physical development while we care for children during the day. The second comprises the curriculum we plan that encourages children to understand, cherish, and care for their bodies. Both approaches, however, should have the same basic goals: keeping children safe and healthy, feeding them well, teaching them to understand and value life, and providing plenty of pleasurable opportunities for the growth of physical expertise.

KEEPING CHILDREN SAFE

Good teachers must be unceasingly aware of what children are doing and occasionally move quickly to forestall an accident, because unfortunately every year in the United States one child in three is injured severely enough to require medical attention (Children's Safety Network, 1996). In the year 2003 more than 1 million children under the age of 5 required emergency treatment due to falling, and more than 2,000 died from accidental injuries (Centers for Disease Control and Prevention, 2004a). The problem for beginning teachers is to know when to intervene and when not to. It is easy for them to be so overprotective that the children absorb their apprehension and, interpreting this as a vote of no confidence, lose confidence in themselves. This is surely undesirable. On the other hand, there is no doubt that children must be stopped quickly before running in front of a moving swing or stepping backward off the playhouse roof. The question is: How can you as a teacher tell when an activity should be stopped and when it should be allowed to continue?

The answer is: *Use common sense* and learn to worry about the right things. If the child is doing something that is likely to seriously hurt him or someone else, then it is time to stop him; but if the danger is relatively slight and he is likely to learn something valuable from the experience (such as that it is a good idea to keep your fingers out of the way when using a hammer), then let him continue. Anytime you are truly dubious about the safety of a particular activity, it is wiser to stop it temporarily and then evaluate the situation with the child. Certainly it is better to be safe than sorry.

Another point to remember is to *teach children to think about safety for themselves*. This is probably the best way to keep them safe. Help them anticipate consequences and evaluate *beforehand* what the result will be of what they want to do. This is hard to accomplish without moralizing. A frightened teacher finds it easy to blame a child for an accident by saying something like, "See, I told you not to run with your socks on. I told you the floor is slippery—I was right, wasn't I? See, you hurt yourself, didn't you?" How much better it would have been if the teacher had said before the accident, "Our rule is, 'We only dance in bare feet.' Now why do we have that rule?" The teacher also should demonstrate how slippery the floor is when wearing socks. Or, when out of doors, she might say, "That looks pretty high to me. Try jumping from lower down first and see what that feels like, then we'll decide together whether it's safe to jump from higher up in the tree."

A Safe Play Yard

Keeping the play area safe is a top priority. Look over the play yard with a critical eye for safety before the children arrive. Tricycle handle bars unprotected by rubber end guards can deliver nasty cuts to the forehead of a child who tips over on them, wooden swing seats can loosen teeth, and rickety climbing equipment can come to pieces and really harm youngsters. Glass bottles (no matter how small and sturdy) at the water table may cut, as may rusty cans and metal toys in the sandbox. Splintery boards literally leave painful reminders behind. Constant vigilance is needed to make certain that all decaying equipment is either removed or repaired immediately (Aronson, 2001a; Frost, Wortham, & Reifel, 2005).

It is particularly important to make certain all swing seats are made of canvas or rubber, because 25% of all playground injuries result from children being struck by or falling from this piece of equipment. In addition, it is vitally important to maintain a resilient surface under swings and climbing equipment. Falls are the number one reason why children under the age of 5 end up in the emergency room (Centers for Disease Control and Prevention, 2004a). Most of us do not realize that "when a 4-foot-tall child falls from a height of 5 feet, he may hit the ground at 16 miles per hour" (Frost, 1992, p. 239). This fact explains why falls often produce serious head injuries. A number of commercially developed products on the market are available to cushion falls safely, or many utility companies will provide large quantities of shredded plant materials free of charge. The amount of shredded bark needed to prevent injuries varies from 6 to 12 inches depending on the

Allowing children to test themselves by taking mild physical risks encourages confidence in their physical abilities.

On the other hand, sometimes the teacher must move quickly!

height of equipment, but it is always better to have too much than too little (Consumer Product Safety Commission, 1997). Sand can also be used but tends to create problems because children like to play in it and may put themselves in dangerous proximity to equipment as they play.

A Safe Community

Enlist families and the community in the campaign to keep children safe. Two examples of possible safety programs that parents should attend include fire safety in the home and the use of safety car seats for young children.

Fire departments are usually delighted to send speakers and pamphlets on fire safety. All families should discuss and practice ways of leaving their homes in emergencies, and all children should be taught to "stop, drop, and roll" rather than run should their clothing catch fire. If a parent program presents this material in a calm, matter-of-fact way, it can be done without arousing too much anxiety, and, more important, it may save lives or the terrible pain and disfigurement resulting from burns.

Automobile accidents are the number one cause of accidental death in young children (Centers for Disease Control and Prevention, 2003; Frost, Wortham, & Reifel, 2005). Fortunately, in the past few years many states have passed legislation encouraging the use of safety car seats. Early childhood teachers who see families deliver children by car every day are in an excellent position to remind and encourage all adults to obey this law. The teacher should become acquainted with the resources in the community that make these seats available free to families who could not otherwise afford them. An evening program could emphasize this information and make it available to all.

Safety in an Emergency

Prepare an emergency plan in advance. These plans need to cover a variety of possibilities, such as what to do when a child is seriously hurt, how to leave the building safely and where to go should a fire break out, and how to deal with other sudden emergencies such as earthquakes, hurricanes, or tornadoes. An excellent resource for making emergency plans is the American Red Cross, listed at the end of this chapter (see Related Organizations and Online Resources).

Emergency instructions should be posted in several places throughout the school, together with emergency phone numbers by the telephone—and *these must be periodically reviewed during staff meetings*. Families, in particular, need to be reassured about how their children will be kept safe and where the children will be taken for safety and pickup should a crisis occur.

Both staff and children must have regular opportunities to practice how to behave in a potential disaster. This crisis-proofing, if carried out in a matter-of-fact manner, does a lot to prevent panic. For example, if the children have heard the fire alarm before and know they should drop everything and go immediately to the door where the teacher is standing, they are not as likely to be paralyzed into inaction, and if the teacher practices in advance taking the attendance sheet and family reference file with her, she is more likely to remember them when they are sorely needed.

Of course, it is impossible to anticipate all catastrophes in advance, and there are additional, long-term aspects of coping with them that space does not permit discussing here. The most important thing to remember is that having an emergency plan and practicing it are essential parts of keeping children safe that must not be put off or ignored.

KEEPING CHILDREN HEALTHY

Following Simple Rules of Health and Hygiene

Perhaps because health and cleanliness do go together and as some people believe that "cleanliness is next to godliness," teachers tend to get preachy when they talk about health. At least at the early childhood level, good health practices are generally better taught by example than in such units as "Our Friends, the Teeth" or "Milk Makes Strong Bones."

Very young children are largely unaware of their bodies as such and completely ignorant of how to care for them, so teachers can help them learn about good health care by setting a good example and by making sure the children follow certain basic rules of health and hygiene. Older children, too, will benefit from teachers who model good hygiene routines for them.

Rule 1: Hand Washing

One of the most important rules of hygiene is washing hands after toileting and before handling food. The importance of washing hands and learning to keep them away from eyes, noses, and mouths cannot be emphasized strongly enough for both children and adults (Aronson, 2001b; Kendrick, Kaufman, & Messenger, 2002). Doing this not only sharply reduces the number of colds in children's centers but also has been shown to lower the number of hepatitis A infections. Yet teachers frequently supervise hand washing by the children and fail to take advantage of this opportunity to wash their own, or they allow children to prepare food without scrubbing up first. If teachers get in the habit of washing their hands whenever they have children do so, it not only sets a good example but also helps teachers to remain healthy.

The American Association of Pediatrics (2002) recommends that teachers and children wash their hands with soap and water (not alcohol-based hand rubs) as follows:

- Upon arrival for the day or when moving from one child care group to another

- Before and after eating, handling food, or feeding a child; giving medication; or playing in water that has been used by more than one person

- After diapering; using the toilet or helping a child use the toilet; handling bodily fluids from noses, mouths, or sores; handling uncooked food, especially meat and poultry; handling pets and other animals; playing in sandboxes; and cleaning or handling garbage

Rule 2: Disinfecting Common Areas and Equipment

Following the Procedures for Taking Standard (Universal) Precautions where appropriate will help keep everyone safe. Because of possible risks associated with exposure to fresh blood, it is important to follow the recommendations for disinfecting exposed areas when blood or body fluids that might contain blood are present. Here, again, thorough hand washing is very important—even when hands have been protected with latex gloves. Using absorbent disposable materials such as paper towels for cleanup is also important, as is disinfecting any equipment that could have blood on it. The best disinfectant to use is a *freshly made* mixture of 1 part chlorine bleach to 10 parts water—or if a larger quantity is needed, 1/4 cup bleach to 1 gallon of water (Aronson, 2001b; Canadian Child Care Federation, 1999).

Rule 3: Preventing the Spread of Contagious Diseases

Conducting a health check as children arrive is a mandatory part of the regulations of many states and should be carried out whether mandated or not. Families are often hurried in the morning and fail to take a close look at their children in the rush of getting off to school or to the provider's home. Moreover, a sick child presents a terrible dilemma for parents who may be torn between needing to go to work and needing to stay home to care for an ailing

Everyone at school—including teachers—should wash their hands throughout the day.

child. This is a dilemma for teachers, too. However, we must remember that the welfare of the group must be taken into account, as well as the needs of a particular family. Children who are contagious cannot be allowed to stay in the group even if they seem to feel up to doing so. (Refer to appendix C for a chart of communicable diseases and methods of control.)

Some schools attempt to resolve this problem by maintaining lists of people who will care for children in such emergencies, but most schools just encourage families to make plans in advance to handle such emergencies. When these resources fail or when the child becomes ill during the day, he should be isolated from the other children and kept comfortable and quiet until he can be taken home.

Rule 4: Keeping Immunization Records Up-to-Date

Keeping immunization records up-to-date also prevents the spread of various contagious diseases in the school and protects the community at large. Children's centers are typically the first institutions entered by young children; therefore, they can act as the first line of health checks for immunizations provided that they enforce their licensing requirements for admission. Teachers often take immunizations for granted and do not realize that it is still necessary to be very careful to make sure every child entering the program is fully immunized.

One of the great public health triumphs in the United States has been the increase in immunizations of young children, from slightly more than half in 1991 (Children's Defense Fund, 1996) to more than 90% of children currently protected (UNICEF, 2003). This increase is due in part to the increased availability of free vaccinations, but also to the increased vigilance of early childhood and kindergarten authorities as they enforce state regulations requiring immunizations before enrollment. However, there is still more to be accomplished, as the missing 10% attest.

In recent years a disease nicknamed HIB (*Haemophilus influenzae*, type B) has come to the attention of pediatricians because of its potential seriousness for children of preschool age. HIB attacks 1 of every 200 children in the United States before age 5 and is responsible for more than half of all cases of meningitis in children. It also produces joint infections that result in arthritislike conditions and is thought to be responsible for the majority of ear infections as well. Fortunately, a safe vaccine is available for this disease. Teachers should be aware of this potentially serious disease and remind families that four doses of the vaccine should be given before the age of 2 years.

Teachers should also encourage families to vaccinate their children each year for the flu. Nationwide, only 4.4% of children between the ages of 6 months and 2 years were fully vaccinated for the 2002–2003 flu season, when 152 children died from complications of the virus (Centers for Disease Control and Prevention, 2004b).

Rule 5: Taking Special Care When Children Have Been Sick

The fifth important health rule to follow is to take special care of children who have been sick. When a child returns to school following a bout of flu or an earache or something as serious as chicken pox or measles, he must be watched carefully for signs of complications, be kept warm, and not be allowed to become overtired. Even though his doctor has said that he can come back, this does not mean that he is in tip-top shape.

FEEDING CHILDREN WELL

Children, like the army, march on their stomachs. Yet all too many schools still rely on the old juice-and-cracker routine to see youngsters through the morning. Often today this is not even real fruit juice but some dye-laden, sugar-saturated synthetic. The only advantages of this policy are that it is quick and cheap, neither of which is in the best interests of children. Instead of settling for such trash, think of food as being one of the most important parts of the curriculum and plan for it accordingly.

Problems of Malnutrition

Perhaps the reader thinks that the significance of good food is being emphasized unnecessarily because in many parts of the world children suffer from malnutrition to a much greater extent than they do in the United States. However, it is also true that hunger is far from unknown in our own land (Center on Hunger, Poverty, & Nutrition Policy, 1998). This is the case particularly among families of the poor (Cheung, 1995), but malnutrition also exists in special forms among more well-to-do families who allow their children to feast on the junk foods so persistently touted on television. Such inadequate diets result in poor appetites at meal time, decaying teeth, lowered resistance to infection, a reduced ability to pay attention, and (in more severe cases) general lethargy and slower-than-normal physical development (Center on Hunger, Poverty, & Nutrition Policy, 1999).

In the United States, two aspects of malnutrition among children of all economic levels deserve special discussion: dental decay and iron deficiency.

Dental Decay

Tooth decay is one of the most common infectious diseases among U.S. children. A little more than half of all children have experienced decay by the age of 8, and 78% of all American children have dental decay by the age of 17. In addition, tooth decay is of particular concern for children of the poor in that it often leads to other serious problems. Some 50% of low-income children with dental decay do not receive any treatment, which can result in pain, missed school, underweight, and poor appearance—adversely affecting the child's chances to succeed in school (Centers for Disease Control and Prevention, 2005).

Although decay is related to a number of factors, including a child's inherent ability to resist infection, it is well substantiated that a diet high in refined sugar is *directly associated* with increased tooth decay. The most destructive sweetener is sucrose (common table sugar), the same sugar that occurs in brown sugar and molasses (Cottrell & O'Brien, 1999). Sweet food that is sticky, such as candy, should be particularly avoided, because it stays on the teeth for a long time.

It is also important to realize that it is the *frequency* of eating sugar, rather than the total amount consumed, that makes the difference. If a child eats jam or sweetened cereal for breakfast, then is fed a snack of graham crackers (think of how sticky they are), and then has pudding for lunch, sugar has been added at convenient 2-hour intervals to nourish the bacteria that secrete the acids and enzymes that make teeth vulnerable to decay. This is the reason it is worthwhile to plan snacks of popcorn, homemade peanut butter (most commercial peanut butter contains sugar), or carrot sticks with cottage cheese dip. Desserts of fresh fruit should also be featured. Reducing the sugar intake by these means controls bacteria by starving them. Schools also should require toothbrushing after lunch so that teeth are cleaned at least once a day. The brushes should be stored out of reach and exposed to light and air so that they dry as quickly as possible.

Iron Deficiency

Iron deficiency anemia is the most prevalent nutritional deficiency in the United States today, especially among children younger than 3, adolescent girls, and women during the childbearing years. It is also common among preschool children, particularly African American and Hispanic youngsters, of whom 1 in 10 is likely to be anemic (Poskitt, 1998).

Insufficient iron produces pale, apathetic children who tire quickly and who catch cold easily. Teachers should watch for children who match this description. When this condition is suspected, it should be drawn to the families' attention so that they can discuss it with their physician. Meanwhile, the school can do its part in preventing anemia by planning meals that include meats, egg yolks, whole wheat, organ meats (especially liver), seafood, green leafy vegetables, nuts, dried fruit, and legumes.

Problems of Obesity and Overweight

Childhood overweight and obesity has become a national health crisis as the number of overweight children has tripled over the past 20 years (Buch, 2005; Stengle, 2005). Overweight children are at risk for developing serious health conditions including diabetes, heart disease, high blood pressure, and arthritis. Much of the problem arises from a lack of physical activity, which will be discussed further in chapter 9.

Health professionals do not recommend dieting for young children. In addition to promoting exercise, we must be vigilant in providing a well-balanced, nutritious diet for children that is low in unhealthy sugars and fats and high in fruits, vegetables, and fiber-rich grains. Our role as teachers of young children is especially important in creating a healthier nation. The American Academy of Pediatrics suggests that we focus more attention on prevention so that later treatment is not necessary. As pediatric cardiologist Dr. Reginald Washington states, "Once you become obese it's very difficult to lose that weight and keep it off. If you are in the habit of not eating large portions, if you are in the habit of being physically active, that's going to stay with you" (Stengle, 2005, p. A13).

Planning Nutritious Food

One of the best things about children's centers is that many of them still retain the privilege of planning their own meals and snacks. This is ideal because it allows the director and staff to combine what they know about the food preferences of young children (plain familiar food, small portions, and finger foods are preferred) with knowledge of good nutrition.

The Food Pyramid

Use the Food Guide Pyramid for children under age 6. The Food Guide Pyramid (in the Chapter Spotlight on page 132) reminds us that well-balanced meals for children and adults should rest on a strong foundation of bread, cereal, and pasta and that the inclusion of fruits and vegetables is very important, too. These foods are generally low in fat and high in vitamins, minerals, and fiber and are important sources of sustained energy. Note that fats, oils, and sweets should be kept at a minimum. Although this balanced approach remains important throughout our lives, it is particularly important to honor when feeding young children. This is true not only because they are growing so fast but also because food preference habits formed in childhood persist into adulthood.

At first glance the number of portions listed in some segments of the pyramid may seem extreme—for example, a total of five fruit and vegetable servings each day—unless it is understood how small the portions are intended to be, as Figure 8.1 reveals. Americans are so accustomed to larger portions served in restaurants and many homes that it can also be helpful to picture equivalent sizes of common objects—such as an ounce of cheese being about the size of a film canister, half a cup of most foods equaling the size of a tennis ball, and 3 ounces of meat being the size of a deck of playing cards (Oklahoma Child Care, 2000b). Perhaps we would all be better off if we followed the advice of many Chinese parents, who teach their children to always stop eating a little before they feel full!

131

Food Guide Pyramid for Young Children

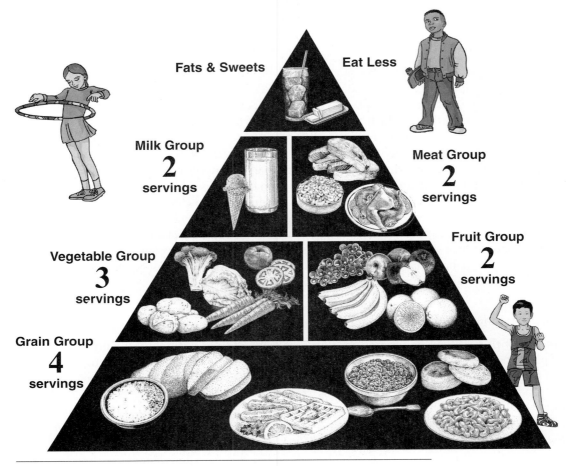

Source: U.S. Department of Agriculture, Center for Nutrition Policy and Promotion, 1999.

MyPyramid for Kids

Use the revised MyPyramid for Kids for children ages 6 to 11. In 2005 the federal government released its revised system to offer nutritious advice to Americans. The new program, MyPyramid, was designed as a customized, interactive food guidance system that comes in 12 versions depending on a person's activity level and caloric need. An online resource is available for individuals to enter their age, sex, and activity level to receive dietary recommendations. Teachers of children over the age of 2 can use the MyPyramid online system for specific nutritional recommendations (see Related Organizations and Online Resources).

The Chapter Spotlight on page 134 shows the pyramid, which is now a series of vertical bands of varying widths. The bands of fruits and vegetables combined use the most space and should be the most consumed. The narrowest band is that of oils and should be eaten the least on a daily basis. Another notable change is that of the stairs on the side of the pyramid,

What Counts as One Serving?		
Grain Group	**Fruit Group**	**Meat Group**
1 slice of bread	1 piece of fruit or melon wedge	2–3 ounces of cooked lean meat, poultry,
1/2 cup of cooked rice or pasta	3/4 cup of juice	or fish
1/2 cup of cooked cereal	1/2 cup of canned fruit	1/2 cup of cooked dry beans or 1 egg
1 ounce of ready-to-eat cereal	1/4 cup of dried fruit	counts as 1 ounce of lean meat
		2 tablespoons of peanut butter count
		as 1 ounce of meat
Vegetable Group	**Milk Group**	**Fats and Sweets**
1/2 cup of chopped raw or	1 cup of milk or yogurt	Limited calories from these
cooked vegetables	2 ounces of cheese	
1 cup of raw leafy vegetables		

Figure 8.1

"One Serving" on the Food Guide Pyramid

Note: Four- to 6-years-olds can eat these serving sizes. Offer 2- to 3-year-olds less, except for milk. Two- to 6-year old children need a total of 2 servings from the milk group every day.

Source: U.S. Department of Agriculture, Center for Nutrition Policy and Promotion, 1999.

emphasizing the equally important need for physical activity in maintaining a healthy body. Teachers can get more information about using MyPyramid with children at the Web site listed at the end of the chapter (see Related Organizations and Online Resources).

Cultural Food Preferences

Be sensitive to cultural food preferences. For meals to have maximum appeal, they should reflect the children's cultural backgrounds as well as be nutritious. Nothing fills a newcomer's heart with such despair as the sight of bowls and bowls of food he does not recognize and fears to eat. With a little imagination and sensitivity on the teacher's part, the misery of this experience can be avoided.

Young African American children, for example, may find mustard, turnip, and collard greens especially appealing and may like black-eyed peas and hominy grits. Mexican American children, on the other hand, may find tortillas, *pan dulce*, salsa, and chili more to their taste. Youngsters of Japanese heritage may prefer food flavored with soy sauce and may particularly enjoy fish, rice crackers, and soba (whole-wheat noodles). Although these dishes are likely to be special favorites of children from these backgrounds, it is probable that all the children will come to enjoy them if they are gradually included in the menus. Because the majority of the group may be unfamiliar with these foods, the best approach may be to serve only one unfamiliar item at a time.

Be sensitive to cultural food preferences.

133

MyPyramid for Kids

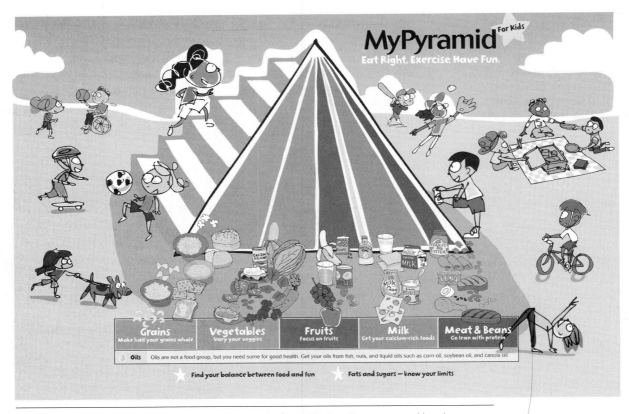

Source: U.S. Department of Agriculture, Food and Nutrition Service, 2005 (http://www.mypyramid.gov).

Remember that to some of the children who come from different backgrounds, most of the food at the center may be unfamiliar, at least at first.

Table 8.1 shows how a daily menu can offer multicultural foods and adhere to the food pyramid recommendations.

Food Safety Precautions

Keep some special food safety precautions in mind. For instance, it is important to consider the age of the children when planning their meals. For younger children in particular, slice round foods such as hot dogs lengthwise and cut grapes and large pieces of dried food in half to avoid choking. Peanut butter, if used at all, should be spread thinly on crackers or toast to avoid gagging on a large spoonful all at once.

And, speaking of peanuts, the recent publicity about potentially lethal though rare allergic reactions to peanuts reminds us how important it is to pay attention to family requests to honor food allergies. Food *allergies* differ from food *intolerances* because allergies involve an immune system reaction that produces physiological responses ranging from nausea, hives, rashes, nasal congestion, diarrhea, and wheezing to anaphylactic shock where the

Table 8.1

Sample Lunch and Snack Menus for Preschoolers

Menus for Preschoolers: Lunch and Snack				
Day 1	**Day 2**	**Day 3**	**Day 4**	**Day 5**
Beef/vegetable stew	Stir-fry chicken with celery, carrots, and bok choy	Lean roast pork	Baked chicken	White beans and ham
Molded salad with orange sections		Sweet potato	Broccoli	Cooked greens
Whole-wheat bread	Orange slices	Baby lima beans	Cooked tomatoes and pasta	Fresh broccoli with fat-free ranch dressing
Margarine	Spinach salad with fat-free dressing	Carrot sticks	Whole-wheat bread	Apple slices
2% milk		Whole-wheat bread	Margarine	Cornbread
	Whole-wheat bread	Margarine	2% milk	Margarine
	2% milk	2% milk		2% milk
Snack:	Snack:	Snack:	Snack:	Snack:
Hard-cooked egg	Pineapple chunks	Grapefruit sections	Dried fruits—peach slice, apricot slice, dates	Grapes (green)
Blueberries	2% milk	2% milk		2% milk
2% milk			2% milk	
Day 6	**Day 7**	**Day 8**	**Day 9**	**Day 10**
Soy-enhanced chicken patty	Chili with tomato sauce, beans, and hamburger	Roast turkey	Vegetable burger with tomato, pickle, lettuce	Seafood chop suey with bean sprouts, bamboo shoots, water chestnuts, and green pepper
Baked potato		Sweet potatoes	Oven-baked potatoes	
Fresh cantaloupe	Spinach salad with fat-free dressing	Cranberry salad	Baked beans in tomato sauce	Brown rice
Brussels sprouts	Grapefruit	Whole-wheat bread	Apricots	Fresh fruit salad
Whole-wheat bread	Whole-wheat crackers	Margarine	Whole-wheat bun	Whole-wheat bread
Margarine	2% milk	2% milk	2% milk	Margarine
2% milk				2% milk
Snack:	Snack:	Snack:	Snack:	Snack:
Pineapple	Sliced peaches	Citrus cup	Apple slices	Strawberries
2% milk	2% milk	Toasted wheat germ	Peanut butter	2% milk
		2% milk	2% milk	

Source: From *Food, Nutrition, and the Young Child* (5th ed.), by J. B. Endres, R. E. Rockwell, & C. G. Mense, 2004, Upper Saddle River, NJ: Merrill/Prentice Hall. Reprinted with permission.

entire body goes into a serious, sometimes fatal reaction. According to Schardt (2001), "The commonest allergic reactions are caused by nuts (walnuts and almonds), peanuts (which are actually legumes), milk, eggs, fish, shellfish, soybeans, and wheat" (p. 10).

Because of the rare but potential seriousness of some allergic reactions, parents should be encouraged to list these on application forms. They should also tell the teacher about any food allergies their children have and should provide an anaphylactic kit for the school to keep on hand, together with a release, so that staff may administer that shot should it become necessary to do so.

Fluid Intake

One final word on nutrition: Provide plenty of fluids. Children and adults need to drink plenty of fluids. Children do not always realize they are thirsty, and so they often translate their discomfort into crabbiness. Although teachers may have to discourage children from filling up on milk and skipping the rest of their lunch, they should make certain that plenty of liquids are offered during the day. It is especially wise to be aware of this on hot afternoons and to offer every child a *cup* of water—a few swallows from a drinking fountain are insufficient.

INCLUDING COOKING IN THE CURRICULUM

Feeding children well in terms of snacks and lunches is important, but this is only half the nutrition story. The other half relates more directly to the children, because it centers on involving them in understanding about good food through cooking activities.

The value of providing such experiences frequently in the school is extraordinary because cooking offers so many different kinds of learning for all the child's selves, as Table 8.2 reveals. For the cognitive self there is learning how to measure and weigh, learning temporal sequence (first break the egg, then beat it, then mix it with the margarine), and learning the different flavors, textures, and consistencies that teachers love to bring to the attention of children. Much cause-and-effect learning also is related to cooking, such as "Is it the water or the heat that made the egg hard? How can we be sure?" Many plain facts are presented, too, such as the fact that eggs come from chickens.

Information about health and nutrition can be incorporated casually, but persistently, into cooking activities. This helps children understand the value good food has for keeping their bodies in good condition and helps them learn to take care of their physical selves.

Other, even more basic values than those listed here are inherent in the preparation of food, and these are closely bound up with the psychological value of nourishment. Young children equate food with love. This arises from their early feeding experiences in which love was embodied by the mother relieving the child's hunger with milk. What better ways, then, to continue to express caring and love to children than by feeding them well and allowing them to cook for themselves and other people? Cooking permits children not only to satisfy their own needs but also to experience the satisfaction of nourishing others—an excellent opportunity for encouraging the development of the social self.

Moreover, because of the intense gratifications involved, cooking is one of the most ideal ways to incorporate multicultural values into the lives of young children. What better way to learn that Jewish or African American or Italian or Mexican people are attractive than by preparing and eating something delicious that is typical of their culture?

Basics for Choosing a Recipe

Pick a recipe that is not too delicate. Part of the cooking experience for children inevitably includes tasting everything, and this does take its toll in proportions. For this reason, it is often best to begin the cooking year with some items whose proportions do not matter much. For example, scrambled eggs with cheese, fruit salad, green salad, spaghetti, and vegetable soup all turn out well no matter what gets sampled along the way. (Incidentally, a good base for vegetable soup is tomato juice; this provides body, color, and flavor, without requiring that meat be added.)

Pick a recipe that has a lot of things for the children to do. Many recipes for children seem to concentrate only on stirring, which usually means that everyone waits impatiently while each child takes two whacks with the spoon. To counteract this, look the recipe over and note whether there is enough variety to it. For example, compare the following cookie recipe with that of an instant pudding package. The two steps in making instant pudding

Table 8.2
What Can Children Learn from Experiences with Cooking?

Physical	Emotional	Social	Creative	Cognitive/Language
Encourages:	Encourages:	Encourages:	Encourages:	Encourages:
Good physical health produced by sound nutrition	Sense of satisfaction with life because of eating well	Working together to produce a result	Experimentation with changing flavors	Understanding of cause-effect relationships (application of heat, cold, additional liquid; effect of different cooking methods on same food—whipping or boiling eggs)
Learning through many sensory channels (tastes, smells, textures, temperatures)—Can you hear it? How does it sound when you chew it?	Taking pleasure in activity—cooking is fun	Satisfaction of doing something to benefit the group	Use of own ideas with some foods: pizzas, tacos, fruit salad	Understanding of measurement by various methods: temperature, liquid and dry measures (cups, spoonfuls), length of time, weight, development of increased vocabulary
Development of fine-muscle skills (chopping, peeling, mashing, stirring, kneading)	Development of self-control while using kitchen tools, working with hot pans, etc.	Satisfaction in doing real, meaningful work (both cooking and cleaning up)	Arranging prepared food attractively	Practice in temporal ordering (sequence)
Understanding that good food helps you grow healthy and strong	Ability to take (well-supervised) risks while handling tools such as knives, hot plates, etc.	Widening positive acquaintance with other cultures by experiencing their good-tasting foods	*Note:* Many people think of cooking as a creative experience; however, to purists there is a difference between "making" something and "creating" something. "Creativity" implies more self-expression than is intended by many recipes.	Practice in classification skills
	Willingness to risk trying new flavors and unfamiliar foods	Learning that people meet the same need in different ways (e.g., make bread and compare with other kinds of breads)		Development of emergent literacy skills: "reading" picture recipe left to right; understanding value of number: How much, and how many?
		Trying out adult role of parent in kitchen		Acquisition of facts about various foods (milk comes from cows; it provides butter, cheese, yogurt, ice cream, etc.)
		Idea that food is important to everyone in the world—we must share and not waste it		Acquisition of facts about nutrition
				Extended experiences: gardening; toothbrushing; going to the market; visiting ethnically oriented delicatessens; visiting a farm; seeing a cow milked at county fair

are: 1) beating the mix with milk, and 2) pouring it into dishes. The main ingredients of instant pudding are sugar, dextrose, artificial flavor, salt, and food coloring. Ask yourself these questions: How many different things will the children be able to do in each? What is the learning potential of each recipe? What is my opinion of the nutritional benefits to be obtained from each? Which would I choose as providing the most desirable curriculum opportunities for the children?

Nutritious-Delicious Cookies*

Measure and stir together the dry ingredients:

1⅓ c flour (unbleached)
1 t baking soda
½ t salt
½ t cinnamon
½ t (or less) nutmeg
¼ t (or less) cloves

Put the following in bowl and beat, combining first margarine and honey, then adding egg, and last the zucchini:

½ c margarine, softened
⅔ c honey
1 c grated zucchini
1 egg, beaten

Combine blended ingredients with dry ingredients. Then add the following:

½ c rolled oats
1 c dates, finely chopped
1 c walnuts, chopped
½ c coconut (optional)

Drop by heaping spoonfuls onto an oiled cookie sheet. Bake at 325° for 15 minutes until cookies are golden brown. Makes 36 cookies.

Whenever possible, choose recipes that avoid refined flour and sugars because these have a deleterious effect on teeth and digestion. The use of whole grains, fresh fruits, and vegetables provides good sources of fiber while also providing wonderful opportunities to talk with children about eating foods that both taste good and are good for them. Two good cookbooks that stress nutrition are Katzen & Henderson's *Pretend Soup and Other Real Recipes: A Cookbook for Preschoolers on Up* (1994) and Wilson's *The Good-for-Your-Health All-Asian Cookbook* (1995). But nourishing recipes can be found anywhere and teachers owe it to the children to seek them out.

Age-Appropriate, Multicultural Cooking Activities

Recipes must also be appropriate for the developmental levels of the child, and even children as young as 2 enjoy cooking. Table 8.3 offers some examples of activities that are appropriate for children of various ages.

In addition to being durable, nutritious, age-appropriate, and providing opportunities for participation, the recipe should be multiethnic if possible. Teachers should make use of the wealth of multicultural recipes now readily available in libraries and online (see also References for Further Reading at the end of this chapter).

---

*From *Zucchini Cookbook*, by V. Lemley and I. Lemley, 1976. Cave Junction, OR: Wilderness House. Copyright © 1976. Used by permission.

Table 8.3
Cooking Activities for Young Children of Different Ages

Ages of Children	Suggested Cooking Activities	Comments
2- to 3-year-olds	Washing and scrubbing vegetables Peeling hard-boiled eggs Tearing lettuce for salad Fruit milkshakes (mash fruit, shake in plastic bottle) Mixing cottage cheese dips Fondue (grating cheese, etc.) Squeezing orange juice (press-down-type electric juicer) Potato salad (begin with boiled potatoes) Bananas rolled in honey and wheat germ Arranging pizza ingredients Deviled eggs Kneading bread Nachos	Utensils that work well with 2s include wooden spoons, dull knives (for spreading things and for cutting soft substances, such as bananas), vegetable brushes, graters (particularly four-sided plastic ones), and sieves. Twos are interested in contrasting substances, such as cornmeal compared with unbleached flour and molasses with milk. Be prepared for a great deal of tasting and touching. Although fairly conservative about trying new foods at the table, they are often willing to taste bits of less familiar items while cooking them. Although these rules are important for all ages to remember, 2s must be taught the simple rules of hygiene—you must wash your hands before cooking, and you must not touch your nose and then touch food the group is going to eat.
3- to 4-year-olds	Vegetable soup Scrambled eggs French toast (with whole-wheat bread) Fruit salad Grilled cheese sandwiches Frozen juice bars (allow them to squeeze oranges first) Applesauce Filled celery stalks Meatballs Tacos Tabouli Asian dishes that require chopping and cutting Hamburgers Greens with bacon Yogurt sundaes	Threes are able to use utensils, such as measuring cups and spoons, sharper knives, graters, peelers, juice squeezers, manually operated rotary egg beaters, and rolling pins. They like to mash, mix, measure, and talk about the order in which things go together. They can use recipes that require more heat, although they will need close watching. They are able to wait a bit longer for results. They enjoy doing things that help the entire group, such as making part of the snack for everyone to enjoy later.
4- to 5-year-olds	Bread Quiche Ice cream Anything grown in their garden Butter Beef jerky Fruit leather Read-for-yourself recipes Recipes from other cultures	Fours, particularly if this is their second year in school, are accomplished cooks and can do just about everything except deep fat frying. They are able to use tongs and pancake turners, assemble equipment, such as ice cream freezers and food grinders, use a barbecue grill, and even separate eggs. If recipes are illustrated with cups, spoonfuls, and labels, they will enjoy following these with only minimal help from the teacher.

Note: We want to thank Donna Coffman, former Director of the Santa Barbara City College Children's Center, for some of the suggestions included in this table.

As well, families are a great resource and should be invited to cook and share recipes with the children. Sometimes a member of a child's family will join the class and reminisce about how people cooked when he or she was little, and this intensifies the children's interest when they make the same recipe. Children also enjoy bringing some special foods from home to share with the group.

Suggestions for Making Life in the Kitchen Easier

When cooking, overcrowding should be avoided because this means that each child gets to take only one stir. It may even be dangerous if the children start shoving for the knife or arguing over a hot pan. Overcrowding can be prevented if at least one other, very attractive activity is deliberately offered at the same time—preferably as far away from the cooking area as possible. Crowding can be reduced also if two adults make the same recipe at separate tables or if one adult repeats the recipe twice so that additional children can participate the second time. Choosing a recipe that offers many things to do that do not require close supervision or a recipe that an additional staff member can supervise also alleviates crowding. Finally, the best way to reduce overcrowding is to offer cooking frequently enough that the novelty wears off, while the satisfaction remains. When children know there are plentiful opportunities to take part in an experience, they lose that desperate "I gotta do it now" feeling.

Avoid recipes that are too difficult, and allow plenty of time for the children to participate fully. The test of whether a recipe is too difficult is how much of the work the teacher ends up doing and whether most of the children remain interested throughout the process.

It is always wise to try out a recipe at home before using it with the children. This enables the teacher to anticipate problems and also provides a time line. It is a pity to hurry children through a cooking experience that has such rich learning possibilities, so it is wise to plan plenty of time on cooking days.

Remember that cleanup is half the fun, and plan enough time for children to participate in this process. Children love to do dishes and mess about with soapy sponges, and cooking gives them a fine opportunity to do this while experiencing the satisfaction of meaningful work as well. Think of cleanup as being an integral part of the cooking experience and plan so that children can usually participate in this satisfying aspect of the activity.

Integrate Information About Food into the Curriculum

Besides actually cooking, it is desirable to talk about food and good nutrition during the day. So many delightful books about food are available that it is impossible to mention them all here, but such treasures as *Blueberries for Sal* (McCloskey, 1948), *Sip, Slurp, Soup, Soup Caldo Caldo Caldo* (Bertrand, 1997), *Tiger Soup: An Anansi Story* (Temple, 1998), *The Enormous Turnip* (Parkinson, 1986), *Gregory the Terrible Eater* (Sharmat, 1980), *Tops and Bottoms* (Stevens, 1995), *If You Give a Mouse a Cookie* (Numeroff, 1985), and *Bread and Jam for Frances* (Hoban, 1964) tie in well with cooking and eating and are great fun besides.

Families appreciate knowing what their children are eating during the day, so posting menus in a prominent place helps assure them that the children are being well fed. At the Institute, where we have a policy of serving no-dye, sugar-free, low-fat, and low-salt foods, we have made a point of telling families about the policy and why we follow it. We couple this with suggestions of nourishing treats they can supply in place of the sticky birthday fare so often provided. Most families are pleased to comply with our requests for these wholesome substitutes that can include popcorn, trail mix, fresh and dried fruits, and nuts.

SUMMARY

There are many ways of developing the physical well-being and competence of young children. This chapter stresses two of them: keeping children safe and healthy and feeding them well. When considering physical safety, teachers must use their common sense to decide when to intervene and when not to intervene. They must also continually assess the condition of school equipment to make certain that it has not deteriorated, and they should teach children gradually to think about safety for themselves.

Basic rules of health include consistent hand washing by children and adults, disinfecting common areas and equipment, excluding children from school when they are contagious, maintaining up-to-date immunizations, and taking special care of children who have been ill.

Feeding children well is best approached from two points of view—planning meals and snacks that are nutritionally sound, and offering cooking as a continuing part of the curriculum. Eating well deserves a good deal of attention in children's centers because problems of malnutrition—particularly dental decay and iron deficiency anemia—are widespread among children in the United States. In addition, teachers must help children avoid obesity and overweight through healthful eating habits.

The Food Guide Pyramid for Young Children and MyPyramid for older children are featured as the Chapter Spotlights because they clarify what children (and adults) need to eat every day to stay healthy and develop well.

When choosing recipes to cook with the children, the teacher should select ones that are not too delicate, that offer many things for children to do, that are nourishing and age appropriate, and that come from a variety of cultures.

Recipe for a Happy Day*

1 cup friendly words
2 heaping cups of understanding
4 heaping teaspoons time and patience
A pinch of warm personality
Dash of humor

Mixing:

Measure words carefully. Add heaping cups of understanding. Use generous amounts of time and patience.

Cook on front burner, but keep temperature low; do not boil.

Add generous dash of humor and personality. Season to taste with the spice of life.

Serve in individual molds.

**From Recipes for Busy Little Hands, by D. J. Croft, 1967. Palo Alto, CA: DeAnza College. Copyright © 1967. Used by permission.*

Food for Thought and Group Discussions

1. Hannah's mother arrives with her child in tow and says, "Oh, by the way, Hannah threw up in the middle of the night, but she seems to be all right now—I'd appreciate it if you'd keep an eye on her today." How would you handle this situation? Should Hannah be allowed to stay at school? Should she be sent home? What would you say to the mother?

2. Suppose you are in charge of planning snacks for the coming week. As a consciousness-raising activity, develop five different snacks that have minimal food value but that the children would like a lot. Now develop five with sound nutritional values that children would also relish.

3. Share a recipe with the class that represents your own cultural background.

4. Maintaining adequate immunity against infectious diseases is important for everyone. What are some of the most important steps teachers can take to help the spread of illness at school? How up-to-date are your own immunizations? Investigate the services of your county health clinic and report to the class. Which immunizations are available there at nominal cost?

Self-Check Questions for Review

Content-Related Questions

1. What is a good rule of thumb to follow when deciding whether an activity is safe for a child to continue?
2. What is HIB? And how is it best controlled?
3. List some valuable ways of keeping children healthy.
4. What are the two most important health problems related to malnutrition among children of all economic levels in the United States?
5. What are the changes recommended for food selection and preparation that could lead to better health for everyone?
6. Explain some helpful points to consider when choosing a recipe to cook with young children.

Integrative Questions

1. A father is enrolling his child in your school and explains that although the child's immunizations are not up-to-date, he will take care of them as soon as he can get around to it. Would you or would you not allow that child to enter school? Explain the reasons for your decision.
2. Give an example of something you might say to a child after an accident that would be moralizing. Then rephrase it in a more appropriate form.

References for Further Reading

Pick of the Litter

Berman, C., & Fromer, J. (1997). *Meals without squeals.* Palo Alto, CA: Bull. A user-friendly book that should not be missed—it includes recipes, information on nutrition, cleanliness, recycling, feeding practices, and more.

Health and Safety

Kendrick, A. S., Kaufmann, R., & Messenger, K. P. (Eds.). (2002). *Healthy young children: A manual for programs* (Rev. ed.). Washington, DC: National Association for the Education of Young Children. This manual offers a comprehensive, practical mix of information ranging from safety and preventive health to nutrition and caring for children with special needs. *Highly recommended.*

Nutrition—General Information

U.S. Department of Agriculture. (1999). *Tips for using the Food Guide Pyramid for young children 1 to 6 years old.* Washington, DC: Center for Nutrition Policy and Promotion, U.S. Department of Agriculture. The guide is well worth sending for—just request it from your state office or download it (http://www.fns.usda.gov/cnd/care/Publications/kidspyramid.htm). It includes lists of foods qualifying for inclusion in the subsections of the pyramid as well as menu ideas for young children. *Highly recommended.*

Menu Planning

Marotz, L. R., Cross, M. Z., & Rush, J. M. (2005). *Health, safety and nutrition for the young child* (6th ed.). Albany, NY: Delmar/Thomson. This text contains an outstanding emphasis on nutrition and includes a chapter on menu planning.

Teaching About Good Nutrition and Cooking with Young Children

Katzen, M., & Henderson, A. (1994). *Pretend soup and other real recipes: A cookbook for preschoolers and up.* Berkeley, CA: Tricycle. Mollie Katzen of *Moosewood Cookbook* fame has produced a delightful, well-illustrated, child-tested cookbook. Each recipe is pictured so that very young cooks can "read" what to do. Sensible advice is also included.

Lakeshore Learning Materials. (n.d.). *Multicultural cooking with kids.* Carson, CA: Lakeshore Equipment. This spiral-bound, plastic-coated book offers two to three recipes from each of several diverse cultures—Mexican, Japanese, and German, for instance—plus a cultural fact about each recipe.

Satter, E. (2000). *Child of mine: Feeding with love and good sense.* Palo Alto, CA: Bull. Everything you could possibly want to know about feeding a child up to age 5 is included here.

Information About Obesity

Paxson, C., Donahue, E., Orleans, C. T., & Grisso, J. A. (Eds.). (2006). Childhood obesity [Entire issue]. *The Future of Children, 16(1).* This journal discusses trends, causes, and prevention of childhood obesity. It can be downloaded free at http://www.futureofchildren.org/

Information About Allergies

Jalongo, M. R. (2000). Editorial: On behalf of children. Firsthand experiences with children's food allergies and intolerances. *Early Childhood Education Journal, 28(2),* 75–77. This article is important because the results of some allergies are life threatening for children.

Taking Cultural Good Preferences into Account

Bermúdez, M. T. (2001). *Mexican family favorites.* Phoenix: Golden West. This cookbook, now in its 21st reprinting, offers authentic, basic recipes with readily obtainable ingredients.

Cox, B., & Jacobs, M. (1991). *Spirit of the harvest: North American Indian cooking.* New York: Stewart, Tabori, & Chang. This book features attractive American Indian recipes classified according to region. Overviews of Native American tribes and handsome photographs of some recipes are included. Every effort has been made to keep the material as authentic and respectful as possible.

Parham, V. R. (1993). *The African-American child's heritage cookbook*. South Pasadena, CA: Sandcastle. Parham provides a good array of recipes including ones specifically identified as African, Creole, Jamaican, soul food, and healthy ways to fix old favorites.

Wilson, M. (1995). *The good-for-your-health all-Asian cookbook*. Washington, DC: Tuttle. This book has 220 recipes drawn from Korea, Indonesia, Malaysia, Pakistan, India, the Philippines, Singapore, Thailand, Vietnam, Japan, and China.

For the Advanced Student

Center on Hunger, Poverty, and Nutrition Policy. (1998). *Statement on the link between nutrition and cognitive development in children*. Medford, MA: Tufts University, Center on Hunger, Poverty, and Nutrition Policy. This concise publication presents a summary of research documenting the serious consequences of undernutrition and its relationship to reducing growth and functioning of the brain.

Consumer Product Safety Commission. (1997). *Handbook for public playground safety*. Washington, DC: Author. This document lists numerous safety guidelines for all kinds of "public" playgrounds—including children's centers. *An indispensable resource.*

Related Organizations and Online Resources

The American Academy of Pediatrics (AAP) Web site provides many excellent resources for parents and teachers with many useful downloads. http://www.aap.org

The American Red Cross is an indispensable resource for developing emergency plans. http://www.redcross.org/

The Child Care Nutrition Resource System provides information to persons working in USDA child nutrition programs. The Web site has many useful resources from the federal government, including menus for children's centers, information on health issues such as choking and emergency preparedness, and information about guidelines for centers to receive food assistance. http://www.nal.usda.gov/childcare

Child Health Alert is an organization committed to the health and well-being of all children. The Web site provides a quick way to keep up-to-date on a wide variety of child health issues. http://www.childhealthalert.com/

The Web site of the Food and Nutrition Service, USDA, is the central government site for all information related to nutrition, including access to the Food Guide Pyramid for Young Children (ages birth–6) and the new MyPyramid for Kids (ages 6–11). http://www.fns.usda.gov/. Specific nutritional recommendations starting at 2 years of age can be accessed at http://www.mypyramid.gov

DEVELOPING PHYSICAL COMPETENCE

Have you ever . . .

- Wondered what teachers can do to promote children's physical fitness?
- Wondered what should be offered to enhance motor skills?
- Wondered not only how to start a dance experience but also how to prevent it from turning into chaos?

If you have, the material in this chapter will help you.

Sitting still is overrated. It makes sense for the opera or for meditating, but in most class-rooms and child care centers, it's given far more honor than it deserves. Children need to move. Movement is one of the ways brains develop. Dendrites grow, connecting this part of the brain to that one and complementing this function with another. Sitting still makes us dumber. The brain doesn't grow.

—Tom Hunter (2000, p. 50)

In addition to making sure that children's bodies are well nourished and that the children are learning to cherish and care for them, teachers also need to do all that they can to en-courage sound physical development through exercise. U.S. Surgeon General Richard H. Carmona has stated, "The crisis is obesity. It's the fastest-growing cause of disease and death in America. And it's completely preventable." Lest we feel the crisis only affects adults, Carmona continues:

> The fact is that we have an epidemic of childhood obesity. . . . The bad news is that an unprecedented number of children are carrying excess body weight. That excess weight sig-nificantly increases our kids' risk factors for a range of health problems, including diabetes, heart disease, asthma, and emotional and mental health problems. (U.S. Department of Health and Human Services, 2003, p. 1)

It is estimated that 1 in 5 children in the United States is overweight (National Institutes of Health, 2005; U.S. Department of Health and Human Services, 2003). This situation seems bound to become worse as children continue to stuff themselves with unwholesome foods and spend longer and longer hours squatting in front of television sets and playing with computers.

Nor is it correct to assume that just because children are in school every day that they are in-volved in enough vigorous exercise. Activity levels of young children have been declining sig-nificantly in recent years (Buch, 2005; Oliver & Klugman, 2005). The rise in electronic media use such as television, computers, and video games—at home *and* in school programs—has re-sulted in a nation of sedentary children. Even children as young as age 2 spend at least 2 hours a day sitting in front of an electronic screen (Kaiser Family Foundation, 2003). In addition, since the passage of the No Child Left Behind Act, the trend in elementary schools is to reduce or eliminate recess in an attempt to focus more attention on academics (Lynn-Garbe & Hoot, 2005; Zygmunt-Fillwalk & Bilello, 2005). Clearly, if we want to instill a taste for healthy, vigorous exercise in the children we care for, we must do more than turn them loose on the playground for a few minutes or allow them to sit for hours at the computer.

THE GREAT OUTDOORS

It is an unfortunate fact that as our society becomes more "plugged in," children lose out on the benefits of outdoor play. As stated in a recent *New York Times* article, "The days of the free-range childhood seem to be over" (McKee, 2005, p. D1). Recent research confirms the fact that children spend less time outdoors and more time in sedentary, indoor activities which has led to a host of physical—and avoidable—problems (Buch, 2005; Kaiser Family Foundation, 2003; U.S. Department of Health and Human Services, 2003). The antidote to this sad trend is for teachers to provide large blocks of time for outdoor play that is sometimes free play, sometimes organized as movement activities, but *always* exuberant and robust, in accordance with the nature of childhood.

Keep in mind that many activities are enhanced when they go outdoors. This includes dress-up play, fine motor activities, painting, dancing, and reading just to name a few. Teachers should continually search for creative ways to get the children outdoors—where fresh air and the freedom to move about are integral to a healthy childhood. Simply by taking children for walks, teachers can help them develop a healthy lifestyle that not only reduces illness but also leads to a longer life (Stein, 2005).

PHYSICAL ACTIVITY BENEFITS ALL THE SELVES

As Table 9.1 illustrates, no other kind of activity offers such rich opportunities for the development of all the selves. Obviously the body benefits—and so does the emotional self, as the child acquires feelings of competence through the acquisition of new skills, or uses physical activity as an acceptable channel for aggressive feelings, or becomes involved in creative dance and explores a wide range of emotions. The cooperative interplay between children and the satisfaction of doing things together develop the social self. The cognitive self is enhanced as children learn about body image and spatial relationships, and the creative self is provided with opportunities for original thinking that are encouraged by movement exploration activities and also nourished by the marvelous creative opportunities inherent in dance experiences and play.

Life is enhanced by the great outdoors.

Because of all these benefits, physical activity is of great value to the young child, and it behooves teachers to think carefully about its educational potential to help children make the most of its possibilities (Gallahue & Ozmun, 2005; Sanders, 2002; Zygmont-Fillwalk & Bilello, 2005). What is needed is the development of a comprehensive physical development program that does not regiment the children but does provide opportunities to practice many different kinds of skills using different parts of the body.

The best way to achieve this lies in acquiring general knowledge of the likely ages for acquisition of various skills and specific knowledge of the developmental needs of the individual children. This information should then be used to plan a comprehensive program using perceptual-motor activities, movement exploration, and creative dance. Older children in elementary school enjoy organized games that involve running, chasing, jumping, and ball play. These experiences should be offered in attractive forms so that children will seek them out rather than having to be coerced into participation.

IDENTIFYING LEVELS OF DEVELOPMENT

It only makes sense to plan physical activities that fit the developmental abilities of the children. Threes, for instance, are a lot more likely to be interested in simple climbing skills and

Table 9.1

How Can Physical Activity Promote Development of the Whole Child?

Physical	Emotional	Social	Creative	Cognitive/Language
Encourages:	**Encourages:**	**Encourages:**	**Encourages:**	**Encourages:**
Development of skills:	Positive attitude toward attempting challenges (trying new things)	Cooperative play	Vigorous pretend play	Coordination of language with physical activity (Miss Mary Mack; finger plays; simple singing games)
Locomotion	Being persistent	Cooperative use of equipment (trike and wagon; round tire swing; rocking boat)	Unusual ways to use familiar equipment	Knowledge of fundamental principles of good health; e.g., exercise makes bodies strong
Dynamic and static balance	Sense of physical competence		Generation of tricks and stunts	
Body and space perception	Ability to channel aggression	Social give-and-take (sharing trike track)	Expression of own ideas in dance	Knowledge of spatial relationships (in, under, etc.)
Rhythm and temporal awareness	Relief of tension through acceptable physical activities	Acknowledgment of other children's physical skills	Use of imagination	Ability to estimate in advance: depth and distance; potential risks
Rebound and airborne activities	Safe expression of wide range of feelings in dancer	Development of competitive attitude toward other children under some circumstances	Original solutions to "problems" in movement exploration activities	Ability to conform to simple rules for safety
Projectile management	Willingness to take moderate risks	Development of conflict resolution skills	Aesthetic appreciation of combined music and movement experiences	Ability to understand rules of simple group games, such as Farmer in the Dell
Fine-motor skills				Use of movement to communicate ideas
Physical fitness:				
Endurance				
Heart rate				
Muscular strength				
Flexibility				
Good health				
Development of coordination:				
Eye–hand				
Eye–foot				
Kinesthetic awareness (knowledge of what body is doing as it moves; body "cues")				
Sensory awareness				
Bilateral and cross-lateral physical activities				
Ability consciously to relax				

Plan physical activities that fit the developmental level of the children.

riding tricycles than they will be at catching balls or skipping rope. For the approximate ages at which the average child attains various skills, Table 9.2 provides a useful index.

Once the teacher has an idea of the general level of ability in the group and is also aware of children who have special talents or who lack motor skills that most children have acquired by their age, a solid foundation exists for knowing what level of activities should be included in the program. One word of caution is in order, however. Although the sequence in which children develop physical skills remains fairly constant, the time of acquisition varies considerably, and this must be taken into account when evaluating developmental status (Bredekamp & Copple, 1997; Copple & Bredekamp, 2006). Just because a child seems a bit ahead or behind the time listed in Table 9.2, the teacher should not conclude that she is either an athletic genius or a potential klutz. Gross deviations, on the other hand, should be cause for further investigation by a pediatrician.

EQUIPMENT FOR PHYSICAL DEVELOPMENT

It was stressed in previous chapters that equipment should be durable, safe, and well maintained. (See also the discussion of outdoor equipment in chapter 4, and note particularly the discussion of simple, complex, and super play units there.) We often think of *equipment* as meaning large, permanent structures, and some sorts of vigorous activity do require this kind of installation. However, many activities suggested later in this chapter in Tables 9.3 to 9.8 do not require large, elaborate equipment at all.

The best resource for physical play activity remains the child's ideas and body, combined with a variety of readily obtainable accessories, such as boards, ladders, tires, barrels, boxes, and blocks. These kinds of materials have the capacity for infinite rearrangement necessary for the generation of creative, large-muscle play (Frost, Wortham, & Reifel, 2005; Rivkin, 1995; Sanders, 2002).

Some of these items, such as hollow blocks, are best purchased, though we once saw a very substantial painted set that had been made from old whiskey boxes. However, much portable equipment can be built. Some can even be wheeled for free from businesses such as milk companies that donate old milk crates or tire companies that give away worn tires.

When large structures are needed, there is no other place in the preschool where one can spend so much money so quickly. There is no denying there are some beautiful, physically satisfying structures available for purchase, but fortunately there are also many ways of achieving equivalent play value without spending a fortune. Each community offers its own potential for free materials for such construction—including things like railroad ties, logs sawn into various heights, boulders for climbing, chipped sewer pipes for tunnels, and strong dead trees.

People, too, are good resources. Park and street department people are often generous with advice and surplus materials if contacted by child-care centers. Park and recreation people, in particular, are deeply interested in and knowledgeable about large-muscle play

Table 9.2
Age at Which Most Children Perform Locomotor Skills

By the End of the 1st Year, the Child:	By the End of the 2nd Year, the Child:	By the End of the 3rd Year, the Child:	By the End of the 4th Year, the Child:	By the End of the 5th Year, the Child:	Between the 6th and 8th Years:
Reaches sitting position by himself	Walks independently	Climbs well	Hops and stands on one foot up to 5 seconds	Balances on one foot for 10 seconds or longer	Development slows compared to the preschool years
Crawls forward on his stomach	Climbs stairs (sometimes needs support)	Walks up and down stairs using a rail	Goes upstairs and downstairs independently and alternating feet	Walks backward	Can sequence a series of movement skills
Pushes up into hands-and-knees position	Enjoys climbing structures (and climbing on furniture)	Jumps off steps or structures	Kicks ball forward	Hops	Somersaults with ease
Creeps on hands and knees or crawls	Carries objects while walking	Throws, kicks a ball	Throws ball overhand	Jumps rope	Develops competency in skills for team sports (throwing, catching, etc.)
Pulls himself up to standing; may stand alone for a short time	Trots and runs	Runs easily	Catches a bounced ball	Somersaults	Takes physical risks
Walks while holding onto something; may take a few steps alone	Stands on toes	Pedals a tricycle	Jumps rope	Swings	Develops quick reaction time
	Throws, kicks a ball	Bends over without falling	Moves forward and backward easily	Climbs	Coordinates more advanced physical development with more advanced mental development; begins to enjoy games with rules
		Engages in physical play with full energy, then gets tired, sometimes cranky		Rides a bike	
				Swims	
				Skips	
				Usually is independent in toileting	
				Has a high level of physical energy	

149

equipment. Ask them for suggestions about planning and for community sources of free materials—they are used to making dollars stretch.

It is of utmost importance to ensure that whatever is built is safe and that it is twice as strong as you think it should be. Never assume that just because the children are small, equipment need not be well braced and firmly built. In fact, young children are very hard on equipment. They use apparatus vigorously and constantly, and construction must take this into account if the equipment is to be safe and to last more than a few months.

Finally, every school has its own unique potential for physical experiences. It may be a large, blank wall to bounce balls against, or a gentle slope for children to roll down, or something as seemingly undesirable as a completely paved playground that also means a quickly drying surface in almost all weather. The point is that every situation has hidden assets if teachers will take a fresh look at their environment from time to time and then put these possibilities to work.

MAKE A PLAN FOR COMPREHENSIVE PHYSICAL DEVELOPMENT

Does Practice Make Any Difference in Physical Development, or Do Children Just Develop Anyway?

Nowhere is there more interesting evidence that both nature (heredity) and nurture (environment) play an interactive role than in the realm of physical development. For example, as Table 9.2 and the chart of normal development in appendix A remind us, the sequence in which various physical skills are acquired is reasonably similar for children from a variety of cultures. We know, also, that babies first gain control of their head and trunk muscles and more gradually learn to coordinate their arms, legs, and hands. Thus children learn to sit before they stand and stand before they walk. Physical development also proceeds from head to toe—babies are able to reach and grasp before they crawl and walk. These kinds of activities are primarily due to the development of the brain stem (nature) and are not much influenced by practice (Eliot, 1999).

On the other hand, practice *does* improve these new skills as they develop. Anyone who has watched a baby make repeated attempts to grasp a rattle dangling above her or tirelessly though fretfully pull herself upright and fuss to be helped down again understands the role that experience and practice play in the acquisition of new skills.

These examples, and innumerable ones like them, make it plain that both inheritance and environment play significant roles in how children develop. This is true, of course, for all the selves, but is particularly evident when discussing the physical self. Perhaps the clearest way to sum up the effect of the heredity-versus-environment debate is to remember this simple saying: Heredity (nature) determines what one *may* become, but environment (nurture) determines what one *does* become.

Although teachers may have no influence on the hereditary portion of the development equation, we *can* influence the environmental–experience part of

Practice improves new skills as they develop.

that equation (Ceci & Williams, 1999; Frost et al., 2005; Sanders, 2002). That is the reason it is important to become aware of the different categories of physical skills that preschool children should acquire. We need to know what the major categories are so we can make certain that opportunities for practicing them are included in the curriculum.

Which Skills Should Be Included?

Making plans involves having two kinds of information. The first is knowing what individual children in the group already can do. The easiest way to find that out is to keep track of each child's developing skills through observation and by using physical development checklists such as those described in chapter 6.

The second source needed for planning is an outline of basic physical skills to make certain the plan is comprehensive and provides appropriate practice in the most important skills. These lists (taxonomies) vary from author to author but our favorite remains the outline proposed by Arnheim and colleagues (Arnheim & Sinclair, 1979; Arnheim & Pestolesi, 1978) because it is reasonably comprehensive and is easy to understand. There are eight categories:

1. Locomotion
2. Balance
3. Body and space perception
4. Rhythmic activities
5. Rebound and airborne activities
6. Projectile management
7. Fine-muscle coordination
8. Tension and relaxation strategies

Locomotion.   Locomotion includes the enormous variety of ways children have of getting from one place to another. In the beginning it can be as seemingly simple as learning to roll over, or it can be as complex as pulling oneself up a rope ladder or sliding down a pole. It also includes jumping, hopping, and skipping. In Table 9.3, for instance, note how long it takes to develop into an adequate skipper.

Table 9.3
Perceptual-Motor Activity: Locomotion

Locomotion	Easier	More Challenging	Movement Education Activity
Rolling (5 months) (mats are nice but not essential)	Roll over and over, sideways—both directions. Roll downhill (and try rolling up).	Roll with arms overhead or do forward roll somersault (age 5), arms around knees—roll "butterball" style. Roll about, balanced on top of very large ball. Be rolled by someone else while braced in large tire.	Roll to music "I roll myself over and over." Roll toward sound of drum with eyes closed—changing direction as drummer moves.
Creeping and crawling (10 months)	Can use legs straight or bent.	Crawl while pushing a ball with head or following a line.	Play at being various crawly animals—snakes, lizards, turtles, bears, cats, etc.

(Continued)

151

Table 9.3
(*continued*)

Locomotion	Easier	More Challenging	Movement Education Activity
Creeping and crawling (*continued*)	Crawl with arm and leg on same side of body parallel or in opposition (X) movement. Encourage crawling on textured surfaces for increased sensory input.	Wriggle across floor using only arms (GI crawl).	For control, creep slowly and then pounce—while singing "Old Grey Cat Goes Creeping"—or be spider singing "Eensy Weensy Spider." Ask children whether they can crawl under, over, through, and so forth. Try big cardboard boxes for this.
Climbing (as early as age 2; proficient at 4; ladder climbing mastered by age 6)	Slide ladder is often only fixed ladder on playground; can also use jungle gyms, arched climbers, cargo nets, or A-frames—good to encourage hand-over-hand, foot-over-foot activity.	Rope ladder or fireman's ladder. Ladders with more distance between rungs are more difficult. Steeper is harder. Ramp to top of sewer pipe, jump off. Attach rope to top of slide and climb up hand-over-hand.	For children who know the story, "Jack and the Bean Stalk" provides lots of pretend climbing.
Jumping (28 months)	Jumping easier than hopping. Jump over lines or off low heights.	Jump over low objects. Jump off higher things onto mattress. Jump rope swung in half arc slowly, or whirled in circle on ground. Jump and land "on target" marked with tape or carpet square.	Rabbits, grasshoppers, popcorn, and birds all jump. Can act out motions of animals, such as a scared rabbit. Position in space by jumping in and out of hoops; more advanced form, one child jumps in as another jumps out; be a frog jumping on a lily pad; jump in something sticky like molasses.
Hopping (age 3—hop two or three times, same foot)	Hop one or two steps on one foot, over lines, etc.	Hop several times, same foot.	For alternate hopping activity, Claire Cherry suggests Native American dancing. What can you do on one foot? On one arm?
Running and leaping (children are accomplished runners by age 4)	Very desirable to have large open space for this—conveys marvelous feeling of pleasure and freedom.	Can foster agility by encouraging figure-8 runs; this is quite difficult for 4s. Run and then jump as far as possible.	Crouch down and "explode" on signal by leaping up; run and stop in time to music or play "freeze"; leap over "puddles" on floor. Can you run like a mouse? Like an elephant? Run as if the wind is pushing you. Run as butterflies fly. Do shadow running and leaping, moving as partner does.
Skipping		14% of 4s and 22% of 5s can skip; therefore, not appropriate to stress at nursery school level.	

Balance. Balancing basically comes in two forms—balancing while holding still (*static balance*) and balancing while moving around (*dynamic balance*). Playing the game of "freeze" is not only a nice variation for practicing static balance but can also be a pleasant way to regain control of a group during an overly exciting episode of dance. Scooters are a good way to provide practice for dynamic balance. If possible, it is wise to encourage the children to try alternating feet from time to time to enhance balancing skills on each side of their bodies. Table 9.4 suggests balance activities for a range of developmental levels.

Body and Space Perception. This is the area, in particular, where movement-education activities really shine. This is because adding names to what the children are doing generates additional connections between neurons in their brains. This, in turn, enriches their understanding of the activity by enabling them to talk about it, and also calls their attention

Table 9.4
Perceptual-Motor Activity: Balance

Balance	Easier	More Challenging	Movement Education Activity
Static (balance while still)	Stand on tiptoe; try balancing lying on side.	Balance on hollow block. Balance on one foot. Stand still with eyes closed.	Hold still as long as drum doesn't beat. Can you balance on three parts of your body? Without touching the floor? Without using your feet? Play "statues."
Dynamic (balance while moving) (both feet on beam, walk partway, 38 months).	Use a balance board—wider is easier. Walk with one foot on, one foot off beam; walk along log, curb, edge of wall, or thin chalk line.	Both feet on beam (4-inch beam or, if proficient, use narrow side of beam), or walk sideways, foot-over-foot on beam. Visit a "clatter" bridge (may overwhelm some children). Walk on well-anchored gangplank between A-frames. Skate on one roller skate. Use a scooter. Walk around an edge of tire or "toober" (big inner tube). Step over thin ropes laid across balance beam. Walk on edges of ladder. Roll a hoop.	How can you get to end of balance beam without walking on it? Imagine you're on a tightrope. Dance on tiptoe—slowly for greater challenge. Use hollow block as "stones" to step across the river.
With object	Roll a tire. Crawl with beanbag on back. Walk with beanbags, arms extended from sides.	Balance beanbag on back of hand. Balance balloon or small ball on hand. Walk on wide plank—with one weighted pole on one side or carrying bottle of sand on one side. Walk carrying something spillable in bowl.	Dance with hoop or paper parasol or very large fans (can be obtained from stores specializing in oriental goods) and retain balance. What can you do with the fan? How far can you bend over with it?

153

to how their bodies feel. (How a movement feels is sometimes termed the *kinesthetic* sense.) As we will see later in this chapter, such bodily knowledge is also valuable when teaching children the fundamentals of relaxation. For ideas on incorporating body and space perception activities in the classroom, see Table 9.5.

Rhythm and Temporal Awareness.   All regularly repeated patterns of activity qualify for inclusion in this category, but the ones with a definite "beat" seem to be most pleasurable. This beat can be provided by a drum, music, or clapped hands—and remember that chants and rhymes also qualify and can be used to very good effect spontaneously out on the playground. Table 9.6 suggests activities to enhance children's rhythm and temporal awareness.

Rebound and Airborne Activities.   Rebound activities, in particular, go hand in hand with rhythm and temporal activities. Jumping on bouncy mattresses and swinging are good examples of how activities can provide two-in-one practice opportunities. Hanging and stretching also double up well with the relaxation category and feel wonderful besides. Rebound and airborne activities are described in Table 9.7

Table 9.5
Perceptual-Motor Activity: Body and Space Perception

Body and Space Perception	Easier	More Challenging	Movement Education Activity
	How many people can fit in the box? Guess, then try it.	Play "Simon Says." Use screen that just lets shoes show—guess who the shoes belong to. Guess about bare toes and hands, as well.	Any activity requiring movement in space, varied in *tempo* (pace and rhythm); *force* of motion, particularly where awareness is stressed.
	How high can you reach? Any activity that fosters knowledge of body parts such as "Head, Shoulders, Knees, and Toes" will do.	Shut eyes—guess who you are touching by touch alone. Do something with body and tell what you did in words. Work on identifying more difficult body parts—eyebrows, elbows, toenails, eyelids. Traffic course on bikes requiring careful steering.	All body–object relationships— "on," "under," "behind," and so on (directionality). How slow can you creep? How fast can you run? Practically any kind of finger play. Move in water if a pool is available. All activities where expression of emotion or physical states is encouraged—a "tired" dance, for example. Have child move like an animal of his choosing—ask others to guess animal. Use "mirror" or shadow dancing. How close can you get to your partner and not touch him? Ask "What can you do with your toes?" and "Anything else?" Have children propose ways to use the parachute.

Table 9.6
Perceptual-Motor Activity: Rhythm and Temporal Awareness

Rhythm and Temporal Awareness	Easier	More Challenging	Movement Education Activity
(Even newborns are sensitive to different rhythms) For further discussion, see text: "Movement Education" and "Help Children Enjoy Creative Dance"	Any activity that has a regularly recurring rhythm to it—rocking boats, swings, even tricycles, rocking chairs. Any kind of bouncing equipment (see Table 9.7). Finger-paint to music. Ride bouncy horses to music.	Jump over rope. Jump rope swung in half arc. Galloping has definite rhythm (rudiments acquired by age 4). Can clap hands in pattern—knees, hands, head.	Rock with partner—singing "Row, Row, Row Your Boat." March and do other moving-to-music activities that emphasize response to "beat." Shaking activities—like wet dog, like salt shaker, "Looby Lou" (rhythm band is a conforming, not creative, rhythmic activity). Dance to holiday music—contrasting rhythm of "Jingle Bells" to "White Christmas," for example. Move according to poetic chants—"John Brown's Body" has a lot of appeal. Marching and using instruments at same time is more difficult.

Table 9.7
Perceptual-Motor Activity: Rebound and Airborne Activities

Rebound and Airborne Activities	Easier	More Challenging	Movement Education Activity
Jumping activities	Involves jumping skills combined with timing. Equipment such as mattress, box springs, bouncing boards are appropriate. *Do not use trampolines;* they require too much supervision and training. (Many insurance companies refuse insurance on this equipment.) Bouncing has added value as an aggression reliever.	Jump on "toober." Try turning while jumping. Jump on and off low mattress.	Can you bounce another way? Sitting down? Squatting? Bouncing activities are particularly satisfying when music is added. Vary tempo to encourage variety of kinds of bounces.
Hanging and stretching activities	Simply hang and stretch from exercise bar.	Use hand-over-hand exercise ladders. Use trapeze for swinging and hanging. Hang by knees from exercise bar.	How far can you reach? How high can you reach? Can you hang with one hand? How else could you hang?

155

Projectile Management. This is just a fancy name for throwing and catching! This category is often overlooked at the early childhood level—perhaps because young children are not very skilled at it. Then, too, some teachers think of "projectiles" as being dangerous, but as the activities suggested in Table 9.8 demonstrate, there are many low-risk opportunities for working on throwing and catching skills. Moreover, children need these skills particularly as foundations for later game sports at the primary school level.

Fine-Muscle Skills. It is particularly important to be aware of fine-muscle skills. (*Note:* the fine-muscle skills related to writing are discussed in chapter 16 on literacy.) These skills are so inherent to and pervasive in activities in the early and later school years that teachers sometimes fail to think of them as being *psychomotor* (mind–body related) skills and take them more or less for granted. We must realize however that such fine-muscle skills are not

Table 9.8
Perceptual-Motor Activity: Projectile Management

Projectile Management	Easier	More Challenging	Movement Education Activity
Throwing (easier than catching—children not really proficient until 5)	Roll large balls to partner. Throw soft balls, such as Nerf balls.	Roll at target—large empty bleach bottles. Throw at target or through hoop. For advanced children, try combination of running and throwing.	Pretend you are rolling something big and heavy—or as light as thistledown. Use scarves and streamers for waving in air.
Catching (also not well developed at preschool level)	Begin with catching a rolled ball between legs; encourage child to keep eyes open. Requires adult to throw ball to child for proper chance of catching; best to use large ball. Offer a large quantity of bean bags with target or box to throw at. Bounce ball with two hands.	Catch slightly smaller ball. Bounce and catch ball. Try a pitchback net. Make target farther away or box smaller.	Catch soap bubbles (watch out for slippery floor). Try blowing feathers and/or down.
Kicking (requires ability to poise on one foot)	Kick large, still ball.	Kick gently rolling ball. Roll faster to increase challenge.	
Striking (makes teachers nervous but children enjoy it even though it takes close supervision)	Keep balloons in air with hand. Hit punching bag mounted on spindle. Hit whiffle ball poised on traffic cone with plastic bat.	Hit balloon with paddle. Hit ball hung from string with paddle. Use large plastic bat and ball; adult pitches.	Dance with balloons.

equally easy for all youngsters to master and that *expecting young children to work at such skills for too long without relief can be a real source of strain.*

Moreover, teachers should regularly take a careful look at the children as they are handling small manipulative items, such as beads or puzzles, and be on the alert for undue clumsiness, excessive frustration, and for children who habitually hold such work too close to their eyes or who avoid such activities altogether. All these behaviors are indications that children may be having special eye–hand coordination problems. Such youngsters should be referred promptly to their pediatricians, ophthalmologists, or optometrists for further identification of the difficulty.

What about handedness? Statistics show that 85% to 90% of adults in the United States are right-handed, although now that left-handedness is more accepted, the number of left-handed people appears to be increasing somewhat. This preference for right-handedness begins as early as 13 weeks after conception, where sonograms reveal that most fetuses prefer to suck their right thumbs! Why this preference for using the right hand appears to be the most frequent choice remains open to debate, and theories abound (Eliot, 1999).

Children sometimes switch back and forth a number of times during the early years before finally settling on a preferred hand. By age 4, a great majority of the children have become either definitely right- or left-handed, although some youngsters do not reveal a consistent preference for one or the other until age 7—and of course, a few continue to use either hand with seemingly equal dexterity (Eliot, 1999).

Tension and Relaxation Strategies. Early childhood teachers have long recognized the necessity of having quiet times during the day, such as nap or midmorning rests. The ability to make good use of these times by genuinely relaxing varies from child to child. The more tense the child, the more difficulty she will have letting go—and the more she needs to do so. We often think of tension as being revealed by restlessness or a strained facial expression, but there are many other signs to look for. These are seen in children who hold their bodies in tense positions (hunched shoulders or clenched jaws), who appear immobile, or who are awkward or inhibited in movement. Other familiar indicators of tension include the inability to eat or a compensatory need to eat more than necessary, breathing difficulties, blushing or turning pale, cold hands or feet, the need to urinate frequently, tension headaches, and insomnia. When one reviews this list, the value of freeing a child from such burdens by teaching her to relax becomes apparent.

Teachers can help children learn to relax by using the simple method advocated by Jacobson (1976). Described in general terms, this method involves helping children learn to perceive how their bodies feel when they are tense and how they feel when they are relaxed, and then helping them learn to relax at will. Young children can grasp this fairly readily if asked to make themselves as stiff and tight as possible or to walk like a robot, and then to make themselves as floppy as a soft rag doll or to melt like a Popsicle. Mirrors are helpful accessories because the children can observe their faces when they scrunch them up tight and then let them go soft. They can also be encouraged to look at other children and tell when they are tensing or relaxing. Emphasis should be placed on repeatedly contrasting tense and relaxed states until the children identify them easily and produce each state at will. Once they have mastered whole-body relaxation, they can work on isolated areas, such as legs or arms or hands.

Stretching and yawning are excellent relaxation inducers, as are simple yoga exercises for breathing that can be used with older 4s and above. Of course, using soothing music and reducing extraneous stimulation, such as that caused by children and staff going in and out of the room during rest period, are basic to achieving success when teaching relaxation.

There are so many interesting, informal, playful ways to provide practice in these skills it would be a pity to reduce them to "drill-like" exercises. It is also simple to provide variety by making them easier or more challenging as the children become more competent and/or to include them when planning movement education activities during dance time.

Some kinds of activities, such as climbing and swinging, are best included through informal, spontaneous play and are usually available in most schools. Others, such as relaxation strategies, balancing techniques, and beginning throwing and catching skills, may be less familiar and require planned inclusion.

In general, the more informal the presentation of such activities, the more ideal—because an easygoing, casual approach is the antithesis of regimentation. However, teachers should not construe *informal* to mean *unplanned*. A good physical development program requires careful planning to make certain that opportunities for practice are provided for developing each of the listed skills at various levels of challenge.

Of course, planning should remain flexible and subject to change in accord with what the children spontaneously attempt. There is no better place in the curriculum to practice sensitivity to their ideas than in the realm of physical activity. Teachers who see their role as listening and responding to the children's ideas as well as taking responsibility for proposing possibilities themselves will find their physical activities program vastly enriched.

Teachers should supply appropriate vocabulary along with each activity because children are unlikely to possess such language without such assistance. This helps children identify what they are doing, extends their range of information, and may enhance, in some fashion that is not yet completely understood, their motor-planning skills by tying the cognitive/verbal component to the action. This vocabulary may be as simple as the statement "Jumpy, jump, jump!" to a young 2 or as elaborate as the comment "See how your toes are gripping the edge of the tire underneath—they're inside, and you're outside" to a 4-year-old. Either statement identifies and enriches the child's experience at an appropriate level.

Include Obstacle Courses

Another way to present perceptual-motor activities is to offer obstacle and action courses once or twice a week. This can put both the teacher's and children's ingenuity to work if the teacher asks, "Let's see, what could we use to jump into today?" or "What would be fun to balance on?" It is interesting to note that the children often concoct things to do that are a lot harder than what the grown-up considers reasonable.

Some general things to remember about obstacle courses are that they require a large, maneuverable area, that they should be supervised carefully (particularly if the teacher has some specific skills in mind for the children to practice), and finally that it is fun to change them while they are being used.

Honor Developmental Tastes and Preferences

Two-year-olds love to crawl (through tires, plastic snap-together blocks, and large, open pipes), climb (sets of stairs and A-frames), and jump from low heights onto mattresses or other spongy materials. They love balancing tasks on low, wide boards but are easily frightened of being too high up or of being shut in tunnels or boxes. Repetition of basic physical activities can be such a passion with 2s that it may seem almost obsessive to the adults in charge. (*Note:* Thanks to Paula Machado, former specialist in 2-year-olds for the Santa Barbara City College Children's Center, for these comments.)

Three-year-olds enjoy activities similar to those enjoyed by 2s, but they are much more competent, particularly in the domain of balance and coordination. They like to develop their own ideas of how to build tunnels and construct other exciting physical experiences. Whereas 2-year-olds require careful supervision because they are inexperienced and cannot always anticipate results adequately, 4-year-olds require supervision because they enjoy taking risks and doing daring stunts. It is as though, now that they have acquired basic physical competencies, they feel impelled to test these to the utmost. They enjoy tumbling activities, balancing on more difficult beams, hanging upside down by their knees, and jumping from considerable heights. Of all the ages of children, 4s are the ones for whom teachers need to offer the most challenge and variety.

Young children in elementary school have improved motor skills that are reflected in their flexibility, balance, and agility. They enjoy games that showcase these skills but often encounter challenges that push them *too* far, as the incidence of injury at this age increases. Physical activities enjoyed in the early grades include jump rope, tag, soccer, hopscotch, and hide-and-seek.

Help Children with Disabilities Participate

Teachers sometimes overlook the pressing need for physical activity felt by children who have various physical disabilities and tend to assume the children do not mind being so immobilized. However, their limited opportunities for physical activity mean that, if anything, these children need more, not fewer, chances to use their bodies in every way that can be made available to them.

For example, sand tables and water tables at waist height can be used by youngsters in wheelchairs if the chair is turned sideways to favor use of the child's dominant hand, or well-anchored trays can be fastened to the chair itself (although this is not as much fun as using the larger table). Or handholds can be provided on the edge of tables to enable children to pull themselves to a standing position. Or a slide can be installed on the slope of a hill with handrails and an easy-to-climb ramp beside it lined with textured material for traction. Children who have difficulty with small-muscle activities can be more successful if magnetic "sticky" blocks are provided. Youngsters with impaired vision can use a lot of outdoor equipment such as hanging bars, swings, and climbing equipment once they have had a quiet chance to investigate such equipment by feeling it and having it described to them. Remember, though, that it is *even more important than usual* to shield these activities so that partially sighted youngsters cannot possibly walk in front of them and be struck—this is *especially* important to remember to do with swings.

What it mainly takes to increase the participation of such children is a teacher who is sensitive to their needs and willing to look for creative solutions and who remembers to ask the families and the other specialists associated with the children's care to contribute their ideas also.

Provide Movement Education

In addition to the kinds of activities that have already been discussed, an additional activity teachers often use to foster the physical development of children is termed *movement education*. Tables 9.3 to 9.8 offer many examples of how this approach can be used with young children.

Although not as free as creative dance, movement education does have creative aspects, because teachers using this approach stress creative thinking on the part of the children. Movement education also helps children become more conscious of their bodies and what their bodies can do. Thus, the teacher might ask the children to demonstrate all the ways they can balance a beanbag or how they might get from one corner of the room to the other without using their feet. Because this approach often uses music, it is pleasurable to children and thus can make physical development seem less like exercise and more like fun. A combination of movement exploration activities and creative dance makes a good blend—movement education helps ensure that the range of perceptual-motor activities is complete and that concepts of body image are developed, and dance (discussed next in this chapter) ensures opportunities for rhythmic improvisation and self-expression.

Movement education can easily be corrupted and misinterpreted if the teacher is insensitive and allows the experience to degenerate into an instructional situation intended only to teach the meaning of adverbs. Teachers should be careful that this kind of direction ("Can you put your body behind something or in front of something?") does not become overly academic and dull.

Help Children Enjoy Creative Dance

By far the freest method of providing experiences that use some of these motor abilities is through creative dancing. This requires combining some open-ended suggestions from the teacher with spontaneous activity generated by the children. Beginning teachers (and more experienced ones, too) sometimes approach creative dance with apprehension. They usually fear two things: losing control of the group and not being able to get the children to participate. The problem may also be compounded by their feeling self-conscious about dancing themselves.

Maintaining Control of the Group

To keep control of the creative dance group, draw the line between active movement and wild running around. Fortunately, several things will help. Among them are keeping the group a reasonable size and always having an idea about what you intend to do next. It is important to employ a variety of slower and quicker rhythms and to provide relaxation periods so that the dance session does not keep building and building to a disastrous climax. It will also help teachers retain control if they incorporate movements that involve sitting and lying down part of the time, as well as those that require standing and moving about. Life will generally be easier if an assistant is available to help with shoes, music, and so forth. (If dance activities are offered toward the end of the morning or afternoon, often a family member can be prevailed on to return early and assist before picking up a car pool.)

How to Begin

Getting children to participate need not be difficult if the teacher does some planning and also participates in the activities with them. Such enthusiasm is contagious. It often works out well to begin a dance session with some simple, sitting-on-the-floor activities such as finger plays, dancing with the arms to music, and movement education activities. These "beginners" help overcome self-consciousness by not making everyone be up on their feet moving around right away. Sad to admit, even as early as preschool, some little boys have already decided that dancing is sissy. If this is the case, it is wiser to call it *movement time* or some other less prejudice-laden term than *dancing*.

Using simple props can help start the dance session also; scarves, balloons, tubes of stretchy jersey material, crepe paper streamers, tie-on skirts made of tulle sewn to ribbon waistbands, capes, and even piles of dry leaves may help distract the self-conscious child from focusing on herself. It is better not to depend on props too much, though, because they can become distracting.

In cases where it is the teacher and not the child who feels awkward, thinking about the children instead of oneself is a good basic remedy for overcoming personal self-consciousness, but other activities will help, too. Taking a dance class where everyone is moving together is one way of working through this feeling. Another way to reduce the overall sense of anxiety is by planning everything well and having a reassuring reservoir of ideas on which to fall back. Some beginning teachers prefer to be left completely alone with the children and provided with the assurance that absolutely no one will interrupt them; others feel more comfortable if they pair with another person at the start.

Incidentally, dance experiences provide excellent opportunities for identifying children with possible hearing difficulties. Watch for children who do not respond at all to changes in rhythm, who lose interest as soon as softer music is played, or who seem to stay consistently close to the source of the sound. These behaviors may be indicators that the child is not hearing well and would benefit from a referral to a physician.

Using Music

Music contributes a great deal to the satisfaction of a dance experience. A piano and accompanist are ideal but not necessary. Probably the best solution is to make compilations of your own to fit various moods and rhythms. It is also possible to purchase CDs to fit these categories, but be sure you plan in advance which tracks you wish to use so children aren't waiting around while you hunt for the perfect song.

Be wary also of a multitude of so-called children's music that features vocals that are arch, condescending, and insincere. When listening to these recordings, it is obvious that the people who produced them do not know much about young children, because so often the tempo is too fast, the pitch is too high, the lyrics inane, and the activities inappropriate. Remember that children's tastes are being formed by the music you use; do not settle for second-rate tripe when there are performers like Ella Jenkins, Marcia Berman, and Raffi available.

It is not necessary to use music the entire time. Percussion instruments, such as drums and tambourines, are very effective, and chants and songs are useful also.

Never forget that music offers fine opportunities for incorporating multiethnic materials into the school day. Every culture has its own tradition of folk dances, drum patterns, and songs. Music can also bring the culture of the home to the school if children are invited to bring recordings of popular music from home to share. After all, most popular music is written to be danced to.

Folk dances have both strengths and weaknesses for dancing with young children. Because they follow prescribed patterns, we cannot deceive ourselves that they are creative, and they may also be too complicated or move too quickly if presented in their original form. It is important to remember that they can be simplified, that they do provide a way of honoring other people's culture, and that they offer opportunities for children to accomplish something together in a group. Therefore, they deserve their place in the dance experience as long as teachers realize their limitations as well as their virtues.

Expressing Ideas and Feelings

Once the children are moving freely, the time is ripe to draw suggestions from them about what the music is saying to their feet. From here it is but a short step to encouraging children to express their feelings and helping them make contact with those feelings, whose presence they may otherwise deny. For example, the teacher might move from playing an action game based on the song "Here We Go 'Round the Mulberry Bush," featuring the things done at school (swinging, eating snack, hammering wood), to dancing the way they would dance if they felt sad when their parent left them at school, or if they felt a little angry about being left, or if they were happy to come. During the activity, the teacher also can comment casually that children often feel all these ways—a mixture of feelings. The same approach could be applied to going to the hospital, receiving a measles shot, or dealing with the arrival of a new baby.

To sum up, then, a good plan for dancing includes some nonthreatening warm-up activities to begin with, some multiethnic music for cultural richness, at least one idea that encourages the expression of feelings related to the children's life experiences, and plenty of encouragement for the children to dance freely to a variety of tempos and rhythms (Stinson, 1990). A good plan also includes a reserve of ideas in the teacher's head in case something does not go as well as hoped and a good selection of CDs with which the teacher is so familiar that the needed music can be located quickly.

Evaluate the Activities to Increase the Children's Success

Keeping an eye on what is happening and making quiet changes where possible while the activity is in progress can help the children have a more successful experience right away. Of course, it is always valuable to think about the activity at a later time, too, not only to improve the same activity another day but also to think about how to vary it—perhaps making it a little more difficult or changing it to attract other participants.

SUMMARY

Activities that enhance their physical skills are very dear to young children, as well as vital to their growth and development. For this reason, it is well worth teachers' time and attention to plan a comprehensive program that develops each kind of basic perceptual-motor skill. In addition, it is crucial that we impart to children a sense of joy in partaking in vigorous physical activity—especially outdoors—to stave off the temptations of sedentary pursuits (television, computers, etc.). With the crisis in childhood obesity and overweight, it is imperative that teachers develop movement activities for the children every day.

To do this successfully, teachers must know about general developmental levels and also know specific facts of physical development about each child. Once they have this information, they should refer to a thorough outline of perceptual-motor skills to make certain that their curriculum plans are truly comprehensive.

It is valuable to offer both portable and solidly fixed apparatus to encourage the growth of physical skills. Although all these items may be purchased, it is also possible to build many of them for reasonable sums of money.

The needed activities can be incorporated into the school's day in several ways: offering perceptual-motor activities per se, constructing changeable obstacle courses, and including movement education and creative dance activities on a regular basis. Learning how to relax should also be included as an important aspect of exercise.

Food for Thought and Group Discussions

1. Suppose you wanted to make certain that all the children participated in every physical activity each day. Explain to the class what the value of doing this might be and what the drawbacks might be.

2. If you could add only one piece of outdoor equipment to the school where you teach, what would it be? And why would you select it? How could you obtain it for the least cost?

3. Is there a piece of equipment where you observe or teach that the children rarely use or always use the same way? Suggest two things you might try to make it more attractive to them.

4. The weather has been very bad for the past 4 days—so bad that no child or teacher has ventured outdoors. Can you suggest a number of large-muscle activities that could be used indoors to provide relief? What if you put all the furniture out in the hall? Or could you use the hall?

5. Share with the class the most successful things you have done with the children so far to encourage creativity in dance.

Self-Check Questions for Review

Content-Related Questions

1. Give some examples of how physical activity benefits each of the five selves.
2. Name some movable types of equipment that are inexpensive and useful, to offer when developing a play space for children that stimulates large-muscle play.
3. Why is it important to teach children how to relax? Suggest some strategies for teaching relaxation that are helpful to use with young children.
4. List some helpful principles to remember when leading children in a creative dance experience.

Integrative Questions

1. Think of several outdoor play yards you have seen in children's centers or primary schools. What were their strong points? Were there pieces of equipment you think would be particularly valuable to add?
2. Tables 9.3 to 9.8 provide many examples of activities children can use to develop various physical abilities. Suggest an activity not included in the chart for each of the abilities. Explain how you could make the activity easier or more challenging, depending on the skill and age level of the children.
3. How do movement education and creative dance differ from each other? What are the benefits of each of these activities?

Coordinating Videotape

By leaps and bounds. Tape #2. The whole child: A caregiver's guide to the first five years. The Annenberg/CPB Collection, P.O. Box 2345, South Burlington, VT 05407-2345. *By Leaps and Bounds* surveys children's physical development, including large- and fine-muscle groups and motor skills, and provides instruction on good health practices, environmental safety, and appropriate developmental activities.

References for Further Reading

Pick of the Litter

Weikart, P. (2000). *Round the circle: Key experiences in movement for young children* (2nd ed.). Ypsilanti, MI: High/Scope. In this very good book, Weikart explains the fundamentals of basic movement development, ties the material to the High/Scope philosophy, and describes how to foster movement in sensible, attractive ways.

Overviews

Sanders, S. W. (2002). *Active for life: Developmentally appropriate movement programs for young children.* Washington, DC: National Association for the Education of Young Children. This sensible guide stresses suiting physical education instruction to the individual child while also recognizing that children progress through a series of phases and stages. Includes a list of national physical education standards and an example of a checklist that could be used for evaluating children's progress.

Information About Physical Development

Gallahue, D. L., & Ozmun, J. D. (2005). *Understanding motor development: Infants, children, adolescents, and adults* (6th ed.). New York: McGraw-Hill. Replete with charts and illustrations, this clearly written book on physical development remains the bible of motor development. *Highly recommended.*

Suggestions of Activities

Sluss, D. J. (2005). *Supporting play: Birth through eight.* Clifton Park, NY: Thomson/Delmar. This comprehensive book provides a wealth of physical play activities for all early childhood ages and programs. There is also an excellent chapter regarding children with special needs.

Wellhousen, K. (2002). *Outdoor play every day.* Albany, NY: Delmar/Thomson. Many age-appropriate, attractive, fresh suggestions for outdoor activities are included here.

Thomas, P., & Shepherd, W. (2000). Relaxation: Every child's right to be. *Child Care Information Exchange, 131,* 42–48. The authors describe how to introduce the elements of Tai Chi to young children in a practical way, so they may benefit from this ancient approach to achieving a restful state.

Movement Education

Pica, R. (2004). *Experiences in movement: Birth to age eight.* Albany, NY: Thomson/Delmar. This book is replete with ideas for activities based on developmental levels. It covers just about everything the teacher needs to know when presenting movement experiences and integrating them throughout the curriculum.

Including Children with Disabilities

Hurley, D. S. (2001). *Sensory motor activities for the young child.* Brisbee, AZ: Imaginart Press. The author presents activities—for those who are developing typically and those who are not—that help children ages 3 to 7 process sensory experiences.

Greenstein, D., Miner, N., Kudela, E., & Bloom, S. (1995). *Backyards and butterflies: Ways to include children with disabilities in outdoor activities.* Cambridge, MA: Brookline. This well-illustrated book describes numerous ways that equipment can be adapted to include everyone in the joys of outdoors.

Children and Nature

Louv, R. (2005) *Last child in the woods: Saving our children from nature-deficit disorder.* New York: Algonquin Books. The author presents current research and trends, stressing the importance of nature play in children's development.

For the Advanced Student

Frost, J., Wortham, S., & Reifel, S. (2005). *Play and child development* (2nd ed.). Upper Saddle River, NJ: Merrill/Prentice Hall. The chapter on creating play environments should not be missed.

Related Organizations and Online Resources

The American Alliance for Health, Physical Education, Recreation and Dance offers many materials related to an astonishing range of physical activities on its Web site. http://www.aahperd.org/

P.E. Central is a Web site that provides the latest information about developmentally appropriate physical education programs. http://www.pecentral.com

P.E. Central's list of Adapted Physical Education Web sites provides links to resources on adapting physical education for children with disabilities. http://www.pecentral.org/adapted/ adaptedsites.html

HELPING CHILDREN UNDERSTAND AND VALUE LIFE

The nursery school is a place where the pulse of life is sensed and celebrated. Encountering the wonders of existence, the beauty and mystery of life and birth, the joy of music, and the fun of movement, pulses life-enabling energies. One of the goals of nursery school is to help a child feel life pulsing within, and animating his community and his world.

—Martha Snyder, Ross Snyder, and Ross Snyder Jr. (1989, pp. 33–34)

Teaching children to understand and value life may seem too abstract or advanced a subject for such young children, but when it is broken down into specific topics, it becomes clear that we have many opportunities to establish basic attitudes toward life (and death) at this early age.

For example, even very young children are interested in their own bodies and what goes on inside of them. They often ask such questions as these: If we eat watermelon seeds, will they grow out of our ears? When I want a baby sister, why can't I buy one of those little jars at the market, take it home, and just water it real good? (The child who asked this was convinced that babies came from baby food jars.) Why doesn't the bird fly anymore? Why can't we wake him up?

These and innumerable questions like them provide evidence that questions about life and its cycle come up frequently and naturally in early childhood classrooms. The difficulty with this subject matter is that some adults feel uncomfortable dealing with it themselves, much less discussing it with young children. Then, too, despite the fact that many families want schools to discuss sex education in particular, some continue to feel strongly that such material should be handled only within the family, and not in the school. For these reasons, individual teachers must decide what the appropriate approach is for their particular group of children and community and use the material in this chapter accordingly. It is to be hoped that most teachers will be able to include information about life and death in a matter-of-fact and wholesome way as the opportunity arises.

TEACHING REVERENCE FOR LIFE

The most fundamental concept to bear in mind when teaching about the cycle of life is that the living things in the world around us should be valued and cherished for their beauty. The world is filled with exquisite life-forms, and every time you teach children to step over a spider, or point out the fragile beauty of the rat's paw, or share the delicate wonder of a sprouting seed, you are helping them acquire this concept.

Our obligation to conserve and protect nature's wonders should also be a part of teaching reverence for life. Such mundane activities as building a compost heap, digging rabbit droppings into the garden, and returning a rotten pumpkin to the earth can all help children realize they can participate in a simple, practical effort to sustain natural life cycles.

Best of all, teaching reverence for life can be woven beautifully into cross-cultural learnings from Native Americans. These people have understood better than most how to live in harmony with nature, abusing neither animals nor earth.

In no other area of subject matter are so many books available that can be used to extend the child's feelings for the beauty of the world. Even when the text is too advanced, as is the case with the books by Holling Clancy Holling, the illustrations alone may be worth the price of the volume. The National Wildlife Federation publishes three magazines by age group for toddlers through the elementary grades that stress conservation and understanding nature (see References for Further Reading at the end of this chapter). Teachers can make quite an occasion of this attractive magazine's arrival each month.

A practical and enjoyable way to help children learn a reverence for life and living creatures is to include animals in the classroom. The Chapter Spotlight on page 168 offers suggestions of various ways for presenting animals to young children.

Teaching about reverence for life also involves teaching about the entire life cycle of human beings. Children love the idea that they are growing bigger and stronger every day. They relish visits by babies, and they are quicker than people of many ages to appreciate the value of older adults, who can become treasured participants in the life of the school. Not only do older people need children, but children also genuinely need older people to enrich their understanding of the stages of human life. Most communities have organizations composed of older adults who can be approached in the search for congenial volunteers.

Living creatures enhance young children's lives and teach them reverence for life.

HELPING CHILDREN LEARN TO CHERISH THEIR BODIES

One of the most meaningful areas of life education for young children is learning about their own bodies and how to cherish them. Children like to know what is inside themselves. They are interested in seeing X-rays of arms and legs, listening to heartbeats, and comparing parts of their bodies that are soft such as ears and tongues with parts that are hard such as fingers and heads. They love drinking a glass of water and then rocking in a chair to feel the splash inside, and they are fascinated with blood—what it is and what it does.

They are also interested in urination and bowel movements because they went through toilet training not long before. Children often attach strong feelings to defecation, because toilet training remains a point of strain in some families. Indeed, some psychologists and teachers with Freudian backgrounds maintain that one of the most significant values of offering mud, play dough, and finger painting is that these materials allow children opportunities to express some of their more hostile feelings about toileting in a socially acceptable (sublimated) way. For this reason, they recommend that children's remarks likening these substances to bowel movements should be accepted casually rather than deplored, because such remarks are frequently a part of such play. On the other hand, a reasonable line must be drawn so that children do not spend their lunch time talking about how the gravy is made of poopoo, lest it make the food seem unpalatable to the listeners.

Discussions about excretions should be frank, as should discussions about anatomical differences between boys and girls. The usual preschool practice of using the same bathroom for both sexes is a great aid in dispelling the mystery of sexual differences. Using correct vocabulary for various body parts and functions also is more desirable than using slang or

Helping Children Understand and Appreciate the Wonder of Animals

Having animals at school can be a delight or a pain in the neck, depending on the manner of presentation. Most children love animals and are likely to be very excited when one comes to visit. The advantage of having the visitor stay a few days or at least several hours is that as some of the newness wears off, the children have time to become more familiar with the animal. This allows them to overcome either their intense excitement or possible apprehensions. Remember, never force an animal on a reluctant child or vice versa.

When presenting an animal, choose not only one that you enjoy yourself but also (if possible) one that is fairly slow moving and emotionally placid. Always consider safety first, and prepare for safety in advance. This is essential. Make certain that the animal can be adequately confined (we once had an octopus that escaped through an incredibly small hole in the mesh screen). A tippy, temporary cage increases the teacher's anxiety and the consequent number of warnings that she or he must naggingly give the children. Make certain that cages are secure and steady and that they require adult assistance to open. Because tired animals, like tired children, are more apt to lose control, make provisions so that the animal can be withdrawn from circulation when it needs a rest.

When presenting the visitor, it is very important to have firm control over the situation. *Insist* that the children sit down and be as calm as possible. It can be helpful to have carpet squares arranged in a circle to mark where they should sit (chairs can also be used for this purpose). Remind the children of what gentleness means—sometimes telling them to "Remember, use soft hands and quiet voices" helps them understand this concept better than using the word *gentle*. Remind them also to move slowly.

Crowd control will need to be considered as well. Older 4s can manage suggestions and rules for themselves, but the younger children will need more direct teacher control. Offering something else of equal interest at the opposite end of the room, for example, will help. Perhaps water play with some new equipment can be offered, or having some children play outdoors while a few at a time come in may reduce pushing. Presenting the animal during large-group time is still another effective method of crowd control. When all else fails, the rule of "only three or four at a time—please come back later" can also be enforced.

Discussion before the animal arrives should include instructions about whether it can be held or should be watched, how to hold the visitor if this is possible, and how to refrain from frightening it. Animals that can be handled are the most desirable kind to have at school. Rabbits, guinea pigs, rats, land turtles, slow-moving snakes, puppies (who have had their shots), and even baby goats and lambs are all good candidates. If a young animal is to be studied, taking pictures as it grows or, better yet, measuring and weighing it every few days helps children relish and understand the growth process. In some instances, it works well to have the animals live at school during this time, but sometimes, particularly with puppies, it is best to have them visit periodically.

Give some thought to what you want the children to gain from the animal experience. The title of this Spotlight intentionally contains the word *appreciate*. Think about how you can help children take time to really look at and appreciate the animal's wonderful qualities, to examine the delicacy of its paws, the beauty of its markings, the softness of its fur, and the whiteness of its teeth. (Children are extremely interested in teeth and whether the animal will bite.)

Books on natural history, such as the Golden Book series, are good sources of information on wilder forms of animal life, but often the adequate sources for more domesticated animals are the pamphlets found in pet stores or the local library. The 4-H Clubs sponsored by county extension programs also offer useful information on caring for various barnyard animals.

Whatever the source of information, you should be prepared to offer the children fascinating factual tidbits as they watch and hold the animal: Isn't it interesting that snails have 10,000 little, rough teeth on their tongues to rip up leaves? Imagine—that whole duck came out of a shell just this big! Do you know that some birds carry shells away in their beaks and drop them far from their nest to keep predators from finding their chicks?

Children love feeding animals, so it is wise to have an ample supply of food on hand. Guinea pigs and rats make very desirable pets, since their appetites are almost insatiable.

But with feeding inevitably comes the problem of keeping the animal clean. Nothing is sadder or smellier than a forgotten animal living in a cage badly in need of cleaning. Such a beast cannot help itself; it is up to us to care for it and keep it clean. If you wish to have animals as permanent tenants, you must be willing to work with the children in keeping the animals in immaculate condition.

street language, though teachers certainly need to understand what a child means when he urgently whispers "kaka" or "peepee."

The most wholesome attitude to encourage is that our bodies are sources of pleasureful feelings and that they deserve good care. It feels good to stretch and yawn, it feels good to eat and be satisfied, it feels good to wake refreshed from sleep, and it feels good to go to the toilet. Our bodies are not parts of us to be punished by being ignored or mistreated; they should be cared for and cherished. This includes allowing our bodies to rest when they feel tired, nourishing them well, and appreciating the joys of good health—pleasures that all too often are taken for granted. Teachers must help children learn to honor their bodies and treat them well so that they remain a source of delight to them all their lives.

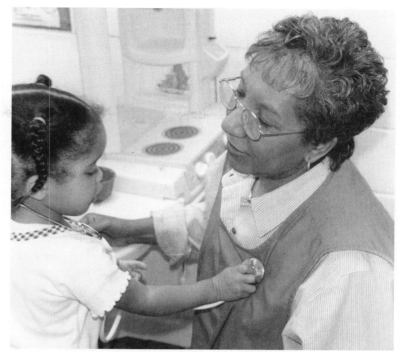

Even young children are interested in their bodies and what goes on inside them.

What to Do When Children Masturbate

Sooner or later most children discover that one source of physical pleasure comes from masturbation. They may do this almost absentmindedly while watching television or listening to stories; they may masturbate as part of lulling themselves to sleep or as a means of passing time during a sleepless nap period; they may retreat to this activity when feeling anxious and insecure in new surroundings.

The difficulty is that this behavior, although natural, is not socially acceptable. Besides that, many adults feel very uncomfortable when we discover a masturbating child. On one level, we are acquainted with research about masturbation that reveals the practice is commonplace among children and adults (both men and women) (Kinsey, Pomeroy, & Martin, 1948; Kinsey, Pomeroy, Martin, & Gebhard, 1953; Masters, Johnson, & Kolodny, 1994). We also know that masturbation is neither perverted nor self-destructive, that penises do not drop off as a result of it, that dark circles do not show under eyes because of it, and so forth. Therefore, at least intellectually, we would like to regard masturbation as being a simple, natural part of human sexuality. But, on an emotional level, our feeling selves may respond in quite a different way, and we may feel embarrassed, disapproving, flustered, and perhaps even angry when coming across a masturbating child (Honig, 2000; Lively & Lively, 1991).

The problem is how to handle these reactions in a way that does not mortify children or make them feel guilty and yet realistically takes into account society's expectations and our own feelings. At present, the best solution seems to be to teach children as calmly as possible that masturbation is something people do only in private, just like nose picking—neither activity is socially sanctioned behavior done in front of other people. Simply take the child aside and quietly explain this without making him or her feel like a criminal.

We must also be aware that many adults (both parents and teachers) would not agree with this point of view—they condemn masturbation entirely. But it is to be hoped that these people can at least learn to refrain from issuing those dire threats that some of us were subjected to in our own childhoods—threats about what happens to little boys and girls who "do that."

Teaching Children to Protect Themselves from Sexual Abuse

We cannot leave this discussion of caring for our bodies without including information on how to teach children to protect themselves from sexual advances. From evidence that has accumulated in the past decade about the sexual abuse of children, it becomes clear that such experiences happen far more frequently than we might expect.

Many children are sexually assaulted every year: 1 in 7 victims of reported sexual assault are under the age of 6. Although the standard advice about never taking candy from strangers or getting into a car with someone you do not know remains sound, research reveals that in most cases of sexual abuse the perpetrator is well known to the child and is often a relative or family friend; among rape victims under the age of 12, some 90% knew their attackers (Childhelp USA, 2005).

In conducting education about sexual abuse, teachers must walk a delicate line between frightening children unduly and instructing them on what to do if they are approached. Children should be taught that their bodies belong to them alone and that their genitalia are private areas that no one has the right to invade in any way. If someone tries to do this and offers them presents or threatens them or their families, their best protection is to refuse and to tell their parents, teacher, or another adult immediately, regardless of how frightened they are.

Children need to understand there is a big difference between an abusive kind of touch and the physical affection of hugs and cuddling that both children and those who love them rightfully enjoy and require in order to feel emotionally fulfilled. Children need to be taught to discriminate between nurturant behaviors and those of a more frightening and unusual nature.

Teachers need to know that when they suspect abuse has taken place, whether it be due to sexual or other types of injury, law requires them to report it to the correct authority (Austin, 2000). Working with such cases requires skill and delicacy and is best handled by people who have special training, so teachers should avoid confronting parents directly with their suspicions. Remember that abuse is highly likely to be repeated, so possible evidence *must not be overlooked or brushed aside*. It is reassuring to remember that reporters of possible child-abuse cases, including possible instances of sexual abuse, are protected under law as long as the call has been made in good faith.

Nunnelley and Fields (1999) recommend that the best place to look for help is a published hotline for such reporting. These are often listed in the telephone book under Child Protection Services. Various mental health agencies and public health nurses are also excellent sources for advice and resources. The National Child Abuse Hotline can also offer assistance (1-800-4-A-CHILD).

Because of occasional flurries of publicity about sexual abuse taking place in child-care centers, some adult caretakers have become hesitant about showing physical affection to children. Fortunately, it appears that most trained early childhood educators understand that expressing affection is not only natural but also a necessary part of building sound relationships between adults and the children they care for. Years of research indicate that positive touch is a crucial element for healthy child development (Carlson, 2005).

Protecting Teachers from Accusations of Sexual Abuse

The sensational publicity about incidents of sexual abuse in child-care centers has caused both parents and teachers to worry about this possibility (Mikkelsen, 1997). Although careful study of the prevalence of such incidents reveals that these episodes are rare, occurring at the rate of 5.5 children for every 10,000 children enrolled in such centers (Stephens, 1988), everyone agrees that even one such episode is too many.

Besides that, there is the problem of false accusations. Experts tell us we should never ignore reports by children that they have been abused because it is unusual for children to make up such stories (Hewitt, 1999). However, such false allegations have been known to occur. Of course, such misunderstandings or false accusations can be disastrous for the accused staff member and the school, too, unless people are able to defend themselves by documenting the steps taken to protect both children and staff.

It is essential that children experience healthy, "good" touching. We must also teach them to report "bad" touching.

Basic precautions include making certain that families know they are always welcome and encouraged to visit at any time, that they do not need to call ahead or alert the school in any way that they are coming. Families should be educated about the difference between sexual abuse and the affectionate hugging and cuddling so necessary to children's well-being. They should be encouraged to become well acquainted with their children's teachers so that a bond of confidence can develop between them. They should be informed that staff always work in pairs, so there is always a "witness" to what is going on.

Arrange rooms and play yards so they are open to view, with no hidden corners or out-of-the-way unsupervisable spots. Stall doors in bathrooms (if they are used at all) should either be half-height or not go all the way to the floor. Finally, directors must be careful about whom they hire. They should follow up written references with telephone inquiries, and they should make background checks of criminal records in states where this is either required by regulation or at least permitted.

The suggestions given here concerning operation of the center should always be followed as a matter of course. If all these procedures are followed consistently, it is probable that both children and staff will be well protected and can go their happy, affectionate way without worrying that their behavior will be misconstrued (National Association for the Education of Young Children, 1997).

ANSWERING QUESTIONS ABOUT REPRODUCTION

Many adults feel uneasy about discussing sex and reproduction with children. (The development of sex roles and nonsexist curriculum is discussed in chapter 13.) Fortunately for those of us who feel awkward about this subject, the questions young children ask are likely to be simple and not very distressing to answer. Young children often do not even realize that dogs always have puppies and cats always have kittens.

They typically want to know where babies come from or why that lady is so fat. The answer to these queries is simple enough: A baby grows inside its mother in her uterus until old enough to be born and then comes out of a special place between the mother's legs called the vagina.

What teachers usually fear is that youngsters will also want to know how the baby got in there in the first place. In case it should come up, it is accurate to say that the father and mother start the baby growing in the mother by being very loving and close to each other. When they are feeling this way, the father fits his penis inside the mother's vagina and a fluid passes into her that helps start the baby growing. This kind of explanation is desirable because it incorporates both the importance of affection and biological facts.

It often confuses children to talk about planting seeds in relation to human babies. When teachers use this analogy, youngsters naturally think of gardening, which can lead to very odd misconceptions about conception.

In discussions about reproduction, teachers should find out what the children really want to know, make answers truthful and simple, encourage children to say what they think, and help them understand that warmth and caring should be important elements in the experience of intercourse. When children are very curious about the topic of babies—and the teacher really listens to the children's questions and theories—it could evolve into an in-depth exploration in the form of emergent curriculum. The Emergent Curriculum in Action box on page 173 describes exactly that: the investigations of children intent on finding out how baby geese are made.

ANSWERING QUESTIONS ABOUT DEATH

No discussion of the life cycle would be complete without including information on the topic of death. Yet, for many people, this remains a subject even more taboo than sex and one that they prefer to avoid completely when teaching young children. They may believe that children should be shielded from experiencing sadness or that death is too difficult for children to understand. Perhaps the whole subject of death is so frightening and distasteful to them that the thought of mentioning it to children seems overwhelming.

If we face reality, however, we must admit that death is all around us, just as life is: Animals die, insects die, flowers die, and people die—even people children know. If, as adults, we are able to acknowledge to ourselves that death is part of life, then we may be more willing to include the subject of death when talking about the cycle of life with children. This comes up very naturally when animals die, roses fade, or pumpkins rot. Even young children can be allowed to investigate how a dead animal differs from a living one and to mourn its passing (Westmoreland, 1996). Moreover, this experience provides sound opportunities to learn that grief is more endurable when shared and that it does not last forever.

It is helpful to understand that young children view death as being a temporary condition from which people may return and continue living (Shelov & Hannemann, 2004; Sprang & McNeil, 1995), a viewpoint unhappily encouraged by animated cartoons that feature exactly this happening. When discussing death with children, the early childhood teacher has to take this kind of magical thinking into account and realize that it is not necessarily an attempt to deny the reality of death but merely an indication that children do not grasp the irreversibility of the event. Because this idea of returning to life appears to be a developmental characteristic, about all the teacher can do is to reiterate patiently the fact that death is permanent.

Young children also tend to equate death with sleep—another concept unfortunately reinforced by some adults, which may induce a certain reluctance for bedtime among sensitive youngsters. For this reason, comparing death to sleep should be avoided.

Emergent Curriculum in Action

How Does the Gosling Get in the Egg?

by Pam Oken-Wright

St. Catherine's School, Richmond, Virginia

Context Information:

- The experience took place in a classroom of 14 5-year-olds with two teachers.
- The experience was documented through photographs and notes. Videotaping was also used as a source of documentation. Documentation panels were created and displayed throughout the classroom.

In the beginning, I placed six goose eggs in the incubator. Throughout the day, small groups of children gravitated to the eggs. We (the teachers) listened to their conversation and conjecture without interrupting. When the interest seemed widespread, I initiated the first class discussion by noting their interest and repeating a few of the comments the children had made. Stories about broken eggs continued and then developed into discussion about what comes *out* of the eggs when they break. None of the children seemed to know about anything other than the yolk in the egg.

Study of the transcript of the first group conversation yielded three ideas for consideration: (1) the children were interested in what's inside eggs. (2) They had co-constructed four possible theories about how a baby bird gets in the egg. (3) In order to cull the implausible and hone the plausible theories, the children needed some firsthand experience with the inside of eggs.

The next day I invited the children to break and explore unfertilized chicken eggs—on trays, with hand lenses, and, at their request, spoons. From the tape of the discourse during exploration, I distilled a page of words the children used, both scientific (membrane) and not so scientific (slimy). That page became part of the ongoing documentation of the project.

I initiated a second whole-class conversation by presenting to the children the four theories extracted from their first conversation: (1) There is nothing in the egg. The gosling magically appears. (2) There is a fully formed gosling in the egg when it is laid. (3) The yolk "becomes" the gosling. (4) There is a seed inside the egg and that becomes the gosling.

Following this conversation, I asked the children to draw their theories. When children represent their theories, as they do in drawing, the theories often become more complete in their minds. The children used their drawings as referents as they explained their theories and I transcribed at the computer.

During the 4 weeks of incubation, the children pored over books with wonderful photographs of developing chicks. We had many more discussions, and the children represented about and around the topic continually and passionately. Periodically I offered small bits of information as provocation for further discussion.

On the 29th day, we finally found a crack in one of the eggs. Another significant discussion ensued as the children watched the slow hatching process. Some children thought the gosling would necessarily be yellow because of the yolk. If it were not yellow, they reasoned, then their theory that the gosling eats the yolk would have to be false. The following day, with all present, our lone gosling emerged wet and exhausted. We saw no yellow on its soggy down.

After the hatch, I asked for another set of drawings of how the gosling gets in the egg. These drawings were physical evidence of the children's shift in their view of this process away from one of static states to one of progression. It appeared that they were now attending to the transformation of chick embryology. In addition, many children drew the stages of development linearly unlike the more random placement of elements in earlier drawings. How interesting that without having been told how the gosling gets in the egg in the first place, these 5-year-olds actually constructed an ultimate theory that was not only plausible but remarkably accurate!

Source: From "How Does the Gosling Get in the Egg? Five Years Olds and the Co-Construction of Theory," by P. Oken-Wright, 1998, *Innovations in Early Education: The International Reggio Exchange, 5* (4) pp. 5–8.

Children are very interested in funerals and enjoy participating in burying pets and school animals that have died. This activity should be permitted because it contributes to understanding the life cycle and the process of mourning. Such interest should not be regarded as morbid or macabre—it is natural. It becomes morbid only when shocked adults force it to be clandestine.

These participatory understandings can be supplemented with books that touch on the subject of dying. Teachers can use such books to introduce matter-of-fact discussions that may dispel some of the more bizarre misconceptions children harbor about death—the worst one being that death is unmentionable. Several good books that serve this purpose, ranging from *Charlotte's Web* (White, 1952) for older children to *The Tenth Good Thing About Barney* (Viorst, 1972) for some of the youngest ones.

Helping Families When Death Occurs

Inevitably there will be occasions during the year when a member of one of the children's family dies. Since families frequently turn to the teacher for advice about how to handle this situation with young children, it seems wise to include a few basic principles here. Some additional books on this subject are included in the references at the end of the chapter.

The most important thing for families to realize is that the death should be neither restricted from conversations nor concealed from youngsters. Children always know when something is wrong (Trozzi, 1999; Willis, 2002) and their fantasies can be much more frightening to them than reality would ever be. Truthful statements are generally the best approach (Shelov & Hannemann, 2004; Willis, 2002).

If possible, families should prepare children in advance for the death of a loved one. This may be done by saying such things as "The doctors are doing everything they can to help your granny, but sometimes there's just nothing else to do, so she may die."

It is not necessary to try to conceal all grief from children—seeing others cry may help them express their own sadness and learn to cope with it (Perry, 2001; Willis, 2002). As time passes, they also have the chance to realize that gradually the pain of losing someone lessens and life can continue.

A beautiful example of how an African village includes children in the mourning process is illustrated in the Chapter Spotlight on page 175.

Some Special Things to Caution Families About

Families should be informed that children (and adults) experience more than pain when someone dies. They are often angry at being abandoned. Sometimes this anger is mixed up with guilt. This may develop because children feel guilty about being angry—"I shouldn't feel mad"—or because they perceive themselves as having caused the death—"If only I hadn't stamped my foot" or "If only I'd been quiet like Mommy said." When families and parents discuss these feelings with children, the youngsters are able to recognize that the feelings are acceptable and natural and that they are in no way responsible for the person's demise.

It may take quite some time for children to grasp that the person is truly gone. For example, one child who seemed to have understood his aunt's death surprised his teachers one day by telling them what he thought she would be sending him for his birthday.

Children also require honest reassurance about who will take care of them and how the family structure may change. They wonder: What will happen? What if the other parent dies? What about life will be the same? Occasionally, adults are shocked at what seems to them to be such a self-interested attitude. But young children are self-centered.

The following paper was written by Haram S. Jameel about her experience as a child in Sudan when she participated in the ceremonies following the death of a village chieftain.

The Death of the Chief

I was eight years of age when my grandfather died. His death was a big thing in our village and no wonder. He was a husband of four wives, a father of more than twenty children, a grandfather of . . . oh only God knows how many . . . let's just say that he had many, many grandchildren by the time of his death. But what was more important than all of this was the fact that he was the CHIEF of the village; he was the man, the one who handled affairs and took care of business.

I remember that his oldest son, who was his personal assistant too, and the next chief in line, called for a big meeting to be held in his compound. There was a separate meeting for my grandfather's spouses and adult children. The children of the family were also called for a special meeting. An elderly man who referred to my grandfather as "the legend," told us about his death. He also told us that his time, though too soon, had come to an end, and that he was going to join the former kings, who run matters from high above; we were also told that his presence would be "felt but not seen." And that the next day was going to be "the drum salutation day." The man went on to explain the drum salutation day, and it goes as follows:

> Tomorrow, when the drums play, we are going to dance, we are going to dance and celebrate the life of a legend, we are going to pay our last respects. You're not allowed to cry out loud, scream, or disturb the presence of the legend's spirit. You can weep if you feel like weeping but not loud, tears but no sounds. There will come a time when you will be able to cry out loud, but that day is not tomorrow.

The meeting was over. The next day came and it was the celebration day. The women who were the first in line danced for "his manhood and generosity," the men who were next danced for "his wisdom and unique leadership." Last came the children who were to dance for "his fatherhood and divine heart" and we all wept. It was easy for us, the children, to weep because we saw our parents weep. It was accepted and it was fine and we did it without fear or hesitation. It was a great therapy for all of us.

At the end of the ceremony, the old man came forward again to announce that there would be another drums dancing the next day, after the burial, and that was going to be the day for everybody to be able to express his feelings however he sees fit.

I am sharing this experience with you to show you how some of the other cultures view things and how seriously they take children into account: What do they do to include children in crisis that any given family might experience, particularly in serious crisis such as death? To see what simple ways they follow to realize inclusion of the children. And how they invite them openly to participate in feelings of concern and grief because it is important and it is healing for them.

In my family's case, the children were considered a major part of the family—the future of the village—therefore they were treated accordingly. They were called for a meeting. The crisis was explained to them, and the procedures were explained, too. They were told what part to play and why; what they were allowed to do and what they were not allowed to do. They were able to weep and then cry out loud when it was necessary. I, personally, think that the way the villagers handled this crisis as far as I was concerned as a child was superb, considerate, and effective because:

- I was able to understand right away what my family was faced with and anticipate what was going to happen next.
- I saw my father and other adult relatives cry, which confirmed to me that "it is OK to cry when you need to."
- It helped us as children to express and clarify feelings about our grandfather's death.
- And finally, it absolved us from any guilt we might have had about the crisis itself.

And this is what inclusion of children during time of crisis, whether the crisis is sudden or of long duration, happy or sad, happens in a cosmopolitan city or in a small distant village, is all about . . . I think.

Note: Thanks to Barry Bussewitz, Solano Community College, California, for sharing this wonderful paper.

Their experience is extremely limited, and the world as they know it does orbit around them. They also know very well how young and helpless they are. When life is disturbed in such a significant way, it is only natural that they require repeated reassurance and explanations that someone will continue to take care of them (Shelov & Hannemann, 2004; Willis, 2002).

Finally, families should know that children benefit from recalling memories of the person who has died. Adults sometimes avoid doing this with children because it may also reawaken the pain of loss, but if the life cycle is to be understood and human relationships valued, recalling happy times with departed family members is most worthwhile. This also provides valuable opportunities to finish working through grief and clear up any misunderstandings or concerns the child may be harboring.

SUMMARY

Teaching children to understand and value life should be a basic element of curriculum intended to stress physical well-being. It includes often taboo subjects such as death, sex, sexual abuse, and learning about other aspects of children's bodies—what is inside them, how they work, and how good they feel. In addition, even very young children can begin to develop a reverence for life; the chapter includes several suggestions of ways to teach this reverence.

Food for Thought and Group Discussions

1. One of the 3-year-olds in your group comes to school in tears because a neighbor has run over his kitten with her car. How do you think this situation should be dealt with at school? The family also wants to know whether they should stop at the pet store on the way home from school and get another kitten. What would you advise?

2. You suddenly realize that you are missing two or three of the 4-year-olds from your group. When you investigate, you find them hiding in the playhouse comparing differences in their sexual anatomies. How do you think this situation is best handled? What approaches do you think should be avoided? Why?

3. You are now teaching in a parent cooperative preschool, and the program committee has decided that the group would like a program on what all young children and their parents should know about sex. They want you to lead the group. Three families are very conservative and believe all sex education should take place in the home, and others believe the school should play a part in such education. What kind of program would you present? What do you believe yourself?

Self-Check Questions for Review

Content-Related Questions

1. What is the wholesome attitude we want children to have toward their bodies?

2. Should masturbation be discouraged at all times? What is the recommended way to deal with a child who masturbates?

3. Why is it valuable to cuddle and hug little children? How have reports on sexual abuse in children's centers affected the behavior of some teachers in those centers?

4. Discuss some practical ways teachers can protect themselves from accusations of sexually abusing young children.

5. What is "reverence for life"? Give some examples of how this principle can be taught to young children.

6. How does the young child's concept of death differ from that of grown-ups? Why is it important not to conceal death from children?

Integrative Questions

1. Families are rightfully concerned about their children's safety while attending school. What will you do and say to reassure families that their children will be safe in your care?

2. Compare the funeral ceremonies for the village chief described by Haram S. Jameel in the Chapter Spotlight with the traditional funeral ceremonies observed in your own community. Were some aspects of the funeral customs very different? Were there some aspects in both cultures that were similar?

References for Further Reading

Pick of the Litter

Oken-Wright, P. (1998). How does the gosling get in the egg? Five-year-olds and the co-construction of theory. *Innovations in Early Education: The International Reggio Exchange, 5*(4), 5–8. This article is *highly recommended* as an example of provocative questioning and theory building related to sexual reproduction.

Overviews

Carson, R. (1956). *The sense of wonder*. New York: Harper & Row. Rachel Carson was one of the first to awaken us to our responsibilities for maintaining the earth in a healthy state. In this classic, she is concerned with helping children learn to wonder about the world around them.

Eyre, L., & Eyre, R. (1980). *Teaching children joy*. New York: Ballantine. This book expresses a wonderfully positive point of view toward children and toward life.

Helping Children Appreciate Life

Kramer, D. C. (1989). *Animals in the classroom: Selection, care, and observation*. Menlo Park, CA: Addison-Wesley. This very good book includes interesting facts and excellent advice on the care of animals ranging from earthworms to rabbits.

Rockwell, R. E., Williams, R. T., & Sherwood, E. A. (1992). *Everybody has a body: Science from head to toe: Activities book for teachers of children ages 3–6*. Mount Rainier, MD: Gryphon House. A wealth of appropriate activities based on experiences with the body are included here.

Education About Sex

Chrisman, K., & Couchenour, D. (2002). *Healthy sexuality development: A guide for early childhood educators and families*. Washington, DC: National Association for the Education of Young Children. The authors explain typical development and how adults can help young, inquisitive children develop healthy attitudes.

Honig, A. S. (2000). Psychosexual development in infants and young children: Implications for caregivers. *Young Children, 55*(5), 70–77. In this article Honig covers most of the basic questions about sexuality and young children that sometimes puzzle early childhood teachers.

Sexual Abuse

Austin, J. S. (2000). When a child discloses sexual abuse: Immediate and appropriate teacher responses. *Childhood Education, 77*(1), 2–5. This article offers helpful suggestions about how to approach this problem in a practical, serious way.

Nunnelley, J. C., & Fields, T. (1999). Anger, dismay, guilt, anxiety—the realities and roles in reporting child abuse. *Young Children, 54*(5), 74–70. This article examines in detail the emotional quandaries teachers may experience when coming across evidence that a child in their care has been abused.

Helping Children and Families Cope with Death

The Dougy Center. (2000). *35 ways to help a grieving child*. Portland, OR: Author. This booklet provides excellent practical advice—a good reference to acquire before an emergency arises.

Goldman, L. (2000). *Life and loss: A guide to help grieving children* (2nd ed.). Philadelphia: Accelerated Development. This book is a mixture of short chapters combined with discussions of specific situations related to loss and lists of ways to help. Of special interest is the section titled "Especially for Educators."

For the Advanced Student

The Future of Children: Protecting children from abuse and neglect. (1998). *Future of Children, 1*, entire issue. This issue covers many aspects of child maltreatment, with the primary focus on how to make child protective services more effective. The issue is available online at http://www.futureofchildren.org/pubs-info2825/pubs-info_show.htm?doc_id=75332

Related Organizations and Online Resources

The Centering Corporation is one of the trail-blazers in the area of bereavement counseling. Its Web site offers a treasure trove of resources for people of all ages. http://www.centeringcorp.com/

The Childhelp USA National Child Abuse Hotline (1-800-4-A-CHILD) is staffed 24 hours daily with professional crisis counselors. It is an invaluable resource for teachers and people who need to make referrals to agencies. http://www.childhelpusa.org/

The Dougy Center for Grieving Children and Families provides help in various forms, including publications, for children who have experienced a death. http://www.grievingchild.org/

The National Wildlife Federation (NWF) provides a wealth of resources for teaching reverence for the earth and wildlife. NWF publishes three monthly magazines appropriate for children ages 1 through elementary school—*Baby Animals, Your Big Backyard*, and *Ranger Rick*—as well as a free online newsletter. http://www.nwf.org/kids/

CHAPTER *eleven*

ACHIEVING EMOTIONAL COMPETENCE

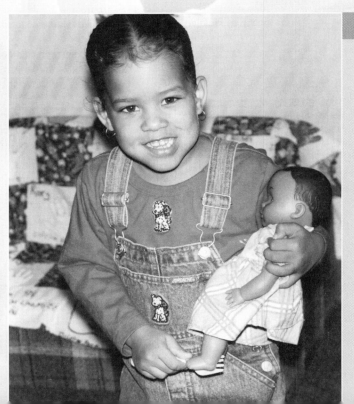

Have you ever . . .

- Wondered how to help children express their feelings without hurting other children?
- Wanted to know some practical ways to reduce feelings of tensions and aggression in children?
- Worried over how to help a child through a family crisis?

If you have, the material in this chapter will help you.

It takes time and faith to get over our own conditioning, and feel comfortable with children's emotions. But it is deeply touching and rewarding to see children move through difficult, painful feelings and come out the other side happy, active, and fresh.

—Herley Jim Bowling and Saro Rogers (2001, p. 81)

Sensitivity, responsive care, involvement, and emotional communication are important aspects of supportive relationships with infants and young children. . . . Teachers should find ways to spend special time with each child in their care, times when the focus is just on the child and the adult. Adults can share their feelings with children and encourage them to express their feelings, too. Caregivers can look for opportunities to make one-to-one moments with each child happen every day. Greeting children as they arrive in the morning, playing in the sandbox, pushing the swing, talking over juice, getting ready for naptime, taking time to share feelings when a child approaches to show that special creation—these are all opportunities to become more involved with a child, when relationship building is a priority.

—James Elicker and Cheryl Fortner-Wood (1995, p. 76)

The difficulty with talking about curriculum for the emotional, or affective, self is that the very word *curriculum* has an academic ring that can lead us to overintellectualizing our teaching if we are not careful. We must guard vigilantly against this tendency by remembering that the most effective kind of learning and teaching about the emotional self is embedded in the everyday happenings of life rather than in self-conscious discussions of feelings in artificially contrived group times. To deal with feelings in the most effective way, we must seize teachable moments as they occur to help children perceive and cope with their feelings so they can lead comfortable, emotionally healthy lives.

Sometimes such learning is best accomplished at school by capitalizing on opportunities as they spontaneously arise between children and other children or between children and staff. Sometimes it is best accomplished by working with families to deepen their understanding of their children's emotional needs and how to meet them at home. But whichever approach is used, the emotional competencies we wish children to attain are basically the same.

COMPETENCE ONE: FOSTER BASIC ATTITUDES OF TRUST, AUTONOMY, INITIATIVE, AND INDUSTRY

The first fundamental goal of curriculum for the emotional self is encouraging the child to be trustful, independent, and able to reach out and investigate the immediate world. Erik Erikson (1963, 1982, 1996; Friedman, 1999) has made a valuable contribution to our understanding of the significance of these attitudes in the emotional life of the child and how to encourage their development. What he first hypothesized in the early 1960s continues to describe what early childhood teachers see today as they watch young children develop emotionally.

Erikson theorized that during their life span, individuals pass through a series of stages of emotional development in which basic attitudes are formed. Early childhood encompasses four of these stages: (1) trust versus mistrust, (2) autonomy versus shame and doubt, (3) initiative versus guilt, and (4) industry versus inferiority. Regardless of the age group you are teaching, it is important to understand the implications of the other stages, also. This is because Erikson theorizes that the resolution of each stage depends in part on the successful accomplishment of the previous one.

Trust Versus Mistrust

In the stage of trust versus mistrust, the baby learns (or fails to learn) that other people can be depended on and also that she can depend on herself to elicit needed responses from them. This development of trust is deeply related to the quality of care that the family provides and is often reflected in feeding practices, which, if handled in a manner that meets her needs, help assure the infant that she is valued and important. Although by the time she enters school, the balance between trust or mistrust will have been tipped in favor of one attitude or the other, the need to experience trust and to have it reaffirmed remains with people throughout their lives. This is also true for the other attitudes as they develop.

Therefore, it is vital that the basic climate of the center encourage the establishment of trust among everyone who is part of that community. If the teacher thinks of establishing trust in terms of letting the children know that they can depend on him, it will be fairly easy for him to implement this goal. For example, consistent policies and regularity of events in the program obviously contribute to establishing a trustful climate. In addition, if he is sensitive to the child's individual needs and meets them as they arise, the teacher can confirm the message of the child's infancy once again that she is worthy of love and thus further strengthen trust and self-esteem.

Autonomy Versus Shame and Doubt

In our society the second stage, in which the attitudes of autonomy versus shame and doubt are formed, occurs during the same period in which toilet teaching takes place. During this time, the child is acquiring the skills of holding on and letting go. This fundamental exercise in self-assertion and control is associated with her drive to become independent and to express this independence by making choices and decisions so often couched in the classic imperatives of the 2-year-old: "No!" "Mine!" and "Me do it!" Erikson maintains that children who are overregulated and deprived of the opportunity to establish independence and autonomy may become oppressed with feelings of shame and self-doubt, which result in losing self-esteem, being defiant, trying to get away with things, and, in later life, developing various forms of compulsive behavior.

The desirable way to handle this strong need for choice and self-assertion is to provide an environment at home and at the center that makes many opportunities available for the child to do for herself and to make decisions. This is the fundamental reason that self-selection is an important principle in curriculum design. At the same time, the teacher must be able to establish decisive control when necessary, because young children often show poor judgment and can be tyrannized by their own willfulness unless the adult is willing to intervene.

Initiative Versus Guilt

Gradually, as the child develops the ability to act independently, she embarks on building the next set of basic attitudes. Around the age of 4 or 5, she becomes more interested in reaching out to the world around her, in doing things, and in being part of the group. At this stage, she wants to think things up and try them out: She is interested in the effect her actions have on other people (witness her experimentation with profanity and "bad" language); she formulates concepts of what her family feels are appropriate sex roles; she enjoys imaginative play; and she becomes an avid seeker of information about the world around her. This is the stage Erikson has so aptly named initiative versus guilt.

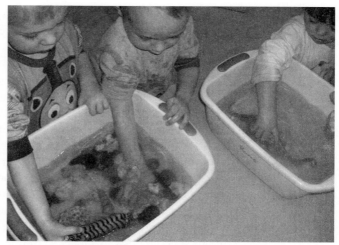

To feel emotionally satisfied, a child must be allowed to explore, to act, and to do.

To feel emotionally satisfied, a child of this age must be allowed to explore, to act, and to do. Children's centers are generally strong in meeting the children's need to explore and create, but they often underestimate the ability of 4- and 5-year-olds to participate in making plans and decisions for their group, or to attempt challenging projects. Encouraging the ability to initiate plans and take action will enhance children's feelings of self-worth and creativity, as well as their ability to be self-starters—all highly desirable outcomes necessary for future development and happiness.

Industry Versus Inferiority

This stage applies to children from about age 5 or 6 to 12 years old, and represents a transition to elementary school where the child learns to master the more formal skills necessary in life. In this stage self-discipline increases (hence homework is appropriate for this age) and the child connects her perseverance with a sense of accomplishment with a job well done. The child works through this stage by mastering the skills necessary for success in our society: relating with peers; learning teamwork; participating in group activities with formal rules such as sports; and achieving academic skills in reading, writing, arithmetic, and the sciences. When the child passes through this stage successfully, she develops competence.

COMPETENCE TWO: HELP THE CHILD LEARN TO SEPARATE FROM THE FAMILY

The second competency the child must acquire to survive away from home is the ability to separate from her parent or caregiver with a reasonable degree of ease so she feels comfortable at school.

The ideal way to make the home-to-school transition as painless as possible is to accomplish separation gradually. This allows youngsters to make friends with their teacher and possibly one or two of the children and be involved in activities before the caregiver "abandons" them. Occasionally schools have the opportunity to make friends by having staff visit the child at home, or they send the child a personal letter of welcome to school (children get so little mail and enjoy it so much).

In situations where the school begins anew in the fall, small groups of children can be invited to attend at different times of the morning for the first day or two to provide personal attention for each youngster and reduce feelings of being overwhelmed.

More typically the separation happens rather abruptly due to employment requirements of the family, and the child enters an ongoing group with possibly little opportunity for preparation. Under these circumstances it is particularly important to be sensitive to buffering the separation experience in as many ways as possible for both family and child.

Helping Children Cope with Their Feelings

It is important to explain to the family how desirable it is for their child to have the chance to become at least a little acquainted before being left all day in an unfamiliar setting. Perhaps the child could come for a visit during the parent's lunch hour or after work, or a friend could bring her by for a visit, or the teacher could send an e-mail greeting and picture or make a friendly phone call to welcome her to the group.

Transition to school is also made easier if beginning days are kept simple and uncomplicated and if standards for behavior are not set too high—eating, for example, is often especially difficult for an anxious newcomer, as is nap time, and the sensitive teacher will make reasonable adjustments as those circumstances require (Perry, 2000a).

Sometimes it helps if the parents leave something tangible that belongs to them for the child to keep. (In one instance, a child wrapped himself in his mother's old sweater for several days.) Sometimes a surrogate comfort object, such as a favorite blanket or stuffed animal, helps bridge the gap. If the child is generally accustomed to toting such an item around, the first days of school are *not* the time to separate her from it. Sometimes a grandparent or other family member can substitute for the parent, or the child has a friend in the group and can carpool after a few days.

Helping Families Cope with Their Feelings

No matter who brings the child to school, the caregiver should be encouraged to stay as long as possible for the first few times until the child has settled in. *Under no circumstances* should the adult be allowed to depart without telling the child. There is no surer way to foster distrust and prolong the separation anxiety situation than to vanish without saying good-bye. *Teachers should be careful to see that this does not happen.*

On the other hand, when it is time to leave, the adult should also be encouraged to be matter of fact and definite, since it increases separation difficulties considerably if the adult debates and vacillates between leaving and staying. Families as well as children benefit from the teacher's assurance, and it can comfort worried parents if they are invited to telephone later to check on whether the child is still crying.

Helping Teachers Cope with Their Feelings

Teachers who allow themselves to feel frightened and guilty when a child is upset surely add to the child's anxiety, whereas teachers who take these upsets in stride convey their own sense of security to the child and are thus reassuring.

Unfortunately, feeling secure in the midst of a disturbing scene is more easily recommended than attained by beginning teachers. This is particularly true because such upsets so often take place while other families are coming and going. The way to become more at ease with these situations is to (1) resolve to see them through as calmly and confidently as you can, (2) comfort the child as well as you are able without pleading or acting apologetic, and (3) while acknowledging her grief, distract her as quickly as possible from her grief.

COMPETENCE THREE: HELP CHILDREN LEARN TO CONTROL WHAT THEY DO ABOUT THEIR FEELINGS

Unfortunately, much of our culture appears dedicated to teaching children to suppress and deny feelings. As early as age 2 or 3, some children have already learned that certain feelings are not acceptable. These vary according to family standards and may include jealousy in one family, anger toward adults in another, or fearfulness expressed by crying in a third. Whatever they are, such denial, if imposed firmly enough, causes a child to disown part of herself and believe that some part of herself is not acceptable.

The reason for such denial and suppression seems to be that people assume that feeling inevitably leads to acting or that acknowledging a feeling will make it stronger. But repressing, denying, or ignoring feelings increases the probability that the child will act them out—either directly or indirectly. In other words, the child who is unable to *tell* someone how she feels is almost inevitably driven to *show* that person how she feels. Perhaps she hits someone; perhaps she messes her pants; perhaps she knocks over the block construction of an innocent bystander; perhaps she retreats to a quiet place and rocks there, endlessly, in a solitary way. None of these behaviors is an emotionally or socially productive solution, and many of them could be avoided if adults would take the risk of helping children recognize their feelings and express them safely.

Hodges (1987) terms this process *active listening* and describes it beautifully:

> Active listening requires giving undivided attention to children and accepting what they say without blame, shock, or solving their problems for them. Giving undivided attention is signaled by positioning squarely in front of a child, getting close to the child's eye level, and leaning forward without crowding. Active listening enables us to reflect the feelings of the child, respond appropriately, and to check to see if we understand. Active listening communicates respect, warmth, and empathy. Children know that they are important and that they belong when they are heard. (p. 13)

Help Children Express Their Feelings

The clearest way to show the child that you have really listened is to take time to describe her feelings before saying anything else. This *paraphrasing* what you surmise she is feeling helps her substitute words for action, thereby fostering self-control. When attempting this, remember to keep sentences describing feelings short, uncomplicated, and tentative. It is particularly important to be tentative because identifying feelings involves sensitive guesswork. To avoid hurting the child through misunderstanding her, it is best to begin interpretations with such phrases as "You seem to me . . ." "I wonder if you're feeling . . ." or "Is your face telling me that . . .?" In short, always remember that such interpretations should be offered as caring guesses rather than as dogmatic labels. Another advantage of concentrating on the child's feelings is that this also begins the lengthy task of teaching her the difference between self-report (telling another person how one feels inside oneself) and verbal attack (hurting the other person's feelings by name calling and so forth)—a valuable distinction, albeit difficult to learn.

Also, because young children's comprehension of language is so limited, it is better teaching to go beyond using an adjective such as *mad* or *happy* or *jealous* to describe the emotion. These words are only beginning to acquire meaning to children of such tender years. Expert teachers try to be more descriptive than that, so they may say, "You look to me like your stomach's all churned up inside" or "I think your eyes are telling me you wish you hadn't done that!" rather than telling a child she looks excited or remorseful.

If two children are in conflict, it is important to identify the angry feelings of each child so that both youngsters hear them stated plainly. This should always be one of the first steps in settling a fight. Once the teacher has stopped the actual battle, it only takes a minute extra to say something as simple and caring as, "Jason, you really want that rabbit badly, and, Jasmine, you aren't ready to give it up, and you don't want him to grab it—is that right?" Such teaching has to be done again and again, but if the teacher is persistent, this technique will gradually bear fruit. These brief descriptions of feelings let both children know the adult cares enough to understand and recognize their respective feelings without passing judgment

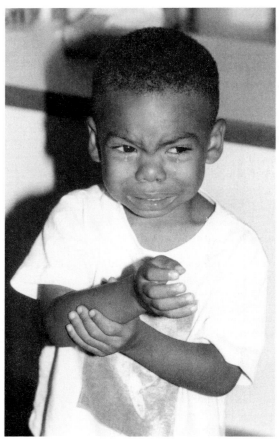

What could you say to this child to acknowledge his feelings and help him cope with them?

on their worth—feelings are neither good nor bad, they simply *are*. But what we do about them is another matter, and so we are reminded once again of the importance of the second part of the basic mental health principle: "Feel what you wish, but *control what you do.*" Recognition does not imply permission.

Young children frequently require clear reminding, sometimes coupled with physical restraint, that it is not all right to act out a feeling by socking or biting somebody, no matter how angry they feel. To continue with the rabbit incident, the teacher might say, "Jason, I know you want that rabbit badly, and you, Jasmine, aren't ready to give it up, and you don't want Jason to grab it. I know it's hard to wait and hard to share, but I can't let you pull the rabbit's leg that way—it hurts him too much." In other words, the pattern of intervention from the teacher should include a statement of the children's feelings, a statement of what they can or cannot do, and a simple, clear reason for the restraint.

In addition to implementing sound mental health practices, this particular strategy has the added advantage of instilling the beginnings of internalized consciences in children. Research indicates that an effective way of building an internal conscience is combining warmth and control with simple reasons why a child must not act a particular way (Coopersmith, 1967; Hoffman, 1970). These occasions are not the time to moralize and talk about how good little girls would feel or what nice little boys would do. The teacher should state the reason firmly and briefly why the child cannot do as she wishes and move on with her to something else.

Avoid Long, Drawn-Out Discussions About Motives or Forcing an Apology

One more thing about describing and discussing feelings must be emphasized: It just does not work to ask young children *why* they did a particular thing. Occasionally well-intentioned students inquire, "Why did you hurt the puppy like that?" or "Why did you cry when your mother left?" It is a rare child who can deal with this question effectively and explain in any depth why she hurt the puppy or why he poured paint all over his neighbor's picture.

Insisting that a child apologize is equally ineffective with young children. An apology is meaningful only if it is authentic and comes from the heart—as anyone who has received an insincere apology can confirm. Many children learn that if they simply offer a rote "I'm sorry" immediately after doing someone harm, they are excused—is this really what we want children to learn?

COMPETENCE FOUR: HELP CHILDREN USE PLAY AND CREATIVE MATERIALS TO RESOLVE EMOTIONAL PROBLEMS

Describing children's feelings to them is one valuable method of helping children remain in touch with their emotional selves, but its effectiveness depends on the sensitivity of the

These New York City first- and second-graders designed a memorial for the World Trade Center victims. Through various creative media such as drawing, painting, and sculpture, these young children were able to process their emotions after experiencing tragedy.

teacher, as well as on her being right on the spot. Fortunately, additional activities can be provided in the curriculum that also serve this purpose and do not require such close attention from the teacher. These are primarily pretend-play situations and self-expressive creative activities (Alat, 2002; Frost, 2005; Koplow, 1996). When such activities are provided, children make use of them in a very natural way to work through troubling situations, repeating them until they have diluted their impact to manageable proportions and have attained some mastery over them.

For example, children often play out hospital experiences, enact scenes from home in which they assume adult roles, or retreat to infantile behavior and roles as their feelings dictate. It is common—and therapeutic—for children to use play and creative arts to act out their feelings after experiencing a crisis. For instance, after the 9/11 terrorist attacks, teachers in New York City noted children's intense interest in representing the planes crashing into the twin towers of the World Trade Center (Fenichel, 2002; McGinn, 2005). The Emergent Curriculum in Action box on page 186 offers a powerful description of how children's feelings were handled through an emergent curriculum offering a wealth of expressive art experiences.

Use Pretend Play to Strengthen the Emotional Self

Children can use almost anything that comes to hand for pretend play, and to help them exercise their imaginations, it is best to choose equipment that lends itself to many possible uses. Blocks, for example, can be used to represent roads, cars, baby bottles, buildings, or fences. Scarves can be made into aprons, diapers, reins for horses, veils, or elegant sashes. Of course, it also facilitates certain kinds of play if some items of a more structured nature, such as dolls and dress-up clothes, are provided. These lend themselves beautifully to playing out episodes of domestic happiness as well as contention. Then, too, special circumstances can warrant inclusion of other structured items (we added leg braces and crutches shortly after a youngster with a disability joined our group), and equipment for general hospital play is always valuable to offer.

Emergent Curriculum in Action

The World Trade Center Memorial Park for Children

by Brigid McGinn

The World Trade Center Memorial Park for Children is a park designed by New York City children for the children of victims of the World Trade Center attacks. In September 2002, a class of 6- and 7-year-old New York City school children embarked on a study of playgrounds in the wake of the first anniversary of the September 11th attacks and emerged with a comprehensive memorial design, creating an imaginary place for them to address their fears and find answers to their questions.

The children designed their park as a group collaboration and created it in various media—including sketches, blueprints, and clay models. Finally, the children's design was entered in the World Trade Center Site Memorial Competition. Of the 1,501 submissions from 63 nations, it was the only design by children.

The children were able to create meaningful places that were sensitive to the needs of grieving children and, at the same time, offer possibilities for them to explore what happened. The children live and play downtown and were very aware of all that was going on, not to mention the trauma they personally experienced on September 11th.

The classroom teachers recorded the children's conversations, and it was apparent that the children's minds were on the World Trade Center and all the social and political activity that was buzzing around their homes and communities.

Michael: I remember I watched TV when the World Trade Towers went down. My mom's best friend, he died.

This focus had not been the intention behind the curriculum prepared by the classroom teacher but, with respect to the children's frames of mind she approached me, the studio teacher, about possible ways to engage the children in work that more directly addressed the children's concerns.

This group of children and I knew each other very well, and so their work all year on this World Trade Center Memorial Park for Children was spontaneous and enthusiastic. As a group, the children were in agreement about their goals for the project. The park was to make children happy and safe.

Jamila: People feel good if they have nice benches to sit and think about the parents that died. You want children to be happy because the people that died still have feelings. So, you want a place that their children will be happy so then their parents can feel happy in heaven.

Rebecca: Grownups think about grownups, so we made a place where kids can think about kids. It is easier for grownups to be sad because they are already grown up. But children have to go through a lot of changes. We have to grow up and be sad. That is why we made our park.

The model was built to help the jury see their ideas but, as the model neared completion, it became a pretend play zone for the children. The first time it was set up, Emma, Eleanore, and Journey used their fingers like little people walking through the model. They pretended that their little finger people were a mommy and children and they walked over the bridge to play in the park. They played for a long while.

The children are proud to be represented in the exhibit on the Lower Manhattan Development Corporation website. For some of them, seeing their work on the Internet meant they were "in" as Michael put it. For some others, the competition was secondary. They want to get their park built. Alex said, "Okay, so if they don't want to build our park and the Mayor hasn't called . . . let's send a letter to Donald Trump."

Note: The final result of the children's project was a submission in the World Trade Center Site Memorial Competiton and can be viewed at www.wtcsitememorial.org (click on "Exhibition" and enter the name McGinn). To see more documentation of this project, visit the *Making Learning Visible* Web site at http://www.pz.harvard.edu/mlv/visual_essay.cfm.

Encourage Storytelling by Children

Still another way of using imagination to help children understand how they feel is by encouraging them to dictate stories. Young children often relish dictating such accounts, and these are clearly influenced by their personal concerns. Sometimes the teacher can help focus the child's concern by starting the story in a particular vein. Perhaps he might begin,

"Once upon a time there was a child named Henry who went to the doctor and he said, 'Henry, you're going to have to have your tonsils out.' Well, that was quite a surprise to Henry. . . ." (Cook, 2001).

As well, children's play and storytelling can be drawn out through the addition of little rubber dolls, miniature animals, or puppets.

Use Self-Expressive Materials to Express Feelings Safely

In addition to supplying materials for imaginative play and storytelling, teachers can provide for the socially acceptable expression of various emotions by offering expressive art materials such as paint and dough. These substances have additional cardinal virtues as outlets for creative ideas and aesthetic satisfactions, but they are without peer in the realm of expressing feelings. (Chapter 14 presents an extensive discussion of the creative possibilities offered by paint and dough.)

It is not realistic to expect most young children to use these materials to produce actual pictures of their problems. Nevertheless, the youngster who uses her fingernails to scratch tensely through the finger painting paper or who limits herself to using only the center of the paper is expressing her feelings, just as the child swooping and squishing his way through a finger painting is expressing his happiness and lack of constriction. Some of these materials lend themselves particularly well to the sublimated expression of aggression, and some to the relief of more generalized tension.

Aggression-Relieving Activities

We may as well realize that the world is full of frustrating circumstances for young children. Their wants are immediate, intense, and personal, and inevitably they are prevented numerous times every day from satisfying their desires. Such frustrations range from seeing that another child already has the ball they want, to having a passerby stumble over their blocks, or to finding that lunch time has cut short their play on the swings. The intensity of frustration and amount of ensuing anger and aggression vary from child to child, but all children need to learn to redirect their aggressive feelings into channels that harm neither themselves nor others.

Ways to Relieve Anger Harmlessly

The most effective way to relieve anger, as already discussed, is dealing with it directly by letting the child know that you are aware of the anger and that you will help her confront it squarely and deal with it safely. (Chapter 12 discusses additional ways to cope successfully with angry behavior.)

There are also some other less direct activities that can be substituted for more direct expressions of aggression when the cause of the anger is not known. Sometimes, for example, the child just seems to arrive with a chip on her shoulder or have a general grudge against the world. Occasionally during such play the real reason for the anger comes out and can be talked about—sometimes not—but at least the child will be more comfortable temporarily.

Examples of harmless, aggression-relieving activities might include boisterous physical activity, jumping hard on a mattress or throwing beanbags at a target. Vigorous crying can be an outstanding way to achieve relief. Dancing—particularly if offered with therapeutic questions such as "What's the strongest dance you do?" or "What's the angriest thing you can think of to be? Show us what that would look like"—provides a valuable avenue of expression. Hammering is still another excellent aggression-redirecting activity, particularly if large peg-and-hammer sets are used, because these can take brutal punishment while not requiring close supervision. Beating large drums also offers a safe aggression reliever, if the teacher can tolerate the noise (outdoors is infinitely preferable to indoors for this activity). Squirting water is still another satisfying, though milder, way of getting feelings of frustration and anger out of the system.

187

Regardless of what aggression reliever is provided, teachers should bear in mind that they need to be on hand to exert control if necessary. Children using these materials forcefully must still stay within the bounds of safety. It is important to be very clear with them about the rules, before they start. The hammer may be used only with the peg set, no matter how the child feels, and the water may be squirted on the fence or the tree, but not on another child or the teacher. (More direct methods of preventing and controlling aggression are discussed in the next chapter.)

Although such restraints are obviously necessary, it is important to remember also that the basic intention of such activity is to reduce frustration, not build it. For this reason, it is best to select materials that do not require much skill to use. This is why it is better to use a peg-and-hammer set rather than a hammer and nails for relieving aggression. Having to fiddle with a pesky nail in itself contributes to rage.

Soothe Feelings by Offering Tension-Relieving Activities

Some general tension-relieving activities are also of great value. Two of these are so practical that we often forget about them: (1) taking children who are acting restless to the toilet, and (2) offering children something to eat or drink when they are out of sorts. I would not want these suggestions to be misconstrued so that every restless boy is continually escorted to the bathroom or that food is used as a means of continually placating children, but sometimes these solutions are worth trying. Children are often unaware that physiological needs are making them cranky; they just know that nothing feels quite right, and sometimes this gets them into unnecessary trouble.

The value of crying as a tension reliever is often underestimated by adults, both for themselves and for children. But crying, as Solter (1992) points out, can "be a healing mechanism, a natural repair kit that every person has. It allows people to cope with stress" (p. 66).

Other tension-relieving activities include rhythmic ones such as swinging and rocking, which are very soothing to young children. The close physical contact while rocking in the teacher's lap, in particular, provides its own special relaxing comfort. Other, more specific relaxation techniques discussed in chapter 9 are also valuable. Finally, finger painting and dough, mud, and water play offer excellent opportunities for children to relax and mess about to their heart's content. (Finger painting and dough are discussed in chapter 14.)

Whatever is offered in the way of materials that relieve feelings, it must be remembered that such items are intended to help children over the inevitable humps and hollows of growth. As such, they are only temporary measures—first aid, not long-term cures. It is the overall environment of the school, where frustration is kept to a tolerable level by careful planning and by sound knowledge of children's needs and where overstimulation is avoided, that produces the basic facilitative climate that helps children gradually attain understanding and mastery of their feelings.

COMPETENCE FIVE: HELP CHILDREN LEARN TO FACE REALITY

On first thought, it might seem to be ideal for children to experience childhood as a perfect, golden time devoid of frustration and anxiety, but children can benefit from experiencing at least a certain amount of frustration and anxiety particularly if families and teachers help them learn to cope with these situations in a productive way. Part of this learning to cope involves facing reality and accepting what cannot be changed.

Everyone has to learn at one time or another that some things in life cannot be changed. No amount of tears can affect the fact that the cut must be stitched, any more than tears can bring about a reconciliation of parents determined to separate. This does not mean that the child should not protest or mourn. Such behavior is natural, but at the same time adults can provide reassurance and comfort by taking the position, "You may not like whatever is happening, and I can understand why you feel bad, but it is something that cannot be changed. It's going to be tough, but we'll see it through together. After a while, you'll feel better again."

Learning to Accept Alternative Satisfactions

There can even be a silver lining to the dark cloud of learning to accept what cannot be changed. It is that children can learn to extend their coping abilities by creatively seeking alternative solutions. For example, one alternative strategy they can acquire is the ability to accept compromises to get part of what they want. The child who wants to build a tower of blocks, for instance, may be willing to substitute the oblongs in place of the cylinders for this purpose if the cylinders are all in use. Or she can be encouraged to strike bargains with another youngster: She will let him use her truck if he will share some of the blocks with her.

One additional comment about providing alternative satisfactions is in order here: Sometimes when a serious crisis strikes a family, the teacher is tempted to "make it up" to the youngster by becoming a surrogate parent. The teacher should realize, however, that it is neither possible nor desirable to fill this void by behaving this way. For one thing, the relationship between teacher and child is only temporary; it draws to a close at the end of the year, and so its value is necessarily limited. Besides that, the teacher has the obligation to be involved with all the children, not with one in particular. Finally, allowing such a relationship to become established is unfair to the family, no matter how kindly the teacher's intention, because doing this robs parents of their right of parenthood.

Using Mechanisms for Protecting the Emotional Self from Too Much Reality

Neither children nor adults learn to face reality in one fell swoop or with unwavering consistency. All people develop ways of protecting themselves from time to time, and these methods of protection (or coping) serve the useful purpose of reducing stress to tolerable limits. All children develop their own personal repertoire of coping skills for everyday life situations. It can be fascinating, as well as enlightening, to pick a particular event (such as arriving in the morning or settling down for sleep) and then note how individual children manage this event each day. A sensitive observer will find that there are likely to be as many different ways of making these transitions as there are children attending school. Part of the purpose of teaching is to help children extend their repertoires of adaptive coping responses, which thereby will increase their ability to adjust more easily to changing life circumstances.

Withdrawal and Regression

Using the strategies of withdrawal and regression can also help children cope with reality when life circumstances overwhelm them. These mechanisms warrant special comment here because they appear so commonly in early childhood and are often regarded with undue alarm by teachers. Both of these responses are indicators that the child feels overwhelmed and needs to retreat for a bit. The goal of the teacher should not be to deprive the child of these strategies but to recognize them when they occur, appreciate their value, and also perceive them as signals by the child that all may not be well in her world.

Sometimes withdrawal is quite literal: The child hovers behind an easel, dabbling idly with a brush, or builds a corral of blocks and sits inside, or even hides under a table. Such children should not be forced into participation before they are comfortable, no matter how unsocial the behavior may appear to the teacher. Indeed, the more the teacher pushes, the more resistance may be incited. On the other hand, patience combined with enticing materials and a low-key approach that does not reward nonparticipation with attention will almost always draw such youngsters into activities.

Regression, the second of these two defense mechanisms, occurs when the child retreats to behavior appropriate for a younger child. Thus, we see examples of bed wetting when the new baby arrives, or wanting to be pushed on the swing, or insisting on being helped with boots and coat when only a week before putting these on herself was a jealously guarded prerogative.

Teachers are so growth oriented that they seem especially threatened by this kind of emotional backsliding. However, if they relax and meet this dependency in an understanding way by satisfying the child's emotional hunger rather than trying to starve it to death, the child will almost always return to a more independent status as soon as she is emotionally able to do so. Children have a compelling desire to grow, and wise teachers count on this fact as their most useful ally.

COMPETENCE SIX: HELP CHILDREN COPE WITH CRISIS SITUATIONS

Give Children Credit for Being Resilient

Crises of one sort or another happen to all children from time to time. They can be as serious as the death of a parent or a devastating hurricane, or as relatively mild as moving to a new neighborhood or starting school. Sometimes crises are of long duration; sometimes they are as brief as getting stitches in the emergency room. What is interesting about this subject is the fact that some children crumble under such experiences whereas others cope more effectively and recover quickly. What is it about these survivors that causes them to come through such difficulties sunny-side up?

Werner (2000) has identified a number of protective factors that evidently help answer that intriguing question of why some children in high-risk situations such as poverty, illness, and family turmoil survive in reasonable emotional health whereas others do not. Although space does not permit a complete listing of factors, a sampling of personal characteristics contributing to resiliency includes low emotionality, sociability, an "easy" temperament, and the ability to emotionally distance oneself and control impulses. Fewer than four children in the family, a relatively high level of education and competence in the mother, close bonds with a primary caregiver, and supportive grandparents, siblings, and teachers were identified as family and community factors favoring the development of resilience.

Prepare Children in Advance for Crises Whenever Possible

Some crises, such as accidents, occur so suddenly that advance preparation is not possible, and child and parent must simply see them through with whatever fortitude they can muster. Other potential emergencies can be prepared for, at least to a degree, by using a technique called *crisis proofing* (Furman, 1995).

Crisis proofing seeks to arm the child against crises by providing the child with a mild, diluted form of the experience before a more serious crisis occurs. One example of such crisis proofing is the use of pet funerals, discussed in chapter 10. The opportunity to experience death in moderately saddening but not devastating circumstances can help prepare a child for a more serious experience later such as the death of a family member or friend.

Other crisis-proofing activities might involve having an ambulance visit the school so that the children can see what is inside, visiting a kindergarten before actually attending, or touring the children's ward before having surgery. Such experiences are included in the curriculum to provide opportunities for children to gain advance understanding and knowledge, which

All too many children have run in terror from a masked firefighter trying to save their lives. Crisis proofing can forestall that panic reaction.

thereby reduces their fear of the unknown and partially prepares them for similar but more powerful situations.

Reading topical books to children is an additional way to provide advance preparation for a crisis. (These can also be read after one has occurred.) This technique is called *bibliotherapy*, and it can be an excellent way to free children to ask questions and become involved in discussion. Some good reference resources for these books are included at the end of the chapter.

Before presenting such a book, it is important to read it through carefully. Make certain that it is appropriate for the particular group and situation. Anticipate questions that may arise from the children and consider how you might best handle these. Prepare some discussion questions of your own that would encourage the children to talk about the material. Perhaps you might want to supplement the book with some pictures or with poetry. Plan to repeat the story or theme on additional days, just as you would any other theme. Children need time to understand new information; they need time to consider what was said and to ask questions that may occur to them later.

The purpose of crisis proofing and bibliotherapy is to help children gain strength and understanding without causing them to be excessively anxious. For this reason, it is important to point out the positive as well as the negative aspects of a situation. For example, when discussing hospitalization, although you should not gloss over the possibility of pain with false reassurances, you should explain that hospitals help children feel better and get well.

Teachers' efforts at crisis proofing can have effective and powerful results. Just 2 weeks before the deadly tsunami of 2004 struck, Tilly Smith, age 10, had studied them at school and had watched a videotape of an actual tsunami. While on vacation in Thailand, she noticed unusual patterns of the waves as she walked along the beach. She warned her parents and hotel staff who evacuated the beach of 100 people, saving their lives. Tilly Smith was honored at the United Nations and met with former President Bill Clinton who stated, "All children should be taught disaster reduction so they know what to do when natural hazards strike" (Dobnik, 2005, p. 33A). As teachers we bear particular responsibility for crisis proofing our children to the best of our ability—and we never know when our efforts might result in heroic efforts by our students.

As mentioned in the discussion about death, it is important to include children as part of the family when crises arise. Children will sense tension and problems in the family anyway, and the uncertainty they experience of not knowing the reason for the strain is likely to be worse than the certainty of knowing what the trouble is. However, young children should not be expected to bear the burden of feeling responsible for either causing or helping cure the problem. We do not want them to blame themselves for the situation or feel that they must do something to correct it. Still, they do benefit from simple explanations about what the emergency is and what is being done to relieve it. If there is some way that they can be helpful, this will also provide comfort to children by enabling them to feel somewhat in control.

Children also benefit when adults share their own feelings. Families should be informed that it is not necessary or desirable to shield children from all expressions of dismay, grief, or feeling upset *as long as reassurance is provided along with the expression of feelings.* Children learn about handling strong emotions partly by seeing how others cope with them. Sharing concerns, revealing a moderate amount of feeling, and showing children how to cope with that feeling is recommended. Exposing children to floods of adult emotion is not.

Provide Children with Chances to Ask Questions

Sometimes questions about crises arise at home, sometimes at school. Whenever they come up, the adults should make every attempt to answer them simply and truthfully: "Yes, when they take the stitches out, it will hurt a little—it will feel like a sharp little pinch, but then it will be over and your cut will have grown together again."

Rather than plunging into a lengthy explanation, it often works best to ask questions in reply to a question to find out what the child really wants to know. Does Jeremy really want to know all the details of the divorce, or is he actually most worried about whether he will see his father again?

Remember That Play Is the Great Healer

Earlier in this chapter, and in chapter 3 as well, considerable time was devoted to discussing how to use play to promote emotional health. When children are undergoing a crisis, provision for working through their feelings via play can bring them great relief (Frost, 2005; Monahon, 1993).

Curriculum that is particularly worthwhile to use with children in times of emotional stress includes tension-relieving activities and sublimated ways of expressing aggression. Pretend play involving relevant themes can often be sparked by the inclusion of items suggesting that theme in play.

Sometimes when families are troubled, play can also alert the teacher to the fact that the youngster needs special help. Signals to watch for include playing out themes not appropriate for the child's age, too-intense feeling associated with the play, extreme repetitiveness of themes, and unusual topics.

Keep the Environment as Stable and Reasonable as Possible

Children's centers and schools can make a wonderful contribution to the child's well-being in the area of stability. The steadiness of routine, calm affection, and confident control by the teacher can provide a haven for children who are living in stressful situations at home or due to a local crisis. Simply knowing what is going to happen next and what is expected in the way of behavior at school is comforting. When this is combined with the use of play to clarify feelings, children can return to their family situation strengthened and reassured.

While keeping the environment as stable as possible, it also may be necessary to reduce expectations of good behavior for children experiencing crises who may be feeling miserable. They may cry more easily or fly off the handle more readily; they are more likely to tire sooner; they may be unable to settle down at nap; and anxiety may reduce their appetites, making them feel even more fatigued.

When children display these behaviors, they require extra comforting combined with reasonable but not excessive toleration. Yet, at the same time they cannot be allowed to become tyrants—a difficult balance to maintain. The best approach to balancing routines and expectations with children's special needs is to use common sense, mercy, and patience. As their lives return to normal, expectations can be readjusted accordingly.

Other Children May Be Aware of the Crisis

In numerous situations, families confide in teachers about intimate problems, and *teachers need to keep such information completely confidential.* However, a crisis often becomes known to other children in the group, as when someone's house has burned down, a car pool parent has fallen ill, or a child has had an accident. The children may feel quite distressed or anxious at the news, and they often wonder if such a thing could happen to them or their families.

Be aware that these children need much of the same kind of help as that recommended for the individual child to enable them to come to terms with their anxieties. This includes crisis proofing, chances to discuss their concerns, and opportunities to deepen their understanding through play.

In addition, remember that such crises can provide very desirable opportunities to help children do something thoughtful for the child with the trouble. If the teacher asks children how they could help, they often have quite delightful ideas: "We could draw him a get-well picture," "We could give her hugs," "We could be nice and let her choose first at snack time." Children can generate nice, practical ideas for expressing concern and offering comfort. Moreover, these expressions benefit the children in the group by allowing them to do something kind for someone else.

COMPETENCE SEVEN: HELP CHILDREN BUILD EMPATHY FOR OTHER PEOPLE

Throughout this chapter we have been concentrating almost exclusively on how children feel and how to help them gain understanding of their feelings, as well as competence in dealing with them. The chapter would not be complete, however, without discussing a different kind of goal, even though it is one that can be only partially achieved by such young children. This is the goal of instilling empathy—the ability to put oneself in another's place and feel as that person is feeling. This ability is related partly to the emotional self and partly to the social self.

As Piaget (1983) theorized, putting oneself in another's place is a difficult task because young children are essentially centered on themselves and have great difficulty realizing that other people do not feel the same emotion or have the same ideas that they do.

More recent research on what is termed the *theory of mind* maintains that the recognition of "otherness" begins earlier than Piaget realized. Lillard and Curenton (1999) cite many research projects that document the development of that ability. For example, they cite evidence that children may begin as early as a year-and-a-half to realize that different people have different desires, and this ability to differentiate between themselves and others continues to grow throughout the preschool years.

When we realize that the development of empathy requires the child not only to understand that other people have feelings different from her own, but also to set aside her personal feelings and feel another person's feelings instead, it becomes clear how patient teachers must be when attempting to build empathy in such young children.

Bearing these limitations in mind, there are three practical ways of beginning to foster empathy in young children: (1) self-report, (2) role-playing in pretend situations, and (3) "remember when" experiences.

Using Self-Report

Self-report, which in this case really should be called "other" report, can be used in two ways to foster empathy when teaching young children. The first is to encourage other children to tell the child how they feel. Thus, you can ask a child being pushed off the bench by another: "Do you like what he's doing? Well, tell him how you feel about it." Or: "Do you want him to do that? Well then, tell him you don't."

The second way to use self-report is to make a point of honestly reporting your own feelings to the children. This is valuable as long as you are not too forceful or use the report of a "bad" feeling as a threat to induce better behavior. An example of an undesirable threat is: "You'd better watch out—I'm getting angry!" On the other hand, an appropriate self-report statement might be: "I'm worried you children won't remember to wait with me when we get to the curb." It is even all right, when stopping a fight, to say, "Just a minute—I haven't decided what to do about this yet; I need some time to make up my mind." This is more satisfactory than making an impulsive decision that you regret later but cannot change without losing face. Honest self-reporting not only helps the children understand the teacher better but also sets a model for them to copy.

There are some reasonable limits to the use of self-reports by adults. One is that care must be taken so that they are not used as a means of justifying the expression of rage or abandonment to grief, since such flood tides of feeling from grown-ups frighten children too much. When properly used, self-reports allow adults to present themselves as human beings who experience a range of feelings, just as children do. The books of Greenspan (1999), Koplow (1996, 2002), Faber and Mazlish (2000), and Samalin (1991) contain many wonderful examples of sincere communication between children and adults and can be read with benefit by every parent and teacher.

Using Role-Playing

The cultivation of insight through imaginative role-playing, which happens so often in dramatic play, is a second valuable way to help the child begin building empathy for other people. Although it is true that the child who is feeling brave while being the firefighter or petulant while being the baby is playing out her own feelings and ideas of that role, it is also true that she is obtaining a little insight into how other people act and respond in particular instances. This helps lay a framework on which to build later understanding.

Using "Remember When"

Finally, it is possible to build understanding of how another child feels by using the "remember when" approach. This remembering approach is a much stronger teaching method to use with young children than saying, "What if you were Tyler—how would you like it if he took your truck?" Phrasing the question in this way is too difficult for a young child to grasp because it requires him to (1) imagine himself as Tyler and (2) imagine Tyler as being him—a difficult task indeed for a child who has not yet decentered. No wonder that the usual response to such a query is one of baffled indecision.

It is far more effective to ask, "Remember when your father left you here for the first time? Remember how you cried? Well, that's how Tanya feels right now. [Wait a bit for this to sink in.] What do you think we could do to help her?" Or, "Remember how mad you got when Sean took that red car from you? Well, that's how Rico is feeling." Note that no moralizing is attached to these questions; they simply remind the children of how they felt, in order to help them understand that someone else feels that way, too.

SUMMARY

The emphasis in curriculum for the emotional self should be on helping children become as resilient as possible by using everyday life situations as the medium for teaching. Such situations should be used to build the following competencies in young children:

- Attaining basic attitudes of autonomy, initiative, and industry
- Learning to separate from their families with a reasonable degree of ease
- Remaining in contact with all their feelings while learning to control what they do about them
- Using play and self-expressive materials to clarify feelings and resolve emotional problems
- Facing reality
- Learning to cope with crises
- Beginning to build empathy, and understanding that other people have feelings, too

Food for Thought and Group Discussions

1. Can you remember being allowed (or forbidden) to play with mud, sand, and water when you were a young child? How did you feel about this experience then? How do you feel about it now?

2. Do you think that parents are sometimes right in setting limits on what they allow their children to say to them to express their feelings? If limits should be set, at what point should they occur? And what kinds of limits would you suggest?

3. You have had a 3-year-old girl in your school every weekday for 5 weeks, and every time she comes she cries bitterly for at least half an hour after her father departs. Both you and the father are quite concerned. Do you think this child should stay in school?

4. With a tape recorder, record yourself talking with various children. Listen to the results carefully, and identify some of your replies that were insensitive to what the children were feeling. Explain what you plan to say next time to respond more effectively to their real feelings.

Self-Check Questions for Review
Content-Related Questions

1. Which stage of emotional development comes first— the stage of initiative versus guilt, or autonomy versus shame and doubt? What is the name of the first stage babies go through? Describe some characteristics of each stage.

2. How can play and other creative materials be used to help children resolve emotional problems?

3. Suggest some nonviolent alternatives you could suggest to a child who wants something another child won't let her have.

4. What is self-report, and why is it a useful strategy to use with young children?

5. Why is it more effective to use "remember when" instead of saying to a child, "What if you were Tyler? How would you like it if he took your truck?"

Integrative Questions

1. Why should teachers be optimistic about the inner strengths many children possess?

2. Describe a situation where someone you know was upset or lost her temper. Then put that person's feelings into words by describing to her what she felt or would like to do.

3. There are some principles that are helpful to follow when dealing with almost any crisis. Think of a particular crisis situation you have come across, and explain how you would apply the principles in that situation.

Coordinating Videotape

Dealing with feelings. Tape #4. The whole child: A caregiver's guide to the first five years. The Annenberg/CPB Collection, P.O. Box 2345, South Burlington, VT 05407-2345. *Dealing with Feelings* shows practical activities that promote a child's emotional health in areas including working with the child's family, encouraging self-expression, dealing with frustration, identifying stress, and managing short- and long-term emotional issues.

References for Further Reading
Pick of the Litter

Greenspan, S. I. (1999). *Building healthy minds: The six experiences that create intelligence and emotional growth in babies and young children.* Cambridge, MA: Perseus. In friendly, clear language Greenspan traces the social/emotional development of children from birth to age 5 and explains how to form mutually satisfying relationships with them.

Overviews

Goleman, D. (2005). *Emotional intelligence: 10th anniversary edition.* New York: Bantam Books. For an interesting, diverse book about emotions and their effects on children and adults, this book is hard to beat.

Hyson, M. C. (2003). *The emotional development of young children: Building an emotion-centered curriculum* (2nd ed.). New York: Teachers College Press. Hyson presents a good review of recent research on emotional development. The second half of the book provides sound advice on ways to honor and support the role of emotions in the classroom.

Stages of Emotional Development and Emotional Needs of Children

Erikson, E. H. (1963). *Childhood and society* (2nd ed.). New York: Norton.

Erikson, E. H. (1982). *The life cycle completed: A review.* New York: Norton. These publications detail Erikson's concepts of the eight stages of man and the emotional attitudes of paramount importance at various stages of development.

Communicating with Children (and Other People)

Faber, A., & Mazlish, E. (2000). *How to talk so kids will listen, and listen so kids will talk.* New York: Avon Books. Numerous examples of describing and sharing feelings make this book a treasure trove of helpfulness.

Alleviating Common Emotional Difficulties

Cook, J. W. (2001). Create and tell a story: Help young children who have psychological difficulties. *Young Children, 56*(1), 67–70. Cook provides a step-by-step outline of how to develop a story with therapeutic benefits when that is necessary.

Miller, K. (2003). *The crisis manual for early childhood teachers: How to handle the really difficult problems* (Rev. ed.). Beltsville, MD: Gryphon House. The author provides practical advice on subjects as diverse as death, divorce, and natural disasters. Good suggestions for crisis proofing are included.

Bibliotherapy

Sullivan, A. K., & Strang, H. R. (2003). Bibliotherapy in the classroom: Using literature to promote the development of emotional intelligence. *Childhood Education, 79*(2), 74–80. The authors explain emotional intelligence and how bibliotherapy can promote development of the socioemotional competence.

Zeece, P. D. (2001). Meeting children's needs with quality literature. *Early Childhood Education Journal, 28*(3), 175–180. This list features new, good-quality books for preschool children.

Use of Specific Materials to Foster Emotional Competence

Hendrick, J., & Weissman, P. (2006). *The whole child: Developmental education for the early years* (8th ed.). Upper Saddle River, NJ: Merrill/Prentice Hall. The chapter titled "Tender Topics: Helping Children Master Emotional Crises" deals with general and specific recommendations related to various kinds of crises.

For the Advanced Student

Greenman, J. (2005). *What happened to my world? Helping children cope with natural disasters and catastrophe.* Watertown, MA: Comfort for Kids. This comprehensive guide explains typical children's reactions to stressful events and how adults can foster resiliency and a sense of security in young children. An outstanding resource. Available online at www.brighthorizons.com./talktochildren/

Lillard, A., & Curenton, S. (1999). Research in review: Do young children understand what others feel, want, and know? *Young Children, 54*(5), 52–57. This is a good place to begin further research investigations for students seriously interested in pursuing "theory of mind" studies.

Related Organizations and Online Resources

The FEMA for kids web page of the Federal Emergency Management Agency (FEMA) has many excellent resources to help teachers use crisis proofing as a strategy to help children through emotionally difficult times. http://www.fema.org/kids

Zero to Three, the National Center for Infants, Toddlers, and Families, offers many resources for promoting emotional health and publishes the journal *Zero to Three*. It stresses emotional health and covers all kinds of topics relevant to working with the infant-toddler age group, but the practices it advocates are sound to follow for older children as well. http://www.zerotothree.org

GETTING ALONG TOGETHER

Achieving Competence in Interpersonal Relations

Have you ever . . .

- Worried about what to do next when children refuse to stop a dangerous activity?
- Wished that you knew how to teach children to get what they want without just grabbing it?
- Wanted to know how to help children get along well together in a group?
- Tried to think of ways children could be genuinely helpful?

If you have, the material in this chapter will help you.

The important point to emphasize is that punishment does not teach a child self-discipline. Second, while fear of punishment may restrain the child from doing wrong, it does not make children wish to do right.

—Karen Owens (1995, p. 194)

Rewards and punishment is the lowest form of education!

—Chuang Tzu (399–295 BC)

Our society has a long history of thinking of discipline as an either/or phenomenon—either adults win or children will walk all over us. It seems that we think that learning appropriate behavior is different from learning any other skill, and, as a result, we believe that we can force children to learn how to behave, when we wouldn't use force to teach them anything else which is important for them to learn.

—Louise Porter (1999, p. 2)

One of the most frequent reasons families give for sending their youngsters to a children's center is that they want them to learn to get along with other children and generally be "fit to live with." But social competence goes far beyond those general abilities and embraces many subskills. For example, one research study listed some 32 different social abilities, ranging from wanting to be with other children, to showing someone else how to do something, to waiting for a turn and making suggestions that facilitate group play (Babcock, Hartle, & Lamme, 1995). Another study that identified prosocial qualities valued by teachers and parents included cheerfulness, sensitivity, friendliness, and expressing affection (Bergin, Bergin, & French, 1995).

Such lists are valuable because they broaden our views of what constitutes friendly, prosocial actions, thereby helping us be more aware of the many positive behaviors young children exhibit. At the same time, it is necessary to single out a few of the more basic skills to work on with the children that provide the underlying foundation for social competency. These include knowing they are able to control their aggressive impulses much of the time. Socially competent children also know how to use alternative ways of getting what they want from other children. They are able to form friendships, and they understand what constitutes acceptable behavior at the lunch table or during large group. They find satisfaction in helping other people from time to time, and they relish the ego-enhancing experience of occasionally performing what they think of as being grown-up work.

Of course, most children do not arrive at school possessing all these skills. It is up to us, the teachers, to help them acquire these. How to accomplish this is the subject of this chapter. (For a developmental chart that traces the growth of social and self-help skills from birth to age 6, please refer to appendix A.)

HELP CHILDREN LEARN IMPULSE CONTROL

The ability to control unsocial or asocial impulses is absolutely basic to getting along with others (Bronson, 2000; Levin, 2003). When the recommendation is phrased in this way, however, it may sound simpler than it really is. In actuality, we must never forget or underestimate the fact that children's wants are *immediate*, *intense*, and *personal*. This means that when a young child wants something, he wants it right now, he wants it very much, and he wants it because *he* wants it. Yet, we continually expect him to wait, to defer gratification, and even to be pleasant while doing this.

The most effective way to keep our demands and expectations within reason so that the child is not driven to desperation over the conflict between what *he* wants and what *we* want is to be quite clear in our own minds about what behavior must be stopped and what can be overlooked. The rule of thumb to apply here is that *we must not allow the child to seriously hurt himself or someone else or damage anyone else's property.* The word *seriously* is used to make it clear that we should not err on the side of being overly protective. Children learn best through experiences—unpleasant as well as pleasant ones—and if the consequences are not too dangerous, it may be desirable to let children simply experience the consequences of their actions. For example, a child who shoves another youngster down in the play yard may learn more from getting shoved back than from our preventing this relatively harmless encounter. On the other hand, if it looks as though he is going to push someone off the top of the slide or poke another child in the face with a stick, immediate action must be taken to forestall this.

Besides the rule-of-thumb standard, it is also necessary to have a set of well-defined rules that are agreed on and enforced by all the staff. These classroom rules should always be discussed with the children, and large group times are an excellent opportunity for doing so as well as soliciting children's input—which makes following the rules so much easier (Gartrell, 2004; Harris & Fuqua, 2000; Levin, 2003).

SHORT-TERM METHODS FOR CONTROLLING UNDESIRABLE BEHAVIORS AND BUILDING INNER CONTROLS IN CHILDREN

Behaviors that require immediate, short-term control generally include the ones mentioned previously—that is, they involve situations that may be dangerous to the child or those around him, or involve the destruction of property.

Both Physically and Emotionally Hurtful Behaviors Require Control

The saying "Violence is the means of the inarticulate" should ring true for teachers of young children. In addition to teaching children to express their emotions in acceptable ways, as discussed in chapter 11, teachers must also stand firm against allowing violence at school. The goal is to establish a peaceable classroom where children learn to express their feelings in the knowledge that everyone is safe and has their rights respected. There are simply times when teachers must step in to protect children from harm—and then follow up when things have calmed down to maximize the learning potential from the experience.

Violent acts, such as the sand-throwing situation depicted in Table 12.1 later in this chapter, are obviously hurtful behaviors, but it is important to realize that there are many additional less obvious kinds of behavior that are potentially just as hurtful and require control. At the preschool and elementary levels they include a wide gamut of bullying behaviors such as ridicule ("You look like a duck in those dumb shoes—waddle, waddle, stupid duck"), ostracism ("You can't play!"), teasing and taunting ("Yeah, yeah! I've got the trike—yeah! Yeah!"), threats ("You'd better not tell or you can't come to my birthday party"), and insults ("Snot nose! Snot nose—yuck, ugh—you snot nose!"). Note that racial insults are particularly harmful and are discussed in chapter 13.

Unfortunately, as Goldstein (1999) points out, these behaviors are rarely dealt with in American schools. This is particularly regrettable because research reveals that, if unchecked, bullying behavior continues and can translate into more serious criminal acts as the bully matures as well as having permanently damaging effects on the child who is abused (Crawford, 2002; Gartrell, 2004; Goldstein, 1999). Perhaps when these ugly behaviors are seen in their true colors as acts of aggression teachers will make the effort to prevent them by following steps 1 through 6 described next, and also teaching children how important it is to be kind to one another. It is hoped we do not need another Columbine to convince us that bullying behavior has long-term, harmful effects on developing personalities and must be stopped.

What Are the Six Steps Recommended When Short-Term Control Is Needed?

Because beginning teachers are usually most concerned about handling situations that require immediate control, it seems best to begin with these, and then discuss how to work toward longer-term ways of enhancing children's social skills. Note that both short- and long-term approaches have the same goal in mind—teaching the child to control, to regulate his own behavior rather than depending on someone else to do it for him.

The six steps for short-term control are as follows:

1. Redirect the child to more positive behavior and remind him of the right thing to do (the rule, and the consequence for violating it).
2. Remove the child and keep him beside you.
3. Help the child put his feelings into words and discuss the rules.
4. Wait for the child to decide when he is ready to return.
5. Help him return and be more successful in an acceptable way.
6. When all else fails and the behavior persists, take firmer action.

Aren't These Steps Just the Same as Using Conventional Time Out?

Although both procedures involve the teacher's taking the child away from what he's doing for a period of time, in conventional time out, he is typically sent to sit by himself and made to stay there until the teacher says he may return. Under these circumstances it is the teacher who makes all the decisions.

On the other hand, when the preceding six steps are followed, the focus is on the *child's feelings* and on *making his own decision* about when to return. These steps shift the responsibility for his behavior from the teacher to the child, thereby fostering the growth of the child's inner controls. (See the Chapter Spotlight for more in-depth discussion about time out.)

Usually it is necessary only to warn a child, say his feelings and/or intentions out loud, and tell him the acceptable thing to do instead. When it is necessary to take firmer action, there are some special reasons why it is so important to follow the recommendations outlined in steps 2, 3, and 4 to help the youngster build inner self-control.

Step 2 stresses that the teacher should keep the child with her rather than sending him off to the time-out chair. The Chapter Spotlight makes it clear why doing this is so much better than isolating the youngster. Keeping the child with the adult interferes with what he is doing in a mildly unpleasant way, maintains a bond between teacher and child, and prevents feelings of complete abandonment. And, finally, having the child right beside the teacher ensures that the teacher won't forget he is there and make the intervention last too long.

Step 3, taking time to describe the child's feelings to him by putting them into words, is vital because this says to the child: "I understand what you're feeling, even though I have to stop what you're doing. I care enough about you to take time to show you I understand by putting your feelings into words." This also means, as explained in the previous chapter, that the child does not need to continue *showing* you how he feels by acting out the angry feeling, which helps bring his behavior under control. In addition, telling him a simple rule helps the child see the sense and reason for the restriction.

Step 4, having the child decide when to return, is equally important because this puts the responsibility for his behavior on *his* shoulders, not yours. If you want children to become *self-* controlled, waiting for them to make these decisions for themselves has great significance.

What's Wrong with Time Out?

From the teacher's point of view, using the conventional kind of "time out" as a form of discipline is certainly better than spanking children, threatening to lock them in closets, or denying them the respite of outdoor play. It is convenient, nonviolent, and allows for a cooling off period for both teacher and child.

Why, then, with so many virtues, is it *not* recommended as the method of choice in *Total learning?* Why is time out with the teacher advocated instead? The answer is that there is little difference between sending the child away to "the quiet chair" and sending him to the corner with a dunce cap on his head. Either way the child is isolated and often left for way too long by himself—partly because the teacher may forget about him and, partly because it can be so convenient! Moreover, in such situations, the child is rarely encouraged to decide for himself when to return and explain what he's going to do once he gets there.

Besides these problems, there is something else to think about that is rarely considered. That is how the children feel about it. To find this our, Readdick and Chapman (2000) conducted a study where 42 2-, 3-, and 4-year-old children were interviewed after they had been sent to time out. About half the sample were girls and half boys and about two-thirds of the children were Caucasian and one-third African American. *Time out* was defined as "an occasion in which the child is removed from an activity or group for performing an act deemed unacceptable or undesirable by an adulr, and spends time in a designated spot isolated from others at the request of the adult" (p. 83).

After the children were released from time out they were interviewed and asked a series of questions about the experience. The results were that about three-quarters of the children reported feeling alone, disliked by their teacher, and ignored by their peers during that experience, and, not surprisingly, 9 out of 10 said they didn't like it. Only two-thirds of the children had been told why they were in time out, and slightly more than half of them thought they deserved the punishment. Of particular interest is the fact that, when asked what they would have to do to get out of time out, the children replied "be quiet," "be good," "do what I'm told," "don't know," and so forth—apparently not one child had to make a decision for himself about when to return and how to behave after returning there.

The other findings that are of particular interest are the actual reasons determined by the observers why the children were sent to time out. Although Readdick and Chapman point out this strategy is typically recommended only for serious cases of misbehavior such as children being really out of control or posing imminent threats to others, in actuality teachers used it mostly when children simply refused to comply with what the teacher told them to do and had nothing to do with hurtful behavior.

How sad that such a well-intentioned discipline strategy is misunderstood and misused with the consequence that many children feel isolated, do not understand what they have done wrong, and are not expected to decide for themselves when to return and try again. As Readdick and Chapman comment, that misuse certainly "turns the time out experience into a punitive rather than an instructional one" (p. 87).

Note: For the purposes of simplicity and conciseness, the research by Readdick and Chapman was summarized in general terms and figures. For a more complete description refer to "Young Children's Perceptions of Time Out," by C. A. Readdick and P. L. Chapman, 2000, *Journal of Research in Childhood Education, 13*(1), 81–87.

Table 12.1 offers a sampling of possible things teachers might say to carry out this short-term method of controlling behavior. Bear in mind that steps 2 through 6 should be used only when other methods, such as distraction and redirection, have failed.

LONGER-TERM METHODS OF BUILDING INNER CONTROLS: USING PREVENTION RATHER THAN CURE

As the sandbox example in Table 12.1 demonstrates, it is not always easy for children to control their immediate, intense, and personal impulses, and adults must be ready to take swift,

Table 12.1

Six Steps Toward Acquiring Self-Control: Dealing with Behavior Problems on an Emergency Basis

General Principles	Examples of What to Say
Step 1 Remind the child, and redirect him if he will accept such redirection. For example, you might warn a youngster that if he continues to throw sand, he will lose the privilege of staying in the sandbox; then suggest a couple of interesting things he could do with the sand instead of throwing it. It is important to make the child understand that his behavior is up to him. It is *his* choice, but if he chooses to continue throwing sand, see to it that you carry out your warning.	What could we get out that would be fun? How about some water? Or could you put the sand in the dump truck? Remember, Zac, keep the sand down—when you throw it that way, it hits the other children. Why not turn around and dig the other way? Make sure you put the sand beside you here—if you throw it, it might get in someone's eyes. Do you need something to put the sand in? Let's look around and find something so you don't have to throw it. Our rule is "You have to keep the sand down so it's safe." If you throw it, you might get some in Beth's eyes. Then she'll feel bad and you'll lose the privilege of playing here for a while. Mae, I'm going to warn you once about keeping the sand down so it's safe—if you do that again, you'll have to come sit with me for a while until you decide you can control yourself.
Step 2 Warn only once. If he persists in doing what he has been told not to do, act calmly and promptly. Remove him and insist that *he stay with you,* telling him he has lost the privilege of playing in the sand. This is much more valuable than just letting him run off. Having him stay beside you interrupts what he wants to do—a mildly unpleasant consequence of his act, which also prevents his substituting another, more pleasant activity. We prefer this method to putting the child off by himself, because as the Chapter Spotlight emphasizes, it allows the teacher to stay bonded to the child. This feeling of closeness seems to lend the child additional ego strength. He is also less likely to feel punished by being ostracized and less abandoned.	Well, you decided you would throw it again, so you've lost the privilege of using the sand. Come and sit with me and we'll talk about it. That's really against our safety rules—up you come! [Pick up the child.] Sit over here with me until you can control yourself. Jennifer, you've been warned about that, but you chose to keep right on doing it. You've lost the privilege of staying here for now—come sit with me awhile. I told you boys, we just can't have that kind of behavior with sand. It hurts too much when it gets in people's eyes. You'll have to come over here with me until you calm down.
Step 3 Take time to describe his feelings in an understanding way, but state the rule and the reason for it clearly and firmly. Do not moralize or rub it in too much. Do not talk too much.	I guess you wanted to see whether I really meant what I said when I warned you. I can see you were very mad at Janie and you wanted to get even, but I can't let you hurt her. You must keep the sand down. It looks to me like you were so busy with that hole you just couldn't remember to think about where you were tossing the sand. I can understand why you feel that way—it's OK to be mad at Janie or me, but it isn't OK to hurt somebody. Throwing sand can hurt if it gets in people's eyes. We have to keep the sand down in the sandbox.
Step 4 Allow the child to decide when he is ready to return to the activity. Many teachers say something like, "Now you sit here until lunch is ready," thus shifting the responsibility for the child's behavior to their own shoulders instead of putting the child in command of himself. it is better to say, "Now, tell me when you can	When you can remember to keep the sand down, tell me and then you may go back and play. It's up to you. [To a child who is too shy or young to put the intention into words] Are you ready to go back now? [Perhaps he just nods or looks ready.] Good, your eyes tell me you are. What would you like to do for fun there?

Table 12.1
(continued)

General Principles	Examples of What to Say
Step 4 (*continued)* control yourself, and I will let you go back." Some children can actually say they are ready. but others need help from the teacher, who can ask them when they look ready if they are ready to go back.	When you decide you can use sand the safe way, nod your head and we'll think of something that it's all right to do with it.
Step 5 Return with the child and help him be successful so that he has the experience of substituting acceptable for unacceptable behavior. It will probably be necessary to take a few minutes to get him interested. Be sure to congratulate him when he has settled down. [Perhaps, if the teacher had done and said some of these things earlier, she might have avoided steps 2 through 4.]	Well, let's seen what you've decided to do that's fun and safe. I'll help you get another bucket so that you don't need to take Lashonda's. Would you like to use these little red cars? Maybe they need a tunnel to run through. That's the way to do it—now everyone's safe. Show me what's the safe way. That's right. Good for you! Now you're doing the right thing. I'm proud of you!
Step 6 Occasionally, the teacher will come across a more glib customer who says hastily when removed from the sandbox, "I'll be good, I'll be good!" but then goes right back to throwing sand when he returns. At this point, it is necessary to take firmer action. Have him sit beside you until he can think of something acceptable to do, but do not permit him to go back to the sandbox. After he has calmed down, have him select a different place to play. Go with him or alert another teacher to be sure that he becomes involved in an acceptable activity. The same may be done if two or more children are involved. However, it may be wiser to separate them. In this case, take them to different activities and provide an explanation to the attending teacher. Comment favorably on his regained self-control as soon as you possibly can.	What you did [be explicit] shows me that you haven't decided to do the right thing, so you'll have to come back and sit with me until you can think of somewhere else to play. You've lost the privilege of playing in the sandbox. [To the other teacher] Leah and Maggie have lost the privilege of playing in the sandbox. They have decided they'd like to push each other on the swing awhile. Could you get them started on that?

effective action. Helping children establish inner controls goes far beyond this immediate action, however. Teachers and families can follow many longer-term policies that will make life easier and more pleasant for everyone and, at the same time, build self-control within the children.

Emphasize Activity Centers That Foster Friendly Prosocial Interchanges

When planning activity centers, it makes sense to bear in mind that different centers elicit different kinds of positive social behaviors and some produce more positive social interaction than others do. Although we are likely to assume that pretend-play situations would produce the most opportunities and, hence, the largest number of positive interactions, it may be surprising to find out that, at least in one study, that was not the case. When Babcock and colleagues (1995) kept track of such behaviors, they found that the creative activity centers (art, woodworking, and writing) produced 42% of the positive social interchanges they observed. This was followed by 19% at group activity centers (discovery,

If you were their teacher, what do you think you should do or say?

water play, and blocks). Just 8% of such activity occurred in the pretend-play centers (mainly housekeeping), with 7% taking place in the process centers (primarily reading). The individual activity centers that featured listening and computers had the lowest rates of interchange at 3%. They also reported that different kinds of positive social behaviors were common to different activities. For example, blocks elicit more proximity seeking and leadership behaviors, whereas the creative centers facilitated a lot of sharing and helping each other. Teachers who wish to foster positive social activities would, apparently, do well to make sure they are including plenty of art, woodworking, and writing activities to generate the greatest amount of social interchange.

Analyze the Reasons for Repeated Behavior Problems, and Correct or Prevent Such Conditions When You Can

Some "discipline" situations have a way of recurring. For example, teachers may find themselves constantly telling two or three of the children not to run into the wall with their trikes or to stop tapping the table with their cups or not to poke their neighbor at group time.

When such situations happen again and again, *change the situation rather than nag the child.* A board on sawhorses in front of the wall or passing the cups just before milk is poured, for instance, will eliminate some of the difficulties. Shortening group time or rescheduling it for when children are less tired makes it easier for the children to be in better control of themselves. Why make it harder than necessary for children to follow the rules?

Teachers should also be sure to include the children in frequent discussions about the rules and expectations for classroom behaviors. When children contribute their ideas about what the rules should be and why, they feel listened to, empowered, and more inclined to follow the rules (Gartrell, 2004; Levin, 2003). If the same problems with following classroom rules keep occurring, a small- or large-group discussion is called for.

Take Individual Needs into Account

Children act out for a variety of reasons—fatigue, illness, social inexperience, and immaturity are among them. Some of these causes can be mitigated with the teacher's help. For example, careful scheduling of activities can reduce the effects of fatigue, and inexperience can be modified by seizing on social learning experiences as they arise and by gradually teaching children how to handle these without resorting to fighting. Other causes of difficult behaviors must be remedied by the processes of time, growth, instruction, and patience.

Realize That Children Often Resort to Difficult Behaviors Due to Problems or Crises at Home

We have already spoken in chapters 10 and 11 of the effect family crises may have on behavior, but even when not dealing with crises, puzzled parents may resort to ineffective child management techniques. Sometimes, too, they feel at their wit's end and simply do not know what to do. Teachers can offer real help in these situations, particularly if they are sympathetic rather than seeming antagonistic or condescending by implying that the families are to blame for all the child's problems. Chapter 2 provides many suggestions for offering such guidance to families when this is needed.

Warn Ahead

Many noncompliance situations (and much "misbehavior" can simply be thought of as noncompliance with teacher expectations) can be avoided by giving children advance notice of what will be happening next. Doing this gives children time to adjust to the new idea. Perhaps the teacher might say, "Pretty soon it's going to be time for snack. I wonder what it will be today?" or "It's almost time to go in. Would you like to leave the snowman up and work on it some more after nap?" or "In a few minutes I'll be back to help you finish the puzzle because it's going to be group time."

Tell Children What They *Should* Do: Provide Positive Instructions Instead of Negative or Neutral Ones

This is another tactful way of encouraging desirable behavior. The teacher who says, "Put the sand in the truck" or "Keep the sand down" rather than "Don't throw the sand" helps children behave well because she has provided positive guidance before they get in trouble.

Be Alert to Potential Difficulties, and Step in Before Disaster Strikes

This advice to intervene promptly must be balanced against the value of letting children learn from direct experience. However, when teachers know that they ultimately will have to intervene, it is far better to do it when everyone is still relatively calm and no one has experienced gratification from aggressive action. Children learn much better under such circumstances than after everything has blown sky high.

This advice also means that teachers must pay consistent attention to what is going on around them. Particularly for beginners, it can be a real temptation to focus on only one amiable child and avoid watching a wider area—but good teachers learn to do both things at once. They retain a kind of peripheral awareness of the entire yard or room, no matter what other adult is present, and also pay attention to individual children at the same time. It is an art—but a very necessary one to learn.

Make a Point of Recognizing Positive Behavior

This does not have to be fulsome praise. Such simple statements as "Thank you" or "That's exactly the right thing to do!" or "I appreciate your help" are satisfying without being gushy or overdone.

Convey a Feeling of Warmth Along with a Sense of Firmness

Admittedly, this can be tricky advice to give novice teachers, because some misinterpret it and attempt to buy good behavior from the children by being too friendly or "chummy" with them. The role of teachers is different from this: They must set a tone of warmth and caring concern while also maintaining a posture of firm reasonableness that is quite different from being the children's buddy.

Children (and adults) flourish in this climate of sincere approval and warmth. When they sense the teacher likes them, they try harder to retain this approval by behaving in accordance with her wishes. On the other hand, if they feel continually criticized and attacked, they gradually abandon hope and give up the effort of behaving well (Gartrell, 2004).

They will also feel more secure and trustful if they know that the teacher cares enough about them to prevent them from doing anything seriously out of line. This is why there is often a feeling of comfort between child and teacher after they have worked through a "scene." Although an inexperienced teacher often fears that the child will avoid or dislike her following an encounter, usually an increased sense of closeness and confidence between teacher and child is the result—but it certainly takes courage on the teacher's part to see the first two or three such storms all the way through. Perhaps it is not only the child who feels more secure following such an encounter.

Be Reasonable

By this we do not mean reasonable in the sense of not expecting too much, although that is certainly important, too. *Reasonable* here means that a simple reason for conforming to the rules should always be included along with the prohibition. Supplying a simple, clear-cut reason not only makes it plain that the rule is not just a whim of the teacher but also puts into practice some well-supported research findings that firm control combined with warmth and *accompanied by a reason* are the most effective agents in building inner controls and establishing the beginnings of conscience in young children (Bronson, 2000; Gartrell, 2004; Hoffman, 1970).

Be a Good Example Yourself

It is true that children learn from models and that they may express more direct aggression when they have witnessed a model behaving aggressively (Bandura, 1986; Coloroso, 2003; Molitor & Hirsch, 1994) or have been exposed to actual aggressive behavior (Knutson & Bower, 1994; Levin, 2003). Therefore, to reduce aggressive behavior, it is important to remain in control of yourself so that you do not model such behavior for the children to copy. Unfortunately, it is all too easy to pull two struggling children apart and angrily dole out instant punishment to both of the culprits as a way of relieving your own aggressive feelings—and then regret the severity of that punishment a few moments later. How much more desirable it is to stop what the children are doing immediately and give a self-report about your own feelings before doing anything more: "Wait just a minute. I need to calm down myself and think this over—then we'll talk about it." Doing this stops the action, gives everyone a minute to draw breath, and allows you to proceed in a less aggressive, better considered way while presenting an example of how to control oneself.

Profit by Your Experience

Of course, not all discipline situations work out perfectly, and adults often feel bad about this. Although mishandling a situation cannot be condoned, it is also valuable to realize that one poorly handled encounter will not result in permanent damage to child or teacher.

The important thing to do when this has happened is to avoid sinking into the depths of self-abasing despair but rather to think the situation over carefully, learn from it, and decide what you will do differently next time. Doing this helps prevent the useless repetition of ineffective responses to difficult behaviors, and planning ahead confers an invaluable sense of assurance on the teacher.

When children resort to force, it is often because they know of no other way to get what they want. This is why it is so worthwhile to teach children the alternative strategies that are discussed next. Children who possess a number of these advanced social ploys are less likely to resort to violence or bullying to get what they want. Moreover, having these skills increases their feelings of being competent and masterful.

Teach Alternatives

If teachers keep on the lookout for potential confrontations, they can use them as a basis for practical social teaching provided they are aware of the range of alternative solutions that can be proposed to children. These strategies include teaching children to:

- Ask to use something when the other child is done ("Ask him, 'Can I have that when you're through?' ").

- Suggest that the child use something else as a substitute, or encourage him to do something else while waiting ("Tony's using the elephant puzzle right now. How about doing the giraffe while you're waiting?").

- Trade one thing for another ("Maybe if you gave him your hat, he'd let you use the cane.").

- Work out some kind of compromise in which each child obtains some satisfaction ("I know she's holding both crayons. Perhaps she'd let you use the orange while she's using red, and then you could trade" or "Tell you what—you cut and let her choose!").

- Work out a genuinely cooperative arrangement in which the play is enriched by the newcomer's contribution ("Anna, if they let you play, would you help them carry the blocks? Well, why don't you tell them that?").

When children are old enough (around age $3\frac{1}{2}$ to 4), it is even possible to ask them to tell you what they could do instead. This helps them think up their own alternatives. For example, the teacher might ask, "It sure didn't work to tip over her trike, did it? Now she's mad and won't let you play. The next time you want Tricia to let you ride, what could you do instead?"

Any of these alternatives generally work better than insisting that the children take turns regulated by the teacher or expecting that a youngster will gladly surrender something he is using just because someone else has asked for it. After all, why should he? Moreover, these alternatives are more desirable than the adult making the decision because they do not depend so much on adult enforcement, nor do they place an unreasonable expectation of generosity on either of the children involved.

Of course, these approaches do not always work—and when a youngster just begins trying them out, teachers need to remain with the child and lend their support to make them as effective as possible. It is also helpful to preface the suggestions with such phrases as "*Maybe it would work* if you tried trading him this truck for that little car," or "*Perhaps* he'd let you play if you'd sit on that side of the swing to balance it." This leaves the way open, if the other child simply refuses, to say, "Well, I guess she needs that herself right now. We'll just have to find something else for you to do instead. Maybe she'll come and tell you when she's through—would you do that, Keiko? That would be very kind of you."

Finally, it is important to show approval when you see children accepting and using these alternatives: "I'm sure glad to see you ask Dylan for that instead of biting him the way you used to—and he likes you better, too!" or "Well, that trade worked out pretty well, didn't it? Both you children got something you wanted." This makes the children more aware of what they are doing, and the positive reinforcement makes repetition of that behavior more probable.

Help Children Respond Generously

Children are more likely to feel generous about welcoming newcomers into their play or sharing equipment with them if they know that their own rights are protected. This is the reason many children's centers observe the rule that "You can keep something until you're done with it, but if you've stopped using it, then someone else can have a turn." This policy helps reduce the need to cling jealously and vigilantly to things lest they be arbitrarily taken away by the teacher. It also means that when children are finished and have had enough, they give the item up willingly instead of grudgingly. In other words, they are sharing because they *want* to, not because they *have* to. There is a world of difference in what children learn in those two circumstances.

Children should also be taught how to stand up for their own rights because this, too, is an aspect of being socially competent, and, paradoxically, children who know they can protect themselves are likely to be less defensive and protective of their possessions. For example, the teacher might encourage a child to defend himself by asking an indecisively whimpering 3-year-old, "Do you want her to take your buggy? Well, then, tell her you don't," or say to another child, "Hang on! You don't have to let him have that, you know. Tell him the rule!"

Generous behavior will be encouraged if the teacher occasionally points out to a youngster who has shared something that the other child is now feeling gratified and friendly: "Gee, you really made her feel good" or "Look how he's smiling at you. I think he's feeling friendly because you let him use that box." Perhaps a quick hug can be used to show pleasure in the child's altruistic behavior.

Finally, simply having enough equipment and materials to go around makes a difference that cannot be overlooked. As frustration increases, constructiveness in play decreases and nothing is more frustrating or breeds more closehandedness than having only enough blocks to build one tower or enough dough for tantalizing little fistfuls. It is not always necessary to have a large budget to provide plentiful amounts of materials and equipment. Many can be made or scrounged at reasonable cost if teachers and parents are willing to make the effort.

HELP CHILDREN MAKE FRIENDS

What Makes a Good Friend?

One of the reasons it is valuable to teach children to get along easily with other children is that they are more likely to have friends when they are able to do this—and even for children of preschool age, having friends contributes to happiness.

Although some may have the impression that friendships between young children are largely temporary and haphazard, teachers know this to be untrue, and studies of actual behavior bear this out as well (Axtmann & Bluhm, 1986; Dunn, 2004; Howes, Unger, & Matheson, 1992). It is obvious that in most groups there are children who prefer each other's company, as well as those who are more likely to be shunned or shut out of play.

Research has shown that children give several reasons for friendship, including liking to play with the child, nearness (propinquity), and possession of interesting toys to play with (Hayes, 1978). Some additional qualities that make a young child more likely to be selected as a friend include being physically attractive and acting friendly and outgoing (Hartup,

1983). On the other hand, Hayes (1978) reported that youngsters disliked children who were aggressive, behaved in unusual ways, or broke the rules.

Increase Children's Ability to Make Friends by Increasing Their Likability

Teachers can do simple things to help children form friendships. One is pairing children for special experiences. Asking a pair to help set up a cooking experience may lead to their cooking together afterward, for instance. Others include restructuring a car pool or suggesting that a family invite a child regularly to play after school. Sometimes finding a common interest helps generate a bond.

Occasionally, providing a clear explanation of how the child is offending other children becomes necessary: "You know, when you walk into the block corner and kick over their things, they feel really mad at you. That's why they won't let you play. Maybe if you got that truck, you could deliver some blocks when they need them. When you help people, they like you better."

As they help children make friends, teachers must realize that they can help with some factors but that others are part of the child's temperament. Some children, by nature, are quiet and less outgoing than others are and so appear to be less friendly. Some children seem to feel most comfortable with one or two good friends, whereas others manage well with a number of different playmates.

Learning to Control the Way They Express Anger

While taking temperament into account, teachers can do some things that may increase a child's likability. One of the most important of these is helping children learn to control the way they express anger because research confirmed by common sense and experience shows that other children dislike the perpetrators of hostile aggression (Gartrell, 2004; Levin, 2003). It is because learning to control the expression of hostile aggression is such a fundamental social skill that the steps toward acquiring self-control discussed earlier in the chapter are so important. The emphasis on fostering self-decision and self-regulation emphasized in those steps is intended to increase the child's ability to regulate his own behavior rather than relying entirely on the teacher to do that for him (Eisenberg, Fabes, Carlo, & Karbon, 1992).

Developing Alternative Ways to Get What They Want

Children who have developed a repertoire of alternative ways to get what they want are also less likely to resort to socially unpopular methods of snatch and grab and so are more likable. Generally speaking, increasing children's feeling of competence in any area helps them feel more confident, and this confidence helps them be more open, less defensive, and more friendly to others.

Valuing Others' Ideas

Help children learn to value and accept each other's suggestions. Really listening to everyone's ideas is a hallmark of the schools in Reggio Emilia and does much to foster friendly feelings among the children. No one is ever ridiculed or put down because of a suggestion, and the ensuing respect generated between the children helps them all feel valued and cordial toward each other.

The value of teaching such respect for others' ideas combined with an open-minded ability to compromise is also supported by some research from Trawick-Smith (1988), who investigated the actual leaders in a play group that he was observing. Defining *leadership* as having one's ideas accepted, he found that it was not the outspoken youngsters who forced their ideas on others or those who agreed to everyone else's ideas with no resistance who had the greatest success leading the group. Instead, to his surprise, he found that the children who accepted directives and suggestions from other children were also the ones whose ideas were most frequently accepted.

Help Children Cope with Rejection

Although all children experience occasional rejection and exclusion by others, sometimes more extreme cases occur. The child continually hangs around a particular child, and the harder he presses the issue, the more vehement the rejection becomes. After trying some of the alternatives listed previously, the teacher may just have to help the child accept the fact that a particular child does not want to be friends with him. There is no way to force such relationships. If he chooses to continue his wistful pursuit, that is his own decision, but the teacher can point out that other children are available to play with if he chooses to do that instead.

INCREASE THE CHILD'S ABILITY TO FUNCTION SUCCESSFULLY AS PART OF A GROUP

Use Play Situations to Help Children Develop Group Social Skills

Children learn a lot about getting along with people by playing with them (Frost, 2005; Frost, Wortham, & Reifel, 2005; Koralek, 2004; Levin, 2003). They learn what others will tolerate and what they will not, how to maintain a balance of satisfaction so that everyone has enough fun that they want to stay and play, when to give in, and when to assert themselves. Maintaining this delicate balance between compromise and getting one's own way is an essential social skill that seems to come more easily to some children than it does to others.

Playing with other children varies in accordance with children's age, temperament, and amount of social experience. Two- and 3-year-olds play more frequently by themselves or alongside each other, whereas older 3s and 4s play more frequently together, often instructing each other quite specifically in the roles they should assume ("You be the mommy, and I'll be your little girl"), stipulating conditions ("I'll play, but you don't give me no shots!"), and using their imagination to set the stage ("This stuff over here is the tree, and we're the lions who live there"). Twos and 3s tend to focus more on playing with objects and play materials, investigating their properties, sometimes investing them with imaginary play themes and sometimes not, whereas older 3s and 4s participate in more interactive dramatic play. Young children in elementary school have become adept at cooperative as well as competitive play.

Once play has begun, teachers should bear in mind the value of prolonging and extending the interaction so children benefit from maximum social experience. It does take a delicate hand to know when to intervene and when not to. Some inexperienced teachers tend to participate too fully by acting childlike or make themselves the center of attention or become the source of too many of the ideas, all of which rob the children of the initiative.

On the other hand, some teachers lean too far in the other direction and do not encourage the children enough, with the result that the play falls apart too quickly or lacks richness. These people should acquaint themselves with the landmark research by Smilansky and Shefatya (1990), which reports that intervention is particularly necessary with children from underprivileged families, who may lag behind in the development of their sociodramatic play skills and who need special modeling and encouragement in how to play to develop these skills more fully. Of course, limited richness of play may not be restricted to those children who are living in poverty. As more and more youngsters of all economic classes spend longer hours in front of television sets, their play may also require added support from teachers.

Such intervention may take the form of suggestions ("Perhaps you boys need a bag if you're going to go to the market. Let's see, I wonder what you could use?"), supportive comments ("You children are really busy in there" or "My goodness, little kitten, you *do* look snuggly—your mother is sure taking good care of you!"), or even direct participation and modeling ("Yum, yum, yum! Thanks for that delicious mashed potato cake! Should I feed some to the baby until you're not so busy?").

In general, if teachers remember that the purpose of intervening is not to dominate but to sustain and continue the play, as well as to foster positive social interaction among the children, they will not go far wrong.

Table 12.2 provides many suggestions for ways teachers can foster positive social interaction among children. Two areas of curriculum have been singled out to illustrate their potential for doing this. Actually, all areas of curriculum have equivalent potentials for positive and negative social learning. Consider what these might be when setting up each area—whether it be the block corner, the water play table, or the sandbox. Good planning facilitates desirable social learning.

Use Mealtimes to Foster Social Competencies

Sometimes we lose sight of the fact that eating together is one of the most profoundly social activities available to human beings. In many cultures around the world, the act of breaking bread together is a sign of peace and also lies at the heart of many celebrations. These lofty practices may seem far removed from a group of 3-year-olds spooning up fruit and yogurt. Yet, it is valuable for people working with children to keep the more profound social value in mind even while mopping up milk and showing children how to scrape their plates because it will help the adults remember that the fundamental goal of eating together is to have a congenial experience in which everyone is both physically satisfied and socially replenished.

Moreover, if well presented, mealtimes offer the best opportunity of the day to foster the feeling of home and family so important to young children and all too often missing from large child-care situations. This feeling of "familiness" can be generated not only by the overall climate of warmth and human interchange but also by attention to such details as serving food that is culturally familiar (note that *familiar* comes from the same root as *family*) and by encouraging families to participate in meals at school by occasionally having lunch with their youngsters or sending birthday goodies or sharing their surplus garden produce with the school (though there is a limit to the amount of zucchini even a center can willingly consume).

Creating a Climate of Intimacy and Calm

In addition to linking home and school, three other practices will help achieve a climate of easy comfort right from the start of the meal. First, the group at the table needs to be kept as small as possible. What should be avoided at all costs is putting all 15 or 16 children around one table with no adult present, because pandemonium results. The children have to wait too long for food to be passed to them, and there is almost no way to generate conversation in such bedlam.

Second, the food should be right there on the table, ready to be passed as soon as all the children are seated. The only drawback to this is that it may cool a little more than desired, but having a meal ready is infinitely preferable to nagging at children to sit still and stop tapping their cups or poking their neighbor until the food finally arrives.

Finally, it is very desirable for adults to be present and sitting down as the children come to the table. It is not the function of these adults to get up and run after sponges, go to the

211

Table 12.2

Ways to Increase Positive Social Interaction Among Children

Approaches Likely to Induce *Positive* Social Action	Approaches Likely to Induce *Negative* Social Action
Dramatic Play Centering on the Home	
Be prepared to suggest ongoing ideas from time to time when play appears likely to lag or fall apart. ("Hmmm, do I smell vegetable soup?")	Make the play area too small and congested so that the children get in each other's way much of the time.
Provide both male and female items to welcome both sexes and provide opportunities to try out other-sex roles. These might include shaving equipment, tools, wedding dresses, or boots.	Allow clothing or other equipment to accumulate on the floor so that the children stumble over it, mistreat it, or cannot find what they need.
Stimulate variety in the play by varying the equipment. Offer market supplies, hospital things, or the large blocks and boards.	Offer only female-type items, with the result that the boys feel subtly excluded. This makes attacks by the boys more likely.
Vary the location. Move equipment to a new area—perhaps outside or into a large bathroom for water play.	Do not set up the homemaking area before the children arrive. Leave it as it was the day before.
Include items that attract children particularly, such as water, several large empty boxes, or guinea pigs.	Provide no physical barriers, so that children who are passing through intrude either intentionally or unintentionally.
Foster cultural respect by offering multiethnic equipment, such as wooden bowls from Africa, a bedspread made of Guatemalan material, or dolls of various ethnic backgrounds, and speak casually, but respectfully, of such things as our "Mexican chair," our "Zambian bowl," and so forth.	Keep equipment skimpy so that children have to wait too long for a chance to use it.
Offer more than one piece of the same large equipment, such as two baby buggies or two suitcases.	Allow equipment to become broken or dirty. This tells the children that this play area and what happen there are not really important and that you do not care about them.
Split the housekeeping equipment into two households, and encourage the children to improvise additional needed items.	
Set up an office or a market in conjunction with the housekeeping area.	
To encourage role-playing, offer items large enough for the children to get into themselves, such as a regular high chair and a child-size bed.	
Increase the reality-information base of the play by having a baby visit, going to a real market, or actually visiting places where parents work to see what their mothers and fathers do there.	
Offer a simple cooking experience, such as making peanut butter sandwiches, in the housekeeping corner.	
Encourage more than one age to play together. This is fairly easy to do in housekeeping because of the variety of family roles that are available.	
Encourage the children to solve problems together. How could they turn the house into a camper? What could they use for bananas?	
Pay attention to the children's requests and ideas. This helps them feel valued and important and encourages children to listen to each other, also.	
When necessary, help new arrivals enter the group successfully by suggesting how they could help, what they could be, or what they might say to the children who are already playing there.	
Put all the regular equipment away and encourage the children to develop their own house, using blocks, boards, and accessories.	

Table 12.2
(continued)

Approaches Likely to Induce *Positive* Social Action	Approaches Likely to Induce *Negative* Social Action
Outdoor Large-Muscle Play:	
Whenever possible, select equipment that invites or requires more than one child's cooperative use for best success, such as double rocking boats, a hammock, large parachute activities, jump ropes, wagons, and horizontally hung tire swings.	Provide no focus for the play— let the children mostly just run around.
Offer several of one kind of thing, not only to reduce bickering but also to induce social play. Several bouncy horses together facilitate social congeniality, for example.	Keep the children indoors so long that they are pent up and desperate for physical activity when they do get out.
Provide plentiful equipment for dramatic play. In particular, a good assortment of blocks, ladders, sawhorses, and boards encourages the children to build things together. Smaller equipment, such as ropes, hats, and horses, also encourage this kind of social play.	Sit idly by. Offer the same kind of large-muscle activities every day. This lack of variety breeds boredom and fighting.
Think of the sandbox as providing an interesting social play center (particularly for younger children), and provide things to do together, such as a fleet of little cars or a good supply of pans and sturdy spoons and shovels.	Store equipment in inaccessible places so that it is difficult to get out and hence will not be frequently used.
Stay alert and aware of what is going on to provide input and control in time when it is needed.	Suggest competitive activities— who can run fastest, get there first, and so forth. This breeds ill feeling and hurt feelings.
Occasionally encourage more physically proficient children to teach less skilled children how to do something.	Encourage games with many rules. This baffles the younger children, increases frustration, and reduces spontaneity and creativity.
Encourage children to help each other—push each other on the swing, for example.	Permit the older, more powerful children to monopolize the equipment.
Review chapter 4 and apply what Kritchevsky, Prescott, and Walling (1996) have to say about developing complex and super play units rather than simple ones.	
Offer outdoor sand, mud, and water play whenever possible. This encourages peaceful social interaction for lengthy periods of time.	
Offer large-group projects that involve doing something together, such as painting a large refrigerator box to make something to play in, or gardening. This is not exactly play, but it is so much fun it feels like play to the children.	

kitchen for refills, and so forth. The sponges should already be available on the service trays, and children should be allowed the social opportunity of going for refills. The adults are present to help generate a peaceful, welcoming, happy atmosphere in which each child has the chance to talk with the teachers and friends and also the opportunity to help others by passing food, mopping up, and so forth.

Keeping Mealtime Policies Consistent with the Basic Educational Philosophy of the School

Nowhere in curriculum is the fundamental educational philosophy of the teacher revealed more plainly than in the way the food situation is handled.

Who makes the final decision on what to eat? Does the teacher decide by arbitrarily doling the food out on each plate and making the child eat everything? Or do the children decide by serving themselves and being allowed to go easy on food they do not like or are suspicious of?

Who passes the food around the table? Does the teacher move from child to child, or are individual children allowed to serve themselves and pass it on to their neighbors, learning social consideration by taking some and leaving some?

Who generates conversation? Is it always teacher centered, or does it become talk *between children* as a result of the adult encouraging that focus? Remember that conversation is thought to be one of the earliest (if not the earliest) forms of turn taking that children learn. Learning to allow space and time for others to reply is an intensely valuable social skill.

Use Group Time to Foster Social Competencies

Too often teachers think of group time as being primarily a time to read a book or two to the children, and books do have a valuable place in that activity, as discussed in chapter 16. But, in addition to the opportunities for language and cognitive growth inherent in group time, teachers should also use it to foster positive social interaction and learning (Gartrell, 2004; Harris & Fuqua, 2000; Levin, 2003).

This time of day offers excellent opportunities for children to become interested in other youngsters and what they have been doing. Perhaps someone has brought his pet mouse from home, or perhaps three or four of the children have just returned from seeing a poodle get its hair clipped at the groomer's. Such experiences are of genuine interest to children and delightful to share in the group. However, teachers get in trouble with having children share their experiences when they assume it is necessary to go entirely around the circle and have each child tell something each day. This takes too long, and instead of generating interest, this practice generates seething boredom because the children are pushed beyond their limits of self-control for holding still. Yet, if groups are kept small and experiences are shared naturally by different children on different days, group time can be interesting and can also provide another opportunity to value things from home at school.

Occasionally discussing social problems also fosters social learning at group time (Beaty, 1997b; Gartrell, 2004; Levin, 2003). For example, on the day before a new tricycle will be made available, the group might discuss how to work things out so that everyone will have a chance to use it, or they might discuss how to keep children from picking the tomatoes in the garden before they are ripe enough to eat. It is important that this kind of discussion not center on the past misdeeds of some small sinner in particular but focus instead on making a group decision that will bring about socially positive behavior.

The teacher who leads such a discussion should know that, as in many other aspects of child development, children's ideas of right and wrong (and hence their ideas of what constitutes justice) change as the child develops. She should not be surprised if the rules they suggest are quite severe, definite ones, because children of this age believe what is right is right and what is wrong is wrong. Their idea of justice is one of reciprocity, the eye-for-an-eye and tooth-for-a-tooth variety, so the teacher may need to help the children temper their suggestions with mercy. However, if such group discussions are not overdone, they can help children think about the effect individual actions have on the group as a whole and what should be done about it.

ENCOURAGE CHILDREN TO BE KIND TO EACH OTHER, HELP EACH OTHER, AND HELP THE GROUP

Encourage Kindly Actions

Encouraging children to be kind to each other is an important yet sometimes overlooked way to encourage positive social behavior and learning. Even though young children are largely self-centered in the sense that they see the world in terms of their own needs and point of view, they are also capable of offering comfort and help to other people if properly encouraged and if the example has been set for them in the past (Gartrell, 2004; Levin, 2003; McGinn, 2005; Miller, 2000; Smith, 1993).

Help Children Gain Insight into How Other People Feel

Many opportunities arise every day at the center for children to experience the satisfying rewards of taking kindly, prosocial action in someone else's behalf—action that usually involves being considerate of other people's feelings and making efforts to help them feel comfortable and/or happy.

To do that, children have to realize that other people feel differently from the way they feel, and they also must be able to think up kindly ways to respond to those different feelings. One way to help children develop these skills is to follow Beaty's (1997b) advice. She advocates asking a child directly, "How do you think he is feeling?" and then "How could you help him feel better?" Note that, as we discussed in chapter 11, this is very different from using the more confusing question, "What if you were him? How do you think *you* would feel?"

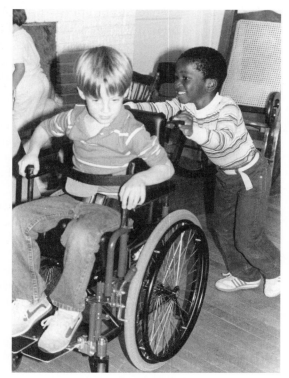

A simple act of unexpected kindness helps everybody feel good.

Encourage Children to Help and Comfort Each Other

Another approach, as exemplified in Smith's (1993) book *The Peaceful Classroom*, is to incorporate various activities into self-select or small-group time that sensitize children to being more compassionate and loving toward others. For example under "Kindness Skills," Smith includes skills related to caretaking, gentleness, helping, generosity, rescue/protection, and respect/encouragement. Once these are identified it becomes easier to generate activities for practicing them. A *gentleness* activity, for example, centers on handling pets in a sensitive way, and *caretaking* might involve making pinecone feeders for birds, or putting bandages on a scraped knee.

Doing meaningful work is a particularly satisfying *helping* activity. Some examples include almost any kind of cleaning up that involves water, such as scrubbing easels, doing dishes, hosing off sidewalks or sandy toys, scrubbing chairs, or washing doll clothes. Working by fixing things, such as repairing pages from torn books, breaking up dried potter's clay with a hammer so it can be moistened and reconstituted, sawing off the handles of paintbrushes that are too long, tightening tricycle seats, decorating the picture file box with collage, and putting up the swing seats in the morning are other possibilities. Still another kind of work that contributes to the well-being of the group might be fetching second helpings from the kitchen, taking old material down from bulletin boards, spreading out the plastic door mats on snowy days, helping set up cots, feeding the fish, or reassembling a puzzle that the teacher finds too difficult. When more than one child has to cooperate to accomplish a task, the value is even greater. Perhaps two are needed to fold the larger blankets, or several children can work together to wash the teacher's car or carry the housekeeping equipment outside.

These opportunities should be available every day and will be most enjoyed by the children if the teacher allows them to choose how they want to help, keeps the jobs short, is not too critical of the results, and remembers to say "Thank you" afterward. It is particularly valuable to help children enjoy their feeling of accomplishing something genuinely worthwhile, which means that the job cannot be "make-work." Children love the sense of competence that comes from hard work well completed. It is one of the finest avenues for building self-esteem while also contributing to the welfare of the group.

If not overdone, older children can benefit by helping younger ones at school. This willingness to help others, however, need not be limited to assisting younger children. The child who volunteers to open a door for a teacher whose hands are full or who helps his friend push a wagon up the hill is also demonstrating his ability to care for and help other people.

Children also feel very positively about caring for animals, and it is nice to give them this opportunity. Baby animals, in particular, elicit a kindly feeling in younger children, who are also likely to be concerned and critical about the quality of care the mother animal is providing.

Then, too, as early as 18 months of age children are quick to worry and feel concern when they see another child crying or when someone is hurt. If the teacher welcomes this concern and involves the child in providing comfort and fixing the small injury, this not only helps reassure him but also lets him experience the benefit of helping another child feel better.

SUMMARY

If we want children to learn to balance their own needs and desires with concern for those of other people, we must have a clear grasp of the most basic social skills to teach them so they will become happy, well-liked, social people.

Among the most important of these competencies is the ability to control unsocial impulses and use alternative ways of getting what they want that do not hurt anyone else. Short-term recommendations for controlling unsociable behavior involve six steps for establishing inner controls. These should be combined with longer-term policies including provision of centers that foster friendly interchanges, warning ahead of transitions, giving positive directions to children, and profiting from experience.

Children need friends, and there are many practical ways to increase a child's likability—one of the most important being the ability to listen to other's suggestions and incorporate them in the play.

Three group situations offer particularly fruitful opportunities for developing social skills: sociodramatic play, eating together, and small-group sharing and learning times. Finally, children should be encouraged to find satisfaction in helping each other and doing things to help the group as a whole.

Food for Thought and Group Discussions

1. Picking up the small blocks is often regarded as a real chore by both teachers and children. Suggest some things to do that would make this task more palatable and the children more cooperative.

2. Describe some situations you have recently seen at your center in which it was not necessary to intervene in an argument between two children.

3. This book talks quite a lot about fostering alternatives to physically aggressive action. Pick out some of the

more aggressive situations you have witnessed, and propose two or three alternative solutions that the children might have been encouraged to use.

4. Are there times when you now realize that you helped a child do something when another child might have helped instead?

Self-Check Questions for Review

Content-Related Questions

1. What is the rule of thumb about when to stop behavior?
2. Why is it important to be consistent in enforcing center rules?
3. List and discuss the six recommended steps for dealing with behavior problems. Illustrate each step with an example.
4. There are also many longer-term methods of building inner controls. What are some of those practical methods? Again, illustrate each with an example.
5. What are some things teachers can do that may help a child be better liked by the other children?
6. Discuss some ways teachers can foster social competencies in the children during play, group times, or at meals.

Integrative Questions

1. Sarah has just snatched some train track from Mia and is holding onto it fiercely while Mia is trying to tug it back. Both girls are crying loudly as they struggle. Describe how you would go through the six learning steps about discipline with Sarah, giving actual examples of what you would do or say. Then describe how you would use the situation to teach Mia what she needs to do next time.
2. Bullying behaviors include making fun of someone, ostracizing them, taunting them, or threatening them. Give a real-life example of each of these kinds of behavior.
3. Maggie and Michael are making dinner in the housekeeping area. Both children want to use the teapot to pour cups of water for the doll children. Give an example of an alternative solution—(1) a compromise, (2) a trade, or (3) a cooperative arrangement the children could use instead of fighting over it.

Coordinating Videotape

Building inner controls. Tape #9. *The whole child: A caregiver's guide to the first five years.* The Annenberg/CPB Collection, P.O. Box 2345, South Burlington, VT 05407-2345. *Building Inner Controls* provides the basis for guiding young children to control themselves and to find acceptable ways of expressing their aggressive feelings. Discipline management and aggression prevention techniques are described.

References for Further Reading

Picks of the Litter

Levin, D. (2003). *Teaching young children in violent times: Building a peaceable classroom* (2nd ed.). Washington, DC: National Association for the Education of Young Children and Educators for Social Responsibility. This is one of the best resources, full of practical examples, for teachers who wish to help children develop the inner controls necessary for positive social interactions.

Zarzour, K. (2000). *Facing the schoolyard bully: How to raise an assertive child in an aggressive world.* Buffalo, NY: Firefly. This is absolutely the best, most practical book available on this subject.

Overviews

Katz, L. G., & McClellan, D. E. (1997). *Fostering children's social competence: The teacher's role.* Washington, DC: National Association for the Education of Young Children. An excellent book offering practical classroom suggestions for enriching children's social development.

Maag, J. W. (2001). Rewarded by punishment: Reflections on the disuse of positive reinforcement in schools. *Exceptional Children, 67*(2), 173–186. Maag provides a first-rate explanation of negative and positive reinforcement strategies and makes practical recommendations about ways to implement the positive approach.

Building Inner Controls in Young Children

Gartrell, D. (2004). *The power of guidance: Teaching social-emotional skills in early childhood classrooms.* Clifton Park, NY: Delmar/Thomson and National Association for the Education of Young Children. This book offers a combination of sensible advice supported by a solid foundation of research.

Marion, M. (2003). *Guidance of young children* (6th ed.). Upper Saddle River, NJ: Merrill/Prentice Hall. Marion's book is filled with a sound combination of research, theory, and practical advice on this subject.

Corporal Punishment

Hyman, I. A. (1997). *The case against spanking: How to discipline your child without hitting.* San Francisco: Jossey-Bass. Written primarily for parents of school-age youngsters, this very good book is filled with practical advice about controlling adult anger and aggression and instilling self-control in children.

Paintal, S. (1999). Banning corporal punishment of children: A position paper: Association for Childhood Education International. *Childhood Education, 76*(1), 36–39. The title is self-explanatory.

Bullying and Children with Disabilities

Smith, P. K., & Sharp, S. (1994). *School bullying: Insights and perspectives.* London: Routledge. This book describes an

217

actual program instituted in some English schools to reduce bullying. It includes a chapter on bullying of children with disabilities.

For the Advanced Student

Brooks, R., & Goldstein, S. (2001). *Raising resilient children: Fostering strength, hope, and optimism in your child.* New York: McGraw-Hill. Written by child psychologists and directed at parents, this gem of a book offers practical suggestions that teachers can also use to teach and model empathy, create opportunities for children to act responsibly and compassionately, and help them build inner resources.

Related Organizations and Online Resources

National Association for the Education of Young Children (NAEYC) offers many resources related to children's social development. http://www.naeyc.org/

The National Youth Violence Prevention Center is a federal resource for teachers, parents, and youth to prevent violence against children. The Web site includes a comprehensive section on bullying and anti-bullying resources. http://www.safeyouth.org/

WHO AM I?
WHO ARE YOU?

Coming to Terms with Multicultural, Gender, and Disability Issues

Have you ever . . .

- Wished that you knew how to help a child feel better about herself?
- Wondered what to do about racial insults?
- Racked your brain for what you could do to reduce sex stereotyping in children?
- Wanted to welcome a child with a disability into the group but felt worried about how to do it?

If you have, the material in this chapter will help you.

In order to give other people the right or privilege of maintaining their own values, you have to confront what you do when those values conflict with yours. It's a two-layered process. One is to recognize what your own biases and belief systems are, and the other is to accept the possibility that they may not be right for everyone else. That's the hard one.

—Barbara Bowman (1995, p. 40)

To be truly culturally responsive, we must continually challenge ourselves to reevaluate and rethink our practice.

—Carol Copple (2003, p. 165)

As we continue to learn about the most appropriate ways to approach multicultural education in early childhood, new issues arise. Experts say we should spend less time thinking about holidays, food, and dress (the surface features or isolated activities of culture) and more time thinking about values, interaction patterns, and child rearing practices (the deep structural features of culture). As Carol Brunson Day (2000) said, "Let's worry less about teaching cultures to children, and more about teaching children in a culturally consistent context."

So far we have been talking about social competence in terms of the interpersonal social skills that families and teachers can help children develop. This chapter considers some additional aspects of social development that, though more subtle, are equally important. These include young children's perceptions of themselves, how those perceptions develop, and practical ways to foster a wholesome sense of self-esteem within them. Because children's awareness of other people also develops during this period, this chapter also discusses ways to cultivate positive feelings about ethnic and racial heritages, gender identities, and disabilities.

HOW DO YOUNG CHILDREN SEE THEMSELVES?

Harter (1999) reports that young children tend to see themselves in terms of concrete attributes related to what they look like (physical), what they can do (active), or how they feel (psychological). For example they will say, "I have blue eyes," "I can run real fast," "I have a brother named Kenny," or "I am happy." Or sometimes they define themselves in terms of preferences such as "I like pizza." What they do *not* do is integrate these separate aspects together into a coherent self-portrait. In other words, they are unable to put three statements together and arrive at an overall perception of how they see themselves.

In addition, Harter singles out two other characteristics that set young children's self-perceptions apart from those of older youngsters. Their self-descriptions are likely to "represent a litany of talents that may transcend reality" (1999, p. 38)—for instance, "I can count all the way to 100." Harter reminds us that this "overstated virtuosity" is not due to vanity or unseemly boasting but is only a normal stage of intellectual development: According to Piaget's findings, such young children are intellectually unable to keep their own performance in mind while comparing it to someone else's.

HOW DO CHILDREN DEVELOP A SENSE OF SELF?

Theories about how the sense of self—of who am I?—develops remains a matter of debate (Harter, 1999; Owens, 1995). In the beginning, it is thought that infants experience a sort of global oneness with their mothers and that an early task of infancy is to achieve a sense of separateness and a realization that the mother, as she comes and goes, continues to exist even when she is not within the baby's sight. As the infant gradually achieves this concept of mother separateness and continuing permanence, she also begins to sense herself as a separate, individual being. Piaget (1954) has called this sense of the "separate other" the concept of *object permanence*, and he regards it as being a fundamental prerequisite in the formation of later intellectual processes.

After infancy, children add to the sense of who they are by gaining identity from the people around them and becoming like them. This is the way children learn what constitutes basically acceptable ways for them to be and behave in their society.

Freud (1962) postulated that this process of identification initially resulted from children being dependent on their mother and wanting to incorporate their strength into themselves. He maintained that the child gains security by acting as the mother acts—switching, if a boy, at about age 4 to identify with his father instead. Identification, then, as Freud sees it, is a complicated kind of substitution whereby a child comes to think, feel, and behave as though the characteristics of another person were her own. In a sense, she becomes as the other person is.

Proponents of behaviorism, on the other hand, subscribe to a different explanation of how children achieve a sense of identity and become like the people around them. Their approach, as exemplified in the work of B. F. Skinner (1954, 1974), favors the idea that, once the genetic endowment has been set, the individual's behavior is determined by external events. Put very simply, pure behaviorists maintain that behavior is repeated only if it has been rewarded in some manner. Parents and other members of the larger society reward behavior they approve of, causing children to repeat it and gain a sense of how they should behave.

Albert Bandura (1977, 1986) makes use of this theory of behaviorism but also notes that some behavior is internalized by children even when external reinforcement for repeating it is not evident. He theorizes that children learn to be like adults in their society by observing them and imitating what they do, as well as by having their behavior reinforced. Apparently this kind of imitative learning takes place simply because children want to be like their parents, and this is a gratification itself.

Whether one subscribes to the Freudian, Skinnerian, or Banduran point of view, it is worth noting that all of them emphasize that adults are powerful influences in establishing the child's identity. Both Freud and Bandura stress that nurturing, attractive adults are the ones most likely to be imitated, and considerable additional research supports this contention (Baumrind, 1989; Harter, 1999; Kostelnik, 2004). The implications of these findings for us as parents and teachers, who are all strong power figures in children's lives, is that if we want children to identify with us so that they want to "do as we do," we should be as warm and nurturing as possible, as well as being good examples.

One more factor worth mentioning is not directly discussed in these theories but also helps children develop a sense of self and of how to behave in their society. That factor is direct instruction. It is worth pointing out to teachers because adults frequently use it. Teachers and parents often tell children directly what are the acceptable and unacceptable ways to behave. How often adults say in essence: "We just don't do that. We never hurt animals." "It isn't right to bite people!" "Our family always . . ." or "Our family never . . ."

To sum up self-development theory, after infancy children appear to gain their basic sense of who they are and what their place is in the world partly through the process of identifying with admired others and behaving as much like them as possible, and partly through conforming to the expectations of others to obtain their support and approval. Both these factors contribute to children's ideas of what it means to be a boy or a girl, what it means to be a member of a particular ethnic group—and even as early as 3 or 4 years of age, what they can look forward to becoming when they grow up. Witness this chilling statement from a

4-year-old who was asked what he would be if he were a girl: "A girl?" he asked. "A girl? Oh, if I were a girl I'd have to grow up to be nothing!" (Leifer & Lesser, 1976, p. 18).

And these attitudes do not necessarily change over time. In 1994, Sadker and Sadker reported that although 42% of the girls could see there would be some advantages to being a boy, 95% of the boys could see *no* advantage to being a girl. When they asked children how they would feel if they woke up and found they were members of the other gender, some of the boys replied, "If I were a girl my friends would treat me like dirt," and "I would *kill* myself *right away* by setting myself on fire so no one knew" (pp. 83–84).

But teachers and parents must realize that, in addition to these basic processes of identity development, many other factors contribute to children's developing sense of self as they become aware of the world outside their homes. These include many elements over which teachers and families may have little control. Current usage speaks of such influences as being part of the ecology of childhood (Brim, Boocock, Hoffman, Bronfenbrenner, & Edelman, 1975; Cortés, 2000; Werner, 2000). Bansavage (1978) quotes Brim as defining this ecology as "the natural setting of developing children—the types of families, the types of communities, the friendship groups, the characteristics of their schools, contact with the adult world and similar environmental factors" (p. 119). This focus is useful, not only because it helps pinpoint influences but also because it reminds us that we must not underestimate the significance of slums, television, the neighborhood children, family size and income, an urban or rural setting, persistent high levels of noise, overcrowding, climate, population density, and so forth, on the development of the children and their sense of who they are.

PRACTICAL WAYS TO ENHANCE CHILDREN'S FEELINGS OF SELF-ESTEEM

Beware of Overusing or Misusing Praise

If we define the sense of self as being the child's gradually developing idea of who she is, we can say that self-esteem is present when she feels this self to be valuable and worthwhile.

Many teachers think of self-esteem as being something they bestow on children by praising them or making them feel important, and it is true that merited praise and recognition are valuable ways of building self-esteem, because in the beginning these positive feelings come from outside the child. However, we certainly do not want children to remain eternally dependent on a constant barrage of "You're wonderfuls" and gold stars to feel good about themselves (Kohn, 1999, 2001; Wilt, 1996). Over a period of time, children need to develop feelings of self-worth and motivation that come from within rather than from outside themselves.

The question is: What can teachers do to help children depend less on external, extrinsic rewards such as praise and depend more on internal, *intrinsic* rewards for satisfaction?

For one thing, teachers should avoid praising a child by comparing her with someone else—either by saying, "I sure wish Cedric behaved as well as *you* do," or using her as an example to the other children: "Look how well Mariko is putting the blocks away!" At best, this kind of praise generates a priggish satisfaction in the praisee and dislike from peers. At worst, it violates some cultural attitudes of children from Native American and Asian backgrounds who have been taught never to stand above or surpass the accomplishments of their companions.

Another kind of praise to avoid is the gushing, insincere type. All this "blanket-type" praise does is smother children who soon learn that it really does not count for much.

When you do use praise, make it as specific as possible. For example, instead of telling a restless child, "You were a good kid at group time today," it is better to say, "You sat by Jose a whole 5 minutes without poking him at group time—that's terrific." This kind of praise has two virtues rolled into one: It singles out specific behavior, and, because it is specific, the child knows you *really* cared about him enough to see what he was actually doing. It also provides encouragement as well as recognition of accomplishments.

Show Children That You Respect Them as People

Showing a child respect may seem like a difficult or intangible thing to do, but, actually, teachers translate that attitude into real behavior in many ways every day of their lives.

Taking time to really listen without interrupting to what children are dying to tell you, respecting their opinions, honoring their choices when they have been offered a choice, and not talking about them as if they aren't there are all examples of respectful behavior.

Prevent the Use of Insults to Express Anger

In chapter 11, a big point was made about the importance of knowing what you are feeling and being able to say it out loud without hurting anyone else.

Now, it is time to consider a special aspect of talking about feelings—not hurting anyone else—because there is a vast difference between saying how you feel ("I'm really mad at you—you took my car") and verbally attacking someone else by calling them an inflammatory or racist name.

There are three reasons that insults like this must be stopped. The first, most obvious, is that it is an example of hateful prejudice that wounds the other person's feelings—just as it is intended to do. The second is that it lowers the self-esteem of the child who is insulted (Jalongo, 1999b).

The third reason for preventing such remarks is more subtle but is, in the long run, even more important: It is vital for children to know and admit to themselves why they are *really* angry. This is because we do not want them to displace their anger on a false reason. Arvin is not mad at Jeff because he is black, but because Jeff took his red car. If the teacher allows Arvin to substitute a false reason why he is angry, *the teacher is responsible for helping lay the foundation for further prejudice* by not getting to the heart of the matter. After all, Arvin has every right to be angry—Jeff *did* take his car.

For example, the teacher needs to say to Arvin, "I know you're mad at him, but we don't use mean words like that. We tell kids *why* we're mad instead [pause]. What did Jeff do that you don't like? "Well, tell him that—tell him you don't like it and want the car back."

Next he turns to Jeff: "Remember, Jeff, just because somebody says you're something doesn't make it true! You and I know you're a good kid [pause]. Did you like what he called you? Well, tell him, 'Don't you call me that! I'm a good kid!' [pause]. Why do you think he's really mad at you?" Well—tell him that. Say, 'You're just mad cuz I took your car.'"

Then, to both boys, the teacher says, "Now, how are you going to settle this fight?"

Provide Children with Skills So They Feel Competent

The child who is well coordinated and able to balance her way along a narrow wall or hang by her knees has a pleasant feeling of competence that "I'm good—I can do it," as does the youngster who can pull up her pants herself or carry the pitcher without spilling it. Acquisition of these skills requires that the teacher provide sufficient time and plentiful opportunities for practice and that he keep the level of challenge difficult enough to make things interesting, but not so hard that it scares children off from trying. If he also provides chances to carry out meaningful work and to help other people, as discussed in chapter 12, the teacher will enhance the children's feelings of mastery and satisfaction even further.

The goal in all these areas is to provide opportunities for children to feel successful so that they know deep inside that they are capable, adequate people.

Help Children Do Things for Themselves So They Feel Powerful

To paraphrase a better known statement, children should be encouraged to do things "of themselves, by themselves, and for themselves" to increase their autonomy and gain a positive sense of self. This is really another facet of competence. Allowing this independence to develop can be especially difficult for teachers of young children, because they must balance the children's needs for dependence and independence with their own need to keep the daily routines operating at a reasonable pace. It is not easy to tread the narrow path between lending a loving hand when it is needed so that children know we care and waiting quietly by when it is better for them to help themselves. Actually, waiting for a child to accomplish something by herself can be one of the hardest parts and most important skills in teaching. Even though teachers theoretically agree that the ultimate gains make waiting worthwhile, it may still be necessary for them to firmly remember this as they stand poised by the door while a group of 3s fumble endlessly with their sweater buttons.

Offer Creative Experiences

Early childhood teachers are generally quite strong in providing creative opportunities for children, although they do not always think of these as being esteem builders. Yet expressing ideas and feelings that come from within through the use of self-expressive materials can be a powerful source for enhancing self-esteem. Because creative activities are such esteem builders, it is particularly valuable to preserve the children's confidence that they are creative people so that this attitude and the resulting sense of personal worth can be retained in later life. What a pity it is that so many people, as they mature, come to feel apologetic and uncreative and close themselves off from one of the safest and potentially most rewarding avenues to self-satisfaction and self-esteem. Helping people retain the freedom to be creative probably is best accomplished by teaching children that the most important aspect of creating something is to be satisfied with pleasing themselves rather than other people. We will learn more about how to do this in chapter 14. In addition, the Emergent Curriculum in Action features throughout this text illustrate how using a wide range of self-expressive experiences enhances children's feelings of self-esteem. For instance, one can easily imagine how powerful and capable those 6-year-olds felt after designing their memorial for the World Trade Center victims of 9/11, as described in chapter 11.

STRENGTHEN CHILDREN'S POSITIVE BODY IMAGES

The whole subject of body image as it relates to people's sense of self is a fascinating one, and research reveals that children as young as age 5 or 6 are concerned about their appearance (Gilbert, 1998). Nor is it related only to feelings of attractiveness. Just being aware of the body and what it can do has been found to vary a good deal with different children. For example, it is necessary with some children to begin by teaching them to point to their eyes and ears and hair before going on to the fun of identifying eyebrows, cheeks, and ankles. Children also enjoy naming things inside their bodies, such as bones and blood. We even had one youngster who wanted to know where his gallbladder was.

In addition to developing body awareness by learning the names of various parts, we also want children to appreciate what the body can do and to gain skill in its control. Movement education is probably the best way of accomplishing this. It makes children aware of their bodies' position in space and relation to other people and objects, as well as encouraging them to devise creative ways of moving around in that space. Moreover, physical prowess is much admired by other children and becomes even more important in elementary school, where proficiency in games is a basic key to popularity. Chapter 9, which deals with the development of physical competence, provides many suggestions for helping children gain confidence and competence in controlling physical movement.

Finally, there is the whole delicate matter of what children actually think of their bodies. At such an early age, this is not often a conscious matter, although there is evidence that young children are already aware of the color of their own skin and other people's (Copple, 2003; Holmes, 1995), as witnessed by the little girl's remarks in the Chapter Spotlight later in the chapter, on pages 232–233. Nevertheless, even young children are affected by how attractive they feel they are and by the influence their physical appearance has on the way people respond to them.

Think how adults respond differently to the exquisite little girl with naturally curly hair, or the child whose nose is always runny, or the frail little boy with dark circles under his eyes. There is really no clear action teachers can take except try to see through the physical appearance of the child to the personality inside and encourage other people to do that, too.

It is not only physical characteristics that influence people's responses to children. Body postures influence responses and tell teachers a lot about how the child feels about herself. The child who shrinks behind her mother's skirts on the first day reveals more of her feelings than she possibly could with words. Often increased emotional and physical well-being is reflected in the easier, more open stance of children as the year progresses. Teachers respond continually to these physical signals, sometimes termed *body language*, just as children respond to theirs. Since these postures reveal so much about children (and adults), it would be wise for teachers to make a deliberate effort to take time to look closely at what the children's body language is telling them.

CULTIVATE POSITIVE FEELINGS ABOUT SEXUAL IDENTITIES, ETHNIC AND RACIAL HERITAGES, AND CHILDREN WITH DISABILITIES

Many principles of presenting curriculum intended to widen horizons and reduce negative attitudes apply equally well to nonsexist and multicultural education and to incorporating children with disabilities into the classroom. That is the reason a great deal of information is condensed into Table 13.1.

Be on the Lookout for Opportunities to Confront Bias of All Sorts

Although this chapter confines itself to discussing nonsexist, multicultural, and antidisability education, we must remember that many other kinds of prejudice also exist (Adams et al., 2000; Copple, 2003). Some people are prejudiced against old people (witness the dearth of elderly characters on television), while others assume that overweight people lack self-control, poor people are always dirty, or that early educators are "just babysitters."

Pacific Oaks, a college in Pasadena, California, has been a leader in advocating that even children as young as 2 or 3 years old should be presented with an antibias curriculum that actively takes a stand against all these forms of prejudice (Derman-Sparks, 1987, 1992, 1995; Derman-Sparks & the ABC Task Force, 1989; Derman-Sparks & Ramsey, 2006).

To make this both real and relevant, the antibias curriculum links such teaching to the children's lives and approaches the subject three different ways. To begin with, children are encouraged to explore physical differences and similarities. For example, Derman-Sparks (1987, 1995) suggests that 3-year-olds might be encouraged to note the differences in skin

Table 13.1
Creating Equal Learning Opportunities

Nonsexist Possibilities	Multicultural Possibilities	Special Needs Possibilities
Human Relations		
Employ teachers of both sexes who participate equally in the majority of activities; that is, the male teachers do not always supervise carpentry and female teachers do not always present cooking. Everyone pitches in to teach everything, clean up, take children to the toilet, and so forth.	Employ teachers from a variety of ethnic backgrounds. Make certain minority people are not relegated only to aide positions but are placed in positions of authority also. Children are shrewd assessors of such power rankings.	Make every effort to see past the exceptional to what is typical in the child, and treat her accordingly.
Know the families well, and be on the lookout for members who have transcended the gender barrier in various occupations (female police officers, male nurses) and ask them to visit and acquaint children with what they do.	Know the families well. Encourage them to share interesting customs and traditions with the children at school as they do with their children at home. This might have to do with favorite ethnic foods, holidays, trips, and so on.	If the child is accompanied by an aide or parent, integrate that person into the staff as much as possible. Encourage the person to relate to all the children.
Be sensitive to men who have custody of their children. Offer assistance when they want it, but do not treat them as curiosities or objects of pity or condescension.	Make certain that all families are genuinely welcome. Help people meet each other, pick up each other for potlucks, and plan together for workshops.	Be sensitive to family fears that their child is being rejected or that they feel blamed for the child's condition. Realize they are comparing their youngster to other more typical children in the group and are perhaps feeling pain as a result.
Arrange realistic visiting times at school when parents who work outside the home and siblings are free to attend—a Saturday morning play session, for example.	Remember that older family members are viewed somewhat as a culture apart in our society by some people. Make a point of including them and valuing their ideas and services.	Foster understanding and empathy in the children. Be truthful and matter-of-fact with other children about the child's disabilities.
Encourage children of both sexes to have access to the full range of their feelings (see chapter 11).	Visitors and field trips: Be on the lookout for people from many ethnic groups in a variety of occupations—particularly occupations thought of as professional or skilled ones. Be casual about this, but make sure children have a chance to become acquainted with such people.	Facilitate child–child relationships by encouraging communication and inclusion (provide techniques for talking with a child who is hard of hearing, explain to a partially sighted child what the children around her are doing so she can join in, etc.).
Visitors and field trips: It is worth mentioning once again that a point should be made of providing contacts with members of both sexes participating in a variety of occupations.	Take a small group and visit the homes of different families from time to time. This can emphasize both the things families have in common and special attributes, too.	
Many children have no idea what their parents do when they go to work. Take a few youngsters to visit so they can find out what both mothers and fathers do who work outside the home.	Take the children to interesting places with a special ethnic favor—the Greek delicatessen, the Chinese market, the Japanese kite shop.	

Room Climate and Environment

Use pictures that show both boys and girls doing active things—beware of sweet little toilet paper–type ads showing girls with kittens. Include pictures of boys in caring roles and pictures showing boys expressing feelings. Include pictures of fathers with children, mothers working outside the home, and so forth.

Follow a policy of "open toileting" (boys and girls using same bathroom together) to reduce clandestine sexual interests.

Manipulative materials, such as lotto games, puzzles, and block accessories, should be scrutinized to make certain they include men and women in a wide range of occupations. Make certain an equal number of boys and girls are pictured.

Offer boy and girl dolls and boy and girl dress-up clothes, and encourage both sexes to use all the equipment.

Use pictures that include children of all ethnic groups doing things the children in your school also do. (Incidentally, NAEYC offers a nice selection of multiethnic posters for sale using illustrations from *Young Children* covers.) Collect and use pictures of children in integrated groups doing things together.

Accumulate series of pictures showing how people of various cultures meet a universal need in a variety of ways—children taking baths in different ways, for example, or families eating together.

Make certain multicultural activities are consistently present throughout the curriculum and not confined to a week's unit on Indians or the Cinco de Mayo celebration.

Make certain pictures of older people in active roles are included. Beware of using only the grandparent stereotype.

Whenever possible, use furnishings and equipment at the school that come from a variety of countries—perhaps a Mexican child's chair in housekeeping or a bedspread from India with deer and elephants on it. Speak of these appreciatively to the children.

Manipulative materials, such as puzzles and block accessories, should include people from different ethnic groups.

Dolls of various ethnic groups should be consistently available. Take a good look at these—are they true to ethnic type or just white dolls with different-colored paint on their faces? Many manufacturers are guilty of this sort of racial insult.

Include clothing typical of various cultures. Point out which culture they represent. Children's clothes are particularly appropriate.

Use pictures of children and adults who have various disabilities—show them participating in familiar activities.

Make necessary physical adjustments in the room—ramps, pathways for wheelchairs, equipment on low shelves.

Adapt equipment to increase usability: puzzles with knobs on nonskid mats or carpet squares, brushes with handles enlarged with wrapped masking tape.

It may be necessary to keep arrangement of furniture more static than usual, and make certain the floor is kept clear of clutter.

Avoid offering equipment that stimulates unusual behavior (such as things that spin readily if a child with autistic behaviors is attending).

Include dolls with disabilities in the housekeeping corner.

Include books about children with disabilities.

Post important sign language words at strategic places in the room to facilitate their use by everyone.

(Continued)

Table 13.1
(continued)

Nonsexist Possibilities	Multicultural Possibilities	Special Needs Possibilities
Activities		
In general, encourage children of both sexes to try everything—involve girls in science and boys in washing up, for example. Encourage both sexes to engage in vigorous outdoor play, self-expressive activities, and blocks.	If the school operates on a bilingual basis, consider alternating days of each language rather than only translating back and forth.	Think of the child's abilities and be sure to include activities he *can* do easily and with satisfaction, as well as more challenging ones.
Occasionally keep a checklist to see if one area of the school is used more consistently by one sex than the other. Analyze why this is true, and attempt to correct it.	Foster children doing things together. When opportunities present themselves, pair ethnically different children together. Encourage intergroup mixing—sometimes, particularly when two languages are in use, children speaking the same language group together. Although this tendency is understandable, it is desirable to encourage children of all backgrounds to communicate as best they can while playing together. They manage surprisingly well.	Encourage children to include the child with the disability by finding him a role, helping him enter the group, etc.
Story time: Examine books with care. Train yourself to spot books that present boys as heroes and girls as passive admirers. Check bibliographies listed in References for suggestions of nonsexist books available for purchase. Check appendix D for guidelines on assessing books for sexist content.	Story time: Examine books carefully for racial stereotypes and overly quaint out-of-date presentation of unfamiliar cultures, and also make certain that a balanced collection of books is purchased representing as many different kinds of children and adults as possible. Include ethnic folk tales. Check bibliographies in References for suggestions of resources, and also check appendix D for assessment guidelines.	Story time: Encourage children who have vision or hearing problems or who need special control to sit close to you.
Music and dance: It may be necessary to call *dance* something else if boys have already learned to be wary of that "girl stuff." Widen the kind of material presented in dance so that it appeals to both sexes (see chapter 9).	Offer an occasional folk dance, keeping it simple and bearing in mind it takes considerable repetition for the children to learn it. Beware of perpetuating such stereotypes of ethnic dancing as putting feathers in the children's hair and dancing around doing war whoops.	Be particularly aware of including opportunities for intensified practice of skills—for example, many children with differing disabilities benefit from extensive language stimulation; children who are blind need plentiful opportunities for vigorous physical activity.

Take special scheduling needs into account. This might involve extra toileting, keeping routines very predictable, or providing for rest periods for children who become exhausted more quickly than is typical. |
| Make certain to use male and female singers, ranging from Pete Seeger to Marlo Thomas. Also listen to what the lyrics are saying. Some of them are surprisingly sexist. | | Invite adults with disabilities to visit and demonstrate their prosthesis if they are comfortable doing this. Ask them to visit several times and involve them in attractive activities with the children. |

Cooking: Although books on nonsexist education keep stressing that boys should participate in cooking, there are few schools in which this kind of participation is a problem. If it *is* a problem, boys should be deliberately drawn in to participate.

Blocks and other three-dimensional construction activities: For reasons described in the section titled "Foster Positive Attitudes Toward Gender Roles," it is particularly valuable to encourage girls to use blocks more frequently than they may have done in the past.

Do not shun the music used in the children's homes. Popular music is very much a part of many families' culture.

There are many excellent folk music records available from all sorts of cultures and suitable to use with young children. Ella Jenkins, for instance, has made a rich contribution to this area. Some resources for these are included in the References.

Cooking: This is a wonderful way to learn to value other cultures as we discussed in chapter 8. Make certain ethnic food is not presented as peculiar or unappetizing. Remember, cooking can include going to specialty markets, cooking with culturally correct utensils, and eating in culturally appropriate style, such as using china spoons to eat egg noodle soup.

Provide experiences using assistance equipment, such as crutches, wheelchairs, and hearing aids for all the children to use.

colors among children in their group, matching those colors with paint or crayons; hear and talk over a related story; take color photos of children and staff; and make a poster of the different colors of their skins.

As opportunities arise, other situations that have a potential for confronting bias can be included. Children can try out a child's crutches, for example, and then list all the things they do that do not depend on running around.

The second approach advocated in the Pacific Oaks antibias curriculum is to explore cultural variations and integrate material into the curriculum based on the cultural backgrounds of the children in the group. This might include cooking favorite family foods, sharing accounts of trips back to Mexico to visit relatives, or comparing hairstyles. Books that reflect stereotyped ethnic or sex roles can be read and then discussed—the teacher may ask children whether it is true that only men can be police officers or only women can take care of children.

Finally, the antibias curriculum of Pacific Oaks suggests that children learn to take direct action that challenges stereotypes and discriminatory behavior. For example, one group wrote a letter to a bandage manufacturer protesting the use of the term "flesh colored" to describe its product, and another group scrubbed offensive graffiti from a playground wall. Direct action of this kind, providing it is developmentally appropriate, empowers children and teaches them they can take an active role in protesting unfair or biased behavior.

FOSTER POSITIVE ATTITUDES TOWARD RACIAL AND CULTURAL BACKGROUNDS

All too often it appears that teachers think of multicultural education only in terms of using integrated pictures in their rooms or making certain that the books they are reading to the children are not racially biased or that tortilla making is included as a multicultural experience. No one denies that this approach has value, and some suggestions for incorporating such ideas into the curriculum are included in Table 13.1.

What is disturbing is that some teachers fail to understand that the real purpose of offering multicultural materials should be to foster positive attitudes in children about their own and others' racial and cultural backgrounds. The purpose, then, of inviting a Mexican mother to help the children make tortillas is not just to teach them that tortillas are made of a special kind of cornmeal called *masa harina* or that Mexican people eat tortillas and that tortillas taste good. The purpose is to provide a real, involving experience that is so much fun for the children that they attach pleasant feelings to being Mexican and eating Mexican food. In other words, making tortillas is merely the medium through which the message of positive respect for someone's culture is conveyed.

Attitudes Are Caught, Not Taught

Because it is attitudes that matter most and children can sense teachers' feelings so keenly, teachers must search their own hearts and monitor their behavior to make certain that they are controlling the expression of their prejudices as much as possible. Of course, everyone prefers to believe they do not possess any prejudices, but it is more probable than not that we all possess feelings of prejudice in some area (Derman-Sparks & Phillips, 1997; Van Ausdale & Feagin, 2001). For example, studies reveal that some teachers do not believe that Latino children are capable of academically demanding work and that instructional programs for such children tend to be remedial (Artiles & Zamora-Durán, 1997). The effects of segregation and prejudice on the self-esteem of various groups including African Americans, Latinos, and Native Americans have also been well documented (Adams et al., 2000). Finally, after the terrorist attacks of 9/11, only about 5% of the elementary teachers interviewed in one study said they would be willing to teach children that not all Muslims were terrorists (Hoot, Szecsi, & Moosa, 2003).

Although it may not be possible to overcome deep-seated feelings of prejudice entirely, it is still valuable to know they exist inside oneself because once bias is recognized and "owned," it can also be controlled. Every time a prejudiced remark is suppressed, a tiny blow for fairness has been struck.

For those who wish to go further and weed such uncomfortable feelings from their hearts, a fairly effective way of overcoming prejudice is to learn more about people of other groups by taking courses on their culture—but getting to know them personally is best of all. Attempting to learn their language reduces the feeling of distance. Some local groups also work toward the goal of increasing racial understanding, as do presentations at educational conferences.

Remember, Families May Not Always Cherish the Same Values You Hold Dear

There is increasing recognition in the past few years that teachers do not always know what is best for every child, and so we must understand and incorporate the cultural values of the home if we intend to provide a truly multicultural environment. We must recognize that sometimes these values differ from our own and that we may need to reconsider our own convictions from time to time (Barrera, Corso, & Macpherson, 2003; Gonzalez-Mena, 2004; Gonzalez-Mena & Shareef, 2005; Grieshaber & Cannella, 2001; National Association for the Education of Young Children, 1995).

The question is: Once differences between home and school are recognized, what can we do about them? There are some times when parenting styles are in direct conflict with what we know is best for children. For example, just because a family advises the teacher to "slam him one when he don't behave" does not mean that the teacher should do that at school. Teachers must be committed to working through differences with families and communication is always key. According to Gonzalez-Mena and Shareef (2005), trying to reach a compromise is less important than trying to refrain from judgment and attempting to gain a deeper understanding of others' points of view.

Help Children Learn That Everyone Has Some Things in Common

Young children need to learn that people of every ethnic background have some human needs and characteristics in common: Everyone needs shelter, rest, and food; everyone's knees hurt when they get skinned; everyone bleeds when cut; and everyone's blood is the same color (Derman-Sparks & Ramsey, 2005). Children can begin to gain an appreciation of these truths from such simple activities as leafing through a scrapbook of pictures showing children of various cultures all sleeping, but sleeping in all sorts of beds, ranging from hammocks to trundle beds.

Be aware that, although matters have improved somewhat in regard to multiethnic materials, many manufacturers still seem to interpret "multiethnic" to mean only African American. It is still very difficult to find educational materials that picture people with accurate Latino, Japanese, or Native American features. Even many of the "black" materials are just white faces painted a different color. Multiethnic books also require careful evaluation and selection.

Learning will be even more meaningful if the group is a racially integrated one, because opportunities to teach about common needs and likenesses abound when children are together.

Sometimes teachers who feel quite comfortable when teaching about similarities are confused about whether to teach children that people are not completely alike. They seem to fear that mentioning cultural diversity, sometimes termed *teaching cultural pluralism*, encourages the formation of prejudice or that it somehow "isn't nice" to talk about such things. Perhaps these teachers hope that if they avoid mentioning differences, the children will not notice them—but this is not true.

Considerable research reports that children as young as age 3 are aware of the skin color of African and Mexican Americans (Edwards & Ramsey, 1986; Holmes, 1995; Ramsey, 1995; Wardle, 1999; York, 1998a, 2003). Beuf (1977) states that this is also true for preschool Native American youngsters of the Southwestern and Plains tribes. Moreover, as children become older, awareness of ethnic group differences increases (Ramsey, 1995).

Because children do become aware of racial differences between people during their early years, it is only reasonable to conclude that teachers should be prepared to deal with questions about such differences in a positive way so that children learn to view diversity as a valuable part of being human (Derman-Sparks & Ramsey, 2005; Gonzalez-Mena, 2004).

The Chapter Spotlight illustrates how one teacher helped a child appreciate this truth as it relates to ethnic diversity. As this example demonstrates so clearly, the closer to home we can bring cultural diversity and richness to the actual lives of the children in our

CHAPTER SPOTLIGHT

You Mean You're Black All Over?
A Student Teacher's Lab Experiences with "Isabella"

My experience in the lab was an interesting and memorable one. I was brought very close to a 5-year-old girl named Isabella. From our relationship, the impression I received is that she had never been in any contact with Blacks at all in her life.

My first contact with her was in the locker room. Isabella and Lynn were finger-painting, and they had put it all over their faces. Afterwards I helped them wash up. Isabella then said, "You're a Black, you have Black hands."

I replied, "Yes," and that was the end of it. She didn't make any further comments for a while.

One day I sat down at the puzzle table with her and watched her complete a puzzle. She asked, "Were you born Black?"

"Yes, and my mother and father are Black, too."

She seemed shocked that I had parents, "You have a mother and father?"

"Yes, I also have a son, too, Isabella."

"Is your baby Black, too?"

"Yes."

Another day I wore my wig, and she was the only child that really noticed my hair was different.

"Why is your hair curly?"

"I'm wearing a different hairstyle today."

A week later I wore a semi-Afro hairstyle, and she said, "Why did you wear your hair like that?"

"I like it this way."

"I don't like it."

Every week or so I would change my hairstyle, and every single time she always noticed the change. She might say, "Your hair looks different," or "How come you changed your hair?"

During all this time I had been telling Mrs. W. about this situation, and she later had a conference with Isabella's parents on their daughter's new discovery. After the talk Mrs. W. informed me that Isabella's mother had bought her a Black doll and said she was going to buy some books with Black people in them.

A few weeks later, Isabella and some other girls were in the locker room switching clothes, and I had come out of the bathroom buttoning up my pants. My blouse was up enough that she could see my stomach. Isabella went on to say, "You have on nylons."

"No, I don't. See, I'm wearing knee socks," as I pulled up my pants leg so she could see. All the other girls just sat and listened.

"Oh, you're Black all over!"

"Yes, I am." I was totally shocked by her statement. I took it for granted that she knew I was Black all over. From here on in it was definite to me that she knew absolutely nothing about Blacks. She did not seem to correlate the Black doll to human Black people, which means children need concrete evidence at times.

When we left the locker room, she asked me to help her zip up the jump suit she was wearing. She watched me intensely as I zipped it up. Out of the blue she said, "Some are Black, huh?"

I didn't want to put any ideas in her head so I asked, "Some of what are Black?"

"Some skins are Black."

"Yes, they are, and some are White."

This statement showed me that Isabella's parents had been talking to her about Black people at home.

Many times when the class was outside on the playground, she would run past me and hit me on the arm and say, "Hi, Black."

And I would reply, "Hi, White." This did not affect her one bit.

Toward the end of the semester the class was being split up into four reading groups, and the children were assigned to different teachers every day. While they were assigning them she yelled out, "I wanta go with the Black."

During this same week my neighbor had cornrowed my son's and my hair. I came to school the next day and many of the children made many comments.

"Why did you wear your hair like that?"

"What happened to your hair?"

"I don't like it that way."

"How did it get like this?"

And Isabella, to my surprise, said in a cool and calm way, "That's how Blacks wear their hair, huh?"

"Sometimes," I answered.

"The next day I brought my son to the lab, and again the children noticed his hair was just like mine. Mrs. W. asked Isabella if she had seen my son.

She replied, "Oh, yeah, the Black down there." She didn't really come around him much, but came over to the block area and said, "Your baby is Black, too," and left.

One more thing she said that I almost forgot was on a day I was head teacher and I was pinning on children's name tags. She hung around the table for a long while talking to me, at the same time keeping her face real close to my face whenever she got the chance. With a puzzled look on her face, she stuck out her lips and without sticking them back in their normal position she asked me, "Why do your lips stick out like this?"

Not really knowing how to answer her question, I said, "That is the way some Black people's lips are made."

Thinking about what she had asked me, I asked her why did her lips stick in. She answered, she didn't know why. She hung around a little bit more, examining my face, and then left to get involved in an activity.

At a picnic I wore my wig again and she ran past me and said, "You got curly hair," and kept on running past.

One thing that sticks in my mind about the whole thing is that there was not any trace of viciousness in any of Isabella's comments. She never felt I was inferior compared to herself, which I felt was excellent, because many times I have come in contact with many White children, outside the lab, that are either frightened to death of Blacks or have some negative comments to make, which they probably picked up from their family or the street. I honestly believe she was very fond of me, and I too was very fond of her.

Isabella's mother talked to me one day and expressed she was embarrassed about the whole situation. I told her not to be, for Isabella had never tried to hurt my feelings. She went on to tell me that she had never been in contact with Blacks until she was in college, at the age of 20. She later went to teach at an all-Black elementary school.

"I was so amazed by these Black children that I went around patting all their heads. And they are so rhythmic. But all in all I feel that you have been a great help to our daughter."

When she said that the children were "so rhythmic," I thought I would die. She sounded so typical of this day and age.

Since this situation has happened here and I know it has happened elsewhere, I hope it will help the present educator and future educators to see the importance of having multiethnic teachers and multiethnic education, for these types of children need to be exposed to people and cultures outside their own, along with this preschool experience. It is sad to see these same children go into adulthood and get jobs where they have to deal with society on the whole and not have any insight into any other race of people than themselves. I cannot see how they can represent all the people when they know nothing of all the people.

In conclusion, it was a good experience for me and I hope it was for Isabella also. I wish her all the luck in her future experiences and hope she keeps her beautiful curiosity and accepts all the new information as openly as she received my differences.

Note: The child's name was changed to protect her privacy. Thanks to the author, Reba Gordon, as well as to Helen Ross and Mary Warner of San Diego State University for sharing this material from their classes.

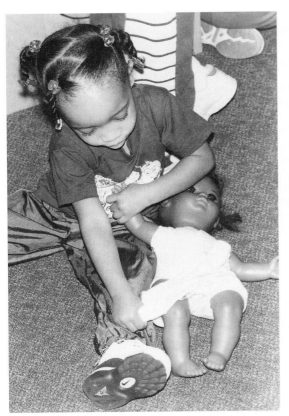

Although pictures, books, and equipment reflecting the ethnic heritage of the children are desirable to include, the most important ingredient in any cross-cultural curriculum is fundamental respect for every individual.

schools, the better will be our chances of substituting understanding and appreciation in place of prejudice. We do this in part by teaching each child that her own family and culture are worthwhile and in part by helping her enjoy the contributions of other families and cultures.

For instance, it can be interesting during holidays such as Thanksgiving to talk about the different ways families celebrate. Do they have friends in or go to their grandparents'? Do they have mincemeat or pumpkin pie? How do some Native American families feel about celebrating this day? Is there a special way their family celebrates birthdays? Are there religious occasions, such as Hanukkah or Ramadan, that the family observes and would be willing to tell the other children about (Bisson, 1997; Fitzjohn, Weston, & Large, 1993; Gonzalez-Mena, 2004)? Might some of the children be invited to a home for a Japanese bath, or might a Hopi youngster be encouraged to bring some of his or her kachina dolls and tell the children about the characters they represent? Perhaps grandparents would come and tell stories to the children about what it was like when they were little ("You mean you didn't never even have television?"). All these opportunities have the potential for convincing a child that her own cultural background is interesting and admirable, and they also help children see youngsters from different cultural backgrounds as being special and having special things to share with the group.

Use Comparison to Demonstrate the Positive Aspects of Cultural Pluralism

Cultural comparison activities can be added to a multicultural curriculum. These activities are intended to show the children that there is more than one way of reaching a common goal and that these ways are equally satisfactory. They provide opportunities for real involvement and for positive comparisons to be made, too.

Some of the comparisons can be quite simple, others more elaborate—but all should encourage young children to compare their culture with another culture in a participatory experience, see the advantages of each, and enjoy them both. These activities could include making the following comparisons:

1. African American hair care with Anglo hair care

2. Cooking methods and eating styles of the West with those of Japan

3. Children's undergarments from the West with those from China

4. The open market of Jamaica with the supermarket of the United States

5. White bread (made into "French" toast) with Indian fry bread

6. A futon with a sleeping bag

Children love participating in these types of experiences, and the adults benefit, too. Our own horizons widen as we learn about the customs of other groups so that we can present them in an authentic way to the children.

Support Multicultural Learning Through Play

Play presents delightful possibilities for including multicultural materials and instilling positive attitudes about ethnic and cultural differences into the lives of children. For instance, the multicultural addition one week might be Hawaiian clothes in the dress-up area. These should be introduced casually to the children: "Aren't these pretty? You're welcome to put them on. Leilani's family is sharing these for the fun of it this week. Did you know that she was born in Hawaii?" Or a hammock from Guatemala could be hung outside, and as the children enjoy swinging in it, the teacher could explain that it comes from another country, Guatemala, where it is so hot that people sleep this way to stay cool. He might say, "See, the air comes right through when you swing. Isn't that a practical idea? And it's fun, too."

Another aspect of multicultural play is the occasional problem encountered by teachers who have groups of children from different cultures in the same room. Of course, it is understandable that children who speak the same language find it convenient to play together. Sometimes teachers appear to make no effort to encourage the children to intermingle as they play. In fact, they sometimes seem completely unaware of the split in the group. However, children can and *should* be encouraged to overcome language barriers while playing, as well as while participating in more structured situations. A child does not have to speak fluent English or Spanish to enjoy building a block tower with another child, and the noises little boys make while pushing toy cars around the sandbox appear to stem from some universal reservoir of language.

Teachers should search for multicultural learning possibilities and encourage play among all the children whenever possible. Children are basically friendly, and teachers who provide tactful encouragement add one more building block to the bridge of interracial friendliness among people.

FOSTER POSITIVE ATTITUDES TOWARD GENDER ROLES

We all know there are physiological differences that make each sex unique, and it is necessary to help children understand genital characteristics and cherish their inherent sexuality, as discussed in chapter 10. The ability to feel good about his or her sexual role as it relates to procreation and childbearing should be a fundamental element in every child's sense of self.

Nonsexist Education

In addition to valuing the sexual aspects of the self, teachers should attempt to widen the horizon of both boys and girls so that they are no longer constrained and limited in their ideas about what activities are appropriate for children of either sex. This is what nonsexist education is all about. It teaches that people have many abilities, as well as needs, in common, no matter what their gender. Girls and women are encouraged to do things formerly the sole prerogative of boys and men, and vice versa.

At its best, nonsexist education opens new avenues for both boys and girls and helps them be complete, whole people. For example, girls are encouraged to see themselves as possessing a variety of potentials in addition to being wives and mothers, and boys are urged to remain sensitive to their caring and emotionally expressive side—a side that, in the past, our culture has frequently taught them to repress.

Many sexist attitudes are conveyed to children by their environments, as well as by other people's attitudes and behavior, and children's centers and schools can make a positive contribution by being aware of this (Crawford, 1996; Fagot, 1994; Mercurio, 2003; York, 1998a, 1998b, 2003). Although our schools are generally quite open to both sexes in offering such activities as outdoor play or cooking, there is still a long way to go in building sensitivity to the content of books, which continue to show a preponderance of boys as heroes taking an active role in stories and girls taking more passive ones (Wellhousen, 1996).

Inspection of many equipment catalogs also supports the claim that the majority of toys and teaching materials related to occupations continue to be sexist. For example, those stand-up cutout models of people frequently used in the block corner teach all too well the lesson that girls are nurses, teachers, and mothers and that boys are doctors, police officers, and motorcycle riders.

Moreover, teachers (often unintentionally) foster such attitudes, too. Many young female student teachers approach the carpentry table with trepidation. Although it is true that such an activity requires careful supervision, there is little reason for it to arouse the degree of concern and even distaste often reflected on their faces. They often protest that the children will hurt themselves with the saws or hammers, but more likely, they are the victims of their own previous sexist education. It may be necessary time and again to entice the adult students, as well as the girls and boys, to use carpentry materials. Otherwise, they may help perpetuate this particular kind of instrumental incompetence in the next generation. (Chapter 14 provides information on effective ways to present carpentry to all the children in the group.)

To encourage a variety of role models, do your best to encourage men to participate at the center. Unfortunately, the preponderance of early childhood teachers is overwhelmingly female. Boys find themselves in a predominantly female environment and we must take care that male needs and perspectives are taken into consideration (Gartrell, 2005; Sandberg & Pramling-Samuelsson, 2005). Sometimes this is as brief as asking fathers to schedule an hour in the morning once a month when delivering their child and stay to share a book or an interest with whomever is interested. Sometimes older male volunteers can be included on a weekly basis. Of course, when it is possible to employ male staff members, this is even more satisfactory because of the regularity and consistency of their contact with the children.

Suggestions from Research That May Enhance Nonsexist Teaching

Research also provides suggestions for ways to reduce sexist practices in addition to simply encouraging cross-gender activities. A classic study by Honig and Wittmer (1982) documented that toddler boys more frequently used negative ways to elicit responses from teachers than the girls did. The caregivers, in turn, responded to this behavior from boys proportionately more often. Thus, the boys' less desirable behavior was reinforced by the caregivers' attention in such circumstances—and so perpetuated itself. There is much value in recommending that teachers make more of a point of responding to the *positive* behavior of boys.

Another study reveals that parents of both sexes interrupt girls when they are speaking more frequently than they interrupt boys (Grief, 1980). And the same behavior was found to be true of women teachers when they were observed talking with 4-year-old boys and girls during snack (Hendrick & Stange, 1991). Not only did the boys interrupt the teachers more frequently than the girls did and were not corrected for doing this, but *the teachers interrupted the girls much more often than they did the boys.* One may well ask what boys and girls learn from such subtle but consistent responses. Quite possibly, the boys are learning that it is their role to be heard without interruption and also that it is acceptable for them to be assertive and interrupt adults, or at least female adults, when they wish to do so. And what of the girls?

A full-spectrum curriculum makes certain that participation in all activities is encouraged for all children.

What might they be learning? As modeled by a wide variety of teachers, that role was to accept being interrupted more and also to interrupt less themselves when talking with males. Because what they had to say was treated with less respect, they may also have been learning that they are less important than their male counterparts.

Finally, a series of studies by Serbin (1980) indicates that there are some three-dimensional materials, such as blocks, that are generally preferred by boys. It is believed that using these materials contributes to the ability to solve the kinds of cognitive problems that require spatial visualization. (Visual-spatial ability is the ability to picture in the mind's eye how to rotate an object or mentally transform its shape. Remember those items on intelligence tests that ask you to predict how many blocks there are in an irregular stack or whether a hand seen from an unusual angle is the right or left one?) As Serbin points out, these visual-spatial skills are the ones most needed by people who become pilots, engineers, physicists, and architects—all fields in which few women currently excel. The question yet to be answered is: If girls used these materials more often, would their visual-spatial skills increase? And would new fields of endeavor be open to women as a result? Although we do not know the answers to these questions, we can reasonably assume that it would be worthwhile to encourage girls to play with blocks more often. Perhaps this early experience would help equalize their chances; certainly it could do no harm.

FOSTER ACCEPTANCE AND UNDERSTANDING OF CHILDREN WHO HAVE DISABILITIES

Nowhere is the teacher's own attitude more important or infectious than when he is welcoming a child with a disability into his group. Frequently that attitude is an uncomfortable mix of apprehension and uncertainty combined with the good-hearted willingness to do one's best—if only one knew what "the best" was!

To complicate matters further, not only must the inexperienced teacher cope with his own feelings, but he must also help the children in his group and the newcomer and the newcomer's family come to terms with theirs as well.

The Place to Start: Identify and Face Possible Feelings About Associating with a Person Who Has a Disability

Until quite recently, it has been true that children and adults who had disabilities spent their lives in relatively segregated circumstances, but, as we have pointed out in previous chapters, this is no longer the case. We must realize that the previous segregation had a two-way effect: It not only isolated the disabled person from contact with many other people, but it also isolated so-called normal or "differently abled" people from contact with our disabled peers. Many of us have known hardly anyone who has a disability, and for that reason we are uncomfortable and apprehensive when we meet them because we do not know how to behave. Indeed, we may even feel aversion or distaste when coming in contact with them. Or, possibly, we feel pity mingled with a certain relief we are not so afflicted ourselves. Because feelings like these are not attractive, many of us prefer to deny their presence, but it is more emotionally healthy to get them out in the open and confront ourselves about them. Doing this allows us to cope rather than use up energy attempting to conceal them from ourselves and other people. It is hoped that gaining insight into ourselves will help us appreciate how the children in our group may feel, too.

Familiarity and Information Can Help Overcome Initial Feelings of Apprehension

This holds true for teachers, families, and children. Whether the group should be prepared in advance about the new child remains an open question. Does the teacher follow that practice for all newcomers? Is there something so unusual about the child's appearance that it will cause a lot of immediate curiosity? Or should explanations be provided gradually and more casually as the need arises? Specific circumstances will dictate different answers to these questions at different times.

When questions do come up, of course, it is important to be truthful: "Ben's ears don't work very well. He'll hear you better if you stand right in front of him and make sure he's looking at you before you say something to him." "I know you told Marcella before not to grab your brush and she keeps doing it—it takes Marcella longer to remember things like that. Hold on to the brush, and tell her 'I'm using this one.' Then hand her another one instead."

One question children are likely to wonder about, particularly in the case of highly visible disabilities, is how the child got that way. Sometimes they are fearful the same thing might happen to them. Once again, the truthful, simple answer is best: "He was born that way—some people are," or "She had an accident," or—and this is often the case—simply "I don't know!" Explanations, of course, need to be combined with reassurance that things like that don't happen very often and that there are always ways to help the person overcome the disability.

Encourage Sensitivity to Other People's Feelings

Even young children know how it feels to have someone hurt their feelings, and they can learn to be sensitive to the effect cruel remarks have on the feelings of other people, also. "When you tell Nick he walks funny so he can't play Power Raiders, it makes him feel bad. Remember when Shawntel said your shoes were weird? You felt bad, and we asked Shawntel not to say that again. Well, that's how Nick feels now. His feelings are hurt. I agree he can't run fast with those braces on, but isn't there some way he can play? Maybe he could be a motorcycle rider instead. There's a trike over here that nobody's using."

Above all, remember to be on guard for signs of rejection by the other children. Do your best to counteract that behavior or prevent it before it occurs. The basic point to emphasize firmly is that a child who has a disability is a lot like the other children—more like them than different from them. *Everyone* is better at doing some things and not as good at doing other things—and accompany that statement with examples.

Do Everything Possible to Integrate Children with Disabilities into the Group

Positive attitudes are certainly an important aspect of welcoming children with disabilities into the group, but we must realize that attitudes are not enough. Once the child is admitted, it is very important to make certain that she is genuinely included in as many activities as possible—and this requires constant monitoring on the part of the teacher. Otherwise, many of the children will either ignore her or, sometimes, regard her as an irritating intruder if she lacks the social skills they have come to expect. True inclusion must go beyond just having the child present (Favazza, Phillipsen, & Kumat, 2000).

Unfortunately, space does not permit detailed attention to the wide variety of other concerns and strategies needed for successful integration of children with disabilities into the ordinary preschool classroom. Suffice it to say here that, in addition to positive attitudes and deliberate efforts to facilitate participation, successful inclusion requires adequate support staff, an informed teacher, cooperative families, and appropriate, adaptable, developmental curriculum (Bricker, 1995; Cook, Tessier, & Klein, 2004; Daniels & Stafford, 1999; Hendrick & Weissman, 2006). It is a wise teacher with the best interests of the child at heart who makes certain these ingredients are available before gathering such a youngster into his group.

SUMMARY

The children's sense of who they are and of their place in the world has important ramifications for building their sense of social competence. Children gain their basic sense of who they are by identifying with the people around them whom they admire and want to be like. As they enter a center or school outside the home, the models teachers provide may socialize children into additional ways of coping with their worlds. Teachers can influence children's feeling of self-esteem, their ideas of what constitutes appropriate sex roles for themselves, and what it means to belong to a particular ethnic or cultural group.

Teachers as well as families can help children build inner sources of self-esteem by (1) providing them with skills so that they feel competent, (2) including opportunities for them to do meaningful work, (3) helping them do things for themselves, and (4) encouraging them to be creative. A positive body image also contributes to children's sense of identity and can be developed in various ways.

In teaching about sexual and ethnic identity, the most important learning for children to internalize is a positive attitude toward members of the opposite sex and toward their own sex and toward their own and other's racial and cultural backgrounds. Children need to accept other youngsters with disabilities and see past those disabilities to the child within who is like themselves, just as they learn that people of both sexes and various ethnic and cultural backgrounds are both alike and different from each other. There are many ways to make this teaching both positive and real for young children, as the work done by Pacific Oaks College demonstrates.

Food for Thought and Group Discussions

1. List several new skills you have seen children in your school learn this week that increased their feelings of competence.

2. Have your ideas changed in recent years about what constitutes appropriate ways for men and women to behave? Are there still some activities you think is only all right for one sex to do, such as asking for a date or changing a tire?

3. You are now the director of a children's center, and a father comes to school somewhat concerned about your nonsexist approach to early childhood education. He is quite frankly worried, as are many people, that letting his son dress up in skirts may encourage him to become homosexual. How would you reply to this concern? Might he be right?

4. Some students view themselves as having no cultural or ethnic heritage. They just say they are American. To demonstrate that you are more sophisticated than this, propose a project to do with the children that is based on some aspect of your own family's cultural or ethnic background.

5. As the children are assembling for group time, one of the little girls says distastefully, "I don't want to sit by Angelina—her skin's dirty!" (Angelina is brown because she is Puerto Rican, not because she is dirty.) How would you handle this incident? Be sure to think of practical, immediate, and long-term approaches.

Self-Check Questions for Review

Content-Related Questions

1. Give an example of a way to increase self-esteem that comes from outside the child. Now list several other strategies teachers can use that will help generate self-esteem within the child.

2. Cite an example illustrating how body image might affect an individual's sense of self.

3. What does the antibias curriculum developed by Pacific Oaks College advocate?

4. What is the fundamental concept on which nonsexist education should be based?

Integrative Questions

1. A Navajo child and a Hopi child are in your center, as well as a number of Anglos, and you have invited the Native American mothers to come and make Navajo fry bread and Hopi blue cornbread with the children. Explain what you want the children and their families to gain from this learning opportunity.

2. Ivan is an unpopular 3-year-old who has been hovering wistfully at the edge of the sandbox. Terrel looks up, smiles at him, says "Hi, Ivan—wanna dig tunnels?" and offers him a shovel. Later on, when the teacher has a quiet moment with Terrel, what might he say if he were going to recognize and praise Terrell's kindly action in a general way? How could he change that praise to make it more specific?

Coordinating Videotapes

Respecting diversity. Tape #10. *The whole child: A caregiver's guide to the first five years.* The Annenberg/CPB Collection, P. O. Box 2345, South Burlington, VT 05407-2345. *Respecting Diversity* examines how prejudice develops in both children and adults. It promotes the principle of equity in dealing with children and shows how to recognize and respect cultural differences, deal with racial insults at the preschool level, and honor both the similarities and uniqueness of individuals.

Everybody's special. Tape #7. *The whole child: A caregiver's guide to the first five years.* The Annenberg/CPB Collection, P. O. Box 2345, South Burlington, VT 05407–2345. *Everybody's Special* provides guidelines for working with families whose children have special educational needs. This program suggests what teachers can do to help parents identify problems and recommends ways to integrate children with special needs into the classroom. Viewers will see specific ways of working with children who have special educational requirements.

References for Further Reading

Picks of the Litter

Copple, C. (Ed.). (2003). *A world of difference: Readings on teaching young children in a diverse society.* Washington, DC: National Association for the Education of Young Children. A rich assortment of articles about diversity, and multicultural and nonsexist education.

Pelo, A., & Davidson, F. (2000). *That's not fair! A teacher's guide to activism with young children.* St. Paul, MN: Redleaf. Pelo and Davidson clarify that opportunities for activism extend far beyond dealing with questions of racial prejudice. Many age-appropriate examples are provided, plus an excellent reference list.

Overviews

Derman-Sparks, L., & the ABC Task Force. (1989). *Antibias curriculum: Tools for empowering young children.* Washington, DC: National Association for the Education of Young Children. This book explains in practical terms how that approach can be integrated into the early childhood curriculum. A classic.

Shade, B. J., Kelly, C., & Oberg, M. (1997). *Creating culturally responsive classrooms.* Washington, DC: American Psychological Association. This outstanding publication discusses the impact of culture and variations in points of view of Mexican, Asian, African, and Native Americans.

Developing a Positive View of the Self

Harter, S. (1999). *The construction of the self: A developmental perspective*. New York: Guilford. This scholarly book is so readable and is recommended even for newcomers to the field of self-identity.

Sources for Information About Specific Cultures

Mindel, C. H., Habenstein, R. W., & Wright, R. (Eds.). (1998). *Ethnic families in America: Patterns and variations* (4th ed.). Upper Saddle River, NJ: Merrill/Prentice Hall. For readers who wish to substitute accurate information about cultures in place of stereotypes, this collection of information about a wide variety of ethnic groups will be helpful.

Wardle, F. (2001). Supporting multiracial and multiethnic children and their families. *Young Children*, 56(6), 38–39. This article offers practical advice for including multiracial children—helpful material on a rarely discussed subject.

Promoting Gender Equity

Cunningham, B., & Watson, L. W. (2002). Recruiting male teachers. *Young Children*, 57(6), 10–15. Title is self-explanatory.

Gurian, M., & Stevens, K. (2005). *The minds of boys: Saving our sons from falling behind in schools*. San Francisco: Jossey-Bass. The authors investigate the "male learning style" that is often at odds with female-dominated educational practices. They provide advice about avoiding common pitfalls of teaching boys, such as expecting them to fill particular gender stereotypes.

Examples of Multicultural and Nonsexist Curriculum

Moomaw, S. (2002). *Nobody else like me: Activities to celebrate diversity*. St. Paul, MN: Redleaf. Excellent developmentally appropriate activities are presented to create a multicultural curriculum.

Ramsey, P. G. (2004). *Teaching and learning in a diverse world: Multicultural education for young children*. (3rd ed.). New York: Teachers College Press. The author defines what multicultural education means in a range of settings. Includes practical examples and activities to challenge children's prejudices about race, social class, gender and sexual orientation, and disabilities.

Information About Integrating Children with Disabilities

Cook, R. E., Tessier, A., & Klein, M. D. (2004). *Adapting early childhood curricula for children in inclusive settings* (5th ed.). Upper Saddle River, NJ: Merrill/Prentice Hall. This comprehensive textbook offers a wealth of information about disabling conditions and what the teacher in the inclusive early classroom can do about them.

Smith, R. M., Salend, S. J., & Ryan, S. (2001). Watch your language: Closing or opening the special education curtain. *Teaching Exceptional Children*, 33(4), 18–23. This article provides many examples of deficit-oriented language unwittingly used by insensitive teachers and also suggests more positive approaches to be used instead. *Highly recommended*.

For the Advanced Student

Eagly, A. H., Beall, A. E., & Steinberg, R. J. (Eds.) (2005). *The psychology of gender*. (2nd ed.). New York: Guilford. This volume provides a broad survey of issues relating to gender identity, differences, and similarities.

National Association for the Education of Young Children (NAEYC). (1995). *National Association for the Education of Young Children position statement: Responding to linguistic and cultural diversity: Recommendations for effective early childhood education*. Washington, DC: Author. The title is self-explanatory.

Related Organizations and Online Resources

The Council for Exceptional Children, Division for Early Childhood, publishes *Young Exceptional Children* and sponsors an annual conference. It is a subsidiary of the Council for Exceptional Children, which also publishes journals of interest and provides an annual conference. The Web site has many resources for including children with disabilities. http://www.cec.sped.org

Head Start Bureau is a nationwide early childhood program of the Administration for Children and Families, U.S. Department of Health and Human Services, serving children from families of low income or with disabilities. The Web site has many resources related to diversity and inclusion. http://www.acf.hhs.gov/programs/hsb/

MenTeach is a national nonprofit organization that serves as a clearinghouse for research, education, and advocacy to increase the number of men teaching in early childhood and elementary education. http://www.menteach.org

FREEING CHILDREN TO BE CREATIVE

Have you ever . . .

- Dried up completely on ideas for creative activities?
- Wished you could explain more clearly why coloring books are not creative?
- Had trouble explaining to a parent the difference between creating something and making something?

If you have, the material in this chapter will help you.

All children have the right to have their interests and abilities affirmed and nurtured; all children deserve opportunities for creative thought and expression. . . . It is incumbent upon all who work with children not only to see the genius in every child but also to advocate for every child's creative development.

—Mary Renck Jalongo (2003, p. 218)

Creativity, as practiced by young children, is a dynamic, changing, fluid experience that derives its greatest satisfaction from the process, not the product. It is, in the best sense of the word, a state of "becoming." It is also an intensely personal process, since the wellspring of creativity lies within the child. For this reason, it contains the potential for both self-enhancement and self-despair. Because its manifestations are easily withered by disapproval, adults must be particularly careful to nourish rather than discourage creative self-expression in children, lest their criticism or domination blight its growth.

WHAT IS CREATIVITY?

Definitions of *creativity* vary widely according to the aspect being defined (Davis, 1983; Jalongo, 2003). For our purposes, the one first proposed by Smith (1966) is most useful because it does not include the process of critical evaluation that is more appropriate to apply when working with older children and adults. He defines *creativity* as being the process of "sinking down taps into our past experiences and putting these selected experiences together into new patterns, new ideas or new products" (p. 43).

In early childhood, this putting together of new ideas and products based on past experience is expressed primarily through imaginative pretend play, through the use of self-expressive materials, and through creative thought. This chapter focuses on self-expressive materials and imaginative play. Creativity in thought is discussed in detail in chapter 17.

SOME GENERAL PRINCIPLES FOR FOSTERING CREATIVITY

Later in this chapter we will discuss some specific approaches that apply to the presentation of particular kinds of self-expressive materials, but there are also seven general principles that apply to all of them. These will be covered first.

Create a Climate That Encourages Children to Feel Creative

A climate that encourages creativity is composed of a number of things; keeping anxiety low is certainly basic to it. When children feel they are living in a predictable environment where they know what is expected of them and the teacher is a reasonable person, they feel secure and so have more energy to devote to the pleasures of creativity.

Added to this is the general attitude of the teacher that could be summed up as "Let's try it!" or "Why not?" This attitude is expressed as an openness to suggestions from the children and a willingness to venture with them as they explore various creative media. It tells them that it is all right to try something new and experiment with the possibilities of the materials being offered.

Teachers who wish to generate a creative climate must also be prepared to live with a certain amount of messiness. When children are caught up in the fever of creating things,

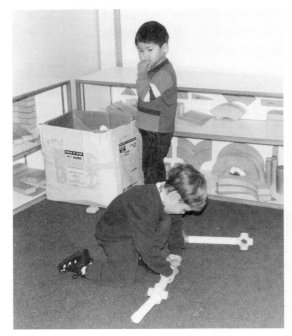

Providing open, unstructured materials encourages children to express their own ideas. You can almost see the "Ah-ha" experience taking place as he thinks about how to make a hockey stick.

their behavior is often somewhat helter-skelter, and it can really interfere with the creative process to insist that self-expressive or play materials be maintained in nearly perfect order at all times. (Note also that comments on cleaning up are sprinkled liberally through this chapter to balance this behavior.)

Finally, a general air of approval and interested inquiry about what the children are doing does much to set the creative atmosphere for the group. This should be more a feeling of enjoying the experience *with* the children rather than singling out specific products for praise. A child once confided after finger-painting, "You know, this experience was udderly dewightful!" Surely this is the climate we should aim for when building competence in the children's creative selves.

Remember That Process Is More Important than Product

One reason it is better to emphasize the process is that young children are not skillful users of materials. Much of their creative effort is expended in the manipulative experience of trying things out and becoming acquainted with them (Miller, 2003; Schirrmacher, 1998). The other very important reason to emphasize process is that this reduces the temptation to provide models for children to copy. Copies are not originals, and it is originality that is the hallmark of creativity (Cartwright, 2001; Thompson, 2005).

Remember That Encouraging Choices Fosters Creativity in Children

For an experience to be creative for children, it must be generated from within them, not be an experience "laid on" from outside. Amabile and Gitomer's study (1984) substantiates that it is important to encourage children to make choices about the materials and activities for themselves. For example, rather than setting out three colors at the easel, why not suggest that each child choose which of four or five colors he wants to use, or select the nails she prefers, or pick accessories he requires in the block corner?

Encourage Children to Explain What They Mean by Illustrating Their Ideas Graphically

Of course, these depictions may not be on the advanced level of the youngsters at Reggio, but they can be a valuable beginning, nevertheless. For example, a child might use a felt pen to make streaks of blue showing how water streamed off the roof, or demonstrate with his body how the rain felt when it hit him, or roll clay into "pipes" to show what happened when his father installed new roof gutters. All of these activities are examples of using creativity to translate an idea into a different form to explain what they mean to someone else.

Offer Support When Needed, but Interfere as Little as Possible

Children are entitled to assistance with creative materials when they need it, just as they are entitled to help with their shoelaces or having their meat cut up. If materials are too difficult to manage, the result is frustration, not creative satisfaction and children abandon the effort. Teachers should offer technical help when necessary but not usurp the children's right to make their own creative decisions.

Teachers can also offer support by providing enough time for children to have thoroughly satisfying experiences. It takes awhile for them to become deeply involved in play or get deeply into finger painting, and if the scheduled time for such activities is too short, the children are deprived of the leisurely richness they require to lose themselves in it entirely (Jalongo, 2003; Miller, 2003).

Still another important kind of support to offer is the provision of sufficient quantities of materials, as well as plenty of opportunity to use them. Children should be allowed to paint as many pictures or make as many collages as their fancy dictates rather than "just making one so Ashley can have a turn, too."

Fortunately, many materials that are appropriate for self-expressive activities and for dramatic play are available free for the asking, and their reuse has the added virtue of helping children appreciate the value of recycling (Redleaf & Robertson, 1999; Topal & Gandini, 1999). All it takes are an imaginative eye, the courage to ask for them, and the energy to collect them regularly.

Provide Enough Variety in Creative Activities

Providing variety is important because different activities appeal to different children. Variety can be obtained in many ways. Sometimes simply moving an activity from one place to another will attract different children. Boys, for example, who may shun dramatic house play activities indoors often participate more readily if the equipment is moved outside, or young 3s may use the large hollow blocks more freely if they are placed around a corner of the building where the older children are less likely to intrude on them.

It is also valuable to make a point of varying the activities themselves, not only by varying such basic materials as dough and paint recipes, but also by offering different levels of difficulty that suit different levels of maturation and skill.

One of the joys of offering creative, self-expressive materials to children with disabilities is that they offer an open invitation to experience and learn without judgment about the "right" way to do it. Creative self-expression is always right, and usually results in satisfying feelings about oneself (Karnes, 2005). Visually impaired youngsters gain information about the physical world through manipulating various materials, and they can be used with delight whether or not a child hears well (Anderson, 1996; Karnes, 2003). Adjustments can also readily be made for children with coordination problems. For example, adjustments might entail providing a table with a U-shape cutout so a child in a wheelchair can reach the art materials without stretching, or planning a particularly appealing collage experience for a youngster who needs lots of simple fine-muscle practice.

Make the Activity as Creative as Possible

Finally, when curriculum is developed that is intended to foster the creative aspect of the child's self, it is helpful for teachers to be quite clear in their own minds about just how creative the contemplated activity is likely to be. Table 14.1 provides some examples of materials that offer varying degrees of freedom of self-expression.

Those activities with the greatest potential for creative self-expression are characterized by requiring the least amount of control and instruction by the teacher. In Table 14.1, there is more opportunity in Column 1 activities for direct involvement of the children with the materials, and there is more room left for them to express their intentions and feelings (their own, personal, creative selves), because they are not caught up in how to use the materials to such a marked degree. Because they are so satisfying, these materials can be offered over and over again, and they should constitute the mainstays of the creative, self-expressive curriculum in the school.

Table 14.1
Creative Potential of Self-Expressive Activities

Column 1: Maximum Potential	Column 2: Moderate Potential	Column 3: Minimum Potential
Easel Painting (and its variations) Using materials as child wishes, provided he follows simple rules for positive social behavior, such as not painting his neighbor's picture or dripping paint on the floor. (Experience is varied by using several shades of same color, different-size brushes, painting to music, and so on.)	Painting in ways that allow less control by child, such as string painting, blowing paint around with straws, dropping food coloring on damp paper towels. Painting an object the child has made. Opportunities for genuine self-expression are sharply reduced because child cannot control the medium and express his own feelings and ideas.	Painting or coloring in coloring books or worksheets. Copying something the teacher has made, such as a sun, stick figure, or house.
Finger Painting (and its variations) Finger painting as it is usually presented. (Experience is varied by presenting different textures of paint, a variety of colors, and so on.)	Food painting, because it requires sitting down and needs careful control to avoid slipping. Taking "negative" prints from tabletop finger paintings.	No example. One teacher commented that teachers are usually so busy helping the children "set up" that they do not have time to think up more managing strategies.
Drawing Drawing with simple materials such as chalk, crayons, soft pencils, crayon "relief," chalk with starch, or felt-tip pens.	Child encouraged to illustrate an experience, such as a previous field trip.	Drawing around stencils of animals, circles, triangles, and so forth. Using coloring books or duplicated worksheets, keeping carefully within the lines.
Dough Play Manipulating dough as child wishes and as an emotional release. (Variety is provided by many different kinds of doughs, colors, and so on.)	Selecting whatever cookie cutters he wishes to make Christmas ornaments, decorating them as he desires with red and green felt-tip pens.	Making a bowl or vase according to a model provided by the teacher. Following a recipe for making biscuit dough.

Column 2 (moderate creative potential) also offers some valuable activities for children. However, these kinds of activities might be characterized as being more craftlike than creative. They generally require more skill on the part of the children and more instruction (at least initially) by the teacher. They tend to have more of a definite focus and direction, even though the teacher may meticulously avoid providing an actual model. To be successful, these materials usually require repeated presentation so that the children can practice and gain skills in their manipulation, yet they are frequently offered as only "one-shot" deals.

Column 3 (minimum creative potential) presents activities at the restricted end of the creative continuum. The advantages of offering these kinds of activities are that they teach children to follow directions, to conform, and to learn something the teacher has decided is valuable for them to learn. We would heartily agree that it is necessary for children to learn how to follow directions. However, this kind of activity is all too often passed off as being "creative" by teachers who do not grasp the difference between *creating* something and *making* something. Such an activity may be creative for teachers who invent the instructional idea, but it offers children almost no latitude for expressing their own responses, ideas, and feelings and hence should not be thought of as providing opportunities to develop their creative selves.

Column 1: Maximum Potential	Column 2: Moderate Potential	Column 3: Minimum Potential
Collage Making Child chooses from assortment of materials. (Teacher encourages child to consider qualities of design by asking what he thinks would look good together. Infinite variety is available in this medium through use of different materials and collage bases.)	Collage making centered on a theme—seaweed, shells, and sand after a visit to the beach; cotton balls, colored crushed egg shells, and Easter grass on lavender paper at Easter.	Cutting out pictures at the teacher's behest of all the chairs the child can find in a magazine and pasting them in a scrapbook. Gluing precut eyes, nose, and mouth on a precut pumpkin head.
Dancing Dancing freely as the music suggests or feelings dictate.	Participating in movement education activities—"How many ways can you . . .?"	Folk dancing.
Puppet Play Using puppets just to "fool around with" and to express feelings.	Making up a story together and using puppets to present it after considerable practice.	Presenting a puppet play of a well-known story, such as "The Three Bears."
Woodworking Using different kinds of wood, nails, and so forth. (Technical advice is provided when necessary, but children are left free to use materials as they wish, provided that safety is observed.)	Making an airplane or boat at the teacher's suggestion with no model provided and materials chosen by child. (Advanced tools are provided that require considerable teacher instruction and supervision for successful use. As skill is gained, this activity probably moves over to Column 1.)	Nailing together a precut bird house or shoeshine kit.
Unit Block Play Playing with blocks that are available and well sorted and with accessories that are brought out at child's request or with several different kinds of accessories that are available on nearby shelves for self-selection.	Playing with rubber zoo animals that are deliberately set out after trip to children's zoo to provide focus for play.	Teacher setting up cages made of blocks with animals inside them after a trip to the zoo and encouraging children to do likewise.

Gaspar (1995) sums it up well:

> Many "art projects" are really fabrication activities. Children enjoy copying and constructing, and there can be other developmental or educational value as well as their enjoyment. *However, it may be helpful for teachers to clarify which type of experiences they have designed for children in order to understand if their students are getting art experiences or copying and fabricating activities.* (p. 46, Gaspar's italics)

A Note About Expense

Throughout this book, suggestions are included about ways to save money while presenting a first-rate curriculum for the children. Nowhere is it more important to know how to stretch money than in the area of self-expressive activities, because children can use up materials faster than the blink of an eye when they are involved in creative endeavors. For this reason, teachers need to develop their scrounging instincts.

One common problem is the way materials seem to pile up in an unsorted mess once they are collected. The most practical remedy (in addition to having adequate space for storage) is to take 5 minutes at the beginning of every staff meeting for everyone to sort out what has accumulated and toss it into the appropriate containers.

A number of economy measures are included with many of the discussions on materials in the rest of this chapter. Following these suggestions will help keep expenses down while providing the children with the plentiful amount of materials they require.

SOME NEW IDEAS ABOUT CREATIVITY FROM REGGIO EMILIA

In the past decade, interest in young children's artistic expression has been stimulated by an exhibit touring the United States called the "Hundred Languages of Children." This exhibit features the work of preschool-age children from the municipal schools of Reggio Emilia, Italy, and has led many of us to be more aware of an additional benefit to using graphic materials, besides the expression of children's feelings and aesthetic satisfactions: the use of graphic materials to communicate to other people what the children are thinking about and what they know.

Indeed, the title "Hundred Languages" is intended to emphasize the multitude of possible materials children can use to communicate their knowledge. For example, if the children are interested in constructing a playground for birds, they might first draw their ideas of how to make a fountain for the birds to enjoy or construct a model of their ideas about that while using clay. The reader will notice that in the Emergent Curriculum in Action features throughout this text, this building of experience through varying creative materials is employed in U.S. programs as well with wonderful effect.

Some Contrasts Between the American and Reggian Points of View

Because various aspects of the Reggio Emilia philosophy have been discussed in previous chapters and will be touched on again in the cognitive sections later in this book, we will confine ourselves here to talking about some different emphases in the Italian approach to fostering creativity compared with the American approach. The most obvious one is the result—the advanced quality of the children's work. This is due partly to plentiful opportunities for repeated practice with materials from a very early age and partly from teachers deliberately showing the children how to use materials successfully. But although these factors are important, there is a third factor of even greater significance: Every lecture by Reggio educators begins with the statement that children are "rich, strong, and powerful"

They see children as possessing great potential—potential that is the privilege of the teacher to perceive and empower. They see children not as having needs, but rather as having rights—as being entitled to good care and sound teaching because of who they are, not because of what they need.

How does this differ from the American point of view? On the surface, at least, we would certainly agree with it. But underneath, do we really see children as having such extraordinary ability at such an early age? It seems that we view them from a much more protective and possibly restrictive vantage. For example, we often discuss "meeting children's needs" and "strengthening their weaknesses." Perhaps we have been so wrapped up in defending children's right to authentic childhoods that we may have unintentionally carried this defense too far, which has led us actually to underexpect what children can do. Certainly the accomplishments of the youngsters in Reggio Emilia offer many interesting examples of realizing creative potential many of us have not dreamed possible in the United States. As well, the American programs highlighted in the Emergent Curriculum in Action features of this text, demonstrate that all children—whether in the United States or Italy—can create extraordinary work when teachers base their curriculum on respect for children's abilities and rights.

Attitudes About Creativity

Besides this most significant difference in attitude toward children, it is interesting to single out just a few of the many other differences between the Reggian and traditional American approaches to creativity (Hendrick, 1997). One of the most obvious is the multitude and variety of materials the Italians make available for the children combined with the special work areas, typically separate rooms, they call *ateliers*—or studios—where children come to construct their ideas. Moreover, a special staff person (an *atelierista*) is provided to facilitate that process. Although the majority of school staff in the United States would not find it difficult to extend the range of creative materials made available to children if they just thought about it, it is a rare school that could find the wherewithal to support the salary of an *atelierista* much less provide a permanent space for that person to hold forth. Nevertheless, as visitors behold the results made possible by this support, it leaves us hungering to provide similar opportunities for our children. And fortunately many U.S. programs are now finding ways to include *ateliers* and *atelieristas* in their schools (see the Emergent Curriculum in Action features in chapters 1, 10, 11, and 16 for some program descriptions).

The admiration for the color, beauty, and quality of the Italian products often blinds the visitor to another real difference between American and Italian purposes in providing graphic materials. We value the creative process because it comes from within the child, is unique and original, and provides for the expression and possible relief of feelings. The Italian setting, on the other hand, appears to have a more cognitively oriented approach. The purpose of providing graphic materials leans more toward enabling children to express their ideas—to explain, for example, how the water actually gets to the fountain or what they think causes rain to fall. In Reggio, the children use creative materials to explain their hypotheses about the world, and teachers use their creations as a means of documenting what the children think.

We Americans hesitate to make suggestions to the children about what they are making, fearing we may stifle the children's spontaneity and creative original ideas if we intervene. We emphasize discovery and learning or figuring out how to use materials by trying them out. Therefore, we scrupulously leave children to discover on their own how to use materials effectively. The Italians, on the other hand, think nothing of showing a child how to wipe the brush on the edge of the cup to avoid dripping or how to wet the edges of clay so it will stick better.

This creation done by children in the Reggio Emilia schools illustrates how permission to experiment combined with a variety of materials can enrich creative play.

The educators in Reggio maintain that lending adult assistance when needed—whether it be bending a recalcitrant piece of wire or hammering in a nail—empowers youngsters to move ahead with their creations in a satisfying way. Indeed, there is a vast difference between showing a child how to use a brace and bit to make a hole, and telling him where to put the hole or what to do with it once drilled. Although the Reggio teachers unhesitatingly teach skills and lend a helping hand when needed, they would never tell the child where to put the hole (though they well might ask him why he is putting it in a particular place).

What Can We Learn from the Reggio Approach?

What does this exciting example of children's creative potential mean to American preschool teachers? Does it mean that what we have been doing should be abandoned or regarded as undesirable practice? Of course not—our essential treasuring of the creative process is quite correct, just as the value of fostering originality and the unique self-expression of feelings and ideas remains sound. Certainly we must retain these values.

At the same time, we can also welcome and include the more cognitive approach favored by the Reggians and encourage children to communicate their ideas through a variety of self-expressive materials. Even more significantly, we can strive to see children as they really are—not as unformed, weak, vulnerable people who require our protection, but rather as strong, capable people.

USING PRETEND PLAY TO FOSTER CREATIVITY

No matter what else is discussed in relation to the various selves of the child, discussions of play keep cropping up in almost every chapter. This is because play is the great medium through which children learn about and understand their world. In this chapter, once again, it is essential to talk about play to explain how it contributes to the development of the creative self. (The reader also may wish to review chapter 3 at this point.)

Creative, dramatic play provides limitless opportunities for children to imagine and pretend themselves into roles ranging from parents to babies to ogres to bears. Within a matter of minutes, their imaginations can transform a simple object such as a piece of wood into a little car, a baby bottle, a gun, or a bit of roof. Thus, imagination enables children to become in play what they cannot be in real life, and doing this exercises their intellects, because there is an obvious mental operation involved in substituting symbols for reality (Gowen, 1995; Piaget, 1962, 1976). Such play allows children to be masterful. It permits them to experiment with tentative solutions to problems, and it provides unparalleled opportunities for them to use their own ideas.

In their classic work, Sylva, Bruner, and Genova (1976) list some additional characteristics of play that are worth noting here because they apply particularly well to a discussion of the creative aspects of play. As they phrase it, "The essence of play is the dominance of means over ends" (p. 244)—a statement that certainly sounds familiar and comfortable to process-not-product devotees. They cite other characteristics of play, cite including a lessening of the risk of failure and an increased freedom because people involved in play are less preoccupied with specific, focused tasks and so are more open to the world around them. Finally, the authors point out that play is voluntary and self-initiated; that is, it comes from within the person. These qualities of freedom and self-initiation are what teachers wish to favor in creative play situations. The problem for beginning teachers is how to translate these high-sounding purposes into actual, down-to-earth practice. Fortunately, providing for such play need not be expensive, as Table 14.2 illustrates.

Table 14.2
Sources of Free or Almost-Free Materials for Imaginative, Dramatic Play

Materials	Sources
Large appliance boxes for houses, markets, trains, or whatever; also nice for group painting projects	Appliance stores—kitchen, radio, and TV stores
Discarded furniture, cut down and repainted, for pretend-play corner—high chairs, small beds, and so forth	Attics, rummage sales, thrift stores
Sandbox and housekeeping equipment	Rummage sales, thrift stores; ask families to donate extras
Telephones for promoting social interaction in play	Often on loan from public relations office of telephone company
Props for play, such as used envelopes, aged typewriters, pieces of hose, rose, discarded backpacks, hats of all descriptions	Families, paint stores, fast-food places, workers, thrift stores, garage sales
Used gift wrappings—fun to use to play birthday party	Ask families to save
Dress-up clothes—provide a good assortment of clothes for both sexes; add multiethnic touches if possible: cut garments down to reasonable size so children can move freely in them	Ask families to save; garage sales, thrift shops
Large outdoor blocks	Milk companies sometimes donate old cases; computer packers and shippers sometimes donate foam, packing blocks
Crutches, braces, canes, blindfolds, ear plugs for hearing aids, and wheelchairs	Sometimes hospital rental supply places will donate worn equipment, or it can be borrowed temporarily

No matter what the budget, schools can use the following suggestions to enhance students' creative play experience:

- Provide a background of actual experiences that may suggest possibilities for the children to pretend, such as a trip to a doctor's office.

- Provide plentiful equipment of the right kind (unstructured materials lend themselves to imaginative play most readily).

- Allow children to use this equipment in creative, possibly unconventional, but harmless ways to meet the needs of their play.

- Provide accessories to enhance play when children request them or to suggest a possible theme for play.

- Provide unusual rearrangements and juxtapositions of equipment to stimulate and extend play (combining the unit and hollow blocks, for example).

- Keep the play area appealing and the materials accessible.

- Most important of all, support but do not dominate the children's play by offering whatever assistance is necessary to continue or enrich it.

USING BLOCKS TO EXPRESS CREATIVE IDEAS

Unit Blocks

Unit blocks are those small hardwood blocks so dear to the hearts of children and so filled with potential for creative play. Designed by Caroline Pratt more than half a century ago, they remain one of the most enduring media for early childhood education.

> Unit blocks are an open-ended toy, a system of related shapes. Children decide how blocks can be used—there is no right or wrong way to build. Their versatility and flexibility make them useful companions in all areas of the classroom. They expand all areas of the curriculum—science, math, dramatic play, art, and physical development. More than any other single toy, they stimulate curiosity, expand imagination, promote exploration and invite discovery. (Oklahoma Child Care, 2000a, p. 17)

Blocks are valuable because they suit the developmental needs and capabilities of a wide range of children, and they lend themselves to achieving large, spacious effects rather quickly. In imaginative play, unit blocks have another special quality that they share with models of animals and dolls: To use them for pretend purposes, children must project their imaginations even more than they do when involved directly in housekeeping play, because blocks are less structured. Table 14.3 includes many additional ways all the selves of the child may benefit from using this wonderful equipment.

Hardwood blocks are expensive but well worth the investment, and a school should add more every year, if at all possible, until they have a plentiful supply and a variety of shapes available. The various-size blocks should always be multiples of each other to facilitate comprehension of mathematical concepts of equality and to make building with them more satisfactory. If new blocks are waxed with heavy-duty paste wax upon arrival, they will stay much cleaner and more appealing over the years.

A temporary set can be made from softwood with an electric saw, but unit blocks undergo such vigorous use that these softwood substitutes are not permanently satisfactory because they splinter and their corners get knocked off. In a real financial pinch, teachers can use flat-topped milk cartons or sealed detergent boxes for blocks rather than offer no blocks at all.

Table 14.3
What Can Children Learn from Playing with Large and Unit Blocks?

Physical	Emotional	Social	Creative	Cognitive/Language
Encourages development of:	Encourages children to:	Encourages children to:	Encourages:	Encourages:
Eye–hand coordination	Play through emotional concerns	Share space	Use of imagination and pretend play	Use of symbols to replace reality (emergent literacy skill)
Fine-muscle control	Express feelings safely	Share resources	Generation of large, creative effects quickly	Use of comparison to determine same or different (matching—emergent literacy skill)
Large-muscle control	Relieve aggression safely (knocking blocks down)	Play together and cooperate (negotiate, bargain, wait, accept other people's ideas)	Problem solving ("If I can't build it this way, maybe I could . . .")	
Specific perceptual motor skills, such as stacking, grasping, lifting, shoving	Feel masterful because of potential for achieving large results quickly	Practice the art of persuasion	Generation of creative ideas in three-dimensional space	Conceptualization of ideas
Sense of spatial relationships	Exercise patience to try again when blocks collapse	Put their ideas of how social world operates into concrete form (highways, trains, houses, etc.)	Aesthetic pleasures of handling beautiful wood	Use of language to explain ideas to others
Following safety rules (stack blocks no higher than head, except for cardboard ones)	Feel delight with structures they build	Do meaningful work together (cleanup)		Understanding principles of physics: balance, gravity, momentum, cause–effect
		Enlarge their gender roles (both girls and boys can build block structures)		Understanding of mathematical/Piagetian concepts of equality—transitivity, conservation (4 is 4 no matter how blocks are arranged), reversibility
				Use of estimation ("How many blocks will it take to . . .?")
				Planning what to build in advance (older children)

Storing and Presentation. Unit blocks should always be stored, same size together, long side in view, on shelves—not in tubs or bins. If they are dumped in bins, children cannot find just the size they want when they need it; they also have no opportunity to perceive the relationships among the different sizes.

If children are taught to build slightly away from the shelves, fighting and stress will be reduced as other youngsters try to reach in for blocks also. The construction area needs to be shielded from traffic to discourage children from delivering a kick at some treasured structure as they pass by, and it should be as large as possible and capable of being extended when necessary. A carpeted space is nice to use for this activity because it is warmer to kneel on while working and also quieter for play.

Getting Play Started. It often does require attention from the teacher to draw children into block play. One way of doing this is to use the "nest-egg" approach—perhaps setting out a few of the cars on the beginning of a road made of blocks or stacking up some of the blocks in an inviting way before the children arrive. This is not intended to provide a model for the children to copy but to attract them and prompt the beginning of their play.

The teacher who quietly pulls up a chair and sits near the block corner while keeping an eye on the room in general will also draw children to that area and can encourage the play with an occasional supportive comment or question. Drawing diagrams occasionally of their constructions also stimulates such play, as does taking photographs of the children's block creations and posting them in the area.

In addition to unit blocks, tabletop blocks of various descriptions cultivate the use of smaller muscles, facilitate eye–hand development, and foster creative play, particularly if they are combined with little plastic figures of animals and people. Lego toys, log-type blocks, and similar toys appeal to 4s and 5s, and Bristle Blocks can be used even with 2s and 3s because the pieces fasten together in such an easy, satisfactory way. Once again, it is important to have a large enough supply of these so that children can really build something with them and not run out of what they require.

Helping Children with Disabilities Enjoy Playing with Blocks. Phelps and Hanline (1999) extol the sometimes overlooked values of block play for children with disabilities by pointing out block play's ability to foster social interaction, generate ideas, and promote conversation. Many of their suggestions, such as allowing for plenty of space and adequate amounts of time plus interesting accessories, apply to block play in general—but they also suggest providing pieces of painted plywood (3 feet by 4 feet each) to emphasize specific spaces for building and walking, high-contrast block color with floor surface, plenty of light, blocks within easy reach, active involvement by the teacher to stimulate and guide the activity where necessary, and textural or high-contrast cues on shelves to help children see where to replace the blocks at pickup time.

Cleanup. The block area is much more appealing if blocks are not allowed to accumulate in a jumbled mess, so it makes sense that the children be encouraged to pick them up before leaving the area. Yet if this rule is enforced too rigidly or if the teacher refuses to help with the task, it certainly does discourage play. It seems better to strive for a general effect of tidiness without being disagreeable about it—thanking the children who do help and pitching in oneself to provide a good example. Children do not mind picking up so much if they can make a game of delivering the blocks to the shelves on trucks or shoving them over, train style, and they do experience satisfaction in getting them all marshaled neatly back in place.

Some Suggested Variations for Unit Block Play

Following are additional ideas to enhance children's block play:

- Widen the variety of shapes of blocks as the year progresses—include cylinders, pillars, and ramps, gothic arches, switches, and triangular blocks.

- Add cubical counting blocks; the touches of color these provide are exquisite.

- Use a dollhouse and furniture and dolls to go with it.

- Offer little cars and trucks.

- Provide a small wood train and tracks (a wonderful accessory for such play).

- Include additional transportation toys, such as boats and airplanes.

- Include wooden or rubber animals.

- Combine unit blocks with blocks of other kinds; they work well with both larger and smaller ones.

- Suggest that children incorporate tables into their block structures, particularly when combining them with smaller blocks.

- Offer the long boards as accessories.

- Move the block cases to other areas in the room; this often stimulates play by children who have not been attracted to them before.

Large Hollow Blocks and Boards

Simply nothing matches the value of boards and large hollow blocks for fostering creativity in play. Their manipulation requires children to involve both their minds and bodies together in a total way as they lug them about and hoist them into position. Their very nature and size suggest construction of structures large enough to play in when completed. Play periods should be long enough that there is time for this activity, as well as for actual building.

Hollow Blocks. Hollow blocks are expensive and do require protection by using them either on carpeting inside or on grass or some other resilient material outdoors. (One center, for instance, uses artificial grass laid over cement as a cushioning surface to keep the blocks from breaking when they fall.) If used outdoors, they also require sanding and painting once a year with quick-drying lacquer to preserve them.

Once again, the nest-egg approach can prove useful as a starting point for large block play. The "egg" can be as simple as arranging four boards leaning against a few blocks to suggest a ramp, or setting up a ladder to bridge two walls.

Providing accessories—such as ropes, lengths of hose, ladders and telephones, dolls, or housekeeping furniture—will also suggest possibilities and attract children. If the blocks are used in conjunction with other outdoor equipment such as a boat, trikes, or a climbing gym, or are used around the sandbox to make a house, play in those areas will increase rapidly.

The teacher should be attentive to what is going on and be willing to serve as helper and supplier of needs rather than as dominator and controller of ideas. It facilitates play if such objects as sawhorses, hats, telephones, and old bedspreads are stored nearby so they can be produced at a moment's notice. To tell a child, "I can't get it right now—you'll have to wait until tomorrow," is unsatisfactory, as it is likely that the play will have moved on to something else by then.

Hollow blocks and boards should be used both indoors and out, because they generate different kinds of play when moved around. A nice, inexpensive large block that is satisfactory for use indoors where it is dry is the kind made of corrugated cardboard. Children can help assemble these and glue them closed, and a goodly supply can be obtained for a reasonable sum of money. Some computer firms also ship their products wedged between large blocks of spongy plastic. These make very light, surprisingly tough blocks.

Boards. Boards are one of the most useful and underrated pieces of equipment in schools. They should be made of $5/8$- or $3/4$-inch all-weather plywood and cleated on the ends so that they hook safely over the edge of blocks and A-frames. They should be cut to fit other playground equipment when this exists. For example, it increases their usefulness if they hook across the bars of climbing gyms so that the children can use them to build floors within the gym for "tree houses."

Boards are indispensable, and their usefulness is increased even more when sawhorses, barrels, tires, and large boxes are provided along with them. An adequate supply consists of 25 to 30 boards, of whatever two lengths adapt best to existing equipment. All it takes is one bake sale to raise enough money to purchase the wood and a handful of adults to cut, make, and finish them. The children's delight should be ample repayment for this effort.

Storage and Cleanup. Blocks and boards are cumbersome to move, although children are often of considerable help in doing this, particularly if they use a wagon. There are large, low carts made for this purpose, and if these materials must be stored far from the play area where they are used, such a cart can be a worthwhile investment. It is ideal to have the storage closet near a large, level area appropriate for large block play; it is also best to store the boards in racks, tray style, along one side of the storage wall rather than behind the blocks, so they will be used more freely. For added convenience, ladders can be hung on the wall also and sawhorses and A-frames stacked nearby.

USING SELF-EXPRESSIVE MATERIALS TO FOSTER CREATIVITY

Easel Painting

One of the classic materials in almost all children's centers is the easel with its offering of tempera paint. Children of all ages enjoy this activity, and there are numerous ways to provide enough variety to sustain interest throughout the year.

Presentation of the Material. Needed equipment includes mixed paint, small containers for paint that fit the easel tray as nearly as possible, brushes, paper, a bucket, sponges and towels for washing hands, aprons, and a felt-tip pen for labeling the paintings.

Large newsprint paper is best so that the children have plenty of scope to paint. Soft, floppy camel-hair brushes allow the children to swoop about the paper most freely; the stiff, flat kind of brush makes it harder to produce wavy lines. Although mixing paint in large quantities saves the teacher's time, the children enjoy making it so much and this is so educational for them to do that mixing a fresh batch each day with one or two children helping stir is generally better. A surprisingly large amount of tempera is needed in relation to the quantity of water to make rich, bright, creamy paint; thus, it is best to dump the tempera into a pint container first and then add water bit by bit. Instead of water, some teachers prefer using liquid starch because it thickens the paint mixture (although it does increase the expense). It is helpful to add a dash of liquid detergent, since this makes cleaning up easier.

A couple words of caution: Some blue paints smell like rotten eggs if mixed in advance, so it is best to mix blue fresh each day. Also, the use of a small electric hand mixer expedites paint mixing but is best used by the teacher before the children arrive.

It will expedite matters if several pieces of paper are clipped to the easel at once. Many teachers prefer to write the child's name and date on the back of the paper to avoid the problem of having him paint over it. If a developmental portfolio is kept at school for each child, dating a few paintings and saving them delights families at conference time because it enables them to see how the child's skills have developed during the year.

Cleanup. Children often enjoy helping clean up this activity. They can spend considerable time squeezing the colored, soapy water through sponges, wiping off easels and aprons, and so forth.

Economy Measures. Putting a small amount of paint in a can at a time is one way to avoid waste. Ordering bulk paint in quantity once a year is another way to make money go as far as possible, and if schools combine their orders, sometimes an even lower cost per can is offered. Children should be taught some practical techniques for handling paint to avoid waste, such as wiping the brush on the edge of the container and returning paintbrushes to the same color paint each time. (There is a difference, however, between teaching children enabling techniques like these and limiting their ideas by suggesting what they should paint.)

Some Suggested Variations of Easel Painting

Other variations of easel painting include the following:

- Use a number of shades of one color.
- Use colored paper—colored newsprint comes in pastel shades, or the backs of faded construction paper can be used.
- Use the same color of paint with same color of paper.
- Use black and white paint (fun at Halloween).
- Use various sizes of brushes, or both flat and floppy ones, with the same colors of paint.
- Paint objects the children have made in carpentry or paint dried clay objects.
- Paint large refrigerator-type boxes.
- Work on a long piece of paper together to produce murals.
- Paint the fence with water and large brushes.
- Draw firmly on paper with crayons and then paint over it to produce "crayon resist" art.
- Paint with undiluted food coloring (this is expensive but lovely).
- Use all pastel colors (start with white and add color a bit at a time when mixing).
- Use cake watercolors (teach children to wash brush before changing colors).
- Cut paper into various shapes—leave a hole in the middle or cut it like a pumpkin, a heart, and so forth.
- Set up a table with many colors of paint and encourage the children to select the colors they prefer.
- Paint to music.

Finger Painting

Jean Stangl (1975) summarizes the value of finger painting very well:

> One cannot measure the satisfaction finger painting brings to the child who is tense, timid, autistic, shy, fearful, aggressive, or hyperactive. It allows the child to get involved. It requires no help or skill, there is no fear of competition and the student is always successful. (How can the lesson fail?) Finger painting enables the individual to explore, to experiment, to be imaginative and creative, to be expressive and to get rid of many frustrations. It provides an opportunity for growth in self-confidence by allowing the student complete control over the paint. (pp. 4–5)

257

Finger painting seems to produce feelings of joy and peace more than any other activity. Thus, teachers should offer it frequently, even though cleanup is somewhat time-consuming.

Methods of Presentation. The quickest, simplest way to make finger paint is to combine liquid starch with dry tempera. This may be done by pouring a generous dollop of starch onto the paper and then sprinkling it with dry tempera. Alternatively, some teachers like to stir the dry pigment into an entire container of starch base. Another method is to put spoonfuls of various plain bases onto the paper and then shake on whatever colors the children desire. No matter how the paint is originally prepared, teachers need to be ready to add more ingredients as the children work. The results to strive for are rich, brilliant color and sufficient paint to fill the paper completely if the child so wishes. Table 14.4 provides a number of tested finger paint recipes.

Needed materials include *waterproof* aprons (*old shirts are not satisfactory* because they allow paint to soak through onto the children's clothing), large sheets of glazed finger paint paper, starch or some other medium to carry the color, pigment (either tempera or food color), and buckets of soapy water, sponges, and towels for cleanup.

Helping Children Who Feel Uncomfortable Enjoy the Experience. Although reluctant children should not be pressured unduly to participate in finger painting, those who are uneasy about getting their hands "dirty" can often be induced to try soap painting. This is a variation of finger painting using Ivory Snow whipped with a rotary beater until light and fluffy. It is best presented as tabletop painting rather than paper painting because it cracks and flakes as it dries, and parents do not welcome getting this all over their cars on the way home from school.

Table 14.4
Tested Finger Paint Recipes

Method	Comments
Standard Finger Paint Pour a puddle of liquid starch on glazed paper that is sufficient to cover it when spread, and shake on 1 to 2 tablespoons dry tempera to make a rich bright color. It may be necessary to add more starch or color as the children finger paint. Add more than one color in separate corners so children can enjoy blending them.	This is the quickest and easiest way to prepare finger paint. It dries dull and does not flake off. Liquid starch is somewhat costly. Try out the brand before buying a lot of it—a few off-brands curdle and are not satisfactory.
Cornstarch Finger Paint Dissolve ½ cup cornstarch in 1 cup cold water. Pour mixture into 3 cups boiling water (it thickens suddenly). Stir constantly until shiny and translucent. Allow to cool and use as finger paint base, adding whatever color the children desire, or put in jars and stir in tempera or food coloring. This cornstarch recipe does not store particularly well. Recipes that *do* keep several days without caking follow:	This is the least expensive form of finger paint base to make and is very satisfactory. It feels slick, spreads well, and is not sticky. If it is colored with food coloring, it should be stored in the refrigerator. *It can only be kept 1 or 2 days* before caking occurs and is best used the day it is made. This paint has an attractive "clear" but not shiny look when dry provided it is used when fresh. It also works well mixed with tempera.
Easy-to-Store Finger Paint 1 Combine 2 cups water and ½ cup cornstarch, and boil until thick, stirring constantly. Add 1 cup Ivory Snow and coloring (if desired), cool, and use.	The addition of soap makes the base appear slightly curdled; material feels creamy when spread. Paintings, when dry, are dull and rich looking. Can be kept several weeks without refrigeration. Soap makes the cleanup easy.

Children who are wary of becoming involved in such a messy activity also need plenty of opportunity just to stand and look, plus the assurance that they can wash the paint right off whenever they want to. For these youngsters, teachers should avoid using permanent colors, such as purple or orange. Occasionally, a very shy child, who seems torn between wanting and not wanting to participate, is willing to begin by placing his hand on top of the teacher's as she paints. However, most children find this expressive medium irresistible—and teachers need only make sure that the children are clad in waterproof aprons before they plunge in.

Economy Measures.   There are a few noteworthy ways to save money on materials for finger painting. Because finger painting paper is expensive, teachers may wish to substitute butcher paper, which also has a special finish (but does soak through faster than finger paint paper does). Because it comes in rolls, butcher paper has the added advantage of being any size the teachers wish to cut. Painting directly on a plastic tabletop or large tray makes paint go further, requires less restriction of the children than painting on paper does, and can be very satisfying for children to clean up with lots of soapy sponges and warm water.

Method	Comments
Easy-to-Store Finger Paint 2	
Dissolve 1 cup cornstarch in 1½ cups cold water. Soak 2 envelopes plain unflavored gelatin in an additional ½ cup water. Add cornstarch mixture quickly to 4 cups hot water. Cook over medium heat, stirring constantly, until mixture is thick and glossy. Blend in gelatin and 1 cup powder detergent until dissolved. Store in refrigerator. This makes a whiter base than the other recipes do.	This recipe seems like a lot of trouble, but if you need one that keeps, this is it! It cleans up easily because of so much detergent in it.
Thicker Finger Paint (modified Rhoda Kellogg recipe)	
Combine 2 cups flour with 2 teaspoons salt; beat in 3 cups cold water with rotary egg beater. Add 2 cups hot water, and boil until mixture looks shiny. (Start it on low heat to prevent lumping.) Stir in 2 tablespoons glycerine. (The glycerine prevents this heavy mixture from being too sticky to spread and use easily.)	Use of dry laundry starch makes a thicker paint, but because it is often hard to find, try this recipe instead. If food coloring is used with this (and it takes a lot to make it bright), it eventually dries shiny. Tempera is also satisfactory. This paint is thick and takes a long time to dry, but it looks rich.
Soap Finger Painting	
Ivory Snow works well. Simply add water gradually while beating with a rotary egg beater until mixture is light and fluffy. Children enjoy making this as well as using it.	This mixture often appeals to children who resist getting their hands in "dirty" paint. It is best to use it directly on a plastic tabletop. Scrape it up and reuse it as different children want a turn. If it is used on paper, it flakes off as it dries and is very messy. It is lovely when tinted in pastel tones with food coloring. It cleans up more easily if vinegar is added to the cleanup water. Dispose of soap mixture by flushing it down the toilet or putting it in the garbage (it clogs sinks). Material turns slimy if kept.
Shaving Cream	
This can be used by several children it squirted on a plastic tray.	Shaving cream feels and smells nice, though it is expensive. When dry, it is dull and flakes off easily.

Note: Ready-made premixed finger paint is also available for purchase but is generally too expensive to use as frequently as the children need it. Thanks to Cené Marquis, head teacher, Institute of Child Development, for retesting these recipes.

In addition, it is much less expensive for teachers to make their own paint than to buy it ready-made. To prevent waste, they should shake on the tempera themselves rather than allowing the children to do this, though the children should be allowed to select the colors that they prefer. On the other hand, teachers should not economize by using small sizes of paper and insufficient quantities of base and tempera. The purpose of finger painting is to encourage deep, sensual, expressive pleasure in rich, bright, large, free painting. Skimpy, restricted dryness of the paint should be avoided at all costs.

Additional Drawing Materials: Chalk, Crayons, Felt-Tip Pens, and Pencils

Teachers should not overlook the potential of chalk, crayons, pencils, and felt-tip pens, which are two-dimensional materials requiring fine-muscle activity—although these do require practice for successful use. All of them have the advantage of being easy to get out and clean up, and at the end of a long day this is important. Unfortunately, in a few schools they are the only expressive media readily available to the children, and this is certainly undesirable.

Sometimes teachers have unrealistic expectations about the drawing and writing abilities of young children. Table 14.5 provides a helpful list of what children at different ages can produce in the way of shapes and forms.

Table 14.5
Developmental Continuum in Children's Drawings

Preschool (ages 2–5)
- Scribbles, loops, zigzags, wavy lines, jabs, arcs—often partially off the paper at first
- Chance forms or shapes
- Trying out different effects
- Meaning in the act itself, not in results or product
- Experimenting with leaving a mark, with colors and motions to leave a sign or have an effect
- Reflecting motion of hand/arm
- Separate lines, circlelike shapes, combined straight and curved lines
- Other basic forms, controlled marks, first schematic formulae, mandalalike shapes

Sources: Physical act of moving a hand and arm, basic concepts such as the circle, exploration of possibilities of line

Early Primary (ages 4–6)
- Shapes combined, becoming schemas; intentional image repetition of schemas; development of preferred schemas
- Beginnings of representation, often of people; letterlike forms; basic forms represented consistently—houses, flowers, boats, people; animals in profile
- Meaning (subject matter) increasingly readable
- Repertory or symbolic forms repeated, practiced, and new elements added
- Beginnings of individual style (e.g., typical way of drawing a house)

- Figures isolated, no context or baseline; each discrete (no overlapping of whole or of parts); size and details according to perceived importance or interest (e.g., long arms)
- Several figures on the page; beginning representing of events or narratives; schematic figures placed in a larger concept, for example, knowing an elephant is a four-legged animal with a trunk, the child uses a well-established routine, or schema, for drawing animals—cats, dogs, and so forth—and adds a trunk

Sources: Child's concepts and knowledge about the world, which take precedence over direct perception

Middle Primary (ages 5–8)
- Elaboration and variation of schematic figures and experimentation: repetition of imagery, practicing "set pictures" (always drawn the same way), such as racing cars
- Details often traditional or formulaic, such as windows with tie-back curtains, chimneys with smoke coming out at an angle, girls defined by skirts and long hair
- Narrative, illustrative, inventive; baselines often multiple; "see-through" houses; most figures in own space without overlapping

Sources: Copying conventional renderings by other children, imagination, book illustrations, TV, cartoons, and so on

Source: From *Considering Children's Art: Why and How to Value Their Work* (p. 35), by B.S. Engel, 1995, Washington, DC: National Association for the Education of Young Children.

Are Worksheets Creative?   Sometimes teachers succumb to the use of prefabricated materials, which could be termed, quite aptly, "dictated art." Even though children are often permitted to use whatever colors they wish, such experiences are almost bound to stress staying within the lines, coloring in only one direction to "make it pretty," and using preselected subject matter. The result is a lesson in conformity, not in exploring one's own ideas and feelings and putting these down on paper.

Beleaguered teachers say that they hate using worksheets but that the parents expect it. Perhaps parents expect photocopied worksheets because that is what they recall from their own early schooling experiences. Once teachers explain the educational value of self-expression and originality and also what constitutes developmentally appropriate activities for young children, families no longer desire the photocopied materials.

Chalk.   Chalk is inexpensive and comes in pretty colors. Its most typical use is with chalkboards, but children do not seem to use it very effectively there. They do better if allowed to mark on the sidewalk with it—perhaps because the rougher texture of the cement more easily pulls the color off the stick, and the children seem more able to tell what they are doing as they squat down and draw and can press harder with the chalk. It is, of course, necessary to explain to them that they may "write" with chalk only on special places.

Chalk is also available in larger squares in a range of marvelous colors (be sure not to purchase oil pastels, which are beautiful but will not wash away). These can be used with rough paper and a liquid starch base for an interesting variation halfway between finger painting and drawing. Liquid tends to seal the chalk, so teachers must rub it occasionally on a piece of old sandpaper to break this seal so the color will continue to come off readily.

Crayons and Nonpermanent, Nontoxic Felt-Tip Pens.   Crayons are much more economical than pens (and who has not felt the thrill of pleasure over a new box of these), yet pens do come in beautiful clear colors. Compared with paint, they have the additional advantage of staying bright and unsullied until the children use them up.

Most schools set out crayons or pens jumbled together in a basket, but if they are kept in sets in plastic bags so that each user has an individual set, there is less arguing and all the colors are available as the children require them. The use of thick crayons is general practice in preschools because they do not break as easily as thin ones do and, theoretically, because they are easier for children to hold. However, it is often the case that thinner crayons are probably easier to hold and manipulate. Perhaps early educators should offer both varieties or try out both and decide for themselves.

Pencils.   These require careful supervision. Children must not be allowed to run around with them, for they are somewhat dangerous. Some children have almost no experience with them at home. Since they are widely used in kindergarten, the children need practice with them, so it is wise to add them to the curriculum. For maximum success, teachers should purchase pencils with rich, soft graphite cores and instruct children on the rules about where these can and cannot be used.

Printing and Stamping

Printing and stamping have some value in helping children develop a sense of design and understand cause-and-effect relationships, but the materials of these activities do not allow as much latitude for creative self-expression as other forms of self-expressive materials do. Nevertheless, information is presented here because so many questions are asked about how to use them effectively.

Several kinds of stamps are simple enough for young children to use, although any printing that involves paint is likely to change into finger painting as it smears—an indication of what the children would probably prefer to do. Commercially made rubber stamps work well with ink pads of various colors. Cookie cutters dipped in shallow paint trays print without distortion and can be used to stamp paper for various holiday events. Bits of sponges cut into different shapes can also be used effectively to create stamped designs. Clothespins make nice handles for these when clipped to one end of the sponge. Potato stamps can also be dipped in shallow paint and used for printing. These seem to work best if the design is incised very deeply rather than cut out.

Dough and Clay

As is true with finger painting, play with dough or clay offers direct contact with the material and provides particularly rich opportunities for the expression and relief of feelings as children push, squeeze, and pound. These materials are three-dimensional in effect—and clay, in particular, provides opportunities for "clean" smearing, which many children enjoy.

Suggestions for Making Dough. Children should participate in making dough whenever possible (the only exception being cooking the cornstarch mixtures, which become stiff so suddenly that they really require the teacher's strong arm and careful use of very hot materials). If allowed to help make the dough, children learn about measuring, blending, and cause and effect and also have the opportunity to work together to help the school.

The doughs that require no cooking are best mixed two batches at a time in separate deep dishpans. Using deep ones keeps the flour within bounds, and making two batches at a time relieves congestion and provides better participatory opportunities. Tempera powder is the most effective coloring agent to add because it makes such intense shades of dough; adding it to the flour *before* pouring in the liquid works best. Dough can be kept in the refrigerator and reused several times. Removing it at the beginning of the day allows it to come to room temperature before being offered to the children; otherwise it can be dishearteningly stiff and unappealing. The addition of flour or cornstarch on the second day is usually necessary to reduce stickiness.

Variations. In schools where process, not product, is emphasized, the dough and clay are generally used again and again rather than the objects made by the children being allowed to dry and sent home. For special occasions, however, it is nice to allow the pieces to harden and then to paint or color them. Two recipes are included in Table 14.6 that serve this purpose particularly well (Ornamental Clay and Baker's Dough).

Presenting Dough. Once made, dough is easy to get out and simple to supervise. Usually all the children have to remember is to keep it on the table and out of their mouths. It is a pleasant material to bring out toward the end of the morning or in late afternoon when children and teachers are tired and cleanup needs to be quick and easy.

For dough to be truly satisfying, children need an abundance of it rather than meager little handfuls, and they should be encouraged to use it in a manipulative, expressive way rather than in a product-oriented manner. For this reason, the usual practice of offering it with cookie cutters should be varied by offering it alone or only with rolling pins.

Cleanup. The cooked cornstarch recipes are the only ones that are particularly difficult to clean up because they leave a hard, dry film on the pan during cooking. However, an hour or two of soaking in cold water converts this to a jellylike material that is easily scrubbed off with a plastic pot-scrubbing pad. If pans are soaked during nap time, the children will be quite interested in the qualities of this gelatinous material when they get up.

Table 14.6
Tested Play Dough Recipes

Ingredients and Method	Comments
Basic Play Dough 3 cups flour, $\frac{1}{4}$ cup salt, 6 tablespoons oil, enough dry tempera to color it, and about $\frac{3}{4}$ to 1 cup water. Encourage children to measure amounts of salt and flour and mix them together with the dry tempera. Add tempera *before* adding water. If using food coloring, mix a 3-ounce bottle with water before combining with salt and flour. Combine oil with $\frac{3}{4}$ cup water and add to dry ingredients. Mix with fingers, adding as much water as necessary to make a workable but not sticky dough.	Many basic recipes do not include oil, but it makes dough softer and more pliable. It also makes it slightly greasy, and this helps protect skin from the effects of the salt. Dry tempera gives the brightest colors, but food coloring may be used instead if desired. Advantages of this recipe are that it can be totally made by the children, since it requires no cooking and it is made from ingredients usually on hand that are inexpensive. This dough stores in the refrigerator fairly well. It gets sticky, but this can be corrected by adding more flour. This is a good, standard, all-purpose, reusable dough.
Cornstarch Dough Mix thoroughly 1 cup salt, $\frac{1}{2}$ cup cornstarch, and $\frac{3}{4}$ cup water to which food coloring has been added, and cook in a double boiler until thick and translucent. This happens suddenly, and it is very difficult to stir but worth it. Allow to cool to lukewarm on an aluminum pie plate.	This is one of the prettiest doughs. It sparkles while moist and resembles gumdrops! It has little grains of salt throughout so it feels mildly grainy but not unpleasant. For "gumdrop" effect, food coloring, *not* tempera, must be used. Quantity is sufficient for one child. It dries to a dull finish and does not break easily. Stirring *must* be done by an adult. It will keep overnight.
Ornamental Clay Mix 1 cup cornstarch, 2 cups baking soda, and $1\frac{1}{4}$ cups water. Cook together until thickened, either in double boiler or over direct heat—*stir constantly.* When it is cool enough, turn it out and let children knead dough and make it into whatever they wish. If used for ornaments, make hole for hanging ornament while it is still moist.	This is a brilliant white dough that does well if dried overnight in an oven with pilot light on. It is quite strong when dry. If dried in air, it does not seem to be quite as strong. It has a kind of crisp though malleable texture when handled. Ideally it should be used same day it is made, preferably while still warm. If it is saved for next day, it can still be used, does not get sticky, but does become somewhat drier, crumbly, and a little stiff. It can be rolled very thin and cut with cookie cutters. Makes enough for one child or perhaps two, depending on what they do with it. When dry, it has a slight sparkle and is snowy white. It can be drawn on easily with felt-tip pens and is very lightweight.
Baker's Dough Mix 4 cups flour, 1 cup salt, and 1 to $1\frac{1}{2}$ cups water as needed to make dough nice to handle. Knead and handle as desired. Bake at 350°F for 50 to 60 minutes. Material will brown slightly, but baking at lower temperatures is not as successful.	This recipe makes enough for two or three children and keeps well in refrigerator. When baked, it becomes very light and very strong. It can be painted or drawn on with felt-tip pens to add color and requires no cooking, except for final baking if preservation is desired.

Note: Thanks to Cené Marquis, head teacher, Institute of Child Development, for retesting these recipes. Remember, flours vary. Adjustments, therefore, are sometimes necessary as dough is made. If too sticky, add more dry ingredients. If too dry, add more liquid.

Sources: Basic Play Dough recipe from Santa Barbara City College Children's Center.
Cornstarch Dough recipe modified from *A Curriculum for Child Care Centers,* by C. Seefeldt, 1973, New York: Merrill/Prentice Hall.
Ornamental Clay recipe from *Recipes for Busy Little Hands,* by Doreen J. Croft, 1967, Palo Alto, CA: Author. Reprinted by permission of Doreen J. Croft.
Baker's Dough recipe from *A Curriculum for Child Care Centers,* by C. Seefeldt, 1973, New York: Merrill/Prentice Hall.

Potter's Clay.   Potter's clay may be purchased at any art supply store in moist form. This is much easier to deal with than starting with dry powder. It is typically available in two colors, gray and terra cotta (terra cotta looks pretty but seems harder to clean up). Clay requires careful storage in a watertight, airtight container to retain its malleable qualities. When children are through with it, form it into large balls, press a thumb into it, and then fill that hole with water and replace in container. Clay that is too soft for easy handling can be kneaded on a plaster "bat" board to remove excess moisture.

If oilcloth table covers are used, they can simply be hung up to dry, shaken well, and put away until next time. Formica-covered boards (sink cutouts left over from new countertops) also make nice large surfaces to use with dough or clay.

Self-Expressive Materials Requiring Glue: Collage, Assemblage, and Wood and Box Gluing

Collage and assemblage (three-dimensional collage) offer the best available media in the center for helping children think about such qualities of design as the way colors, textures, and forms look when arranged together. For this reason, collage should not be considered primarily a paper-on-paper experience. Instead, it is best thought of as being a three-dimensional expressive experience that provides opportunities for children to become acquainted with innumerable materials and build their appreciation of and sensitivity to color, substance, and design.

Presentation. Collages and assemblages require a firm base of some sort for their construction. This can be anything from construction paper to large pieces of tree bark, scraps of wood shingles, meat trays, discarded mat board from frame shops, or bolt boards from fabric stores. The base should be large enough to allow plenty of space for the arrangement of materials; therefore, such picayune things as cottage cheese lids are unsuitable.

The only substance that really sticks well enough that it can be used to glue all kinds of collage is white glue. Though not cheap in any size, it is least expensive when bought in gallon jugs. It cleans up readily with hot water until it dries. After that, it is very difficult to remove, so be sure to clean up carefully when the collage experience is finished—and this includes *wiping the neck of the glue bottle*.

Children should be taught that glue is not paint (the use of brushes and its thick appearance encourage this notion) and that it should be used with care. It can be set out in flat, untippable TV dinner trays or in little flat pans. Some schools use squeeze bottles, but these have to be watched closely and cleaned very carefully so they do not clog. Children should brush the glue onto the place where they want something to stick, but not all over the paper. An alternative to brushing is dipping the object to be glued lightly into a shallow pan of glue and placing it on the paper—but this tends to get fingers stickier and stickier!

Collage materials should be placed on a *separate* choosing table and sorted into shallow containers, such as baskets, so that the children can readily appraise the kinds of things that are available and consider how they will look when arranged together. Teachers can foster this awareness—particularly with 3s, 4s, and older children—by asking them what they think would make an interesting contrast, what colors would be attractive together, and so forth. Children also should be encouraged to modify the materials to suit their needs. Perhaps they want to cut off just a snippet of packing foam to use, or scrunch up a twist of tissue paper rather than leaving it flat, or bend a piece of wire to just the right shape.

Some Suggested Variations for Collage

The range of materials for collage is almost endless, and teachers should devote careful thought to selection of the materials presented together so that variety, contrast, and harmony are all present. The following are some possibilities for materials:

- All shades and colors of yarn, strings, ribbons, pipe cleaners, and colored wire
- All varieties of paper—corrugated, tissue, dull rough cardboard, old blotters, gilt papers from greeting cards, print shop papers, can labels, used gift wrapping papers, and so on

- Buttons of all sizes and colors

- Bottle caps and corks

- All forms of foam packing (the white makes a nice contrast to other materials), including broken-up foam egg cartons

- Rock salt sprinkled on as the collage is completed for a snowy effect (can be colored by shaking it in a bottle with a little food color)

- All kinds of natural materials are exquisite—small pinecones, seeds, berries, leaves, twigs, bits of bone, bits of bark, small lustrous pebbles, feathers (though these can be difficult for small, gluey fingers), shells, pods, starfish, and so on

- Small tiles (require a strong collage base)

- Leather scraps and trimmings

- Spongy materials

- Wood chips and interesting wood shavings

- Netting and other see-through materials, such as cellophane, and old theatrical gelatins

- Beads from broken strings (colored beads make handsome accents)

- Cloth and wallpaper for adding patterns and textures—particularly fleeces, burlaps, velvets, and cloth and paper with interesting patterns

- Scraps and trimmings (such as rickrack), lace, and embroidery ends

- Colored glue with tempera for an interesting accent

The following are additional variations closely related to collage:

- Offer wood gluing, using foam meat trays or roofing shingles to provide firm support. Painting or shellacking these later is a real pleasure and extends the experience for 4s who can endure waiting for their constructions to dry before going on to the next step.

- Small boxes (hearing aid boxes and film boxes, for example), combined with other bits and pieces of things, provide satisfying, quick methods of "assemblage."

- Arrange flat materials such as bits of tissue paper between layers of waxed paper and iron. The melted wax intensifies the colors. The result can be taped to a window and can be quite beautiful.

- Use felt pieces of a flannel board for a more temporary kind of collage. Many children like to do this, and it fosters an interest in design.

Woodworking

Some schools shun presenting carpentry, perhaps because some teachers have had little experience with woodworking tools and therefore think they are dangerous. But the activity is so satisfying for children that teachers should learn to use tools with care and competence so they can help children be successful, too. Further, women teachers who use tools in a confident, competent way provide good behavioral models for the children to emulate—models that may be particularly important for girls who, in the past, have all too frequently been instrumentally incompetent in the area of woodworking.

Tools can be frustrating and tempers can mount as a result, so it is important to provide continual, attentive supervision for safety's sake. Teachers should be aware of children who are finding the activity too frustrating and offer help and encouragement in time to prevent explosions. As with the other self-expressive activities, it is possible to help children learn *techniques* in working with wood without restricting *what* they are creating with it.

Basic Tools. The most basic woodworking tools are hammers and saws. The hammers should be good, solid ones—*not* tack hammers. The saws should be crosscut ones so that they can cut with or across the grain of the wood, and they should be as short as possible. A well-made vise in which to place wood securely while sawing is invaluable. Preferably, there should be two of these, one at each end of the table. (C-clamps also can be used for this purpose and are less expensive, or a board can be nailed to the table while the child saws it, but this leaves the troublesome chore of removing the nails afterward.)

As the year progresses, additional tools should be added from time to time. A brace and bit are desirable (much better than "egg beater" drills, which are almost hopeless for little children to use); the brace and bit can be taken apart by the children, and different-size bits can be inserted for variety. Rough and fine rasps and a light plane are also worthwhile. (Stanley Surform rasps are particularly good because they can be held with two hands and are very safe.) A general and important principle to remember is that, whatever tools are selected, they must be of good quality and really work. *Never* give children miserable little toy replicas; they are too unsatisfying to use.

Young children enjoy sawing up the large pieces of foam that come as packing for electronic equipment. Hammering into such material or into plasterboard is also quick and easy and does not require more force than 2s and 3s can muster. Older children need plentiful amounts of soft wood to work with. This is commonly available as scrap at construction sites and at some lumber mills. Cabinet shops are also good sources of wood; however, many of their scraps are hardwood and are more suitable for gluing than carpentry because they are too tough for children to saw through. Plywood is too tough and hard to be satisfying for children to manipulate. An old tree stump is great fun for children to pound countless nails into.

Some Suggested Variations for Woodworking

Following are more ideas for a creative woodworking experience:

- Remember to vary the tools the children use as their skill (and self-control) increases.
- Purchase a variety of nails by the pound, not by the little box, from a hardware store. Children love an assortment of these. They can be set out in small foil pie plates to keep them from getting mixed up. Some schools nail these pie plates to a long board to prevent spilling.
- Offer various kinds of trims to go with woodworking, such as wire, thick colorful yarn, and wooden spools (with nails long enough to go through the spool).
- Offer round things for wheels, such as bottle caps, buttons, or the lids of 35mm film containers.
- Provide dowels of various sizes that will fit the holes made by the different sizes of bits.
- As previously mentioned, children like to paint what they have made, but this must be done another day or supervised by a second person because it is vital to stay right beside the carpentry table at all times.

SUMMARY

Young children express their originality and creativity primarily through the use of self-expressive materials, imaginative play, and creative thought. This chapter discusses methods of fostering creativity by means of imaginative play, blocks, and expressive materials.

Some principles of teaching that foster creative self-expression include (1) maintaining a climate that encourages children to feel creative, (2) remembering that process is more important than product, (3) encouraging children to make choices, (4) interfering as little as possible with the children's creative activities but offering support and encouragement when necessary, (5) providing enough variety to the activities and keeping them developmentally appropriate, and (6) making certain that the activities are genuinely creative.

Specific recommendations are offered related to fostering imaginative, pretend play, using blocks to promote creativity, and presenting a variety of self-expressive art materials in ways that enable children to make the best use of their creative powers.

Food for Thought and Group Discussions

1. It is hard to really appreciate the individual merits of the dough recipes unless they are actually available for inspection and experimentation. As a class project, have volunteers make them up and bring them to class to try out.
2. Every community has its own special resources for free self-expressive materials. Gather these tidbits of information from members of the class and compile a resource list of these for everyone to use.
3. What are some general principles you can employ to promote children's creativity?

Self-Check Questions for Review

Content-Related Questions

1. How is creativity usually expressed by young children?
2. Imagine you are preparing to present easel painting or finger painting to the children in your group. How can you set it up most efficiently? What are some variations you could use to add variety to the experience? Answer the same questions for dough, collage, and woodworking.
3. The principal of your school has asked you to explain why you want to purchase blocks for your classroom. Think of each of the child's five selves (physical, emotional, social, creative, and cognitive) and list at least two ways block play would help each of those selves develop.

Integrative Questions

1. The text points out there is a difference between suggesting that a child bear down on a brace and bit and telling him where to drill the hole. Please explain just what the difference is.
2. What is the difference between *creating* something and *making* something? Explain how carpentry could be presented to fit either of these verbs.
3. Suppose there is a child in your class who is very afraid of thunder and lightning. He has drawn a picture of a thunderstorm (consisting of purple and black patches and lots of little specks of black for raindrops). How could you honor the American value of using his painting to relieve his fears and also incorporate some of the cognitive values reflected in the Reggian approach?

Coordinating Videotape

Creativity and play. Tape #11. The whole child: A caregiver's guide to the first five years. The Annenberg/CPB Collection, P. O. Box 2345, South Burlington, VT 05407-2345. *Creativity and Play* outlines the role of creativity in healthy child development, provides examples of how to encourage it, and devotes the second half of the tape to explaining why play is vital for healthy development and how to encourage it to flourish.

Reference for Further Reading

Pick of the Litter

Gandini, L., Hill, L. T., Cadwell, L. B., & Schwall, C. (Eds.) (2005). *In the spirit of the studio: Learning from the atelier of Reggio Emilia.* New York: Teachers College Press. This book, full of beautiful photographs and examples, explores how the use of expressive materials and ateliers in the Reggio schools leads to deep levels of thinking, self-expression, and creativity.

Overviews

Isenberg, J. P., & Jalongo, M. R. (2001). *Creative expression and play in the early childhood curriculum* (3rd ed.). Upper Saddle River, NJ: Merrill/Prentice Hall. The authors present a comprehensive discussion of the theoretical and practical aspects of creativity—best in the field.

Koralek, D. G. (Ed.) (2005). *Spotlight on young children and the creative arts.* Washington, DC: National Association for the Education of Young Children. This collection of articles discusses how crucial the creative arts are to children's development and includes resources and developmentally appropriate activities.

Collections of Creative Activity Suggestions

Note: Newcomers to the field of early childhood education should bear in mind that, when looking for resource books of creative activities, it is strictly buyer beware. Many so-called creative books are really collections of highly structured craft ideas that leave little or nothing to the child's imagination. The books included here are happy exceptions to this rule.

Bos, B. (1982). *Please don't move the muffin tins: A hands-off guide to art for the young child.* Roseville, CA: Turn the Page Press. Nicely illustrated, this book has many practical suggestions and draws a clear distinction between crafts and art.

Chenfield, M. B. (2002). *Creative experiences for young children* (3rd ed.). Orlando: Harcourt Brace. Chenfield divides activities according to topics such as bodies or people we meet. She suggests creative activities, including art, movement, and discussion activities related to the topic.

Including Children with Disabilities

Anderson, F. E. (1996). *Art-centered education and therapy for children with disabilities.* Springfield, IL: Thomas. Teachers will find the chapter on art adaptations for children with disabilities to be particularly helpful.

Money Savers

MacDonald, S. (1996). *Squish, sort, paint & build: Over 200 easy learning center activities.* Beltsville, MD: Gryphon House. The book presents a multitude of equipment and accessories teachers can make for almost no money, which generate activities that provide variety and new experiences for the children—a superior example of creativity.

Redleaf, R., & Robertson, A. (1999). *Learn and play the recycle way: Homemade toys that teach.* St. Paul, MN: Redleaf. This book offers many ideas for free or inexpensive materials that teachers can make.

Visual Arts

Epstein, A. S., & Trimis, E. (2002). *Supporting young artists: The development of the visual arts in young children.* Ypsilanti, MI: High/Scope. In addition to providing theoretical background and research, the authors provide practical information for supporting children's artistic experiences including drawing, painting, paper, and found and recycled materials.

Clay

Kohl, M. F. (1989). *Mudworks: Creative clay, dough, and modeling experiences.* Bellingham, WA: Bright Ring. A tremendous variety of mixtures are included together with estimates of appropriate age, palatability, and variations.

Woodworking

Huber, L. K. (1999). Woodworking with young children: You can do it! *Young Children, 54*(6), 32–34. Encouragement and advice is provided here for first-time venturers in woodworking.

Blocks

Wellhousen, K., & Kieff, J. (2001). *A constructivist approach to block play in early childhood.* Albany, NY: Delmar/Thomson. A wealth of information is supplied here, including a rare chapter on using blocks in the primary grades and one on including children who have disabilities in block play.

For the Advanced Student

Kohn, A. (2000). Art for art's sake. In S. Nagel (Ed.), *Creativity: Being usefully innovative in solving diverse problems.* Huntington, NY: Nova Science Publishers. This chapter conveniently summarizes research on creativity conducted by Teresa Amabile, a foremost researcher in this field.

Related Organizations and Online Resources

The National Art Education Association (NAEA) is a nonprofit organization supporting art educators. http://www.naea-reston.org/

The North American Reggio Emilia Alliance (NAREA) is an organization that supports the exploration of the Reggio Emilia approach worldwide. The Web site has information about the Reggio schools in Italy, the "Hundred Languages of Children" exhibit, and North American programs that are exploring the Reggio approach. http://www. reggioalliance.org/

CHAPTER *fifteen*

DEVELOPING VERBAL COMPETENCE

Have you ever . . .

- Worked in a multiethnic classroom and wondered whether you should make all the children speak English all the time?
- Worried what to do about a 3-year-old who hardly ever says a word?
- Wished that you could get the children to sing more?

If you have, the material in this chapter will help you.

There is no better play material in the world than words. They surround us, go with us through our work-a-day tasks, their sound is always in our ears, their rhythms on our tongue. Why do we leave it to special occasions and to special people to use these common things as precious play material? Because we are grownups and have closed our ears and our eyes that we may not be distracted from our plodding ways! But when we turn to the children, to hearing and seeing children, to whom all the world is as play material, who think and feel through play, can we not then drop our adult utilitarian speech and listen and watch for the patterns of words and ideas? Can we not speak in rhythm, in pleasing sounds, even in song for the mere sensuous delight it gives us and them even though it adds nothing to the content of our remarks? If we can, I feel sure children will not lose their native use of words: What's more, I think those of six and seven and eight who have lost it in part—and their stories show they have—will win back their spontaneous joy in the play of words.

—Lucy Sprague Mitchell (1948)

Language and vocabulary represent the very foundation of learning to read and write. . . . Language is not just talk. Prominent psychologists, such as Jean Piaget and Lev Vygotsky, recognized the importance of the relationship between language and thought. In other words, children use words as a way to understand important concepts. In fact, language actually drives cognitive development, with words standing for increasingly sophisticated ideas.

—Susan B. Neuman (2006, p. 12)

HOW DO CHILDREN LEARN TO TALK?

Arguments continue over how children actually acquire the ability to use language, and no definitive answer has been settled on yet (Bohannon & Bonvillian, 2001; Gleason, 2001; Han, Roskos, Christie, Mandzuk, & Vukelich, 2005). However, it is valuable for teachers to be acquainted with the current state of theories of language acquisition, because this field of study is very active at present and the conclusions about how language is learned have important implications for teaching.

What is known so far is that the development of language is a gradual process that proceeds in predictable order and that families and teachers (as representatives and conveyers of culture) can be powerful influences in fostering the acquisition of vocabulary and the growth of fluency as they help children acquire concepts and attach words to those concepts (Han et al., 2005; Neuman, 2006).

One school of thought favors the importance of imitation and reinforcement as the most probable acquisition device (Bandura, 1986; Cattell, 2001; Skinner, 1957, 1974), but many people think these theorists have difficulty explaining how children can produce novel, previously unheard utterances by means of these processes. Another group postulates that children develop a language in accordance with a basic, universal linguistic structure inherent in all people that is gradually acted on by different cultures to produce diverse languages (Cattell, 2001; Chomsky, 1987, 1999; McNeill, 1970). According to this linguistic theory, novel utterances are the result of applying abstracted linguistic rules rather than merely imitating what has been heard. Still another theory is that children simply derive abstract rules of language structure as they use it and hear it spoken around them (Maratsos, 1989). Such formulations of rules are not deliberate and consciously determined. It is impossible to picture little children saying to themselves, "If I want to tell my mother I see more than one cat, I must add an s at the end of *cat*." As Herriot (1987) puts it, "They use the rule though they cannot describe it" (p. 427).

Because anyone who has worked with young children can cite numerous examples of their acquiring language through imitation and equally numerous examples of spontaneous, novel speech, it seems probable that several factors operate together in language learning and that teachers should take them all into account. If imitation and reinforcement play a part in language acquisition, it behooves teachers to provide good examples for children to imitate and to make the process of using language to communicate satisfying for them. Such gratifications need not be elaborate. Paying attention to what children are saying, for instance, is a very effective way of encouraging them to con-

Teachers can be a powerful influence in fostering the child's language acquisition.

tinue speaking. If teachers also believe that children use experience with language to somehow arrive at linguistic rules for speaking, they will want to expose them to hearing a great deal of language and encourage them to use language in return. They should also encourage the children to use it in expressive, spontaneous ways as often as possible.

The Effects of Early Education on Children's Language Development

One of the most important learnings that takes place in the child's early years is learning to express herself with words. Children who communicate well end up doing better in school and in their social relationships later in life, as early language development is correlated with later academic and social success (Bredekamp, 2005; Goldstein, 2004; Han et al., 2005; Hart & Risley, 1995, 2003). Early language learning also affects the child's ability to read in elementary school. Researchers have consistently found that children with greater language proficiency become better readers. For children with less fluency, their reading comprehension will likely fall below grade level in elementary school. Thus, researchers Han and colleagues (2005) conclude: "Creating vocabulary learning opportunities for children in the early years is one of adults' most critical responsibilities" (p. 333).

The amount of time that adults talk with young children affects their language learning. Studies have shown that the more time parents spend talking to their children, the more words and language skills the children pick up (Bredekamp, 2005). Unfortunately, studies have also shown that teachers spend surprisingly little time in actual conversations with individual children, spending more time discussing routine matters (Han et al., 2005). Since children's later success is dependent upon early language learning, it is crucial that teachers develop curricula that are rich in opportunities for children to speak and be heard. This is particularly important for children with disabilities who show a higher prevalence of language delay and need early language intervention in order to keep up with their peers (Goldstein, 2004). (The Chapter Spotlight offers further insight into the importance of developmentally appropriate language teaching in the early years.)

Teachers also need to have in mind a developmental timetable of when various language skills appear. Table 15.1 and Table 15.2 provide a list of readily observable behaviors that can help teachers and parents identify children who are lagging too far behind or who are exceptionally advanced. These youngsters can then be offered the special help and opportunities they require.

CHAPTER SPOTLIGHT

Language and the Brain

Although acquisition theories remain a matter of debate, there are some solid facts about language development and the brain that can be summed up under the headings of *location, maturation,* and *education.*

Location and Maturation

Location and maturation play an important role in language acquisition. We all know that when babies start to talk they begin with one word "sentences" and then gradually add more complicated ones as they grow older. This progression from simple to complex seems logical, but what most of us do not know is that, logic aside, there is a *physiological* reason for the progression from words to grammatically constructed phrases because of the pattern of how the brain grows. The part of the brain that enables children to acquire vocabulary is located toward the back (Wernicke's area) and is the first language area to develop—hence the baby develops single-word sentences. The second important language area (Broca's area) is located much closer to the front of the brain and matures later. Broca's area enables children to apply grammatical rules to adjust the form of words to enrich their meaning (for example, in English adding "ed" to indicate the past tense, or "s" to indicate more than one) as well as to arrange words into meaningful sentences. This grammatical ability begins about age 2 and is largely in place by age 4 (Eliot, 1999).

In addition to this new information about the developmental time line for Wernicke's and Broca's areas, research also substantiates the fact that there is a *critical period* in development that constitutes the most ideal time for children to acquire language skills. Of course, people can and do improve their native and foreign language skills beyond that period, but researchers agree that the optimal period for acquiring language extends from infancy to age 7 or 10 at the latest (Eliot, 1999; Gleason, 2001).

Implications for teachers and parents: The interesting information accumulating about why and when children are capable of using different language areas of the brain and the sequential timetable for that development makes clear the futility of pushing children too soon to learn skills they are not capable of using. Obviously, it does no good and possibly some discouraging harm to struggle to teach children something before their brains are capable of using it.

On the other hand, the critical period research that identifies age 7 and younger as providing the best window of opportunity for most easily learning language suggests how important it is to provide plentiful language stimulation during those early years for children to develop their skills most completely.

Education

This is *education* used in the broadest sense of the word—it includes all the external experiences that the child is exposed to that influence which language, or languages, she learns and what she does with what she has learned. This learning begins in the very earliest stages of life—some research indicates perhaps even before the child is born—and certainly within the first 6 months following birth, when research reveals that babies become more "tuned" (educated) to hearing the sounds (phonemes) used in a particular language and less sensitive to those not heard regularly (Gleason, 2001).

During the preschool years and the critical language learning period that time includes, the influence of the environment and the education it provides becomes increasingly important. A landmark study undertaken by Hart and Risley (1995) provides an example of just how important. They were concerned about the differences in language ability they found among children from different economic levels in the United States. They studied a group of preschool-age youngsters in their homes to find out why the children from the lowest economic group had the smallest vocabularies. After 2½ years of extensive investigation, their findings were that the parents from the upper socioeconomic group talked to their children more than twice as much as the disadvantaged parents did and also used more different words and more elaborate sentence structures. The higher socioeconomic parents also used more positive discipline techniques based on guiding rather than demanding, and they were more responsive to the children's behavior.

Implications for teachers and parents: As Hart and Risley demonstrated, the quality of the language environment that children are exposed to really does affect how well their language develops. It is vital to expose them to a wide variety of words and language usage and provide that experience in as positive an environment as possible if we want to foster the greatest growth of verbal ability.

Although we adults must wait on nature's timetable for certain signs of language readiness to appear, we must also realize how important the early years are for building receptive and expressive language skills, since that time largely covers the critical period for language development. This chapter discusses many practical, developmentally appropriate approaches teachers and parents can employ that will empower children to use language richly and well as their abilities mature.

Table 15.1

Milestones in the Development of Language Ability in Young Children

Average Age	Question	Average Behavior
3–6 months	What does he do when you talk to him?	He awakens or quiets to the sound of his mother's voice.
	Does he react to your voice even when he cannot see you?	He typically turns eyes and head in the direction of the source of sound.
7–10 months	When he can't see what is happening, what does he do when he hears familiar footsteps? The dog barking? The telephone ringing? Candy paper rattling? Someone's voice? His own name?	He turns his head and shoulders toward familiar sounds, even when he cannot see what is happening. Such sounds do not have to be loud to cause him to respond.
11–15 months	Can he point to or find familiar objects or people when he is asked to? **Example:** "Where is Jimmy?" "Find the ball."	He shows his understanding of some words by appropriate behavior; for example, he points to or looks at familiar objects or people, on request.
	Does he respond differently to different sounds?	He jabbers in response to a human voice, is apt to cry when there is thunder, or may frown when he is scolded.
	Does he enjoy listening to some sounds and imitating them?	Imitation indicates that he can hear the sounds and match them with his own sound production.
1½ years	Can he point to parts of his body when you ask him to? **Example:** "Show me your eyes." "Show me your nose."	Some children begin to identify parts of the body. He should be able to show his nose or eyes.
	How many understandable words does he use—words you are sure *really* mean something?	He should be using a few single words. They are not complete or pronounced perfectly but are clearly meaningful.
2 years	Can he follow simple verbal commands when you are careful not to give him any help, such as looking at the object or pointing in the right direction? **Example:** "Johnny, get your hat and give it to Daddy." "Debby, bring me your ball."	He should be able to follow a few simple commands without visual clues.
	Does he enjoy being read to? Does he point out pictures of familiar objects in a book when asked to? **Example:** "Show me the baby." "Where's the rabbit?"	Most 2-year-olds enjoy being "read to" and shown simple pictures in a book or magazine, and they will point out pictures when you ask them to.
	Does he use the names of familiar people and things such as *Mommy, milk, ball,* and *hat?*	He should be using a variety of everyday words heard in his home and neighborhood.
	What does he call himself?	He refers to himself by name.
	Is he beginning to show interest in the sound of radio or TV commercials?	Many 2-year-olds do show such interest, by word or action.
	Is he putting a few words together to make little "sentences"? **Example:** "Go bye-bye car." "Milk all gone."	These "sentences" are not usually complete or grammatically correct.
2½ years	Does he know a few rhymes or songs? Does he enjoy hearing them?	Many children can say or sing short rhymes or songs and enjoy listening to records or to mother singing.

(Continued)

Table 15.1

(continued)

Average Age	Question	Average Behavior
2½ years	What does he do when the ice cream man's bell rings, out of his sight, or when a car door or house door closes at a time when someone in the family usually comes home?	If a child has good hearing, and these are events that bring him pleasure, he usually reacts to the sound by running to look or telling someone what he hears.
3 years	Can he show that he understands the meaning of some words besides the names of things? **Example:** "Make the car go." "Put the block in your pocket." "Find the big doll."	He should be able to understand and use some simple verbs, pronouns, prepositions, and adjectives, such as *go, me, in,* and *big.*
	Can he find you when you call him from another room?	He should be able to locate the source of a sound.
	Does he sometimes use complete sentences?	He should be using complete sentences some of the time.
4 years	Can he tell about events that have happened recently?	He should be able to give a connected account of some recent experiences.
	Can he carry out two directions, one after the other? **Example:** "Bobby, find Susie and tell her dinner's ready."	He should be able to carry out a sequence of two simple directions.
5 years	Do neighbors and others outside the family understand most of what he says?	His speech should be intelligible, although some sounds may still be mispronounced.
	Can he carry on a conversation with other children or familiar grown-ups?	Most children of this age can carry on a conversation if the vocabulary is within their experience.
	Does he begin a sentence with *I* instead of *me, he* instead of *him?*	He should use some pronouns correctly.
	Is his grammar almost as good as his parents'?	Most of the time, it should match the patterns of grammar used by the adults of his family and neighborhood.

Source: From *Learning to Talk: Speech, Hearing, and Language Problems in the Pre-School Child* by the National Institute of Neurological Diseases and Stroke, 1969, Washington, DC: U.S. Department of Health, Education, and Welfare.

Table 15.2

Milestones in the Development of Language Ability in Early Elementary School Children (6–8 Years)

- Movement from oral self-expression to written self-expression.
- Receptive vocabulary increases not just by listening but by reading.
- By age 8, typically has about 20,000 words.
- Can learn almost 20 words a day in a language-rich environment.
- Understands that words can have multiple meanings.
- Engages in interactive, reciprocal conversations with adults and other children.
- Realizes there are multiple points of view and uses language to think, explain, and influence others.
- More effectively uses the power of verbal communication, including humor.
- Has capacity to acquire bilingual or multilingual competence.

Source: From *Developmentally Appropriate Practice in Early Childhood Programs* (rev. ed.) by S. Bredekamp and C. Copple (Eds.), 1997, Washington, DC: National Association for the Education of Young Children.

Language as a Two-Way Street

Language is best thought of as a two-way street, with the traffic of listening and talking going back and forth in a sharing way. One direction, which requires speaking skills, is called *expressive language*, and the other, which requires listening and understanding skills, is called *receptive language*. Because many teachers are less adept at encouraging children to use expressive language, ways of fostering it are discussed first and are then followed by enjoyable ways to build receptive language skills by enticing the children to listen.

PRACTICAL WAYS TO ENCOURAGE CHILDREN TO USE THEIR EXPRESSIVE LANGUAGE SKILLS

Chapter 11 on emotional health has already discussed how important it is for the teacher to "hear" the children's feelings and, by describing these to them, let them know that he understands what is going on inside them. This kind of interested concern is also a fundamental way of encouraging children to talk, because the teacher who truly listens draws forth conversation from children as a magnet attracts iron.

Of course, if teachers have packed the day too full so that everyone must be pushed from one activity to the next or if there is not enough teaching staff, the leisure that good conversational opportunities require is hard to come by. But even in centers where these circumstances prevail, teachers can encourage children to chat with them, if they realize how valuable such opportunities are for encouraging verbal fluency.

Provide Real Things for the Children to Talk About

Language without experience and experience without language are almost meaningless to children. The work of Eve Clark (1983) on how children learn to attach meaning to words reminds us of the importance of tying experience to language. She points out that children originally establish word meanings on the basis of salient perceptual features of objects: shape, movement, size, sound, taste, and texture—all sensory experiences. The moral for early childhood teachers (even though they are dealing with children slightly older than the ones in Clark's studies) is that they must be careful to offer language activities related to those tangible, concrete things children know about because of their direct sensory experience with them.

It makes no sense to read a poem about snow to California children, many of whom have no idea of what it is, unless teachers also liken it to hail and include such experiences as taking them to visit an ice skating rink, showing them pictures of snow, and talking about how it feels when they put their hands in the refrigerator. Even then, these children do not really have the meanings associated with snow that youngsters in wintry climates do. Just because children can mouth a word does not mean they necessarily grasp the concept.

Use Discussion and Conversation Whenever Possible

Some examples of possible discussion openers include asking children to offer suggestions ("Visiting day is coming up. What activities do you think we should set up for your brothers and sisters to do? What would they enjoy?"), to consider alternatives ("It's such a beautiful day! Do you think we should have water play after snack, or would you prefer to walk to the park?" "Would you rather have Officer Thompson visit us at school or go to the police station and meet her there?"), to make plans in advance ("You know, Ciara is bringing her puppies to visit again tomorrow. Let's put our heads together and make a plan to keep them from being handled too much."), and to solve social problems ("We've been having so many fights over that trike with the license plate on it. I want to know what you children think we should do about it.").

Note that most of these gambits also require follow-up questions that encourage children to give the reasons for their opinions. Once all the possibilities, opinions, and reasons have been aired, it is best to reach a democratic group consensus—working out compromises where possible and, in the end, following the democratic principle of doing what the majority thinks best.

These decision-making opportunities should only be offered when the choices are real and are truly appropriate for children to evaluate. For example, it would not be appropriate to ask the children to decide what to do about a youngster who is wetting his pants or to expect them to make a decision on whether school fees should be raised, but it would be within their ability to ask them to suggest a number of ways Halloween might be celebrated or how they would help their friend Ciara feel better because her puppy died.

An alternative to taking the risk of abiding by a group decision, if you feel the children are too immature to reach an adequate one, is to tell them you want some ideas and suggestions that will help you arrive at a fair or good decision.

Conduct a Conversation, Not an Interrogation

Teachers frequently see themselves as being primarily information givers and getters; that is, they are forever using their own expressive language and telling children important facts or asking them questions so the children will prove they already know the facts or are thinking about them. Good conversation, however, rarely dwells on such matters.

Witness the following variations on the same topic, then ask yourself which of the two you would prefer to take part in if you were the child. Also, ask yourself what the child learned from each of the two encounters and which one fostered the greater fluency and development of thought.

EXAMPLE 1

Child: Guess what, Teacher, I got new shoes!
Teacher: No kidding! My, my! They're really pretty!
Child: They got chuckles!
Teacher: Chuckles?
Child: Yeah, you know! *Chuckles!* Here on the side. (points to buckles)
Teacher: (light dawning) Oh, you mean *buckles!* That word sounds like buck-buck-buck-buck-buck-buck-a-luck buckles!
Child: (amused) Buck-buck-buck-buck-buck-a-luck buckles!
Teacher: That's right—buckles. (pause) Are they hard to get through that hole? (meaning the straps)
Child: Yeah, but I don't mind. I just worm 'em through!
Teacher: Yeah, just wiggle the edge that way—into the side place!
Child: I can do it! Into the side place! (pause) They make marks on my socks!
Teacher: Oh, yeah, I see. Does it hurt?
Child: Nope. My foot's sweaty, that's all—makes the red come off.
Teacher: You take those shoes off at night, you'll still have little red feet on!
Child: (thinks this over, laughs) Well, yeah—little *pink* feet! Just like wearing shoes to bed! (laughs) My momma sure won't like that, no way! (runs off to play)

EXAMPLE 2

Child: Guess what, Teacher, I got new shoes!
Teacher: Yes, I see you did. They're pretty, Tania. What color do you think they are?
Child: (pause) Red.
Teacher: And what else is special about them?
Child: (shakes head) I don't know.

Teacher: Oh, yes, now—think a minute. What's that on the side of your red shoe? Right there? (pointing to the buckle)

Child: It makes red marks.

Teacher: That isn't what I mean! What's *this* called? (pointing to the buckle again)

Child: Don't know.

Teacher: It's called a *buckle*. *Buckle*—can you say that?

Child: Fix it for me!

Teacher: What's the magic word?

Child: (pause) Please.

Teacher: Please what?

Child: Please fix that.

Teacher: (persistently but not unpleasantly) What's that called? I just told you.

Child: (says nothing)

Teacher: (patiently) Buckle—remember? That's a buckle!

Child: Buckle!

Teacher fixes the shoe while child stands silently, then runs off.

In comparing these examples, it should be clear that there is a place for fun in talking with children and that it is not always necessary to use high-pressure techniques to obtain valuable educational results. Note also how in example 1 the ideas build on each other and the talk flows freely and increases in quantity. These are the most important goals to work toward when building language skills in young children. They are certainly more important than driving and driving to add one new word, *buckle,* to the child's vocabulary.

Listen as Well as Talk

Of course, to conduct a genuine conversation, it is essential to pay real attention to what the child is saying—both with her body and with her words. Sensitive teachers (when working with children from most but not all cultures) show they are listening by bending down and looking eye to eye, providing a pause of "wait time" for the child to formulate her reply, and not preformulating what to reply before the youngster has even had a turn to speak.

Ask Questions That Invite Children to Respond

Questions should relate to topics that children are interested in and that they know something about—preferably, even more than the teacher does. For example, "Where did you get that wonderful hat?" and "How come you like this book so much?" and "I saw you helping your mama in the market yesterday. Were you telling her what to get?" all invite replies that will tell the teacher something he does not already know, and they cast the child in the role of the authority.

If these invitations to chat are coupled with nonjudgmental replies to what the children say, they will encourage talk even further. For example, consider the effect of the two kinds of teacher responses in the following dialogues:

EXAMPLE 3

Teacher (playfully picking up the child and hugging her): I saw you helping your mama in the market yesterday. Were you telling her what to get?

Child: Yeah! I told her to get pickles, and ice cream, and sugar buns!

Teacher: Why did you do that? You know that isn't good for you! You ought to tell her to get cereal and vegetables and the things that we talked about at lunch that are good for you to eat! They'll make you grow up strong like your brother!

Child: (says nothing—just wiggles to get down)

Teacher (playfully picking up the child and hugging her): I saw you helping your mama in the market yesterday. Were you telling her what to get?

Child: Yeah, I told her to get pickles, and ice cream, and sugar buns!

Teacher: I guess you were really hungry!

Child: I sure was—and those little crackers, and chicken, and corn . . .

Teacher: That's what makes you grow—good stuff like that. [meaning chicken and corn]

Child: And shoe polish!

Teacher: Shoe polish! (playfully) I don't want to eat that!

Child (grinning and with great emphasis): And *shoe* polish! We had *shoe* polish frosting for dessert!

Teacher (laughs): Yum, yum. It must have looked like chocolate!

Child: Yeah, chocolate shoe polish frosting. (laughs)

Teacher: Well, it's *real* chocolate pudding for lunch today. Want to set out the napkins?

Child: Sure! (wiggles to get down)

PRACTICAL WAYS TO ENCOURAGE CHILDREN TO USE THEIR RECEPTIVE LISTENING SKILLS

Developing an Attractive Speaking Voice

It is really true that teachers' voices set the tone of the children's day, and it makes sense that the children are more likely to want to listen to voices that generally sound warm and cheerful. Sad to say, when teachers are under stress, their voices sometimes rise in pitch or take on a hard, nasal quality that is unpleasant to listen to and that creates tension in the children, too. Other teachers may have monotonous voices and thereby fail to attract or hold the children's attention.

The best remedy for these problems is for teachers to tape-record themselves regularly during group or lunch time and actually listen to what they are saying and how they sound while saying it. This is because it is impossible to correct a voice-quality problem until becoming aware of it. The next step for teachers is catching themselves in the act and consciously modulating the tone of voice to a more pleasant level. One way teachers can keep track of voice quality is to put five pennies in a pocket at the beginning of the day and transfer one to another pocket every time they hear their voices rising too far. It takes only a few days to keep all the pennies in the beginning pocket.

Presenting Songs and Records

Music should be part of the life of the school throughout the day and definitely not relegated just to group time. The use of a simple, familiar song can ease transitions between activities and deepen pleasure in activities themselves. Such a simple thing as singing the words, "Swing, swing, swingy, swing" to the tune of "Row, Row, Row Your Boat" can enchant a 2½-year-old, for example. Singing can pass the time while waiting for lunch or bind a group of parents and children together at a party. It can introduce the children to their cultural heritage, whether it be early American folk songs or ones from Africa or Germany or Japan. It is the perfect medium for opening group time because children can join in as they arrive without feeling they are interrupting or that they have been left out.

Choosing a Good Song

A good song for young children is one that is simple, short, and repetitive. It should have a range of only a few notes. If it can be personalized by inserting the children's names, so much the better. Careful thought should be devoted to the quality of the song, also. There is no need to settle for trivial material when we have people like Raffi (1987), Thomas Moore (1991), and Hap Palmer (n.d.) providing good-quality pieces.

Traditional music should be included also. Many children today no longer hear nursery rhymes unless they are presented at school, yet many of these are set to tunes that have stood the test of time and are already familiar. "Twinkle, Twinkle, Little Star," "Jack and Jill," and "Mary Had a Little Lamb" come instantly to mind.

American folk songs, although less familiar to some of us, offer another rich resource for singing with children. These are often written in a minor key—a useful quality, because it extends the children's "ear" for melody. Some folk songs are surprisingly funny and frank, also qualities that both children and adults appreciate (Seeger, 1980).

Remember, too, that many children hear music all day long in their own homes where radios or television sets are continually turned on. Although one might not want to use all such material, there certainly are many popular songs that will fit in, and because popular music is so much a part of the life of the children's homes, it makes sense to include it.

Finally, singing simple songs from many cultures offers an excellent way of fostering positive feelings toward other peoples. A child can glow with importance when the teacher mentions that a particular song comes from Puerto Rico—the same place her own family comes from. The records of Ella Jenkins are prime examples of how various cultures can be presented to young children in a pleasurable, participatory way, but it is desirable to explore even further than that. There are many recordings available today that are authentic and appropriate to use with children. Adding musical instruments that come from the same culture as the song is a delightful touch. These need be neither elaborate nor expensive.

Here are five excellent books containing appropriate music for young children:

Church, E. B. (2000). *The great big book of classroom songs, rhymes, and chants.* New York: Scholastic.

Haines, J. E., & Gerber, L. L. (2000). *Leading young children to music* (6th ed.). Upper Saddle River, NJ: Merrill/Prentice Hall.

Jenkins, E. (1997). *The Ella Jenkins song book for children.* New York: Music Sales Corporation.

Moomaw, S. (1997). *More than singing: Discovering music in preschool and kindergarten.* St. Paul, MN: Redleaf.

Seeger, R. C. (1980). *American folk songs for children.* Garden City, NY: Doubleday.

The books by Church, Haines, and Moomaw go far beyond presenting songs per se. They are also rich sources of information on presenting all forms of music to young children with the added advantage of providing *very simple* arrangements scored for piano, Autoharp, or guitar. The Seeger book is an authentic resource for folk songs.

Teaching a Song to Children

Be prepared to repeat a song several times on several days for the children to learn it well enough to enjoy singing it freely. This is one of the primary reasons for choosing simple, repetitive songs of good quality. However, the children will be able to join in right away if there is a short chorus in which first the leader and then the group sing the same refrain (Wolf, 1994).

Sing slowly, and teach only one verse at a time. It will contribute to the pleasure if the song is accompanied by an instrument, such as a guitar or an Autoharp, but this is not essential. Indeed, unless done with care, using something like a piano can be more trouble than it is worth if it means the teacher must turn her back on the children while playing it. The advantage of using an Autoharp is that children can be invited to strum it in time to the singing, because all one must do to control the note is press down firmly on the correct key.

Remember, too, that one of the nicest things about singing with children is the freedom it gives the teacher to improvise and adapt a song to the circumstances of the day. Clare Cherry's book (1971) on movement is full of examples of how topical words can be set to tunes everyone knows.

Presenting Poetry

Like singing, poetry should not be reserved just for group time, although it should always be part of the experience (Norton, 1999). Teachers who take the trouble to commit some short poems to memory and who can quote these as the occasion arises can make literature an integral, pleasurable part of the children's lives. There is great value for teachers to memorize poetry: It can be a source of real delight for the children.

For teachers who do not wish to memorize verse, a poetry file is recommended as the quickest and best way to obtain access to poetry as it is needed. Relying on books as a resource really does not work out well. It is too hard to find just the right poem at the right time.

Our teachers type out or photocopy appropriate, good-quality poetry as they come across it and mount it on mat board obtained as "scraps" from picture frame shops. This preserves the poem on a durable, hard-to-lose background and also makes it easy to file by topic so it can be immediately located when needed. Then when we need something on rain, or worms, or going to sleep, or shadows, we can put our hands right on it.

We have found the poetry of Dorothy Aldis, Marchette Chute, Aileen Fisher, Myra Cohn Livingston, Walter de la Mare, Miriam Clark Potter, Christina Rosetti, and Robert Louis Stevenson particularly appropriate—and of course Mother Goose should not be forgotten. Many fine editions of her rhymes are available.

No matter how complete the file, there will inevitably be times when no poem can be found that exactly suits a particular occasion. When this happens, try writing one yourself. The children will appreciate its timeliness. Its appropriateness for the occasion more than makes up for any potential lack of literary merit.

Presenting Finger Plays

Although the poetic quality of finger plays often leaves much to be desired, their ability to involve children instantly makes them a valuable addition to the language development arsenal. It is the old story of doing while saying—linking language and action—that helps children learn and enjoy this activity.

Finger plays, like songs, are excellent ways to begin a group time because they are so attractive to children. They also can provide relief in the middle of a group time by offering a change of pace and recentering the children's attention. Finger plays make good "time fillers" when the schedule goes awry and the children have to wait awhile for something to happen. If the same one is presented repeatedly, they also enjoy saying it along with the teacher as they go through the actions. The actions themselves need not be limited just to fingers. Many successful "finger plays" actually involve larger muscles, such as getting up and sitting down. They can either be sung or recited.

Presenting Books and Stories

Choosing a Good Book or Story

Choose only the very best quality books to share with the children. Reading books aloud to children presents two wonderful opportunities for developing their aesthetic tastes. One, of course, is the quality of the literature presented. The other is the quality of the illustrations. In these days of violent, often hideous television cartoons and trite, "cute," cheapie books, the only opportunity some children ever have to come in contact with the excitement and good taste of a fine picture book is in the school's book corner and at group time. Therefore we teachers have an extremely important responsibility to provide only the best.

Fortunately, the best need not be prohibitively expensive—in fact, it's free for anyone willing to take the time to go to the library. Should that prove inconvenient, major booksellers carry paperback versions of many excellent preschool books complete with the original illustrations. Scholastic Books also offers book clubs with additional titles that appeal to children and are in good taste.

Good books for young children generally have brief texts, beautiful pictures, and subject matter that is interesting to children and presented in good taste. When possible they should have a multiethnic, culturally accurate look and have a nonsexist approach. Excellent books also have that extra note of originality combined with quality writing and a good story that enshrines them in the hearts of children forever.

Some outstanding examples of excellent children's books are *Roadrunner's Dance* (Anaya, 2000), *Alejandro's Gift* (Albert, 1994), *Curious George* (Rey, 1941), *Owl Moon* (Yolen, 1987), *Imogene's Antlers* (Small, 2000), *Kitten's First Full Moon* (Henkes, 2004), *Wizzil* (Steig, 2000), *Anansi the Spider* (McDermott, 1972), *Baby Goose* (McMullen, 2004), *Abuela* (Dorros, 1991), *The Hello, Goodbye Window* (Juster, 2005), and *Zen Stories* (Muth, 2005).

Books should be readily available throughout the day and varied from time to time—new ones brought out and more familiar friends put away. Variety is as close and inexpensive as the nearest public library.

It is always important to provide a cozy oasis where children can withdraw and leaf through their favorites without interruption. Opening a book to an especially beautiful or interesting picture and placing it in a holder by the bookshelf often entices children to that area. Children should be taught to handle books with care. Never permit them to leave books lying on the floor for children to walk on or otherwise abuse.

Reading Stories

Reading stories is a good example of an activity in which volunteers can excel with only a moderate amount of instruction from the staff. Encourage them to settle down in a comfortable place with several well-chosen books. This provides wonderful opportunities for one-to-one and one-to-two contacts that both children and volunteers find meaningful and satisfying.

Teachers often think of reading stories to children as being primarily a receptive language situation where the children are expected to sit quietly and "receive" the story—but it should be both a receptive and expressive language opportunity. If stories are presented with this goal in mind, teachers no longer have to struggle to keep the children quiet. Instead, they can welcome the children's comments and questions and invite discussion about what may happen next in the story.

Teachers should read with expression and enthusiasm and should be familiar with the text so that they do not stumble over words. They should take time to enjoy what is happening with the children and allow them to add their own comments. Bos (1983) describes this process well:

> Slowly I started letting the children discuss many pages of the book as I read. I would stop. We would examine a picture, asking questions about what they could see. Often they would see details I hadn't. If I would ask them what they thought would happen next, they could frequently come up with wonderfully creative ideas. As this process continued, I began to see marvelous results. I started to see the children themselves emerging—attempting their language, attempting to communicate with me—and at the same time I could see that they were discovering that they were capable of complicated and delightful communication. (p. 7)

Reading aloud is a wonderful way to extend everyone's vocabularies.

Of course, a balance is needed between encouraging children's comments and maintaining the momentum of the plot. Sometimes saying something such as "Just one more comment and then we'd better find out whether the Circus Baby could really sit on that chair" or "Well, let's go on now and see what's on the next page" will usually lead the children back to the book without hurting anyone's feelings.

Encouraging Children to Tell Stories

We have already spoken of the value that telling stories can have for children in terms of expressing their feeling and clarifying their ideas (chapter 11). Providing them with opportunities for doing this also develops language fluency.

To avoid long, rambling accounts at group time, which usually produce uncontrollable restlessness in the other children, it is best to pick times during the day when child storytelling can be done on a one-to-one basis between a youngster and a staffperson or volunteer. Children particularly enjoy dictating stories in their own special books that the teacher has made by stapling a few sheets of paper together. They may also enjoy adding illustrations to emphasize what they mean.

There are various ways of starting things off with the child. The teacher can simply ask the child what she wants to tell about today, inquire if she wants to have him write down how her puppy learned to stop barking, or even begin a story himself for the child to continue, perhaps using those magical words, "Once upon a time . . ."

Another way to encourage children to tell stories is to use pictures from the picture file. Younger children tend to use such single pictures more as opportunities simply to tell what is happening in the picture itself than as a starting point for a more extended story. Older children can go beyond that limited approach. Many times a picture of two little girls on a climbing gym or a lonely-looking boy holding a puppy can spark a long tale that uses the illustration as a takeoff point, particularly if the teacher encourages such storytelling by asking occasional questions or making comments such as "Then what do you think happened?" or "After she caught the fish, what did she do next?"

Suggestions for Telling Stories

Like the children, teachers can also learn to tell stories with a little practice. This often has a liberating, creative effect, since it allows them to tailor the tale exactly to the requirements of the youthful audience. Telling stories also offers the opportunity to include the children themselves as characters. A teacher's story can recapitulate something the children themselves have done, or it can be based on one of the teacher's experiences that he thinks the children will enjoy. Stories can be based on books as well as on personal experience, and this is a particularly useful technique to employ when the illustrations are delightful but the text too difficult for the children to comprehend. Learning to "edit" as they go along is also a useful strategy for teachers to cultivate when material is sexist or conveys an undesirable racist slant. (Guidelines on identifying sexist and racist materials are found in appendix D.)

If you are insecure about storytelling, remember that children's librarians are often excellent storytellers and can frequently be prevailed on to present story hours for visiting children. Furthermore, many of them are also happy to impart their skills to other teachers if invited to participate in training workshops for this purpose.

BLACK ENGLISH AND BILINGUALISM

Because many youngsters come to school speaking only the language of their homes, which may differ from what is spoken at school, it is important for teachers to be well informed about Black English and bilingualism.

Black English

Because the structure of Black English differs from that of Standard English, in the past some teachers have assumed that it was an inferior

Puppets are a delightful way for children to tell their own stories.

form of Standard English (Hill, 1977). However, Black English has been analyzed and shown to possess a sophisticated grammatical structure different from, but not necessarily inferior to, that of Standard English (Labov, 1970; Smitherman, 2000b).

Such research has helped teachers understand that this lect has a definite place in the culture of African American people and that it is not "baby talk." Actually, anyone who has been privileged to be included in the conversations, vivid and friendly insults, and other verbal games that go on between older African American children or adults really cannot fail to acknowledge the quickness of verbal wit and humor displayed at these times (Smitherman, 2000a).

Teachers must also be aware of the negative effect that disapproval of something so personal as the child's means of expressing herself could have on her self-image. Because Black English is not an inferior form of Standard English, and because it is important to sustain the child's self-esteem, many authorities now suggest that teachers not deplore or attempt to suppress this form of speech (Hale, 1992).

Perhaps the most effective way for teachers to regard Black English is to think of it as being another language instead of a lower-class lect. To function successfully in our world today, African American children need to acquire proficiency in both Black and Standard English, because, as they mature, they will need to shift gears back and forth between them depending on whom they are talking to. As is true in other bilingual situations, teachers must realize that for African American children (or Spanish-, or French-speaking youngsters) it is not necessary to abandon their first language in order to acquire a second one (Smitherman, 2000a, 2000b; Tabors & Lopez, 2005).

Bilingualism

The pros and cons of bilingualism and bilingual education are simply too vast a subject to be discussed in detail in a general education text of this kind. Suffice it to point out here that, although no one can deny the value and necessity of knowing English if families intend to live in the United States, it is also true that speaking two or more languages often opens the doors to lucrative employment opportunities for adults—which makes the home language an important educational asset to preserve during childhood (Fernandez, 2000).

In addition, studies have shown that bilingualism increases children's cognitive achievement (Gonzales, 2005).

Another reason for preserving the home language is that it is such an important part of identity that it is vital to honor it just as we do other aspects of children's cultural heritage (Head Start Performance Standards, 2004; Lundgren & Morrison, 2003; National Association for the Education of Young Children, 1995; Tabors & Lopez, 2005). Respect for their native language also helps children maintain closeness to their families by supporting the cultural values of the home—a very worthwhile goal (Gonzales, 2005; Lundgren & Morrison, 2003; Wong, 1991).

Bilingual education is a fact of life as the number of English-language learners continues to grow across the United States. For example, the Hispanic population has grown faster than the overall U.S. population for more than a decade. Areas in the country with little or no experience with ethnic or racial diversity, such as parts of the Midwest, are experiencing the greatest influx of Spanish speakers in the nation (Lundgren & Morrison, 2003). Unfortunately, many communities are ill-prepared for addressing the needs of English language learners, and English-only policies have been instituted in schools where children can be suspended for speaking Spanish (Reid, 2005).

In contrast, early childhood programs have been on the forefront of developing excellent bilingual programs to address the needs of English-language learners. Since 1972, Head Start has required that all classrooms support home languages and ethnic pride (Hill, 2005). Teachers who wish to support English-language learners in their classroom can learn from the established Head Start Program Performance Standards which include the following:

- Provide an environment of acceptance that supports and respects gender, culture, language, ethnicity, and family composition.
- Serve foods that reflect cultural and ethnic preferences.
- Communicate with families in their preferred or primary language or through an interpreter to the extent feasible.
- Hire staff, whenever possible, who speak the home language of infants and toddlers, and when a majority of children speak the same language, hire at least one classroom staff member or home visitor who speaks their language.
- Promote family participation in literacy-related activities in both English and the home language (Plutro, 2005, p. 4).

The main goal for the teacher is to encourage the development of the second, typically English language, while preserving the first one.

Helping the Non-English Speaking Newcomer Feel Comfortable in the Group

The most typical situation encountered by teachers of non-English-speaking students involves anxiously smiling parents, a small, bewildered child, and a tongue-tied teacher—who do not speak each other's languages. In addition to following the recommendations listed in chapters 11 and 13 for integrating all youngsters into the life of the school, here are some additional suggestions that are helpful to use with a non-English-speaking child:

- Remember—speaking louder does not help, but speaking *slowly* probably will. When speaking with the family, writing down what you mean can also make a difference.
- Language learning is a two-way street. Make certain you have written down some basic words to learn in the child's language before the family (and possibly the interpreter) depart.
- Encourage the family to stay as long as possible—sometimes families new to the United States worry that they are in the way or will not be welcome.

- Be warm and friendly without being overwhelming.

- It is very easy, especially with a shy child, to give up speaking directly to her. Be sure to include each youngster and speak to her, even though you know she may not understand what you are saying.

- Use gestures and take the risk of pantomiming even if you feel a little silly doing it— laughing really helps bridge the language gap.

- Accompany your gestures with nouns and verbs, but don't insist the child repeat them to you.

- Honor the "silent period" that often accompanies learning a new language, and don't insist she use English to tell you what she wants—at the same time, let her know you're pleased when she does attempt English.

- Children are wonderful gap-bridgers—encourage the other youngsters to include the newcomer in their play.

Using Bilingual Classrooms To Support Language Retention

At the preschool level, the bilingual approach is usually accomplished by employing teaching staff who are bilingual. In earlier years, the skills of such staff were most often used for interpretation rather than for preservation of the children's native tongue. It frequently happened that, as the children gained facility in English, the school dropped the use of the other language.

Now in some areas of the country there is more of an attempt to operate truly bilingual classrooms, in which a genuine effort is made to teach and sustain both languages and to perpetuate other cultural values, too. This kind of bilingual education is often termed a *maintenance bilingual model*. Barrera (1996) describes this succinctly: "In *maintenance* programs, both languages are equally valued and equally maintained throughout the education. Sometimes these are called *dual language* programs" (p. 46). A variation of this is the two-way model in which native English speakers learn a second language while native Spanish or French speakers acquire English (Zanger, 1991). Still another model uses only the child's dominant language while providing a family-centered, quality educational program. When children reach kindergarten age, they transfer into a transitional bilingual education model (Campos, 1995).

Even though such programs may still be relatively rare in public schools, this need not be the case for children's centers, which have much greater opportunities for autonomy. If teachers so choose, they can make a point of combining the multiethnic educational model and environment discussed in chapter 13 with a balanced bilingual program, thereby providing good-quality language maintenance programs for the children they serve (Fernandez, 2000).

At the very least, as Umberto Eco (1993) advocates:

> Work needs to be done among the young, from a very early age, three or four onwards, if only to teach them that there are different languages, so that they grasp the idea of diversity, to show them, for example, that in different languages there are many different names for a rabbit, and that those who call a rabbit by some other name are not necessarily barbarians. (p. 4)

THE CHILD WHO IS NOT FLUENT IN ANY LANGUAGE

The foregoing discussion assumes that children who are not speaking Standard English do speak some other language or lect fluently. However, some youngsters who arrive at the center are not verbal at all. Teachers must be on the lookout for such youngsters and not make the mistake of assuming, for example, that because they do not speak in English they must be fluent in their "home" language. This is not always the case. It is particularly valuable to check about such nonverbal behavior with the children's families. This will help determine whether they do not talk at school but do talk at home, or whether they say very little in either circumstance.

Children who are generally nonverbal both at home and at school need special attention and stimulation to develop their verbal and mental capacities. When these are provided, they often make very dramatic progress at school. However, if they are still not talking after 2 to 3 months of regular attendance, it is vital to seek the help of specialists, because there is often a significant reason for the delay.

Perhaps the child is hard of hearing or is developmentally delayed in some way (Patterson & Wright, 1990). Referrals should be made to the child's pediatrician, an otolaryngologist (a physician specializing in diseases of the ear, nose, and throat), or a speech pathologist. If developmental delay is suspected, referral should be made to a child psychologist for testing. Once the reason for the delay in speech has been determined, a plan for remediation should be developed, and the teacher should make certain the specialist provides information about what should be done to help carry the plan out. The sooner these conditions are identified, the sooner they can be treated. *Teachers must never wait an entire year with a nonverbal 3- or 4-year-old* in the hope that she will suddenly blossom forth and begin talking. All too often this fails to happen.

Summary

Recent research on brain development confirms the important role that the preprimary years play in children's acquisition of receptive and expressive language. Because learning language during these early years is so crucial, teachers and parents need to do all they can to facilitate its growth.

Strategies include encouraging children to put their ideas into words as frequently as possible, stimulating their listening skills, maintaining the children's home language in the school while also teaching them English, and being aware of developmental timetables so that children who require special help can obtain it promptly. Conducting conversations rather than interrogations and asking questions that prolong conversations are particularly valuable ways of facilitating the growth of language. Specific curriculum activities to promote such growth include the use of songs and records, poetry and finger plays, and books and stories.

Food for Thought and Group Discussions

1. You are teaching in a Head Start center, and you have a 4-year-old Mexican American girl in the group who replies only in single English words when asked a question. What factors and possibilities would you want to consider before deciding how to deal with this behavior?

2. Is it possible to ask children too many questions? What might be some alternative ways of keeping conversation going instead of always asking questions?

3. Go to your local library and look over the books there for children. Select a desirable and an undesirable one for the age you are working with, and bring them to class. Be ready to discuss their strong and weak points.

Self-Check Questions for Review
Content-Related Questions

1. List some average, "milestone" language behaviors typical for 2-, 3-, and 4-year-old children. Why is it important for teachers to know what these "milestones" are?

2. What are the three different theories explaining how children acquire language? Is there anything teachers can do, according to these theories, to help children acquire language?

3. Should teachers require bilingual children to speak only English while they are at school? What about children who speak Black English?

4. Explain what teachers should do about the child who is not fluent in any language.
5. Name three skills teachers should develop that will foster the development of children's language skills.

Integrative Questions

1. Suppose that two 4-year-olds are investigating the let's-find-out table. They are putting ice cubes in tubs of warm and cold water to see which temperature water makes the ice melt faster. They are also sucking on the ice cubes from time to time. Give several examples of controlling comments the teacher might make. Then cite some additional information that the teacher could give or ask about.
2. Pick out a song you think would be appropriate to teach young children. Then explain why you selected it, basing your explanation on the criteria recommended in the book for selecting children's songs.
3. You have a new child in your classroom from Puerto Rico who speaks no English. Since you speak no Spanish, explain several principles you would follow to help her feel comfortable in your room and, perhaps, begin to speak a little English, too.

Coordinating Videotape

Let's talk about it. Tape #12. The whole child: A caregiver's guide to the first five years. The Annenberg/CPB Collection, P.O. Box 2345, South Burlington, VT 05407–2345. *Let's Talk About It* reviews the process of language acquisition and demonstrates methods for increasing language competence in young children including those with special language or hearing problems, bilingual children, and children who speak a language unfamiliar to the teacher.

References for Further Reading

Pick of the Litter

Weitzman, E., & Greenber, J. (2002). *Learning language and loving it: A guide to promoting children's social and language development in early childhood settings* (2nd ed.). Toronto, Canada: Hannen Centre. This book has everything! It combines accurate, practical information with delightful illustrations and a positive, sensible approach to developing two-way communication.

Overviews

Koralek, D. G. (2003). *Spotlight on young children and language.* Washington, DC: National Association for the Education of Young Children. This excellent collection of research-based articles describes ways to promote language development in the early childhood curriculum.

Norton, D. E. (2003). *Through the eyes of a child: An introduction to children's literature* (6th ed.). Upper Saddle River, NJ: Merrill/Prentice Hall. Each chapter includes suggestions for involving children and annotated bibliographies of excellent children's books.

Children's Literature

Lenox, M. F. (2000). Storytelling for young children in a multicultural world. *Early Childhood Education Journal, 28*(2), 97–110. This article is a treasure trove of information about how to select stories to tell, and helpful annotated bibliographies of how-to resources and appropriate stories from various cultures.

Isbell, R., & Raines, S. (2000). *Tell it again 2: More easy-to-tell stories with activities for young children.* Mt. Rainier, MD: Gryphon House. This is a useful resource for teachers that includes 16 multicultural tales and accompanying activities.

Trelease, J. (2001). *Read-aloud handbook* (5th ed.). New York: Penguin Books. A sensible, easy-to-read paperback that is filled with good advice on enjoying books with children. Excellent bibliography.

Poetry and Finger Plays

Dowell, R. I. (1987). *Move over, Mother Goose: Finger plays, action verses, and funny rhymes.* Mount Rainier, MD: Gryphon House. This nice mix of materials is divided into topics such as animals and family.

Orozco, J. L. (1997). *Diez deditos: Ten little fingers and other play rhymes and action songs from Latin America.* New York: Dutton. Title is self-explanatory.

Prelutsky, C. (Ed.). (2000). *The Random House book of poetry for children.* New York: Random House. This is an invaluable collection of 500 poems with delightful illustrations, organized by subject matter.

Music

Moomaw, S. (1997). *More than singing: Discovering music in preschool and kindergarten.* St. Paul, MN: Redleaf. This is an excellent, practical book that explains ways to include music throughout the day and contains advice on helping children enjoy singing and incorporate other musical experiences during group time.

Bilingualism and Ebonics

Meier, D. R. (2004). *The young child's memory for words: Developing first and second language and literacy.* New York: Teachers College Press. The author gives examples, activities, and resources for teachers of multilingual children from birth through age 8.

Smitherman, G. (2000). *Black talk: Words and phrases from the hood to the Amen corner* (Rev. ed.). Boston: Houghton Mifflin. This updated version can be extremely useful when learning to understand what young African American children and their families are telling you.

Speech Difficulties and Delays

Hall, B. J., Oyer, H. J., & Haas, W. H. (2000). *Speech, language, and hearing disorders: A guide for the teacher.* Boston: Allyn & Bacon. This is a clear, quick-reading, concise book that offers practical recommendations for what the classroom teacher can do to facilitate good language habits.

For the Advanced Student

Gleason, J. B. (Ed.). (2001). *The development of language* (5th ed.). Boston: Allyn & Bacon. This comprehensive textbook is an indispensable resource for the serious student of language acquisition. Each chapter is written by a well-known authority in the field.

Hart, B., & Risley, T. R. (1995). *Meaningful differences in the everyday experience of young American children*. Baltimore: Brookes. This landmark study identifies factors that influence the quality of language development in children's families of different economic levels.

Related Organizations and Online Resources

The Early Childhood Research Institute on Culturally and Linguistically Appropriate Services (CLAS) promotes appropriate intervention practices that are sensitive and respectful to children and families from culturally and linguistically diverse backgrounds. http://www.clas.uiuc.edu

Eric Clearinghouse on Languages and Linguistics (CLL) provides services and materials for language educators, including early childhood teachers. Bilingual education, language development, and English as a second language are some of the topics covered. http://www.cal.org/ericcll/

Kane/Miller Book Publishers (P.O. Box 8515, La Jolla, CA 92038) specialize in foreign children's books translated into English and in their native language, such as Spanish. http://www.kanemiller.com/corp/main.asp

Smithsonian Folkways Recordings (Center for Folklife Programs and Cultural Studies, 955 L'Enfant Plaza, Suite 7300, Washington, DC 20560) offers many children's records of classic folk singers including Pete Seeger, Ella Jenkins, Suni Paz, and Woody Guthrie. It is a wonderful, little-known resource well worth pursuing. http://www.folkways.si.edu/index.html

TAKING THE FIRST STEPS ON THE ROAD TO LITERACY

Have you ever . . .

- Felt uncertain how to explain to a critic how you "teach reading" with young children?
- Wondered what people meant by "emergent literacy"?
- Worried about how to control restless children while you were reading to them?
- Needed help in planning language experiences for two different age groups?

If you have, the material in this chapter will help you.

Play is like a gold mine in its potential for facilitating literacy. First, it provides lots of clues for sorting out aspects of written language. For example, play might help children to figure out what an unfamiliar sign means, how a list is used, what a map is for, or what a word says. Children's play is about what is familiar to them, so play typically provides a meaningful context for children to construct new knowledge and for teachers to facilitate this construction.

—Gretchen Owocki (1999, p. 3)

Pre-K and Kindergarten teachers should not be expected to teach children to read; they should, however, be expected to build the foundation for success in learning to read. They, more than teachers at other levels, can help ensure long-term success in learning to read and the prevention of failure.

—John J. Pikulski (Speech, 2005)

Parents (and other members of the public, such as legislators) often think of reading as being the first and fundamental building block of school success, and, in a way, they are right. The ability to read and to grasp the meaning of what is read is basic to school success.

What many people fail to realize, however, is that reading is actually just one link in a long developmental chain of broader literacy skills the child must forge from infancy onward. The concept of literacy extends far beyond the conventional idea of being able to read (Bowman, Donovan, & Burns, 2001; Burns, Griffin, & Snow, 1999; Hart & Risley, 1995, 2003; Pikulski, 2005). If teachers are to protect the children from inappropriate expectations and prescriptions for "teaching reading" it is very important to know and explain to others what *is* appropriate and be ready to provide many examples of how emergent literacy skills are fostered at the early level (Bredekamp, 2005; Neuman, Copple, & Bredekamp, 2000). After passage of the No Child Left Behind Act of 2001, which emphasizes standardized testing, it has become more incumbent upon teachers to understand the developmental process of language learning so that inappropriate methods to "teach the test" are avoided (Kirkland & Patterson, 2005).

THREE IMPORTANT PRINCIPLES ABOUT LITERACY

Literacy Begins with Adequate Language Skills

The acquisition of receptive and expressive language provides the indispensable foundation on which all other emergent literacy skills are built (Goldstein, 2004; Hart & Risley, 1995, 2003; Kirkland & Patterson, 2005). Therefore, a great deal of time and attention is devoted to building adequate language skills in early childhood. In discussions of teaching reading it is very important to emphasize this fact because, judging from a recent examination of a number of emergent literacy texts, language adequacy is frequently taken for granted when all too often such proficiency is not the case. If such knowledgeable people as reading specialists fail to recognize this, just think what the public does not know!

Indeed, as Hart and Risley (1995, 2003) chillingly warn, there are far too many preschool children who have not developed adequate language skills. These are the children most at risk for later reading and school failure: "By age three, children from privileged families have heard 30 million more words than children from poor families. By kindergarten the gap is even greater. The consequences are catastrophic" (2003, p. 4).

Early childhood educators can have a great effect on children's language acquisition and on their chances for later school success. Although remedial reading programs by the time the child is in elementary school are ineffective (Hart & Risley, 2003; Pikulski, 2005), developmentally appropriate preschool programs significantly enhance children's language learning. This early language ability leads to the development of reading that is so necessary for later academic achievement. One recent study found that children who attended preschool programs showed gains in vocabulary scores that were 31% greater over a year than children who had not attended preschool (National Institute for Early Education Research, 2006).

Literacy Depends on Learning a Set of Subskills

Literacy doesn't just happen—it depends on learning a huge repertoire of subskills usually referred to as *emergent literacy skills*. And *emergent literacy* means just what it says! It means that literacy skills (both reading and mathematical ones) emerge gradually. Learning to read is not something that happens suddenly or is enhanced by using flash cards and rote drill of the alphabet. Instead, it happens bit by bit as skills link together to strengthen children's understanding of the printed word. Children must master many of these emergent skills—ranging from learning to hold a book right side up to hearing the difference between "dog" and "bog"—before they can begin to master the nuances of the mysterious world of print.

Emerging Readers Need to Practice Their Literacy Skills

The most effective way to "teach reading" is to know what the subskills are and to include lots of opportunities to practice them throughout the day. The inclusion of practice opportunities is an important principle to draw to the attention of families and other concerned people because, unless the purposefulness of the activities is explained, people often do not understand how such skills contribute to future reading ability. For example, unless teachers take time to explain the reason for having potential grocery lists and pencils provided in the housekeeping corner, their presence can elicit comments from parents and caregivers ranging from "Isn't that cute! It's just like my kitchen!" to "You'd better watch out or they'll write all over your walls with that stuff!"

WHAT KINDS OF LITERACY-RELATED BEHAVIORS CAN REASONABLY BE EXPECTED FROM YOUNG CHILDREN?

The lists provided by the National Association for the Education of Young Children (Neuman, Copple, & Bredekamp, 2000) and the National Research Council (Snow, Burns, & Griffin, 1998) include many examples of literacy-based behaviors that it is reasonable to expect from children of preschool age through second grade (see Table 16.1). Lists such as these not only are useful for teacher reference—particularly for those who must adhere to mandated standards and testing—but they also come in handy when discussing emergent literacy skills with families to help them know what to expect as their child develops.

Note how language development is intertwined with other abilities that are more obviously related to literacy.

Table 16.1

Examples of Typical Literacy-Related Accomplishments by Preschool-Age and Early Elementary School Children

Birth to 3-Year-Old Accomplishments
- Recognizes specific books by cover.
- Pretends to read books.
- Understands that books are handled in particular ways.
- Enters into a book-sharing routine with primary caregivers.
- Vocalization play in crib gives way to enjoyment of rhyming language, nonsense word play, etc.
- Labels objects in books.
- Comments on characters in books.
- Looks at picture in book and realizes it is a symbol for real object.
- Listens to stories.
- Requests/commands adult to read or write.
- May begin attending to specific print, such as letters in names.
- Uses increasingly purposeful scribbling.
- Occasionally seems to distinguish between drawing and writing.
- Produces some letter-like forms and scribbles with some features of English writing.

3 to 4-Year-Old Accomplishments
- Knows that alphabet letters are a special category of visual graphics that can be individually named.
- Recognizes print in the local environment.
- Knows that it is the print that is read in stories.
- Understands that different text forms are used for different functions of print (e.g., a list for groceries is different than the list on a menu).
- Pays attention to separable and repeating sounds in language (e.g., in Peter, Peter, Pumpkin Eater: Peter Eater).
- Uses new vocabulary and grammatical constructions in own speech.
- Understands and follows oral directions.
- Is sensitive to some sequences of events in stories.
- Shows an interest in books and reading.
- When being read a story, connects information and events to real-life experiences.
- Questions and comments demonstrate understanding of literal meaning of story being told.
- Displays reading and writing attempts, calling attention to self: "Look at my story."
- Can identify about 10 alphabet letters, especially those from own name.
- Writes (scribbles) message as part of playful activity.
- May begin to attend to beginning or rhyming sounds in salient words.

Kindergarten Accomplishments
- Enjoys being read to.
- Retells simple narrative stories or informational texts.
- Uses descriptive language to explain and explore.
- Recognizes letters and letter-sound matches.
- Shows familiarity with rhyming and beginning sounds.
- Understands left-to-right and top-to-bottom orientation and familiar concepts of print.
- Matches spoken words with written ones.
- Begins to write letters of the alphabet and some high-frequency words.

First Grade Accomplishments
- Reads and retells familiar stories.
- Uses strategies (rereading, predicting, questioning, contextualizing) when comprehension breaks down.
- Uses reading and writing for various purposes on own initiative.
- Orally reads with reasonable fluency.
- Uses letter-sound associations, word parts, and context to identify new words.
- Identifies an increasing number of words by sight.

First Grade Accomplishments

- Sounds out and represents all substantial sounds in spelling a word.
- Writes about topics that are personally meaningful.
- Attempts to use some punctuation and capitalization.

Second Grades Accomplishments

- Reads with greater fluency.
- Uses strategies more efficiently (rereading, questioning, and so on) when comprehension breaks down.
- Uses word identification strategies with greater facility to unlock unknown words.
- Identifies an increasing number of words by sight.
- Writes about a range of topics to suit different audiences.
- Uses common letter patterns and critical features to spell words.
- Punctuates simple sentences correctly and proofreads own work.
- Spends time reading daily and uses reading to research topics.

Source: Information relating to birth through age 4 is from *Preventing Reading Difficulties in Young Children,* by C. E. Snow, M. S. Burns, and P. Griffin (Eds.) 1998, Washington, DC: National Academy Press. Reprinted by permission.

Practical Ways to Enhance Emergent Literacy Skills

Begin by Substituting Picture-Symbols for Concrete Objects

For very young children, particularly those who have had little or no experience with picture books, it may be necessary to begin at the picture-symbolic level—to help them understand that a two-dimensional picture can take the place of an actual object. In addition to using simple books, a nice place to start with these children is asking them to select a little picture to put in their cubby identifying it as their own.

Seize Every Opportunity to Read to the Children

As the previous chapter has already emphasized, reading aloud to children, which should be done both at home and school, is the most significant and satisfying way to convince children that print is important. At school such reading involves not only stories but also poetry, nonfiction books, and alphabet books. Other opportunities can be seized as well. These might include directions on packages, environmental signs such as Stop and Exit, and anything else that catches the children's attention and interest.

Remember that reading is a two-way street. Particularly when reading aloud, adults are inclined to resist interruptions by the children unless they understand that such "interruptions" provide useful opportunities for finding out whether the children actually understand what they are listening to. And it is not necessary to wait for the children to interrupt! Readers should interrupt themselves, too, and ask the children what they think is happening in the picture, or what will happen next in the story, or what their opinion is about what's happening, or whether they can think of another way to solve a problem in the story.

Catch the children's interest with fun literacy opportunities such as a classroom mail system.

293

Of course, reading should be encouraged at home too, because when parents are encouraged to make a point of regularly reading to their children and talking over what they are reading with them, children increase their language skills and do better at school (Barbarin, 2002; Bredekamp, 2005; DeTemple, 2001; Hart & Risley, 1995, 2003). Although research shows that more parents are doing this currently than was formerly the case, the Hart and Risley study described previously reminds us that a distressing difference in language capability still exists between children from upper- and lower-income families. For this reason teachers should encourage parents to read even more than they may be doing. It is perhaps the simplest way to enrich the children's vocabulary and foster the foundations of literacy at the same time (Barbarin, 2002; Bredekamp, 2005; Dickinson & Tabors, 2001).

Encourage Families to Participate

Teachers should encourage and guide families in supporting their children's language development. Hart and Risley (1995) pinpointed five quality features that appear to enhance the child's language skills, and families should be educated about how they can adopt similar practices in their home. These qualities of family interaction include:

1. "Just talking" with the child
2. Listening to the child
3. Trying to be nice to the child
4. Giving the child choices
5. Telling the child about things

Unfortunately, when families do not engage in these types of interactions, the child tends to develop less language proficiency than those who have a more language-enhancing home life. By third grade, the child with less language ability is at risk to fall below grade level in reading skills (Hart & Risley, 1995, 2003; Pikulski, 2005).

Create a Print-Rich Environment

Actually, the world of early childhood education abounds in opportunities for demonstrating the usefulness of print—these range from reading the message on a youngster's T-shirt to reviewing the directions on a recipe, checking out what a book recommends about feeding the rabbit, or pointing out the street signs during an excursion. It certainly should not be limited to sticking printed labels around the room:

> Young children's learning environments should be rich in print. But more doesn't always mean better. In a room cluttered with labels, signs, and such—print for print's sake—letters and words become just so much wall paper. . . . Put labels, captions, and other print in the places that count: where they catch children's attention and where they serve a genuine purpose. (Neuman, Copple, & Bredekamp, 2000, p. 38)[*]

Asking the children what to write is another satisfying way to enrich the print environment. Children can dictate stories ("My dad and me made a birthday cake for my mom and . . .") or list what they did during the morning ("First Jessie threw up and then . . .") or write instructions to other youngsters ("Leave my stuff alone!").

Print-rich environments should also include many opportunities for the children to attempt writing themselves. Of course the provision of a special drawing and writing area should be included, but writing their own names on their art projects, scribbling orders for fast food, addressing envelopes when the teacher is sending a note home, sending get-well messages to a tonsillectomy patient, or labeling block structures are also examples of such opportunities. Because these early attempts at writing may seem like scribbles of jumbles of letters to the adult,

---

[*]Reprinted with permission from the National Association for the Education of Young Children. www.naeyc.org.

it is perfectly all right to ask the children what they are writing, providing the inquiry is phrased in respectful, interested terms.

The examples of Emergent Curriculum in Action features in this chapter (p. 305), and in chapters 1, 10, and 11 (pp. 17–18, 173, and 186), show how children's attempts at writing and drawing are supported during the course of an investigation. These products are then used in documentation panels within the classroom to further create a *child-produced*, print-rich environment.

Draw Children's Attention to the Conventions of Print

Some conventions observed by Western cultures include reading from right to left and top

Print-rich environments also include many opportunities for the children to attempt writing themselves.

to bottom, grouping letters to form words, and grouping words to form sentences. Of course, tracing print with a finger as the teacher reads is the most obvious way to encourage children's awareness, but writing as they dictate their intentions can be even better—particularly when the teacher says, "Let's write down what you want to say about your picture. Let's see—I guess we always start over on this side and then . . ."

Teach Children the Concept of *Same and Different*

The easiest way to present this concept to young children—even to 2s and 3s—is to call it *matching* and ask the children whether something matches or whether it doesn't. Chapter 18 discusses many ways to present this concept in its most basic form, so the discussion here will be limited to pointing out two kinds of same/different discrimination that are specifically related to emergent literacy: auditory discrimination skills and visual discrimination skills.

Building/Auditory Discrimination Skills

Auditory discrimination is simply a fancy term for teaching children to pay attention to sounds and encouraging them to become discriminating so they can tell when the sounds are the same and when they are different. Being able to distinguish between sounds is an important skill because it can help sensitize children who do not speak clearly to differences in the way words are pronounced—and, even more important, it draws attention to the 44 different sounds or phonemes used in the English language—obviously an important early ability to develop.

Unfortunately, many teachers seem unaware of the value of sharpening children's ears. Perhaps they believe this skill can only be taught through a lot of drill work, but this is untrue. Many activities that can be used to build auditory discrimination skills are just plain fun. Actually, anything that encourages children to listen closely to sounds and to signal in some way that they distinguish between them comes under this heading. The following are some suggestions:

- Let the children pull pictures of animals or model animals out of a "secret box." Next, make various animal sounds. When a child hears "his" animal, he jumps up and shows it to the other children. This activity can be made somewhat more challenging by using a tape recording instead of making the sounds yourself. This helps emphasize the aspect of sound more strongly.

- Tape-record various common household sounds—a car starting, a toilet flushing, food frying, door shutting, an electric mixer, and so forth—and ask children to guess what they are hearing.
- Make up paired sets of sound canisters (35mm film cases are good free containers to use) with different contents, and see if the children can pair the ones together that sound just alike. (Experience proves that it is important to seal the tops of these so that children use their ears, not their eyes or fingers, to determine the source of the sound.)
- Fill a set of sturdy glass jars with different amounts of water, and encourage the children to strike them gently with a spoon and arrange them from lowest to highest tone. (This activity is appropriate for older 4s and requires careful supervision because of the glass containers.)
- Divide a few children into two groups. While one group hides behind a sheet or screen, have one of them say something out loud and ask the other group to guess who is talking. Asking them to say a nursery rhyme will help overcome their self-consciousness about what to say.
- Have fun with poetry and rhyming words such as this traditional southern example:

Carolyn bombarolyn, seearolyn gofarolyn!

Tee-legged, tie-legged, bow-legged Carolyn!

or

Peter, bombeter, seacreter, gofeter!

Tee-legged, tie-legged, bow-legged Peter!

- Let the children think up ways to make sounds using their bodies (such as stamping or clapping or yawning), and ask the other children to shut their eyes and guess what they are doing.

When the children have enjoyed all the preceding exercises, they can try these more difficult discrimination activities:

- Have a small group of objects or even pictures and ask children to pick out the one that begins with "buh" or "a-a-a." A more advanced form of this activity is to ask them to look for something in the room that starts with a particular sound and point it out or ask the children to point out something that starts with the same sound as "baby" or "Mama."
- Have children listen to a series of words that are the same or almost alike, such as *dog, log, fog, dog, dog.* Every time they hear the same word they can take a marble from the pot. See how soon the children can empty the pot.

Building/Visual Discrimination Skills

Encourage children to look closely at objects, pictures, symbols, and ultimately letters, and decide whether they are the same or different. Activities can range from playing picture dominoes and lotto to discussing identical and nonidentical twins, matching fabric swatches, or comparing children's printed names. Chapter 18 includes many suggestions for providing enjoyable practice in acquiring this skill.

What About "Teaching the Alphabet"?

When alphabet books are used appropriately they present wonderful opportunities to con-solidate auditory and visual discrimination skills by using them together. Because these books traditionally emphasize beginning sounds of words and associate the printed letter with that sound and then combine the letters with often glorious illustrations, the result can be most attractive to the children—providing the teacher does not attempt to wade through the entire book at one sitting. Perhaps the teacher could say, "Yvonne's family just adopted a new kitten they named 'mouse.' Let's see what we can find in the alphabet book with those sounds—what do you think? Should we look for the 'mmm-mouse' sound or the 'kuh-itty' sound?"

What About Using Computers?

One of the most useful applications for computers involves the children indirectly. Chapter 6 already pointed out how much quicker and easier it is to keep weekly notes about youngsters on the computer than writing them out by hand—but there are other, even newer benefits coming into use. One of these is keeping records of what the children have created by using a scanner. Scanning not only reduces the volume of stored materials but also means that treasured creations can be sent home rather than hoarded in the teacher's file. Of course, the use of new technology need not be limited to such things as paintings and collages. Keeping a digital camera close at hand is a convenient and quick way to record interesting activities as they develop step by step. These can be used for discussion later with the children, for individual records, and for documentation boards (Trepanier-Street, Hong, & Bauer, 2001).

Since computers were first introduced into classrooms, much has been learned about effective ways to use them directly with the children although some objections remain. Chief among the objections is the problem of finding good, developmentally appropriate programs and programs that offer worthwhile learning opportunities (Armstrong & Casement, 2000; Cordes & Miller, 2000; Haugland & Wright, 1997). Then, too, it will always be the case that, no matter how good the programs are, they do not promote learning through all the senses because they do not involve the manipulation of concrete objects. Instead they are limited to cognitive-visual experiences which, although useful, are generally not as satisfying as learning acquired through several sensory channels.

If computers are to be offered as one of the self-select opportunities, then it is necessary to bear some additional important points in mind. Teachers and staff need training and practice in using the programs themselves so they can teach the children how to use them. Children will also require considerable instruction either one by one or in small groups, as well as considerable patient repetition of that instruction to use the programs successfully (Craig, 2000). All too often this is not been the case, and it is common to see a child crouched at a keyboard repeatedly tapping one little pattern or even just one key to make a single symbol skitter endlessly across the screen—surely not a worthwhile learning experience.

Something else to consider is the question of fairness. Computers and programs are expensive, and if they are to be provided for some youngsters then it is important to make them available to all kinds of centers, both rich and poor, to avoid "replicating inequalities" as Healy (1998) puts it. And, speaking of inequities, research has shown that three times as many boys as girls are drawn to computers (Cassell & Jenkins, 1998), so this becomes another potential source of unfairness unless efforts are made to understand why this is so and programs are written to redress that imbalance.

Despite these objections and problems, it appears that computers are making a place for themselves in some classrooms because they also have a number of positive attributes: They are impersonal and do not scold about "wrong" answers; the programs can be adapted to the level and ability of the individual child; they sometimes foster children working and talking together, particularly if there are two computers side by side; they can empower youngsters who have physically limiting disabilities; they can help prepare children for later literacy; and their early use prevents children from becoming "computer shy" (Hendrick & Weissman, 2006).

For all these reasons it seems likely that computers are here to stay. It is up to us to use them wisely in order that children may truly benefit from their addition.

USING GROUP TIME TO DEVELOP LITERACY SKILLS

Group times present an opportunity par excellence for developing language, literacy, and cognitive skills. Well-presented group times provide golden opportunities for learning. Children are expected to focus their attention, to listen while others speak, to participate in discussions, to control wiggly impulses, and to keep themselves from being distracted by rambunctious neighbors—and they are expected to practice all these skills while also developing their emergent literacy and cognitive abilities! When so much is expected of the children, surely the least the teacher can do is to manage such occasions well and include content that is both interesting and developmentally worthwhile.

Essential Elements of a Successful Group

It is such a temptation just to say to the reader, "All you need to know about group is to read why some children hate it and then don't do that stuff!"—and that certainly is good advice to begin with. But in addition to avoiding the negative aspects mentioned by the children (see the following Chapter Spotlight), there are a number of more positive recommendations for conducting good group times, generally involving good management skills and interesting content.

Keep Groups as Small and Stable as Possible

The larger the group, the less personal attention each child receives, the fewer opportunities he has to participate, and the more waiting he must do. If stated as an equation, it would look like this:

$$\text{Less personal attention} + \text{More waiting} =$$

$$\frac{\text{Reduced}}{\text{learning}} + \frac{\text{Control}}{\text{problems}} + \frac{\text{Increased}}{\text{discipline}}$$

Some teachers try to solve this by having a second adult do "police duty" on the fringes of the group, but it is more effective to split the group and give half the children to the other person.

If the same children are divided into the same groups each day, it is easier to continue interests from time to time as these build. Keeping the group population stable also fosters a sense of belonging among the children.

Choose a Time and Place That Minimize Tension and Distractions

Just before lunch is about the most stressful point of the day to offer group time. It is such better to choose a time when the children are rested and not hungry. For example, many teachers begin the day with this experience as soon as all the children have arrived.

Stress can also be reduced by locating groups as far away from each other as possible. Try to shield each group from the others by placing a low barrier between them, such as a screen or bookcase. Choose a place that offers few distractions. If you sit in front of a shelf of toys, for example, children's eyes are bound to wander to the delights on the shelves

Why Do Some Children Dislike Group Time So Much?

Research Question: There are numerous studies categorizing child-care centers according to standards determined by adult observers, but researchers Wiltz and Klein tried a different approach. They asked the children what they thought of the centers they were participating in—what they did during the day, and what they liked or disliked about the centers they were attending. They also wanted to know whether children in high-quality centers answered these questions differently from children in low-quality centers.

Research Method: To find the answers to these questions the researchers selected eight centers, four of which scored as being high quality and four as being of low quality according to standards identified by knowledgeable adults. They used *The Early Childhood Environment Rating Scale* (Harms & Clifford, 1980), and the *Classroom Practices Inventory* (Hyson, Hirsh-Pasek, & Rescorla, 1990).

Next, Wiltz and Klein selected 120 children from these eight centers who came from various ethnic and economic backgrounds and were mainly 4 years of age. Once the children were identified, the centers were observed, and each child was interviewed a number of times and the child's comments carefully recorded.

Question One: "What do you do at child care?" An interesting difference in replies to this question was revealed. The children in the low-quality centers simply recited the order of the daily activities, whereas the children in the high-quality centers talked about how they themselves participated—for example, they described what they actually did in the writing corner compared with only naming the activity.

Question Two: "What do you like best about child care or school?" Children from all the centers agreed that their favorite activity was playing.

Question Three: "What don't you like about child care or school?" Although the replies included many more "likes" than "dislikes," the children reported a number of things they particularly disliked—among them nap and time out. The most common dislike in both high- and low-quality centers was "meanness" by peers and teacher. The children gave many examples of what they meant by this—pushing, biting, name calling, teasing, and "being talked to" by the teacher.

But what is of particular interest to this chapter are the responses to group or circle time. The researchers reported that "there were three times as many negative responses to circle time in LQ (low-quality) centers as in HQ (high-quality) ones" (p. 225). In fact, 25% of the children in the LQ centers reported they hated circle time, whereas only 8% of the children from the HQ centers did.

The question then becomes: What was different about the group time activities in the low-quality centers that caused so many of the children to dislike it so much? Fortunately, we have the answer to this because of the classroom observations that were also part of this study.

In three of the four LQ centers, Wiltz and Klein sum up the differences as follows: "Circle time lasted between 30 to 40 minutes and focused predominantly on the calendar, rote memorization of letters, numbers and shapes, reviewing classroom rules, and reading stories that had no thematic connection to other classroom activities" (p. 229).

Source: Wiltz, M.W., & Klein, W.L. (2001). "What do you do in child care?" Children's perception of high- and low-quality classrooms. *Early Childhood Research Quarterly, 16* (2), 209–236.

behind you. It is also wise to seat the children far enough away from any equipment so that it is out of their reach. An ideal site is a cozy corner with rugs and a feeling of softness about it.

Plan Carefully and Be Flexible

An important part of promoting harmonious learning at group time is being relaxed yourself. Nothing fosters this as much as *careful planning and preparation*. Always assemble the ingredients of the group time curriculum beforehand, and have them in reach but as much out of the children's sight as possible. Be sure to read books and poetry all the way through in advance to make certain that they are what you really want and to familiarize yourself thoroughly with the material.

Peace of mind is increased if more materials are selected than there will be time to use (two cognitive activities, for example, or several books), because it is almost impossible to know, in the beginning, what will be effective in group time and what will not. There is no sin in simply setting a book aside that the children do not enjoy and going on to something else.

Readiness to extend or contract an activity, to change the order of presentation, and to improvise spontaneously in response to the children's interests as needed is the hallmark of the truly master teacher.

Start Group Time as Soon as Children Begin to Gather

Do not expect the children to sit quietly and wait until the last straggler appears. Having to wait encourages youngsters to think of all kinds of things to do! It is far better to begin group immediately with a song or finger plays. These activities are so attractive that laggards will want to hurry over. Moreover, these particular activities are easy for children to join as they arrive.

Prepare Children for What You Intend to Present Next

The children will participate more if they understand what is going to happen next during group. So many times inexperienced teachers suddenly launch into song or pick up a book and begin reading without introducing it first. The look of bewilderment on the children's faces as they struggle to shift gears makes it obvious that a simple introduction is helpful. Perhaps the teacher can say, "Now we're going to sing that funny song about 'Hop Se Hi.' Do you remember what we did yesterday while we sang it?" or "I'm going to share a story with you today that I bet a lot of you have heard before. It's a story about a little rabbit named Peter who has a special adventure in Mr. McGregor's garden."

Present Difficult or New Experiences Early

Decide in advance what activity is likely to require the most concentration or effort by the children. Perhaps this is a cognitive game or learning a new song. Present this early when the children are still fresh and attentive.

Change the Pace and Include Variety

Group time should generally be upbeat; do not allow anything to drag on too long. Because it is so taxing for young children to sit still for extended periods, some kind of exercise and movement should be provided as part of this experience. Typically this takes the form of finger plays and body movement ideas. It also might involve a relaxation exercise in which the children practice stretching out and letting go.

Encourage Discussion Among the Children

It seems that new teachers in particular fear being interrupted by the children during the group experience, so they read breathlessly through a book, brushing the children's interested comments aside as distractions. This is probably because they dread losing control—but allowing the children to respond to questions and volunteer information increases their interest in what is happening. It also encourages them to put their ideas into words and to share experiences with the group.

Kindergarten teachers often plan for this deliberately by including a sharing time when every child contributes something. At the preprimary level, doing this usually causes the other children to fidget and lose interest because it takes too long. For this reason, it seems best to allow time for children to interject spontaneous remarks and comments as group progresses. Often such remarks can be developed into a valuable discussion that involves many of the children. When it is time to return to the story, all the teacher has to do is say, for example, "Well, that certainly was interesting hearing about how Anselmo caught that fish. Now let's go back to Curious George and see if he caught one, too."

Move with the Children's Ideas

Of course, it is not always possible to shift the group time focus immediately in accord with an interest expressed by the children. However, if the teacher is paying close attention to what the children say, sometimes their discussions reveal an interest that is both unanticipated and surprising. Such an event can be a godsend when thinking about where the curriculum should move next.

Draw the Group to a Close Before It Falls Apart

It is always better to stop a little too soon than to go on and on until the children end up frantic to get away. Quit while you are ahead; then everyone will want to come back next time.

What to Do When a Child Continues to Distract the Group

Even when these strategies are practiced faithfully, all teachers encounter children from time to time who are unable to conform to reasonable standards of behavior during group. The first thing to consider under such circumstances is whether the child is physically able to conform. Does he see well? How is his hearing? Consider also whether he might be developmentally younger than the other children so that the material presented is inappropriate for his interests.

When such problems create group time difficulties, special plans have to be made that will enable the child to participate. Perhaps he needs to sit closer to the teacher to see or hear, or perhaps he can be dismissed early from the group or be read to by himself. Sometimes a number of such youngsters can be gathered into a separate group by another staff member so that the material is more appropriate to their age and interests.

Many children, however, do not seem to suffer from any of these problems, but they continue to be disruptive. The solution to this depends a lot on the philosophy of the particular teacher. Some teachers believe it is acceptable for children who do not want to be part of group time to play by themselves, as long as they are quiet and do not disturb the group. It is often, but not always, the case that such youngsters gradually return and join the others as they become aware of the fun going on in the group.

Other teachers believe this time of being together is so important that all children should attend. They have the restless one sit beside them, separating him from particular friends who may be drawn into misbehavior and then giving him a special role in the group. Perhaps he can turn the pages during story reading or hold the flannel board while others put on special items. Firm expectations of desirable behavior have to be projected to such a child as well.

If all else fails, it is occasionally necessary to have another adult remove the obstreperous one from the group. That person should explain to the child that he has lost the privilege of staying and may return only when he has made up his mind to be more cooperative. (This essentially is an application of the six learning steps described in chapter 12.)

Finally, Enjoy the Children

There is no substitute for your interest and enthusiasm. Be well enough prepared that you do not have to worry about how group time will go. Forget about the little irritating things

Above all, group time should be a time for enjoyment.

that do not really matter, and concentrate on relaxing and letting the children know you like them and that you are excited about what you are going to do together. This will make group time a pleasure for everyone.

Planning Group Time Curriculum

Plan group time curriculum that has variety and holds the children's attention. The basic educational goals of a good group time should be the development of receptive and expressive language and related literacy skills, the enhancement of thinking ability, and the provision of a positive social experience while this is taking place.

To achieve these goals the following ingredients should be included at least once during the week—and the more of them that are used every day, the better!

1. Stories (not necessarily a book)

2. Songs

3. Poetry

4. Finger plays and action activities

5. Practice in cognitive skills (discussed in chapters 17 and 18)

6. Discussions

7. Practice in auditory and visual discrimination skills

8. Some aspect that is multiethnic or nonsexist

Unfortunately, as the research by McAfee (1985) reveals, all too often this kind of variety is not provided. For example although she found that teachers listed 14 activities that should be included in good group times, when observed, the majority of the teachers used only books, a little music, show-and-tell, calendar, and taking attendance. The activities did not vary according to the children's ages, and planning to realize long-term educational goals was "not typical." With this quality of group being so commonplace, is it any wonder that so many children in the Wiltz and Klein study reported they hated group? Who wouldn't be bored with this sort of irrelevant repetition day after day?

And what an opportunity is wasted when a well-planned group experience can offer such rich opportunities for a multitude of language, literacy, social, emotional, and cognitive learning experiences to take place—opportunities that are unsurpassed during the rest of the center day.

Basic Principles to Follow When Planning Curriculum for a Group

When planning curriculum for group time that is both interesting and worthwhile, it is helpful to bear in mind the following guidelines:

• Group times are precious—do not waste them. Regard group as one of the most important activities of the day and discipline yourself to make a plan every single time!

• Make a list of the kinds of experiences that should be included and make certain all eight ingredients are included several times a week. Remember, one selection can serve several purposes. For example, *Stellaluna* (Cannon, 1993), a delightful story about bats and birds, provides a wholesome message about sameness and differentness while also presenting bats in a sympathetic light, including some information about how they live—all presented in the context of a beautifully illustrated, good story.

- Make certain every activity is there for a purpose. Avoid boring time fillers such as calendar and attention destroyers like show-and-tell!

- *Always* be sensitive to the importance of including multicultural and nonsexist materials—and *always* check the materials you are using for possible bias before presentation. If such material is included, be prepared to discuss the bias with the children and how that might be changed.

- It adds to the fun and helps tie learning together if you include one or two activities that are related to the children's current focus of interest, but don't beat that interest to death!

- Make certain many opportunities are included for children to both talk and listen.

- Seize the opportunity to build emergent literacy skills—such as discrimination skills, understanding that writing turns words into print, conventions about print, and so forth.

- Keep the materials appropriate for the age you are working with. A group of 3s (or 2s) does best with short and simple stories, large picture books, and considerable repetition of material. They appreciate beginning with a familiar activity each time—perhaps "Head, Shoulders, Knees, and Toes" or "Where Is Thumbkin?" Group times should be kept fairly short for such young children and should include active participation whenever possible.

- Older 4s can sit for fairly long periods of time, especially when they are interested in the materials. They enjoy some repetition but also relish diversity. They are thirsty for information per se and can deal with experience on a more verbal level. For example, they can grasp the idea that different languages can have different words for the same thing, and they enjoy learning some of these words. They are also partial to "nonsense" rhymes. Fours are able to talk about their feelings and can deal with simple social discussions of such things as the pleasures and perils of giving and receiving gifts. They are also interested in the concept of growing up, and they are developing strong ideas about appropriate gender roles.

- Good group times require not only careful planning and preparation but also the freedom to deviate from the plan when something special comes up.

- Practice may not make perfect, but doing group over and over really helps. Seize every opportunity you can to practice this valuable skill.

SOME ADDITIONAL SUGGESTIONS FOR ENHANCING LITERACY WITH PRIMARY SCHOOL CHILDREN

Many of the principles for language and literacy curriculum in preschool should be maintained in the early elementary grades as well. However, additional activities and goals are appropriate for these older children, as follows:

- Provide a carefully planned environment that promotes opportunities for children to engage in conversations. Classrooms should be print rich and filled with the children's own writing, rather than with purchased, adult-made materials. Children should also be responsible for functional representation that is posted in the room, such as signs. Libraries should teach children self-selection and respect for books.

- Connect the classroom with literature. It is unfortunate that, unlike in preschools, read aloud time gets short shrift in the elementary grades. Teachers must systematically plan for read aloud times every day that include high-level, open-ended questions and discussion, as well as specific vocabulary development. Children can now take concepts they have been exposed to through literature even further in their play, art, music, drama, and dance. Children should be encouraged to extend their reading experiences through all forms of creative expression.

- Develop curriculum that is relevant and interesting to the children, and their language development will follow! When children's minds are engaged and their curiosity is piqued, they can't help but talk. Teachers must allow ample time for free-flowing discourse among the children during the course of projects or investigations. In the Emergent Curriculum in Action features in chapters 1, 10, 11, and 16 (pp. 17–18, 173, 186, and 305) it is clear how much back-and-forth dialogue and sheer vocabulary development took place during the investigations, regardless of the age of the children. These language-enhancing curriculum experiences are even more relevant in the elementary grades as children become more adept at self-direction and expression.

The following Emergent Curriculum in Action feature demonstrates how children's literacy learning can be woven into the daily curriculum—without the use of preformulated writing activities such as alphabet worksheets. The children's understanding of the power of words, in discussion and in written form, is deepened through their involvement in developing relevant and appropriate classroom activities. By being sensitive to children's real interests, teachers can develop a curriculum that is engaging to the children. Through emergent curriculum practices like those described in Our Birds project, teachers support children's mastery of important academic skills such as writing.

Develop curriculum that is relevant to the children and their language development will follow. These first and second graders are discussing their "zillion ideas" for their design for World Trade Center Memorial Competition.

Emergent Curriculum in Action

Our Birds

by Leslie Gleim
Carousel Center, Portsmouth, Ohio

Context Information:
Our Birds project unfolded over the course of 3 months in an integrated classroom of 8 children with special needs and 4 typical children aged 3 to 5 years. The following describes one portion of the project, specifically the way in which literacy learning was enhanced. Through listening to the children, following their real interests, and developing curriculum plans that were truly emergent, the children's understanding of the power of words was realized.

Throughout the year, the children could be found observing the birds that often visited the school. One day, the children discovered a nest. The teachers placed a ladder close to the nest. As each child climbed to the top, they were asked, "Tell me what you are seeing." The children were asked to draw what they had seen from the ladder.

The children revisited the nest and listened to their peers' verbal outpouring about their drawings and what they observed in the nest. At the group meeting, the teachers read back to them a dialogue centering on disagreement about the number of birds. The children decided to go back to the nest to look again. The first child up the ladder exclaimed, "They're gone!" An emergency group meeting was held on the sidewalk. Questions were raised about what happened to the birds; the children were confident that the birds were lost and could still be nearby. A search of the school yard was made, but their birds were not found.

The children expanded their search and asked people on the street if they had seen the birds. After asking several people without success, Adam said to his friends, "We need to put words on paper and put them on the wall."

Three other children joined Adam to help create a "paper with words to tell people about the lost birds." The children discussed which words needed to be on the "paper with words." They wanted some of their words handwritten, and some printed on the computer. The words they wanted to write on the paper "really big" were: "My school's birds ran away." The other, typed words were: "Call if you see and catch our birds. Put it in a cage. Carousel Center Kids."

The four children who composed the "paper with words" ranged in age from 4.5 to 5.3 years. They worked for nearly 2 hours. After they finished their work, they took the "paper with words" back to the entire group for approval. In their discussion, a child mentioned, "We need lots of paper with words!" The teachers asked how to make lots of paper with words. Another child responded, "I know—we can use the machine in the office. It makes lots of pictures. We need enough to go around the block—16 would be enough."

Discussion followed about where to post the signs. The children wanted the signs "all around the city where people are going to see them." The copies were made and the children posted them. Adam summed up their next step, "Well, we did it. They are up—now we have to wait for someone to find the birds. I know this is going to work!"

SUMMARY

Three important principles everyone should know about literacy are:

1. Literacy begins with adequate language skills.

2. Literacy depends on learning a repertoire of subskills called *emergent literacy skills*.

3. The most effective way to "teach reading" is to provide practice in those subskills every day.

There are many practical, developmentally appropriate ways to enhance emergent literacy skills. These include substituting pictures for concrete objects, reading aloud, providing a print-rich environment, and using the concept of *same and different* to provide practice in building auditory and visual discrimination skills. There are also contributions to be made by computers and by using alphabet books. The chapter concludes with recommendations for managing a successful group time and suggestions about what kinds of content should be included therein, including additional suggestions for primary school children.

Food for Thought and Group Discussions

1. The Wiltz and Klein study about why some children said they disliked group time mentioned (1) calendar; (2) rote memorization of letters, numbers and shapes; (3) reviewing classroom rules; and (4) hearing stories that had no thematic connection to other classroom activities. Provide examples of typical ways teachers present each of these activities.

2. You have a little girl in your group who constantly interrupts what you are saying in group time. You believe children should participate in that experience, but this is too much! How would you solve this problem?

3. You want to present some group times that focus on water play, but you cannot find even one poem or finger play on that topic. Take 20 minutes and write one to share with the class.

Self-Check Questions for Review

Content-Related Questions

1. What are the three principles about literacy that everyone should know?

2. Give several examples of items you might include in the housekeeping corner that would enhance the print-rich opportunities in that area.

3. List several things children have the opportunity to learn during group time.

4. There are some fundamental principles to bear in mind when presenting group times that will help make them more successful. What are these principles?

5. List the eight ingredients for enhancing literacy skills that should be included as often as possible during a week of group times. Do most teachers include them when presenting group time? Why or why not is this the case? Why should they be included?

Integrative Questions

1. If you were the director of a center and realized that the teachers under your supervision were relying only on stories and songs for group time, how would you go about changing their behavior? Would just telling them they should do better be enough? If not, what kinds of practical help and motivation could you offer?

2. How do you expect the behavior of 2- and 4-year-olds to differ from each other during group time? Based on these differences, explain how you would adjust your group time plans to take those differences into account.

3. Why must children be able to tell the difference between "dog" and "bog" before they can "begin to master the mysterious world of print"?

References for Further Reading

Pick of the Litter

Burns, M. S., Griffin, P., & Snow, C. E. (Eds.). (1999). *Starting out right: A guide to promoting children's reading success.* Washington, DC: National Research Council, National Academy Press. This book is filled with sound information about learning to read and write while also providing numerous practical activities that enhance children's skills at developmentally appropriate levels.

Overviews

Fields, M., Spangler, K. L., & Groth, L. (2004). *Let's begin reading right: Developmentally appropriate beginning literacy* (5th ed.). Upper Saddle River, NJ: Merrill/Prentice Hall. The authors discuss the underpinnings of literacy as well as the development of reading and writing with older youngsters.

Neuman, S. B., Copple, C., & Bredekamp, S. (2000). *Learning to read and write: Developmentally appropriate practices for young children.* Washington, DC: National Association for the Education of Young Children. Beginning with the IRA/ National Association for the Education of Young Children position paper on this subject, the authors document relevant research and learning goals for children from preschool through grade 3 and illustrate many appropriate ways to foster reading and other literacy skills in young children.

Owocki, G. (1999). *Literacy through play.* Portsmouth, NH: Heinemann. This book is filled with innumerable ideas of developmentally appropriate ways written language can be drawn to the children's attention and/or incorporated into their pretend play experiences.

Group Times for Children with Special Needs

Hut, V., Dennis, B., Koplow, L., & Gerber, J. (1996). Lesson plans for emotional life. In L. Koplow (Ed.), *Unsmiling faces* (pp. 289–307). New York: Teachers College Press. The authors include a great many examples of meeting-time activities with emphasis on topics appropriate for children who need to build particular emotional and social relationship skills.

Linder, T. W. (Ed.). (1999). *Read, play, and learn! Storybook activities for young children: Teacher's Guide.* Baltimore: Brookes. Of particular value are two chapters on visual and hearing impairments that provide practical information about linking books and language to youngsters with these disabilities.

Supporting Literacy for African American Children

Bowman, B. (Ed.). (2002). *Love to read: Essays in developing and enhancing early literacy skills of African American children.* Washington, DC: National Black Child Development Institute. This collection of essays addresses the disparity between African Americans and Caucasians in reading achievement and makes recommendations for closing the gap.

Resources for Group Time Activities

Church, E. B. (2000). *The great big book of classroom songs, rhymes, and cheers: 200 easy, playful language experiences that build literacy and community in your classroom.* New York: Scholastic. While no one could mistake these poems for great literature, they do offer the advantages of brevity, familiar melodies, and categories sorted according to teacher need such as multicultural, circle time, transitions, and so forth.

Morrow, L. M., & Gambrell, L. B. (2004). *Using children's literature in preschool: Comprehending and enjoying books.* Newark, DE: International Reading Association. In addition to offering suggestions for using books at group time, there is a wealth of information for including literature in all aspects of the curriculum.

Rhoten, L., & Lane, M. (2001). More than the ABCs: The new alphabet books. *Young Children, 56*(1), 41–45. This very good review of alphabet books recommends using them in developmentally appropriate ways by inviting involvement with the children.

Computers

Behrman, R. E. (Ed.). (2000). Children and computer technology. *Future of Children, 10*(2), entire issue. This publication presents an unbiased assessment of the pros and cons of computer use by children.

Haugland, S. W. (2000). Early childhood classrooms in the 21st century: Using computers to maximize learning. *Young Children, 55*(1), 12–18. Haugland discusses current advances and potential difficulties and includes practical suggestions on the purchase, integration, and use of computers in the preschool classroom.

Trepanier-Street, M. L., Hong, S. B., & Bauer, J. C. (2001). Using technology in Reggio-inspired long-term projects. *Early Childhood Education Journal, 28*(3), 181–188. The authors explain the benefits of using scanners and digital cameras to record children's work.

Position Papers on Learning to Read and Write and on Technology

Note: These papers are worthwhile because they spell out "best practices" and are written in language the public can understand. They are available online at the NAEYC Web site (http://www.naeyc.org).

International Reading Association and National Association for the Education of Young Children. (1998). *Learning to read and write: Developmentally Appropriate Practices for young children.* Washington, DC: Authors.

National Association for the Education of Young Children. (1996). *Position statement on technology and young children—Ages three through eight.* Washington, DC: Author.

For the Advanced Student

Roskos, K. A., & Christie, J. F. (Eds.). (2000). *Play and literacy in early childhood: Research from multiple perspectives.* Mahwah, NJ: Erlbaum. This is a collection of research reports on how literacy skills develop. Many of the projects contain ideas of ways teachers could add to their literacy-building repertoires.

Related Organizations and Online Resources

The American Library Association promotes information services and public access to information. The Web site has a good list of recommended children's books. http://www.ala.org/

The International Reading Association (IRA) is the world's leading organization of literacy professionals. Many resources are available at the Web site. http://www.reading.org/

Reading Is Fundamental (RIF) is a good resource for articles, classroom suggestions, recommended reading lists, and even free books for families and programs that can't afford them. http://www.rif.org/

HELPING CHILDREN LEARN TO THINK FOR THEMSELVES

Using the Emergent Approach

Have you ever . . .

- Heard the term *emergent curriculum* and wondered what it meant?
- Wondered just who Vygotsky was and why people are talking about him?
- Thought that teaching facts was not enough but did not know how else to get the children to think?
- Heard the words *Reggio Emilia* and wondered what they meant?

If you have, the material in this chapter will help you.

Education is not the filling of a pail, but the lighting of a fire.

—William Butler Yeats (1865–1939)

Whatever you can teach a child from the nature of things themselves, do not teach by words. Let the child see, hear, find, stumble, rise again, and be mistaken. Give no words when action or deed is possible. What a child can do, let the child do.

—Johann Pestalozzi (1746–1827)

It is often difficult for caregivers to resist providing help as soon as they see a child struggling. However, working through difficulties to solve a problem or master a task independently increases children's persistence and feelings of competence. It is important that the challenge be appropriate for the child's level of skill so that she has a good chance of ultimate success.

—Martha B. Bronson (2000, p. 210)

One of the most interesting aspects of teaching young children lies in the area of mental development, because young children usually come to school filled with curiosity, wonder, and the wish to learn. This eagerness makes cognitive education a delight for both teachers and children, if the teachers have a clear idea of the children's capabilities and how to develop these further in an appropriate way.

To accomplish this most effectively, teachers must take time to clarify their own educational values and decide for themselves what the real purpose of educating the children's cognitive selves should be. Should mental development consist only of learning a large array of facts, recognizing the alphabet, and parroting memorized replies to questions? Or should such education foster the ability to think and reason, to generate new ideas, to relish learning about a fascinating world, and to feel confident and enthusiastic when approaching new intellectual challenges?

While acknowledging the value of factual knowledge, the majority of teachers want to include opportunities for thinking and reasoning in the curriculum, too. They want to nourish that spark of intellectual curiosity, develop that ability to think, and sustain that interest in the world and all it contains, as well as provide the children with facts and information.

THREE APPROACHES TO FOSTERING MENTAL ABILITIES

This book takes the position that there are three ways to foster the development of mental abilities. And, as Table 17.1 makes clear, they each enhance different kinds of mental processes and abilities in the children.

The first, most typical approach is engaging children in acquiring facts about their world and so is called the *information approach*. The second, termed the *emergent creative approach*, fosters the development of higher-order mental abilities such as problem solving. The third approach is termed the *conventional approach* because it focuses on some skills already familiar to many early childhood teachers. It provides practice in some mid-level mental abilities that form a foundation for later success in such academic areas as reading and certain mathematical processes. The conventional approach is discussed in detail in chapter 18.

Table 17.1
A Comparison of Cognitive Learning Opportunities Using the Three Approaches

	Information Approach	Emergent Creative Approach for Teaching Creative Thinking and Problem Solving	Conventional Approach for Teaching Mid-Level Mental Abilities
Value of approach	Provides information base needed as foundation for mid-level and problem-solving skills. Widens knowledge of world.	Allows children to develop full range of mental powers. Encourages application of prior knowledge to solving new problems. Empowers children to try out ideas and explain what they know to other children and adults.	Makes certain diversified practice in apply mid-level mental ability skills (concepts) is provided. These are valuable emergent literacy and mathematical skills.
Examples of kinds of mental ability skills developed by approach	Pay attention. Process information. Retain information. Recall information. Reconstruct information.	Generate ideas on own. Form hypotheses (reasons) why something happens and try them out. Assess and evaluate possibilities. Pursue interests in depth.	Apply specific concepts to specific activities: matching, grouping, perceiving common relations, seriated and temporal ordering, cause-and-effect relationships, and conserving.
Teacher's role	Supply information to children and/or help them find information for themselves.	Listen to children; follow their lead to select pathway to investigate. Plan curriculum ahead but alter and adjust plans as direction of pathways becomes apparent. Encourage generation of ideas by "provoking" children to consider problems and solve them. Develop opportunities with children to try out their ideas.	May use children as source to determine interest around which to build a theme. Plan ahead to think up and present activities and experiences for children that provide opportunities for practice and application of specific concepts.
Child's role	Soak up interesting information and store it in memory. Be able to recall, reconstruct, and repeat information when needed.	Collaborate (toss ball of ideas back and forth) with teacher to pursue interests. Think up ways to express ideas and solve problems. Try ideas out. Express ideas and what is found out through language, graphics, and child-constructed models.	Participate in learning activities provided by teacher, thereby practicing various mid-level mental ability skills. Acquire mental ability concepts and apply them by reasoning. Express what he knows by manipulating teacher-provided materials.
Examples of typical questions	What color is this? What did we talk about last time? Tell me what happened? Can you find the round one?	Your opinion is that . . . ? How could we . . . ? What could we use to . . . ? What would happen if . . . ?	Is this the same? What belongs together? What should come next? What made that happen?

Comparing the Approaches

The Information Approach

To begin with, we must acknowledge that many well-intentioned teachers still see cognitive learning as mainly helping the children acquire a lot of interesting facts about a subject—and it is true that if you are going to think about something, you really *do* need facts to base your thinking on. In addition, with the necessity of meeting government-mandated standards and testing requirements, many teachers find themselves preparing children for assessments that emphasize their factual knowledge (Rector, 2006).

As an example of how to implement the information approach, let's suppose a rabbit has come to school (Table 17.2). The teacher might get out a book that talks about characteristics of rabbits or share an amusing story about them. She might also encourage the children to try feeding him various things to find out what he eats and help them dig his droppings into their garden for fertilizer.

The benefit of the information approach is that the children are probably interested, and they are acquiring factual information. The drawbacks are that it can lead to branching out in a helter-skelter kind of webbing in which topics are at best moderately and at worst too loosely related to the subject of rabbits, so that a central focal point is lost. For instance, "rabbits" might lead to "springtime," and "spring" to "rainy weather" and "what makes thunder," and then to "ways to keep our feet dry so we stay healthy," and so on and so on.

Moreover, teachers who use only this approach are cheating the children because young children are capable of doing so much more thinking beyond learning facts. If given the opportunity, they are also capable of having creative ideas, solving problems, and acquiring some mid-level figuring-out skills as well.

The Emergent Creative Approach

As we see in Table 17.1, in the discussion of the Reggio Emilia schools, and in the Emergent Curriculum in Action features highlighted throughout *Total Learning*, this approach is characterized by the teachers and children collaborating together to pursue a common interest. Sometimes an idea for investigation comes directly from the children, sometimes from the teacher—but whatever the initial inspiration may be, there is always back-and-forth communication about the direction the curriculum will take.

Lilian Katz (2006), one of the originators of the *project approach* discussed later in the chapter, describes the difference between using *themes* (the information approach) versus *projects* (the emergent creative approach):

> Themes often mean that teachers look for something to represent (through math, words, shapes, etc.). The goal seems to be to find a topic around which to apply some basic skills. This approach is not in any way harmful, but likely not to be as interesting to the children as a project focused on finding things out about a topic. . . .
>
> In contrast to themes, projects involve investigation of a topic, making predictions about what the findings will be, explaining the bases for the predictions, and then conducting research and reporting their findings. A large part of project work is children testing their own predictions and hypotheses.

This does not mean that the teacher's role is only to follow the children's lead, although this is *sometimes* a part of emergent curriculum. What really happens, as Tables 17.1 and 17.2 indicate, is that the teacher may (or may not) have in mind some possibilities to begin with. He discusses potentially interesting subjects with the children and pays careful attention to their comments and questions. Then he analyzes what these reveal so he can selectively choose what he thinks might be the most productive possibilities to pursue further. As the project develops, he repeats this process many times and adjusts the curriculum accordingly.

311

Table 17.2
Example of Using Three Approaches Together to Facilitate Learning for the Cognitive Self

Source of Interest	Information Approach Featuring Acquiring Facts	Emergent Approach Featuring Problems to Solve	Conventional Approach Featuring Mid-Level Cognitive Skills

White, pink-eyed baby rabbit donated to center's group of 4-year-olds by one of the families	**What do children already know and/or think is true?**
	
	• Rabbits can hop straight up in the air.
	• They like lettuce.
	• They have long ears and a fluffy tail.
	• All rabbits are white and have pink eyes.
	• Rabbits hatch from Easter eggs.
	
	Additional facts they might acquire:
	
	• Rabbits are easily frightened.
	• There are many different kinds and colors of rabbits.
	• They can be housebroken.
	• They like to gnaw on things.
	• They are mammals—mothers give birth to babies.
	• Rabbits have strong hind legs and can scratch if frightened.
	• Rabbits get sick if they eat too many greens at one time.
	• Rabbits are very good diggers and like to make tunnels to live in.
	• There are different words meaning "rabbit" in different languages.
		Basic question: How can we take very good care of this young rabbit and make him happy?
		
		Children's concerns and potential solutions:
		
		• He misses his mother.
		  Borrow his mother to visit.
		  Put guinea pig in same cage.
		  Act friendly and be gentle with him ourselves.
		• His cage is so small—he needs to hop around some more— . . . but if we let him out, we can't catch him!
		  Build corral of blocks indoors.
		  Build rabbit pen outdoors.
		    What would it look like? Can we draw something (or model it from sticks or clay or something) to show how we could make it?
		    What can we make it out of?
		    How can we find out how much chicken wire to buy?
		    How many stakes will we need?
		    How high must it be to keep him from jumping out?
		    What if he digs under the fence?
		• What could we use temporarily outside until the pen is ready? Would the wading pool work? A big box?
			Matching: Play "Bunny Bingo" made from Easter rabbit stickers.
			
			Grouping: Are all rabbits white with pink eyes? Compare a variety of pictures of rabbits with several pictures of guinea pigs. Why do rabbits belong in one group and guinea pigs in another?
			
			Common relations: Pair live rabbit with picture in book. Pair baby animal pictures with mother animals—who goes with which mother?
			
			Temporal ordering: Use documentation board of children's plans, comments, and progress during pen building to show progress over time.
			
			Seriation (graduated ordering): Keep track of how far rabbit can hop as he matures. Compare with how far the children can hop.
			
			Cause and effect: Why *do* rabbits have long ears and big hind legs? What makes rabbits run and hide? What makes the rabbit cuddle down in your lap?
			
			Emergent literacy activities: Measuring and recording his growth; listening to rabbit stories and looking up information; telling rabbit food label apart from guinea pig label.

One of the most important tasks of the teacher is to *observe* and *listen* to the children in order to base curriculum on their ideas and theories about the world.

Perhaps the children comment that they think the rabbit is unhappy because he keeps bumping his head as he tries to jump in his cage. Then the teacher could ask them how to make his home better for him, which in turn could lead to taking the rabbit out on the grass, and the new problem would need to be solved about how to confine him there. Perhaps a pen of chicken wire would work—what would that look like? How will we know how much wire to buy? And what can we use to hold the chicken wire up? What could we use for his home until we can build that enclosure? Although this project has stemmed from the children's concern for the rabbit's well-being, it is the teacher who poses the problems ("What can we do to make him happier?" and "How could we keep him from bumping his head?") and who foresees the learning opportunities that could come from needing to figure out how the children might draw or model their suggestions, how to measure the amount of chicken wire required, how to keep the rabbit warm at night, and so forth.

The Conventional Approach

Returning to Table 17.1, we see that in contrast to the emergent approach, the conventional approach is much more teacher-determined. The teacher decides in advance which mid-level skills (such as matching or grouping) should be included in the curriculum, and he plans theme-related activities for the children to enjoy that provide opportunities to practice those skills.

Because the activities that make this approach possible are discussed in more detail in chapter 18, we will only take space here to describe it as an approach that singles out a handful of specific mental abilities and provides opportunities for practicing those abilities by including them in theme-related activities for the children to use. Although this approach is valuable and definitely a step up from just emphasizing facts, it really does only part of the mental development job because it does not make use of the children's ideas and creative intellectual capabilities. Therefore, it is best used when it is included along with the more stimulating emergent approach.

Curriculum: Putting It All Together

Teachers should keep in mind that all three curriculum approaches add important pieces to the children's learning. Curriculum can be thought of as "what to teach" and "when to teach it" (Bredekamp, 2005). When early childhood curriculum has clearly defined, developmentally appropriate aims, children benefit and tend to have greater school success. Because there is no single "best" curriculum approach, teachers must develop flexibility and their own creativity. Learning standards must be met, specific knowledge must be acquired, and at the same time children's curiosity and power to construct their own knowledge must be encouraged. (Who ever said teaching was easy!) If we think of curriculum as a means for providing investigation and *focused intentional teaching*, we will be offering our children an education that is worthwhile and growth-enhancing.

CONTRIBUTIONS OF LEV VYGOTSKY

Vygotsky (1978) was a Russian psychological theoretician and teacher whose works have become increasingly well known in the West in the past few years. His interest in the effect of the sociocultural world on the child's development and its implications for the role of the teacher, in addition to his emphasis on the significance of language in fostering cognitive development, have provided a balance to the Piagetian view that children construct knowledge from within themselves.

Because many of his ideas are a "good fit" with the current interest in emergent curriculum, which emphasizes collaboration between teacher and child, it is helpful for early childhood teachers to understand some of his basic premises, so some of his most relevant ideas are briefly presented here. Readers who desire more in-depth information are referred to several excellent references at the end of this chapter.

The Impact of Society on the Child's Development

Fundamental to Vygotsky's theory is the assertion that all knowledge is socially constructed and that learning cannot be separated from the social context in which it takes place. For this reason, the influence of both adults and peers is seen as crucial to facilitating the child's development. It is what they say and do and what the child does in response that facilitates the child's mental development.

The Concept of the Zone of Proximal Development

Perhaps the best-known aspect of Vygotskian theory is what he termed the *zone of proximal development* (often spoken of as the ZPD). By this he means that children's abilities exist along a continuum of development within a zone of possible achievement. At one end of the continuum is what they are capable of doing on their own. At the other end, which is nearly (or proximately) within their reach, is the level they could move on to with the guidance of another more informed person. Each child has her own personal, unique zone of readiness that the teacher must detect to guide her most effectively in that direction.

The Role of the Teacher

Vygotsky's emphasis on the significance of external influences on the child's advancement emphasizes a particular aspect of the teacher's role—the importance of being a sensitive observer and guide. The ideal teacher is envisioned as being exquisitely aware of what the child already knows, what could be proposed next to further her learning, and how to conduct a dialogue that would facilitate that next step. By offering this support, or *scaffolding*, the teacher empowers the child to actualize her potential (Berk & Winsler, 1995). As the child gains competence, this support is gradually withdrawn, leaving her able to operate at a higher level than she was formerly capable of achieving by herself.

Specifically, what does Vygotsky say the teacher can do to encourage development? During the preprimary and early elementary years, children are shifting from what is termed *lower mental functions* (abilities held in common with other mammals) to the *higher mental abilities* unique to human beings. These include the use of mediated *perception* (typically using language to gain understanding), focused attention, deliberate or intentional memory, and symbolic thought (using words to think with).

The teacher facilitates the development of higher mental abilities by providing *leading activities;* in early childhood, Vygotsky maintains that the primary leading activity is play. He sees play as being particularly valuable because during play the child is always extending herself and moving beyond her usual operating level of development (Bodrova & Leong, 1996). According to Vygotsky play fosters the development of self-regulation, focused attention, and deliberate memory. But for it to enable the child to move toward the growing edge of her understanding and ability, Vygotsky maintains it must be play of a particular kind. Namely, it should involve imaginary situations in which the child participates in role-playing and uses language and social rules as components of that experience.

In addition to providing opportunities for imaginative pretend play to take place, Vygotsky suggests that the teacher can facilitate development in a second way: by using discussion between the child and the adult and with other children to explore and share ideas on a subject.

For example, the group might share ideas about how a gosling "gets inside the egg" (chapter 10, Emergent Curriculum in Action, p. 173) or where shadows go in the rain (chapter 1, Emergent Curriculum in Action, pp. 17–18). This could be followed by trying out some of the ideas—are shadows hiding behind the trees? When it is sunny outside, do we see shadows? When it is cloudy? And so forth.

It is this emphasis on teacher–child collaboration we see put into practice in the emergent curriculum of the Reggio Emilia schools.

USING THE EMERGENT APPROACH: AN EXAMPLE FROM REGGIO EMILIA

From time to time we have singled out aspects of the preprimary schools in Reggio Emilia in the hope that the examples will broaden the reader's points of view and teaching repertoires. For instance, in the chapter on designing the environment (chapter 4), the beautiful atmosphere of the schools was described. Part of that ambiance was due to planning and good design selected by adults, but part of it was the result of the wondrous things the children had made. The schools abounded with remarkable murals, collages, clay figures, and other constructions all done by children from toddlers to age 6.

The attractive results convey an impression of beauty and happiness that entices visitors from abroad to seek answers to questions such as: How is it possible for such young children to produce such beautiful and advanced work? How are these children taught, and what do they learn?

Some Basic Tenets of the Reggio Approach to Emergent Curriculum

The Basic Educational Theme Stresses Interaction and Expression

Despite the abundant evidence of artistic creativity, it is important to understand that the Reggio Emilia children's centers are not intended to be art schools. Rather, Loris Malaguzzi, the founder, intended them to be places where children and teachers interact—listening and talking with each other—to explore subjects in depth by exchanging ideas and trying those ideas out. That is the reason the discussion of the Reggio philosophy is placed in this chapter on cognitive development rather than in the chapter on creative self-expression.

The results of these joint investigations between teachers and children are then transformed by the children into visible results to communicate what they know to other people. As the staff often says, "You don't know it until you can express it." Because the children are too young to write, the staff encourages them to express what they know by using all sorts of other "languages." It might be the language of paint, or clay, or cardboard structures, or concoctions of bent wire bedecked with tissue paper, or shadow plays acted out behind a lighted screen. That is why the exhibit of their work currently touring the United States is termed the "Hundred Languages of Children." It illustrates the almost numberless ways children can use various materials to express what they know if only they are provided with that opportunity (Edwards, Gandini, & Forman, 1993, 1998).

Children Are Viewed as Competent, Strong, and Powerful

For many years early educators in the United States have fought and *must continue* to fight against push-down curriculum that focuses on learning the alphabet, using worksheets, and so forth (Bredekamp & Shepherd, 1990). That necessity has made us so wary of pushing children out of their depth (Dahlberg, Moss, & Pence, 1999; Elkind, 1990a, 1990b) that we may have underestimated what they *can* do.

The Italians are also wary of developmentally inappropriate curriculum but at the same time have retained an openness to young children's abilities and a willingness to guide them

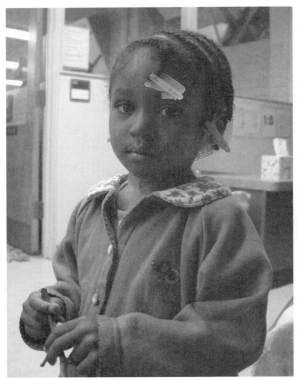

The image of the child is that she is competent, strong, and powerful.

to the edge of their ZPDs. By following their intellectual leads, proposing problems for them to solve, and encouraging them to use developmentally appropriate kinds of symbolization to express what they have learned, the teachers have empowered the children while not straining them beyond their capacities.

The Curriculum in the Reggio Schools Is Truly an Emergent One

Although many early childhood teachers in the United States make a point of selecting a theme of genuine interest to the children, all too often that theme remains the same year after year—transportation, baby animals, or dinosaurs, for example. Although this generic approach has certain conveniences, it is a far cry from the recording and transcribing of the children's comments that is done daily in Reggio Emilia. That close listening and consequent analysis is what enables the Reggio teachers to tailor curriculum to the children's concerns as these emerge and generate plans to further stimulate their thinking.

The Curriculum in the Reggio Schools Encourages the Children to Pursue a Subject in Depth

Because we cannot possibly teach any child a little about every subject in the world, why not concentrate on fewer subjects and experience the satisfaction of knowing more about a particular one in depth? The topic might be "Who Measures What in Our Town?" (Katz, 1992) coupled with how to measure a table and convey the results to an adult who will make a new one for the school (Scuola Diana, 1991), or how to make an amusement park for the birds involving making a fountain that actually works (Gambetti, 1992), or an investigation of shadows, or making puddles disappear, or any number of other possibilities. As we see in this and the following chapter, any subject can be used to provide practice in all sorts of broad and/or more closely targeted thinking and reasoning skills—so why settle for the smattering of information so common in American schools that Katz (1992) deplores?

Careful Documentation Is an Important Part of the Reggio Approach

As projects develop, recordings of the children's discussions are made and transcribed. These are used for two purposes. The first is that careful study of the written transcriptions often helps teachers spot interests and ideas they might otherwise have overlooked while the discussion was taking place. The second purpose is keeping track of the progress of projects as they develop.

Children's and teacher's comments are included on documentation boards, along with photographs and other graphics contributed by the children that explain what is happening. It cannot be emphasized enough that these boards form an integral part of the learning and assessment process because they record ongoing experiences, not just the final result. Families and visitors are kept current by this means, teachers are more aware of what is happening, and the boards are used with the children to help them recognize what they formerly thought or are currently pursuing. In addition, the presence of these aesthetically pleasing boards, which are hung at strategic points in the school, adds a spirit of engagement, enthusiasm, and beauty to the environment that is very different from the materials usually seen on American bulletin boards (Helm, Beneke, & Steinheimer, 1998).

The Role of the Teacher

Because a Reggio teacher sees the child as strong, rich in potential for constructing her own thought, he sees himself not as a transmitter of knowledge (a doer *to*) but as someone with whom the child collaborates in figuring things out (a doer *with*). The teacher helps the child construct a situation in which she can use her own competencies combined with the competencies of other children and the teacher to explore experiences and reach conclusions. In this approach, the teacher becomes a compass that may point the child in a particular direction, and education is seen as a process that cannot be determined in advance because it develops organically.

Close and repeated observation of the natural world is encouraged and accompanied by a wealth of self-expressive materials that are kept readily available for the children's use. Families are welcomed as a vital part of this process and are expected to participate very actively in these experiences.

How Do the Teacher and Children Work Together to Develop the Emergent Curriculum?

In the Reggio schools, learning proceeds as investigative pathways down which the children, teachers, and families venture together, hand in hand. Sometimes the direction of the pathways is anticipated in advance by the teachers; sometimes the direction shifts in unanticipated ways as the interests of the children point to a particular direction and the teachers pick up on that change.

But this sensitivity to the children's interests should not be interpreted as permissively letting them do whatever they wish. What the teachers do is select an aspect of the children's interests to develop further. Ideally, that aspect is one that presents problems for the children to consider and solve. For example, their comments about the battered condition of a worktable might lead to figuring out how to explain to a volunteer carpenter what to build to replace it. This, in turn, might require deciding on units of measure, how to "write" down the ensuing dimensions, and how to draw diagrams to clarify their vision.

Although not pursued every day and rarely with the entire group, the majority of these interest pathways continue for a long time, sometimes as long as several months. How different this is from our American way of having a theme a week and providing children with what Katz (1992) characterizes as teaching a "smattering of information."

The Reggio teachers take the principle of following the children's lead very seriously for, as they say, "If you wish to follow, you have to see where the children are going." Therefore, they listen with close attention to what the children say, often recording discussions and meticulously analyzing them after school with other teachers. This requires a great deal of time and dedication, but the results are worth it because such careful listening provides insight into what the children are thinking and understanding. The result is a day-by-day development of a truly emergent curriculum—one that inspires an enthusiasm for learning in both the children and adults of the school.

The closest analogy to American education is to think of the Reggio approach as using a kind of "project approach." But we must take care when using the word *project* because in many U.S. schools *project* means making something the teacher has thought up for the children to do, such as making suet balls for the birds or get-well cards for a sick friend. This kind of "project" is typically teacher instigated and controlled.

When using *project* in the emergent curriculum context, as Katz does (2006) and Helm and Katz (2001) and Katz and Chard (2000) do, we mean something quite different from that. In this context, *project* means an ongoing investigation of a topic agreed on by the children and teacher together that develops gradually over a period of time. This kind of project should be pictured as a pathway along which everyone journeys together.

For instance, such a project emerged in one of the Reggio schools when the children saw a puppet show that featured a monster—always an attractive, intriguing subject to 4- and 5-year-olds. The children produced a number of monster puppets of their own, and then some of them recalled the myth about the minotaur who was hidden in a labyrinth (or maze) on the nearby island of Crete. Much discussion about labyrinths and mazes ensued. The teachers encouraged the children to develop their interest further by making maps of paths in their own classroom as being a kind of maze. Some youngsters used clay to do this; others used strips of tape or colored pens. They were also encouraged to develop plans for pretend mazes as well. After much discussion and some controversy, the group settled on a maze drawn by a particular child to translate into an actual maze out on the playground.

Here a difficult problem developed: how to turn a plan, a diagram on paper, into an actual larger maze—how to change a symbol back into a real maze they could walk through. Ultimately the children solved this problem by requesting a ladder on which some of them stood so they could look at the plan and then direct their friends where to set the markers and draw the chalk lines to indicate the walls of the maze. The teachers said the final step would be for a group of parents to use the same plan to construct a three-dimensional maze in front of the school for everyone to enjoy.

As the children's investigations progressed, the teachers regularly took photos of what they were doing. These pictures were mounted, along with children's transcribed words and examples of their creative work, on documentation boards to remind the children of what they had already accomplished and to keep families informed of what was happening. As previously explained, these documentation boards are an integral part of the Reggio approach (Hall, Oleson, & Gambetti, 2001; Tarini, 1997).

Is There Any Common Ground?

Perhaps after reading descriptions contrasting the emergent and conventional curriculum approaches—particularly, the emergent approach as practiced in Reggio Emilia—the reader is feeling a mixture of inspiration mingled with despair. The discouraging part is that, as attractive as it is, it is unlikely the Reggio philosophy and practice could ever be transplanted in its entirety to our culture—nor do the people at Reggio advocate that happening. For example, it is difficult to imagine there would be a city in the United States willing to devote a substantial portion of its municipal budget to the education of its youngest children or that teachers' pay would include several hours a week dedicated to consulting with each other about the curriculum!

On the other hand, it is inspiring to realize that the Reggio approach and some U.S. schools share many values. For example, the labyrinth investigation just described involved the children and teachers in many higher-order mental processes and skills. Translated into "Americanese" educational terms, the skills include fostering creativity in thought, child-centered learning, cooperative learning, learning by doing, problem solving, basing learning on real experience, observing, reflecting on what has been learned, predicting outcomes, hypothesis forming and testing, using symbolic representation, inquiry learning, and so forth.

Perhaps the best solution to this quandary is to regard the Reggio schools as an inspiring example of what another culture is producing, and benefit from their experience and ideals where possible, while also retaining what we currently identify as being "best" emergent practices used in U.S. schools. We are pleased to present in this edition of *Total Learning* so many excellent examples of emergent curriculum taking place in the United States.

USING THE EMERGENT APPROACH IN U.S. SCHOOLS: SOME RECOMMENDATIONS

Model Joy and Interest in Learning Yourself

The verve and interest in a subject that teachers feel themselves are among the most valuable ways to encourage children's enthusiasm for cognitive learning. When teachers are excited about whatever topic is used as a basis for developing mental ability, the children sense this and respond to it with their own enthusiasm.

But sometimes over the years as teachers become fatigued and stressed, they lose that vital edge:

> Embalmed curriculum originates . . . with the teacher and all her years of experience. She started out with enthusiasm—writing her lessons plans, collecting her resource materials, working every night and all weekend. She can't work like that every year—so for every set of fresh faces, she brings it all out and dusts it off and is ready to roll. (Jones & Nimmo, 1994, p. 77)

One of the best rewards for using the emergent, evolving method of curriculum development is that it keeps the interest of the teacher as well as the children stimulated because there are always unanticipated, fresh elements to pursue as new pathways develop.

Be Prepared to Take Risks

Allowing curriculum to "emerge" sounds so easy in theory but actually can make teachers *uneasy* in practice because they dread the insecurity of not knowing what they should plan ahead of time. This anxiety can be alleviated if the teacher realizes that allowing curriculum to emerge does *not* mean that he does not plan in advance. The teacher *does* plan, but he remains sensitive to the children's concerns and adjusts his plan to pursue those concerns in an educationally beneficial way.

The real risks involved, then, do not lie in forgoing planning. It seems to have more to do with the teacher's underlying point of view about children. Does he really risk trusting them, relying on them to be competent and to collaborate with him in making decisions about the learning process? Or does he see them as fundamentally incompetent, helpless beings who require constant control and guidance to make sure they really learn something? Is the teacher really able, as Confrey (1995) advocates, "to walk softly, ask without telling, and rely on the child's actions as much as on his or her words" to determine the direction the curriculum should take (p. 205)?

Keep Cognitive Learning Appropriate to the Children's Age and Abilities

For those of us who see children as truly competent, there remains a delicate balance between challenging and empowering young children to think, reason, and express their understanding through a variety of media and not overstressing them by driving them too hard.

If we are not careful, we can easily be led astray. For one thing, most of us went to elementary schools that may have used overly academic models of instruction, and we tend to repeat what we learned there—particularly in the academic realm. For another, the pressure from other non-early childhood teachers, administrators, families, and even politicians to conform to an academically inappropriate model can be difficult to resist for someone who is newly employed (Rector, 2006).

Nowadays still a third factor may lead us astray if we are not careful. *Some people misinterpret what Vygotsky intended.* They overlook his emphasis on the importance of imaginative play and the value of sensitive interchanges between child and teacher that allow the teacher to empower the child to reach a slightly more advanced level. The result can be (and in some instances already has been) domineering teachers providing inappropriate, too-difficult curriculum in the name of advancing the child's ZPD.

We must remember that there is a risk to misinterpreting an individual child's zone of potential development. Pushing children beyond their depth breeds discouragement, saps motivation, reduces opportunities for learning what the children should be learning at that particular age, and results in tension and unhappiness (Rescorla, Hyson, & Hirsh-Pasek, 1991; Steffe & Gale, 1995). (For a developmental chart that includes cognitive skills, see appendix A.)

On the other hand, curriculum that is developmentally appropriate intrigues children and leads them to express further interest (Bredekamp, 2005; Bredekamp & Copple, 1997). Some good indicators of developmental appropriateness are whether children are attracted to a subject or activity when it is presented, whether they persist in working on it, whether they show progress in learning to master it, and whether they contribute their own ideas to continue the interest. In short, cognitive curriculum should be difficult enough to invite interest but not so difficult that it produces despair.

Keep Cognitive Learning a Part of Real Life

This book frequently extols the virtue of basing learning on concrete, actual involvement with the physical manipulation of materials—a position that is well supported in the literature (Piaget, 1983; Vygotsky, 1978). Besides actual involvement, however, a second aspect should be emphasized when discussing cognitive learning. Intellectual learning should not only be based on the physical manipulation of materials but also be integrated into the everyday, real life of the center whenever possible. This is best achieved by selecting the focus of interest for developing thinking opportunities based on the *children's current concerns*. The way the labyrinth topic developed from the Italian children's concerns with monsters provides a good example of how such an interest could emerge *for them* because of their cultural knowledge base about the minotaur.

Keep cognitive learning a part of real life. Here children explore New York City to get ideas for designing their memorial park for the World Trade Center victims of September 11.

For children in the U.S., the subject might be birds after a nest is discovered on the playground (see chapter 16, Emergent Curriculum in Action, page 305), or they could be interested in weather because school has been closed during a snowstorm. Or, like the children in New York City who experienced the World Trade Center attacks on September 11, it could be a focused and serious year-long pursuit to design a memorial park (see chapter 11, Emergent Curriculum in Action, page 186).

As we can see in this chapter and the next, any of the topics explored in emergent curriculum could be used to develop higher-level and mid-level thinking abilities. Additionally, one can go through each of the projects described in the Emergent Curriculum in Action features and list all the learning standards that are addressed. All the topics will assuredly be relevant because they come from the youngsters themselves.

Keep Feelings a Part of the Experience

Remember, too, that part of reality is having feelings. *Feeling and knowing properly belong together.* Even when the accent is on developing an intellectual skill, whenever human beings are involved, feelings are there, also. Indeed, unless the emotional life of the child is reasonably calm and she has been able to achieve some degree of peaceful social coexistence with the other children, it is unlikely that she will be free to focus much of her energy on the more difficult task of intellectual learning. Therefore, teachers should be prepared to recognize feelings as they arise and not try to brush them aside "because we're playing lotto now." Teachers should also appreciate the opportunities for special emotional or social learning that some subjects afford and deliberately include these as part of that curriculum area. Learning should take place for many selves on many levels at the same time.

As demonstrated in the Emergent Curriculum in Action feature in chapter 11(p. 186), when teachers are sensitive to the children's emotions and support the expression of those feelings through curriculum, a deeper learning experience ensues. Studio teacher, Brigid McGinn (2005) describes one child's reaction after the destruction of the World Trade Center towers and how the child was offered the opportunity through school curriculum to work through his feelings:

> Jake lives just a few blocks north of Ground Zero. He spent 3 days in the winter of 2001 building a wooden pair of towers and destroying them with every big ugly sharp tool he could find. He worked up a sweat for 2 hours each day and on the 3rd day he piled up the pieces on a shelf, put his name on it and said he would be back. He didn't return [to the *atelier* or art studio] until spring. That afternoon he ever so gently put his towers back together and soothed them as he painted them silver.

Encourage Children to Show You as Well as Tell You What They Mean

Many times when children are developing an idea about how things work or how they might solve a problem by making something work, words fail them. But anyone who has seen the "Hundred Languages of Children" exhibit knows there are many ways besides verbal language to express what one knows. In that display, everything from paints and drawing materials to bent wire, modeling clay, and dance are used to explain the children's ideas.

Moreover, as we all know, it is one thing to talk about something and quite another to represent it in graphic, visual form. We often think of using symbolic language as the highest form of understanding, but moving from one symbolic system such as language to another representational system, the way the Reggio youngsters did in their maze project, is a very advanced form of mental activity and should always be encouraged. Of course, this also means that a wide variety of materials, teacher support, and the time to use them must be consistently available to the children.

Use Questions to Promote Discussion and Facilitate Learning

Because the remainder of this chapter concentrates on using questions in appropriate ways, it is important to emphasize here, as we did in chapter 15, that there is a difference between having a *conversation* versus conducting an *interrogation*. Discussions are not question-and-answer sessions—they should be talks in which everyone shares their ideas and opinions together. This means (Lindfors, 1999) that the teacher needs to concentrate on understanding what the child is trying to explain, not on whether what the child says is right.

Special provisions are made in the Reggio Emilia schools for numerous small-group discussions in which interested children will pursue a particular topic over weeks or months—returning again and again to recall past work and ideas as well as to pursue new material. In U.S. schools the most likely opportunities for such interchanges are during self-select activity times when the teacher can move about and talk individually or with small groups of children, or perhaps during large-group time, though it takes practice to follow individual lines of thought from the children under such circumstances.

A teacher can ask the best, most interesting, and age-appropriate questions in the world and still experience discouragement if he fails to allow enough time for the children to reply before rushing on to the next question or, worse yet, answering it himself.

Rushing ahead of the children's ability to think is more typical of teachers than we would like to believe. When Rowe (1974) studied how long teachers typically waited for an answer after asking the children a question, she found that they waited only *a second or less* between asking the question and answering it themselves! Fortunately, this research has a happy ending because Rowe went on to demonstrate that when these same teachers learned to wait only a little bit longer (3 seconds instead of just 1), the participation and quality of the children's responses increased dramatically—and the quality of the teacher's follow-up questions improved, too.

As this landmark study reveals so clearly, there are tremendous benefits for the children when teachers discard the pressured, hurry-up approach and substitute a more extended period of wait time between questions. And wait time between questions and answers can be extended even longer than a few minutes with benefit. For example, when teachers in Reggio speak of wait time, they sometimes mean waiting several *days* while ideas percolate in the children's brains.

Encourage Children to Ask and Answer Questions Themselves

Coe (1987) puts it well when he says, "The best school, after all, for the world of childhood is not the school where children know the most answers, but the school where children ask the most questions" (p. 70). Teachers can do several practical things to encourage question-asking and wondering behavior in their classrooms. Staying open and listening for questions are fundamental parts of such encouragement. Sometimes, particularly when the question is not clear, the teacher might ask the child to repeat or rephrase it, which helps both child and teacher understand what is being asked. Finally, as Rowe's research reminds us, waiting and resisting the impulse to provide the answer oneself can stimulate the child to answer and ask more questions on her own.

These responses are highly desirable because every time a child figures out an answer for herself, she has gained independence, confidence, and self-esteem because she has been able to rely on herself instead of on someone else. Of course, sometimes there is just no way for a child to learn something unless she is told—names of things or certain facts fall into this category. But there are many other times when, *if the teacher asks the right question* in reply to the child's question, the child can have a pleasurable "Aha!" experience as she discovers or thinks through an idea on her own. These learning experiences are to be cherished, because they contribute much to the child's sense of happiness and feeling of intellectual competence.

With young children, such opportunities should be uncomplicated and straightforward. When something is tried out, the experiment will be most successful if it provides chances to figure out the answers to such questions as "Why do you think that happened?" "What would happen if . . . ?" or "How could we find out if . . . ?" These questions should be followed by "Let's try it and see!"

The experiments can be as informal as seeing how a dog reacts when scratched in different places, or finding out how to make a kitten purr, or discovering what happens when red and yellow are mixed together. Perhaps it is a hot day, and the metal slide is hot, too. The teacher might ask the children, "How can we cool the slide?" If the children suggest pouring water down it, the teacher might respond, "Well, let's find out. How can we get the water there? What if the hose won't reach? Then what?" These opportunities for thinking and reasoning abound for the teacher who is on the lookout for them.

Remember that part of the learning experience should always include having the children put their conclusions into words. ("Well, what did make the kitten purr?" "Did the squirt bottle or the bucket of water work better? How come, do you think, the bucket was better?") The following are examples of spontaneous situations in which the children could formulate reasons (hypotheses) for something happening:

- What makes the play dough so sticky? How could we make it drier?
- Can we turn Jell-O back to water? And then back to Jell-O again?
- How did you make that shadow? Can you make it go away?

The children may need to be helped along in their thinking by questions posed by the teacher or by other children, but the test of a truly successful experiment is that the children can answer most of their own questions as a result of their experience trying out possibilities with the materials.

Use Children's Questions to Help Them Learn

Answering a child's information-seeking questions requires two skills. First, it requires asking the right kind of question in reply to the child's query. Second, it requires waiting for the child's reply. Witness the differences in the following dialogues:

EXAMPLE 1

The children, who have returned from a visit to the veterinarian, have found the doctor's kit all set up for them in the housekeeping corner. The teacher begins to unpack it.

Erin (to the teacher): What are you doing with those things?
Teacher: I'm getting out the stethoscopes. They help us hear noises in our bodies. Doesn't your doctor ever listen to your chest with one of these?
Erin: He listens to my heart. Where *is* my heart?
Teacher: In your chest. (he points) Right there! Here, Erin, listen! (He puts the stethoscope on the child's chest.)
Erin (whining): I can't hear it. What does it sound like?
Teacher: Listen to mine. Don't you hear it go thump-thump?
Erin: Oh, yeah, now I do. It *does* go thump!
Teacher: Now listen to yours. What does *it* do?
Erin: It goes thump, too.

This situation may not seem limiting to the child, until you contrast it with the following one:

EXAMPLE 2

On the way back from a trip to the veterinarian, Hank and Maggie decide they want to play hospital when they return to school. Upon arrival, they hurry to get out the medical kits.

Maggie (to the teacher): What's in that box?
Teacher: This one? Want to look? (hands the box to Maggie)
Maggie: Oh, it's that thing my doctor uses. It's a—what's it called?
Teacher: Anybody know? (total silence) It's called a stethoscope (pause). Does it tickle when your doctor uses it?
Maggie: Yes, and it's cold, too. What good is it anyway?
Hank: He listens to your heart. I've heard it—it goes kuh-thump. There, I'll show you. (They listen to each other's hearts and to the teacher's, too.)
Teacher: But how come the dog doctor had one?
Maggie: Do dogs have hearts?
Teacher (pause): Well, *you* know a dog. [The children's center is frequently visited by a forbearing springer spaniel named Lady.]
Hank: Lady! Let's get Lady! (The children proceed to the director's office where, providentially, Lady is stretched out, snoring.)
Teacher: Now, don't surprise her. Speak to her first.

Maggie: Hi, there, Lady, old girl. (Lady looks up and wags her tail.) (to Hank) Where's her heart?

Hank (authoritatively, pointing to Lady's hindquarters): Down there!

Teacher: Is it?

Maggie (putting stethoscope on Lady's rear): I don't hear nothing. She hasn't got one!

Teacher: Are you sure?

Hank: Let me listen! Nope, nothing there.

Teacher: Gee, I thought dogs had hearts. Where could it be?

Hank: On her back maybe.

Maggie: I want a turn. Let me do it. (She slides the stethoscope around Lady's chest.) I hear it! I hear it! Here it is! (Lady, gratified by the attention, licks her hand.) Yuck, her mouth is sticky—yuck, yuck! I gotta wash.

Hank: But lemme hear her heart first. (Maggie runs off, but Hank continues to listen, ultimately distinguishing the sounds of the dog's breathing and stomach growling, also.)

Note that this kind of teaching does not mean that the teacher never provides information or never makes a suggestion in the form of a guiding question (the teacher in example 2 did both), but it does mean that he continually asks himself "How can I help the children discover the answer for themselves?"

Ask Children to Think of Ways to Solve Problems and Propose Alternative Possibilities

One final function of asking questions must be added. To encourage the generation of ideas, teachers should cultivate the ability to ask questions that cause children to think about how to solve problems or even to propose alternative solutions. Such questions are intended to encourage original solutions and so are called *creative thought* or *open-ended questions.*

Creative thought questions are characterized by having more than one "right" (alternative) answer because a number of possible replies may be of equal worth. This sort of open-ended thinking has been christened *divergent thinking* by Guilford (1981), who contrasts it with its opposite, *convergent thinking,* which could be defined as thinking in which only one correct answer is possible. When teachers are developing *convergent* thinking in children, they ask questions that require information in reply. Such questions as "How old are you?" "What's your name?" "What's that picture on your T-shirt?" and "What's that called?" anticipate one correct, factual response. Note that much "discovery" learning, which fosters reasoning and process thinking, also produces convergent replies. For example, in the dialogue about finding Lady's heart, the children figured out the *facts* that a dog does have a heart and that it is located in its chest. However, if the children had been asked to figure out additional ways to hear Lady's heart, then it would have been an example of creative problem solving.

The following are examples of questions that stimulate *creative* problem solving and *divergent* thinking:

- How could we fix it?
- What else could we do?
- What do you think would happen if . . . ?
- But what if that won't work. What else could we use?
- What could you use to make it?
- What do you think? What's your opinion?

Such creative thought questions invite a multitude of answers and possibilities. Children relish thinking about funny problems (What if everybody had a tail like a monkey? or What if we lived under water the way fish do?) as well as solving more serious ones (How can we keep the rabbit from getting too warm? or Where should we hang all the bulky coats now that winter is here? or What is the best way to dry the dog after her bath?).

Young children usually come up with one idea each, but if these single ideas are pooled in a group discussion, children can learn to appreciate that there is often more than one good way to solve a problem.

Reinforce the Production of Creative Ideas by Recognizing Their Value

It is all too easy for adults, who have had so much more experience, unintentionally to discourage creative thinking by evaluating the results too critically too soon, or by applying unreasonably high standards of accomplishment to what the children are doing, or by showing amusement at the unexpected novelty of a suggestion or by "just fixing it a little to make it nicer." Children are extraordinarily sensitive to these "put-downs" and quickly learn to hold their tongues and stop sharing their ideas when this occurs. Perhaps they may even stop thinking up alternative solutions to problems when subjected to such negative responses or, worse yet, to what they sense is subtle ridicule.

On the other hand, children will continue to be adventurous if teachers provide positive reinforcement by paying attention to their ideas, treating them with serious respect, encouraging them to try out their suggestions whenever possible, and offering help when needed. Even an idea that does not turn out to be practical can have a beneficial result if it is used to teach the children that making an attempt is worthwhile and that failure just means it is time to propose another alternative.

Often, of course, the children's ideas are sound ones, and when this is the case and the group adopts the suggestion, the delight of the children is obvious. Their self-esteem, as well as their mental ability, has been enhanced.

SUMMARY

When curriculum is generated for the cognitive self, the most important goal toward which to work is helping children feel confident, happy, and enthusiastic when engaged in mental activity.

There are three approaches to developing cognitive curriculum, all of which have merit. They include (1) teaching facts to provide a foundation of information, (2) using the emergent approach to facilitate the development of thought, and (3) including practice in some mid-level mental ability skills that underlie later academic learning. Good cognitive curriculum offers opportunities for investigation and focused intentional teaching.

Emergent curriculum, which advocates that curriculum be based on the children's evolving interests and abilities combined with thoughtful support and guidance by their teacher, should provide the overall framework in which cognitive learning takes place. Using that approach provides the most interesting challenges for the children while making it possible for them to acquire information and practice mid-level skills at the same time. The schools of Reggio Emilia, the educational philosophy of Vygotsky, and the Emergent Curriculum in Action features of this text provide interesting examples and a theoretical base showing how this can be achieved.

Some practical points to remember when developing emergent curriculum include modeling joy and interest in learning yourself, being prepared to take risks, keeping cognitive learning appropriate to the children's age and abilities, keeping it part of real life, and keeping feelings a part of the experience. Encouraging children to show as well as say what they mean and using questions to promote discussion and facilitate learning are additional important ingredients in sustaining effective cognitive learning.

Food for Thought and Group Discussions

1. In examples 1 and 2 on pages 323 and 324, identify the teacher's statements that provided factual answers. Were some of these necessary? Is it any better for another child to tell a child a fact than for the teacher to do it? Consider the incorrect information Hank gave Maggie about the location of Lady's heart—do you think the teacher should have said anything about that?

2. Try some brainstorming yourself. What else might a potato masher be used for? A rubber tire? A piece of cloth? A box of matches, contents included? Try to go beyond ordinary uses: Have fun, take risks! (And if this exercise is especially difficult for you, analyze what has made it so hard and not fun.) What are ways you can use these insights when teaching children to foster a more positive response from them?

Self-Check Questions for Review

Content-Related Questions

1. Explain why children should not be pushed beyond their depth in any area of learning.

2. Define *emergent curriculum*. Explain why the Reggio Emilia curriculum is said to be emergent.

3. What are three important things teachers can do that will help children enjoy cognitive learning?

4. Explain what the zone of proximal development is. What is the name of the educational theorist who developed that concept?

5. What are three purposes of documentation boards in the Reggio Emilia schools?

6. List four practical points to remember when developing emergent curriculum.

Integrative Questions

1. Explain why the staff of Reggio Emilia maintains that children have a hundred languages at their disposal.

2. Provide an example of an emergent possibility you have come across in recent weeks while working with children. How was that possibility handled at school (or home)? Would you describe the curriculum in your current school as emergent, conventional, or informational?

3. The children have been playing with beanbags, and one of the bags has got stuck in a tree beyond reach. Propose a dialogue between teacher and child that would discourage the child from thinking of a way to retrieve the beanbag. Now rewrite the dialogue demonstrating how the teacher might ask a series of questions that could help the child figure out ways to retrieve the beanbag.

Coordinating Videotape

Growing minds. Tape #13. *The whole child: A caregiver's guide to the first five years.* The Annenberg/CPB Collection,

P.O. Box 2345, South Burlington, VT 05407-2345. *Growing Minds* describes two approaches to developing mental ability. The program offers basic ways teachers can encourage young children to think creatively by using emergent curriculum with an emphasis on the inquiry method as a means of stimulating thought. It also touches on the more conventional approach as teachers set up activities that provide practice in specific mental abilities such as matching and grouping.

References for Further Reading

Pick of the Litter

Cadwell, L. B. (2003). *Bringing learning to life: The Reggio approach to early childhood education.* New York: Teachers College Press. The sense of fresh adventure and inspiration conveyed by this book should encourage all of us to translate some of that inspiration into our own school environments.

Overviews

Jones, E., & Nimmo, J. (1994). *Emergent curriculum.* Washington, DC: National Association for the Education of Young Children. This book describes the agony and the ecstasy of providing emergent curriculum for a group of young children throughout a year. Honest and inspiring.

Perry, B. D. (2001). Curiosity: The fuel of development. *Scholastic Early Childhood Today, 15*(6), 22–23. Perry briefly reviews ways to inhibit or encourage curiosity by young children.

Applications

Helm, J. H., Beneke, S., & Steinheimer, K. (1998). *Windows on learning: Documenting young children's work.* New York: Teachers College Press. This book details the ways documentation—particularly documentation boards—can be used to keep track of what children are doing and explain it to other people.

Helm, J. H., & Katz, L. (2001). *Young investigators: The Project Approach in the early years.* New York: Teachers College Press and National Association for the Education of Young Children. The authors describe an American approach to emergent curriculum. Down-to-earth information, recommendations, and an actual example make this book practical and helpful.

About the Schools and/or Philosophy of Reggio Emilia

Edwards, C., Gandini, L., & Forman, G. (Eds.). (1998). *The hundred languages of children: The Reggio Emilia Approach—Advanced reflections* (2nd ed.). Greenwich, CT: Ablex.

Gandini, L., & Edwards, C. P. (2001). *Bambini: The Italian approach to infant/toddler care.* New York: Teachers College Press.

Gillespie, C. W. (2000). Six Head Start classrooms begin to explore the Reggio Emilia Approach. *Young Children, 55*(1), 21–27.

Hendrick, J. B. (Ed.). (1997). *First steps toward teaching the Reggio way.* Upper Saddle River, NJ: Merrill/Prentice Hall.

Hendrick, J. B. (Ed.). (2004). *Next steps toward teaching the Reggio way.* Upper Saddle River, NJ: Merrill/Prentice Hall.

Information About Vygotsky

Berk, L. E., & Winsler, A. (1995). *Scaffolding children's learning: Vygotsky and early childhood education.* Washington, DC: National Association for the Education of Young Children. This readable book clearly explains the basic principles of the theory, cites research related to it, and explains how it can be applied to preprimary and early elementary school.

For the Advanced Student

Vygotsky, L. S. (1978). *Mind in society: The development of higher psychological processes.* Cambridge, MA: Harvard University Press. Originally written in 1934, this book sets forth some of Vygotsky's most fundamental ideas about learning.

Related Organizations and Online Resources

Early Childhood Research and Practice is a free, bilingual online journal on the development, care, and education of young children. Each issue highlights a project—complete with photos—using the emergent curriculum approach. http://ecrp.uiuc.edu/

Innovations in Early Education: The International Reggio Exchange (Merrill-Palmer Institute/Wayne State University, 71-A East Ferry Ave., Detroit, MI 48202) is a quarterly newsletter that encourages the exchange of ideas from around the world as they relate to the Reggio approach. Includes information on conferences and the "Hundred Languages of Children" exhibit. The entire collection of back issues is available on CD as well. Subscription information and how to join the online discussion group, REGGIO-L, can be found online. http://www.mpi.wayne.edu/earlychildhood.htm

The North American Reggio Emilia Alliance (NAREA) is an organization that supports the exploration of the Reggio Emilia approach worldwide. Information about programs in the United States that are exploring the Reggio approach can be found at the Web Site. http://www.reggioalliance.org/

The Project Approach home page is a wonderful resource for discovering the project approach and seeing examples of projects from a variety of classrooms. There is also information about joining the online discussion group. http://www.project-approach.com/

HELPING CHILDREN DEVELOP MENTAL ABILITIES AND ACADEMIC COMPETENCE

Using the Conventional Approach

Have you ever . . .

- Heard people refer to Piaget but did not really understand why his theories are so valuable?
- Wondered how to go about developing mental abilities in the children without pushing them beyond their depth?
- Wished that you knew more about presenting "pre-academic" skills so the children would find them fun?
- Wondered whether such young children could learn arithmetic?

If you have, the material in this chapter will help you.

HELPING
CHILDREN
DEVELOP
MENTAL
ABILITIES AND
ACADEMIC
COMPETENCE

Academics is a term that is widely used but rarely defined. If academics are understood to mean important foundational skills and knowledge in early literacy, mathematics, science, and other subjects, then academics definitely are an essential part of developmentally appropriate early childhood programs. Of course, to be developmentally appropriate these learning domains must also be addressed in ways that fit children's ways of learning. It is when academics are defined very narrowly as a set of specific facts and when these facts are taught by "drill and kill" or other such methods pushed down from older grades that they are less relevant to young children's overall development and learning.

—Carol Copple and Sue Bredekamp (2006, p. 62)

In general, start science from the child's touchable, viewable, immediate environment. Go to the park, even if they've been there many times before. Learning takes place with repeated experience. Collect stuff. Look at stuff. Be the wind and blow a seed. Bring back a feather. How does the water look when a duck is swimming? What happens when you throw in a stone?

—Dorothy Peters (2000, p. 32)

In addition to helping children sustain a zest for intellectual learning by fostering the global skills of investigation and problem solving inherent in the emergent approach, it is also valuable to incorporate curriculum that targets some narrower, more specific mental abilities and emergent mathematical and science-related skills. This is particularly important for teachers who must meet state or federally mandated educational standards, such as Head Start and publicly funded programs, and elementary schools.

Some of these skills are of a more general nature and apply particularly to emergent literacy, mathematical, or science discovery skills. These include matching, grouping, seeing common relationships, seriated and temporal ordering, and having a rudimentary understanding of cause/effect relationships. Other skills are more specific and apply mainly to emergent mathematical understandings. These include such skills as attaching meaning to counting, perceiving simple number relationships, realizing how useful mathematics is and how its concepts are all around us, and understanding general quantifying terms such as more and less.

CONTRIBUTIONS OF JEAN PIAGET

Jean Piaget has contributed a great deal to our understanding of many mental ability skills and their value. To understand more about such mental abilities, it is first necessary to review the most basic conclusions of Jean Piaget (1983) because his work has made such a significant contribution to what is known about the development of cognitive structures in childhood—cognitive structures that form the foundation for the development of more advanced thinking and reasoning skills as children mature.

Piaget has long maintained that children's mental growth is the result of dynamic *interaction* between children and their environments and that the activity of play and actual, involving experience are vital ingredients in fostering mental development. He also maintains that the thought processes of children differ from those of adults and that these processes pass through a series of developmental stages as the child matures. He has demonstrated the truth of this contention quite convincingly in several areas, the most familiar being his demonstrations of young children's inability to master the principle of conservation (the fact that the total amount or quantity of material remains unchanged even though the shape or number of parts may be altered). Young children will maintain stoutly, for instance, that the amount of water in a tall, thin beaker is greater than an identical amount of water in a squat jar, even though they may have just witnessed that the quantities were originally the same. As Charles (1974) puts it, preschool-age children lack "the ability to consider, at the same time, the whole and various arrangements of its parts" (p. 14). In our culture, it is not until about age 7 that children grasp the principle of "reversibility" and can, in their mind's eye, return a substance to its original state while viewing it in its altered state. This is, of course, only one of numerous examples Piaget and other scholars of the Genevan school have investigated over the past 60 years that demonstrate the perception-bound quality of thinking characteristic of young children. For children of this age, seeing is, quite literally, believing.

Piaget's research is very different in style from the more typical research studies cited in this book. To study children's thinking, he used a combination of interview and observation to develop and then confirm his theories.

This has caused him to be criticized because it is not possible to repeat a Piagetian experiment exactly (Centre for Educational Research and Innovation, 1977; Siegler, 1998) since his data often lack precise ages and numbers and are not statistically analyzed. Moreover, instead of using control groups and carefully presenting exactly the same situation to every child, he thought it was more valuable to conduct open-ended discussions with children on a one-to-one basis—so every interview was somewhat different, because he followed the child's lead as he formulated his questions.

Despite these criticisms, Piaget's clever investigations have blazed new trails in the study of children's development, particularly in the realm of cognition. Nowadays this approach has acquired new admirers as we gain an added appreciation of his ability to sense and follow the development of children's ideas by asking them suitable and ingenious questions. Teachers as well as children owe him a debt of gratitude for the remarkable insights he contributed (Singer & Revenson, 1998).

Piaget's Stages of Mental Development

Piaget has divided mental development roughly into four stages—the sensorimotor, preoperational, concrete operational, and formal operational stages—as shown in Table 18.1. Although the age of onset and discreteness of these stages varies somewhat from culture to culture, the order in which the stages occur appears to be fairly regular (Kamii & Ewing, 1996; Siegler, 1998). The main value for the teacher of knowing about such stages and the characteristics of children who are in them lies in perceiving how children gradually construct their understanding of the world and in suiting learning opportunities to what they are able to grasp at each stage.

All children benefit from such learning opportunities, but it is particularly important to offer them to children who come from families of the poor (Sigel & Cocking, 1977), because these kinds of activities may not be part of the culture of their homes. Special attention should also be paid to other children whose life experiences may have been restricted because of such things as extensive hospitalization or overexposure to television.

Conditions That Favor Optimal Development

According to Piaget, development is influenced by (1) physical maturation, (2) experience, (3) interaction with other people (socialization), and (4) equilibration. This information

Table 18.1
Summary of the Piaget Model

Basic Stages	Behavior Commonly Associated with the Stage
Sensorimotor stage (0–2 years) Understanding the present and real	Composed of six substages that move from reflex to intentional activity involving cause-and-effect behavior Involves direct interactions with the environment
Preoperational stage (2–7 years) Symbolic representation of the present and real Preparation for understanding concrete operations	Uses signifiers:mental images, imitation, symbolic play, drawing, language Understands verbal communication Believes what he sees—is "locked into" the perceptual world Sees things from his own point of view and only one way at a time ("centering") Thinking is *not* reversible Busy laying foundations for understanding concrete operations stage, which involves grasping concepts of conservation, transitivity, classification, seriation, and reversibility
Concrete operational stage (7–11 years) Organization of concrete operations	Has probably acquired the following concepts:conservation, reversibility, transitivity, seriation, and classification; that is, now believes that length, mass, weight, and number remain constant; understands relational terms such as "larger than" and "smaller than"; is able to arrange items in order from greatest amount to least amount; can group things, taking more than one quality into account at the same time
Formal operational stage (11–15 years) Hypothesis making Testing the possible	Age of abstract thinking Able to consider alternative possibilities and solutions Can consider "fanciful," hypothetical possibilities as a basis for theoretical problem solving Sees the world not only as it *is* but as it *could* be

has important implications for teachers and families, because adults can influence all these elements, at least to a degree, thereby helping ensure the most favorable climate for the child's growth.

For instance, although physical maturation depends primarily on built-in timetables, the role of good nutrition, adequate health procedures, and ample physical activity should not be ignored. The Romans summed this up to perfection when they spoke of the importance of *mens sana in corpore sano*—a sound mind in a sound body.

The significance of experience—in particular concrete, tangible experience—has been stressed throughout this book as being a fundamental essential component of teaching young children, yet it must be mentioned once again in this discussion of mental growth, lest the reader be tempted to suddenly abandon the real world for the solely verbal-visual one.

The third enhancer of growth, social interactions, requires a bit more comment (DeVries & Zan, 1994; DeVries, Zan, Hildebrandt, Edmiaston, & Sales, 2002). Although teachers of young children are usually well aware of the kind of *social* benefits children gain through interaction with other children, they tend to be less familiar with Piaget's idea that discussion and argument (in the sense of debate) among children is an important avenue of *mental* growth. It is very helpful for children to discuss reasons and thinking problems among themselves, as well as directly with teachers. This encountering of experience together, combined with putting their ideas about it into some kind of symbolic form such as words or pictures and engaging in back-and-forth comparison of their thoughts, is a productive mode of learning that teachers should make greater use of as a teaching method.

Finally, the process of equilibration, or bringing ideas into balance with reality, is valuable to understand. Piaget maintains that there are two ways children deal with information: They either assimilate it or accommodate to it, and both of these processes contribute to equilibration. Quite simply, when children *assimilate* information, they add new facts to what they know already; when they *accommodate* to information, they change what they know to fit the new experience, thereby achieving a new balance or equilibrium.

For example, when some of the teachers in Reggio Emilia were talking with the children about shadows, some youngsters maintained that the reason shadows moved was because shadows of living things moved whereas the shadows of nonliving things did not. The teachers encouraged the children to try out their idea by outlining the shadow cast by a column in the morning and then returning to see what had become of the shadow in the afternoon—had it moved, or was it still where they had drawn it? The fact it had moved contradicted what the children thought they knew and required them to accommodate their knowledge about shadows to fit the observable facts. The movement of the shadows was not related to whether the shadow caster was alive. What then could have made the shadow move? Figuring that out was the next step.

Mental activity usually involves a combination of accommodation and assimilation working together. For example, years ago a child found his little dog lying dead in the gutter one day, run over by a car. Weeks later, his mother reported that he was insisting on walking along the edge of the curb every time they went somewhere, and this almost fanatical preoccupation was driving her crazy! She commented that he had begun doing that about the same time his grandfather had died. It turned out that the reason he had been so insistent on walking along the curb was that he was looking for his beloved grandpa. Once his mother realized this, she explained to him that dead people are not generally found in gutters and that Grandpa had been buried in the cemetery, which they then visited. This anecdote illustrates that this little boy had formerly *assimilated* his grandfather's dying (that is, he interpreted it in the light of what he knew of death). The additional information required him to *accommodate* to it by changing his prior knowledge to include new experience. The new situation required new learning and a rebalancing of what he already knew about the world with what he had just learned.

Much learning involves this process of rebalancing, and teachers tend to accept this fact routinely. What they may be insensitive to, however, is that sometimes accommodating to new information also requires considerable tact by teachers so that the child can save face while he literally is changing his mind.

According to Piaget, development is influenced by physical maturation, experience, interaction with other people, and equilibration.

A Brief Comparison of Piaget's and Vygotsky's Points of View

Perhaps, having read the brief introductions to Piagetian and Vygotskian theory included in these cognitive chapters, you are wondering, "Well, who is right?"

Before answering that question, we should realize that, despite a number of differences, both Piaget and Vygotsky favor the constructivist point of view. That is, they agree that learning is

HELPING
CHILDREN
DEVEVOP
MENTAL
ABILITIES AND
ACADEMIC
COMPETENCE

generated (constructed) by the child and that, as children mature, a progressive structuring of cognitive processes takes place. They also agree that as that growth takes place, the thought processes become increasingly complex. Both theorists also acknowledge that play is the primary mode by which young children acquire learning.

Where they disagree is in the significance they attribute to the importance of external influences. Piaget sees the child as having the crucial role in constructing his understanding; sometimes this is spoken of as the "child as the little scientist," constructing hypothesis after hypothesis as he assimilates and accommodates information from the world. Because of his emphasis on the individual's role as he constructs what he knows, Piaget is sometimes spoken of as a *cognitive constructivist*. But remember that Piaget does not say that this learning takes place in isolation. As we see in his championing of dialogue and debate, he also acknowledges the influence of society on that learning.

On the other hand, though agreeing that children can attain some cognitive concepts spontaneously (on their own), Vygotsky looks at learning from a different point of view. He stresses the influence society has on children's development and so is sometimes spoken of as being a *social constructivist*. He argues that more difficult concepts can only be acquired by children because of the leadership provided by an adult or better-informed peer. For the child to attain a higher level of conceptualization, instruction is essential. The teacher is an essential part of the learning process as she provides the "scaffolding" that supports the child as he figures something out. She does this by using questions, prompts, and challenging examples that arouse the child's interest and cause him to advance beyond what he can do "on his own," thereby reaching the leading edge of his zone of proximal development. But this should not be envisioned as a one-way street—Vygotsky places considerable emphasis on the importance of *interaction* between child and teacher as they exchange information and ideas.

So the answer to the question "Who is right?" really depends on your point of view, because both men have contributed valuable ideas that we should bear in mind when discussing the child's cognitive self. Piaget's emphasis that learning is done by the child and has to be done for himself lies at the heart of our early childhood philosophy. Nor can we argue with Vygotsky's contention that children require other people to help them learn—that society and the cultural history it transmits preselect what knowledge children are exposed to and hence are able to acquire. Really, as Fosnot (2005) points out, the two constructivist viewpoints are inseparable: You cannot have individuals without society, and society would not exist were it not for the individuals who comprise it.

Children are natural scientists, constructing hypothesis after hypothesis.

WHICH MENTAL ABILITIES ARE PARTICULARLY IMPORTANT?

As you progress through this chapter, you will no doubt realize that you occasionally do provide some practice in one or more of the mental abilities discussed here. Perhaps you play bingo with the children or provide Montessori graduated cylinders for them to use. The trouble is that such practice is often haphazard—fortuitous—rather than deliberately planned so that some skills are practiced and other equally important ones are ignored. The remedy for this is to become aware of what the fundamental skills are and plan for their consistent inclusion rather than depending on "happy accidents" to provide spotty coverage of them (Bredekamp, 2005; Copple & Bredekamp, 2006). As Bredekamp (2005) points out, children learn best through their own investigations as well as "focused intentional teaching."

Piaget (1983) identified various mental abilities that form the foundation for later concrete operational thought in older children. Constance Kamii (1972), who has had an important role in implementing Piagetian principles in early childhood classrooms, lists these early forms of concrete operational abilities as including (1) classification, (2) seriation, (3) structuring of time and space, (4) social knowledge, and (5) representation.

Ways of gaining social knowledge and using such symbols as language, literacy activities, and imaginative play to represent reality have already been discussed in previous chapters, so in this chapter we will first concentrate on the remaining mental abilities that are rather broad in scope and are early steps toward Piaget's concepts of classification, seriation, and structuring time and space. After that, we will focus on some narrower, more focused skills that are specifically related to emergent mathematical ability and scientific understandings.

The more general mid-level abilities include the following:

- Matching
- Grouping
- Pairing common relations
- Graduated ordering (seriation)
- Temporal ordering (what happens when)
- Determining simple cause-and-effect relationships

You will find that the activities suggested later in the chapter for developing the various cognitive abilities are simple ones. These have all been used successfully, not only in our own children's center and Institute but also in many other settings, such as Head Start, so we know that young children enjoy them and are able to perform them satisfactorily.

FOSTERING MENTAL ABILITIES TO DEVELOP CHILDREN'S LITERACY, MATHEMATICAL UNDERSTANDING, AND SCIENTIFIC INQUIRY SKILLS

To foster literacy and children's emergent mathematical and scientific inquiry skills, teachers should begin by developing the youngsters' general mental abilities. Of course the abilities discussed on the following pages are by no means a comprehensive list. However, the six skills selected here are of such fundamental importance that experts agree they merit special attention because they provide the foundation on which so many other skills are built (Carpenter, Fennema, Franke, Levi, & Empson, 1999; DeVries et al., 2002; Geist, 2001; Smith, 1999).

Matching

Matching is the ability to identify which items are the same and which ones are different.

The basic question to ask is: "Can you find the pair that is the same?"

We have already seen how important this skill is for attaining literacy where it is vital to hear and/or see differences and samenesses in sounds and letters, but the ability to discriminate extends far beyond that kind of literacy. Being able to match items that are the same promotes the understanding of mathematical equality, and discriminating between *same* and *different* forms the basis for the more sophisticated abilities of grouping or classifying, common relations, and seriation.

HELPING
CHILDREN
DEVELOP
MENTAL
ABILITIES AND
ACADEMIC
COMPETENCE

Grouping

Grouping is the ability to identify the property that members of a class or group of items have in common—in other words, what makes them a "family" when the items are not completely the same.

The basic question to ask is: "Can you show me the things that belong to the same family?"

In order to do this, children must understand the concept of "same versus different" and then go beyond understanding that concept to reason and analyze the differences and similarities in order to decide which items qualify for inclusion in which group. For example, when given a box of many different plastic animals, a 4-year-old might choose to sort them according to the criteria of wild versus tame, whereas a younger child might sort the ones *he* likes best into one pile and all the others into another one.

As children mature and become more able not only to assimilate information but also to change their minds and accommodate to new possibilities, divergent thinking—that is, producing more than one answer—can be fostered as the teacher asks, "Is there another way you could sort them?"

Classification (the more advanced form of grouping) is a basic aspect of life sciences because it allows scientists to organize knowledge by classifying it—for example, Linnaeus brought order to the field of botany by sorting plants into various categories according to their particular characteristics. In mathematics, grouping is a basic aspect of understanding set theory.

However, the greatest value of grouping is that even at the preprimary level it requires analytical reasoning and thinking even though children of that age may not always be able to put their reasons for placing items into particular groups into words. Piaget speaks of such grouping activity as being on the intuitive level—an apt description of how the children proceed. He states that grouping is the beginning form of the more sophisticated hierarchical classification ability that is the intellectual prerogative of children who have attained the concrete operational stage of development occurring somewhere around the ages of 6 to 8.

Common Relations

This is the ability to identify a common relationship or property between *pairs* of items that do not match but *do* have a particularly strong bond or relationship of some sort between them. It differs from grouping because it includes only a pair of items.

The basic question to ask is: "Which thing goes (or belongs) most closely with what other thing?"

Providing practice in this skill fosters mathematical understanding of one-to-one correspondence and equivalency (one long block equals two half-blocks but have the same length in common). It also encourages understanding and enjoyment of many kinds of pairs such as opposites (hot/cold, up/down, rough/smooth) and associations (ring/finger, sock/shoe, tooth/toothbrush), and ultimately, to "If *a* equals *b* and *b* equals *c*, then *a* equals . . . ?" The use of riddles where often an unexpected relationship is the answer (From a 4-year-old: "What's yellow and tickley?" Answer: "Pee pee running down your leg!") and analogies ("This pumpkin has wet spider webs inside!") illustrate still other examples of the common relations concept.

The term *seriation* sometimes sounds more confusing and mysterious to beginning teachers than is necessary. Seriation just means arranging objects or events in some form of logical order. It might refer to a graduated series such as a series of blocks that go from large to small, for example (*graduated seriation*). Or it could refer to a sequence of events that occur in order over a period of time—hence the name *temporal ordering*. Recipes are excellent examples of temporal ordering because the procedures take place one after another.

The basic question to ask for either a graduated seriated sequence or a temporal ordering sequence is: "What comes next?"

We have all heard children proudly rattle off their numbers from 1 to 10 while not having the slightest glimmer of how many "6" really is. Thus, the reason the concept of graduated ordering is so valuable is because understanding how to arrange items in ascending or descending order helps attach real meaning to counting (enumeration)—that 2, for example, is bigger than 1, that 3 is bigger than 2, and so forth. Graduated ordering also encourages the use of comparison and estimation as well as one-to-one correspondence and understanding opposites (for instance, if one row is big-to-small and the second is small-to-big).

Temporal ordering conveys a sense of time and its effect. It includes the relationship between events—which came first? For this reason it is closely related to another concept, cause and effect, and so has special value in scientific investigations. Did what happened first cause what happened second to occur? In storytelling, temporal ordering draws upon memory and fosters the ability to logically explain why something came first, or second.

Cause and Effect

This is the ability to determine what makes something else happen and so is a special case of common relations as well as temporal ordering.

The basic question to ask is: "What made that happen?"

Piaget points out that young children are unclear about cause and effect and base their deductions on what they see happening. For example, when seeing trees blowing in the wind they may reason, "Trees bending make the wind blow," so the teacher may be in for some delightful surprises when asking "What made that happen?" Remember, such misconceptions can also provide interesting opportunities to test such theories, to ascertain the correctness of the hypothesis, as the Reggio teachers did when they marked how shadows moved as the position of the sun changed.

The basic question of cause and effect is: What made it happen?

Cause-and-effect reasoning forms the basis for all scientific experiments because investigators usually ask themselves "What happened?" "What made it happen?" or, "How can we make it happen?" And these same questions are useful to ask the children, too. Questions like these encourage the use of prediction and generation of hypotheses while also introducing children to an elementary understanding of the scientific method.

ACTIVITIES THAT PROVIDE PRACTICE FOR GENERAL MENTAL ABILITIES

HELPING
CHILDREN
DEVELOP
MENTAL
ABILITIES AND
ACADEMIC
COMPETENCE

Matching Activities

Matching is the easiest of the mental skills described here for children to acquire. For that reason, matching activities are particularly appropriate to use with older 2s and young 3s, although older children also enjoy these activities. When developing specific mental abilities, it is desirable to begin with teaching this concept of "same versus different," because children must be able to perform this basic discrimination task before they can learn the more difficult discriminations required for successfully accomplishing grouping, relational, and ordering skills. Moreover, the ability to perceive sameness and differentness is a vital element in learning to read, because children must be able to perceive such subtle differences as the one between *d* and *b* or *m* and *w* to tell the difference between *dog, bog, god*, and *gob* or *mood, wood*, and *doom*.

Matching Activities That Children Enjoy

- Throw beanbags with pictures pinned on them into boxes with matching pictures.
- Put stickers on hands and have the children hunt for a matching child to sit with at lunch.
- Use "mirror" dancing in which one child imitates the actions of another as closely as possible.
- Put identical objects mixed in with other objects in a feel box or bag and have the child identify the identical pair by feel.
- Put one item in the bag or box and put three choices where the child can see them. The child matches the item in the box or bag with one of the three choices.
- Duplicate hand-clap patterns.
- Match sets of identical pairs of sound shakers.
- Match tastes or smells.
- Cut up varieties of apples and ask children if they can match the pieces by taste. (This is really hard!)
- Match paired pieces of various white vegetables, such as radishes, turnips, jicama, sunchokes, and potatoes.

Making the Task More Challenging. The difficulty level for matching activities can be increased by adding more detail to the pictures or making the differences less conspicuous. Using other sensory modalities adds challenge, too. For example, children as young as 3 enjoy using their hands to search out the differences between two or possibly three objects in a feel bag, with the goal of identifying the one in the bag that is just the same as the one the teacher is holding.

Grouping Activities

Many opportunities arise during the day for grouping activities. If children are asked to sort all the foods they think should go into vegetable soup onto one tray and the foods for fruit salad onto another, that is a grouping activity. Or if they fish all the goldfish out of the aquarium and leave in the others, that too is grouping. If they take a field trip to the dog show and return with the concept that there is a large category "dog" composed of many subclasses such as poodles, spaniels, and terriers, once again they are exposed to the idea of grouping according to common properties. In all these situations, the basic questions the children must answer are: "Which things belong to the same group or family?" and possibly "Why do they belong together?"

Talking About the Result.   Simply doing the activity is not enough. The teacher should clarify what the children have intuitively perceived by asking questions about why things do or do not belong to the same group. For example, she might ask why German shepherds are different from poodles, or inquire whether poodles, and shepherds are cats—and if not, why not. She also might ask why cats are cats and dogs are dogs. The children will be able to give only very simple answers, such as "Dogs bark and cats meow," or "Dogs eat dog food, and cats eat cat food," or "Dogs are bigger than cats." Any of these answers should be accepted by the teacher without a lot of hairsplitting, because they are the result of the children identifying some attribute or quality generally possessed in common by one group and not possessed by the other one.

One of the most frequently used strategies for providing practice in classification or grouping is for adults to identify the group first and then ask the children to add things that belong to this category or to remove items that do not belong. For example, teachers frequently direct children to "Find all the things with fur on them" or to "Give me all the red beads." Unfortunately, this kind of teaching requires almost *no thinking on the children's part*. They only have to know what *red* means or what *fur* is and pick out all the items that possess this quality.

The way to elicit more thinking from children is to ask them to identify the common quality themselves and then to sort items or pictures according to that property. For example, children love to sort buttons of all descriptions, and the opportunities buttons offer for composing groups according to differing properties is large indeed. Younger children will most likely sort them according to color or size or shape, but older ones may sort according to whether the buttons are plastic, metal, or shell or according to how many holes they possess. It is often obvious to the teacher what the basis of the grouping is, and if the children are too young to put it into words themselves, she can clarify what they have done by saying, "It looks to me as if you are putting all the red ones here and all the blue ones there. Is that your idea?"

Slightly older children also enjoy the challenge of guessing what should be added to an already existing group. The teacher might set out pictures of furniture on the flannel board without telling the children the common property (namely, furniture) and then ask the children to select the item that belongs to that same group from an additional group of pictures consisting of a table, a dog, a baseball, and a house.

Grouping Activities That Children Enjoy

- Use the dollhouse and ask children what furniture belongs in which room.

- Supply a large number of wildlife stamps, mounted on cardboard, and ask the children to sort which animals belong together.

- Acquire a large number of buttons, each one different, and encourage the children to sort the buttons into whatever categories appeal to them (egg cartons or muffin tins make good sorting trays).

- Dismiss the children according to whether they are wearing a particular color. To make it more difficult, dismiss according to stripes, plaids, and so forth.

- Provide a grocery store and have the children set it up by sorting empty boxes and cans onto the shelves as "they go together."

- Let them pin up, in one place (such as on a bulletin board), the animals they saw at the dog show and, in another place, the things they did not see there.

- Provide them with flannel board groups, such as vegetables and other foods, and ask them to remove what does not belong.

- At dance time, ask the children what they can do with their arms that they cannot do with their feet.

- There are also many commercially made classification games that can be used to provide practice in this concept.

HELPING
CHILDREN
DEVELOP
MENTAL
ABILITIES AND
ACADEMIC
COMPETENCE

Making the Task More Challenging.   The easiest grouping activities are ones in which the common property or attribute is very obvious, such as color or shape. The less obvious the property, the more difficult the category; thickness, for instance, is an attribute much less commonly identified by little children than color (Hendrick, 1973). Asking the children to name the category also increases the degree of difficulty; so does asking them to regroup the materials another way or to group them according to several properties at the same time.

Pairing Common Relations

It is easiest to grasp the difference between common relations and matching skills if one realizes that, although relations always involve pairs of items as matching does, *these are never identical pairs.*

Common Relation Activities That Children Enjoy

- Children love to pore through a box of mixed items and put pairs together, such as salt and pepper shakers, leash and toy dog, nuts and bolts, and shoe and sock.
- Develop a game that involves putting picture and object together, such as ball with pictured ball and comb with pictured comb. (This provides valuable symbolization practice.)
- Use pictures of things that go together, such as animals and their homes or mothers and babies.
- Use flannel board sets of pairs, such as raincoat with hat or swimsuit and cap.
- Put nonsense pairs together and ask children to identify what is wrong with the pair.
- Have children hold a particular item at group time, then wait suspensefully until you or another child can shout its name out loud.
- Give children a particular picture of an animal and, as you produce a picture of its correct food, have them get up and "feed" their animal its dinner.

Ordering

A reminder: There are two systems for arranging things according to some form of order or regularity that are valuable to include in cognitive curriculum for young children. One is arranging items according to some form of graduated order (*seriation*) and the other is arranging them according to the order in which they occur in time (*temporal ordering*). In both cases the basic question the children must be able to answer to perform these thinking tasks successfully is: "What comes next?"

Seriation Activities

Seriation, or arranging items according to a graduated order, is most frequently thought of in terms of gradations of size, and any kind of nested equipment can be used to teach the concept. Measuring cups, measuring spoons, nested blocks, or those little wooden dolls or eggs that fit inside each other are all examples of seriated ordering. Nuts and bolts come in a wonderful array of sizes, too, and children enjoy arranging these in order and also performing the one-to-one correspondence involved in screwing the right-sized nut onto the correct bolt.

To teach the concept in a broader sense, it is also possible to teach gradations of color (ranging from palest pink to deep red, for example), taste (sweet to sour), or sound (loud to soft).

Cuisinaire rods and unit blocks whose sizes are all based on multiples of one basic unit measurement can also be used to teach seriation, if they are stacked in regular order beside each other for comparison. These are particularly valuable because they help children grasp the idea that 2 is composed of two 1s, 3 of three 1s or one 2 and one 1, and so forth. This results in a much more meaningful concept of enumeration than merely learning to parrot "1, 2, 3, . . ."

Seriation Activities That Children Enjoy

- Make a slot box with slots for different-sized and -shaped objects—a small circle, a larger square, a still larger rectangle, and so forth.
- Gather as many nested objects from around the house or school as possible (for example, sets of spoons and cups), and offer them during house play or at the water table. Talk about how one fits inside another.
- When putting things away, hang them up in graduated order (for instance, in the house play area hang up all the cooking spoons in order from small to large).
- Offer varying shades of the same color paint at the easel, from light to dark.
- Offer a feeling game in which various grades of sandpaper, mounted on cardboard, are put in the bag, then the children try to draw out the smoothest first, the next smoothest, and so forth.
- Ask the children to line up according to size and record the order. Repeat during the year to see if there is any change in the relationship.
- Throw beanbags or balls into larger and gradually smaller rings drawn on the cement.
- Build a family of snowmen according to size.
- Fill plastic eggs with differing amounts of beans or pebbles. Seal tightly. Have children arrange these in an egg carton according to the volume of sound they make when shaken. Have older children do this activity with their eyes shut.

Making the Task More Challenging.   The easiest kind of what-comes-next seriation problem is asking youngsters to continue a trend by showing you what comes at the end of an established row or what comes at its beginning. The problem becomes much more difficult as the number of choices is increased or if all the items are presented jumbled together. More difficult still is having them fill in the spaces left unfilled in a series.

Temporal Ordering Activities

Temporal ordering is the logical order of events as they occur through time. Sometimes a change in size as well as an advance in time occur together when it involves the life cycle. For example, as babies mature, they also become larger, as do young plants and animals. When not dealing with the life cycle, temporal ordering is exemplified in such things as following a recipe (the cake cannot go in the oven until the ingredients have been measured, mixed together, and put in a pan), sliding down a slide (you have to climb up before sliding down), or taking a bath (you have to get wet before you get dry). Remember that children should be encouraged to work from left to right when developing these sequences to help them acquire the left-to-right habit necessary in our culture for learning to read.

Temporal Ordering Activities That Children Enjoy

- Take pictures of a field trip the children went on and put the pictures into a hat, have each child draw one picture out of the hat, then ask them to arrange themselves with pictures in hand in a line according to what happened when.
- Be on the lookout for comic strip stories that can be mounted and used for temporal ordering sequence practice. ("Peanuts" is a good source for these.)

HELPING
CHILDREN
DEVELOP
MENTAL
ABILITIES AND
ACADEMIC
COMPETENCE

- Encourage children to tell stories that involve events happening in order—
  "The Three Little Pigs," for example, or "The Three Bears." (The latter teaches both
  graduated and temporal ordering.)

- Plan with the children in advance what the steps in a process will be and illustrate it
  as they tell you what these are—carving a pumpkin is easily drawn on a blackboard,
  for instance.

- Make a time line, such as showing how the baby rat changes as it grows.

- For church-related schools, advent calendars can be fun. Nonreligious calendars can
  also be made to help children anticipate how many days are left until some important
  event takes place (but do not start too soon).

- Use some of the commercially made sequence puzzles; these are quite good and show
  such sequences as getting dressed and making a snowman.

- Make illustrated recipe cards so children may prepare a snack on their own by
  following these in order.

Making the Task More Challenging.   Temporal ordering depends partly on a knowledge of
circumstances and partly on reasoning and common sense. Difficulty can be increased by
adding more stages in the sequence and by asking children to interject events into the middle of the sequence. Older 4s particularly enjoy being asked to arrange events backward.
They can also be challenged by out-of-order, "silly" questions such as "What would happen
if we ate the birthday cake and then the children came to the party?" or "What would happen if we frosted the cookies before we put them in the oven?"

It stimulates the use of memory and makes the task harder if the children are asked to
recall exactly which step in a process they actually did first. The older children in preprimary school also enjoy simple, illustrated sequences that they can "read" by looking at the
pictures as they follow a recipe. Such a chart for making soup, for example, might show pictures of meat cut up in pieces, a frying pan, 4 cups of tomato juice, and a number of vegetables and their needed quantities. Experienced older 4s love the independence of "reading"
such recipes entirely by themselves, assembling the ingredients, and following the illustrated
steps with little or no additional guidance from the teacher. Cooking, building, and complex
art projects allow elementary school children practice in temporal order.

Cause-and-Effect Activities

Children begin to understand the relationship between cause and effect in infancy when
they first determine that shaking their crib makes a little attached bell jingle, for example.
But as Piaget points out, the distinction of which event is the cause and which is the effect
remains confusing for many years. For this reason, when providing cause-and-effect learning experiences for young children, keep them uncomplicated and quite obvious—obvious
in the sense that the cause and the results can be readily observed.

Cause-and-effect learning is often thought of as being part of the world of science, and
many illustrations of such scientific cause-and-effect relationships are included in the discussion of developing the let's-find-out table later in this chapter. However, many additional, simple cause-and-effect relationships occur everywhere and should be discussed with
children. Following are some common actions that can be used to help children realize that
a particular act brings about a particular result.

Cause-and-Effect Relationships That Children Enjoy
- Squeeze whipped soap through a pastry decorator.
- Blow a whistle.
- Turn on a flashlight.

- Use a garlic press.
- Blow soap bubbles or a pinwheel.
- Squeeze an oil can.
- Use wind-up toys (such as little paddleboat bath toys).
- Grind nuts in a grinder.
- Shoot a squirt gun.
- Use a flashlight to make shadows come and go.
- Weigh objects on a balancing scale.
- Push a swing.
- Turn a kaleidoscope.

Children use these items every day but probably remain unaware of cause-and-effect relationships unless the teacher queries them about the relationships. The questions should be very simple ones, such as "What makes the picture change in the kaleidoscope?" or "What makes the garlic come out?" The teacher should not expect highly technical explanations about energy and force in reply, nor should she attempt to provide these. However, the children are perfectly capable of answering that the picture changes because they are turning the cylinder or that the garlic is coming out because they are squeezing the handle.

In cause-and-effect learning situations, the basic question to ask the children is "What do you think made it happen?" and the basic question for the teacher to ask herself is "How can I help the children figure out the answer?"

OPPORTUNITIES TO LEARN MATHEMATICAL SKILLS

Encourage Children to Experience the Satisfaction of Counting

Sometimes adults ask if it is all right to encourage children when they say proudly, "I know my numbers—want to hear?" and then glibly recite numbers out of order—order that becomes more wonderfully bizarre as they reach higher amounts. Of course it *is* true they aren't "counting right," but the relish with which children recite the series is still worth encouraging because it is so important to sustain their positive attitude toward mathematics.

Establish the Connection Between Rote Counting and the Quantity It Stands For

Of course, the next step in counting is to begin tying number names together with actual concrete quantities, and children require numberless (!) opportunities to do this before they acquire that concept. It is essential to provide concrete, hands-on experience with such quantities while attaching words at the same time, but this needn't be a formal "let's sit down and count how many blocks are required" sort of learning situation. More informal and fun activities abound. For example, the teacher can remind the children, "It's going to be cold outside this morning—how many mittens are you going to need to keep your hands warm? Let's count! And how many hats? And how many boots?" Or, for a change, "It's sure cold outside—do you think it's a three-mitten day? Oh, really? Why not?"

Children also enjoy the ideas of very large quantities of things such as a great big container of buttons or colored lollipop sticks and coming up with words they feel do justice to such amounts. For instance, a 3-year-old at our center chanted, as she poured streams of pegs from one container to another: "Millions of cats, millions of cats!" à la the much-loved story by Wanda Gag (1996).

Teach Terms for Quantities and What They Mean

HELPING
CHILDREN
DEVELOP
MENTAL
ABILITIES AND
ACADEMIC
COMPETENCE

As any parent can attest, even very young children quickly grasp the concept of "more" as in "She has more!" and "I have less"—so it is well within the scope of young children's understanding to use general mathematical terms for quantities. These include such terms as "few," "more," "many," "enough," "same as," "as much as," "lots," "zillions," "hardly any," and "extra," just to name a few. Because these are really relative terms that imply the presence of another quantity they are being compared to, it is sometimes useful to restate what the child has said while adding the implied comparison term to it. For example, the teacher might agree, "Yes—you have lots of mosquito bites but Sam has only a few," or "You're right! Nikki has as many block as you—so you have the same number he does—you've just done some arithmetic!—good for you!" Providing opportunities to vote and abide by the democratic precept of majority rule is still another everyday example of understanding terms describing quantities.

Model the Usefulness of Mathematics Throughout the Day

Just as the center environment should have literacy materials distributed throughout the environment, so, too, should numbers and math materials be included (Clements & Sarama, 2005; Geist, 2001; Sprung, 2006).

Here again, group time provides valuable opportunities for making certain such activities are included every day. "Counting books" come immediately to mind, just as alphabet books do for fostering literacy. But there are many other books that embody mathematical concepts, such as those suggested by Thatcher (2001). Her recommendations range from *The Three Little Pigs* (Galdone, 1970) to *Biggest, Strongest, Fastest* (Jenkins, 1995).

Another possibility is writing down numbers just as you write down words, meanwhile calling attention to them so that children begin to understand that number quantities have names and that there is a symbol that stands for the name just as letters stand for words. Perhaps the children are making a shopping list of how many bananas to buy for fruit salad, so the teacher draws three bananas and then also writes "3" as well.

Pointing to the numbers on a clock face and putting a bit of tape beside the one showing when snack time is draws attention to a different use of numbers, even though telling time per se is too difficult for preschoolers.

Measuring to decide how big something needs to be is another way to demonstrate the usefulness of numbers. Informal, practical ways of demonstrating that usefulness might include holding a sweater up against a little girl to see if it is too small to wear, or seeing how much ribbon will be needed to go around a package before cutting it, or measuring the rat's tail to see if it changes as he grows up. For older children some of this information can be translated into graphs in order to compare changing amounts or differing quantities.

Older 4s and 5s will enjoy thinking of different units of measure, such as how many short blocks are needed to make the road reach, compared to how many long

Ah-ha! Four short blocks equal one long one—a good example of how practical experience can be used to foster the emerging mathematical concept of equality.

blocks would be required. They also can appreciate that thermometers, scales, and speedometers are additional interesting ways to use numbers to measure and find things out.

There are many games that can be used in the elementary grades to promote math learning. Games with number cards ("War" and "Go Fish," for example) can be used to teach number recognition as well as strategic reasoning, pairing, and contrasting. Making large charts and counting graphs ("What's your favorite animal?") and then counting up the subgroups and adding them all together is sure to catch the attention of young children and is an easy way to include math activities in the daily curriculum (Clements & Sarama, 2005; Whitin & Whitin, 2003).

PRACTICAL WAYS TO INCLUDE MENTAL ABILITIES IN THE EVERYDAY CURRICULUM

Now that we understand the kinds and varieties of academic mental abilities and why they are important, it is time to think about the most effective and practical ways to present them to facilitate the children's learning.

Keep Families Well Informed About What the Children Are Learning

Families don't always understand the connection between practicing mental abilities and later school achievement unless it is explained to them, but once they understand what is going on they are both relieved and delighted. Therefore, it is a good idea to have a number of meetings early in the year explaining and demonstrating what the abilities are and why they are important. At such times it can be helpful to demonstrate various kinds of equipment available to the children along with the kinds of questions that accompany them.

Workshops for constructing homemade materials (Moomaw & Hieronymus, 1995) are another useful approach. Of course, once the abilities have been singled out, families also become aware of many informal opportunities that occur at home for enriching the basic concepts. Perhaps they realize the mathematical benefits of letting their children play with the nested measuring cups or spoons, or they begin to point out more cause-and-effect relationships when these occur.

One of the best ways of informing parents on a continuing basis, of course, is the documentation boards previously discussed in the descriptions of Reggio Emilia. One such board might illustrate "What the Children Are Learning About Cause/Effect" and include weekly pictures of them trying out various ideas about how to make water run uphill together with their comments on the attempts. Another less attractive but still very functional "board" might be a blackboard hung near the entry with notes entered from day to day as the children develop a particular idea. When these notes have been dictated or written by the children, it is even more likely to catch the parents' attention.

Incorporate Practice of Mental Abilities Within an Overall Emergent Framework

For example, perhaps the children have been digging in the sandbox and have found, to their surprise, that some grass has sprouted there—this awakens their interest in where it came from and why it has those white, cold strings at one end. At that point the teacher thinks of a number of possible directions the curriculum path might take. She might think of starting beans in jars, or maybe it would be interesting to plant some vegetables or flowers, or take a different investigative pathway altogether and find out what else is under the ground, such as worms, pipes, moles, or rabbits. The children continue their interest in the grass and also find some dandelions that are coming up, so she decides to pursue gardening as the emergent interest to build on.

Once that focus is selected, she makes a point of incorporating related experiences that nourish *all* the selves, not just the cognitive one, in her plans. For example, gardening helps develop the physical self by fostering small- and large-muscle development as youngsters dig and weed, and generates social learning by providing opportunities to do meaningful work by both boys and girls working together. When vegetables that are favorites of families from differing cultural backgrounds are included, even more richness is added to social learning. Finally, a lot of emotional satisfaction is involved in just mucking about with mud, sand, and water as well as feeling satisfaction when the plants come up, mature, and are eaten.

As the interests emerge over the weeks, the teacher thinks of ways to "provoke" the children into thinking of many creative solutions to various problems: How can we keep the garden watered enough so that the plants will grow? How can we water the seeds lightly enough that we do not wash them out of the ground? How do we figure out which plants are weeds that we should pull out and which we should leave in the ground to grow? What shall we do with the extra vegetables—take them home? Give them to the homeless shelter down the street? Freeze them to use later? Is it a good idea to pick the tomatoes when they are still hard, green balls? And so forth.

Finally, as the Chapter Spotlight illustrates, the teacher consistently uses the topic of gardening to provide opportunities to practice various mental ability skills.

Keep It Fun

In chapter 17 we spoke of the importance of helping children feel confident and happy in the cognitive realm by providing them with mental challenges that are appropriate for their developmental level, by relating cognitive learning to their interests and real life, and by enabling children to solve problems and figure out answers for themselves. All these factors contribute to the basic pleasures and rewards related to intellectual learning. Besides these fundamental principles, there are a few additional ones teachers should apply when working with more specific mental skills so that the children's pleasure in that experience will be increased.

For one, teachers should integrate practice in mental skills into regular activities and play situations whenever possible. Many ordinary daily activities at school provide opportunities for practice in various mental skills. Using them for that purpose helps integrate them into the lives of the children and keeps practice informal and pleasurable at the same time (Clements & Sarama, 2005; Sprung, 2006).

For example, when making whole-wheat muffins, gradations of sweetness could be compared by allowing the children to taste the flour, honey, and raisins and decide which is sweetest (graduated ordering—seriation), or the children could arrange recipe cards in order according to the steps in the recipe (temporal ordering), or the children could think about cause-and-effect relationships when figuring out that it is the heat in the oven that turns the soft sticky dough into firm moist muffins.

Another principle is that it is important to realize that just *doing* activities will *not* provide sufficient learning. It is necessary also to *talk about* what the children are doing, so they are aware while they are doing it. Otherwise, learning is likely to remain on the intuitive level longer than need be. For example, while putting the blocks away, you might use terms that young 3-year-olds understand and speak of putting away all the big "daddy" blocks first, the medium "mommy" ones next, and the little "baby" ones last to encourage the concept of graduated (seriated) ordering.

An Example of How Mid-Level Mental Abilities Could Be Included in the Topic of Gardening for a Group of 4-Year-Olds

Make a Plan, But Be Prepared to Seize the "Teachable Moment" When It Occurs

To make certain every mid-level ability is included regularly in the curriculum, it is very helpful—probably even essential—to keep a list of them handy to remind yourself to fit them in as you plan.

Admittedly, with so many aspects of curriculum to consider, remembering to provide practice in these abilities can be difficult for the beginning teacher. The only effective way to make it easier is to discipline yourself to take the time and effort to think of appropriate activities every time you develop a pathway so you can include them. The more you do it the easier it becomes to blend the mid-level activities into the rest of the center day and to make use of spontaneous opportunities as they arise, too.

Suggestions for Practicing Scientific Thinking and Mathematical Literacy Based on Gardening

Mid-Level Mental Ability	Basic Question to Answer	Related Activity
Matching	Are these the same or are they different?	Weed the garden, leaving only lettuce and radish seedlings.
Pairing common relations	Which two things go most closely together?	Offer cooked foods at lunch and ask children to decide which raw vegetable they came from: potato/mashed potato; spinach/cooked spinach; tomatoes/tomato sauce; peas in pod/cooked peas. Or pair can labels with what is inside the can.
Grouping	Which things belong in the same group or family?	At group time or snack time have many samples of food (real or pictures), and ask children to place them in groups and then explain to you why they grouped them together.
Seriation (graduated ordering; ordering in space)	What comes next?	In the garden, ask children to water first the smallest, then find the medium, and then water the largest plants.
Temporal ordering (ordering in time)	What happens next?	Put together a sequential pumpkin puzzle showing its life cycle, or dance through the life cycle of plants at dance time. Ask children how could they be a seed, roots?
		Tell "Jack and the Bean Stalk," encouraging children to tell what comes next in the story.
Cause and effect	What made that happen?	Start bean seeds in pots, some in dark with and without water, some in light with and without water.
		Observe tender plants after a hard frost. What happened to them? What made it happen? (Try putting lettuce in the freezer section of refrigerator.)
		What if we did not weed the garden? (Leave a section and find out.)
Forming a hypothesis or guess	Why do you think he chose that?	Read *Tops and Bottoms* (Stevens, 1995) and discuss Rabbit's deals with Bear.
Using comparative language to consider what is a social "good"	What's important if you really want to be kind to someone else?	Read *Alejandro's Gift* (Albert, 1994) and *The Gardener* (Stewart, 1997); analyze the character's good deeds in each book and compare the results—what is really a good deed and what is not?

Meaningful counting	How many will you need?	We've got 3 pots of beans sprouting—Don, it's your turn to water them—How many cups are you going to need?
Equivalency	What equals what?	We need 5 radishes and the same number of onions for the salad. Now that we've pulled up the radishes, how many onions should we pull up?
Measurement and comparison	Are they the same or how much do they differ?	Measure how tall the beans and radishes are as they grow—Ask the children for a practical way to remember the different numbers (write down numbers—make strips of paper equal in height to various plants—graph it and so forth).
Addition/subtraction	How many are there altogether? How many more have been added?	Count out tokens each day equaling total of seedlings. Place in separate containers. Compare totals each day. Ask how many more and how do they know . . . [use different color tokens each day to prevent possible mix-ups].
Examples of Science Activities		Refer to examples in Grouping, Ordering, and Cause/Effect

Provide Plentiful Opportunities for Practice

Repeated practice is necessary to learn any skill, and mental skills or abilities are no exception to this rule. Not only should opportunities for practice be repeated, using the same materials, but practice in the same skills should be provided over a long span of time, using different topics or themes and offering a range of levels of difficulty so that the children may progress as they become more proficient.

Start with Simple Activities, Then Make Them More Difficult

Very young children who are just beginning to work on developing skills need to start with very simple activities, but they become quickly bored by these as their expertise increases. For this reason, each discussion of specific abilities offers suggestions for designing practice opportunities that range from easy to difficult.

Consider these basic ways to increase the challenge or difficulty of these skills:

- Increase the number of items the child has to work with at one time, such as providing two lotto boards to scan instead of one.
- Require that memory be used as part of the process—turning cards over so that the children have to remember which one is where is enjoyed by many 4-year-olds.
- Shift to a different sensory modality, such as moving to activities that require touching instead of seeing or matching by tasting alone.
- Increase the amount of detail that has to be analyzed while figuring out the answer.
- Asking children to give verbal reasons for their decision will certainly make the activity more challenging, and such answers may be within the ability of many 4-year-olds. However, an extensive explanation will probably be beyond the ability of most of them.

Provide Practice in Mental Skills at the Let's-Find-Out Table

Ideally, as the Chapter Spotlight illustrates, opportunities to ask and answer thought-provoking questions, investigate possibilities, foster problem-solving skills, and practice mental abilities should be incorporated throughout the curriculum and throughout the day in accord with the children's developing interests. However, many conscientious teachers prefer offering a special activity area during self-select time that provides a particular focus on cognitive learning. These are often called "sciencing tables" or "let's-find-out tables." Hopefully, these, too, draw their inspiration from the children's concerns (Moomaw & Hieronymus, 1997).

The drawbacks to providing such an area are that it may be overly teacher-determined and inflexible because it is set up by the teacher ahead of time and because it may focus only on teaching facts and information. On the other hand, if they are well planned the cardinal advantage is that such tables can go beyond teaching facts and encourage the children to practice some thinking skills. An additional advantage is that they combine a number of different learning materials in one place and can draw the children's interest and attention to a subject in a specific way.

Good Topics for the Let's-Find-Out Table. The subject matter used for science tables is often some kind of natural history, but physical science subjects such as pulleys, levers, and objects that sink and float are also effective. Some good topics include the following:

- How are rabbits, gerbils, and guinea pigs the same and different?
- How fast do plants grow? How could we find out?
- What's alive and what isn't? How can we tell?
- What do plants need to grow? Can we make them stop growing?
- Can you make water run uphill? Mix with oil? Mix with food coloring? Mix with salt?
- What makes shadows? Can we make them change shape or go away?
- What do birds eat? Do all birds like to eat the same things?
- Do balls roll faster down steep or shallow ramps? How about rolling *up* ramps? Which lets balls roll faster then?
- How heavy is it? How come some little things are heavy and some big things are light?

Basic Principles for Setting Up a Let's-Find-Out Table. The following guidelines will help ensure that the children's mental abilities will be successfully challenged at your let's-find-out table:

1. It is much more satisfactory for children to learn about something when they can learn from real experience and by doing. For example, the inclusion of live animals enhances both interest and learning.

2. For the sake of comparison and asking questions, it is generally helpful to provide a contrast of some kind—such as between guinea pigs and turtles or between two species of turtle.

3. Provide activities the children can do with what is displayed. For turtles and guinea pigs this might include offering them food, analyzing which animal eats what, taking them out and holding them, and watching them move.

4. Unless you happen to know a lot about a particular subject already, it will be necessary to do at least a little reading about the topic.

5. Be prepared to offer some especially interesting tidbits of information, as well as basic facts, about what the children are studying. For example, did you know that the oldest known turtle lived 152 years? And did you know that in Peru, guinea pig is considered a delicacy? A nearby reference shelf of a few books is a real help.

6. Have in mind various questions you might ask the children to help them think up ways of finding out the answer.

HELPING
CHILDREN
DEVELOP
MENTAL
ABILITIES AND
ACADEMIC
COMPETENCE

7. Be as prepared as possible to let them try out their ideas and suggestions.

8. Do your best to combine beauty with learning: neat printing, beautifully illustrated books, pictures, and touches of color all do their part in making the let's-find-out area appealing.

9. Remember to change the contents of the table as the interests of the children develop. Rather than setting out everything about turtles at once, for instance, it would sustain interest more effectively to introduce the turtle one day with some getting-acquainted activities about what it eats and does, then add guinea pigs for comparison toward the middle of the week, and perhaps add the large turtle shell after that for the children to try out being turtles themselves.

10. The let's-find-out area can also be tied nicely into the rest of the curriculum plan to extend learning further. For example, the children would enjoy moving like turtles and guinea pigs at dance time. The 3s would appreciate hearing the story *Turtle Tale* (Asch, 1978), and 4s would like *Molly's Woodland Garden* (Rockwell & Rockwell, 1971) or *Let's Get Turtles* (Selsam, 1965).

Using the Let's-Find-Out Table to Understand Cause and Effect. One of the joys of providing a let's-find-out table is the practice it may afford in figuring out cause-and-effect relationships, because children can try out their ideas and do simple experiments to find out whether their ideas are correct. Trying out ideas introduces children to the concept of the scientific method, which involves (1) making observations, (2) thinking of possible reasons why things happen, (3) trying out these reasons or potential causes, (4) observing the results, and then (5) drawing conclusions.

To encourage this approach, have some questions in mind to get the children started thinking. For example, if turtles are being investigated, the teacher might ask, "Are all turtles the same size?" The children need only look at the assortment of shells, pictures, and live animals provided to figure out the answer for themselves. What is even more interesting (and fun) is to ask them a question and then follow up with, "How could you find out?" Remember, it is this kind of question that leads to simple experiments in which ideas are tried out and the answer is obtained. Of course, the experiments have to be supervised by the teacher to protect the animals from harm, and they need to be spread out throughout the week's time for the same reason.

SUMMARY

During the past half-century, Jean Piaget has made a tremendous contribution to our understanding of how young children think. He maintained that children's understanding of the world and the way they think about it varies at different ages, that the development of thought results from dynamic interaction between children and their environments, that play is an important means of learning, and that movement from one stage of mental development to the next depends on maturation, experience, socialization, and equilibration.

Among the skills identified by Piaget as being significant are those related to classification, seriation, and understanding cause and effect. This chapter emphasizes how to provide cognitive learning opportunities for young children that contribute to their later understanding of these more sophisticated concepts as well as to their success in school. These learning experiences should include work on the general cognitive skills of matching, grouping, pairing common relations, graduated and temporal ordering, and understanding simple cause-and-effect relationships.

Teaching should also include more specific mental abilities directly related to emerging mathematical concepts. These include enumeration (simple counting), counting with meaning, general terms describing quantities, and awareness of such concepts as measuring, adding, subtracting, and so forth as they occur throughout the center day.

To make developing mental abilities a positive experience for teachers and children, it is necessary to keep families well informed about what the abilities are and how to encourage them, to integrate opportunities to practice them throughout the day, make certain the activities are appealing, provide plentiful opportunities for practice, and offer both simple and more taxing activities to sustain the children's interest and continue their growth.

The ideal way to integrate practice of the abilities into the curriculum is to spread them throughout the day, but some teachers prefer to concentrate opportunities for practice in one activity area, often called the let's-find-out table, so basic principles for planning such a table are included.

Food for Thought and Group Discussions

1. Select a holiday that is coming up and discuss with the class some ways that the mental abilities outlined in this chapter could be practiced using the holiday as the focus of interest.
2. Bring a commercially produced or teacher-made cognitive learning activity to class and explain how you might vary the presentation of the basic materials to make it simple enough for young 3s or difficult enough for older 4s to enjoy.
3. Do you or do you not agree with the chapter's contention that rote counting is acceptable because the children enjoy it? Does this imply that teachers should spend time asking the children to chant their numbers, for example, or sing little songs about them?

Self-Check Questions for Review

Content-Related Questions

1. List each of the basic stages of cognitive development according to Piaget, and give examples of behavior that are commonly associated with each stage.
2. Explain what teachers can do to facilitate the conditions Piaget says are necessary for optimal development to take place. These include physical maturation, experience, interaction with other people, and equilibration.
3. The six broad mental abilities discussed in detail in the chapter include matching, grouping, pairing common relations, seriated ordering, temporal ordering, and determining cause-and-effect relationships. Define each of these abilities; explain how each of them is linked to later school-related skills.
4. Describe an activity you could use with the children that would provide practice in each of the six mental abilities discussed in the chapter. Explain how you would make each one very easy for younger children and more challenging for older ones.

5. Name several emergent mathematical skills young children are capable of acquiring.

Integrative Questions

1. Select an area such as housekeeping or outdoor play and propose activities that could take place there that would provide practice in each of the six mental abilities discussed in this chapter.
2. How could you use the material from this chapter to defend your curriculum when worried families come to you and ask, "Why aren't the children learning the alphabet and how to count so they will be ready for school?"
3. Some teachers prefer to use a let's-find-out table while others prefer to spread practice in mental ability skills throughout the curriculum. What are the advantages and disadvantages of each of these approaches?
4. Explain what the scientific method is, providing an example showing how a young child could be expected to use it when figuring out a cause-and-effect relationship.
5. Describe at least two ways of integrating mathematical concepts into the curriculum that are also recommended when integrating literacy concepts into it.

Coordinating Videotape

Growing minds. Tape #13. *The whole child: A caregiver's guide to the first five years.* The Annenberg/CPB Collection, P. O. Box 2345, South Burlington, VT 05407-2345. *Growing Minds* describes two approaches to developing mental ability. In the conventional approach, teachers set up activities that help children develop specific mental skills such as matching, grouping, and cause and effect. Basic ways teachers can encourage young children to think creatively by using the emergent approach are also illustrated, with emphasis on using the inquiry method as a means of stimulating thought.

References for Further Reading

Pick of the Litter

DeVries, R., Zan, B., Hildebrandt, C., Edmiaston, R., & Sales, C. (2002). *Developing constructivist early childhood curriculum: Practical principles and activities*. New York: Teachers College Press. The authors illustrate how constructivist theory can be used in a developmentally appropriate and practical way throughout the curriculum.

Overviews

Note: Both of the following collections of articles from experts in the fields of math and science provide teachers with a wealth of information and curriculum ideas for young children in preprimary programs through the early elementary grades.

Koralek, D. (Ed.). (2003). *Spotlight on young children and math*. Washington, DC: National Association for the Education of Young Children.

Koralek, D., & Culker, L. J. (Eds.). (2003). *Spotlight on young children and science*. Washington, DC: National Association for the Education of Young Children.

Explanations of Piagetian Thought

Wadsworth, B. J. (1996). *Piaget's theory of cognitive and affective development* (5th ed.). New York: Longman. A good, clearly written introduction to Piaget that also deals with implications for teaching.

Explanations of Vygotskian Thought

Kozulin, A., Gindis, B., Ageyev, V. S., & Miller, S. M. (Eds.). (2003). *Vygotsky's educational theory in cultural context*. Cambridge, UK: Cambridge University Press. This international team of scholars provides comprehensive coverage of the main concepts of Vygotsky's theory and proposes specific classroom applications.

Mental Ability Activities

Hohmann, M., & Weikart, D. P. (1995). *Educating young children: Active learning practices for preschool and child care programs*. Ypsilanti, MI: High/Scope. This revision is a comprehensive description of the Piaget-based program that places emphasis on advance planning by child and teacher and includes helpful information on such key experiences as classification and seriation.

Resources Related to Math

Copley, J. V. (2000). *The young child and mathematics*. Washington, DC: National Association for the Education of Young Children. This is an excellent resource for developmentally appropriate math curriculum.

Epstein, A., & Gainsley, S. (2005). *I'm older than you. I'm five! Math in the preschool classroom*. Ypsilanti, MI: High/Scope. This book presents 50 early math activities that build on young children's concrete thinking and allow them to learn through hands-on explorations.

Resources Related to Science

Harlan, J. D., & Rivkin, M. S. (2005). *Science experiences for the early childhood years: An integrated approach* (8th ed.). Upper Saddle River, NJ: Merrill/Prentice Hall. Meticulous step-by-step directions accompany each activity. Every chapter includes a multitude of ways to extend science learning through all other aspects of curriculum.

For the Advanced Student

Siegler, R. W., & Alibali, M. W. (2005). *Children's thinking* (4th ed.). Upper Saddle River, NJ: Merrill/Prentice Hall. The authors present a balanced discussion and criticism of Piaget's theories.

Related Organizations and Online Resources

High/Scope offers many resources for a Piagetian-based educational curriculum. http://www.highscope.org

The National Association for the Education of Young Children (NAEYC) provides many resources, articles, standards, and publications related to math and science early education all available at the Web site. http://www.naeyc.org

The National Council of Teachers of Mathematics (NCTM) promotes developmentally appropriate mathematics education. In the year 2000, the NCTM published its guidelines for math standards K–12, also available online. http://www.nctm.org/

The National Science Teachers Association (NSTA) provides resources, a discussion board, and an ask-the-expert feature for elementary school teachers. In addition, NSTA publishes *Science and Children*, a professional journal focused on teaching children in the primary grades. http://www.nsta.org/elementaryschool

NSTA also sponsors a site for teachers of preprimary children at http://science.nsta.org/earlyyearsblog/

APPENDIXES

Chart of Normal Development: Infancy to 6 Years of Age

The chart of normal development on the next pages presents children's achievements from infancy to 6 years of age in five areas:

- Motor skills (gross and fine motor)
- Cognitive skills
- Self-help skills
- Social skills
- Communication skills (understanding and speaking language)

In each skill area, the age at which each milestone is reached *on the average* is also presented. This information is useful if you have a child in your class who you suspect is seriously delayed in one or more skill areas.

However, it is important to remember that these milestones are only average. From the moment of birth, each child is a distinct individual and develops in his or her unique manner. No two children have ever reached all the same developmental milestones at the exact same ages. The examples that follow show what we mean:

By 9 months of age Gi Lin had spent much of her time scooting around on her hands and tummy, making no effort to crawl. After about a week of pulling herself up on chairs and table legs, she let go and started to walk on her own. Gi Lin skipped the crawling stage entirely and scarcely said more than a few sounds until she was 15 months old. But she walked with ease and skill by 9½ months.

Source: From *Mainstreaming Preschoolers: Children with Health Impairments,* by A. Healy, P. McAreavey, C. S. VonHippel, and S. H. Jones, 1978, Washington, DC: U.S. Department of Health, Education, and Welfare, Office of Human Development Services, Administration for Children, Youth and Families, Head Start Bureau.

Marcus learned to crawl on all fours very early, and continued crawling until he was nearly 18 months old, when he started to walk. However, he said single words and used two-word phrases meaningfully before his first birthday. A talking, crawling baby is quite a sight!

Molly worried her parents by saying scarcely a word, although she managed to make her needs known with sounds and gestures. Shortly after her second birthday, Molly suddenly began talking in two- to four-word phrases and sentences. She was never again a quiet child.

All three children were healthy and normal. By the time they were 3 years old, there were no major differences among them in walking and talking. They had simply developed in their own ways and at their own rates. Some children seem to concentrate on one thing at a time—learning to crawl, to walk, or to talk. Other children develop across areas at a more even rate.

As you read the chart of normal development, remember that children don't read child development books. They don't know they're supposed to be able to point out Daddy when they are a year old or copy a circle in their third year. And even if they could read these baby books, they probably wouldn't follow them! Age-related developmental milestones are obtained by averaging out what many children do at various ages. No child is "average" in all areas. Each child is a unique person.

One final word of caution. As children grow, their abilities are shaped by the opportunities they have for learning. For example, although many 5-year-olds can repeat songs and rhymes, the child who has not heard songs and rhymes many times cannot be expected to repeat them. All areas of development and learning are influenced by children's experiences as well as by the abilities they are born with.

Table A.1
Chart of Normal Development

MOTOR SKILLS

Gross Motor Skills

0–12 months	12–24 months	24–36 months	36–48 months	48–60 months	60–72 months
Sits without support	Walks alone	Runs forward well	Runs around obstacles	Walks backward toe-heel	Runs lightly on toes
Crawls	Walks backward	Jumps in place, two feet together	Walks on a line	Jumps forward 10 times, without falling	Walks on balance beam
Pulls self to standing and stands unaided	Picks up toys from floor without falling	Stands on one foot, with aid	Balances on one foot for 5 to 10 seconds	Walks up and down stairs alone, alternating feet	Can cover 2 meters (6'6") hopping
Walks with aid	Pulls toy, pushes toy	Walks on tiptoe	Hops on one foot	Turns somersault	Skips on alternate feet
Rolls a ball in imitation of adult	Seats self in child's chair	Kicks ball forward	Pushes, pulls, steers wheeled toys		Jumps rope
	Walks up and down stairs (hand-held)		Rides (that is, steers and pedals) tricycle		Skates
	Moves to music		Uses slide without assistance		
			Jumps over 15 cm (6") high object, landing on both feet together		
			Throws ball overhand		
			Catches ball bounced to him or her		

Fine Motor Skills

0–12 months	12–24 months	24–36 months	36–48 months	48–60 months	60–72 months
Reaches, grasps, puts objects in mouth	Builds tower of three small blocks	Strings four large beads	Builds tower of nine small blocks	Cuts on line continuously	Cuts out simple shapes
Picks things up with thumb and one finger (pincer grasp)	Puts four rings on stick	Turns pages singly	Drives nails and pegs	Copies cross	Copies triangle
Transfers object from one hand to other hand	Places five pegs in pegboard	Snips with scissors	Copies circle	Copies square	Traces diamond
Drops and picks up toy	Turns pages two or three at a time	Holds crayon with thumb and finger, not fist	Imitates cross	Prints a few capital letters	Copies first name
	Scribbles	Uses one hand consistently in most activities	Manipulates clay materials (for example, rolls balls, snakes, cookies)		Prints numerals 1 to 5
	Turns knobs	Imitates circular, vertical, horizontal strokes			Colors within lines
	Throws small ball	Paints with some wrist action; makes dots, lines, circular strokes			Has adult grasp of pencil
	Paints with whole arm movement, shifts hands, makes strokes	Rolls, pounds, squeezes, and pulls clay			Has handedness well established (that is, child is left- or right-handed)
					Pastes and glues appropriately

COMMUNICATION SKILLS

Understanding Language

Responds to speech by looking at speaker	Responds correctly when asked *where* (*when* question is accompanied by gesture)	Points to pictures of common objects when they are named	Begins to understand sentences involving time concepts (for example, *We are going to the zoo tomorrow*)	Follows three unrelated commands in proper order	Demonstrates preacademic skills
Responds differently to aspects of speaker's voice (for example, friendly or unfriendly, male or female)	Understands prepositions *on, in,* and *under*	Can identify objects when told their use	Understands size comparatives such as *big* and *bigger*	Understands comparatives like *pretty, prettier,* and *prettiest*	
Turns to source of sound	Follows request to bring familiar object from another room	Understands question forms *what* and *where*	Understands relationships expressed by *if ... then* or *because* sentences	Listens to long stories but often misinterprets the facts	
Responds with gesture to *hi, bye-bye,* and *up* when these words are accompanied by appropriate gesture	Understands simple phrases with key words (for example, *Open the door. Get the ball.*)	Understands negatives *no, not, can't,* and *don't*	Carries out a series of two to four related directions	Incorporates verbal directions into play activities	
Stops ongoing action when told *no* (when negative is accompanied by appropriate gesture and tone)	Follows a series of two simple but related directions	Enjoys listening to simple storybooks and requests them again	Understands when told, *Let's pretend*	Understands sequencing of events when told them (for example, *First we have to go to the store, then we can make the cake, and tomorrow we will eat it*)	

Spoken Language

Makes crying and noncrying sounds	Says first meaningful word	Joins vocabulary words together in two-word phrases	Talks in sentences of three or more words, which take the form agent-action-object (*I see the ball*) or agent-action-action (*Daddy sit on chair*)	Asks *when, how,* and *why* questions	Exhibits few obvious differences between child's grammar and adult's grammar
Repeats some vowel and consonant sounds (babbles) when alone or when spoken to	Uses single words plus a gesture to ask for objects	Gives first and last name	Tells about past experiences	Uses models like *can, will, shall, should,* and *might*	Still needs to learn such things as subject-verb agreement and some irregular past tense verbs
Interacts with others by vocalizing after adult	Says successive single words to describe an event	Asks *what* and *where* questions	Uses *s* on nouns to indicate plurals	Joins sentences together (for example, *I like chocolate chip cookies and milk*)	Can take appropriate turns in a conversation
Communicates meaning through intonation	Refers to self by name	Makes negative statements (for example, *Can't open it*)	Uses *ed* on verbs to indicate past tense	Talks about causality by using *because* and *so*	Gives and receives information
Attempts to imitate sounds	Uses *my* or *mine* to indicate possession	Shows frustration at not being understood	Refers to self using pronouns *I* or *me*	Tells the content of a story but may confuse facts	Communicates well with family, friends, or strangers
	Has vocabulary of about 50 words for important people, common objects, and the existence, nonexistence, and recurrence of objects and events (for example, *more* and *all gone*)		Repeats at least one nursery rhyme and can sing a song		
			Speech is understandable to strangers, but still has some sound errors		

(Continued)

Table A.1
(continued)

356

COGNITIVE SKILLS

0–12 months	12–24 months	24–36 months	36–48 months	48–60 months	60–72 months
Follows moving objects with eyes	Imitates actions and words of adults	Responds to simple directions (for example, *Give me the ball and the block. Get your shoes and socks*)	Recognizes and matches six colors	Plays with words (creates own rhyming words; says or makes up words having similar sounds)	Retells story from picture book with reasonable accuracy
Recognizes differences among people; responds to strangers by crying or staring	Responds to words or commands with appropriate action (for example, *Stop that. Get down*)	Selects and looks at picture books, names pictured objects, and identifies several objects within one picture	Intentionally stacks blocks or rings in order of size	Points to and names four to six colors	Names some letters and numerals
Responds to and imitates facial expressions of others	Is able to match two similar objects	Matches and uses associated objects meaningfully (for example, given cup, saucer, and bead, puts cup and saucer together)	Draws somewhat recognizable picture that is meaningful to child, if not to adult; names and briefly explains picture	Matches pictures of familiar objects (for example, shoe, sock, foot; apple, orange, banana)	Rote counts to 10
Responds to very simple directions (for example, raises arms when someone says, *Come*, and turns head when asked, *Where is Daddy?*)	Looks at storybook pictures with an adult, naming or pointing to familiar objects on request (for example, *What is that? Point to the baby*)	Stacks rings on peg in order of size	Asks questions for information (*why* and *how* questions requiring simple answers)	Draws a person with two to six recognizable parts, such as head, arms, legs; can name or match drawn parts to own body	Sorts objects by single characteristics (for example, by color, shape, or size if the difference is obvious)
Imitates gestures and actions (for example, shakes head no, plays peek-a-boo, waves bye-bye)	Recognizes difference between *you* and *me*	Recognizes self in mirror, saying *baby*, or own name	Knows own age	Draws, names, and describes recognizable picture	Is beginning to use accurately time concepts of *tomorrow* and *yesterday*
Puts small objects in and out of container with intention	Has very limited attention span	Can talk briefly about what he or she is doing	Knows own last name	Rote counts to 5, imitating adults	Uses classroom tools (such as scissors and paints) meaningfully and purposefully
	Accomplishes primary learning through own exploration	Imitates adult actions (for example, housekeeping play)	Has short attention span	Knows own street and town	Begins to relate clock time to daily schedule
		Has limited attention span; learning is through exploration and adult direction (as in reading of picture stories)	Learns through observing and imitating adults, and by adult instruction and explanation; is very easily distracted	Has more extended attention span; learns through observing and listening to adults as well as through exploration; is easily distracted	Attention span increases noticeably; learns through adult instruction; when interested, can ignore distractions
			Has increased understanding of concepts of the functions and groupings of objects (for example, can put dollhouse furniture in correct rooms), and part–whole (for example, can identify pictures of hand and foot as parts of body)	Has increased understanding of concepts of function, time, part–whole relationships; function or	Concepts of function increase as well as understanding of why things happen; time concepts are expanding into an understanding of the future in terms of major events (for example, *Christmas will come after two weekends*)

SELF-HELP SKILLS

Feeds self cracker	Uses spoons, spilling little	Is beginning to understand functional concepts of familiar objects (for example, that a spoon is used for eating) and part–whole concepts (for example, parts of the body)	Uses spoon, little spilling	Begins to be aware of past and present (for example, *Yesterday we went to the park. Today we go to the library.*)	Pours well from small pitcher	use of objects may be stated in addition to names of objects	Cuts easy foods with a knife (for example, hamburger patty, tomato slice)	Dresses self completely
Holds cup with two hands; drinks with assistance	Drinks from cup, one hand, unassisted		Gets drink from fountain or faucet unassisted		Spreads soft butter with knife	Time concepts are expanding; can talk about yesterday or last week (a long time ago), about today, and about what will happen tomorrow	Laces shoes	Ties bow
Holds out arms and legs while being dressed	Chews food		Opens door by turning handle		Buttons and unbuttons large buttons			Brushes teeth unassisted
	Removes shoes, socks, pants, sweater		Takes off coat		Washes hands unassisted			Crosses street safely
	Unzips large zipper		Puts on coat with assistance		Blows nose when reminded			
	Indicates toilet needs		Washes and dries hands with assistance					

SOCIAL SKILLS

Smiles spontaneously	Recognizes self in mirror or picture	Plays near other children	Watches other children, joins briefly in their play	Joins in play with other children; begins to interact	Plays and interacts with other children	Chooses own friend(s)
Responds differently to strangers than to familiar people	Refers to self by name		Defends own possessions	Shares toys; takes turns with assistance	Dramatic play is closer to reality, with attention paid to detail, time, and space	Plays simple table games
Pays attention to own name	Plays by self, initiates own play		Begins to play house	Begins dramatic play, acting out whole scenes (for example, traveling, playing house, pretending to be animals)	Plays dress-up	Plays competitive games
Responds to *no*	Imitates adult behaviors in play		Symbolically uses objects, self in play		Shows interest in exploring sex differences	Engages with other children in cooperative play involving group decisions, role assignments, fair play
Copies simple actions of others	Helps put things away		Participates in simple group activity (for example, sings, claps, dances)			
			Knows gender identity			

What Are Some Good Toys and Play Materials for Young Children?

Table B.1
What Are Some Good Toys and Play Materials for Young Children?

All ages are approximate. Most suggestions for young children are also appropriate for older children.

	Sensory Materials	Active Play Equipment	Construction Materials	Manipulative Toys	Dolls and Dramatic Play	Books and Recordings	Art Materials
2-Year-Olds and Young 3s	Water and sand toys: cups, shovels Modeling dough Sound-matching games Bells, wood block, triangle, drum Texture matching games, feel box	Low climber Canvas swing Low slide Wagon, cart, or wheelbarrow Large rubber balls Low three-wheeled, steerable vehicle with pedals	Unit blocks and accessories: animals, people, simple wood cars and trucks Interlocking construction set with large pieces Wood train and track set Hammer (13-oz. steel-shanked), Soft wood, roofing nails, nailing block	Wooden puzzles with 4 to 20 large pieces Pegboards Big beads or spools to string Sewing cards Stacking toys Picture lotto, picture dominoes	Washable dolls with a few clothes Doll bed Child-sized table and chairs Dishes, pots, and pans Dress-up clothes: hats, shoes, shirts Hand puppets Shopping cart	Clear picture books, stories, and poems about things children know Records or tapes of classical music, folk music, or children's songs	Wide-tip water-color markers Large sheets of paper, easel Finger or tempera paint, ½" brushes Blunt-nose scissors White glue
Older 3s and 4-Year-Olds	Water toys: measuring cups, egg beaters Sand toys: muffin tins, vehicles Xylophone, maracas, tambourine Potter's clay	Large three-wheeled riding vehicle Roller skates Climbing structure Rope or tire swing Plastic bats and balls Various sized rubber balls Balance board Planks, boxes, old tires Bowling pins, ring toss, beanbags and target	More unit blocks, shapes, and accessories Table blocks Realistic model vehicles Construction set with smaller pieces Woodworking bench, saw, sandpaper, nails	Puzzles, peg board, small beads to string Parquetry blocks Small objects to sort Marbles Magnifying glass Simple card or board games Flannel board with pictures, letters Sturdy letters and numbers	Dolls and accessories Doll carriage Child-sized stove or sink More dress-up clothes Play food, cardboard cartons Airport, dollhouse, or other settings with accessories Finger or stick puppets	Simple science books More detailed picture and storybooks Sturdy record or tape player Recordings of wider variety of music Book and recording sets	Easel, narrower brushes Thick crayons, chalk Paste, tape with dispenser Collage materials

(Continued)

Table B.1
(continued)

All ages are approximate. Most suggestions for young children are also appropriate for older children.

	Sensory Materials	Active Play Equipment	Construction Materials	Manipulative Toys	Dolls and Dramatic Play	Books and Recordings	Art Materials
5- and 6-Year-Olds	Water toys: food coloring, pumps, funnels Sand toys: containers, utensils Harmonica, kazoo, guitar, recorder Tools for working with clay	Bicycle Outdoor games: bocce, tetherball, shuffleboard, jump rope, Frisbee	More unit blocks, shapes, and accessories Props for roads, towns Hollow blocks Brace and bits, screwdrivers, screws, metric measure, accessories	More complex puzzles Dominoes More difficult board and card games Yarn, big needles, mesh fabric, weaving materials Magnets, balances Attribute blocks	Cash register, play money, accessories, or props for other dramatic play settings: gas station, construction, office Typewriter	Books on cultures Stories with chapters Favorite stories children can read Children's recipe books	Watercolors, smaller paper, stapler, hole puncher Chalkboard Oil crayons, paint crayons, charcoal Simple camera, film

Source: From *Choosing Good Toys for Young Children* by S. Feeney and M. Magarick, 1983, Washington, DC: National Association for the Education of Young Children. Copyright © 1983 by National Association for the Education of Young Children. Used by permission.

360

Summary of Communicable Diseases

Table C.1
Summary of Communicable Diseases

Disease	Agent	Incubation	Communicable Period	Transmission	Symptoms	Remarks
Chicken pox (herpes zoster; varicella; shingles)	Virus	2–3 weeks	1–5 days before rash: no more than 6 days after first vesicles	Direct contact with vesicle fluid, soiled articles, or droplets from respiratory tract	Sudden onset; slight fever; malaise; mild constitutional symptoms, followed by eruption of lesions; followed by fluid-filled blisters for 3–4 days; ending with scab	Very communicable; lesions, blisters, and scabbed sores can exist at the same time; lesions are most common on covered parts of the body; vaccine available
Conjunctivitis (pink eye)	Bacteria	24–72 hours	Throughout course of infection	Contact with discharge from conjunctiva or upper respiratory tract, or objects contaminated by those discharges	Tearing and irritation of conjunctiva; lid swelling, discharge; sensitivity to light	Most common in preschoolers
Cytomegalovirus (CMV)	Virus	May be acquired during birth, but show no symptoms for up to 3 months after delivery	Virus may be excreted for 5–6 years	Direct/Indirect contact with membranes or secretions; blood; urine	Usually no symptoms; may show signs of severe infection of central nervous system or liver	Most serious in early infancy; many apparently healthy children in day care have CMV in urine or saliva; *potentially serious for pregnant women*
Giardiasis	Protozoa (a cyst in the inactive form)	5–25 days	Entire period of infection	Hand-to-mouth transfer of cysts from stools of infected person	Chronic pale, greasy diarrhea; abdominal cramping; fatigue; weight loss	Frequently found in day care centers; carriers may be asymptomatic
Hepatitis	Several viruses	Hepatitis A: 15–50 days Hepatitis B: 45–180 days	Hepatitis A: A week before infection to one week after appearance of jaundice Hepatitis B: From several weeks before symptoms until weeks after symptoms; may be a carrier for years	Hepatitis A: Fecal/oral route; direct contact Hepatitis B: Contact with infected blood; saliva, and vaginal fluids; semen	Hepatitis A: Sudden onset with fever, lack of appetite, nausea, abdominal pain; jaundice follows in a few days Hepatitis B: Lack of appetite; nausea, vomiting, and later jaundice	Hepatitis A: Common in day care; severity increases with age; infections in infants may be asymptomatic; vaccine available Hepatitis B: May be present but asymptomatic in young children; HB vaccine available to prevent this type of hepatitis

Disease	Cause	Incubation	Communicability	Transmission	Symptoms	Comments
Measles (hard measles; red measles)	Virus	1–2 weeks before rash to 4 days after the rash appears	Communicable from before fever to 4 days after rash	Direct contact with nasal or throat secretions or freshly contaminated objects	Fever conjunctivitis, cough, Koplik spots; rash appears on 3rd day—usually starting on face	Easily spread; very common in preschool populations; immunization available; potentially serious for ill or young children
Meningitis (viral)	Several viruses	Incubation varies by specific virus	Communicability varies with specific virus	Direct contact with respiratory droplets or excretions of infected person, or objects contaminated by these secretions	Symptoms vary by specific type of virus; usually sudden fever and central nervous system symptoms; may have rash	Symptoms last 10 days with residual symptoms for a year or more
Meningitis (bacterial)	Various bacteria	2–10 days	Until organisms are not found in discharge	Direct contact with respiratory droplets or excretions of an infected person or objects contaminated by these secretions	Sudden onset of fever; severe headache; stiff neck; rash	Early detection and treatment necessary to prevent death
Mumps	Virus	2–3 weeks	6 days before until 9 days after onset of illness	Direct contact with respiratory droplets or saliva of infected person	Fever, swelling, and tenderness of one or more salivary glands	Meningitis occurs frequently; vaccine available
Pediatric AIDS	Virus	Unknown	Unknown	Contact with blood and blood contaminated fluids and objects; sexual contact with semen and vaginal fluids	Early symptoms are nonspecific: loss of appetite; chronic diarrhea; fatigue; symptoms progress to opportunistic infections and central nervous system symptoms	Use universal precautions
Pediculosis (lice)	Lice (adult, larvae or nits)	Eggs hatch in a week; sexual maturity is reached 8–10 days after hatching	Communicable as long as eggs and lice are alive on person or clothing	Direct contact with infected person or indirect contact with contaminated objects	Itching and excoriation of infected head and body parts	Common in school children; check with physician regarding use of over-the-counter products; some are not recommended for infants and young children

(Continued)

Table C.1
(continued)

Disease	Agent	Incubation	Communicable Period	Transmission	Symptoms	Remarks
Ringworm	Fungus	4–10 days	Until lesions are gone and fungus is no longer on contaminated objects	Direct or indirect contact with infected persons or contaminated objects	Lesions appear flat, spreading, and ring-shaped; outer ring may be filled with pus or fluid; inside may be dry and scaly or moist and crusty	Infected children should be excluded from common swimming pools
Rubella (3-day measles)	Virus	2–3 weeks	From 1 week before to 1 week after onset of rash	Droplet spread or direct/indirect contact with objects soiled with nasal secretions, blood, urine, or feces	Symptoms may range from no symptoms to cold-like symptoms such as low grade fever, malaise, and runny nose; not all infections have a rash; if it does exist, it usually starts on the face and spreads to trunk and extremities	Easily spread; high incidence in preschool populations; immunizations available; resembles measles; *potentially serious for pregnant women*
Scabies	Mite	2–6 weeks in person with no exposure; 1–4 days after re-exposure	Until miles and eggs are killed; usually 1–2 courses of treatment, 1 week apart	Skin-to-skin contact, or contact with recently infected undergarments or bed clothes	Intense itching of head, neck, palms, soles in infants; may also involve other body creases	In persons with reduced resistance, infection will be generalized; check with physician prior to use of over-the-counter medications, because some are not recommended for infants and young children

Source: From *Preschool Children with Special Health Care Needs, First Edition* (pp. 179–182), by M. T. Urbano, © 1992. Reprinted with permission of Delmar Learning, a division of Thomson Learning: www.thomsonrights.com. Fax: 800-730-2215.

10 Quick Ways to Analyze Children's Books for Racism and Sexism

Both in school and out, young children are exposed to racist and sexist attitudes. These attitudes—expressed over and over in books and in other media—gradually distort their perceptions until stereotypes and myths about minorities and women are accepted as reality. It is difficult for a librarian or teacher to convince children to question society's attitudes. But if a child can be shown how to detect racism and sexism in a book, the child can proceed to transfer the perception to wider areas. The following 10 guidelines are offered as a starting point in evaluating children's books from this perspective.

1. Check the Illustrations

Look for stereotypes. A stereotype is an oversimplified generalization about a particular group, race, or sex, which usually carries derogatory implications. Some infamous (overt) stereotypes of Blacks are the happy-go-lucky watermelon-eating Sambo and the fat, eye-rolling "mammy"; of Chicanos, the sombrero-wearing peon or fiesta-loving, macho bandito; of Asian Americans, the inscrutable, slant-eyed "Oriental"; of Native Americans, the naked savage or "primitive" craftsman and his squaw; of Puerto Ricans, the switchblade-toting teenage gang member; of women, the completely domesticated mother, the demure, doll-loving little girl, or the wicked stepmother.

While you may not always find stereotypes in the blatant forms described, look for variations which in any way demean or ridicule because of their race or sex.

Look for tokenism. If there are non-White characters in the illustrations, do they look just like

Whites except for being tinted or colored in? Do all minority faces look stereotypically alike, or are they depicted as genuine individuals with distinctive features?

Who's doing what? Do the illustrations depict minorities in subservient and passive roles or in leadership and action roles? Are males the active "doers" and females the inactive observers?

2. Check the Story Line

The Civil Rights Movement has led publishers to weed out many insulting passages, particularly from stories with Black themes, but the attitudes still find expression in less obvious ways. The following checklist suggests some of the subtle (covert) forms of bias to watch for.

Standard for Success

Does it take "White" behavior standards for a minority person to "get ahead"? Is "making it" in the dominant White society projected as the only ideal? To gain acceptance and approval, do non-White persons have to exhibit extraordinary qualities—excel in sports, get A's, etc.? In friendships between White and non-White children, is it the non-White who does most of the understanding and forgiving?

Resolution of Problems

How are problems presented, conceived, and resolved in the story? Are minority people considered to be "the problem"? Are the oppressions faced by minorities and women represented as causally related to an unjust society? Are the reasons for poverty and oppression explained, or are they accepted as inevitable? Does the story line encourage passive acceptance or active resistance? Is a particular problem that is faced

Source: Reprinted with permission from the *Bulletin* of the Council on Interracial Books for Children, Inc., 1841 Broadway, New York, NY 10023.

by a minority person resolved through the benevolent intervention of a White person?

Role of Women

Are the achievements of girls and women based on their own initiative and intelligence, or are they due to their good looks or to their relationship with boys? Are sex roles incidental or critical to characterization and plot? Could the same story be told if the sex roles were reversed?

3. Look at the Lifestyles

Are minority persons and their setting depicted in such a way that they contrast unfavorably with the unstated norm of White middle-class suburbia? If the minority group in question is depicted as "different," are negative value judgments implied? Are minorities depicted exclusively in ghettos, barrios, or migrant camps? If the illustrations and text attempt to depict another culture, do they go beyond oversimplifications and offer genuine insights into another lifestyle? Look for inaccuracy and inappropriateness of the depiction of other cultures. Watch for instances of the "quaint-natives-in-costume" syndrome (most noticeable in areas like costume and custom, but extending to behavior and personality traits as well).

4. Weigh the Relationships Between People

Do the Whites in the story possess the power, take the leadership, and make the important decisions? Do non-Whites and females function in essentially supporting roles?

How are family relationships depicted? In Black families, is the mother always dominant? In Hispanic families, are there always lots and lots of children? If the family is separated, are societal conditions—unemployment, poverty—cited among the reasons for the separation?

5. Note the Heroes and Heroines

For many years, books showed only "safe" minority heroes and heroines—those who avoided serious conflict with the White establishment of their time. Minority groups today are insisting on the right to define their own heroes and heroines based on their own concepts and struggles for justice.

When minority heroes and heroines do appear, are they admired for the same qualities that have made White heroes and heroines famous or because what they have done has benefited White people? Ask this question: Whose interest is a particular figure really serving?

6. Consider the Effects on a Child's Self-Image

Are norms established that limit the child's aspirations and self-concepts? What effect can it have on Black children to be continuously bombarded with images of the color white as the ultimate in beauty, cleanliness, virtue, and the color black as evil, dirty, menacing, etc.? Does the book counteract or reinforce this positive association with the color white and negative association with black?

What happens to a girl's self-image when she reads that boys perform all of the brave and important deeds? What about a girl's self-esteem if she is not "fair" of skin and slim of body?

In a particular story, is there one or more persons with whom a minority child can readily identify to a positive and constructive end?

7. Consider the Author's or Illustrator's Background

Analyze the biographical material on the jacket flap or the back of the book. If a story deals with a minority theme, what qualifies the author or illustrator to deal with the subject? If the author and illustrator are not members of the minority being written about, is there anything in their background that would specifically recommend them as the creators of this book?

Similarly, a book that deals with the feelings and insights of women should be more carefully examined if it is written by a man—unless the book's avowed purpose is to present a strictly male perspective.

8. Check Out the Author's Perspective

No author can be wholly objective. All authors write out of a cultural as well as a personal context. Children's books in the past have traditionally come from authors who are White and who are members of the middle class, with one result being that a single ethnocentric perspective has dominated American children's literature. With the book in question, look carefully to determine whether the direction of the author's perspective substantially weakens or strengthens the value of his/her written book. Are omissions and distortions central to the overall character or "message" of the book?

9. Watch for Loaded Words

A word is loaded when it has insulting overtones. Examples of loaded adjectives (usually racist) are savage, primitive, conniving, lazy, superstitious, treacherous, wily, crafty, inscrutable, docile, and backward.

Look for sexist language and adjectives that exclude or ridicule women. Look for use of the male pronoun to refer to both males and females. While the generic use of the word "man" was accepted in the past, its use today is outmoded. The following examples show how sexist language can be avoided: ancestors instead of forefathers; chairperson instead of chairman; community instead of brotherhood; firefighters instead of firemen; manufactured instead of manmade; the human family instead of the family of man.

10. Look at the Copyright Date

Books on minority themes—usually hastily conceived—suddenly began appearing in the mid-1960s.

There followed a growing number of "minority experience" books to meet the new market demand, but most of these were still written by White authors, edited by White editors, and published by White publishers. They therefore reflected a White point of view. Only very recently in the late 1960s and early 1970s has the children's book world begun to even remotely reflect the realities of a multiracial society. And it has just begun to reflect feminists' concerns.

The copyright dates, therefore, can be a clue as to how likely the book is to be overtly racist or sexist, although a recent copyright date, of course, is no guarantee of a book's relevance or sensitivity. The copyright date only means the year the book was published. It usually takes a minimum of 1 year—and often much more than that—from the time a manuscript is submitted to the publisher to the time it is actually printed and put on the market. This time lag meant very little in the past, but in a time of rapid change and changing consciousness, when children's book publishing is attempting to be "relevant," it is becoming increasingly significant.

Educational Organizations, Journals, and Newsletters Associated with Early Childhood Education

Educational Organizations

American Alliance for Health, Physical Education,
    Recreation and Dance (AAHPERD)
1900 Association Drive,
Reston, VA 20191
(800) 213-7193
http://www.aahperd.org

Association for Childhood Education International
    (ACEI)
Olney Professional Building
17904 Georgia Ave., Suite 215
Olney, MD 20832
(800) 423-3563
http://www.acei.org

Child Welfare League of America, Inc. (CWLA)
440 First St., NW, Third Floor
Washington, DC 20001-2085
(202) 638-2952
http://www.cwla.org

Children's Defense Fund (CDF)
25 E. Street NW
Washington, DC 20001
(800) 233-1200
http://childrensdefense.org

Council for Exceptional Children (CEC)
1110 North Glebe Road, Suite 300
Arlington, VA 22201-5704
(800) 224-6830
http://www.cec.sped.org

National Association for the Education of Young
    Children (NAEYC)
1509 16th St., NW
Washington, DC 20036-1426
(800) 424-8777
http://www.naeyc.org

Prevent Child Abuse America
500 N. Michigan Avenue, Suite 200
Chicago, IL 60611
(312) 663-3520
http://www.preventchildabuse.org

Southern Early Childhood Association
    (SECA)
P.O. Box 55930
Little Rock, AR 72215-5930
(800) 305-7322
http://www.southernearlychildhood.org

ZERO TO THREE: National Center for Infants,
    Toddlers and Families
2000 M Street, NW, Suite 200
Washington, DC 20036
(202) 638-1144
http://www.zerotothree.org

Journals and Newsletters

Child Care Information Exchange
P.O. Box 3249
Redmond, WA 98073-3249
(800) 221-2864
http://www.childcareexchange.com/

Child Development
A Publication of the Society for Research in
    Child Development (SRCD)
350 Main Street
Malden, MA 02148
(800) 835-6770
http://www.srcd.org

Child Health Talk Newsletter
National Black Child Development Institute
    (NBCDI)
1101 15th Street, NW, Suite 900
Washington, DC 20005
(202) 833-2220
http://www.nbcdi.org/

Childhood Education
A Publication of the Association for Childhood
    Education International (ACEI)
17904 Georgia Avenue, Suite 215
Olney, MD 20832
(800) 423-3563
http://www.acei.org/

Dimensions of Early Childhood
Southern Early Childhood Association (SECA)
P.O. Box 55930
Little Rock, AR 72215-5930
(800) 305-7322
http://www.southernearlychildhood.org/

Early Childhood Education Journal
Dordrecht, The Netherlands
(800) 777-4643
http://www.springeronline.com

Early Childhood Research Quarterly
A Publication of the National Association for the
    Education of Young Children
Customer Service Department
6277 Sea Harbor Drive
Orlando, FL 32887-4800
(877) 839-7126
http://www.naeyc.org/

Exceptional Children
A Publication of the Council for Exceptional
    Children (CEC)
1110 North Glebe Road, Suite 300
Arlington, VA 22201-5704
(888) 232-7733
http://www.cec.sped.org

The Future of Children
Brookings Institute
Dept. 029
Washington, DC 20042-0029
(800) 275-1447
http://www.futureofchildren.org/

Innovations in Early Education: The International
    Reggio Exchange
Merrill-Palmer Institute of Wayne State
    University
71-A East Ferry Avenue
Detroit, MI 48202
(313) 872-1790
http://www.mpi.wayne.edu/

Journal of Early Intervention
A Publication of the CEC Division for Early
    Childhood
1110 North Glebe Road, Suite 300
Arlington, VA 22201-5704
(888) 232-7733
http://www.dec-sped.org

Journal of Research in Childhood Education
A Publication of the Association for Childhood
    Education International (ACEI)
17904 Georgia Avenue, Suite 215
Olney, MD 20832
(800) 423-3563
http://www.acei.org/

Nutrition Action Healthletter
Center for Science in the Public Interest
1875 Connecticut Avenue, NW,
    Suite 300
Washington, DC 20009
(202) 332-9110
http://www.cspinet.org/

Scholastic Early Childhood Today
557 Broadway
New York, NY 10012-3999
(212) 343-6100
http://www.earlychildhoodtoday.com/

Young Children
A Publication of the National Association
for the Education of Young Children
NAEYC Publications
P.O. Box 96270
Washington, DC 20090-6270
(800) 424-2460
http://www.naeyc.org

Young Exceptional Children
A Publication of CEC Division of Early
Childhood DEC
634 Eddy Ave.
Missoula, MT 59812-6696
(406) 243-5898
http://www.dec-sped.org

Zero to Three
National Center for Infants, Toddlers, and Families
2000 M Street, NW, Suite 200
Washington, DC 20036
(202) 638-1144
http://www.zerotothree.org/

REFERENCES

Adams, M., Blumenfeld, W. J., Castaneda, R., Hackman, H. W., Peters, M. L., & Zuniga, S. (Eds.). (2000). *Readings for diversity and social justice*. New York: Routledge.

Alat, K. (2002). Traumatic events and children: How early childhood educators can help. *Childhood Education, 79*(1), 2–8.

Albert, R. E. (1994). *Alejandro's gift*. San Francisco: Chronicle Books.

Albreacht, K., Dziadul, L., Gwinn, C., & Harrington, B. (2001). The good, the bad, and the wonderful. *Child Care Information Exchange, 137*, 90–92.

Alexander, P. A. (2000). Humble beginnings, ambitious ends: Special issue on motivation and the educational process. *Contemporary Educational Psychology, 25*, 1–2.

Althouse, R., Johnson, M. H., & Mitchell, S. T. (2003). *The colors of learning: Integrating the visual arts into the early childhood curriculum*. New York: Teachers College Press.

Amabile, T. M. (1996). *Creativity in context: Update to the social psychology of creativity*. Boulder, CO: Westview/HarperCollins.

Amabile, T. M., & Gitomer, J. (1984). Children's artistic creativity: Effects of choice in task materials. *Personality and Social Psychology Bulletin, 10*(2), 209–215.

American Academy of Pediatrics. (2002). *Caring for our children*. Elk Grove Village, IL: Author.

American Association for the Advancement of Science. (1999). *Dialogue on early childhood science, mathematics, and technology education*. Washington, DC: Author.

Anastas, P. (1973). *Glooskap's children*. Boston: Beacon Press.

Anaya, R. (2000). *Roadrunner's dance*. New York: Harper.

Anderson, F. E. (1996). *Art-centered education and therapy for children with disabilities*. Springfield, IL: Thomas.

Apter, T. (1997). *The confident child: Raising children to believe in themselves: A compassionate, practical guide*. New York: Bantam Books.

Arbuthnot, M. H., & Root, S. L. (1968). *Time for poetry* (3rd ed.). Glenview, IL: Scott, Foresman.

Armstrong, A., & Casement, C. (2000). *The child and the machine: How computers put our children's education at risk*. Beltsville, MD: Gryphon House.

Arnheim, D. D., & Pestolesi, R. A. (1978). *Elementary physical education: A developmental approach*. St. Louis: Mosby.

Arnheim, D. D., & Sinclair, W. A. (1979). *The clumsy child: A program of motor therapy* (2nd. ed.). St. Louis: Mosby.

Aronson, S. S. (2001a). Reducing the risk of injury in child care. *Child Care Information Exchange, 138*, 64–66.

Aronson, S. S. (2001b). Six tips for germ control: Maintaining a sanitary child care environment. *Child Care Information Exchange, 137*, 94–96.

Artiles, A. J., & Zamora-Durán, G. (1997). *Reducing disproportionate representation of culturally diverse students in special and gifted education*. Reston, VA: Council for Exceptional Children.

Asch, F. (1978). *Turtle tale*. New York: Dial.

Assets for Colorado Youth (2002). *Educators' forum on asset champions: A discussion of strategies and needs in taking the asset framework into schools*. Denver, CO: Author.

Austin, J. S. (2000). When a child discloses sexual abuse: Immediate and appropriate teacher responses. *Childhood Education, 77*(1), 2–5.

Axtmann, A., & Bluhm, C. (1986). Friendship among infants? Yes, indeed! In D. P. Wolf (Ed.), *Connecting: Friendship in the lives of young children and their teachers*. Redmond, WA: Exchange Press.

Babcock, F., Hartle, L., & Lamme, L. L. (1995). Prosocial behaviors of five-year-old children in sixteen learning/activity centers. *Journal of Research in Childhood Education, 9*(2), 113–126.

Bailey, B. (1997). *There's gotta be a better way: Discipline that works!* Oviedo, FL: Loving Guidance.

Ballinger, C. (1999). *Teaching other people's children: Literacy and learning in a bilingual classroom*. New York: Teachers College Press.

Bambini a Reggio Emilia. (1990). *Tutto ha un' ombra meno le formiche*. Reggio Emilia, Italy: Commune di Reggio Emilia.

Bandura, A. (1977). *Social learning theory*. Upper Saddle River, NJ: Prentice Hall.

Bandura, A. (1986). *Social foundations of thought and action.* Upper Saddle River, NJ: Prentice Hall.

Bansavage, J. C. (1978). Ecology of child development. *Children in Contemporary Society, 11*(4), 119–121.

Barata-Lorton, M. (1987). *Workjobs: Activity-centered learning for early childhood education.* Reading, MA: Addison-Wesley.

Barbarin, O. A. (2002). The Black–White achievement gap in early reading skills: Familial and socio-cultural context. In B. Bowman (Ed.), *Love to read: Essays in developing and enhancing early literacy skills of African American children.* Washington, DC: National Black Child Development Institute.

Bardige, B. (2005). *At a loss for words: How America is failing our children and what we can do about it.* Philadelphia: Temple University Press.

Barhyte, D. M. (2000). Keep volunteers invested in your program. *Child Care Information Exchange, 136,* 12–14.

Barnett, W. S., & Boocock, S. S. (1998). *Early care and education for children in poverty: Promises, programs and long-term results.* Albany: State University of New York.

Baron, R., & Parker, J. D. A. (Eds.). (2000). *The handbook of emotional intelligence: Theory, development, assessment, and application at home, school, and in the workplace.* San Francisco: Jossey-Bass.

Barrera, I., Corso, R. M., & Macpherson, D. (2003). *Skilled dialogue: Strategies for responding to cultural diversity in early childhood.* Baltimore: Brookes.

Barrera, R. M. (1996). What's all the fuss? A frank conversation about the needs of bilingual children. *Child Care Information Exchange, 107,* 44–47.

Barrera, R. M. (2001). Bringing home to school. *Early Childhood Today, 16*(3), 44–56.

Bateman, B. D., & Linden, M. A. (1998). *Better IEPs: How to develop legally correct and educationally useful programs* (3rd ed.). Longmont, CO: Sopris West.

Bauer, C. F. (1977). *Handbook for story tellers.* Chicago: American Library Association.

Baumrind, D. (1989). Rearing competent children. In W. Damon (Ed.), *Child development today and tomorrow.* San Francisco: Jossey-Bass.

Beaty, J. J. (2002). *Observing development of the young child* (5th ed.). Upper Saddle River, NJ: Merrill/Prentice Hall.

Beaty, J. J. (2004). *Skills for preschool teachers* (7th ed.). Upper Saddle River, NJ: Merrill/Prentice Hall.

Beaty, J. J. (1997a). *Building bridges with multicultural picture books for children 3 to 5.* Upper Saddle River, NJ: Merrill/Prentice Hall.

Beaty, J. J. (1997b). *Converting conflicts in preschool.* New York: Harcourt Brace.

Beginnings Workshop. (2001). Field trips. *Child Care Information Exchange, 139,* 39–59.

Behrman, R. E. (Ed.). (2000). Children and computer technology. *Future of Children, 10*(2), entire issue.

Benzwie, T. (1987). *A moving experience: Dance for lovers of children and the child within.* Tucson: Zephyr.

Bereiter, C., & Englemann, E. (1966). *Teaching the culturally disadvantaged child in the preschool.* Upper Saddle River, NJ: Prentice Hall.

Bergen, D. (1997). Using observational techniques for evaluating young children's learning. In B. Spodek & O. N. Saracho (Eds.), *Issues in early childhood educational assessment and evaluation. Yearbook in early childhood education* (Vol. 7). New York: Teachers College Press.

Bergen, D. (Ed.). (1998). *Play as a medium for learning and development.* Olney, MD: Association for Childhood Education International.

Berger, E. H. (2004). *Parents as partners in education: Families and schools working together* (6th ed.). Upper Saddle River, NJ: Merrill/Prentice Hall.

Bergin, C. A. C., Bergin, D. A., & French, E. (1995). Preschoolers' prosocial repertories: Parents' perspectives. *Early Childhood Research Quarterly, 10*(1), 81–103.

Berk, L. (1994). Vygotsky's theory: The importance of make-believe play. *Young Children, 50*(1), 30–39.

Berk, L. E., & Winsler, A. (1995). *Scaffolding children's learning: Vygotsky and early childhood education.* Washington, DC: National Association for the Education of Young Children.

Berman, C., & Fromer, J. (1997). *Meals without squeals.* Palo Alto, CA: Bull.

Bermúdez, M. T. (2001). *Mexican family favorites.* Phoenix: Golden West.

Bertrand, D. G. (1997). *Sip, slurp, soup, soup—Caldo, caldo caldo.* Houston, TX: Arte Publico Press.

Betz, C. (1992). The happy medium. *Young Children, 47*(3), 34–35.

Beuf, A. H. (1977). *Red children in white America.* Philadelphia: University of Pennsylvania Press.

Bisson, J. (1997). *Celebrate! An anti-bias guide to enjoying holidays in early childhood programs.* St. Paul, MN: Redleaf.

Block, M. (1994). *A teacher's guide to including students with disabilities in regular physical education.* Baltimore: Brookes.

Blood, C. L., & Link, M. (1976). *The goat in the rug.* New York: Parent's Magazine Press.

Bloom, B. S., Engelhart, M. D., Furst, E. J., Hill, W. H., & Krathwohl, D. R. (1956). *Taxonomy of educational objectives.* New York: McKay.

Bloom, L. (1998). Language acquisition in its developmental context. In D. Kuhn & R. S. Siegler (Eds.), *Handbook of child psychology: Vol. 2. Cognition, perception, and language* (5th ed.). New York: Wiley.

Bodrova, E., & Leong, D. J. (1996). *Tools of the mind: The Vygotskian approach to early childhood education.* Upper Saddle River, NJ: Merrill/Prentice Hall.

Bodrova, E., & Leong, D. J. (2005). Why children need play. *Scholastic Early Childhood Today, 20*(1), 6.

Bohannon, J. N., & Bonvillian, J. D. (2001). Theoretical approaches to language acquisition. In J. B. Gleason (Ed.), *The development of language* (5th ed.). Boston: Allyn & Bacon.

Bos, B. (1982). *Please don't move the muffin tins: A hands-off guide to art for the young child.* Roseville, CA: Turn the Page Press.

Bos, B. (1983). *Before the basics: Creating conversations with children.* Roseville, CA: Turn the Page Press.

Bowling, H. J., & Rogers, S. (2001). The value of healing in education. *Young Children, 56*(2), 79–81.

Bowman, B. (1995). The challenge of diversity. *Scholastic Early Childhood Today, 10*(3), 40.

Bowman, B. (1997). Preschool as family support. In C. Dunst & M. Wolery (Eds.), *Advances in early education and day care: Vol. 9. Family policy and practice in early child care.* Greenwich, CT: JAI.

Bowman, B., Donovan, M. S., & Burns, M. S. (Eds.). (2001). *Eager to learn: Educating our preschoolers: Executive summary.* Washington, DC: National Academy Press.

Boyd, A. (1999). *Guide to multicultural resources, 1977–1998.* Atkinson, WI: Highsmith.

Bracey, G. W. (1998). *Put to the test: An educator's and consumer's guide to standardized testing: The omnipresence of tests and what you need to know about them.* Bloomington, IN: Center for Professional Development and Services, Phi Delta Kappa International.

Bransford, J. D., Brown, A. L., & Cocking, R. R. (Eds.). (1999). *How people learn: Brain, mind, experience, and school.* Washington, DC: National Academy Press.

Bredekamp, S. (Ed.). (1987). *Developmentally appropriate practice in early childhood programs serving children from birth through age 8: Expanded edition.* Washington, DC:

National Association for the Education of Young Children.

Bredekamp, S. (2005, December). *Principles of effective preschool curriculum.* Paper presented at the conference of the National Association for the Education of Young Children, Washington, DC.

Bredekamp, S., & Copple, C. (Eds.). (1997). *Developmentally appropriate practice in early childhood programs* (Rev. ed.). Washington, DC: National Association for the Education of Young Children.

Bredekamp, S., & Rosegrant, T. (Eds.). (1995). *Reaching potentials: Transforming early childhood curriculum and assessment* (Vol. 2). Washington, DC: National Association for the Education of Young Children.

Bredekamp, S., & Shepherd, L. (1990). *Protecting children from inappropriate practices.* ERIC Clearinghouse on Elementary and Early Childhood Education. Urbana, IL: University of Illinois.

Breig-Allen, C. (1997). Implementing the process of change in a public school setting. In J. B. Hendrick (Ed.), *First steps toward teaching the Reggio way.* Upper Saddle River, NJ: Merrill/Prentice Hall.

Brett, J. (2000). *Hedgie's surprise.* New York: Putnam.

Bricker, D. (1995). The challenge of inclusion. *Journal of Early Intervention, 19*(1), 179–194.

Brim, O., Boocock, S., Hoffman, L., Bronfenbrenner, U., & Edelman, M. (1975). *Ecology of child development.* Philadelphia: American Philosophical Society.

Brittain, G. (1979). *Creativity, art, and the young child.* New York: Macmillan.

Bronson, M. B. (1995). *The right stuff for children birth to 8: Selecting play materials to support development.* Washington, DC: National Association for the Education of Young Children.

Bronson, M. B. (2000). *Self-regulation in early childhood: Nature and nurture.* New York: Guilford.

Bruer, J. T. (1999). *The myth of the first three years: A new understanding of early brain development and lifelong learning.* New York: Free Press.

Buch, L. (2005, December 5). Get kids active at early age. *Denver Post,* p. 3F.

Burns, M. S., Griffin, P., & Snow, C. E. (Eds.). (1999). *Starting out right: A guide to promoting children's reading success.* Washington, DC: National Academy Press.

Bybee, R. W., & Sund, R. B. (1990). *Piaget for educators* (2nd ed.). Prospect Heights, IL: Waveland.

Cadwell, L. B. (1997). *Bringing Reggio Emilia home: An innovative approach to early childhood education.* New York: Teachers College Press.

Cadwell, L., & Fyfe, B. (1997). Conversations with children. In J. B. Hendrick (Ed.), *First steps toward teaching the Reggio way.* Upper Saddle River, NJ: Merrill/Prentice Hall.

Caesar, B. (2001). Give children a place to explore. *Child Care Information Exchange, 138,* 74–79.

Calman, L. J., & Tarr-Whelan, L. (2005). *Early childhood education for all: A wise investment.* New York: Legal Momentum.

Campos, J. (1995). The Carpinteria preschool program: A long-term effects study. In E. E. Garcia & B. McLaughlin (Eds.), *Meeting the challenge of linguistic and cultural diversity in early childhood education.* New York: Teachers College Press.

Canadian Child Care Federation. (1999). Universal precautions. *Young Children, 54*(2), 40.

Cancelmo, J. A., & Bandini, C. (1999). *Child care for love or money? A guide to navigating the parent–caregiver relationship.* Northvale, NJ: Aronson.

Cannon, J. (1993). *Stellaluna.* New York: Harcourt Brace.

Carlson, F. M. (2005). Significance of touch in young children's lives. *Young Children, 60*(4), 79–85.

Carlsson-Paige, N., & Levin, D. E. (1998). *Before push comes to shove: Building conflict resolution skills with children.* St. Paul, MN: Redleaf.

Carpenter, T. P., Fennema, E., Franke, M. L., Levi, L., & Empson, S. B. (1999). *Children's mathematics: Cognitively guided instruction.* Portsmouth, NH: Heinemann.

Carson, R. (1950). *The sense of wonder.* New York: Harper & Row.

Carter, B. C., & McGoldrick, M. M. (Eds.). (1999). *The expanded family life cycle: Individual, family, and social perspectives* (3rd ed.). Boston: Allyn & Bacon.

Carter, M. (1999). Developing meaningful relationships with families. *Child Care Information Exchange, 130,* 63–65.

Cartwright, S. (2001). Why promote process over product? *Child Care Information Exchange, 138,* 68–70.

Cassell, J., & Jenkins, H. (Eds.). (1998). *From Barbie to Mortal Kombat: Gender and computer games.* Cambridge, MA: MIT Press.

Cattell, R. (2001). *Children's language: Consensus and controversy.* New York: Cassell.

Ceci, S. J., & Williams, W. M. (Eds.). (1999). *The nature–nurture debate: The essential readings.* Malden, MA: Blackwell.

Center on Hunger, Poverty, and Nutrition Policy. (1998). *Statement on the link between nutrition and cognitive development in children.* Medford, MA: Author.

Center on Hunger, Poverty, and Nutrition Policy. (1999). *Childhood hunger, childhood obesity: An examination of the paradox.* Medford, MA: Author.

Centers for Disease Control and Prevention (CDC). (2003). Web-based Injury Statistics Query and Reporting System (WISQARS). Retrieved December 11, 2005, at the CDC Web site (http://www. cdc.gov/ncipc/wisqars).

Centers for Disease Control and Prevention (CDC). (2004a). *National estimates of the 10 leading causes of nonfatal injuries treated in hospital emergency departments, United States, 2003.* Atlanta, GA: Author.

Centers for Disease Control and Prevention (CDC). (2004b). *Flu deaths in children.* Atlanta, GA: Author.

Centers for Disease Control and Prevention (CDC). (2005). *Children's oral health.* Retrieved December 12, 2005, at the CDC Web site (http://www.cdc.gov/ OralHealth/topics/child.htm).

Centre for Educational Research and Innovation. (1977). *Piagetian inventories: The experiments of Jean Piaget.* Paris, France: Organisation for Economic Cooperation and Development.

Ceppi, G., & Zini, M. (1998). *Children, spaces, relations: Metaproject for an environment for young children.* Reggio Emilia, Italy: Comune di Reggio Emilia/Ministero della Pubblica Istrazione.

Charles, C. M. (1974). *Teacher's petit Piaget.* Belmont, CA: Fearon.

Charner, K. (1996). *The giant encyclopedia of circle time and group activities for children 3 to 6: Over 600 favorite circle time activities created by teachers for teachers.* Beltsville, MD: Gryphon House.

Chen, J. Q., Kritchevsky, M., & Viens, J. (1998). *Building on children's strengths: The experience of Project Spectrum.* New York: Teachers College Press.

Chenfield, M. (1995). *Creative experiences for young children* (2nd ed.). Orlando: Harcourt Brace.

Cherry, C. (1971). *Creative movement for the developing child: A nursery school handbook for non-musicians* (Rev. ed.). Belmont, CA: Fearon.

Cheung, L. W. Y. (1995). Current views and future perspectives. In W. Y. Cheung & J. B. Richmond (Eds.), *Child health, nutrition, and physical activity.* Champaign, IL: Human Kinetics.

Childhelp USA. (2005). *National child abuse statistics.* Scottsdale, AZ: Author.

Children's Defense Fund. (1996). *Yearbook 1996: The state of America's children.* Washington, DC: Author.

Children's Defense Fund. (2004). *Yearbook 2004: The state of America's children.* Washington, DC: Author.

Children's Safety Network. (1996). *The children's safety network: A resource for child and adolescent injury and violence prevention.* Rockville, MD: U.S. Maternal and Child Health Bureau.

Chomsky, N. (1987). Language: Chomsky's theory. In R. L. Gregory (Ed.), *The Oxford companion to the mind.* Oxford, England: Oxford University Press.

Chomsky, N. (1999). On the nature, use, and acquisition of language. In N. W. Ritchie & T. Bhatia (Eds.), *Handbook of child language acquisition.* New York: Academic Press.

Church, E. B. (2000). *The great big book of classroom songs, rhymes, and cheers: 200 easy, playful language experiences that build literacy and community in your classroom.* New York: Scholastic.

Cicerelli, V. G., Evans, J. W., & Schiller, J. S. (1969). *The impact of Head Start on children's cognitive and affective development: Preliminary report.* Washington, DC: Office of Economic Opportunity.

Clark, E. (1983). Meanings and concepts. In P. Mussen, J. H. Flavell, & E. Markman (Eds.), *Handbook of child psychology: Vol. III. Cognitive development* (pp. 787–840). New York: Wiley.

Clements, D. H., & Sarama, J. (2005). Math play: How young children approach math. *Scholastic Early Childhood Today, 19*(4), 50–57.

Cobb, P. (1996). Where is the mind? A coordination of sociocultural and cognitive constructivist perspectives. In C. T. Fosnot (Ed.), *Constructivism: Theory, perspectives, and practice.* New York: Teachers College Press.

Coe, J. (1987). Children come first. *Childhood Education, 64*(2), 73.

Coll, C. G., Surrey, J. L., & Weinharten, K. (1998). *Mothering against the odds: Diverse voices of contemporary mothers.* New York: Guilford.

Coloroso, B. (2003). *The bully, the bullied, and the bystander.* New York: HarperCollins.

Confrey, J. (1995). How compatible are radical constructivism, sociocultural approaches, and social constructivism? In L. P. Steffe & J. Gale (Eds.), *Constructivism in education: Concerns about Vygotsky's theories*. Hillsdale, NJ: Erlbaum.

Connolly, K., & Bruner, J. (Eds.). (1974). *The growth of competence*. London: Academic Press.

Consumer Product Safety Commission. (1997). *Handbook for public playground safety*. Washington, DC: Author.

Cook, J. W. (2001). Create and tell a story: Help young children who have psychological difficulties. *Young Children, 56*(1), 67–70.

Cook, R., Tessier, A., & Klein, M. D. (2004). *Adapting childhood curricula for children in inclusive settings* (6th ed.). Upper Saddle River, NJ: Merrill/Prentice Hall.

Cooks, R. J., & Watt, H. M. G. (2004). Relationships among perceived competence, intrinsic value, and mastery goal orientation in English and Maths. *Australian Educational Researcher, 31*(2), 81–112.

Cooper, T. T., & Ratner, M. (1980). *Many friends cooking: An international cookbook for girls and boys*. New York: Philomel.

Coopersmith, S. (1967). *The antecedents of self-esteem*. San Francisco: Freeman.

Copple, C. (Ed.) (2003). *A world of difference: Readings on teaching young children in a diverse society*. Washington, DC: National Association for the Education of Young Children.

Copple, C., & Bredekamp, S. (2006). *Basics of developmentally appropriate practice: An introduction for teachers of children 3 to 6*. Washington, DC: National Association for the Education of Young Children.

Cordes, C., & Miller, E. (Eds.). (2000). *Fool's gold: A critical look at computers in childhood*. College Park, MD: Alliance for Childhood.

Cortés, C. E. (2000). *The children are watching*. New York: Teachers College Press.

Cottrell, R., & O'Brien, C. (1999). Dental disease. In M. J. Sadler,

J. J. Strain, & B. Caballero (Eds.), *Encyclopedia of human nutrition*. New York: Academic Press.

Cox, M. (1997). *Drawings of people by the under-5's*. London: Falmer.

Craig, D. V. (2000). Technology, math, and the early learner: Models for learning. *Early Childhood Education Journal, 27*(3), 179–184.

Crawford, N. (2002). New ways to stop bullying. *Monitor on Psychology, 33*(9), 64.

Crawford, S. H. (1996). *Beyond dolls and guns: 101 ways to help children avoid gender bias*. Portsmouth, NH: Heinemann.

Creaser, B. (1999). The place of play for young children with disabilities in mainsteam education. In E. Dau (Ed.), *Child's play: Revisiting play in early childhood settings*. Sydney, Australia: Maclennan & Petty.

Croft, D. J. (1967). *Recipes for busy little hands*. Palo Alto, CA: De Anza College.

Crosbie-Burnett, M. (1994). The interface between stepparent families and schools: Research, theory, policy, and practice. In R. K. Pasley & M. Iniger-Tallman (Eds.), *Stepparenting issues in theory, research, and practice*. Westport, CT: Greenwood Press.

Crosser, S. (1994). Making the most of water play. *Young Children, 49*(5), 28–32.

Cryer, D., Harms, T., & Ray, A. R. (1996). *Active learning for fours*. Menlo Park, CA: Addison-Wesley.

Cryer, D., Ray, A. R., & Harms, T. (1996). *Nutrition activities for preschoolers*. Menlo Park, CA: Addison-Wesley.

Csikszentmihalye, M. (1996). *Creativity: Flow and the psychology of discovery and invention*. New York: HarperCollins.

Curry, N. E., & Arnaud, S. H. (1982). Dramatic play as a diagnostic aid in the preschool. *Journal of Children in Contemporary Society, 14*(4), 37–46.

Curtis, D., & Carter, M. (2000). *The art of awareness: How observation can transform your teaching*. St. Paul, MN: Redleaf.

Dacey, J. S., & Lennon, K. H. (1998). *Understanding creativity: The interplay of biological, psychological, and social factors*. San Francisco: Jossey-Bass.

Dahlberg, G., Moss, P., & Pence, A. (1999). *Beyond quality in early childhood education and care: Postmodern perspectives*. London: Falmer.

Daniels, E. R., & Stafford, K. (1999). *Creative inclusive classrooms*. Washington, DC: Children's Resources International.

David, L., & Keyser, J. (1997). *Becoming the parent you want to be: A sourcebook of strategies for the first five years*. New York: Broadway Books.

David, T., Raban, B., Ure, C., Goouch, K., Jago, M., Barriere, I., & Lambirth, A. (2000). *Making sense of early literacy: A practitioner's perspective*. Stoke on Trent, England: Trenthan.

Davis, G. A. (1983). *Creativity is forever*. Dubuque, IA: Kendall/Hunt.

Day, C. B. (2000). *National Head Start Bulletin, 67*, 29.

DeFelice, C. (2000). *Cold feet*. New York: Dorling Kindersley.

Derman-Sparks, L. (1987). "It isn't fair!" Anti-bias curriculum for young children. In B. Neugebauer (Ed.), *Alike and different: Exploring our humanity with young children*. Redmond, WA: Exchange Press.

Derman-Sparks, L. (1992). Reaching potentials through anti-bias, multicultural curriculum. In S. Bredekamp & T. Rosegrant (Eds.), *Reaching potentials: Appropriate curriculum and assessment for young children*. Washington, DC: National Association for the Education of Young Children.

Derman-Sparks, L. (1995). Children and diversity. *Scholastic Early Childhood Today, 10*(3), 41–45.

Derman-Sparks, L., & the ABC. Task Force. (1989). *Anti-bias curriculum: Tools for empowering young children*. Washington, DC: National Association for the Education of Young Children.

Derman-Sparks, L., & Phillips, C. B. (1997). *Teaching/learning anti-racism: A developmental approach.* New York: Teachers College Press.

Derman-Sparks, L., & Ramsey, P. G. (2005). Anti-bias/Multicultural education with white children. *Young Children, 60*(6), 20–27.

Derman-Spraks, L., & Ramsey, P. G. (2006). *What if all the kids are white? Anti-bias/multicultural education with young children and families.* New York: Teachers College Press.

DeTemple, J. M. (2001). Parents and children reading books together. In D. K. Dickinson & P. Tabors (Eds.), *Beginning literacy with language.* Baltimore: Brookes.

DeVries, R., & Zan, B. (1994). *Moral children, moral classrooms: Creating a constructivist atmosphere in early education.* New York: Teachers College Press.

DeVries, R., Zan, B., Hildebrandt, C., Edmiaston, R., & Sales, C. (2002). *Developing constructivist early childhood curriculum: Practical principles and activities.* New York: Teachers College Press.

Dewey, J. (1966). *Democracy and education.* New York: Free Press. (Originally published 1916)

Dickinson, D. K., & Tabors, P. O. (Eds.). (2001). *Young children learning at home and school: Beginning literacy with language.* Baltimore: Brookes.

Dietz, W. H., & Stern, L. (1999). *American Academy of Pediatrics guide to your child's nutrition: Making peace at the table and building healthy eating habits for life.* New York: Villard.

Diffily, D., & Morrison, K. (Eds.). (1996). *Family-friendly communication for early childhood programs.* Washington, DC: National Association for the Education of Young Children.

Division for Early Childhood. (2000). *IDEA requirements for preschoolers with disabilities.* Reston, VA: Council for Exceptional Children.

Dobnik, V. (2005, November 5). Schoolgirl put tsunami lesson to use, saved 100. *Rocky Mountain News,* p. 33A.

Dorros, A. (1991). *Abuela.* New York: Dutton.

Dougy Center. (2000). *35 ways to help a grieving child.* Portland, OR: Author.

Dowell, R. I. (1987). *Move over, Mother Goose: Finger plays, action verses, and funny rhymes.* Mt. Rainier, MD: Gryphon House.

Downing, J. E., & Peckham-Hardin, K. D. (2001). Daily schedules: A helpful learning tool. *Teaching Exceptional Children, 33*(3), 62–68.

Dunn, J. (2004). *Children's friendships: The beginning of intimacy.* Malden, MA: Blackwell.

Ebel, R. L. (1970, November). Behavioral objectives: A close look. *Phi Delta Kappan,* 171–173.

Eco, U. (1993). Interview by Francois-Bernard Huyghe in the *UNESCO Courier.* New York: UNESCO.

Edelstein, S. (1992). *Nutrition and meal planning in child-care programs: A practical guide.* Chicago: American Dietetic Association.

Edmiaston, R., Dolezal, V., Doolittle, S., Erickson, C., & Merritt, S. (2000). Developing individualized education programs for children in inclusive settings: A developmentally appropriate framework. *Young Children, 55*(4), 36–41.

Edwards, C., Gandini, L., & Forman, G. (1993). *The hundred languages of children: The Reggio Emilia approach to early childhood education.* Norwood, NJ: Ablex.

Edwards, C., Gandini, L., & Forman, G. (Eds.). (1998). *The hundred languages of children: The Reggio Emilia approach—Advanced reflections* (2nd ed.). Greenwich, CT: Ablex.

Edwards, C. P., & Ramsey, P. G. (1986). *Promoting social and moral development in young children: Creative approaches for the classroom.* New York: Teachers College Press.

Eisenberg, N., Fabes, R. A., Carlo, G., & Karbon, M. (1992). Emotional responsivity to others: Behavioral correlates and socialization antecedents. *New Directions for Child Development, 55,* 57–73.

Eisner, E. (1969). Instructional expressive educational objectives: Their formulation and use in curriculum. In W. J. Popham, E. W. Eisner, H. J. Sullivan, & L. L. Tyler (Eds.), *Instructional objectives.* Chicago, IL: American Educational Research Association.

Elicker, J., & Fortner-Wood, C. (1995). Adult–child relationships in early childhood programs. *Young Children, 51*(1), 69–78.

Eliot, L. (1999). *What's going on in there? How the brain and mind develop in the first five years of life.* New York: Bantam Books.

Elkind, D. (1990a). Academic pressures—too much, too soon: The demise of play. In E. Klugman & S. Smilansky (Eds.), *Children's play and learning: Perspectives and policy implications.* New York: Teachers College Press.

Elkind, D. (1990b). *Miseducation: Preschoolers at risk.* New York: Knopf.

Elkind, D. (2005). Early childhood amnesia: Reaffirming children's need for developmentally appropriate programs. *Young Children, 60*(4), 38–40.

Endres, J. B., Rockwell, R. E., & Mense, C. G. (2004). *Food, nutrition, and the young child* (5th ed.). Upper Saddle River, NJ: Merrill/Prentice Hall.

Engle, B. S. (1995). *Considering children's art: Why and how to value their work.* Washington, DC: National Association for the Education of Young Children.

English, D. J. (1998). The extent and consequences of child maltreatment. *Future of Children: Protecting Children from Abuse and Neglect, 81,* 39–53.

Erikson, E. H. (1963). *Childhood and society* (2nd ed.). New York: Norton.

Erikson, E. H. (1982). *The life cycle completed: A review.* New York: Norton.

Erikson, E. H. (1996). A healthy personality for every child. In K. M. Paciorek & J. H. Munro (Eds.), *Sources: Notable selections in early childhood education.* Guilford, CT: Dushkin.

Essa, E. L., & Murray, C. I. (1999). Sexual play: When should you be concerned? *Childhood Education, 75*(4), 231–234.

Eyre, L., & Eyre, R. (1980). *Teaching children joy.* New York: Deseret Books.

Faber, A., & Mazlish, E. (2000). *How to talk so kids will listen, and listen so kids will talk* (20th ed.). New York: Avon Books.

Fagot, B. I. (1994). Peer relations and the development of competence in boys and girls. *New Directions for Child Development, 65,* 53–63.

Faller, K. C. (1998). *Child sexual abuse: An interdisciplinary manual for diagnosis, case management, and treatment.* New York: Columbia University Press.

Farnham-Diggory, S. (1992). Head shakers and mind benders. *Child Care Information Exchange, 85,* 54.

Favazza, P. C., Phillipsen, L., & Kumar, P. (2000). Measuring and promoting acceptance of young children with disabilities. *Exceptional Children, 66*(4), 491–508.

Feeney, S., & Freeman, N. K. (1999). *Ethics and the early childhood educator: Using the National Association for the Education of Young Children code.* Washington, DC: National Association for the Education of Young Children.

Fenichel, E. (Ed.). (2002). Infants, toddlers, and terror: Supporting parents, helping children. *Zero to Three, 23*(3), entire issue.

Fernandez, R. C. (2000). No hablo Inglés: Bilingualism and multiculturalism in preschool settings. *Early Childhood Education Journal, 27*(3), 159–163.

Fields, M., Spangler, K. L., & Groth, L. (2004). *Let's begin reading right: Developmentally appropriate beginning literacy* (5th ed.). Upper Saddle River, NJ: Merrill/Prentice Hall.

Fiese, B. (1990). Playful relationships: A contextual analysis of mother–toddler interaction and symbolic play. *Child Development, 61,* 1648–1656.

Finkelhor, D. (1994). Current information on the scope and nature of child sexual abuse. *Future of Children, 4*(2), 31–53.

Fitzjohn, S., Weston, M., & Large, J. (1993). *Festivals together: A guide to multi-cultural celebrations.* Gloucestershire, England: Hawthorne.

Forman, G., & Gandini, L. (1994). *An amusement park for birds.* Amherst, MA: Peformanetics Press. (Videotape)

Forum on Child and Family Statistics. (2000). *America's children: Key national indicators of well-being, 2000.* Washington, DC: Federal Interagency Forum on Child and Family Statistics. U.S. Government Printing Office.

Fosnot, C. T. (2005). *Constructivism: Theory, perspectives, and practice* (2nd ed.). New York: Teachers College Press.

Fox, S. S. (1985). *Good grief: Helping groups of children when a friend dies.* Boston: New England Association for the Education of Young Children.

Frank, C. (1999). *Ethnographic eyes: A teacher's guide to classroom observation.* Portsmouth, NH: Heinemann.

Frank, L. (1968). *Play is valid.* Wheaton, MD: Association for Childhood Education International.

Franklin, M. B., & Biber, B. (1977). Psychological perspectives and early childhood education: Some relations between theory and practice. In L. G. Katz (Ed.), *Current topics in early childhood education* (Vol. 1). Norwood, NJ: Ablex.

Fredricks, J. A., & Eccles, J. S. (2002). Children's competence and value beliefs from childhood through adolescence: Growth trajectories in two male-sex-typed domains. *Developmental Psychology, 38,* 519–533.

Freud, S. (1962). *Three essays on the theory of sexuality.* New York: Basic Books.

Friedman, L. J. (1999). *Identity's architect: A biography of Erik H. Erikson.* New York: Simon & Schuster.

Fromberg, D. P. (1999). A review of research on play. In C. Seefeldt (Ed.), *The early childhood curriculum: Current findings in theory and practice* (3rd ed.). New York: Teachers College Press.

Frost, J. L. (1992). *Play and playscapes.* Albany, NY: Delmar.

Frost, J. L. (2005). Lessons from disasters: Play, work, and the creative arts. *Childhood Education, 82*(1), 2–8.

Frost, J. L., & Sweeny, T. B. (1996). *Cause and prevention of playground injuries and litigation.* Wheaton, MD: Association for Childhood Education International.

Frost, J. L., Wortham, S. C., & Reifel, S. (2005). *Play and child development* (2nd ed.). Upper Saddle River, NJ: Merrill/Prentice Hall.

Fuller, B., Holloway, S. D., & Bozzi, L. (1997). Evaluating child care and preschools: Advancing the interests of government, teachers, or parents? In B. Spodek & O. N. Saracho (Eds.), *Issues in early childhood educational assessment and evaluation: Yearbook in early childhood education* (Vol. 7). New York: Teachers College Press.

Furman, R. A. (1995). On preparation: "New" perspectives. In E. Furman (Ed.), *Preschoolers: Questions and answers: Psychoanalytic consultations with parents, teachers, and caregivers.* Madison, CT: International Universities Press.

Future of Children. (1994). *Sexual abuse of children, 4*(2), entire issue. Los Altos, CA: Packard Foundation.

Future of Children. (1995). *Long-term outcomes of early childhood programs, 5*(3), entire issue.

Gag, W. (1996). *Millions of cats.* Paper Star reprint.

Galdone, P. (1970). *The three little pigs.* New York: Clarion.

Gallagher, K. C. (2005) Brain research and early development: A primer for developmentally appropriate practice. *Young Children, 60*(4), 12–20.

Gallahue, D. H. (1995a). Transforming physical education curriculum. In S. Bredekamp & T. Rosegrant (Eds.), *Reaching potentials: Transforming early childhood curriculum and assessment* (Vol. 2). Washington, DC: National Association for the Education of Young Children.

Gallahue, D. H. (1995b). *Understanding motor development: Infants, children, adolescents, adults*. Dubuque, IA: Brown & Benchmark.

Gallahue, D. H., & Ozmun, J. C. (2005). *Understanding motor development: Infants, children, adolescents, and adults* (6th ed.). New York: McGraw-Hill.

Gallup, G. H., Jr., Moor, D. W., & Schussel, R. (1997). *Disciplining children in America*. Princeton, NJ: Gallup.

Gambetti, A. (1992). *An amusement park for birds*. Paper presented at National Association for the Education of Young Children, New Orleans.

Gambrell, L. B., & Mazzoni, S. A. (1999). Emergent literacy: What research reveals about learning to read. In C. Seefeldt (Ed.), *The early childhood curriculum: Current findings in theory and practice* (3rd ed.). New York: Teachers College Press.

Gandini, L. (1997). Foundations of the Reggio Emilia approach. In J. Hendrick (Ed.), *First steps toward teaching the Reggio way*. Upper Saddle River, NJ: Merrill/Prentice Hall.

Gandini, L., & Edwards, C. P. (2001). *Bambini: The Italian approach to infant/toddler care*. New York: Teachers College Press.

Garcia, E. E., & McLaughlin, B. (1995). *Meeting the challenge of linguistic and cultural diversity in early childhood education*. New York: Teachers College Press.

Gardner, H. (1993). *Multiple intelligences: The theory in practice*. New York: Basic Books.

Gartrell, D. (1995). Misbehavior or mistaken behavior? *Young Children, 50*(5), 27–34.

Gartrell, J. D. (2004). *The power of guidance: Teaching social-emotional skills in the early childhood classroom.*

Clifton Park, NY: Delmar/Thomson and NAEYC.

Gartrell, J. D. (2005, December). *Building a culture friendly to boys and men in early childhood classrooms: Bringing together what we know*. Paper presented at the conference of the National Association for the Education of Young Children, Washington, DC.

Garvey, C. (1983). Some properties of social play. In M. Donaldson, R. Grieve, & C. Pratt (Eds.), *Early childhood development and education: Readings in psychology*. New York: Guilford.

Gaspar, K. (1995). Liberating art experiences for preschoolers and their teachers. In C. M. Thompson (Ed.), *The visual arts and early childhood learning*. Reston, VA: National Art Education Association.

Gatto, J. (1992). *Dumbing us down*. Philadelphia: New Society.

Geist, E. (2001). Children are born mathematicians: Promoting the construction of early mathematical concepts in children under five. *Young Children, 56*(4), 13–19.

Gelb, M. J. (1998). *How to think like Leonardo da Vinci*. New York: Delacourt.

Gestwicki, C. (1998). *Developmentally appropriate practice: Curriculum and development in early education* (2nd ed.). Albany, NY: Delmar.

Ghafouri, F., & Wein, C. A. (2005). "Give us a privacy": Play and social literacy in young children. *Journal of Research in Childhood Education, 19*(4), 279–291.

Gilbert, K. (1998). The body, young children, and popular culture. In N. Yelland (Ed.), *Gender in early childhood*. London: Routledge.

Gillespie, C. W. (2000). Six Head Start classrooms begin to explore the Reggio Emilia approach. *Young Children, 55*(1), 21–27.

Gillespie, N. (2005, August 25). Connecticut sues over No Child act. *Denver Post*, p. A4.

Gleason, J. B. (Ed.). (2001). *The development of language* (5th ed.). Boston: Allyn & Bacon.

Gleim, L. (2005, November 26). *Re: Putting together the Reggio puzzle*. Message posted to REGGIO-L electronic mailing list, archived at http://ecap.crc.uiuc.edu/listserv/reggio-l.html.

Glennon, W. (2000). *200 ways to raise a boy's emotional intelligence: An indispensable guide for parents, teachers, and other concerned caregivers*. Berkeley, CA: Conari Press.

Goble, P. (1978). *The girl who loved wild horses*. Scarsdale, NY: Bradbury.

Goldhaber, J., Smith, D., & Sortino, S. (1997). Observing, recording, understanding: The role of documentation in early childhood teacher education. In J. Hendrick (Ed.), *First steps toward teaching the Reggio way*. Upper Saddle River, NJ: Merrill/Prentice Hall.

Goldman, L. (2000). *Life and loss: A guide to help grieving children* (2nd ed.). Philadelphia: Accelerated Development.

Goldstein, A. P. (1999). *Low-level aggression: First steps on the ladder to violence*. Champaign, IL: Research Press.

Goldstein, P. (2004). Helping young children with special needs develop vocabulary. *Early Childhood Education Journal, 32*(1), 39–43.

Goleman, D. (2005). *Emotional intelligence: Tenth anniversary edition*. New York: Bantam Books.

Golumb, C. (1992). *The child's creation of a pictorial world*. Berkeley: University of California Press.

Gomby, D. S., Culross, P. L., & Behrman, R. E. (1999). Home visiting: Recent program evaluations—Analysis and recommendations. *Future of Children, 9*(1), 4–26.

Gonzales, P. C. (2005). *Becoming bilingual: First and second language acquisition*. Washington, DC: Head Start Bureau.

Gonzalez, G. (1991). Language acquisition research in Mexican American children: The sad state of the art. *Early Childhood Research Quarterly, 6*(3), 411–425.

Gonzalez-Mena, J. (2004). *Diversity in early care and education: Honoring differences* (4th ed.). New York: McGraw-Hill.

Gonzalez-Mena, J., & Eyer, D. W. (2004). *Infants, toddlers, and caregivers: A curriculum of respectful, responsive care* (6th ed.). New York: McGraw-Hill.

Gonzalez-Mena, J., & Shareef, I. (2005). Discussing diverse perspectives on guidance. *Young Children, 60*(6), 34–38.

Goodwin, W. L., & Goodwin, L. E. (1997). Using standardized measures for evaluating young children's learning. In B. Spodek & O. N. Saracho (Eds.), *Issues in early childhood educational assessment and evaluation: Yearbook in early childhood education*, (Vol. 7). New York: Teachers College Press.

Gordon, T. (1976). *P.E.T. in action: Inside P.E.T. families: New problems, insights, and solutions in Parent Effectiveness Training.* New York: Wyden.

Gordon, T. (1989). *Discipline that works: Promoting self discipline in children.* New York: Wyden.

Görlitz, D., & Wohlwill, J. B. (Eds.). (1987). *Curiosity, imagination, and play.* Hillsdale, NJ: Erlbaum.

Gould, P., & Sullivan, J. (1999). *The inclusive early childhood classroom.* Beltsville, MD: Gryphon House.

Gowen, J. W. (1995). The early development of symbolic play. *Young Children, 50*(3), 75–84.

Graham, A. (1976). *Foxtails, ferns, and fish scales: A handbook of art and nature projects.* New York: Four Winds Press.

Graves, M. (1989). *The teacher's idea book: Daily planning around the key experiences.* Ypsilanti, MI: High/Scope.

Graves, M. (1998). *Planning around children's interests: The teacher's idea book 2.* Ypsilanti, MI: High/Scope.

Greenbaum, S., Turner, B., & Stephens, R. D. (1989). *Set straight on bullies.* Malibu, CA: National School Safety Center.

Greenberg, P. (2000). The value of classroom rituals and routines. *Scholastic Early Childhood Today, 15*(1), 32–39.

Greenberg, P. (2001). The comforting classroom. *Scholastic Early Childhood Today, 16*(1), 47–57.

Greenman, J. (1988). *Caring spaces, learning places: Children's environments that work.* Redmond, WA: Exchange Press.

Greenman, J. (1998). *Places for childhoods: Making quality happen in the real world.* Redmond, WA: Exchange Press.

Greenspan, S. I. (1999). *Building healthy minds: The six experiences that create intelligence and emotional growth in babies and young children.* Cambridge, MA: Perseus.

Greenstein, D., Miner, N., Kudela, E., & Bloom, S. (1995). *Backyards and butterflies: Ways to include children with disabilities in outdoor activities.* Cambridge, MA: Brookline.

Grief, E. B. (1980). Sex differences in parent–child conversations. *Women's Studies International Quarterly, 3,* 253–258.

Grieshaber, S., & Cannella, G. S. (Eds.). (2001). *Embracing identities in early childhood education.* New York: Teachers College Press.

Gronlund, N. E. (2000). *How to write and use instructional objectives* (6th ed.). Upper Saddle River NJ: Merrill/Prentice Hall.

Guilford, J. P. (1981). Developmental characteristics: Factors that aid and hinder creativity. In J. C. Gowan, J. Khatena, & E. P. Torrance (Eds.), *Creativity: Its educational implications* (2nd ed.). Dubuque, IA: Kendall/Hunt.

Guralnick, M. J., & Hammond, M. A. (1999). Sequential analysis of the social play of young children with mild developmental delays. *Journal of Early Intervention, 22*(3), 243–256.

Haigh, K. (1997). How the Reggio Approach has influenced an inner-city program. In J. Hendrick (Ed.), *First steps toward teaching the Reggio way.* Upper Saddle River, NJ: Merrill/Prentice Hall.

Haines, J. E., & Gerber, L. L. (2000). *Leading young children to music* (6th ed.). Upper Saddle River, NJ: Merrill/Prentice Hall.

Hakuta, K. (1998). Improving education for all children: Meeting the needs of language minority children. In D. Clark (Moderator), *Education and the development of American youth.* Washington, DC: Aspen Institute.

Hale, J. E. (1992). Dignifying black children's lives. *Dimensions, 20*(3), 8, 9–40.

Halfon, N., Shulman, E., & Hochstein, M. (2001). *Brain development in early childhood.* Los Angeles: UCLA Center for Healthier Children, Families, and Communities.

Hall, B. J., Oyer, H. J., & Haas, W. H. (2000). *Speech, language, and hearing disorders: A guide for the teacher.* Boston: Allyn & Bacon.

Hall, E., Oleson, V., & Gambetti, A. (2001). Including parents in the process of documentation. *Child Care Information Exchange, 138,* 52–55.

Hammet, C. (1992). *Movement activities for early childhood.* Champaign, IL: Human Kinetics.

Han, M., Roskos, K., Christie, J., Mandzuk, S., & Vukelich, C. (2005). Learning words: Large group time as a vocabulary development opportunity. *Journal of Research in Childhood Education, 19*(4), 333–345.

Harlan, J. D., & Rivkin, M. S. (2000). *Science experiences for the early childhood years: An integrated approach* (7th ed.). Upper Saddle River, NJ: Merrill/Prentice Hall.

Harms, T. (1972). Evaluating settings for learning. In K. H. Baker (Ed.), *Ideas that work with young children.* Washington, DC: National Association for the Education of Young Children.

Harms, T., & Clifford, R. M. (1980). *The Early Childhood Environment Rating Scale.* New York: Teachers College Press.

Harms, T., Clifford, R. M., & Cryer, D. (2004). *Early childhood environment rating scale* (Rev. ed.). New York: Teachers College Press.

Harms, T., Cryer, D., & Clifford, R. M. (2003). *Infant/toddler environment rating scale* (Rev. ed.). New York: Teachers College Press.

Harris, T. T., & Fuqua, J. D. (2000). What goes around comes around: Building a community of learners through circle times. *Young Children, 55*(1), 44–47.

Hart, B., & Risley, T. R. (1995). *Meaningful differences in the everyday experience of young American children*. Baltimore: Brookes.

Hart, B., & Risley, T. R. (2003). The early catastrophe: The 30 million word gap by age 3. *American Educator, 27*(1), 4–9.

Harter, S. (1999). *The construction of the self: A developmental perspective*. New York: Guilford.

Hartup, W. W. (1983). Peer relations. In P. H. Mussen (Ed.), *Handbook of child psychology: Volume IV. Socialization, personality, and social development*. New York: Wiley.

Haugen, V., & Neugebauer, B. (1996). Idea sparkers: Small but powerful ways to teach mathematical thinking. In K. D. P. Wolf & B. Neugebauer (Eds.), *More than numbers: Mathematical thinking in the early years*. Redmond, WA: Child Care Information Exchange Press.

Haugland, S. (1999). Computers and young children: The newest software that meets the developmental needs of young children. *Early Childhood Education Journal, 26*(4), 245–254.

Haugland, S. W. (2000). Early childhood classrooms in the 21st century: Using computers to maximize learning. *Young Children, 55*(1), 12–18.

Haugland, S. W., & Wright, J. L. (1997). *Young children and technology: A world of discovery*. Boston: Allyn & Bacon.

Hauser-Cram, P. (1998). Research in review: I think I can, I think I can: Understanding and encouraging mastery motivation in young children. *Young Children, 53*(4), 67–71.

Hayes, D. S. (1978). Cognitive bases for liking and disliking among preschool children. *Child Development, 49,* 906–909.

Head Start Performance Standards. (2004). *Code of Federal Regulations, 4*(45). Washington, DC: U.S. Government Printing Office.

Healy, J. M. (1998). *Failure to connect: How computers affect our children's minds—for better or worse*. New York: Simon & Schuster.

Helburn, S., Howes, C., Bryant, D., & Kagan, S. L. (1995). *Cost, quality, and child outcomes in child care centers: Executive summary* (2nd ed.). Denver: Economics Department, University of Colorado at Denver.

Helm, J. H. (Ed.). (2000). *The project approach catalog 3*. Champaign, IL: ERIC Clearinghouse on Elementary and Early Childhood Education, University of Illinois at Urbana-Champaign.

Helm, J. H., & Beneke, S. (2003). *The power of projects: Meeting contemporary challenges in early childhood classrooms*. Washington, DC: The National Association for the Education of Young Children.

Helm, J. H., Beneke, S., & Steinheimer, K. (1998). *Windows on learning: Documenting young children's work*. New York: Teachers College Press.

Helm, J. H., & Katz, L. (2001). *Young investigators: The project approach in the early years*. New York: Teachers College Press.

Hendrick, J. (1973). *The cognitive development of the economically disadvantaged Mexican American and Anglo-American four-year-old: Teaching the concepts of grouping, ordering, perceiving common connections, and matching by means of semantic and figural materials*. Doctoral dissertation, University of California at Santa Barbara.

Hendrick, J. (Ed.). (1997). *First steps toward teaching the Reggio way*. Upper Saddle River, NJ: Merrill/Prentice Hall.

Hendrick, J. B. (Ed.). (2004). *Next steps toward teaching the Reggio way*.

Upper Saddle River, NJ: Merrill/Prentice Hall.

Hendrick, J., & Stange, T. (1991). Do actions speak louder than words? An effect of the functional use of language on dominant sex role behavior in boys and girls. *Early Childhood Research Quarterly, 6*(4), 565–576.

Hendrick, J., Weissman, P. (2006). *The whole child: Developmental education for the early years* (8th ed.). Upper Saddle River, NJ: Merrill/Prentice Hall.

Henkes, K. (2004). *Kitten's first full moon*. New York: Greenwillow.

Henniger, M. L. (1985). Preschool children's play behaviors in an indoor and outdoor environment. In J. L. Frost & S. Sunderlin (Eds.), *When children play*. Wheaton, MD: Association for Childhood Education International.

Herman, F., & Smith, J. C. (1992). *Creatability: Creative arts for preschool children with special needs*. Tucson: Communication Skill Builders.

Herriot, P. (1987). Language development in children. In R. L. Gregory (Ed.), *The Oxford companion to the mind*. Oxford, England: Oxford University Press.

Hewes, D. (1998). *"It's the camaraderie": A history of parent cooperative preschools*. Davis: Center for Cooperatives, University of California.

Hewitt, K. (2001). Blocks as a tool for learning: Historical and contemporary perspectives. *Young Children, 56*(1), 6–13.

Hewitt, S. K. (1999). *Assessing allegations of sexual abuse in preschool children: Understanding small voices*. Thousand Oaks, CA: Sage.

High/Scope Educational Research Foundation. (1992). *Child observation record*. Ypsilanti, MI: Author.

Hildebrand, V., Phenice, L. A., Gray, M. M., & Hines, R. P. (2007). *Knowing and serving diverse families* (3rd ed.). Upper Saddle River, NJ: Merrill/Prentice Hall.

Hill, C. A. (1977). A review of the language deficit position: Some sociolinguistic and psycholinguistic perspectives, *IRCD Bulletin, 12*(4), 1–13.

Hill, W. M. (2005). Welcome to the English language learners Bulletin. *Head Start Bulletin, 78,* 3.

Hirsch, E. S. (Ed.). (1996). *The block book* (3rd ed.). Washington, DC: National Association for the Education of Young Children.

Hoban, R. (1964). *Bread and jam for Frances.* New York: Harper & Row.

Hodges, S. (1994). *Healthy snacks: Low fat, low sugar, low sodium.* Everett, WA: Warren.

Hodges, W. (1987). Active listening. *Dimensions, 15*(4), 13.

Hoffman, M. L. (1970). Moral development. In P. H. Mussen (Ed.), *Carmichael's manual of child psychology* (Vol. 2, 3rd ed.). New York: Wiley.

Hohmann, M., & Weikart, D. P. (1995). *Educating young children: Active learning practices for preschool and child care programs.* Ypsilanti, MI: High/Scope.

Holmes, R. M. (1995). *How young children perceive race.* Thousand Oaks, CA: Sage.

Honig, A. S. (2000). Psychosexual development in infants and young children: Implications for caregivers. *Young Children, 55*(5), 70–77.

Honig, A. S. (2002). *Secure relationships: Nurturing infant/toddler attachment in early care settings.* Washington, DC: National Association for the Education of Young Children.

Honig, A. S., & Wittmer, D. S. (1982). Teachers and low-income toddlers in metropolitan day care. *Early Child Development and Care, 10*(1), 95–112.

Hoot, J. L., Szecsi, T., & Moosa, S. (2003). What teachers of young children should know about Islam. *Early Childhood Education Journal, 31*(2), 85–90.

Howe, D. (1995). IEP social goals found lacking: Surprise, surprise! *Journal of Early Intervention, 19*(4), 286–287.

Howe, N., Moller, L., & Chambers, B. (1994). Dramatic play in day care: What happens when doctors, cooks, bakers, pirates, and pharmacists invade the classroom? In H. Goelman & E. V. Jacobs (Eds.), *Children's play in child care settings.* Albany: State University of New York Press.

Howell, N. M. (1999). Cooking up a learning community with corn, beans, and rice. *Young Children, 54*(5), 36–38.

Howes, C., & Clements, D. (1994). Adult socialization of children's play in child care. In H. Goelman & E. V. Jacobs (Eds.), *Children's play in child care settings.* Albany: State University of New York Press.

Howes, C., Unger, O., & Matheson, C. C. (1992). *The collaborative construction of pretend.* Albany: State University of New York Press.

Huber, L. K. (1999). Woodworking with young children: You can do it! *Young Children, 54*(6), 32–34.

Hudson, S. D., Thompson, D., & Mack, M. G. (2001). Safe playgrounds: Increased challenges, reduced risks. *Dimensions of Early Childhood, 29*(1), 18–23.

Hulit, L. M. (1996). *Straight talk on stuttering: Information, encouragement, and counsel for stutterers, caregivers, and speech–language clinicians.* Springfield, IL: Thomas.

Hunter, T. (2000). Some thoughts about sitting still. *Young Children, 55(3),* 50.

Hut, V., Dennis, B., Koplow, L., & Gerber, J. (1996). Lesson plans for emotional life. In N. L. Koplow (Ed.), *Unsmiling faces.* New York: Teachers College Press.

Hyman, I. A. (1997). *The case against spanking: How to discipline your child without hitting.* San Francisco: Jossey-Bass.

Hyson, M. C. (1994). *The emotional development of young children: Building an emotion-centered curriculum.* New York: Teachers College Press.

Hyson, M., Hirsh-Pasek, K., & Rescorla, L. (1990). The classroom

practices inventory: An observation instrument based on National Association for the Education of Young Children's guidelines for developmentally appropriate practices for 4- to 5-year-old children. *Early Childhood Research Quarterly, 5,* 475–494.

Hyun, E. (1998). *Making sense of developmentally and culturally appropriate practice (DCAP) in early childhood education.* New York: Lang.

Impara, J. D., & Plake, B. S. (Eds.). (1998). *The thirteenth mental measurements yearbook.* Lincoln: University of Nebraska Press.

Impara, J. D., & Plake, B. S. (Eds.). (2000). *Supplement to the thirteenth mental measurements yearbook.* Lincoln: University of Nebraska Press.

Isenberg, J. P., & Jalongo, M. R. (2001). *Creative expression and play in early childhood* (3rd ed.). Upper Saddle River, NJ: Merrill/Prentice Hall.

Jacobson, E. (1976). *You must relax* (5th ed.). New York: McGraw-Hill.

Jacobson, M., & Hill, L. (1991). *Kitchen fun for kids.* Washington, DC: Center for Science in the Public Interest.

Jalongo, M. R. (1999a). Editorial: On behalf of children. "'Is Pennsylvania really pink?' Young children as questioners." *Early Childhood Education Journal, 27*(1), 1–4.

Jalongo, M. R. (1999b). Matters of size: Obesity as a diversity issue in the field of early childhood. *Early Childhood Education Journal, 27*(2), 95–103.

Jalongo, M. R. (2000). Editorial: On behalf of children: First hand experiences with children's food allergies and intolerances. *Early Childhood Education Journal, 28*(2), 75–77.

Jalongo, M. R. (2003). A position paper of the Association for Childhood Education International: The child's right to creative thought and expression. *Childhood Education, 79*(4), 218–228.

James, J. C., & Granovetter, R. F. (1987). *Waterworks: A new book of water play activities for children age 1 to 6*. Lewisville, NC: Kaplan.

Javernick, E. (1988). Johnny's not jumping: Can we help obese children? *Young Children, 43*(2), 18–23.

Jenkins, E. (1997). *The Ella Jenkins song book for children*. New York: Music Sales Corp.

Jenkins, S. (1995). *Biggest, strongest, fastest*. New York: Ticknor & Fields.

Johnson, J. E. (1990). The role of play in cognitive development. In E. Klugman & S. Smilansky (Eds.), *Children's play and learning: Perspectives and policy implications*. New York: Teachers College Press.

Johnson, J. E., Christie, J. F., & Yawkey, T. D. (1998). *Play and early childhood development* (2nd ed.). New York: Longman.

Johnson, J. E., & Ershler, J. (1982). Curricular effects on the play of preschoolers. In D. J. Pepler & K. H. Rubin (Eds.), *The play of children: Current theory and research*. Basel, Switzerland: Karger.

Jones, E. (1977). *Dimensions of teaching-learning environments: Handbook for teachers*. Pasadena, CA: Pacific Oaks.

Jones, E., & Cooper, R. M. (2005) *Playing to get smart*. New York: Teachers College Press.

Jones, E., & Nimmo, J. (1994). *Emergent curriculum*. Washington, DC: National Association for the Education of Young Children.

Jones, E., & Prescott, E. (1978). *Dimensions of teaching-learning environments II: Focus on day care*. Pasadena, CA: Pacific Oaks.

Juster, N. (2005). *The hello, goodbye window*. New York: Michael di Capua Books.

Kaiser Family Foundation. (2003). *Zero to six: Electronic media in the lives of infants, toddlers, and preschoolers*. Washington, DC: Author.

Kamii, C. (1972). A sketch of the Piaget-derived preschool curriculum developed by the Ypsilanti Early Education Program. In S. J. Braun &

E. P. Edwards (Eds.), *History and theory of early childhood education*. Worthington, OH: Charles A. Jones.

Kamii, C., & Ewing, J. K. (1996). Basing teaching on Piaget's constructivism. *Childhood Education, 72*(5), 260–264.

Kaminsky, J. A. (2001). A conversation about family and community participation at Chicago Commons with Dorothy Kelsie-Miller, Jenny Seacat, and Miguel Archunda. *Innovations in Early Education: The International Reggio Exchange, 8*(3), 7–21.

Kampe, E. (1990). Children in health care: When the prescription is play. In E. Klugman & S. Smilansky (Eds.), *Children–Children's play and learning. Perspectives and policy implications*. New York: Teachers College Press.

Karnes, M. (2003). Art for children with special needs. *Scholastic Early Childhood Today, 18*(5), 39.

Karoly, L. A., & Bigelow, J. H. (2005). *The economics of investing in universal preschool in California*. Santa Monica: Rand.

Katz, L. (1992, February). *The Reggio approach*. The Hundred Languages of Children Conference, Oklahoma City.

Katz, L. (1998). Hunches from my travels. *Journal of Early Childhood Teacher Education, 9*(3), 307–313.

Katz, L. (2006, January 12). *Themes vs. study vs. projects*. Message posted to REGGIO-L electronic mailing list, archived at http://ecap.crc.uiuc.edu/listserv/reggio-l.html.

Katz, L., & Chard, S. (2000). *Engaging children's minds: The project approach* (Rev. ed.). Norwood, NJ: Ablex.

Katzen, M., & Henderson, A. (1994). *Pretend soup and other real recipes: A cookbook for preschoolers on up*. Berkeley, CA: Tricycle.

Kelly, N. T., & Kelly, B. J. (1997). *Physical education for preschool and primary grades*. Springfield, IL: Thomas.

Kendrick, A. S., Kaufman, R., & Messenger, K. P. (2002). *Healthy*

young children: A manual for programs (Rev. ed.). Washington, DC: National Association for the Education of Young Children.

Keyser, J. (2001). Creating partnerships with families: Problem solving through communication. *Child Care Information Exchange, 138*, 44–47.

Kinsey, A. C., Pomeroy, W. B., & Martin, C. E. (1948). *Sexual behavior in the human male*. Philadelphia: Saunders.

Kinsey, A. C., Pomeroy, W. B., Martin, C. E., & Gebhard, P. H. (1953). *Sexual behavior in the human female*. Philadelphia: Saunders.

Kirkland, L. D., & Patterson, J. (2005). Developing oral language in primary classrooms. *Early Childhood Education Journal, 32*(6), 3991–3995.

Knutson, J. F., & Bower, M. E. (1994). Physically abusive parenting as an escalated aggressive response. In M. Potegal & J. F. Knutson (Eds.), *The dynamics of aggression: Biological and social processes in dyads and groups*. Hillsdale, NJ: Erlbaum.

Kohl, M. F. (1989). *Mudworks: Creative clay, dough, and modeling experiences*. Bellingham, WA: Bright Ring.

Kohn, A. (1999). *Punished by rewards: The trouble with gold stars, incentive plans, A's, praise, and other bribes* (Rev. ed.). Boston: Houghton Mifflin.

Kohn, A. (2000a). Art for art's sake. In S. Nagel (Ed.), *Creativity: Being usefully innovative in solving diverse problems*. Huntington, NY: Nova Science Publishers.

Kohn, A. (2000b). *The case against standardized testing: Raising the scores, ruining the schools*. Portsmouth, NH: Heinemann.

Kohn, A. (2001). Five reasons to stop saying "Good job!" *Young Children, 56*(5), 24–28.

Koplewitz, H. S., Goodman, R. F., & Rosen, M. D. (1999). *Childhood revealed: Art expressing pain, discovery & hope*. New York: Abrams.

Koplow, L. (1996). *Unsmiling faces: How preschools can heal*. New York: Teachers College Press.

Koplow, L. (2002). *Creating schools that heal: Real-life solutions.* New York: Teachers College Press.

Koralek, D. (2004). *Spotlight on young children and play.* Washington, DC: National Association for the Education of Young Children.

Kostelnik, M. J. (2004). Modeling ethical behavior in the classroom. *Child Care Information Exchange, 16,* 34–37.

Kostelnik, M. J., Soderman, A. K., & Whiren, A. P. (1999). *Developmentally appropriate curriculum: Best practices in early childhood education* (2nd ed.). Upper Saddle River, NJ: Merrill/Prentice Hall.

Kramer, D. C. (1989). *Animals in the classroom: Selection, care, and observation.* Menlo Park, MA: Addison-Wesley.

Krathwohl, D. R., Bloom, B. S., & Masia, B. B. (1964). *Taxonomy of educational objectives: Handbook II.* New York: McKay.

Krauss, R., & Johnson, C. (1971). *The carrot seed.* New York: Scholastic.

Kritchevsky, L., Prescott, E., & Walling, L. (1996). How to analyze play space. In K. M. Paciorek & J. G. Munro (Eds.), *Sources: Notable selections in early childhood education.* Guilford, CT: Dushkin.

Kritchevsky, M. (1998). *Project Spectrum: Preschool assessment handbook.* New York: Teachers College Press.

Labov, W. (1970). The logic of nonstandard English. In F. Williams (Ed.), *Language and poverty.* Chicago: Markham.

LaCerva, V. (1999). Adverse effects of witnessing violence. *Child Care Information Exchange, 130,* 44–49.

Lally, J. R., Griffin, A., Fenichel, E., Segal, M., Szanton, E., & Weissbourd, B. (2003). *Caring for infants and toddlers in groups: Developmentally appropriate practice* (Rev. ed.). Arlington, VA: Zero to Three/The National Center.

Ledderose, L. (2000). *Ten thousand things: Module and mass production in Chinese art.* Princeton, NJ: Princeton University Press.

Leifer, A. S., & Lesser, G. S. (1976). *The development of career awareness in young children: NIE papers on education and work, No. 1.* Washington, DC: U.S. Department of Health, Education and Welfare; National Institute of Education.

Lemley, V., & Lemley, I. (1976). *Zucchini cookbook.* Cave Junction, OR: Wilderness House.

Lenox, M. R. (2000). Storytelling for young children in a multicultural world. *Early Childhood Education Journal, 28*(2), 97–110.

Levin, D. E. (2003). *Teaching young children in violent times: Building a peaceable classroom.* (2nd ed.). Washington, DC: National Association for the Education of Young Children and Educators for Social Responsibility.

Levin, D. E., & Lobo, B. (2000). Learning about the world through play. *Scholastic Early Childhood Today, 15*(3), 56–64, 71.

Lillard, A., & Curenton, S. (1999). Research in review: Do young children understand what others feel, want, and know? *Young Children, 54*(5), 52–57.

Linder, T. W. (1999). *Read, play, and learn! Storybook activities for young children: Teacher's guide.* Baltimore: Brookes.

Lindfors, J. W. (1999). *Children's inquiry: Using language to make sense of the world.* New York: Teachers College Press.

Lively, V., & Lively, E. (1991). *Sexual development of young children.* Albany, NY: Delmar.

Livingston, M. C. (1994). *Animals, vegetables, minerals: Poems about small things.* New York: HarperCollins.

Losardo, A., & Notari-Syverson, A. (2001). *Alternative approaches to assessing young children.* Baltimore: Brookes.

Lundgren, D., & Morrison, J. W. (2003). Involving Spanish-speaking families in early education programs. *Young Children, 58*(3), 88–95.

Lynee-Garbe, C., & Hoot, J. L. (2005). Weighing in on the issue of childhood obesity. *Childhood Education, 81*(2), 70–76.

Maag, J. W. (2001). Rewarded by punishment: Reflections on the disuse of positive reinforcement in schools. *Exceptional Children, 67*(2), 173–186.

MacDonald, S. (1996). *Squish, sort, paint, & build: Over 200 easy learning center activities.* Beltsville, MD: Gryphon House.

MacDonald, S. (1997). *The portfolio and its use: A road map for assessment.* Little Rock: Southern Early Childhood Association.

Mallory, B. L., & New, R. S. (Eds.). (1993). *Diversity and developmentally appropriate practices: Challenges for early childhood education.* New York: Teachers College Press.

Maloney, C. (2000). The role of ritual in preschool settings. *Early Childhood Education Journal, 27*(3), 143–150.

Mantzicopoulos, P. (1999). Risk assessment of Head Start children with the Brigance K1 Screen: Differential performances by sex, age, and predictive accuracy for early school achievement and special education placement. *Early Childhood Research Quarterly, 14*(3), 383–408.

Maratsos, M. P. (1989). Innateness and plasticity in language acquisition. In M. L. Rice & R. L. Schiefelbusch (Eds.), *The teaching ability of language.* Baltimore: Brookes.

Marion, M. (2007). *Guidance of young children* (7th ed.). Upper Saddle River, NJ: Merrill/Prentice Hall.

Marotz, R., Cross, M. Z., & Rush, J. M. (2001). *Health, safety, and nutrition for the young child* (5th ed.). Albany, NY: Delmar.

Marshall, N. L., Robeson, W. W., & Keefe, N. (1999). Gender equity in early childhood education. *Young Children, 54*(4), 9–13.

Masters, W. H., Johnson, V. E., & Kolodny, R. C. (1994). *Heterosexuality.* New York: HarperCollins.

McAfee, O. D. (1981). Planning the preschool program. In M. Kaplan-Sanoff and R. Yablans-Magid

(Eds.), *Exploring early childhood: Readings in theory and practice*. New York: Macmillan.

McAfee, O. (1985). Circle time: Getting past "Two Little Pumpkins." *Young Children, 40*(6), 24–29.

McBride, S. C. (1999). Research in review: Family centered practices. *Young Children, 54*(3), 62–68.

McClosky, R. (1948). *Blueberries for Sal*. New York: Viking.

McDermott, G. (1972). *Anansi the spider*. New York: Holt.

McGinn, B. (2005, December). *The World Trade Center memorial park for children: How six- and seven-year-olds created a comprehensive memorial design*. Paper presented at the conference of the National Association for the Education of Young Children, Washington, DC.

McKee, B. (2005, April 28). Growing up denatured. *New York Times*, p. D1.

McMullan, K. (2004). *Baby goose*. New York: Hyperion.

McNeill, D. (1970). The development of language. In P. H. Mussen (Ed.), *Carmichael's manual of child psychology* (Vol. 1). 3rd ed. New York: Wiley.

Mei, Z., Scanlon, K. S., Grummer-Strawn, L. M., Freedman, D. S., Yip, R., & Trowbridge, F. L. (1998, January). Increasing prevalence of overweight among U.S. low-income preschool children: The Centers for Disease Control and Prevention Pediatric Nutrition Surveillance, 1983 to 1995. *Pediatrics Electronic Pages*, Available online at the Web site of *Prediatrics*, the official journal of the American Academy of Pediatrics (www.pediatrics.org). *101*(1), e12.

Meisels, S. J., & Atkins-Burnett, S. (2005). *Developmental screening in early childhood: A guide*. (5th ed.). Washington, DC: National Association for the Education of Young Children.

Meisels, S. J., & Fenichel, E. (Eds.). (2000). *New visions for the developmental assessment of infants and young children*. Washington, DC: Zero to Three.

Meisels, S. J., Jablon, J., Marsden, D., Dichtelmiller, N., Dorfman, A., & Steele, D. (1994). *The work sampling system: An overview*. Ann Arbor, MI: Rebus Planning Associates.

Mendoza, J., Katz, L. G., Robertson, A. S., & Rothenberg, D. (2003). *Connecting with parents in the early years*. Champaign: IL: Clearinghouse on Early Education and Parenting.

Mercurio, C. M. (2003). Guiding boys in the early years to lead healthy emotional lives. *Early Childhood Education Journal, 30*(4), 255–258.

Mikkelsen, E. J. (1997). Responding to allegations of sexual abuse in child care and early childhood education programs. *Young Children, 52*(3), 45–51.

Miller, K. (1989). *The outside play and learning book: Activities for young children*. Mount Rainier, MD: Gryphon House.

Miller, R. (1999). *The developmentally appropriate inclusive classroom in early education*. Albany, NY: Delmar.

Miller, S. A. (1994). *Learning through play: Sand, water, clay and wood*. New York: Scholastic.

Miller, S. A. (2000). Learning to show kindness. *Scholastic Early Childhood Today, 15*(10), 45–47.

Miller, S. A. (2003). How children build skills through art. *Scholastic Early Childhood Today, 18*(5), 26–28.

Miller, S. E. (1999). Balloons, blankets, and balls: Gross-motor activities to use indoors. *Young Children, 54*(5), 58–63.

Mind in the Making. (2005). *What is early learning?* Washington, DC: Families and Work Institute.

Mindel, C. H., Habenstein, R. W., & Wright, R. (Eds.). (1988). *Ethnic families in America: Patterns and variations* (4th ed.). Upper Saddle River, NJ: Prentice Hall.

Mitchell, L.S. (1948). *The here and now story book*. New York: Dutton.

Mize, J. (1995). Coaching preschool children in social skills: A cognitive-social learning curriculum. In

G. Carledge & J. F. Milburn, (Eds.), *Teaching social skills to children and youth* (3rd ed.). Boston: Allyn & Bacon.

Molitor, F., & Hirsch, K. W. (1994). Children's toleration of real-life aggression after exposure to media violence: A replication of the Drabman and Thomas studies. *Child Study Journal, 24*(3), 191–195.

Moller, D. W. (1996). *Confronting death: Values, institutions, and human morality*. Cambridge: Oxford University Press.

Monahon, C. (1993). *Children and trauma: A parent's guide to helping children heal*. New York: Free Press.

Monighan-Nourot, P., Scales, B., Van Hoorn, J., with Almy, M. (1987). *Looking at children's play: A bridge between theory and practice*. New York: Teachers College Press.

Moomaw, S. (1997). *More than singing: Discovering music in preschool and kindergarten*. St. Paul, MN: Redleaf.

Moomaw, S., & Hieronymus, B. (1995). *More than counting: Whole math activities for preschool and kindergarten*. St. Paul, MN: Redleaf.

Moomaw, S., & Hieronymus, B. (1997). *More than magnets: Exploring the wonders of science in preschool and kindergarten*. St. Paul, MN: Redleaf.

Moore, R. C., & Wong, H. H. (1997). *Natural learning: Creating environment for rediscovering nature's way of teaching: The life history of an environmental schoolyard*. Berkeley, CA: MIG Communications.

Moore, T. (1991). *My magical world—I am special: Singing, moving, and learning*. Charlotte, NC: Thomas Moore Records.

Morse, P. S., & Brand, L. B. (1995). *Young children at home and in school: 212 educational activities for their parents, teachers, and caregivers*. Boston: Allyn & Bacon.

Moyer, J. (Ed.). (1995). *Selecting educational equipment and materials for school and home*. Olney, MD: Association for Childhood Education International.

Murphy, L. B., & Moriarty, A. E. (1976). *Vulnerability, coping, and growth from infancy to adolescence*. New Haven, CT: Yale University Press.

Muth, J. J. (2005). *Zen stories*. New York: Scholastic Press.

Nager, N., & Shapiro, E. K. (Eds.). (2000). *Revisiting a progressive pedagogy: The developmental interaction approach*. Albany: State University of New York.

Nakayama, T. K., & Martin, J. N. (Eds.). (1999). *Whiteness: The communication of social identity*. Thousand Oaks, CA: Sage.

Nash, J. M. (1997, February 3). Fertile minds: Special report. *Time*, pp. 48–56.

National Association for the Education of Young Children. (1988). National Association for the Education of Young Children position statement on standardized testing of young children 3 through 8 years of age. *Young Children, 43*(3), 42–47.

National Association for the Education of Young Children. (1990). National Association for the Education of Young Children position statement on school readiness. *Young Children, 46*(1), 21–23.

National Association for the Education of Young Children. (1995). *National Association for the Education of Young Children position statement: Responding to linguistic and cultural diversity: Recommendations for effective early childhood education*. Washington, DC: Author.

National Association for the Education of Young Children. (1996). *Position statement on technology and young children—Ages three through eight*. Washington, DC: Author.

National Association for the Education of Young Children. (1997). National Association for the Education of Young Children position statement on the prevention of child abuse in early childhood programs and the responsibilities of early childhood professionals to prevent child abuse. *Young Children, 52*(3), 42–46.

National Association for the Education of Young Children. (2005). *Early childhood program standards and accreditation performance criteria* (Rev. ed.). Washington, DC: Author.

National Association for the Education of Young Children & National Association of Early Childhood Specialists in State Departments of Education. (2003). *Position statement on early learning standards: Creating the conditions for success*. Washington, DC: Authors.

National Black Child Development Institute. (1995). *Young children and African American literature*. Washington, DC: National Association for the Education of Young Children.

National Institute for Early Education Research. (2006). NIEER multi-state study finds meaningful gains from pre-k. Special Report. *Preschool Matters, 4*(1), 5.

National Institutes of Health. (2005). *Statistics related to overweight and obesity*. Washington, DC: Author.

National Research Council and Institute of Medicine. (2000). *From neurons to neighborhoods: The science of early childhood development*. Washington, DC: National Academy Press.

Neisworth, J. T. (2000). Behavior analysis and principles in early childhood education. In J. L. Roopnarine & J. E. Johnson (Eds.), *Approaches to early childhood education* (3rd ed.). Upper Saddle River, NJ: Merrill/Prentice Hall.

Nelson, E. (1987). Learned helplessness and children's achievement. In S. Moore & K. Kolb (Eds.), *Reviews of research for practitioners and parents*. Minneapolis: Center for Early Education and Development, University of Minnesota.

Nelsen, J., Erwin, C., & Duffy, R. (1998). *Positive discipline for preschoolers: Raising children who are responsible, respectful, and resourceful* (2nd ed.). Rocklin, CA: Prima.

Neugebauer, B. (1988). Raising the issues. *Child Care Information Exchange, 69*, 31.

Neuman, S. B. (2006). Speak up! How to help children build rich vocabulary day by day. *Scholastic Early Childhood Today, 20*(4), 12–13.

Neuman, S. B., Copple, C., & Bredekamp, S. (2000). *Learning to read and write: Developmentally appropriate practices for young children*. Washington, DC: National Association for the Education of Young Children.

Neuman, S. B., & Roskos, K. (2005). What ever happened to developmentally appropriate practice in early literacy? *Young Children, 60*(4), 22–26.

New, R. (2000). Reggio Emilia: An approach or an attitude? In J. L. Roopnarine & J. E. Johnson (Eds.), *Approaches to early childhood education* (3rd ed.). Upper Saddle River, NJ: Merrill/Prentice Hall.

Nilsen, B. A. (1997). *Week by week: Plans for observing and recording young children*. Albany, NY: Delmar.

Norton, D. E. (1999). *Through the eyes of a child: An introduction to children's literature* (5th ed.). Upper Saddle River, NJ: Merrill/Prentice Hall.

Numeroff, L. J. (1985). *If you give a mouse a cookie*. New York: Harper & Row.

Nunnelley, J., & Fields, T. (1999). Anger, dismay, guilt, anxiety—The realities and roles in reporting child abuse. *Young Children, 54*(5), 74–79.

Oden, S., Schweinhart, L. J., & Weikart, D. P. (2000). *Into adulthood: A study of the effects of Head Start*. Ypsilanti, MI: High/Scope.

Ohtake, Y., Santos, R. M., & Fowler, S. A. (2000). It's a three-way conversation: Families, service providers, and interpreters. *Young Exceptional Children, 4*(1), 12–18.

Oken-Wright, P. (1998). How does the gosling get in the egg? Five-year-olds and the co-construction of theory. *Innovations in Early Education: The International Reggio Exchange, 5*(4), 5–8.

Oken-Wright, P. (2001). Documentation: Both mirror and

light. *Innovations in Early Education: The International Reggio Exchange*, 8(4), 5–15.

Oklahoma Child Care. (2000a). Creative construction: Unit blocks. *Oklahoma Child Care, 3,* 16–21.

Oklahoma Child Care. (2000b). Teach "5 a day" and the pyramid for better nutrition. *Oklahoma Child Care, 4,* 8–16.

Olds, A. R. (1998). Essay: Places of beauty. In D. Bergen (Ed.), *Play as a medium for learning and development.* Olney, MD: Association for Childhood Education International.

Oliver, S. J., & Klugman, E. (2005). Play and the outdoors: What's new under the sun? *Exchange, 164,* 6–12.

Olweus, D. (1991). Bully/victim problems among school children: Basic facts and effects of a school-based intervention program. In D. Pepler & K. H. Rubin (Eds.), *The development and treatment of childhood aggression.* Hillsdale, NJ: Erlbaum.

Owens, K. (1995). *Raising your child's inner self-esteem: The authoritative guide from infancy through the teen years.* New York: Plenum.

Owocki, G. (1999). *Literacy through play.* Portsmouth, NH: Heinemann.

Paintal, S. (1999). Banning corporal punishment of children: A position paper of the Association for Childhood Education International. *Childhood Education, 76*(1), 36–39.

Paley, V. G. (2005). *A child's work: The importance of fantasy play.* Chicago: University of Chicago Press.

Palmer, H. (n.d.). *Getting to know myself: Learning basic skills through music—The feel of music.* Freeport, NY: Educational Activities.

Palmer, H., & Cheney, M. (1984). Sittin' in a high chair. *Happy song.* Topanga, CA: Hap-Pal Music.

Pareete, H. P., & Petch-Hogan, B. (2000). Approaching families: Facilitating culturally/linguistically diverse family involvement. *Teaching Exceptional Children, 33*(2), 4–10.

Parkinson, K. (1986). *The enormous turnip.* Niles, IL: Whitman.

Parten, M. B. (1932). Social participation among preschool children. *Journal of Abnormal Psychology, 27,* 243–269.

Parten, M. B. (1996). Social participation among pre-school children. In K. M. Paciorek & J. H. Munro (Eds.), *Sources: Notable selections in early childhood education.* Guilford, CT: Dushkin.

Patterson, K., & Wright, A. E. (1990). The speech, language for hearing-impaired child: At-risk academically. *Childhood Education, 67*(2), 91–95.

Paxson, C., Donahue, E., Orleans, C. T., & Grisso, J. A. (Eds.). (2006). Childhood obesity [Entire issue]. *The Future of Children, 16*(1).

Peisner-Freinberg, E. S., Curchinal, M. R., Clifford, R. M., Culkin, M. L., Howes, C., Kagan, S. L., Yazejian, N., Byler, P., Rustici, J., & Zelazo, J. (1999). *The children of the cost, quality, and outcomes study go to school: Executive summary.* Chapel Hill: University of North Carolina at Chapel Hill, Frank Porter Graham Child Development Center.

Pelo, A., & Davidson, F. (2000). *That's not fair! A teacher's guide to activism with young children.* St. Paul, MN: Redleaf.

Pepler, D. J. (1982). Play and divergent thinking. In D. J. Pepler & K. H. Rubin (Eds.), *The play of children: Current theory and research.* Basel, Switzerland: Karger.

Perry, B. D. (2000a). Creating an emotionally safe classroom. *Scholastic Early Childhood Today, 15*(1), 35–37.

Perry, B. D. (2000b). Curiosity: The fuel of development. *Scholastic Early Childhood Today, 15*(6), 22–23.

Perry, B. D. (2001). Death and loss: Helping children manage their grief. *Scholastic Early Childhood Today, 15*(4), 22–23.

Peters, D. (2000). *Taking cues from kids: How they think. What to do about it.* Portsmouth, NH: Heinemann.

Peterson, C., Maier, S. F., & Seligman, M. E. P. (1993). *Learned helplessness:*

A theory for the age of personal control. New York: Oxford University Press.

Petrakos, H., & Howe, N. (1996). The influence of the physical design of the dramatic play center on children's play. *Early Childhood Research Quarterly, 11*(1), 63–77.

Pfluger, L. W., & Zola, J. M. (1972). A room planned by children. In K. R. Baker (Ed.), *Ideas that work with young children.* Washington, DC: National Association for the Education of Young Children.

Phelps, P., & Hanline, M. F. (1999). Let's play blocks! Creating effective learning experiences for young children. *Teaching Exceptional Children, 32*(2), 62–67.

Piaget, J. (1954). *The construction of reality in the child.* New York: Basic Books.

Piaget, J. (1962). *Play, dreams, and imitation in childhood.* New York: Norton.

Piaget, J. (1976). Symbolic play. In J. S. Bruner, A. Jolly, & K. Sylva (Eds.), *Play—Its role in development and evolution.* New York: Basic Books.

Piaget, J. (1983). Piaget's theory. In W. Kessen (Ed.), *Handbook of child psychology: Vol. 1. History, theory, and methods.* New York: Wiley.

Piaget, J., & Inhelder, B. (1969). *The psychology of the child* (translated by H. Weaver). New York: Basic Books.

Pica, R. (1999). *Moving and learning across the curriculum.* Albany, NY: Delmar.

Pica, R. (2000). *Experiences in movement with music, activities, and theory* (2nd ed.). Albany, NY: Delmar.

Pikulski, J. J. (2005, December). *Principles of effective preschool curriculum.* Paper presented at the conference of the National Association for the Education of Young Children, Washington, DC.

Plutro, M. (2005). Program performance standards: Supporting home language and English acquisition. *Head Start Bulletin, 78,* 4–5.

Pollman, M. J. (2000). Using technology to document children's work. *Journal of Early Childhood Teacher Education, 21*(2), 261–267.

Poole, C., Miller, S. A., & Church, E. B. (1998). Reassuring routines and rituals. *Scholastic Early Childhood Today, 13*(1), 25–29.

Porter, L. (1999). *Young children's behavior: Practical approaches for caregivers and teachers.* Sydney, Australia: Maclennan & Petty.

Poskitt, E. M. (1998). Nutritional problems of preschool children. In M. J. Sadler, J. J. Strain, & B. Caballero (Eds.), *Encyclopedia of human nutrition.* New York: Academic Press.

Power, B. (1999). *Parent power: Energizing home–school communication.* Portsmouth, NH: Heinemann.

Pratt, C. (1948). *I learn from children: An adventure in progressive education.* New York: Simon & Schuster.

Prelutsky, C. (Ed.). (1986). *Read-aloud rhymes for the very young.* New York: Knopf.

Pretti-Frontczak, K., & Bricker, D. (2000). Enhancing the quality of individualized education plan (IEP) goals and objectives. *Journal of Early Intervention, 23*(2), 92–105.

Provenzo, E. F., Jr., & Brett, A. (1983). *The complete block book.* Syracuse, NY: Syracuse University Press.

Puckett, M., Marshall, C. S., & Davis, R. (1999). Examining the emergence of brain development research: The promises and the perils. *Childhood Education, 76*(1), 8–12.

Raffi. (1987). *Down by the bay.* New York: Crown.

Raines, S. C., & Canady, R. J. (1989). *Story s-t-r-e-t-c-h-e-r-s: Activities to expand children's favorite books.* Mt. Rainier, MD: Gryphon House.

Raines, S. C., & Canady, R. J. (1991). *More story s-t-r-e-t-c-h-e-r-s: More activities to expand children's favorite books.* Mt. Rainier, MD: Gryphon House.

Raines, S., & Isbell, R. (1994). *Stories: Children's literature in early education.* Albany, NY: Delmar.

Ramsey, P. G. (1995). Research in review: Growing up with the contradictions of race and class. *Young Children, 50*(6), 18–22.

Rasmussen, M. (1979). *Listen! The children speak.* Washington, DC: OMEP, U.S. National Committee, Region III.

Raver, S. A. (2005). Using family-based practices for young children with special needs in preschool programs. *Childhood Education, 82*(1), 9–13.

Readdick, C. A., & Chapman, P. L. (2000). Young children's perceptions of time out. *Journal of Research in Childhood Education, 13*(1), 81–87.

Rector, S. (2006). Keeping learning alive: No child left behind. *Exchange, 167,* 28–30.

Redleaf, R. (1993). *Busy fingers, growing minds: Finger-plays, verses, and activities for whole language learning.* St. Paul, MN: Redleaf.

Redleaf, R., & Robertson, A. (1999) *Learn and play the recycle way: Homemade toys that teach.* St. Paul, MN: Redleaf.

Reid, T. R. (2005, December 15). School suspension reflects national language debate. *Denver Post,* p. 25A.

Rescorla, L., Hyson, M. C., & Hirsh-Pasek, K. (Eds.). (1991). Academic instruction in early childhood: Challenge or pressure? *New Directions for Child Development, 53,* entire issue.

Rey, H. A. (1941). *Curious George.* Boston: Houghton Mifflin.

Reynolds, G., & Jones, E. (1997). *Master players: Learning from children at play.* New York: Teachers College Press.

Rhoten, L., & Lane, M. (2001). More than the ABCs: The new alphabet books. *Young Children, 56*(1), 41–45.

Rice, M. L., & Wilcox, K. A. (Eds.). (1995). *Building a language-focused curriculum for the preschool classroom: Vol. I. A foundation for lifelong communication.* Baltimore: Brookes.

Rinaldi, C. (1994). *The philosophy of Reggio Emilia.* Paper presented at the Study Seminar on the Experience of the Municipal Infant-Toddler Centers and Pre-primary Schools of Reggio Emilia, Reggio Emilia, Italy.

Rinker, L. (2000). Active learning through art. *Child Care Information Exchange, 135,* 72–75.

Riojas-Cortez, M. (2000). It's all about talking: Oral language development in a bilingual classroom. *Dimensions of Early Childhood, 29*(1), 11–15.

Rivkin, M. S. (1995). *The great outdoors: Restoring children's right to play outside.* Washington, DC: National Association for the Education of Young Children.

Robertson, C. (1998). *Safety, nutrition, and health in early education.* Albany, NY: Delmar.

Rockwell, A., & Rockwell, H. (1971). *Molly's woodland garden.* Garden City, NY: Doubleday.

Rockwell, R., Hoge, D., & Search, B. (1999). *Linking language: Simple language and literacy activities throughout the curriculum.* Beltsville, MD: Gryphon House.

Rockwell, R., Williams, R., & Sherwood, E. (1992). *Everybody has a body: Science from head to toe: Activities book for teachers of children ages 3–6.* Mt. Rainier, MD: Gryphon House.

Roemer, J. (1980). *Two to four from 9 to 5: The adventures of a daycare provider.* New York: Harper & Row.

Roopnarine, J. L., Bright, J. A., & Riegraf, N. B. (1994). Family dynamics and day care children's peer group participation. In H. Goelman & E. V. Jacobs (Eds.), *Children's play in child care settings.* Albany: State University of New York Press.

Roopnarine, J. L., & Johnson, J. E. (1999). *Approaches to early childhood education* (3rd ed.). Upper Saddle River, NJ: Merrill/Prentice Hall.

Roopnarine, J. L., Johnson, J. E., & Hooper, F. H. (1994). *Children's play in diverse cultures.* Albany: State University of New York.

Rosenkoetter, S. E., & Squires, S. (2000). Writing outcomes that make a difference for children and families. *Young Exceptional Children*, 4(1), 2–8.

Roskos, K. A., & Christie, J. F. (Eds.). (2000). *Play and literacy in early childhood: Research from multiple perspectives*. Mahwah, NJ: Erlbaum.

Ross, M. E. (1995). *Sandbox scientist: Real science adventures for little kids*. Chicago: Chicago Review Press.

Rowe, M. B. (1974). Wait time and reward as instructional variables, their influence on language, logic and fate control: Part 1, wait time. *Journal of Research on Science Teaching, 11*, 81–94.

Rubin, K. (1977). The play behaviors of young children. *Young Children, 32*(6), 16–24.

Rubin, K. H. (1982). Early play theories revisited: Contributions to contemporary research and theory. In D. J. Pepler & K. H. Rubin (Eds.), *The play of children: Current theory and research*. Basel, Switzerland: Karger.

Rubin, K. H., & Howe, N. (1986). Social play and perspective taking. In G. Fein & M. Rivkin (Eds.), *The young child at play: Reviews of research* (Vol. 4). Washington, DC: National Association for the Education of Young Children.

Russ, S. S. (1996). Development of creative processes in children. *New Directions for Child Development, 72*, 31–42.

Russell, B. (1926). *Education and the good life*. New York: Boni & Liveright.

Sadker, M., & Sadker, D. (1994). *Failing at fairness: How our schools cheat girls*. New York: Simon & Schuster.

Sadler, M. J., Strain, J. J., & Caballero, B. (1999). *Encyclopedia of Human Nutrition* (Vols. 1–3). New York: Academic Press.

Saifer, S. (1990). *Practical solutions to practically every problem: The early childhood teacher's manual*. St. Paul, MN: Toys 'n Things Press.

Sallis, J. F., Patterson, R. L., McKenzie, T. L., & Nader, P. R. (1988). Family variables and physical activity in

preschool children. *Journal of Developmental and Behavioral Pediatrics, 9*(2), 57–61.

Saltz, R. (1997). The Reggio Emilia influence at the University of Michigan-Dearborn Child Development Center: Challenges and change. In J. Hendrick (Ed.), *First steps toward teaching the Reggio way*. Upper Saddle River, NJ: Merrill/Prentice Hall.

Samalin, N. (1991). *Love and anger: The parental dilemma*. New York: Viking.

Samalin, N., & Jablow, M. M. (1987). *Loving your child is not enough*. New York: Viking.

Sandall, S., McLean, M. E., & Smith, B. J. (2000). *DEC recommended practice in early intervention early childhood special education*. Longmont, CO: Division for Early Childhood of the Council for Exceptional Children.

Sandberg, A., & Pramling-Samuelsson, I. (2005). An interview study of gender differences in preschool teachers' attitudes toward children's play. *Early Childhood Education Journal, 32*(5), 297–305.

Sanders, S. W. (2002). *Active for life: Developmentally appropriate movement programs for young children*. Washington, DC: National Association for the Education of Young Children.

Saracho, O. N., & Spodek, B. (Eds.). (1998). *Multiple perspectives in early childhood education*. Albany: State University of New York Press.

Satter, E. (1987). *How to get your kid to eat . . . but not too much*. Palo Alto, CA: Bull.

Satter, E. (2000). *Child of mine: Feeding with love and good sense*. Palo Alto, CA: Bull.

Schardt, D. (2001). Food allergies. *Nutrition Action Health Letter, 28*(3), 13.

Schirrmacher, R. (1998). *Art and creative development for young children* (3rd ed.). Albany, NY: Delmar.

Schwartzman, H. B. (1978). *Transformations: The anthropology of children's play*. New York: Plenum.

Schweinhart, L. J., Montie, J., Yiang, Z., Barnett, W. S., & Belfield, C. R. (2005). *Lifetime effects: The High/Scope Perry Preschool project through age 40*. Ypsilanti, MI: High/Scope.

Schweinhart, L. J., & Weikart, D. P. (1997). *Lasting differences: The High/Scope Preschool Curriculum Comparison Study through age 23*. Ypsilanti, MI: High/Scope.

Scuola Diana. (1991). *Scarpa E metro I bambini E la nusura*. Reggio Emilia: Author.

Seefeldt, C. (Ed.). (1999). *The early childhood curriculum: Current findings in theory and practice* (3rd ed.). New York: Teachers College Press.

Seefeldt, C., & Barbour, N. (1998). *Early childhood education: An introduction* (4th ed.). Upper Saddle River, NJ: Merrill/Prentice Hall.

Seeger, R. C. (1980). *American folk songs for children*. Garden City, NY: Doubleday.

Selsam, M. (1965). *Let's get turtles*. New York: Harper & Row.

Serbin, L. A. (1980). Play activities and the development of visual-spatial skills. *Equal Play, Fall*, 6–9.

Serbin, L. A., O'Leary, K. D., Kent, R. N., & Tonick, E. J. (1973). A comparison of teacher response to preacademic and problem behavior of boys and girls. *Child Development, 22*, 796–804.

Sharmat, M. (1980). *Gregory the terrible eater*. New York: Four Winds Press.

Shearer, D. E. (1993). The Portage Project: An international home approach to early intervention of young children and their families. In J. L. Roopnarine & J. E. Johnson (Eds.), *Approaches to early childhood education* (2nd ed.). New York: Merrill/Macmillan.

Shefatya, L. (1990). Socioeconomic status and ethnic differences in sociodramatic play: Theoretical and practical implications. In E. L. Klugman & S. Smilansky

(Eds.), *Children's play and learning: Perspectives and policy implications.* New York: Teachers College Press.

Shelov, S. P., & Hannemann, R. E. (Eds.). (2004). *The American Academy of Pediatrics complete and authoritative guide: Caring for your baby and young child, birth to age 5* (4th ed.). New York: Bantam Books.

Shepard, L. A., Kagan, S. L., & Wurtz, E. (1998). Public policy report: Goal 1, Early Childhood Assessments Resource Group recommendations. *Young Children, 53*(3), 52–54.

Shonkoff, J. P., & Meisels, S. (2000). *Handbook of early childhood intervention* (2nd ed.). Cambridge, England: Cambridge University Press.

Shonkoff, J. P., & Phillips, D. Z. (Eds.). (1999). *From neurons to neighborhoods: The science of early childhood development.* Washington, DC: National Academy Press.

Shore, R. (1997). *Rethinking the brain: New insights into early development.* New York: Families and Work Institute and National Association for the Education of Young Children.

Shure, M. B. (1994). *Raising a thinking child: Help your young child to resolve everyday conflicts and get along with others.* New York: Holt.

Siegel, D. J. (1999). *The developing mind: Toward a neurology of interpersonal experience.* New York: Guilford.

Siegler, R. W. (1998). *Children's thinking* (3rd ed.). Upper Saddle River, NJ: Merrill/Prentice Hall.

Sigel, I. E., & Cocking, R. R. (1977). *Cognitive development from childhood to adolescence: A constructivist perspective.* New York: Holt, Rinehart & Winston.

Singer, D. G., & Revenson, T. A. (1998). *A Piaget primer: How a child thinks* (Rev. ed.). Madison, CT: International Universities Press.

Skeen, P., Garner, A. P., & Cartwright, S. (1984). *Woodworking for young children.* Washington, DC: National Association for the Education of Young Children.

Skinner, B. F. (1954). The science of learning and the art of teaching. *Harvard Educational Review, 24,* 86–97.

Skinner, B. F. (1957). *Verbal behavior.* New York: Appleton-Century-Crofts.

Skinner, B. F. (1974). *About behaviorism.* New York: Knopf.

Small, D. (2000). *Imogene's antlers.* New York: Crown.

Smilansky, S. (1968). *The effects of sociodramatic play in disadvantaged children.* New York: Wiley.

Smilansky, S., & Shefatya, L. (1990). *Facilitating play: A medium for promoting cognitive, socioemotional, and academic development in young children.* Gaithersburg, MD: Psychosocial and Educational Publications.

Smith, C. (1993). *The peaceful classroom: 162 activities to teach preschoolers compassion and cooperation.* Mt. Rainier, MD: Gryphon.

Smith, J. H. (1966). *Setting conditions for creative teaching.* Boston: Allyn & Bacon.

Smith, M. S., & Bissell, J. S. (1970). Report analysis: The impact of Head Start. *Harvard Educational Review, 14,* 51–104.

Smith, N. R., Fucigna, C., Kennedy, M., & Lord, L. (1993). *Experience and art: Teaching children to paint* (2nd ed.). New York: Teachers College Press.

Smith, P. K., Morita, Y., Junger-Tas, J., Olweus, D., Catalano, R., & Slee, P. (Eds.), *The nature of school bullying: A cross-national perspective.* London: Routledge.

Smith, P. K., & Sharp, S. (1994). *School bullying: Insights and perspectives.* London: Routledge.

Smith, R. M., Salend, S. J., & Ryan, S. (2001). Watch your language: Closing or opening the special education curtain. *Teaching Exceptional Children, 33*(4), 18–23.

Smith, S. S. (1999). Early childhood mathematics. In *Dialogue on early childhood science, mathematics, and technology education.* Washington, DC: American Association for the Advancement of Science.

Smitherman, G. (2000a). *Black talk: Words and phrases from the hood to the Amen corner* (Rev. ed.). Boston: Houghton Mifflin.

Smitherman, G. (2000b). *Talkin that talk: Language, culture, and education in African America.* London: Routledge.

Snow, C. E., Burns, M. S., & Griffin, P. (1998). *Preventing reading difficulties in young children.* Washington, DC: National Academy Press.

Snyder, R., Snyder, M., & Snyder, R., Jr. (1989). *The young child as a person.* New York: Human Sciences.

Solter, A. (1992). Understanding tears and tantrums. *Young Children, 47*(5), 64–68.

Sonnenschein, S., Baker, L., Serpell, R., & Schmidt, D. (2000). Reading as a source of entertainment: The importance of the home perspective for children's literacy development. In K. A. Roskos & J. F. Christie (Eds.), *Play and literacy in early childhood: Research from multiple perspectives.* Mahwah, NJ: Erlbaum.

Sosna, D. (2000). From our readers: Hurrah! Hurrah! Woodworking! *Young Children, 55*(2), 4, 96.

Southern Early Childhood Association. (1990). *Developmentally appropriate assessment: A position statement.* Little Rock: Author.

Southern Early Childhood Association. (1991). *Position paper: Supporting learning with technology in the early childhood classroom.* Little Rock: Author.

Spaggiari, S. (2004). The path toward knowledge: The social, political, and cultural context of the Reggio municipal infant-toddler center and preschool experience. *Innovations in Early Education: The International Reggio Exchange, 11*(2), 1–5.

Spodek, B., & Saracho, O. N. (1997). *Issues in early childhood educational assessment and evaluation: Yearbook in early childhood education* (Vol. 7). New York: Teachers College Press.

Spodek, B., & Saracho, O. N. (1998). The challenge of educational play. In D. Bergen (Ed.), *Play as a medium for learning and development*. Olney, MD: Association for Childhood Education International.

Sprang, G., & McNeil, J. (1995). *The many faces of bereavement: The nature and treatment of natural, traumatic, and stigmatized grief*. New York: Brunner/Mazel.

Springate, K. W., & Stegelin, D. A. (1999). *Building school and community partnerships through parent involvement*. Upper Saddle River, NJ: Merrill/Prentice Hall.

Sprung, B. (2006). Meeting the challenge of math and science. *Scholastic Early Childhood Today, 20*(4), 45–51.

Sridhar, C. (2000). Bibliotherapy for all: Enhancing reading comprehension, self-concept, and behavior. *Teaching Exceptional Children, 33*(2), 74–82.

Staley, L., & Portman, P. A. (2000). Red Rover, Red Rover, it's time to move over! *Young Children, 55*(1), 67–72.

Stangl, J. (1975). *Finger painting is fun!* Camarillo, CA: Educational Techniques.

Starko, A. J. (1995). *Creativity in the classroom: Schools of curious delight*. New York: Longman.

Steffe, L. P., & Gale, J. (Eds.). (1995). *Constructivism in education: Concerns about Vygotsky's theories*. Hillsdale, NJ: Erlbaum.

Stegelin, D. A. (2005). Making the case for play policy: Research based reasons to support play-based environments. *Young Children, 60*(2), 76–85.

Steig, W. (2000). *Wizzil*. New York: Farrar, Straus & Giroux.

Stein, D. (2005, November 15). You can walk your way to a longer life. *Denver Post*, p. 7A.

Stengle, J. (2005, April 19). Tots take early steps to obesity. *Denver Post*, pp. A1, A13.

Stephens, K. (1988). The first national study of sexual abuse in child care: Findings and recommendations. *Child Care Information Exchange, 60*, 9–12.

Stevens, J. (1995). *Tops and bottoms*. New York: Harcourt Brace.

Stewart, S. (1997). *The gardener*. New York: Farrar, Straus & Giroux.

Stinson, W. J. (Ed.). (1990). *Moving and learning for the young child*. Reston, VA: American Alliance for Health, Physical Education, Recreation, and Dance.

Stipek, D. (2005). Early childhood education at a crossroads. *Harvard Education Newsletter, July–August*. Retrieved October 2, 2005, from http://www.edletter.org/.

Stonehouse, A. (1995). What's love got to do with it? *Child Care Information Exchange, 102*, 18–21.

Sullivan, H. S. (1940). *Conceptions of modern psychiatry: The first William Alanson White Memorial Lectures*. Washington, DC: William Alanson White Psychiatric Foundation.

Sutton-Smith, B. (1987, December 9). Commentary: The domestication of early childhood play. *Education Week*, 28.

Swinney, B. (1999). *Healthy food for healthy kids: A practical and tasty guide to your child's nutrition*. New York: Meadowbrook.

Sylva, K., Bruner, J. S., & Genova, P. (1976). The role of play in the problem-solving of children 3–5 years old. In J. S. Bruner, A. Jolly, & K. Sylva (Eds.), *Play—Its role in development and evolution*. New York: Basic Books.

Szinovacz, M. E. (Ed.). (1998). *Handbook on grandparenthood*. Westport, CT: Greenwood Press.

Tabors, P. O. (1997). *One child, two languages: A guide for preschool educators of children learning English as a second language*. Baltimore: Brookes.

Tabors, P. O., & Lopez, L. M. (2005). How can teachers and parents help children become (and stay) bilingual? *Head Start Bulletin, 78*, 14–18.

Tambourlane, W. V. (1997). *The Yale guide to children's nutrition*. New Haven, CT: Yale University Press.

Tarini, E. (1997). Reflections on a year in Reggio Emilia: Key concepts in rethinking and learning the Reggio way. In J. Hendrick (Ed.), *First steps toward teaching the Reggio way*. Upper Saddle River, NJ: Merrill/Prentice Hall.

Tegano, D. W., Moran, J. D., DeLong, A. J., Brickey, J., & Ramassini, K. K. (1996). Designing classroom spaces: Making the most of time. *Early Childhood Education Journal, 23*(3), 135–141.

Temple, F. (1998). *Tiger soup: An Anansi story from Jamaica*. New York: Orchard.

Thatcher, D. H. (2001). Reading in the math class: Selecting and using picture books for math investigations. *Young Children, 56*(4), 20–26.

Theemes, T. (1999). *Let's go outside: Designing the early childhood playground*. Ypsilanti, MI: High/Scope.

Thomas, P., & Shepherd, W. (2000). Relaxation: Every child's right to be. *Child Care Information Exchange, 131*, 42–48.

Thomas, R. M. (1999a). *Comparing theories of child development* (5th ed.). Belmont, CA: Wadsworth.

Thomas, R. M. (1999b). *Human development theories: Windows on culture*. New York: Conron.

Thompson, S. C. (2005). *Children as illustrators: Making meaning through art and language*. Washington, DC: National Association for the Education of Young Children.

Tobias, E. (1994). The play behaviors of special needs children in integrated and non-integrated child-care settings. In H. Goelman & E. V. Jacobs (Eds.), *Children's play in child care settings*.

Albany, NY: State University of New York Press.

Tomes, R. R., & Fan, C. (2000). A cross-cultural comparison of Draw-A-Person, Draw-A-House-Tree and Piagetian cognitive tasks for Chinese and American children. *Journal of Early Childhood Teacher Education, 21*(2), 295–301.

Tomlinson, C. M. (Ed.). *Children's books from other countries.* New York: Scarecrow Press.

Topal, C. S., & Gandini, L. (1999). *Beautiful stuff! Learning with found materials.* Worcester, MA: Davis.

Trawick-Smith, J. (1988). "Let's say you're the baby, Okay?" Play leadership and following behavior of young children. *Young Children, 43*(5), 51–59.

Trelease, J. (2001). *Read-aloud handbook* (5th ed.). New York: Penguin Books.

Trepanier-Street, M. L., Hong, S. B., & Bauer, J. C. (2001). Using technology in Reggio-inspired long-term projects. *Early Childhood Education Journal, 28*(3), 181–188.

Trozzi, M. (1999). *Talking with children about loss: Words, strategies, and wisdom to help children cope with death, divorce, and other difficult times.* New York: Perigee.

Turbiville, V. P., Umbarger, G. T., & Guthrie, A. C. (2000). Fathers' involvement in programs for young children. *Young Children, 55*(4), 74–79.

Turnbull, R., & Cilley, M. (1999). *Explanations and implications of the 1997 amendments to IDEA.* Upper Saddle River, NJ: Merrill/Prentice Hall.

Tyler, R. W. (1950). *Basic principles of curriculum and instruction.* Chicago: University of Chicago Press.

UNICEF (2003). *The state of the world's children, table 3: Health.* New York: UNICEF House, Division of Communication.

U.S. Department of Agriculture. (1999). *Tips for using the food guide pyramid with young children 2 to 6 years old.* Washington, DC: Author.

U.S. Department of Education. (2005). *No child left behind.* Washington, DC: Author. Retrieved October 30, 2005, from the Web site of the U.S. Department of Education (http://www.ed.gov/nclb/landing.jhtml).

U.S. Department of Health and Human Services. (2003). *The obesity crisis in America.* Washington, DC: Author.

Van Ausdale, D., & Feagin, J. R. (2001). *The first R: How children learn race and racism.* New York: Rowman & Littlefield.

Vecchi, V. (1998). What kind of space for living well in school? In G. Ceppi & M. Zini (Eds.), *Children, spaces, relations: Metaproject for an environment for young children.* Reggio Emilia, Italy: Reggio Children.

Viorst, J. (1972). *The tenth good thing about Barney.* New York: Atheneum.

Vygotsky, L. (1966). *Thought and language.* Cambridge, MA: MIT Press.

Vygotsky, L. (1978). *The mind in society: The development of higher psychological processes.* Cambridge, MA: Harvard University Press.

Wachter, J. V. (1999). *Classroom volunteers: Uh-Oh! Or right on!* Thousand Oaks, CA: Corwin.

Wadsworth, B. J. (1996). *Piaget's theory of cognitive and affective development* (6th ed.). New York: Longman.

Walker, J. E., & Shea, T. M. (1999). *Behavior management: A practical approach for educators* (7th ed.). Upper Saddle River NJ: Merrill/Prentice Hall.

Wallerstein, J. S., Lewis, J. M., & Blakeslee, S. (2000). *The unexpected legacy of divorce.* New York: Hyperion.

Walsh, S., Smith, B. J., & Taylor, R. C. (2000). *IDEA requirements for preschoolers with disabilities: IDEA early childhood policy and practice guide.* Reston, VA: Council for Exceptional Children.

Wardle, F. (1999). *Tomorrow's children: Meeting the needs of multiracial and multiethnic children at home, in early childhood programs, and at school.* Denver: Center for the Study of Biracial Children.

Warner, P. (1996). *Healthy snacks for kids* (Rev.ed.). San Leandro, CA: Bristol.

Wassom, J. (1999). Do sweat the small stuff!! *Child Care Information Exchange, 128,* 24–27.

Weikart, D. (1999). *What should young children learn? Teacher and parent views in 15 countries.* Ypsilanti, MI: High/Scope.

Weikart, P. (2000). *Round the circle: Key experiences in movement for young children* (2nd ed.). Ypsilanti, MI: High/Scope.

Weinstein, C., & David, T. (1987). *Space for children: The built environment and children's development.* New York: Plenum.

Weitzman, E. (1992). *Learning language and loving it: A guide to promoting children's social and language development in early childhood settings.* Toronto: Hannen Centre.

Wellhousen, K. (1996). Girls can be bull riders, too! Supporting children's understanding of gender roles through children's literature. *Young Children, 51*(5), 79–83.

Wellhousen, K., & Kieff, J. (2001). *A constructivist approach to block play in early childhood.* Albany, NY: Delmar/Thomson.

Werner, E. E. (2000). Protective factors and individual resilience. In J. P. Shonkoff & S. J. Meisels (Eds.), *Handbook of early childhood intervention* (2nd ed.). Cambridge, England: Cambridge University Press.

Westermoreland, P. (1996). Coping with death: Helping students grieve. *Childhood Education, 72*(3), 157–160.

White, E. B. (1952). *Charlotte's web.* New York: Harper & Row.

White, R. W. (1968). Motivation reconsidered: The concept of competence. In M. Almy (Ed.), *Early childhood play: Selected readings related to cognition and motivation.* New York: Simon & Schuster.

Whitehurst, G. J., & Valdez-Menchaca, M. D. (1988). What is the role of reinforcement in early language acquisition? *Child Development, 59*, 430–440.

Whitin, P., & Whitin, D. J. (2003). Developing mathematical understanding along the yellow brick road. *Young Children, 58*(1), 36–40.

Wien, C. A. (1995). *Developmentally appropriate practice in stories of teacher practical knowledge.* New York: Teachers College Press.

Williams, L. R. (1999). Determining the early childhood curriculum: The evolution of goals and strategies through consonance and controversy. In C. Seefeldt (Ed.), *The early childhood curriculum: Current findings in theory and practice* (3rd ed.). New York: Teachers College Press.

Williams, R. A., Rockwell, R. E., & Sherwood, E. A. (1987). *Mudpies to magnets.* Mt. Rainier, MD: Gryphon House.

Williams, S. R. (1990). *Essentials of nutrition and diet therapy* (5th ed.). St. Louis: Mosby.

Willis, C. A. (2002). The grieving process in children: Strategies for understanding, educating, and reconciling children's perceptions of death. *Early Childhood Education Journal, 29*(4), 221–226.

Wilson, M. (1995). *The good-for-your-health all-Asian cookbook.* Washington, DC: Tuttle.

Wilt, J. V. (1996). Beyond stickers and popcorn parties. *Dimensions of Early Childhood, 24*(1), 17–20.

Wiltz, M. W., & Klein, E. L. (2001). "What do you do in child care?" Children's perceptions of high- and low-quality classrooms. *Early Childhood Research Quarterly, 16*(2), 209–236.

Wing, L. A. (1995). Play is NOT the work of the child: Young children's perceptions of work and play. *Early Childhood Research Quarterly, 10*(2), 223–247.

Wolchik, S. A., & Sandler, I. N. (Eds.). (1977). *Handbook of children's coping: Linking theory and intervention.* New York: Plenum.

Wolf, D. P., & Neugebauer, B. (1996). *More than numbers: Mathematical thinking in the early years.* Redmond, WA: Child Care Information Exchange Press.

Wolf, J. (1994). Singing with children is a cinch. *Young Children, 49*(4), 20–25.

Wolfgang, C. H. (1999). *Solving discipline problems: Methods and models for today's teachers* (4th ed.). Boston: Allyn & Bacon.

Wong, F. L. (1991). When learning a second language means losing the first. *Early Childhood Research Quarterly, 6*(3), 323–346.

Woodhead, M., Faulkner, D., & Littleton, K. (Eds.). (1998). *Cultural world of early childhood.* London: Routledge.

Workman, S., & Anziamo, M. C. (1996). Curriculum webs: Weaving connections from children to teachers. In K. M. Paciorek & J. H. Munro (Eds.), *Early childhood education* (pp. 96–97). Sluice Dock, CT: Dushkin.

Wortham, S. (1998). *Early childhood curriculum: Developmental bases for learning and teaching.* Upper Saddle River, NJ: Merrill/Prentice Hall.

Wortham, S. C. (2005). *Assessment in early childhood* (4th ed.). Upper Saddle River, NJ: Merrill/Prentice Hall.

Yang, O. S. (2000). Guiding children's verbal plan and evaluation during free play: An application of Vygotsky's genetic epistemology to the early childhood classroom. *Early Childhood Education Journal, 28*(1), 3–10.

Yelland, N. (1998). *Gender in early childhood.* London: Routledge.

Yolen, J. (1987). *Owl moon.* New York: Philomel.

York, S. (1998a) *Big as life: The everyday inclusive curriculum* (Vol. 1). St. Paul, MN: Redleaf.

York, S. (1998b). *Big as life: The everyday inclusive curriculum* (Vol. 2). St. Paul, MN: Redleaf.

York, S. (2003). *Roots and wings: Affirming culture in early childhood programs* (Rev. ed.). St. Paul, MN: Redleaf.

Zanger, V. V. (1991). Social and cultural dimensions of the education of language minority students. In A. N. Ambert (Ed.), *Bilingual education and English as a second language: A research handbook, 1988–1990.* New York: Garland.

Zarzour, K. (2000). *Facing the schoolyard bully: How to raise an assertive child in an aggressive world.* Buffalo, NY: Firefly.

Zeece, P. D. (2001). Meeting children's needs with quality literature. *Early Childhood Education Journal, 28*(3), 175–180.

Zhu, J. (2000, November). *Survey of contemporary preschool education in mainland China.* Lecture presented at the National Association for the Education of Young Children, Atlanta, GA.

Zinn, M. B., Hondagnew-Sotelo, P., & Messner, M. A. (Eds.). (2000). *Gender through the prism of difference* (2nd ed.). Boston: Allyn & Bacon.

Zuckerman, M. P. (1992). Editorial: George Bush: Evening in America. *U.S. News & World Report, 113*(10), 88.

Zukowski, G., & Dickson, A. (1990). *On the move: A handbook for exploring creative movement with young children.* Carbondale, IL: Southern Illinois University Press.

Zygmunt-Fillwalk, E., & Bilello, T. E. (2005). Parents' victory in reclaiming recess for their children. *Childhood Education, 82*(1), 19–23.

ACKNOWLEDGMENTS FOR CHAPTER-OPENING QUOTES

Chapter 1

From A. Stonehouse. (1995). What's love got to do with it? *Child Care Information Exchange, 102*, p. 20.

From Martin Luther King, Jr., as quoted on a YMCA bulletin board.

Chapter 2

From P. Anastas. (1973). *Glooskaps' children* (Boston: Beacon Press), pp. 14–15. Copyright © 1973 by Peter Anastas. Reprinted by permission of Beacon Press.

Chapter 3

From P. Monighan-Nourot, B. Scales, J. Van Hoorn, with M. Almy. (1987). *Looking at children's play: A bridge between theory and practice.* (New York: Teachers College Press), p. 9.

From L. Vygotsky. (1966). *Thought and language.* (Cambridge, MA: MIT Press), p. 16. Used by permission.

From M. W. Wiltz & E. L. Klein. (2001). "What do you do in child care?" Children's perceptions of high and low quality classrooms. *Early Childhood Research Quarterly, 16*(2), p. 222.

Chapter 4

From J. Greenman. (1998). *Places for childhoods.* (Redmond, WA: Exchange Press), p. 109. Reprinted with permission from Child Care Information Exchange, P.O. Box 3249, Redmond WA 98073.

Chapter 5

From O. McAfee. (1981). Planning the preschool program. In M. Kaplan-Sanoff & R. Yablans-Magrid (Eds.), *Exploring early childhood: Readings in theory and practice* (New York: Macmillan).

From C. Breig-Allen. (1997). Implementing the process of change in a public school setting. In J. B. Hendrick (Ed.), *First steps toward teaching the Reggio way.* (Upper Saddle River, NJ: Merrill/Prentice Hall), p. 128.

From Y. Berra, as quoted in M. Zuckerman. (1992). Editorial: George Bush: Evening in America, *U.S. News and Word Report, 113*(10), p. 88.

Chapter 6

From D. Curtis & M. Carter. (2000). *The art of awareness: How observation can transform your teaching.* (St. Paul, MN: Redleaf), p. xiii.

Chapter 7

From "Animal School" (anonymous).

Chapter 8

From H. Palmer & M. Cheney. (1984). Sittin' in a high chair. *Happy song.* Topanga, CA: HapPal Music. Reprinted by permission.

Chapter 9

From T. Hunter. (2000). Some thoughts about sitting still. *Young Children, 55*(3), p. 50.

Chapter 10

From R. Snyder, M. Snyder, & R. Snyder, Jr. (1989). *The young child as a person.* (New York: Human Sciences), pp. 33–34. Used by permission.

Chapter 11

From H. J. Bowling & S. Rogers. (2001). The value of healing in education. From *Young Children, 56*(2), p. 81.

From J. Elicker & C. Fortner-Wood. (1995). Adult-child relationships in early childhood programs. *Young Children, 51*(1), p. 76.

Chapter 12

From K. Owens. (1995). *Raising your child's self-esteem: The authoritative guide from infancy through the teen years.* (New York: Plenum Press), p. 194.

From Chuang Tzu, as quoted on http://en.thinkexist.com/quotes/chuang_tzu/2.html

From L. Porter. (1999). *Young children's behavior: Practical approaches for caregivers and teachers.* (Sydney, Australia: Maclennan & Petty), p. 2.

Chapter 13

From B. Bowman. (1995) *Scholastic Early Childhood Today, 10*(3), p. 40.

From C. Copple (Ed.). (2003). *A world of difference: Readings on teaching young children in a diverse society*. (Washington, DC: National Association for the Education of Young Children), p. 165.

Chapter 14
From J. Coe. (1987). Children come first. *Childhood Education, 64*(2), p. 73.

Chapter 15
From L. S. Mitchell. (1948). *The here and now story book*. (New York: Dutton; republished by Fields, Spangler & Lee, 1991).

From E. Weitzman. (1992). *Learning language and loving it: A guide to promoting children's social and language development in early childhood settings*. (Toronto, Canada: Hanen Centre), p. 268.

Chapter 16
From G. Owocki. (1999). *Literacy through play*. (Portsmouth, NH: Heinemann), p. 3.

From D. K. Dickinson & P. O. Tabors (Eds.). (2001). *Beginning literacy with language*. (Baltimore: Brookes), p. 330.

Chapter 17
From M. B. Bronson. (2000). *Self-regulation in early childhood: Nature and nurture*. (New York: Guilford), p. 210.

Chapter 18
From D. Peters. (2000). *Taking cues from kids: How they think, What to do about it*. (Portsmouth, NH: Heinemann), p. 32.

From S. Bredekamp & C. Copple (Eds.). (1997). *Developmentally appropriate practice in early childhood programs* (rev. ed.). (Washington, DC: National Association for the Education of Young Children), p. 110. Reprinted with permission from the National Association for the Education of Young Children. www.naeyc.org

ABC Task Force, 225, 240
Adams, M., 225, 230
Ageyev, V. S., 351
Alat, K., 47, 185
Albert, R. E., 281, 346
Alexander, P. A., 5
Alibali, M. W., 351
Almy, M., 38
Amabile, T. M., 244
American Association of Pediatrics,
    128, 131
Anastas, P., 22
Anderson, F. E., 245, 268
Anziamo, M. C., 79
Armstrong, A., 297
Arnheim, D. D., 151
Aronson, S. S., 125, 127, 128
Artiles, A. J., 230
Asch, R., 349
Assets for Colorado Youth, 5
Atkins-Burnett, S., 110, 115
Austin, J. S., 170, 177
Axtmann, A., 208

Babcock, R., 61, 198, 203
Bandura, A., 206, 221, 270
Barbarin, O. A., 294
Barbour, N., 2
Bardige, B., 7, 11
Barhydt, D. M., 36
Barnett, W. S., 10, 20
Barrera, I., 231
Barrera, R. M., 25, 59
Bauer, J. C., 297, 307
Baumrind, D., 221
Beaty, J. J., 110, 122, 214, 215
Behrman, R. E., 24, 307
Belfield, C. R., 10
Beneke, S., 16, 20, 316–317, 326
Bentzen, W. R., 110
Bergen, D., 20, 40
Berger, E. H., 22, 36
Bergin, C. A. C, 198

Bergin, D. A., 198
Berk, L. E., 314, 327
Berman, C., 142
Bermúdez, M. T., 142
Berra, Y., 71
Berrera, R. M., 36
Bertrand, D. G., 140
Beuf, A. H., 232
Biber, B., 14
Bigelow, J. H., 10
Bilello, T. E., 145, 146
Bissell, J. S., 107
Bisson, J., 234
Blood, C. L., 281
Bloom, S., 163
Bluhm, C., 208
Bodrova, E., 39, 47, 48, 314
Bohannon, J. N., 270
Bonvillian, J. D., 270
Boocock, S., 10, 20, 222
Bos, B., 267, 281
Bower, M. E., 206
Bowling, H. J., 179
Bowman, B., 5, 106, 220, 290, 307
Bozzi, L., 105
Bransford, J. D., 12
Bredekamp, S., 2, 8, 19, 90, 148, 271,
    274, 290, 291, 293, 294, 306, 313,
    315, 329, 334
Breig-Allen, C., 71
Brett, A., 97
Brett, J., 281
Bricker, D., 121, 239
Brickey, J., 61
Bright, J. A., 41
Brim, O., 222
Brittain, G., 7
Bronfenbrenner, U., 222
Bronson, M. B., 5, 53, 69, 198, 206, 309
Brooks, R., 218
Brown, A. L., 12
Brown, P., 69
Bruner, J. S., 251

Buch, L., 131, 145
Burns, M. S., 106, 290, 291, 306
Bussewitz, B., 175

Cadwell, L. B., 98, 326
Calman, L. J., 10
Canadian Child Care Federation, 128
Cannella, G. S., 231
Cannon, J., 303
Carlo, G., 209
Carlson, F. M., 170
Carmona, R. H., 145
Carpenter, T. P., 334
Carson, R., 177
Carter, B. C., 22
Carter, M., 19, 92, 110
Casement, C., 297
Casper, V., 36
Cassell, J., 297
Cattell, R., 270
Ceci, S.J., 151
Center on Hunger, Poverty, &
    Nutrition Policy, 130
Centers for Disease Control and
    Prevention, 125, 126, 129
Centre for Education Research and
    Innovation, 330
Ceppi, G., 58, 68, 267
Chambers, B., 41
Chapman, P. L., 201
Chard, S., 77, 317–318
Charles, C. M., 330
Cheney, M., 124
Chenfield, 267–268
Cherry, C., 280
Cheung, L. W. Y., 130
Childhelp USA, 170
Children's Defense Fund, 36, 129
Children's Safety Network, 124
Chomsky, N., 270
Christie, J., 270
Christie, J. F., 307
Church, E. B., 279, 307

Greenman, J., 55, 68
Greenspan, S. I., 194, 196
Greenstein, D., 163
Grief, E. B., 236
Grieshaber, S., 231
Griffin, P., 290, 291, 306
Grisso, J. A., 142
Gronlund, N. E., 115, 121–122
Groth, L., 306
Guthrie A. C., 36

Haas, W. H., 287
Habenstein, R. W., 241
Haigh, K., 61
Haines, J. E., 279
Hale, J. E., 283
Halfon, N., 12
Hall, B. J., 287
Hall, E., 17–18, 318
Han, M., 270, 271
Hanline, M. E., 254
Hannemann, R. E., 172, 174
Harlan, J. D., 351
Harms, T., 63, 67, 69
Harris, T. T., 199, 214
Hart, B., 271, 272, 288, 290, 291, 294
Harter, S., 198, 220, 221, 241
Hartle, L., 61, 198
Hartup, W. W., 208–209
Harvey, J. H., 36
Hatton, S. D., 19
Haugland, S. W., 297, 307
Hauser-Cram, P., 20
Hayes, D. S., 208–209
Head Start Performance Standards, 284
Healy, A., 353
Healy, J. M., 297
Helm, J. H., 16, 20, 90, 316–318, 326
Henderson, A., 139, 142
Hendrick, J., 11, 15, 20, 28, 31, 58, 90, 196, 236, 239, 249, 298, 339
Hendrick, J. B., 327
Henniger, M. L., 41
Herriot, P., 270–271
Hewes, D., 32
Hewitt, S. K., 171
Hieronymus, B., 344, 348
High/Scope Educational Research Foundation, 106
Hildebrand, V., 5, 36
Hildebrandt, C., 351
Hill, C. A., 283
Hill, W. M., 284
Hines, M. P., 5
Hines, R. P., 36
Hirsch, K. W., 206
Hirsh-Pasek, K., 8, 320
Hoban, R., 140

Hochstein, M., 12
Hodges, W., 174
Hoffman, L., 222
Hoffman, M. L., 184, 206
Hohmann, M., 351
Holloway, S. D., 105
Holmes, R. M., 225, 232
Hong, S. B., 297, 307
Honig, A. S., 22, 23, 169, 177, 236
Hoot, J. L., 145, 230–231
Howe, D., 115
Howe, N., 41, 47, 61
Howes, C., 42, 208
Huber, L. K., 268
Hunter, T., 145
Hurley, D. S., 163
Hut, V., 306
Hyman, I. A., 217
Hyson, M. C., 8, 196, 320
Hyun, E., 53

Impara, J. D., 94, 106
Inhelder, B., 7
Isbell, R., 287
Isenberg, J. P., 53, 267
Ispa, J., 35

Jacobs, M., 142
Jacobson, E., 157
Jalongo, M. R., 142, 223, 243, 245, 267
Jameel, H. S., 175
Jenkins, E., 279
Jenkins, H., 297
Jenkins, S., 343
Johnson, J. E., 20, 46, 48, 51
Johnson, V. E., 169
Jones, E., 7, 57, 64, 73, 90, 319, 326
Jones, J., 110

Kagan, S. L., 108
Kaiser Family Foundation, 145
Kamii, C., 330, 334
Kaminsky, J. A., 29
Karbon, M., 209
Karnes, M., 245
Karoly, L. A., 10
Katz, L., 5, 16, 22, 77, 90, 217, 311, 316, 317–318, 326
Katzen, M., 139, 142
Kaufman, R., 127, 142
Kelly, C., 240
Kendrick, A. S., 127, 142
Kennedy, M., 268
Keyser, J., 36
Kieff, J., 268
King, M. L., 2
Kinsey, A. C., 169
Kirkland, L. D., 290
Klein, M. D., 60, 239, 241

Klein, W. L., 299
Klugman, E., 45, 145
Knutson, J. F., 206
Kohl, M. F., 268
Kohn, A., 110–111, 222, 241, 268
Kolodny, R. C., 169
Koplow, L., 185, 194, 306
Koralek, D., 210, 351
Koralek, D. G., 287
Kostelnik, M. J., 221
Kozulin, A., 351
Kramer, D. C., 177
Kritchevsky, L., 64, 106
Kudela, E., 163
Kumar, P., 239

Labov, W., 283
Lakeshore Learning Materials, 142
Lally, J. R., 8, 23
Lamme, L. L., 61, 198
Lane, M., 307
Large, J., 234
Leifer, A. S., 222
Lemley, I., 139
Lemley, V., 139
Lenox, M. F., 287
Leong, D. J., 39, 47, 48, 314
Lesser, G. S., 222
Levi, L., 334
Levin, D. E., 47, 198, 199, 204, 206, 209, 210, 214–215, 217
Lillard, A., 193, 196
Linder, T. W., 306–307
Lindfors, J. W., 321
Link, M., 281
Lively, E., 169, 177
Lively, V., 169, 177
Lopez, L. M., 283, 284
Lord, L., 268
Louv, R., 163
Lundgren, D., 284
Lynn-Garbe, C., 145

Maag, J. W., 217
MacDonald, S., 268
Machado, P, 158
Macpherson, D., 231
Maloney, C., 73
Mandzuk, S., 270
Maratsos, M. P., 270
Marion, M., 217
Marotz, L. R., 142
Marquis, C., 259, 263
Martin, C. E., 169
Masters, W. H., 169
Matheson, C. C., 208
Mazlish, E., 194, 196

McAfee, O., 71, 302
McAreavey, P., 353
McBride, S. C., 22
McClellan, D. E., 217
McCloskey, R., 140
McDermott, G., 281
McGinn, B., 185, 186, 214–215, 321
McGoldrick, M. M., 22
McKee, B., 145
McLean, M. E., 8
McNeil, J., 172
McNeill, D., 270
Meier, D. R., 287
Meisels, S. J., 106, 110, 115
Mendoza, J., 5, 22
Mense, C. G., 135
Mercurio, C. M., 236
Merritt, S., 116, 121
Messenger, K. P., 127, 142
Metzger, B., 241
Mikkelsen, E. J., 171
Miller, E., 297
Miller, S. A., 214–215, 244, 245
Miller, S. M., 351
Mind in the Making, 16
Mindel, C. H., 241
Miner, N., 163
Mitchell, L. S., 270
Molitor, F., 206
Moller, L., 41
Monahon, C., 192
Monighan-Nourot, P., 38
Montie, J., 10
Moomaw, S., 241, 279, 287, 344, 348
Moore, T., 279
Moosa, S., 230–231
Moran, J. D., 61
Morrison, J. W., 284
Morrison, K., 25
Morrow, L. M., 307
Moss, P., 315

Nager, N., 20
Nash, J. M., 10
National Association for the Education of Young Children, 8, 9, 28, 63, 69, 106, 107–108, 110, 171, 231, 241, 284, 291, 307
National Association of Early Childhood Specialists in State Departments of Education, 9
National Institute for Early Education Research, 291
National Institute of Neurological Diseases and Stroke, 273–274
National Institutes of Health, 145
National Reading Association, 307
National Research Council, 106, 291

National Research Council and Institute of Medicine, 8, 10
Neisworth, J. T., 115
Neugebauer, B., 83
Neuman, S. B., 7, 8, 9, 270, 290, 291, 293, 294, 306
Nimmo, J., 73, 90, 319, 326
Norton, D. E., 280, 287
Numeroff, L. J., 140
Nunnelley, J., 170
Nunnelley, J. C., 177

O'Brien, C., 130
Oberg, M., 240
Oken-Wright, P., 103, 173, 176–177
Oklahoma Child Care, 131, 252
Olds, A. R., 57
Oleson, V., 318
Oliver, S. J., 45, 145
Orleans, C. T., 142
Orozco, J. L., 287
Owens, K., 198, 220
Owocki, G., 290, 306
Oyer, H. J., 287
Ozmun, J. C., 7, 15, 146
Ozmun, J. D., 163

Paintal, S., 217
Paley, V. G., 7, 53
Palmer, H., 124, 279
Pareete, H. P., 36
Parham, V. R., 143
Parkinson, K., 140
Parten, M. B., 40
Patterson, J., 290
Patterson, K., 286
Paxson, C., 142
Peckham-Hardin, K. D., 90
Peisner-Freinberg, E. S., 10
Pelo, A., 240
Perry, B. D., 174, 182, 326
Pestalozzi, J., 309
Pestolesi, R. A., 151
Peters, D., 329
Petch-Hogan, B., 36
Petrakos, H., 61
Pfluger, L. W., 56
Phelps, P., 254
Phenice, L. A., 5, 36
Phillips, C. B., 225, 230
Phillips, D. Z., 12
Phillipsen, L., 239
Piaget, J., 7, 14–15, 49, 53, 193, 221, 320, 329, 334, 341
Pica, R., 163
Pikulski, J. J., 290, 291, 294
Plake, B. S., 94, 106
Plutro, M., 284

Pomeroy, W. B., 169
Porter, L., 198
Poskitt, E. M., 130
Power, B., 25
Pramling-Samuelsson, I., 236
Pratt, C., 252
Prelutsky, C., 287
Prescott, E., 57, 64
Pretti-Frontczak, K., 121
Provenzo, E. F., Jr., 97

Raffi, 279
Raines, S., 287
Ramassini, K. K., 61
Ramsey, P. G., 231, 232
Rasmussen, M., 49
Raver, S. A., 23, 24
Readdick, C. A., 201
Rector, S., 311, 319
Redleaf, R., 245, 268
Reid, T. R., 284
Reifel, S., 39, 50, 53, 125, 126, 148, 164, 210
Rescorla, L., 8, 320
Revenson, T. A., 330
Rey, H. A., 281
Rhoten, L., 307
Riegraf, N. B., 41
Rinaldi, C., 73, 248–249
Risley, T. R., 271, 272, 288, 290, 291, 294
Rivkin, M. S., 148, 351
Robertson, A., 268
Robertson, A. S., 5, 22, 245
Rockwell, A., 349
Rockwell, H., 349
Rockwell, R. E., 135, 177
Rogers, S., 179
Roopnarine, J. L., 20, 41
Rosegrant, T., 2, 90
Roskos, K., 7, 8, 9, 270, 307
Ross, H., 233
Rothenberg, D., 5, 22
Rowe, M. B., 322
Rubin, K. H., 41, 47, 48
Rush, J. M., 142
Russ, S. S., 48
Ryan, S., 241

Sadker, D., 222
Sadker, M., 222
Salend, S. J., 241
Samalin, N., 194
Sandall, S., 8
Sandberg, A., 236
Sanders, S. W., 146, 148, 151, 163
Santos, R., 110
Saracho, O. N., 39
Sarama, J., 343, 344, 345